THE COUNTRY HOUSE LIBRARY

Mark Purcell

THE
COUNTRY
HOUSE
LIBRARY

PUBLISHED FOR
NATIONAL TRUST BY

Yale University Press

NEW HAVEN & LONDON
MMXVII

First published by Yale University Press 2017
302 Temple Street, P.O. Box 209040, New Haven CT 06520–9040
47 Bedford Square, London WC1B 3DP
yalebooks.com / yalebooks.co.uk

Published for National Trust

ISBN 978–0–300–227406 HB

Library of Congress Control Number: 2017015031

10 9 8 7 6 5 4 3 2 1

2022 2021 2020 2019 2018 2017

Editor: Catherine Gaffney
Designer: Robert Dalrymple
Typeset in Adobe Jenson and MVB Celestia Antiqua
Printed in China

Front cover: The Library at Wimpole Hall, Cambridgeshire
Back cover: Vita Sackville-West's Tower Room at Sissinghurst, Kent
Front flap: Double page from Evelyn's translation of Jean-Baptiste de
la Quintinie, *The Compleat Gard'ner*, London 1693 (Erddig)
Frontispiece: The Library at Chatsworth, Derbyshire

Contents

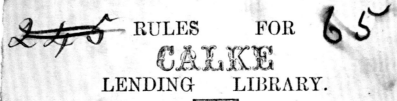

RULES   FOR
CALKE
LENDING   LIBRARY.

1st. Rule. A Penny to be paid every month by the members.

2nd. Rule. Books to be changed every Thursday at Three o'clock.

3rd. Rule. Not more than one book to be taken at a time.

4th. Rule. No Library Books taken by members to be lent to anyone else.

5th. Rule. Any book returned soiled or marked, a halfpenny will be charged.

[1] Early nineteenth-century flyer with the Calke Abbey Lending Library rules

Acknowledgements

My first debt is to the National Trust. As its Libraries Curator from 1999 to 2015, for fifteen-and-a-half years I had oversight of over 160 historic libraries across England, Wales and Northern Ireland. I spent far too much of my time away from home, far too much time driving, and far too much time sitting on often late-running trains. But the rewards were very great, and this book is the result.

A small group of friends and colleagues helped by asking beady questions at the planning stage, and particular thanks go to David Adshead, Robert Harding, Peter Hoare, Simon Jervis, David McKitterick, David Pearson, Paul Quarrie, and to Sally Salvesen. The final book has been greatly enriched by the splendid photographs, many commissioned by Chris Lacey in the National Trust Image Library, and would not have got far without Claire Forbes, of the Trust's Specialist Publications programme.

Many others have helped, and I regret the impossibility of thanking everyone by name: the list of library and archive staff, not to mention house staff, curators, conservators and volunteers working for the National Trust and the National Trust for Scotland would run to many hundreds. I should, however, also like to thank the three Assistant Libraries Curators I worked with at the National Trust – Yvonne Lewis, Ed Potten and Nicola Thwaite – as well as Becci Shanks, Gina Murphy, Cara Wallace and Claire Hollinghurst, who all provided the office back-up without which a nomadic librarian would long since have gone under.

I should like to thank staff of the Bodleian Library in Oxford, where much of this book was written, and my colleagues at Cambridge University Library, where it was finished, as well as: the Duke of Abercorn (Baronscourt), Martha Andrews (Paxton), †Giles Barber, Caroline Bendix, Robert Betteridge, Tom Boggis (Audley End), Sir Brooke Boothby (Fonmon), Donough Cahill, Roger Carr-Whitworth, David Connell (Burton Constable), Timothy Cutts, Kathleen and †Tam Dalyell (the House of the Binns), Hannah DeGroff, Martin Drury, Althea and Henrietta Dundas-Bekker (Arniston), Lord Egremont (Petworth), Dai Evans (Picton), Richard Faircliff, Gareth Fitzpatrick (Boughton), Katie Flanagan, John Gandy, Ian Gow, Daryl Green, David Griffin, John and Eileen Harris, Kate Harris (Longleat), Brian Hillyard, Peter Hughes (Madresfield), Harvey James, Morgan Kavanagh (Borris Castle), Peter Kidd, Tom Lloyd, Owen McKnight, Giles Mandelbrote, the Earl of March and Kinvara (Goodwood), Catherine Maxwell-Stewart (Traquair), †Paul Morgan, Charles Noble (Chatsworth), Crónán Ó Doibhlin, Francis O'Gorman, James Peill (Goodwood), Ruth Peters (Stowe), Vicki Perry (Hatfield), David and Carla Raikes (Treberfydd), Terence Reeves-Smyth, Suzanne Reynolds, Jack Rhoden, Christopher Ridgeway (Castle Howard), Ian Riches, Dunstan Roberts, †Julian Roberts, James Rothwell, Christopher Rowell, Lord Sackville (Knole), Pippa Shirley, Murray Simpson, Susannah Stone, Marjory Szurko, David Taylor, James Towe (Chatsworth), Helen Vincent, Germaine Warkentin, Susie West, Sarah Wheale, Gordon Wheeler, Lisa White, and Nigel Wiggins (Holcombe).

This publication was made possible by the National Trust's Specialist Publications Programme, supported by a generous bequest from the late Mr and Mrs Kenneth Levy. While it does not dwell exclusively on Trust libraries, it does draw extensively on the Trust's collections. The Trust's libraries programme is itself underwritten by the endowment raised by the Campaign for Country House Libraries run by the Trust's US affiliate, the Royal Oak Foundation. The campaign made it possible for the Trust to set its libraries in order and place the catalogue online, and I hope that this appropriately Anglo-American collaboration with Yale is a suitable 'thank you' offering for those who supported the appeal.

I am grateful to William Hale and David Adshead for copy-editing, and for cutting several impossibly long chapters down to size. Above all my wife, Caroline Shenton, challenged, checked, read tricky medieval handwriting and cast a critical eye over a long series of drafts – all way beyond the call of duty. But any errors remain my own. MEP *Cambridge, Christmas 2016*

Note on Access

Pevsner's *Buildings of England* traditionally included a formula thanking owners for admission to their houses, but warning readers that mention in the text did not imply any right of public access. The same is true of books in private libraries.

I am grateful to those who allowed me into their houses, especially when they were under no obligation to do so. Private libraries have filled important gaps in the narrative, and it would have been difficult to write this book without them. A good number of library interiors can, of course, be seen by anyone who cares to visit a house when it is open, though a few of the country houses I have mentioned are rarely or never shown, and rather more have historic libraries which are not on the public visitor route. Access to books and manuscripts is self-evidently more complicated, and certainly should not be taken for granted. Even finding out what is there may be problematic. Though many do not, a few of the grander private houses have professional curators, librarians or archivists, and some even have library catalogues. A few have published or republished them in modern times: a copy of the 1905 catalogue of the Duke of Norfolk's library at Arundel Castle, for example, is helpfully mounted as a PDF file on the castle website, while other libraries – Longleat and Paxton House, Berwickshire, are good examples – have reported their early British books to the online ESTC, the *English Short Title Catalogue* (estc.bl.uk). Other libraries can be investigated using historic catalogues. Sir James Lacaita's four-volume catalogue of the library at Chatsworth, published in 1879, illustrates the problems and pitfalls. In the first place many books have subsequently been sold, and in the second Lacaita was preoccupied with texts, whereas modern researchers are much more likely to want to know, for example, which of the books were annotated by the 3rd Earl of Burlington, or whether Chatsworth still has any Renaissance bindings from the library of Jean Grolier (1479–1565) – it does: there are twenty-three.

In the United Kingdom (though not the Republic of Ireland) an appreciable number of historic books in private ownership have been 'conditionally exempted' for tax purposes. Members of the public have a right to see conditionally exempted chattels. A partial catalogue is available online on the website of HM Revenue and Customs, though often with only limited information about location and provenance. For printed books in country houses, the Revenue specifies that the access requirement is satisfied if the public can see the spines en masse from the visitor route, but access to individual volumes must be available by appointment, and a range of suitable dates must be offered within one month of the original enquiry. My own experience is that some owners are less familiar than they should be with the obligations which they have entered into in return for tax exemptions. A little persistence usually pays off, and failing that, interested parties can always contact the Revenue.

Researchers are on safer ground with National Trust collections, as most of the 300,000-plus books owned by the Trust are described in some detail on the United Kingdom union catalogue, Copac (copac.ac.uk). Access is by appointment (it can take time to find the book, and someone must be on hand to supervise the researcher), but is generally entirely unproblematic, and the Trust's hard-working Libraries Team is always on hand to answer enquiries.

In general I have not shied away from discussing anything which seemed to me to be interesting or important, except when owners and custodians have asked me not to do so, which has been rare. When it has been possible to illustrate a point in my argument by reference to libraries which are visible and accessible, I have done so.

[2] Library steps by Thomas Chippendale the Younger at Stourhead, Wiltshire

On the Country House Library

In many country houses the Library is the most spectacular room in the house. At Blickling in Norfolk the Long Gallery, 123 feet long and lined end-to-end with books, is unforgettable (fig. 4). At Alnwick Castle in Northumberland the double-height Library, shelved from floor to ceiling, is enormous (fig. 3), and at Calke in Derbyshire it is the second largest room in the house. Elsewhere interiors impress less for their size than for their opulence. At Traquair, south of Edinburgh, each bay of shelving has a classical author painted on the cornice above, just as in the seventeenth-century Library of the antiquarian Sir Robert Cotton (1570/1–1631) at Westminster, where the bust of a Roman emperor once sat atop each bookcase.[1] At Abbotsford many of Sir Walter Scott's books remain on the shelves of the great room he created for them, while the library of another bestselling novelist survives at Hughenden, the Buckinghamshire retreat of Queen Victoria's favourite Prime Minister, Benjamin Disraeli.[2]

But the history of libraries in country houses is a history of lost libraries as well as extant collections. Quite apart from books sold by the descendants of their original owners, libraries have always been subject to dissolution in more dramatic fashion. The library of the 3rd Duke of Argyll was described in a lavishly produced catalogue published by the Foulis Press in Glasgow in 1758, and subsequently sold to George III's Prime Minister, the 3rd Earl of Bute (1713–92). It was then destroyed in a fire at Bute's English home, Luton Hoo, in 1771.[3] Nearly two hundred years later the library of the aesthete Ralph Dutton (1898–1985) was destroyed in 1960 in a great fire at Hinton Ampner, near Winchester. So intense were the flames that the books were left 'almost petrified, as if engulfed by a volcanic eruption'.[4] In Ireland many libraries perished in the house burnings which marked the end of the old order during the War of Independence and ensuing Civil War.[5] It was not a new phenomenon. In a

leaflet in circulation during the Land War in the 1880s, beleaguered Irish gentry were already being advised to use heavy ancestral books to barricade windows against attack.[6] In fact by the revolutionary era, many Irish libraries had already been sold following state-sponsored land reforms begun in the dying decades of British rule in Ireland.

In both Britain and Ireland there are many instances where a house survives but its library does not. It comes as a surprise that there was a major library at Castletown in County Kildare as recently as the 1960s.[7] At Sudbury Hall in Derbyshire, probably not one National Trust visitor in a thousand realises that the seventeenth-century Long Gallery was once shelved end to end (fig. 5). At Ettington Park in Warwickshire, now a hotel, the spectacular Gothic Library built by the gentleman-scholar E. P. Shirley (1812–82) remains. Guests can decide whether they believe in the Library poltergeist, but Shirley's books, like those from his Irish house at Lough Fea, County Monaghan, are gone.[8] In both cases, the loss of a remarkable library is a pointer to an important fact. The more magnificent the books and the more quickly the shelves had been filled by an enthusiastic nineteenth-century collector, the more likely it was that they would eventually be removed and sold.

Then there are the many country houses which are today open to the public, but where visitors see little or nothing of books. At Chatsworth visitors are only able to look through the Library door, though even that is spectacular (see frontispiece). At Longleat most of one of the finest private libraries in the world is not seen by ordinary tourists at all. To varying extents the same is true of houses like Holkham, Houghton, Goodwood, Petworth and Knole, where libraries are not in show rooms long open to tourists, but in historically private apartments, in rooms which frequently remain off-limits to casual sightseers. The reasons are not difficult to guess at, but the logic is that

[3] The Library at Alnwick Castle

there are more grand libraries in private hands than many people realise. But there are also many libraries which are, if less spectacular, in many ways just as remarkable. Sometimes in show houses and sometimes in houses very much in private occupation, these smaller libraries may be accommodated in modest and unpretentious rooms. Their books may have been in place for centuries and be of considerable interest. At Gunby Hall the library assembled by the Massingberds, a family of east Lincolnshire squires, goes back to the late seventeenth century. Though battered and now only a partial survival, the books provide a fascinating flavour of gentry life in an often-forgotten corner of England. Elsewhere, quite ordinary eighteenth- or nineteenth-century books may be housed in apartments of some magnificence. At Flintham Hall, in

Nottinghamshire, a double-height Library provides the link between a comfortable Victorian family home and a vast conservatory clearly inspired by the Crystal Palace. At Sheringham Park the books of the Upcher family, high-minded Norfolk squires, remain in the room designed for them by Humphry Repton (1752–1818), a space in every sense the precursor of the modern living room. There is an almost equally elegant Regency Library at Wassand Hall in East Yorkshire, a Catholic house, and like Gunby still with its original books, while similarly interesting books are found in houses like Farnborough Hall in Warwickshire, or Dudmaston in Shropshire.

Other libraries survive, but not *in situ* nor in the hands of their original aristocratic owners. The most spectacular is the vast library of the

[4] The Long Gallery, Blickling Hall

bibliomaniac 2nd Earl Spencer (1758–1834), from Althorp, Northamptonshire, sold en bloc in 1892 to the Cuban-born Enriqueta Rylands as the foundation collection of the new research library she founded in memory of her husband, the Manchester cotton magnate John Rylands (1801–88). There was nothing new in the institutionalisation of aristocratic libraries. The 5th Duke of Norfolk had at the suggestion of John Evelyn given his personal library to the Royal Society in 1667, while Frances, Duchess of Somerset, gave about 1,000 books from her late husband's library to the Dean and Chapter of Lichfield in 1674.[9] The magnificent library from Stoneleigh Abbey, Warwickshire, was bequeathed to Oriel College, Oxford, in 1786. The college showed its gratitude by commissioning an exquisite new building from James Wyatt to house the books, and by quietly selling Lord Leigh's Shakespeare First Folio to Sir Paul Getty in 2002 (fig. 6).[10] Deplorable though this seemed to many, Oriel was not doing anything new in selling to a private collector. As far back as 1811, T. F. Dibdin (1776–1847) had procured three Caxtons from Lincoln Cathedral for the library of his patron Earl Spencer.[11]

Other country house libraries were subject to what amounted to a rather subtle nationalisation in the years following the Second World War. A large number of manuscripts from the library of the Earls of Leicester at Holkham went to the Bodleian Library in Oxford in the 1950s. Other Holkham

books ended up in the British Library, as did books from Chatsworth, including incunabula and the tenth-century Benedictional of St Æthelwold (fig. 7). The transfer of these and other treasures to public ownership was the consequence not only of the enormous death duties of the post-war period, but also of new regulations on export stops.[12] But for some books it was already too late. Had export stops been in place in the early 1930s, it seems inconceivable that two more great Anglo-Saxon manuscripts, the eighth-century Blickling Psalter and the Blickling Homilies (fig. 8), would have been allowed to leave the United Kingdom.[13]

This dovetails neatly into another form of nationalisation. The National Trust was founded in 1895, and its first books were at Coleridge's Cottage, Nether Stowey (Somerset), acquired in 1907. However, its first serious library, at Blickling, was bequeathed along with the house by the 11th Marquess of Lothian (fig. 9) in 1940. It has sometimes been said that Lothian's involvement in the Trust's Country Houses Scheme (1934) was the result of his distress at the sale of books from Blickling and his principal Scottish seat, Newbattle Abbey, in 1932. If this was the case there is no reference to it in Lothian's papers, and no mention of libraries in his correspondence with the National Trust. The crucial point is that Lothian lent his name to the Country Houses Scheme, and subsequently left Blickling and its remaining 12,561 books to the Trust.[14] It was the beginning of a

[5] The Long Gallery at Sudbury Hall in use as a Library in 1906

[6] Lord Leigh's Shakespeare First Folio (now at Wormsley Park)

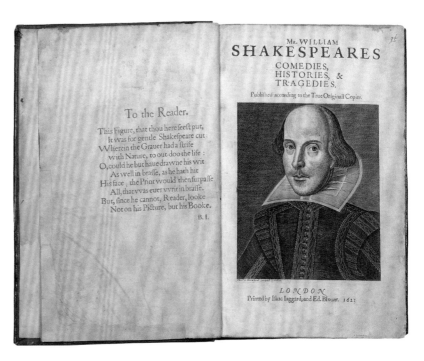

process which would subsequently see the gradual transfer of about 300,000 books to the Trust, whether by gift, bequest, Treasury transfer in lieu of death duties or, later, by purchase. A similar process was repeated on a smaller scale north of the border, where the National Trust for Scotland was founded in 1931.

If there are now far fewer libraries in country houses than there were in the nineteenth century, the number of survivors, in both private and institutional hands, is far from negligible. How many exactly is unclear, but at the most conservative estimate we must be dealing with hundreds of thousands of books in hundreds of locations. So it remains surprising that so many libraries have been so consistently overlooked in modern times. When he died in 1682, the probate inventory of the 1st Duke of Lauderdale reckoned that his books at Ham House made up half the value of all the chattels in the house. One would scarcely guess this when reading the many publications on furniture, pictures and upholstery at Ham (the problem has recently been redressed with the publication in 2013 of a full-scale scholarly study of Ham which *does* includes a chapter on the lost library).[15] Many similar books on other houses resolutely ignore libraries, as do most of the enormous number of general books on country houses, as well as many guidebooks.

The problem was brought very vividly to my attention in 1999 when, as the recently appointed Libraries Curator to the National Trust, I was invited on a private tour of Houghton Hall, Sir Robert Walpole's great house in Norfolk. Our bear leader, the genial and generous John Cornforth (1937–2004), was one of the country's most distinguished architectural historians. After an exhaustive tour of the house, in which every architectural detail, every picture, every tapestry and every stick of furniture was examined with forensic skill, finally we arrived in the Library (fig. 10). There we picked over everything in sight: panelling, window glazing, seat furniture and, of course, bookcases. Finally, I imagined, we might turn to the books. But having discussed every object in the Library except those which it had actually been designed to house, John moved on to the next room, leaving Walpole's books on the shelves. At Houghton and elsewhere, great libraries have survived, but for whatever reason many of the people who might have been expected to be interested in them

have taken surprisingly little notice of them. The increasing professionalisation of scholarship and curatorship in historic houses in the late twentieth century has often seemed to pass them by. In 1988 the National Trust's Gervase Jackson-Stops (1947–95) published an article on country house libraries in *Country Life*. For all his expertise in other areas, nothing could mask the fact that he did so without referring to a single book. A chapter in his 1984 *The English Country House: A Grand Tour* was not much better.[16] Presumably he would have justified this by explaining that he was interested in interiors, but no one would have written about picture galleries or porcelain cabinets without saying anything about the pictures or the porcelain. Jackson-Stops's published work on libraries, like that of John Cornforth, Clive Wainwright and other distinguished figures of the 1980s and 1990s, was undermined by an all-too-evident inability to

[7] The Baptism of Christ from the Benedictional of St Aethelwold, written by the scribe Godeman for St Æthelwold, Bishop of Winchester, in the tenth century (now British Library)

consider Libraries as interiors without treating the books in them as a subsidiary and unimportant part of the interior design scheme.

The reasons for this must remain a matter for debate, but what is beyond question is that country house libraries had by the twentieth century become something of a backwater. The time when country houses were at the centre of the library world has gone, and whole swathes of the books on country house shelves now hold little appeal for many. Theology and classical scholarship, for example, loom large on many ancestral shelves, but these have steadily moved from being matters of central importance for any well-trained mind to subjects widely regarded as irrelevant or abstruse, or even incomprehensible or unutterably boring. At the same time the increasing specialisation of academic disciplines since the middle of the nineteenth century has tended to result in historians and literary scholars of all kinds knowing more and more about less and less. An eighteenth-century gentleman collector of classical sculpture is likely to have taken at least a passing interest in Renaissance editions of Cicero. As late as 1854 the German art historian Gustav Waagen (1797–1868), while primarily interested in pictures, took it for granted that a serious scholar would be interested in illuminated manuscripts, and even occasionally in incunabula (or incunables, books printed before 1501) and early editions of English drama, commenting on all of them in his descriptions of his visits to British country houses.[17]

Only quite recently have things started to change. Over the last thirty years the new discipline of the history of the book has grown and flourished. In the English-speaking world the fusion of a long-established Anglo-American bibliographical tradition with more recent theoretical developments from Continental Europe has produced some conspicuously successful scholarship, from accounts of individual publishing houses, libraries, readers and collectors to multi-volume collaborative works like *The Cambridge History of the Book in Britain* and *The Cambridge History of Libraries in Britain and Ireland*. All this has only underlined how little we yet know about the history, contents, arrangement and use of private libraries. Much of what has been published continues to fall back on

[8] The eighth-century Blickling Homilies (now Princeton University Library)

[9] Sir Herbert James Gunn, *Philip Henry Kerr, 11th Marquess of Lothian (1882–1940)*

a fairly limited number of well-known examples: Bess of Hardwick's six books at Hardwick Hall, the Duke of Lauderdale's Library room of 1672 at Ham House or Lord Chesterfield's lofty disdain for eighteenth-century book collectors. Meanwhile a vast hinterland of other places and experiences has remained substantially unexplored.

If country house historians have tended to ignore libraries, library historians, too, have not always paid as much attention to private libraries as they should have done. Some of this has been a matter of simple practicalities. Until the launch of an online catalogue in 2010, for example, it was remarkably difficult for researchers to find out what was actually in the 170-odd libraries in the care of the National Trust. This is truer still of many private libraries, even those that are on show in buildings which enjoy a high public profile, and which belong to owners who welcome researchers and employ capable and informed staff. Then there is the question of locating former country house books in institutional collections. A researcher investigating the holdings of the British Library for books *about* Holkham or Chatsworth will swiftly find them via the online catalogue, but anyone wishing to find out what books the British Library has that were once *at* Holkham and Chatsworth faces an altogether more formidable task. It can sometimes feel almost as if the curatorial practices of research libraries must have been devised to make it as difficult as possible to investigate which books came from where. Establishments like the National Library of Scotland, which has both the library once at Newhailes in East Lothian and a substantial selection from Castle Fraser in Aberdeenshire, and has kept both collections together, have been unusual.

Broader historiographical trends have also been at work. For much of the twentieth century, most serious historians fought shy of narrative and biographical history. The focus was on analytical, sociological and statistical techniques, and the declared objective was to produce a more rounded, more inclusive and (as it seemed to some at the time) more 'scientific' form of history. All of this was strongly represented in the work of the French *Annales* school, out of which the sub-discipline of the history of the book emerged in the 1950s and 1960s. This style of history was sceptical not just about empirical methodologies, but about the history of elites. Others continued to think about

the rich and powerful, though not necessarily in a way which encouraged in-depth analysis of their lives. In his influential *Crisis of the Aristocracy*, for example, Lawrence Stone included a few paragraphs and a statistical table about private libraries in Renaissance England, derived from work published by the American scholar Sears Jayne.[18] Perhaps more interested in pursuing the 'gentry controversy' vendetta with Hugh Trevor-Roper than dissecting the minutiae of who owned and read what, Stone produced statistics about libraries which present an at-best inadequate summary of an infinitely complex situation.

In other words, libraries have been ignored or misunderstood for reasons which go beyond the fact that country house history is usually written by people who would not know one end of an incunable from the other. Much of the best work in the field of the history of the book itself originated from an intellectual milieu which was sceptical about elite history in the first place. In some circles, there was not only a reluctance to study the minutiae of aristocratic life, but the conviction it would not of necessity yield anything very meaningful or useful. Such things were better left to the 'antiquarian empiricists' denounced by Stone in 1979.[19] History was best studied in terms of macroeconomic trends and inexorable processes. It was not advanced by scraping around in archives, still less by fiddling around with historic bookbindings or reading notes scribbled in the margins of early printed books.

Some light is cast on the origins of this world view in a cartoon published in the Soviet newspaper *Komsomolskaia Pravda* in November 1940. By then the Tsarist nobility had been all-but wiped out, but Stalinist propaganda still saw mileage in a caricature of a lice-ridden nobleman lazing on a *chaise longue*, book in hand, a bookcase of ancient books close by. Despite their libraries, the caption explained, aristocrats were by nature idle and uncultured, and lived in verminous squalor. The charge made little sense, as unlike Britain, where historically oligarchic landowners were in charge, the Russian nobility had been a service nobility, and almost by definition Tsarist intellectuals were members of the privileged orders. In strictly legal terms, Pushkin, Tolstoy, Dostoyevsky and even Lenin were all aristocrats.[20] Few in Britain have ever expressed class hatred with such violence, but in Ireland feelings could run higher. As recently

[10] Library interior, Houghton Hall

as 1990 a professor of geography at an Irish university bizarrely asserted that books in Irish country houses had always been few in number and little used, on the basis that 'the descendants of Cromwell's adventurers were non-literary by nature'.[21] Fox-hunting Irish squires notwithstanding, this would have been regarded with hilarity by W. B. Yeats or Lady Gregory, whose 1931 eulogy to the soon-to-be dispersed books at Coole Park, County Galway, is an especially moving response to the dissolution of a library long central to the lives of the family which owned it (fig. 11).[22] The evidence suggests that there were hundreds of thousands of books in Irish country houses. How these books were used is a matter for research, but the few surviving libraries certainly do show signs of use.

In Britain the rhetoric of an increasingly democratic age was generally less fierce, and the consequences less catastrophic for the descendants of those who had once ruled the roost. Nonetheless, about 1,200 English country houses have been demolished since 1900, and proportionately more in Scotland and Wales.[23] For an iconic image of the era, one can hardly do better than the extraordinary photographs of the landscape park at Wentworth Woodhouse, near Rotherham, strip-mined to the door of the house (fig. 12) on the orders of Clement Attlee's Minister of Fuel, Manny Shinwell. Pushed

through using wartime emergency powers, the operation was widely regarded even at the time as an act of vengeful class warfare. Earl Fitzwilliam's protests were brushed aside, though some of the strongest criticism came from the National Union of Mineworkers, whose members had long used the park for recreation.[24]

Sometimes, however, demolitions and sales were more a matter of retrenchment than of oblivion. Abandoning a decaying Palladian mansion, or sending a large library or an important collection of pictures to auction, was, for some, a mark of desperation. For others it was the route to survival. The descendants of the Fitzwilliams may no longer be at Wentworth Woodhouse, but they are still very much in business.[25] The great library of the 3rd Earl of Sunderland (1675–1722) was sold from Blenheim in the 1880s, but the Marlboroughs are still there.[26] Their library was certainly not the only one to be broken up. Millions of volumes have been dispersed, many going overseas. But the constant flow of books *out* of country houses over the last hundred and fifty years may have had an unexpected side effect. Could it be that all the auctions have reinforced latent assumptions that country house books were always intended primarily for show, unread from one generation to the next? Or that books were mostly about conspicuous consumption, and that non-use can

[11] The Library, Coole Park, County Galway as photographed probably in the early 20th century

[12] Open-cast mining at Wentworth Woodhouse

be assumed unless proven otherwise? I suspect that this is indeed the case. Allied to this, many commentators, the inhabitants of democratic and comparatively equitable societies, find it difficult to shake off a series of unhelpful assumptions when looking at the hierarchical and deferential world of our ancestors. When it comes to thinking about libraries, the chief misapprehensions include the idea that libraries have always primarily been the province of institutions rather than individuals, that cultural patronage has always fundamentally been the preserve of states or organisations, rather than individuals, and that it is normal for books to be available to everyone, as a matter of right, rather than being concentrated in the hands of a minority.

These are bold claims, but I hope it is implicit that I am equally sceptical about the rose-tinted nostalgia that overlays much of what we think and write about country houses. Great houses were an integral part of the world that created them, a world where some lived in luxury and others in slums, and the grandeur of the few was paid for by the labours of the many. As that world changed, many houses either changed or died. Visiting the site of Hamilton Palace (fig. 13), once the largest private house in Scotland and demolished in 1919,

it is impossible not to feel a twinge of regret – not just for the building but also for its contents, which included two great libraries, one inherited from William Beckford, sold in London in 1882 and 1885.[27] But this is to dwell in counterfactuals. For most owners, their houses were not cultural monuments which were the legitimate interest of the world and his wife, but private property. As recently as 1932, the heir to Chatsworth spoke for many when he blustered against provisions for the protection of historic buildings in the Town and Country Planning Act.[28]

It would be possible to spend a great deal of time defining what a country house is. I do not intend to do that, but a few words of explanation are necessary. Traditional definitions tend to focus on three fundamental characteristics: that a country house should be large, should be a freestanding building in its own grounds and should lie at the centre of an income-producing estate. For my purposes these criteria are unsatisfactory. What is more, as Giles Worsley (the scion of a landowning family) pointed out in an important article published in 2005, they are tinged with snobbery.[29] They tend to exclude suburban villas, not all of which had their own estates, or at least not ones which were

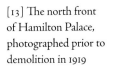

[13] The north front of Hamilton Palace, photographed prior to demolition in 1919

[14] The Library at Burton Constable, East Yorkshire

financially independent. Several of these once contained important libraries. The books formerly in Lord Burlington's villa at Chiswick are today at Chatsworth, and there were distinguished libraries at Ham House and Osterley Park, as well as more modest collections in smaller houses. The traditional definition also causes problems with nouveau-riche houses of the later nineteenth and twentieth centuries, funded by industry rather than agriculture, or indeed Bateman's, Rudyard Kipling's house, financed by the proceeds of his pen.

Then there is the even more vexed question of what constitutes a library. The editors of the *Cambridge History of Libraries in Britain and Ireland* quite reasonably expended a good deal of energy on this, but I am content to sidestep the issue. For my purposes, a library is simply any reasonably substantial assembly of books in a country house, together with its fittings, furnishings and accoutrements. I am primarily interested in the books: their acquisition, arrangement, organisation, use and – often – the process of their dispersal, but I make no value judgements about them. I do not, for example, regard the books at Wimpole Hall to be somehow more library-like than those at Llanerchaeron in west Wales. The first were selected with care and taste by wealthy intellectuals, and the latter by backwoods squires for whom the life of the mind

came a distant second to the self-evidently more important business of hunting. Both are part of the story. For reasons of clarity, a library refers to books (I hesitate to use the word 'collection', which begs a lot of questions), while a Library is a room. I hope that this does not seem too contrived, but clarity on the point is frequently essential to the argument. The spaces in which books are kept are often integral to any understanding of their history, so architecture, fittings and furnishings also loom large. With furniture, my attention tends to focus on library-type kit, so I am more likely to pay attention to library steps, medal cabinets, chairs, sofas, globes, telescopes and bookcases than tapestries, ceramics or the weave of the library curtains. Pictures get an occasional look in, either because they have something specific to say about libraries – their subject matter, for instance, may form part of a particular library iconography – or because their owners clearly regarded their presence alongside their books as particularly significant. As to what I mean by 'reasonably substantial', in practice this could refer to anything from a few dozens to many thousands of books, though the earlier the library, the smaller I am likely to go. (In quoting figures, unless I say the contrary, I am referring to titles and not volumes. The three-volume first edition of *Pride and Prejudice* (1813) is one book, but a single volume containing twenty-three separately published pamphlets is twenty-three.)

Another important question is whether the concept of 'the country house library' is useful at all. I am slightly ambivalent about this. It is arguable that a country house library is best seen as just one sort of private library, and that there was little distinction between, for example, the books of a scholarly landowner, a wealthy clergyman and a rich London collector. There is a good deal to be said for this, and it is an issue which I explored in an article published in 2001.[30] In Scotland, for example, there is a long tradition of the gentleman-lawyer. Elsewhere, dynastic succession notwithstanding, books migrated easily from one sphere to another. At Springhill in County Londonderry, the library contains books which belonged to merchant cousins in the city of Derry at the beginning of the eighteenth century.[31] At Lanhydrock many of the Renaissance books in the Long Gallery belonged to a local clergyman, Hannibal Gamon (1582–1651), who bought them while he was at Broadgates Hall in Oxford, shifting them to Cornwall in 1619.[32] Then there is the question of books in town and country. Many landowners owned or rented a town house, usually in London. Few remain in family occupation, and most were demolished long ago, but many once contained libraries, and several of the greatest country house libraries, including Blickling and the dispersed library from Blenheim, were once kept in London. This raises some important questions, explored in chapter ten. Altogether there are any number of problems with the very notion of the country house library, a term which clearly requires caution. On the other hand, there are country houses that visibly contain libraries, and for the most part houses and libraries alike passed by dynastic inheritance down the centuries.

As Libraries Curator to the National Trust from 1999 to 2015, I found myself in a uniquely privileged position. In leading the long-term project to open up the Trust's libraries, I had in-depth access to a huge number of libraries over many years. I was also welcomed by the owners of many private libraries. My thoughts and conclusions have inevitably been coloured by this, but with it comes the danger of overstating the importance and interest of the libraries with which I am most familiar. I am also aware that there is a risk of dismissing too lightly the opinions of others, confident in the assumption that I have seen more libraries than they have. Nonetheless, it may be helpful to venture a few tentative conclusions.

Fundamentally there has been a tendency to assume that libraries in British and Irish country houses were less numerous, less used and less important to their owners than was actually the case. (I am reluctant to advance similar views on aristocratic libraries in other European countries, for the simple reason that I am insufficiently familiar with them. My own visits to libraries in the Czech Republic and Sweden have in themselves been enough to suggest that there would be real benefits to some sort of pan-European collaborative research project, though this would be hampered by the simple fact that in many countries few if any libraries have survived *in situ*.) My conclusions can be broken down into five broad observations:

— The number of libraries in country houses has almost certainly been underestimated.

— It is often assumed that a library became a standard appendage of a country house from the late seventeenth century, but the story begins much earlier.

— The importance of books to many owners has tended to be understated.

— The extent to which books were read by people other than their actual owners has been underestimated.

— We need to resist the temptation to try to fit the story into neat and tidy models, and to recognise the enormous range of form and function which historically libraries have assumed.

If these conclusions are even partially correct, then the ramifications are considerable. It is perhaps surprising that a full-scale survey of library country houses has not been published before, but I hope that my own, whatever its failings, will at least encourage further work in a curiously neglected field.

CHAPTER ONE

'Reciting my Poems Even in Britain'
From Roman Britain to Magna Carta

Dicitur et nostros cantare Britannia versus.
Martial, *Epigrams*, xi, 3

Villa Libraries in Roman Britain

In the summer of 1754 word reached the Royal Society in London of an astonishing discovery in southern Italy. Excavations had been going on for some years at Herculaneum and Pompeii, buried by the eruption of Vesuvius in AD 79. Now, in a letter addressed to the philosopher and bibliophile Thomas Hollis (1720–74), the Society's Neapolitan correspondent Camillo Paderni outlined the latest find:

> The place where they are digging at present is under *Il Bosco di Sant'Agostino*, … All the buildings discovered in this site are noble: many of the pavements are of mosaic, variously and finely made, disposed with a beautiful symmetry … In one of these buildings there has been found an entire library, compos'd of volumes of the Egyptian Papyrus, of which they have taken out about 250; and the place is not yet clear'd or emptied … These volumes of Papyrus consist of Latin and Greek manuscripts; but from their brittleness, occasioned by fire and time, it is not possible to unroll them, they being now decay'd and rotten.

By 1754 the Royal Society was no longer dominated by scientists or natural philosophers, but by aristocrats, themselves the owners of great houses with magnificent libraries. If, at this point, they pricked up their ears, they were forced to wait another six months for Paderni to elaborate:

> As yet we have only entered into one room … It appears to have been a library, adorned with presses, inlaid with different sorts of wood, disposed in rows; at the top of which were cornices, as in our own times. I was buried in this spot more than twelve days, to carry off the volumes found there; many of them were so perished that it was impossible to remove them.[1]

Buried under 80 feet of debris, the villa which Paderni was describing was an enormous complex, and various candidates have been suggested for the owner of what became known as the Villa of the Papyri. The most likely is Lucius Calpurnius Piso, father-in-law of Julius Caesar, and patron of the Epicurean philosopher Philodemos of Gadara (*c.*110–40/35 BC), who may have been the owner of some of the papyri. The task of deciphering them began in 1753, with the arrival from Rome of the priest Antonio Piaggio (1713–96), who introduced a special machine designed to unroll them without damaging them (fig.16).[2] Publication began in 1793, and is still far from complete.

There has been speculation that the library uncovered in the 1750s, consisting mainly of Hellenistic philosophical texts, was just one of several, and that the villa also had a Latin library. As it is, books were found in locations all over the villa, some on the floor (as if an attempt was underway to save them), some in cabinets or bookcases, and others in *capsae*, the bucket-like containers used to store scrolls in antiquity. The main cache was found in a small chamber in a suite of domestic rooms which also included a bath house. The fact that this room contained a table suggests that it was also used for reading. More papyri, including some

[15] The prophet Ezra in his Study, from the early eighth-century Codex Amiatinus (Biblioteca Medicea Laurenziana, Florence)

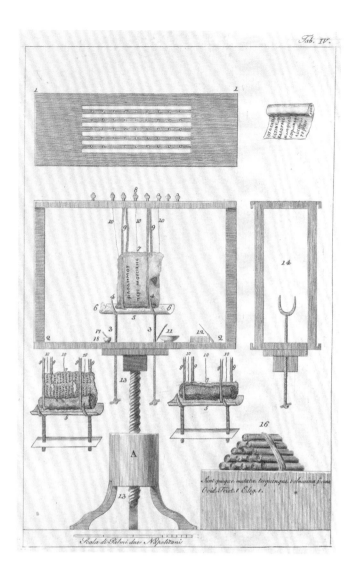

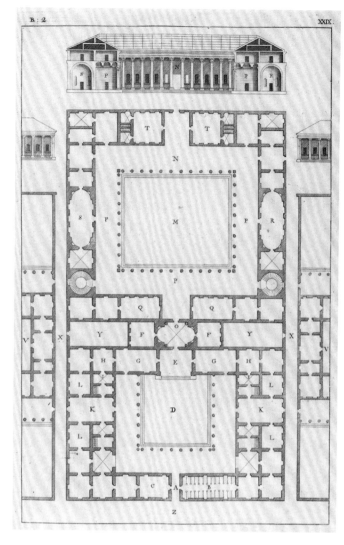

in Latin, came to light in the *tablinium*, a small private room situated between the villa's atrium and its colonnaded entrance garden, or peristyle. According to Roman tradition, the *tablinium* was the proper location for the marital bed, but by the time of the Villa of the Papyri such rooms had assumed several other functions. One was to provide a secluded space into which the master of the house could withdraw for private conversation with privileged guests. But the *tablinium* also served another purpose. It was the place to store valuable books and documents. This twin function – a small high-status private room which was also used to store the owner's books – was one which would recur many times in the centuries that followed.[3]

Despite Paderni's statement that the Herculaneum manuscripts could not be unrolled, his English translator persisted in referring to them as 'volumes', as if each was an eighteenth-century codex, with stitched pages, a spine, and front and back covers. In fact they were papyrus scrolls, in Latin *rotuli*, so severely carbonised by the heat of the pyroclastic flows from Vesuvius that they were at first assumed to be logs.[4] The scroll or roll was the usual format for books in antiquity, usually made out of papyrus from the Nile valley, the reeds sliced into thin strips which could be assembled into sheets. Scrolls were used in conjunction with codices, wooden diptychs covered with wax, which could be written on with a metal stylus, and which were useful for notes and record keeping.

In the 1750s the Royal Society was packed with wealthy aristocrats. Fellows like the Duke of Devonshire and the Earls of Macclesfield and Hardwicke all owned great libraries. They would have known from Pliny and Cicero that the ancients had also kept private libraries in their country retreats. For further information, all they had to

[16] Antonio Piaggio's machine for unrolling papyri, engraved in G. Castrucci, *Tesoro letterario di Ercolano*, Naples 1852, Table IV

[17] Palladio's reconstruction of an ancient Greek house, as published by Isaac Ware in 1738

do was refer to Isaac Ware's 1738 edition of Palladio, where plate 29 sets out Palladio's reconstruction of an ancient Greek house, complete with a peristyle and an atrium, the latter with an elliptical Library opening off it (fig.17).[5] Given the obvious parallels, it would be surprising if no one paused to wonder whether similar libraries had once existed in Roman Britain. In the absence of an avenging volcano, and in a damper climate than the Campagna, could the remnants of such a library still be lurking in a forgotten hole, waiting to be discovered? These questions still cannot be answered with certainty. It seems likely that private libraries did exist in Roman Britain, but no scrolls have ever come to light. Probably such books as existed were either imported from elsewhere in the Roman world, or were written locally on imported papyrus, rather than on parchment, a far more durable material, which climate and the abundance of suitable animals suggest should have been readily available in Britain.

There were many villas in Roman Britain, some from soon after the Roman conquest and others, like the substantial clutch around Bath and Cirencester, dating from the third and fourth centuries A D. At their grandest they were very grand indeed, with mosaics, bath houses and under-floor heating, presumably funded by the estates which surrounded them and serviced by large numbers of slaves. There is no firm evidence that these very large residences contained private libraries. However, the houses of grand provincials in other corners of the late empire certainly did. The fifth-century Gallo-Roman aristocrat Sidonius Apollinaris (c.430–89) chattered enthusiastically in his letters about his library and the libraries of his friends. These included the books in the Villa Octaviana near Narbonne and the library of Tonantius Ferreolus (c.390–453) at Prusianum, in the Gard valley. There Roman classics were arranged on one side of the room, and the Fathers of the Church on the other.[6]

The best evidence for stocks of scrolls in Roman Britannia dates from more than six hundred years after the departure of the legions. By the eleventh century the Roman city of Verulamium was virtually abandoned, a fetid slum infested by thieves and prostitutes. The monks of St Albans, building their great church in honour of the proto-martyr, decided that the nearby ruins needed to be cleared. In the remains of one building their workmen found in a wall recess 'along with a number of lesser books and rolls, a strange book-roll which had suffered but little

in spite of its great age'. It emerged that this scroll was none other than a life of St Alban, written in the language of the ancient Britons, which was read with the aid of an aged priest; the other rolls were found to be full of pagan incantations and were burned.[7] The story is easily dismissed as a pious fraud, but the fact that the books found were described as rolls suggests that it may be based on a kernel of truth.

Two hands were needed to read antique rolls, and while they were good for texts intended to be read from beginning to end, they were less convenient for those which the reader might wish to dip into, cross-referring from one part to another. The Christian scriptures are an obvious example, and indeed in late antiquity, the codex became closely associated with Christianity. The existence of Bibles in late Roman Britain can be assumed, and the commissioner of the fourth-century Hinton St Mary mosaic, which depicts the head of Christ, would have had at least one Bible in his villa. However the only written fragments which have come to light are legal, administrative or commemorative texts. Taken together, these nonetheless contain enough evidence to suggest that more extended texts circulated as well. One example is the Trawsfynydd Codex, a fragment of a wax-covered writing tablet found in a peat bog in Wales in the middle of the nineteenth century. Brought to the British Museum for identification in 2003, it contains fragments of a second-century will, whose formulaic wording suggests that standard Roman legal textbooks were in use in Roman Britain.[8]

Evidence of another kind can be found in the first- and second-century Vindolanda tablets, scraps of military and administrative records written onto wooden leaves. A phrase in one implies familiarity with a now lost text by Pliny the Elder on javelin throwing; in another it seems implicit that the children of the Roman commandant Flavius Cerialis were learning Virgil's Aeneid, as children might have done anywhere in the Roman world. Further south, the wording of a lead cursing tablet found in the Cotswolds suggests that the writer knew the work of Livy. Hearing of Julius Caesar's invasion of Britain, Cicero (106–43 BC) had sneered that the country was barely worth conquering, as there was little prospect of booty, and any slaves captured could hardly be expected to be skilled in music or literature. Martial (A D 40–c.102/4), on the other hand, joked that his verses were so popular that people were even reciting them in Britain, and indeed we know that Demetrius of Tarsus, a Greek teacher of literature, toured

Britain in about AD 83 or 84, presumably intending to sell his services to local notables. Three centuries later, the enemies of the heresiarch Pelagius (c.380–420) agreed that he came from Britain. If so, this makes him the first British author whose books survive, and his stiff but correct Latin implies the existence of a formal system of education in the last decades of Roman rule.[9]

The fourth-century villa at Low Ham in Somerset, discovered in 1938, supports this. There the floor of the *frigidarium* in the bath complex is covered by a magnificent narrative sequence from books one and four of the Aeneid (fig. 18). It is possible that the designs were derived from an imported copy book, and some commentators have argued that their intention was primarily decorative. Others have disagreed, suggesting that the mosaics, which were clearly moved from another location, were copied from a long-vanished illustrated manuscript of Virgil. Virgil is also in evidence in the villa at Otford in Kent, where fragments of a fourth-century wall painting survive labelled with a quotation, *bina manu lato crispans hastalia ferro* ('brandishing in his hand two spears of broad blade'), an obscure corner of the Aeneid, which seems to imply close familiarity with it. We are on firmer ground still with the nearby villa at Lullingstone, where a mosaic in the *triclinium*, or dining room, built in about AD 330, shows a scene from the legend of Europa and the Bull (fig. 19). This mosaic was clearly made for the place where it remains, and is labelled with a tag of poetry,

which reads in translation: 'If jealous Juno had seen the swimming of the bull, with more justification she would have gone to the home of Aeolus.' This couplet is not identifiable as the work of any known author. Stylistically it appears to be the work of an amateur poet who admired both Virgil and Ovid. If so, the villa's owner may not only have chosen his own subject matter, but knocked up his own caption, one suggesting close acquaintance with the Roman literary canon.[10]

All this is far short of the hundreds of papyrus rolls preserved at Herculaneum, but together it does support the idea that the first country house libraries in Britain were in Roman villas.

From Bede to King John

Privately owned books were clearly rare in Anglo-Saxon England, and may have been all but non-existent. Yet ironically one of the most spectacular depictions of a late antique library is to be found in an Anglo-Saxon manuscript. The monumental Codex Amiatinus is the oldest surviving near-complete manuscript of the Vulgate (fig. 15). It was made not in a villa or a private residence, but in Bede's home monastery, the Benedictine abbey of Monkwearmouth-Jarrow, just under a century after St Augustine landed in Kent in 597. Unfortunately the miniature of the prophet Ezra in his Study, his books lying flat on shelves, on their sides, tells us little or nothing about book storage in sixth-century Northumbria, as it was probably copied directly from an Italian original – perhaps the nine-volume Bible once in the library of the late Roman

[18] The mosaic floor of the *frigidarium* at Low Ham, illustrating scenes from Books 1 and 4 of the Aeneid

[19] Scene from the legend of Europa and the Bull at Lullingstone Roman villa

scholar-gentleman Cassiodorus (c.485–c.580), purchased in Italy by the abbey's founder Benedict Biscop (c.628–90) and his friend and successor Abbot Ceolfrith.[11]

By then, much had changed. From reading as a civilised leisure activity and an essential part of a literary education, when books existed at all, they were studied in the context of a curriculum which was fundamentally grounded in theology. Libraries, when they existed, were in monasteries like Monkwearmouth-Jarrow or Canterbury, rather than in private residences. A few were substantial, but most Anglo-Saxon monastic libraries will have consisted of just one or two chests of books. After the collapse of both literacy and urban life in the immediate post-Roman period, there was a modest revival of both, followed by a precipitate decline of letters in the period of the Viking attacks in the ninth and tenth centuries, to the point when some feared for the continuation of literacy even among the clergy.[12] King Athelstan (895–939), however, is known to have owned books, several of which survive today, including the late ninth- or early tenth-century Coronation Gospels, a gift from the Ottonian court, and the MacDurnan Gospels, made in Armagh and apparently a diplomatic gift

[20] A treasure binding, c.1065, on a Gospel Book belonging to Judith of Flanders (The Morgan Library, New York)

from Ireland.[13] It is interesting that just as Athelstan received both as gifts, so, too, he swiftly gave them away to the monks of Christ Church, Canterbury.[14] The same pattern, of aristocratic and gentry owners receiving or commissioning finely decorated liturgical and devotional manuscripts and then presenting them to favourite churches, was one which was repeated many times in medieval Britain.

By the early thirteenth century King John owned a library of French and Latin books, and he had clearly had a taste for books since childhood. In 1208, for example, he demanded the return of a book by Pliny from Reading Abbey, where it had been sent for safekeeping, as well as a copy of the Old Testament and contemporary scholastic texts.[15] Whether many Anglo-Norman magnates shared John's apparent tastes is doubtful. It seems fairly unlikely, though Queen Margaret of Scotland (d.1093), a descendant of the Anglo-Saxon royal house, owned a finely illuminated Gospel book, of talismanic value in an essentially pre-literate society, a book which she may have bequeathed to the monks of Durham.[16] Two more Gospel books survive which belonged to her near-contemporary Judith of Flanders (d.1094), whose first husband was Tostig Godwinson, Earl of Northumbria. They are in jewelled treasure bindings (fig. 20), whose visual effect makes it easy to understand why books around the time of the Norman Conquest were likely to be stowed in a lord's treasure hoard, along with relics and other precious objects, and were too few in number to have been regarded as a special or separate category of object.[17]

As to the use of manuscripts, it is certainly possible to imagine the after-dinner recitation of some epic like the *Chanson de Roland* in the great hall of a Norman castle, though there is little solid evidence for this.[18] It may not be a coincidence that the earliest extant manuscript of the *Chanson* appears to have been made in mid-twelfth-century England, or that the Norman invaders encountered in Anglo-Saxon England the only culture in Europe with a tradition of putting epic vernacular verse into writing.[19] King John's great-grandmother Queen Edith (d.1118) commissioned a translation of the Latin Voyage of St Brendan into French rhyming couplets, presumably for reading aloud at her court.[20] On the other hand, as Christopher de Hamel has observed, it is striking that amid all the many objects illustrated in the Bayeux Tapestry – which of course depicts ecclesiastical and state ceremonies in some detail – there is not a single book to be seen.

CHAPTER TWO

'A *study caullid Paradise*'

The Antecedents of the Country House Library, from the Thirteenth Century to the Early Tudor Period

One thing I likid exceedingly yn one of the towers,
that was a study caullid Paradise.
John Leland, *c.*1540

I · FROM MAGNA CARTA TO THE REIGN OF HENRY IV
Problems and definitions

From the thirteenth century we have more evidence for the private ownership of books, but it is patchy and can be difficult to interpret. Few books survive in or near the great houses and castles where they were kept in the Middle Ages. The largest group is perhaps from Wollaton in Nottinghamshire, where medieval manuscripts which were once in Wollaton Old Hall – the predecessor of the great Elizabethan house still standing today – survived *in situ* into modern times, before being transferred to Nottingham University Library nearby.[1] There are three manuscripts at Alnwick Castle which belonged to the Earls of Northumberland in the sixteenth century, but at least one is a recent re-acquisition. One would like to think that the seven manuscripts now at Coughton Court, Warwickshire, could have belonged to the Throckmorton family in the fourteenth or fifteenth centuries, and their appearance supports this idea (fig. 22).[2] However Coughton was sacked in 1642, when Parliamentarian troops 'burnt many popish books, some of them almost as big as we could lift with one hand', while others 'were thrown into a great moat'. On the other hand the Throckmorton's Buckinghamshire house, Weston Underwood, escaped a similar fate, so some element of continuity is possible.[3]

If books have generally vanished from houses, so, too, have the physical settings in which they were kept. There are no obvious medieval Library rooms extant in great houses, and little or nothing survives by way of fittings and furnishings. Even in ecclesiastical and collegiate settings, rooms frequently described as medieval Libraries are no such thing. The famous chained Library at Hereford was created in 1611, and its Jacobean furnishings are now in a building constructed as recently as 1996. Duke Humfrey's Library and the Library of Merton College, both in Oxford, may be medieval buildings in their bones, but their fittings and arrangement again owe more to the seventeenth century.

A good deal of information about book ownership in medieval England was abstracted from wills by Susan S. Cavanaugh in a doctoral thesis submitted in 1980, an invaluable compilation available in many research libraries. Nonetheless, Cavanaugh's survey was of necessity incomplete, being based almost entirely on records which were available in print. In any case wills only give part of the picture, and Cavanaugh herself was clear that medieval testators often omitted some or even all of their books.[4]

By comparison with France and Burgundy, medieval England produced relatively few inventories of royal and aristocratic libraries.[5] Those which exist were often created for a particular purpose, and should be interpreted accordingly. When the widowed countess Juliana de Leybourne died in 1367, an inventory was taken of the contents of her manor house at Preston-next-Wingham, in Kent. Casual readers of this would not guess that Juliana was the owner of a magnificent illuminated Apocalypse and Coronation Order, made in

[21] A lavishly-appointed medieval Study as depicted in a manuscript made for Edward IV (British Library)

De la cause de l'œuvre emprise.
Premier chapitre.

Our ce que la multi
tude des livres et la
brieueté du temps et
la foiblesse du meore
ne seuffrent pas les
choses qui sont escriptes estre com
prinses ensemble en ung courage
ce mest aduis a moy qui suis le

mendre de tous mes freres en sacre.
Et ce puis ie scauoir en moy mesmes
qui ay veu leu et retourne plusieurs
liures y moult long temps assiduele
ment et curieusement. Et neatmois
par le conseil d'aucuns de mes pl' sou
uerains et seigneurs ausquels ie
que iay esleues y mon petit engin
A bien peu de tous les liures de nře
foy catholique ou des liures payens

England between 1330 and 1339 (fig. 23). It may have been in another house at the time, or been one of the several books mentioned without further detail in her chapel, or it may already have gone to St Augustine's Abbey in Canterbury, to which Juliana bequeathed it and where she was buried.[6]

Some of the most remarkable aristocratic inventories surviving from the Middle Ages were the result of attainders. Unsurprisingly, the officials recording the goods of a man who was already dead in law tended to be preoccupied with what the goods were and what they were worth, rather than with the details which fascinate modern-day historians. The case of Sir Simon Burley (c.1336–88) illustrates this side of the coin. Burley, a man of humble origins, was raised to the ranks of the gentry through his friendship with Edward the Black Prince, becoming tutor to Richard II and one of the most influential men in England. He is known to have owned twenty-six books, mostly in French, including a book of saints' lives, religious books, chivalric romances, the prophecies of Merlin and a multi-lingual dictionary. However, we only know of these because Burley was impeached and executed in the Merciless Parliament of 1388. The episode demonstrates that much of what we know about lay ownership of books is the result of documentary accident. Unless we are prepared to believe that those who were attainted were more likely to possess books, it must follow that contemporaries who were not attainted (and for whom we have

fewer detailed inventories) are as likely to have been book owners as Richard II's disgraced tutor.[7]

Given all these problems, the sceptic might wonder what evidence we do have, and Juliana de Leybourne's Apocalypse provides the answer: we have extant books. Those which survive can be only a small proportion of those which once existed (it has been estimated that some 40,000 Missals existed in churches in England and Wales by the end of the fourteenth century; perhaps ninety now survive).[8] There is no database of medieval book owners, and the private ownership of books has received less attention than books from academic and ecclesiastical libraries. Nonetheless an appreciable number of manuscripts and printed books contain evidence of pre-Reformation aristocratic and gentry ownership. Tracing who owned what is far from straightforward, involving tracking owners through a wide range of catalogues and finding lists. Occasionally a scrap of evidence – a characteristic binding, a note in the margin or a donation inscription – betrays something of the multifarious ways in which an early owner could interact with a book. Much of this sort of evidence, however, will have been destroyed by eighteenth- and nineteenth-century collectors intent on rebinding and washing their books to produce elegant, 'clean' copies. Books which survive are widely scattered, though a large number have ended up in the great research libraries of Great Britain and North America. It is

[22] One of the seven medieval manuscripts today at Coughton Court

[23] The Apocalypse of Juliana de Leybourne, 1330–9, fol.37v (Corpus Christi College, Cambridge)

these books which have most to tell us about the prehistory of the country house library.

With important literary texts or de luxe illuminated manuscripts, scholars, curators and dealers have long taken an interest in provenance. With early printed books, matters are less straightforward. While meaningful statistical analysis is impossible, anyone with the patience to sit down and read through catalogues of manuscripts is likely to conclude that evidence of personal ownership of books is sparse before the mid-thirteenth century, thicker in the fourteenth, and fills out considerably from about 1400. Extant books are more common from England than from Scotland, Ireland and Wales, and from England more survive from the south and east of the country than from elsewhere. A significant number of books survive from a handful of aristocratic dynasties. Other families appear to have left nothing at all, often no doubt the result of historical accident – a sixteenth-century attainder, the destruction of a castle in the Civil War, or an eighteenth- or nineteenth-century house fire. The great manuscript scholar Neil Ker, writing about monastic libraries, warned of the dangers of drawing conclusions from 'the fallacious test of surviving books'. This is equally true of books in the domestic sphere.[9]

[24] An aristocratic household on the move (British Library)

Books from certain families also survive because quirks of inheritance brought them into the Old Royal Library. This near-miraculous survival from the Middle Ages, given to the British Museum by George II in 1757, contains many books of aristocratic as well as royal provenance. Surviving texts are preponderantly liturgical or devotional, and generally either in Latin or in French. As the fifteenth century progresses, we find ever more books in English, volumes on subjects as diverse as law, chivalry and medicine, and others clearly designed to be read out loud for entertainment. In Ireland and Wales, books were produced addressing more local concerns, often in the native languages of those two countries. In England the mid- and later fifteenth century saw a few tentative contacts with Renaissance Italy, as well as the advent of the printed book.

We also have to wrestle with more fundamental conceptual problems. It is easy to talk about 'libraries', and Chaucer used the word in the 1370s, but concepts of 'libraryness' may not be helpful.[10] For the most part, even when we know that a family or individual owned books, we know nothing about where they were kept, how they were arranged or even if they were in one place at all. Medieval lords, like medieval kings, seldom stayed in one place for long. The noble household, or *familia*, moved around, as lord and retinue journeyed from one residence to another. In many cases aristocratic books would have followed their owner as other household goods did, transported by officers well used to packing and unpacking (fig. 24). Liturgical books were generally kept with the accoutrements of the chapel, while devotional books might be placed in an adjacent Closet for the owner's private use. Other sorts of books might have been stowed in boxes or chests, essentially mobile items of furniture, easily moved around the house.[11] Medieval domestic buildings were inherently flexible. Even when certain chambers were in principle set aside for a particular purpose, in practice they could be furnished for a wide range of uses as need required.[12]

As Christopher de Hamel has observed, most medieval folk probably spent their whole lives without handling a book. It is tempting to infer that books were more prominent in medieval society than they really were because they have survived in large numbers compared with other luxury goods.[13] There is, however, evidence of books – and even of a few book rooms – in the medieval great house. Traditionally, manuscript specialists have concentrated first on individual books, and then on books which belonged to individuals or were made by identifiable artists and scribes. Books which belonged to a particular social category, still less books which may have been associated with a particular sort of building, have been less to the fore. In parallel, architectural historians have often been oblivious to the fact that books which once belonged to the men and women who lived in their buildings may still exist. In 1977 a consortium of archaeologists published an account of excavations at Pleshey Castle, in Essex, between 1959 and 1963. Puzzled by an unusual form of chimney, they turned to an illuminated manuscript in the Bodleian Library in Oxford (fig. 25) and found a picture of a castle with similar chimneys. Since the manuscript was made in Flanders, they concluded that the design of their chimney was northern French or Flemish in origin. Whether this was right is immaterial. What is more striking is that no one seems to have thought of the manuscript as anything other than a source for information on medieval buildings. A glance at the Bodleian's catalogue of illuminated manuscripts would have revealed something far more interesting. The manuscript with the castle with the fancy chimneys was actually *in* Pleshey Castle in the fourteenth century (see pp. 38–40).[14]

Richard de Bury and the court of Edward III

The most voracious English book collector of the Middle Ages was the churchman Richard de Bury (1287–1345), the son of a gentry family from Leicestershire, who became Bishop of Durham in 1333. De Bury was an important figure at the court of Edward III, for whom he seems to have acted as tutor, or at least as a father figure and mentor.[15] His *Philobiblon* talks at length about his passion for books and the ways in which he acquired them. It is also laced with critiques of contemporary scholarly and religious practices. Ignorant clergy who damaged books by handling them roughly, by testing their pens on the endpapers, or allowing snotty noses to drip over their pages come in for especially trenchant criticism. But nowhere does the *Philobiblon* provide the slightest hint that the laity either should or did own books.[16]

De Bury's pupil Edward III learned to write, and could read French and administrative Latin.

[25] A page from the Romance of Alexander manuscript once at Pleshey Castle (Bodleian Library)

Books available to him during his youth included Vegetius' late Roman *De Re Militari*, and the thirteenth-century *De Regimine Principum* of Giles of Rome, classic works on warfare and statecraft, both translated into Anglo-Norman.[17] He also received an illuminated manuscript of the *De Regimine* as a wedding gift from his bride Philippa of Hainault when the couple married in 1328. An example of a genre of writing known as 'mirrors of princes', this text was intended for kings and their sons, but similar works were owned by members of the aristocracy, and exercised an important influence on the education of high-born children.[18] Other books available at court included liturgical texts for the chapel and for private prayer, as well as romances containing stories culled from the Bible, the classics and Arthurian legends, usually in Anglo-Norman verse. Again these books resembled closely those owned by members of the nobility.

More strikingly, in the early part of the king's reign there was a substantial cache of 340 manuscripts and unbound quires stored at the Tower of London. The Tower served as a place for keeping records and a strongbox for royal valuables, but these books were not a working library, but rather the by-product of a long period of factional infighting. From Edward II's execution of his cousin Thomas of Lancaster in 1322 and Edward III's coup against his mother Queen Isabella and her lover Roger Mortimer in 1330 there had been a succession of executions and sequestrations, as one magnate after another fell foul of whoever was in charge. Of the 340 books and quires, some are listed by title, but most (211) are described either as 'various books' or as 'parts of books of romances'. Edward III had a policy of rehabilitating disgraced magnates, and by 1341 all but eighteen of the books had either been returned to their original owners or given away. This episode indicates the continuing value of books as gifts and the ease with which books could pass from royal to aristocratic hands, and also provides an insight into the ownership of books by great lords and their dependants.[19]

Books on the move

A Durham chronicler commented that Richard de Bury's massive collection of books would easily have filled five carts, a quantity perhaps equivalent to about 1,500 volumes.[20] At first sight the five carts

look only like a striking way of expressing the size of the bishop's collection, but it is plausible that Richard de Bury's books really were moved from place to place in carts. De Bury travelled extensively and had a large *familia* of clerks and chaplains, the ecclesiastical counterpart of the lay household of a lay magnate.[21] The royal household certainly did move books around. The pipe roll for 1203 records the cost of 'chests and carts to take the king's books overseas', and two hundred and fifty years later Edward IV had a 'carre' in which 'among other things, are caryed suche bokes as pleseth the king to studye in'.[22] It is difficult to know how this might have worked in practice, but since the functioning of noble households changed slowly over the centuries, the household ordinances issued by the 5th Earl of Northumberland in 1512 provide a possible illustration. The earl's household was vast, and it included an ecclesiastical retinue of priests, children and gentlemen of the chapel, as well as numerous gentlemen and yeomen attendants. Custom dictated that seventeen 'carrages' or two-wheeled carts were required 'at every remevall' to shift the goods proper to the various household members. In addition to bedding and other necessaries, the ordinances specify the space that was required for tools and other specialist equipment. Finally, they mention that certain officials had 'a Gret Standert Chist for carrying of ther Bookes with them'. In this case the books were clearly administrative records like account books, but the entry confirms that the books frequently mentioned in inventories of the

[26] Wooden chest made in England in about 1340 formerly in the Chancery Court at Durham (Burrell Collection, Glasgow)

dead could be and probably were moved around on carts.[23]

A good number of medieval chests survive, though it can be difficult to be sure precisely what they were used for. There are numerous examples in the National Archives in London, and they, at least, can generally be associated with the history of record keeping. A spectacular example is now in the Burrell Collection in Glasgow: a large plank-built chest made in England in about 1340, which was for many centuries in the Chancery Court at Durham.[24] It has iron banding, locks and carrying handles, and the inside of the lid is magnificently painted with four coats of arms, one of which is the arms of Richard de Bury as Bishop of Durham (fig. 26). The Durham chest is extremely large and heavy, but given the quantity of muscle available to shift it onto the back of a cart, its use for moving manuscripts or administrative records around the country cannot be ruled out. There is a smaller and plainer example at Hereford Cathedral – an early fourteenth-century chest made of poplar wood, with rings at either end for carrying poles (fig. 27). The pioneering library historian Burnett Hillman Streeter (1874–1937) had 'no doubt' that it was part of the travelling library of a medieval bishop. To prove his point, he referred to the description of an apparently similar chest in a mid-fifteenth-century inventory from the great Beauchamp collegiate church, St Mary's, Warwick: an 'old irebound cofre having hie feet and rings of iron in the endes thereof to heve it bye. And therein liuth certein bokes belonging to the Chapter.'[25]

Chests could also provide static storage for books. Richard de Bury described with delight his raids on chests of long-slumbering books housed in monasteries.[26] As late as 1513, the 13th Earl of Oxford had 'a Chest full of frenshe and englisshe books' stored in his chapel at the recently renovated Hedingham Castle in Essex, alongside the liturgical books and chapel furnishings.[27] Such chests might be internally subdivided, for easier storage. In another later example an inventory of 1566 from Appuldurcombe House on the Isle of Wight mentions 'A Spruce Chest wth divers boxes in hym'. This chest may already have been old in 1566, and the inventory is clearly describing what archivists call *pyxides*, record boxes fitted snugly inside larger cupboards or containers, a phenomenon still visible in fifteenth-century muniment rooms like that in the tower at Magdalen College,

[27] An early fourteenth-century poplar chest with carrying pole at Hereford Cathedral, photographed in use for B.H. Streeter

Oxford.[28] Another example points not just to the connection between chests and record keeping, but also to one reason why books may be less common in early inventories than they were in reality. When in 1566 the compilers of an inventory of Lord de la Warr's house at Offington in Sussex reached a large chest in a gallery leading to the chapel, they were clearly refused access to it, noting laconically: 'not praysed because there are evidences in them'.[29] Administrative records – evidences – and perhaps books, too, were precious, valuable and liable to be regarded as private.

Books for magnates and gentry

The medieval court was a centre of education and cultural exchange. Aristocratic children and royal wards completed their education there, and the heirs of magnates spent time in the royal household and in other noble households.[30] Royal offspring themselves became magnates, intermarrying with members of aristocratic dynasties and founding dynasties of their own. The fourteenth-century Dukes of Lancaster, for example, were descended from a younger son of Henry III, while Edward III and Henry IV both fathered a quiverful of sons. To this extent the books owned by kings and their families provide a context for book ownership by great magnates.

If we know little about where fourteenth-century magnates kept their books, for the most part a distinction was clearly drawn between liturgical and devotional books and secular texts such as romances or chivalric tales. In 1322 Joan Mortimer, Countess of March (d. 1356), had a Psalter and four volumes of secular romances at Wigmore Castle in Herefordshire. Roger, Lord de la Warr (d. 1370), bequeathed to his third wife Eleanor all the books in his chapel as well as the romances which were kept in his private apartment, but these were to revert to the family on his death. On a more modest scale, Henry, Lord Percy (d. 1352), owned both a Psalter and a Bestiary, in French; he may indeed have owned other books as well.

This was a bilingual or even trilingual world, where Latin, French and English co-existed. Depending on education, gender and social status, members of the nobility and gentry might be more or less familiar with all three, and likely to use them for those purposes judged appropriate for each. In Ireland, Wales and Scotland other languages might be added to the mix. Literacy is difficult to define, and the concept is more culturally determined than is sometimes acknowledged. Readers can be literate in one language but not another. They may be able to read but not write, and they may associate the very concept of literacy with particular sorts of texts. In medieval England a *litteratus* was fundamentally a man with letters, in other words one with at least a minimal ability to read Latin. But this term was easily conflated with *clericus* (clerk in modern English), and in practice a *clericus* was

liable to be described as a *litteratus*, and a *laicus* was an *illiteratus*, potentially a source of serious misapprehension in medieval documents.[31] Nonetheless it is striking that when thirteen Norfolk gentleman who were asked during a late thirteenth-century legal dispute whether they could read an entry in a chronicle, ten asserted that they could and two admitted that they could not (the reading ability of the thirteenth is unrecorded).[32] For those unable to handle the necessary languages, help could be provided: for example the earliest extant English Book of Hours has prayers added in French to assist its female owner in navigating the Latin text.[33]

Links with France continued to be important. It is a measure of the relative size of the book trade on either side of the Channel that we know the names of fifty-eight booksellers in thirteenth-century Paris but none at all in London before 1312.[34] Many books were imported from France, not just to England and Wales, but also to Scotland and Ireland. One striking example is the magnificent Breviary (fig. 28) made in Paris between about 1330 and 1342 for the French-born Marie de St Pol (d. 1377), widow of Aymer de Valence, Earl of Pembroke and founder of Pembroke College, Cambridge. It may well have been commissioned

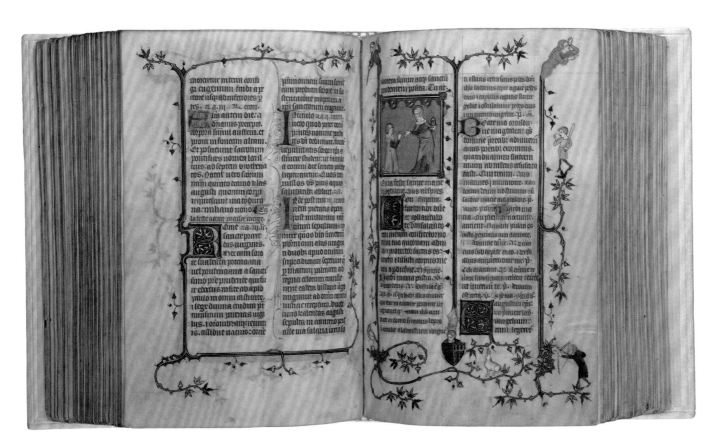

in France via her sister.[35] Luxury manuscripts could also cross the Channel in other ways. One of the most spectacular examples is the great *Bible historiale* (fig. 29) of John II of France (1319–64) captured at the Battle of Poitiers in 1356. It ended up in the hands of the English commander William Montagu, 2nd Earl of Salisbury (1328–97). Later still, the bulk of the French royal library was seized from the Louvre by Henry v's younger brother John, Duke of Bedford (1389–1435), Regent of France for the young Henry vi, taken to Rouen, and then on to London.[36]

Liturgical and devotional books

In the fourteenth century the most common books for magnates and gentry alike were Psalters, derived from liturgical texts but equally suitable for personal use. From the mid-thirteenth century Books of Hours became popular, and by the fifteenth century they were ubiquitous. Earlier generations might have owned an Apocalypse, depicting the tribulations of the last days. These were liable to be richly decorated and might contain inscriptions, dynastic coats of arms and family obits, to allow prayer for family members on the anniversaries of their death.[37] All are likely to have formed part of the prayer regime of a devout layman or woman. Joan, Lady Cobham (1314–43), is memorialised at prayer on a fourteenth-century brass at Cobham church in Kent, and the bishop who preached her funeral sermon noted that 'on no day would she willingly come down from her chamber or speak with any stranger, until she had said matins and the Hours of our Lady, the Seven Psalms, and the Litany'. During the silent parts of the mass she would also say private prayers from her Book of Hours, as well as 'some Paternosters and Hail Maries'.[38] To use a Book of Hours or Psalter meant more than simply reading the text, but savouring it at length, using the illuminated miniatures and historiated initials (perhaps images of the Virgin, the sufferings of Christ, and the saints) as the focus for prayer and meditation.[39] As late as the 1530s, the Carthusian author of a printed devotional manual, *The Pomander of Prayer*, recommended books even to those who could not read them, particularly commending 'lyttel books in the whiche is conteyned pictures of the articles of the lyfe and passion on our Lorde Jesu'.[40]

Since devotional and liturgical books allowed members of the laity to participate vicariously in

[29] *Bible historiale* of John II of France, fol. 1r (British Library)

[30] The Murthly Hours, c.1280, fol. 149v (National Library of Scotland)

the religious life of monastics, it is unsurprising that they were often bequeathed to religious houses. In 1422 John Booth of Barton, Lancashire, an ancestor of the owners of Dunham Massey, bequeathed a large Missal to Eccles church. He also reserved a smaller one for his son.[41] In 1399 Eleanor, Duchess of Gloucester, left a collection of seven books in French to her daughter, a nun in London: a striking example of the transmission of books along lines of kinship and friendship.[42] The Grey-Fitzpayn Hours (c.1315–30; fig. 31) were perhaps made to celebrate the marriage between Joan Clifford of Frampton and John de Pabenham (d.1331) in 1314, members of two Norfolk gentry families.[43] Such richly illuminated religious books may have been conceived as acts of prayer in their own right, with the images of the Virgin and the saints continuing to pray for the owner even after the book was put away. After the owner's death the books reminded his or her descendants, or the clergy of a favourite church, to pray for his or her soul. When the Lincolnshire knight Sir Thomas Cumberworth died in 1450, for example, he divided his devotional books between his chantry priests and three local parish priests.[44]

In a high-status house, Psalters and Books of Hours would often have been read in a Closet, a private space originally no more than a fabric enclosure, in or overlooking a private chapel. At Bodiam Castle in Sussex, begun in about 1385, Sir Edward Dalyngrigge's chapel was overlooked on the south side by a window which gave onto an adjacent chamber, probably a bedchamber.

There was also a window looking onto the chapel from a neighbouring small oratory which led off this chamber.[45] Fashions changed slowly, and the ruins of the chapel at Ashby de la Zouch Castle in Leicestershire, built for Edward IV's favourite William, Lord Hastings, have holes in the wall which seem to have supported balcony closets. That on the first floor once connected through to the castle's great chamber.[46] At the palatial early Tudor house at Westhorpe, built for Henry VIII's favourite Charles Brandon, Duke of Suffolk (c.1484–1545), there was 'a chapel above a fare closett with ij wyndowes openynge in to the said chapell'.[47] Illuminated miniatures of the Virgin at prayer, like that in the magnificent fifteenth-century Book of Hours which belonged to Margaret Beauchamp (1405/6–82), probably give as good an impression as any of the opulence of a grand late medieval chapel Closet.[48]

Quite ordinary gentry families might own spectacular devotional manuscripts. One of the most famous is the Luttrell Psalter, begun before 1340 for the Lincolnshire knight Sir Geoffrey Luttrell (1276–1345) of Irnham, Lincolnshire, who had fought in Edward I's wars with Scotland and was associated with Henry III's grandson Thomas of Lancaster (c.1278–1322). Obits in the calendar suggest that the Psalter swiftly passed through several sets of hands, including those of Richard Fitzalan, 3rd Earl of Arundel (1313–76), and Joan, Countess of Hereford (1347–1419), wife of Humphrey de Bohun, a member of a family noted for its interest in fine manuscripts.[49] Another example is the Madresfield Hours, a fourteenth-century English Book of Hours in its original chemise binding, which was originally made for the North Country gentlewoman Maud de Tilliol (d.1343) of Scalesby in Cumberland. Like the Luttrell Psalter it subsequently passed into other hands: in this case to members of the Neville and Scrope families in the fifteenth century.[50]

Nor was this confined to England. The Murthly Hours (fig. 30), a manuscript once believed to have been made in medieval Scotland, is now thought to be a composite work made in Paris and England round about 1280. Its original owner may have been Joan de Valence (sister-in-law of Marie de St Pol), who certainly had books in her household chapel at Bampton in the 1290s. However, manuscript additions, some in Scots Gaelic, show that it was in Scotland by the late fourteenth or early fifteenth

[31] The Grey-Fitzpayn Hours, c.1315–30 (Fitzwilliam Museum, Cambridge), perhaps made to celebrate the marriage of two Norfolk gentry families

century. It remained in Perthshire in the hands of the descendants of Sir John Stewart, Lord of Lorne (d. 1421), until 1871.[51] A Flemish Psalter of about 1300 survives in the library at Traquair House, another Stewart house, in Peeblesshire. It has been in the hands of the same family since at least the early fifteenth century, and may indeed once have belonged to the same early owners as the Murthly Hours.[52]

Histories, chronicles and romances

If Books of Hours were intended for private meditation, wills and inventories provide evidence of the popularity of books of a different kind: histories, chronicles and romances. The categories involve a degree of overlap, as histories and chronicles could be in any language, while romances were by definition *en romanz*, in other words in the romance language now called French, as opposed to formal, written Latin.[53] While these books might have been used for private reading, they were also suitable to be read out loud, either to an individual or to a small group assembled in a lordly chamber in a castle or manor house. The author of the Romance of Horn, a late twelfth-century Anglo-Norman adventure story, went so far as to begin his tale with the words 'my lords, you have heard the lines of parchment', as if the manuscript itself was addressing its hearers.[54] Histories and chronicles, as the Venerable Bede had noted centuries before, were valued because they provided readers and hearers with examples of virtue for emulation, as well as exposing the misdeeds of the wicked as an exhortation to avoid sin. In recounting the story of humankind from the beginning – drawing on the Bible, classical historians like Caesar, Suetonius and Livy, and stories and examples derived from Christian authors like Augustine or Eusebius, the lives of the saints, or the adventures of Arthurian knights – such books set the entire history of creation in a specifically Christian context.

An early and striking example of this comes from the forty-two books which Guy de Beauchamp, 10th Earl of Warwick (*c.*1272–1315), gave to the Cistercian Abbey of Bordesley in Worcestershire in 1305. Guy was the implacable enemy of Piers Gaveston, who nicknamed him 'Black Dog of Arden' and paid with his life for the insult when Guy was instrumental in the execution of Edward II's favourite in 1312. Despite or perhaps because of this episode, Guy de

Beauchamp was described by contemporaries as a man of probity and wisdom. His books included an Arthurian romance about Lancelot, saints' lives, and the histories of Titus and Vespasian and the Jewish revolt against Rome. Books of more specifically English interest ranged from a life of the royal saint Edward the Confessor to a biography of Henry II's illegitimate son William Longespée (*c.*1176–1226). There was also a copy of the *Brut*, a popular Norman-French verse chronicle of the history of Britain from the time of the mythical Brute the Trojan, based on the *Historia Regum Britanniae* of Geoffrey of Monmouth (*c.*1100–*c.*1155). Some of these books seem rather strange gifts for an abbey of Cistercian monks, suggesting either that Guy was disposing of books that were no longer needed, or that the act of giving was as important as any use which might subsequently be made of them. At any event, the forty-two books which he gave in his own lifetime probably represent only a portion of the books which he actually owned.[55]

Books at Pleshey Castle

The scanty remains of Pleshey Castle stand a little way to the north-west of Chelmsford. Very little of it survives, but in the thirteenth and fourteenth centuries Pleshey was the principal residence of the Bohuns, Earls of Hereford and Essex, and descendants of Edward I in the female line. The detailed history of the Bohun family has no place here, but three facts are worth outlining. Firstly, members of the family collected and commissioned fine manuscripts over an extended period of time. Secondly, when Humphrey de Bohun, 7th Earl of Hereford, died in 1373, he was succeeded as Lord of Pleshey by Thomas of Woodstock, Duke of Gloucester, the owner of the Bodleian Romance of Alexander manuscript (see fig. 25). Thomas married the heiress Eleanor de Bohun, taking over the castle and with it the substantial library that was already in place. He was attainted by his nephew Richard II in 1397, and because of this we have a uniquely rich record of the castle and its contents, including 124 books. Thirdly, Eleanor's younger sister Mary was married in 1380 to Henry Bolingbroke, the son of Thomas's younger brother, who usurped the crown from Richard II in 1399 and became Henry IV. Henry, his wife Mary de Bohun (*c.*1368–94) and his three sons Henry V, John Duke of Bedford and Humfrey Duke of Gloucester were all notable for their interest in books.

Not only are the Pleshey books well documented, but an appreciable number survive. In addition to books which are known to have been in the castle, there are least eleven extant manuscripts which were actually made or altered there for various members of the Bohun family.[56] These books were the product of a manuscript atelier in the castle, a unique arrangement so far as documentary evidence is concerned, but something which could have been quite common. We even know the names of some of those who made the manuscripts, including three household clerks, Piers, Martin and Robin, and the Augustinian Friar John de Teye, who in 1384 asked permission from the head of his order to bring another friar, Henry Hood, to Pleshey to learn the art of illuminating books. The illuminators seem to have enjoyed a close relationship with their patrons, as John de Teye is mentioned prominently in the 6th Earl's will (1361) and a miniature in the Egerton Psalter, now in the British Library, depicts the illuminator as a monkey playing with a bear (the scribe) and a lion (the 7th Earl of Hereford): a piece of jesterly teasing which can only have occurred in the context of friendly relations between employer and employee (fig. 32).[57]

Other manuscripts are extant which can be mapped against Thomas of Woodstock's inventory, some of them described as 'old' and evidently inherited from his wife's Bohun forebears. Among the most famous of these is the so-called Alphonso Psalter. Originally made for Edward I's short-lived

third son Alphonso (d. 1284), it was inherited after his death by his sister Elizabeth, who married Humphrey de Bohun, 4th Earl of Hereford (c.1276–1322), in 1302. This and other liturgical manuscripts give a sense of the splendour of the castle chapel at Pleshey, where the holdings of books equalled those of a large parish or collegiate church. The secular manuscripts were equally impressive. As well as the Romance of Alexander ('un large livre en Fraunceis tresbien esluminez'; see fig. 25), there was an equally grandiose *Roman de la Rose*. This was made in Paris between 1320 and 1340 and sold to Thomas by the executors of its previous owner Sir Richard Stury (c.1327–95), a household knight and trusted adviser to Edward III and Richard II.[58] Another manuscript, Brunetto Latini's *Le Livre du Trésor*, made in Italy in the French style, was given to Thomas of Woodstock by William Montagu, 2nd Earl of Salisbury – the same man who had earlier acquired the French royal *Bible historiale* (see fig. 29) seized at the Battle of Poitiers.[59]

We do not know what the Library was like at Pleshey, if indeed it was a room at all. The royal escheators who took the 1397 inventory were interested in the value of the books rather than their arrangement. They were, however, set out in two separate lists: those 'for the chapel' (forty books) and 'various romances and narratives' (eighty-four), so liturgical books and library books were recognised as being different. To go further than this, the best we can do is refer to some parallel cases. Two years earlier, in 1395, Thomas of Woodstock's nephew Richard II, delighted at the gift of a luxurious illuminated book by the chronicler Froissart, perused it for some while with the author in his outer chamber. According to Froissart, the king then directed a knight of his chamber to take the manuscript 'in to his secrete chamber'.[60] In other words this particular book was to be kept, or at least enjoyed, in a small private room adjacent to the main royal apartment. Other books may perhaps have been there, too. Another pointer comes from Richard II's nemesis Henry Bolingbroke. On seizing the throne as Henry IV, Bolingbroke almost immediately started work on a lavishly appointed 'new study' in his country retreat at Eltham, a project which ran from 1399 to 1407. The earliest known English royal Library (at least as a room), the Study was equipped with a desk for books, and boasted a ceiling decorated with figures

[32] Miniature in the Egerton Psalter, 1356–73, fol. 32v, showing the illuminator as a monkey playing with a bear scribe and the lion 7th Earl of Hereford (British Library)

of angels and windows glazed with images of the saints.[61]

For insights into book storage we can also turn to illuminations in manuscripts. An early four-teenth-century manuscript of the *Roman de Troie* – admittedly Italian and not English – tells the story of the mythical Cornelius, nephew of Sallust, who finds a cupboard full of ancient Trojan romances while hunting for a grammar. The accompanying miniature (fig. 33) shows a sturdy rectangular piece of furniture with doors and, inside, four shelves. The romances within lie flat on the shelves: their pages face outwards, though it is difficult to see whether they are bound or are in unbound quires.[62] For such an arrangement to be viable a household would have needed enough books for them to be seen as a distinct category of object which merited distinct storage arrangements. At Pleshey it seems clear that books were numerous enough for this to have been the case. Elsewhere, books in noble households may have been numbered at most in dozens, and often in handfuls.

II · FROM HENRY IV TO THE DISSOLUTION

The Lancastrians and their courtiers

Descended through their mother from an especially bookish family, Henry IV's children continued the trait into the fifteenth century. Henry V had acquired a substantial library by the time of his death in 1422, while his youngest brother Humfrey, Duke of Gloucester (1390–1447), was a pioneering collector of humanist manuscripts and a benefactor

of the University of Oxford. Another brother, John of Lancaster, 1st Duke of Bedford (1389–1435), was Regent of France for his infant nephew Henry VI, but is at least as well known for his taste in luxury illuminated manuscripts.[63] The most famous of these is perhaps the extraordinarily lavish Bedford Hours, presented by Duke John and his wife Anne of Burgundy to King Henry at Christmas 1430.[64] Bedford also seized books from the French royal collections after 1422. One of them is the so-called Paris Apocalypse, made perhaps in Salisbury in about 1250, which subsequently belonged to Charles V and Charles VI of France.[65] The French royal books were shifted from Paris to Rouen after 1429, but by 1435 they were in London, where they were described as 'a greet librarie that cam owte of France'. None of the dozen or so books made or adapted for Bedford and his wife are listed in the inventories made after his death. Once again, however, it is striking that the Bedfords' chapel books and library books were evidently thought of as being separate.

French influences of another kind came to bear through the twenty-five-year captivity of Charles d'Orléans (1394–1465). Captured at Agincourt, from 1417 the Valois prince of the blood was in the custody of a series of English nobles, including Sir Nicholas Montgomery of Tutbury, Sir Thomas Comberworth of Bolingbroke Castle and William de la Pole, 1st Duke of Suffolk (1396–1450). Charles repeatedly travelled to and from London and his captors' country seats, and assembled a fine library while in England, a collection which went on to form the nucleus of the future French royal library, replacing that taken by the Duke of Bedford.[66] Of his captors, Comberworth owned both devotional books and a manuscript of Chaucer's Canterbury Tales, but the connection with the de la Poles, a new family who also owned great houses at Wingfield in Suffolk and Ewelme in Oxfordshire, is more intriguing. A favourite of Henry VI, William de la Pole, 1st duke of Suffolk, was beheaded in 1450, but his widow Alice, granddaughter of Chaucer, lived on until 1475. In 1542 Ewelme Palace was described by John Leland as 'exceeding fair and lightsum', and a pair of inventories compiled in 1466 give an impression of the richness of its fifteenth-century contents. Unfortunately, this impression is only partial, as the inventories record just a limited number of chattels, some of which had apparently recently been transferred to Ewelme from Wingfield Castle. These included twenty-two books which were listed alongside the chapel goods, though by no means all of them were religious. A hint of their possible deployment comes from the list of rooms in the palace, which as well as a chapel included a 'gentlewomen's closet', 'my ladies closet' and 'my lordes chamber', complete with an attached wardrobe.[67] The books themselves were predominantly liturgical texts, including a Missal, Antiphoners and Graduals, bound to match in 'white lether'. There was also a volume of music ('a large boke of priked songe bounden and covered in rede lether and closped wᵗ latom'), as well as a life of St Radegund, a copy of the romance *Les Quatre Fils d'Aymon* (a text subsequently printed by Caxton) and a manuscript of the *Cité des Dames* (1430) by Christine de Pizan. Some books had metal bosses, or were covered in black damask. Most were evidently written on parchment, though one book, the translation (1426) of the Pilgrimage of the Life of Man by the Benedictine poet John Lydgate (*c*.1370–*c*.1451), was on paper.[68]

Others owned books selected for practical utility. In the early years of the fifteenth century a bound compilation of documents on politics, legislation and royal ceremonial was in the hands of a member of the Mowbray family. It may have been made for Thomas Mowbray, 1st Duke of Norfolk (1366–99), who became Earl Marshal in 1386.[69] Thomas's son John Mowbray, 2nd Duke of Norfolk (1392–1432), owned a manuscript of Thomas Hoccleve's Regimen of Princes, now in the British Library. Hoccleve's poem offers advice on kingly conduct, and the manuscript may have been commissioned

for the duke's coming of age in 1413. An illuminated miniature in it depicts him kneeling at the feet of Henry V to receive it.[70]

Books were not the exclusive preserve of very grand folk. In 1415 officials investigating the possessions of the attainted traitor, Henry le Scrope, a former favourite of Henry V, found a translation of the book of Genesis in French in his manor house at Faxflete in Yorkshire. His will shows that he owned many other books (the wording of the will suggests that they were not all listed in it): there were at least thirty-seven, as well as about a dozen chapel books. As at Ewelme, they were mostly religious and liturgical books, and they included Missals, an illuminated Apocalypse, books of homilies and meditations, a glossed Psalter, and a Psalter illuminated with the Scrope arms. The Apocalypse was bound in linen, a book of meditations in red cloth from Cyprus, and a Bible in red leather.[71]

Fifteenth-century English humanists

We move into rather different territory with the handful of fifteenth-century magnates who cultivated links with Renaissance Italy. John Tiptoft, 1st Earl of Worcester (1427–70), born into a Cambridgeshire gentry family, was an accomplished Latinist, a graduate of the University of Oxford and a ruthless henchman of Edward IV, executed on the short-lived return of Henry VI in 1470. After a pilgrimage to the Holy Land, Tiptoft spent two years studying civil law in Padua between about 1459 and 1461. He also visited Rome and Florence, commissioning books from Vespasiano da Bisticci (1421–98), the Florentine book dealer who advised Cosimo de' Medici. According to his friend Ludovico Carbone (1430–85), Tiptoft 'despoiled the libraries of Italy so that he might adorn England with handsome monuments of books'. Thirty-one of his books have been identified, along with several 'possibles'. Despite a few Books of Hours and a manuscript of John Lydgate, they are overwhelmingly classical.[72] Four very elegant humanistic manuscripts now in Oxford are typical, all made in Padua or Ferrara at the time of Tiptoft's stay in Italy: Basino of Parma's *Astronomica*, a manuscript of Lucretius, a commentary by Ognibene da Lonigo (1412–*c*.1500) on the Satires of Juvenal, and a manuscript of the Histories of Tacitus, an author little known in the Middle Ages and rediscovered by Giovanni Boccaccio (1313–75). Merely to read their titles shows that we are in a different world from that represented by the library of John, Duke of Bedford, just a few years earlier.[73]

If we do not know where Tiptoft kept his books, the more famous library of Humfrey, Duke of Gloucester, appears to have been lodged at Bella Court, his Thameside mansion at Greenwich, six miles downstream from London. Details of the library are still being uncovered, but it is clear that in fifteenth-century England it was something new in scale and in conception. The books which he gave to the University of Oxford were said to have been worth a thousand marks, a vague figure, but indicative at least of contemporary perceptions of the scale and magnificence of the donation. Humfrey apparently donated 274 books, but he may have retained anything up to 700 more for his own use at Greenwich. To date, just 47 have come to light, though further discoveries seem likely. Humfrey typically inscribed his books with a grandiloquent ex libris, which tends to begin 'Cest livre est a moy Humfrey duc de gloucestre', but there were systematic attempts to remove his ownership marks

from the books after his death.[74] The villain of the piece appears to have been Henry VI's physician John Somerset (d.1454), who wrote and collected medical treatises, and passed the life of a country gentleman at Osterley in Middlesex when not at his house in London.[75]

Duke Humfrey's library was clearly rich and varied, and supported by an active programme of book acquisitions in Italy. The duke retained an Italian humanist secretary from the mid-1430s, the Ferrarese Tito Livio Frulovisi (c.1400–after 1456), who was employed as a poet and orator, and also to write a biography of Humfrey's older brother Henry V.[76] One of Humfrey's most famous manuscripts is his Pliny of about 1440, written in Italy at the duke's request by Pietro Candido Decembrio (1399–1477), who was paid an annual stipend of 100 ducats in return for sending a selection of Latin classical texts to England (it is unclear how many were actually sent).[77] However, not all of Duke Humfrey's manuscripts were learned books, not all came from Italy, and not all of them were

[34] The Ellesmere Chaucer, fol. 169r (Huntington Library, San Marino)

[35] The Petworth Chaucer, c.1420–30

of recent manufacture. Others included a twelfth-century Hebrew Psalter, now in Leiden, and a thirteenth-century bestiary, now in Los Angeles.[78] *Les Grandes Chroniques de France* (Paris, c.1332–40), commissioned by John II of France, was another piece of Hundred Years War booty.[79] Humfrey also owned an important manuscript of Matthew Paris's *Historia Anglorum*, made in St Albans in about 1250, which included portraits of the Anglo-Norman kings and a map of an itinerary to the Holy Land.[80]

Books in English
(and other vernacular languages)

None of the Duke Humfrey manuscripts so far identified is in English, but his lifetime coincided with the rise of English as a literary language, with dramatic implications for the private ownership of books.[81] The most magnificent surviving manuscript of Geoffrey Chaucer, a prime mover in this change, is the Ellesmere Chaucer (fig. 34), so called because of its association for many

centuries with the library of Sir Thomas Egerton (1540–1617), whose descendants became the Earls of Ellesmere. Unlike most Chaucer manuscripts, it is lavishly illustrated and was clearly intended for an aristocratic patron, perhaps John de Vere, 12th Earl of Oxford (1408–62), a Lancastrian supporter executed on the orders of John Tiptoft.[82] About eighty Chaucer manuscripts survive, around half of which have some evidence of their fifteenth-century owners. If their social origins seem varied, some of the manuscripts at least were in the hands of noble and gentry owners. Caxton borrowed a Chaucer manuscript from an unknown 'gentleman' to collate his first printed edition of the *Canterbury Tales* in 1478. Henry VII's mother, Lady Margaret Beaufort, bequeathed a manuscript to her chamberlain in 1509, while Sir William Cavendish (1505–57), ancestor of the Dukes of Devonshire, had another at his house at North Awbrey in Lincolnshire in 1540, seven years before he married Bess of Hardwick.[83] The magnificent example at Petworth (c.1420–30; fig. 35) passed by descent through the Percy Earls of Northumberland from the late fifteenth century. If less lavish than the Ellesmere manuscript, it is a large and handsome book, with decorated initials and margins ornamented with sprays of leaves and flowers. It is also one of very few medieval books which have remained *in situ* in a house where it might have been used in the Middle Ages, though in the fifteenth century the Percys were based in the north of England, and Petworth was a secondary residence. The Petworth Chaucer's precise origins are unclear, but the addition after 1474 of the arms of the 4th Earl of Northumberland (c.1449–89) on the verso of the final leaf suggests it may have been acquired by him.[84]

Until its sale in 1928, another important Middle English manuscript, of the Benedictine poet John Lydgate, sat alongside the Chaucer at Petworth.[85] A second Lydgate manuscript (fig. 36), which undoubtedly belonged to the 4th Earl of Northumberland, subsequently found its way into the Old Royal Library, where it remains. In its original form it included his Troy Book and his Siege of Thebes, but it was expanded with the addition of further texts under the 5th Earl. Its original owner was the 4th Earl's father-in-law, the Anglo-Welsh magnate William, 1st Earl of Pembroke (c.1423–69), executed by Warwick the Kingmaker after the Battle of Edgecote Moor. Ironically enough, one of the texts added by the 5th Earl, an elegy by the poet

John Skelton, commemorates yet another fifteenth-century violent death, the lynching of the 4th Earl of Northumberland by a York mob in 1489. The manuscript thus illustrates the history and vicissitudes of a powerful aristocratic dynasty over a period of nearly a century.[86]

Other manuscripts relate to rites of passage of a less bloody kind. One example is a composite volume now at Trinity College, Cambridge, created in the 1480s or 1490s as the direct result of a marriage between two East Anglian gentry families. The first part, which includes copies in the same hand as Lydgate's Troy Book and Siege of Thebes, had previously belonged to the family of the Norfolk gentleman John Thwaites (1457–1507). The second, the Romaunce of Generydes, the tale of Generides, the mythical son of a King of India, came from the family of his new wife Anne Knyvett (d.1541).[87]

One of the most remarkable Middle English manuscripts is the so-called Vernon manuscript, named after the family which owned it in the seventeenth century. Made perhaps between about 1390 and 1400, it contains a huge collection of English prose and poetry. Incomplete though it is, it weighs in at a hefty 22 kilos. In its original form it had over 420 leaves, a book so enormous that it must have been kept on some sort of lectern, and which, because of its size and numerous illustrations, was especially suitable for display. (The term 'coucher book', first recorded in 1434, is sometimes used for a book whose size meant that it had to be laid flat or propped up to be read at all. The term is especially associated with the north of England. Elsewhere, the term 'ledger' was preferred.) The Vernon manuscript's origins are mysterious, and there is no consensus as to whether it was made for a layman or for a religious house. A blank coat of arms (fol. 150r) may suggest that it was originally destined for an armigerous owner. At any event it certainly originated in the West Midlands, and there may be a connection with Sir William Beauchamp, younger brother of the 13th Earl of Warwick. A similar though smaller manuscript, sold in 1937 from Chillington Hall in Staffordshire and now split between libraries in London, Washington and Princeton, belonged to the Warwickshire landowner Sir Nicholas Clopton, a Beauchamp retainer. Intriguingly, it also contains the arms of two other local gentry families, the Crewes and the Throckmortons of Coughton.[88] Another important

manuscript of Middle English verse, made in the 1330s and now in the British Library, seems to have been in the possession of a family in the Welsh Marches, perhaps the Talbots of Richards Castle. Since the pastedowns of the binding were taken from an account book of the 1st Earl of March, there may also have been some connection with the Mortimers of Wigmore.[89]

Vernacular books were not necessarily secular books. Joan, Countess of Kent (1328–85), owned a copy of the Carthusian Nicholas Love's Lyf of Jesu Christ. A century later Elizabeth de Vere, Countess of Oxford (d.1537), by birth a member of the Scrope family (and the widow of a patron of Caxton and possible early owner of the Ellesmere manuscript), owned a manuscript devotional manual. With its description of the Passion, and its practical advice on achieving a pious death, the manuscript highlights the devotional preoccupations of the fifteenth century.[90]

English was not the only vernacular language. In Ireland the Book of Mac Carthaigh Riabach (McCarthy Reagh in English orthography) was written between 1478 and 1506 for Fínghin Mac Carthaigh Riabach, the powerful Prince of Carbery, of Kilbrittain Castle in south-west Cork. A compendium of mostly earlier Irish texts, it includes saints' lives, religious texts, tales of ancient kings and heroes, as well as translations into Irish of the histories of Charlemagne and Marco Polo. The Book of Mac Carthaigh Riabach is one of several similar manuscripts made for late medieval Irish and Hiberno-Norman families: other examples include the mostly fifteenth-century Book of Fermoy, made for the Roche family, again in County Cork.[91] It remained at Kilbrittain until the castle was captured in 1642. The book was then seized by the sons of the Protestant Richard Boyle, 1st Earl of Cork (1566–1643), finding its way to the Boyle stronghold of Lismore Castle (from which it takes its alternative title, 'the Book of Lismore') before passing by descent to the Devonshires at Chatsworth, where it remains. Whether it was the only book at Kilbrittain Castle, or one of many, is impossible to say.[92]

In mid-fifteenth-century Wales Ieuan ap Phylip, constable of Cefnllys Castle in Radnorshire, owned a manuscript containing four poems addressed to him and his wife Angharad by the itinerant bard Lewys Glyn Cothi (c.1420–90). These include a description of the couple's new hall at Cefnllys, which the poet compared to Ehangwen, the mythical hall of King Arthur.[93] In Scotland the fifteenth-century Hay Manuscript includes translations from French into Scots of a range of texts on chivalry, knighthood and kingship, and was written probably for Oliver Sinclair of Roslin, second son of William, Lord Sinclair. It subsequently caught the eye of Sir Walter Scott, and ended up in his library at Abbotsford.[94] An especially famous Scots text, *The Kingis Quair*, a semi-autobiographical poem attributed to James I of Scotland (1394–1437), telling of his capture and imprisonment in England, survives in a single late fifteenth-century manuscript. This belonged to Henry, Lord Sinclair (*c*.1460–1513), a member of the same family.[95]

French texts remained important, as did the translation of works out of French – whether into Irish, Scots or English. Sir John Fastolf's stepson, Stephen Scrope, for example, translated Christine de Pizan's Epistle of Othea to Hector into English, and presented a luxurious French-style manuscript of it (fig. 37) to Humphrey Stafford, 1st Duke of Buckingham (1402–60).[96] Saints' lives, especially, were of great interest to pious aristocratic readers, and a manuscript of a French translation by Jean de Vignay of Jacobus de Voragine's *Legenda Aurea*, made in Paris in 1382, belonged to William Fitzalan, 9th Earl of Arundel (1417–87), and later still perhaps to Henry VII's mother, Lady Margaret Beaufort.

Arundel was a patron of Caxton, who translated the Golden Legend from Vignay's French into English with his encouragement, publishing it in 1483.[97]

The advent of print

Like any late medieval magnate, Henry VIII's Lord Chamberlain Sir William Sandys (1470–1540) not only kept a private chapel (fig. 38), but owned all the liturgical articles necessary for the offices of the Church. At the time of his death, the chapel vestry of his still-extant great house at The Vyne in Hampshire housed a full complement of liturgical books, but nearly a century after Gutenberg, and decades after the introduction of printing into England by Caxton, many were printed. They include 'a fayre masse book in vellom printed', 'iii grayles [Graduals] prentyd' and 'viii Antiphoners printed in paper'.

The advent of printing in England followed, in European terms, a rather unusual pattern. In Paris print was closely associated with the city's ancient university, and in other printing centres, like Venice or Cologne, it was allied with humanistic scholarship or mercantile elites. But at a time when printing in the vernacular was all but unknown, many of the books printed by Caxton in the orbit of the royal court at Westminster were in English, products for which there was a ready market immune to competition from abroad. In 1496

[37] Christine de Pizan's Epistle of Othea to Hector, 1450–60, fol. 1r, translated by Stephen Scrope and presented to the 1st Duke of Buckingham (St John's College, Cambridge)

[38] The Chapel at The Vyne, Hampshire

Wynkyn de Worde produced a finely illustrated reprint of the *Book of Hawking, Hunting and Blasing of Arms*, a compendium originally issued from the press of the Benedictine abbey of St Albans in 1486. As if the intended market was not already obvious, De Worde explained in his preface that he had added a treatise on angling because his new edition was intended for 'gentyll & noble men'. It was not for 'ydle persons which sholde haue but lytyll mesure in the sayd dysporte of fysshynge.'[98] Many of Caxton's chosen texts, too, were books of a type which had long circulated in manuscript among well-born readers. Two of his first books, the romance *The Recuyell of the Historyes of Troye* (*c*.1474–5; fig. 39) and the partly allegorical *Game of Chess* (1474), were issued under the patronage of Edward IV's siblings Margaret of Burgundy and George, Duke of Clarence. Subsequent books included *The Canterbury Tales* (1477), *Reynard the Fox* (1481), the massive English version of *The Golden Legend* (1483) and an attractively illustrated translation of Aesop (1484).[99] To these his successor De Worde subsequently added a series of treatises in English on subjects as various as medicine, husbandry, gardening and cookery, all calculated to appeal to gentlemen and gentlewomen, and all texts which had long circulated in manuscript.[100]

Caxton was clearly aiming at a broader market than that which had previously bought manuscripts, but owing to the poor survival rate of his books it is difficult to draw too many firm conclusions about ownership. Of the 'books for gentleman', thirty-five extant copies contain some evidence of their early owners, but only nine of these owners can be positively identified. Of these, three were from an aristocratic or gentry background: Sir Thomas Lovell (*c*.1449–1524), Chancellor of the Exchequer and Speaker of the House of Commons (he had a house at Elsing in Middlesex and owned a copy of Caxton's 1489 English translation of Christine de Pizan's *Faits d'Armes et de Chevalrie*), the judge Sir Anthony Browne (1510–67), and John Sackville (*c*.1478–1557), a member of the well-known Kentish and Suffolk family which eventually ended up at Knole.[101] Beyond this, further conclusions are problematic. Even when books are listed in early inventories, from the 1460s on, it can be difficult to tell whether the books described in them were printed or in manuscript. Though it is tempting to suggest those with firm dates assigned

by inventory-takers are likely to have been printed, this may be too tidy to be true.

Magnates and their books to 1540

One of the best-recorded aristocratic libraries of the period was in Ireland. The Fitzgerald Earls of Kildare were not only the wealthiest Irish magnates, but one of the ten wealthiest nobles in England or Ireland at the time. In 1534 the family's principal library was lodged at Maynooth Castle, a sumptuously furnished palace-fortress some 15 miles west of Dublin, though the Earls of Kildare also owned other houses, including a town house in the Irish capital. Our knowledge of the collection rests on two library lists, which differ somewhat in detail, though each enumerates the books in four columns by language: English, Irish, Latin and French. The

[39] Raoul Lefèvre, *The Recuyell of the Historyes of Troye*, William Caxton and probably Colard Mansion, Bruges 1473 or 1474

Irish books will all have been manuscripts, as there was no printing in Irish until 1568, but many of the other books could easily have been printed. It is also difficult to say which books belonged to Gearóid Mór, the 8th Earl of Kildare (c.1456–1513), and which were acquired by his son, Gearóid Óg, the 9th Earl (1487–1534). By his time the Kildare books included saints' lives (many, though not all, in Irish, and not all of Irish saints: there is a life of St Bernard), theology (texts of Nicolaus de Lyra, and *Dialogues* of Pope Gregory the Great), classical texts (Virgil, Juvenal, Caesar, Boethius), histories and chronicles, Froissart, Malory's *Morte d'Arthur*, the *Roman de la Rose*, liturgical books, dictionaries (an *Ortus Vocabulorum*) and a manuscript of Gerald of Wales's *Topographia Hiberniae*. Gearóid Mór lived as a hostage at the English court for eight years between c.1495 and 1503, and some of the books may well have been obtained from London booksellers.[102] Only two surviving Fitzgerald books can be matched with any certainty with those in the two early lists: a fourteenth-century manuscript of Thomas Grey's *Scalacronica* (fig. 40), which may have belonged to the Earls of Kildare as

early as the 1390s, and a richly decorated manuscript Psalter made in Rouen in the 1420s. Another manuscript, a late fifteenth-century copy of John Lydgate's Fall of Princes, now in Oxford, may be a Kildare book as well, and several other Kildare books survive which are not in either of the library lists, including an important late fifteenth-century medical book in Irish acquired by the earl in 1500. Remarkably the library seems to have survived the fall of Maynooth Castle to the Crown in 1535.[103]

Was Maynooth typical? In scale the answer must surely be no, but extant manuscripts translated into Irish suggest a growing interest in non-native texts in fifteenth- and sixteenth-century Ireland. Translations were made of *The Travels of Marco Polo* and the legend of Guy of Warwick, for example, while the Gaelic lord Finghin Ó Mathghamhna made a translation of Mandeville's *Travels* in 1475.[104]

By comparison in England, with the exception of the Percy Earls of Northumberland (discussed below), we know less than we might do about books and libraries in magnate households between the Wars of the Roses and the Dissolution of the Monasteries. At present it is difficult to advance much further than inferences necessarily drawn from the survival of individual books, with all the attendant risks which this entails. The Pembroke Hours, made in Flanders between 1465 and 1469, possibly for William Herbert, 1st Earl of Pembroke (d. 1469), was still a treasured family possession in the time of his grandson, who died in 1570.[105] From the Yorkist inner circle, the Hastings Hours, made for Edward IV's Chamberlain William, Lord Hastings (c.1430–83), is almost equally grand.[106] A French translation of Boccaccio's *De Casibus Virorum Illustrium*, made in Rouen in about 1440, belonged to Marie Woodville, widow of Caxton's patron, Earl Rivers.[107]

The library of the Howards, Dukes of Norfolk and Earls of Arundel, is particularly mysterious. There is no sign in an inventory of 1524 of anything approaching a library at Framlingham Castle, though of course the family owned many other houses. On the other hand the chapel at Framlingham housed a large number of manuscript and printed liturgical books, including thirteen Missals bound in crimson or purple velvet, as well as 'a little playne song boke of velyme written for the organs'.[108] The great collection of books and manuscripts at Arundel House in London was

[40] Fourteenth-century manuscript of Grey's *Scalacronica*, fol. 1r (Corpus Christi College, Cambridge), which may have belonged to the Earls of Kildare from the 1390s

donated to the Royal Society in 1667, but although the catalogue includes a substantial number of incunables and early sixteenth-century printed books, these were bought by the 14th Earl of Arundel in the seventeenth century and were not inherited from late medieval dukes.[109] An earlier library was inherited by John, Lord Lumley (c.1533–1609), from his wife's Arundel forebears, eventually passing to James I's son Henry, Prince of Wales (d.1612), and from him into the Old Royal Library.

Personal devotion and reading aloud

In some fifteenth-century aristocratic households it was the custom that formal meals were eaten in silence, but elsewhere pious works were read out loud over dinner, as they would have been in a monastic refectory. Cecily, Duchess of York (1415–95), a member of the Neville family and mother of Edward IV and Richard III, retained Bible clerks for the purpose. Favourite texts at her table included devotional works, the Golden Legend, and lives of St Catherine of Siena and St Brigit, though a more tangible relic of the duchess's piety survives in the form of an extraordinarily lavish Book of Hours which later passed to her granddaughter, Elizabeth of York, Henry VII's queen.[110] Duchess Cecily's dynastic rival Lady Margaret Beaufort was equally devout (fig. 41). Whether at her London house in Coldharbour or her Northamptonshire house at Collyweston, she heard mass repeatedly each day, reciting matins in her Closet with her chaplain and spending a final quarter of an hour at her devotions in her chapel before bed. Her books were evidently a source of both personal solace and relaxation, and her biographer John Fisher recalled that she 'had dyuers bokes in Frensshe wherewith she wolde occupy herself whan she was wery of prayer'. Despite John Fisher's words, Lady Margaret also owned devotional works in the vernacular; a collection of private prayers survives, partly in English, which may have been commissioned by her husband Thomas Stanley. This manuscript later passed to Stanley's descendants, the Earls of Derby. Another of Lady Margaret's books, a Book of Hours now at Lambeth Palace, had changed hands in a more dramatic way. It had previously belonged to her son's enemy Richard III and was a secondhand book already sixty years old when the king owned it. Richard III's Book of Hours was made in London, but the fifteenth century also saw the import of a large number of similar books for

the English market from the southern Netherlands, especially from Bruges.[111]

A much humbler family, the Throckmortons, acquired Coughton Court in Warwickshire in 1409, and the chance survival of a set of Latin instructions written for a layman from his confessor gives something of the flavour of life in a devout household. The owner was enjoined to look carefully at the books in the parish church while the clerks were singing. The Gospel and Epistles for the day were especially recommended, with their expositions, as well as 'a certain *Legenda Sanctorum* which is very old'. Returning home, meals were to be eaten in silence, but a suitable book should 'be brought to the table as readily as the bread'. In place of a Bible

[41] Rowland Lockey (c.1565–1616), *Lady Margaret Beaufort at Prayer* (St John's College, Cambridge)

Clerk, the householder was encouraged to 'expound something in the vernacular which may edify your wife or others', so evidently Latin or French texts would have been glossed into English a line at a time for the benefit of those who would not otherwise have understood what was being read.[112]

Practical books for the gentleman

The increasing profusion of ordinary books on everyday subjects is indicative of the spread of literacy during the course of the fifteenth century. What is more, surviving fifteenth-century English books are commonly well thumbed and covered with jottings and scribblings: clearly many were well used.[113] As well as books on courtesy and conduct, books on warfare were understandably valued. The British Library has a prose translation of Vegetius's *De Re Militari* made for Thomas, 10th Lord Berkeley, in 1408, for example, while Sir Thomas Kerdeston (d.1446), of Claxton, Norfolk, owned a pair of treatises on falconry probably made for him in Norwich in the 1430s (fig. 42).[114] A manuscript treatise on equine medicine apparently belonged to the West Country gentleman Henry Pauncefoot (d.1507) of Hasfield, six miles north of Gloucester. It enjoyed a long shelf-life and was still in use in 1567.[115] Law books, too, fulfilled an obvious purpose: a surviving set of manuscript statutes from Edward I to Henry VI belonged probably to Henry de Beauchamp, Duke of Warwick (d.1445).[116] In Norfolk the Townshends of Raynham owned books at the time of the death of Sir Roger Townshend in 1493, when there were over forty manuscripts and printed books at East Raynham Hall, over half of them legal books. These were kept in large chests in a vaulted room, presumably above ground, as the same room had a chimney.[117] At Wollaton Hall in Nottinghamshire, the late medieval library apparently assembled between about 1460 and 1540 was similarly rich in legal books.[118]

III · HOUSING BOOKS

Studies and evidence rooms

We know far more about the books than about the settings in which they were used. Nonetheless from around about 1400 we start to catch occasional glimpses of Studies, Closets and Libraries: rooms associated with books, prayer and privacy. A quarter of a century after Henry IV's Study at Eltham, Henry Bowet, Archbishop of York (d.1423), had a room called the Library in his house: its total contents were valued at £6.[119] At Wardour Castle in Wiltshire a small self-contained chamber behind the dais of the hall may originally have been Lord Lovel's own private Study or oratory.[120] In 1516 a lock was fitted to the door of the Duke of Buckingham's Closet at his great new castle at Thornbury in Gloucestershire.[121] Conservative moralists like the poet William Langland (c.1332–c.1386) had condemned the quest for privacy as anti-social, but as great magnates travelled less and spent more time in a small number of favourite residences, so they became increasingly inclined to spend money on their own comfort and convenience. Private chambers and lodgings allocated to named individuals multiplied, as did rooms allocated for specific purposes.[122] The desire for privacy went beyond the domestic sphere. The surviving description of the Study at Eltham, with its stained glass and angels, makes it sound remarkably like a lavishly appointed chantry, and today the fan-vaulted side chapels of late medieval churches probably evoke the appearance and feel of a nobleman's Closet or Study more closely than gaunt ruins or sketchy descriptions in household inventories.[123]

At Markeaton Hall in Derbyshire Vincent Mundy (b. *c.*1509), an upwardly mobile Derbyshire lawyer, had a Study in 1545. The son of Sir John Mundy, a wealthy goldsmith who was Lord Mayor of London in 1522, Mundy compiled his own inventory on the birth of his eldest son in 1545, noting against each item its intended destination: his son, his wife or his executors. The unusual circumstances may explain the level of detail.[124] Mundy's Study was 'within … the gret chamber wher we dyne'. If this means that it was an enclosure which stood within (or perhaps off) the great chamber, it may have resembled the Study depicted in a woodcut in Gilles Corrozet's *Les Blasons domestiques*, published in Paris in 1539 (fig. 43). Corrozet's Study was a small chamber which sat on a platform within a larger room. It was sparsely furnished with a chest (books laid on top), a single shelf at head height (also with books), an angled wall lectern, and a bench to sit on.[125] The Derbyshire example contained a range of useful books and articles for business and pleasure:

'a forme for my lady to laye her boke upon' as she meditated with her Book of Hours. Near by, 'My Lordys Studdey' was more lavish still:

> Item a stondyng coubberde wyth viii drawserthes
> Item a coubberd wyth v shelffys to sette the bokys apon
> Item a bourde to sett bokys apon wyth iii threstylles &
>   a shelf under that
> Item a stondying to sett a boke upon.[127]

a booke of parchment of the syege of Troye	xiijs iiij d
a boke of parchement of gower viz.
confessio amantis	vj s viij d
a olde frenche cronycle parchement new bound	iij s iiij d
policronicon and Fabyans cronycle	xx d
ij other lytell olde bookes parchment	xx d
the kings magestys boke new set forth	xij d
a boke of lettres Italyen	xii d
a Roll of lapydary	iij s
a red cofer bowed with yeron with evidences	iiij s
a payr balans and a pyle of troye weights	vj s
desk a sandbox and a payr gold ballancz	xx d
a Standyssh for pen ynk etc. of fyrre	xx d
a wrytynn bord couered and ij formys j cusshyn	ij s iiij d
a payr tables slate and a combe case	ij s

One of the Markeaton books, a manuscript of Lydgate's Troy Book, is still extant, a gift from Sir John Mundy to his son Vincent. It had previously belonged to Sir Humphrey Talbot (d. 1492), and prior to that to William Carent (1344–1422) of Carent's Court, Dorset.[126]

A little earlier, at Stafford Castle in 1537 there was a Closet attached to the castle chapel, which contained a cupboard 'to laye bokeys apon', perhaps some sort of lectern with storage below, as well as

The lodgings at Stafford were destroyed during the Civil War, and little now remains of the castle, but

interestingly Henry, Lord Stafford (1501–63), was the son of the Duke of Buckingham who had fitted a lock to his Closet door at Thornbury in 1516, and who was executed by Henry VIII in 1521. Stafford Castle was the one residence the former ducal family eventually managed to recover.[128]

Studies like this may not have held all that many books. Presumably the books on the five shelves would have lain flat on their sides, as depicted in the Codex Amiatinus (see fig. 15) nearly a thousand years earlier. Many fifteenth- and sixteenth-century books have long since been rebound, but when contemporary bindings have survived, they provide

screw. In the background books stand on a desk which hangs against a panelled wall. In another example a manuscript made for Edward IV shows a book cupboard with a revolving desk mounted on top of it which, again, could be raised or lowered by means of a central screw (fig. 21).[129]

This kind of elaborate kit can only ever have existed in the wealthiest of households. Other images show simpler rooms typically with single or double rows of shelves placed at head height, with books sitting flat upon them. The title page of an English book printed by Richard Pynson, probably in 1518, bears a woodcut depicting a

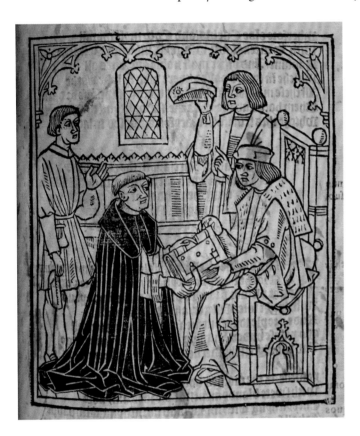

[45] The title page of a book printed by Richard Pynson (1518), showing a Cambridgeshire gentleman in his Study

[46] Caricature of the book fool in Sebastian Brant, *Navis Stultifera*, Basel 1507, illustrating furniture used for storing and reading books

some evidence for their original storage. The Petworth Chaucer manuscript, for example, retains its original fifteenth-century binding (fig. 44), re-covered in velvet in the 1860s. The position of the horn-covered parchment label with the title on the lower board suggests that the book was either kept flat or on a sloping lectern. Either way, it was stored with the back cover face-up. Further insights can be gleaned from visual evidence of one kind or another. An illuminated manuscript made in Flanders for Henry VII shows a book wheel, supposedly in the French royal Library. It consists of a revolving desk which could be raised or lowered by means of a

Cambridgeshire gentleman in his Study (fig. 45). Sir Giles Alington (1483–1522) of Horseheath Hall sits on a wooden seat while Alexander Bercley (1475?–1552), a monk of Ely, presents him with a copy of a book he has translated into English. It is a large book and has metal furnishings. In the background is a lectern, though owing to the vagaries of the perspective it is not clear whether it is a straight lectern like the well-known fifteenth-century examples in Lincoln Cathedral Library, or perhaps a piece of polygonal furniture.[130]

Sometimes the few facts we know about individual Libraries are rather surprising.

In mid-fifteenth-century Norfolk Sir John Fastolf's books were in his 'stew', or bath house, at Caistor Castle. They included a French Bible, chronicles, works by Aristotle, Caesar, Livy, Justinian, Lucretius and St Bernard, books on geomancy, etiquette and military science, as well as the tales of King Arthur. On the face of it an extremely implausible place for books, since parchment is notoriously susceptible to damp, the stew was in fact one of a suite of three private rooms which together constituted Fastolf's chamber.[131] At Whitehall Palace in 1531 Henry VIII had a Library in a tower or turret adjacent to his dressing room, one of several in the palace in the king's lifetime. At the royal retreat at Greenwich the Library was also high up, and in 1531 a table with decorative ironwork was installed in it.[132] At Lacock Abbey in Wiltshire, a three-storey polygonal tower (fig. 47) was added to the recently dissolved Augustinian nunnery by the courtier Sir William Sharington (c.1495–c.1553). There is little documentary evidence as to its original function, but the two upper storeys both have exquisite octagonal stone tables attributed to the carver John Chapman. The iconography of the upper chamber, accessible across the lead roof, suggests that it was a banqueting house, but the middle chamber (fig. 48), with stone cupboards and stone shelves at head height, was probably either a Study or a muniment or evidence room (that is, a room for keeping records).[133] At Caistor, too, Sir John Fastolf kept his papers in his treasury in a tower.[134]

Lesser houses might not run to an evidence room, though record keeping was of the utmost importance, and there must often have been a considerable overlap between evidences, books and other precious objects. In the 1480s Sir John Fastolf's neighbour Sir John Paston kept his deeds in a 'square trussing coffre'. Inside were boxes, pyxes and bags containing personal and legal papers, including a copy of Fastolf's will and maps of his lands.[135] In 1531 the Derbyshire gentleman John Fitzherbert of Norbury had an 'Evidence Cofer' in his private quarters, and in his will took care to see that 'all the evidence belonging to it' went to his male heirs along with the estates which they described.[136] The second- and third-floor chambers of the south-west tower of the inner court at Thornbury castle (completed in 1521) were shelved up to house the Duke of Buckingham's muniments. Their position above the private Closets of the bedchambers of the duke and duchess attested to their importance.

Wressle Castle and the Percys

The most detailed description of a pre-Reformation domestic Library comes from Wressle Castle (fig. 49), the palace-fortress of the Percy Earls of Northumberland, 35 miles south of York. The seventeenth-century antiquary Sir Simonds D'Ewes (1602–50) reckoned the Percys 'one of the greatest families of Christendom'.[137] Wressle was admittedly only half the size of Leconfield Manor, the neighbouring Percy house some 70 miles to the north-east, which with some eighty-three rooms was one of the largest residences in England. Nonetheless the castle was a house of a grandeur commensurate with the Percys' elevated status.[138] Despite partial destruction by the Parliamentarian authorities in 1650, and a serious fire in 1796, about a third of the castle still stands.[139] Set back from the road behind stern 'private' signs, it remains far less well known than other late medieval palatial residences like Bolton Castle, the fourteenth-century seat of the Scrope family in the North Riding, which it closely resembles. In its original form the interiors were lavishly decorated, apparently for Henry 'The Magnificent', the 5th Earl of Northumberland (1478–1527), who, with rent rolls of about £4,700 a year, was one of the richest peers in early Tudor England.[140]

When John Leland (c.1503–52) visited Wressle in 1540, he was noticeably enthusiastic. 'The house is one of the most proper beyond Tr[ente] and semith

[49] Wressle Castle, by T. F. Hampe, c.1600 (Petworth House archive, in the care of West Sussex Record Office)

as newly made', he noted, though in large measure it actually dated from the time of Richard II. He admired the castle's five towers, its moat, gardens and orchards, and commented that 'the haule and the great chaumbers be fair, and so is the chapelle and the closettes'. However, the feature which attracted the most attention was the Earl of Northumberland's Study, or Library, 'Paradise', which occupied the top floor of the four-storey Chapel Tower at the south-east corner of the castle:

One thing I likid exceedingly yn one of the towers, that was a study caullid Paradise, wher was a closet in the middle of 8. squares latised aboute: and at the toppe of every square was a desk ledgid to set books on cofers withyn them, and these semid as yoined hard to the toppe of the closet: and yet by pulling one or al wold cum downe, briste highte in rabettes [grooves], and serve for desks to lay bokes on.[141]

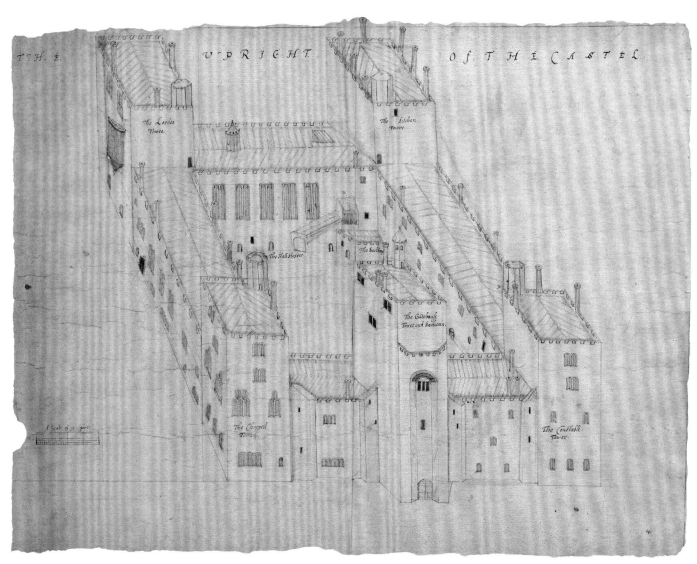

Paradise is a name occasionally found for a favourite room in a great house. A sixteenth-century German visitor to Hampton Court admired 'the Paradise Room', remarking 'it captivates the eyes of all who enter'.[142] There is another example at the sixteenth-century Bramhall Hall in Cheshire; and there was a 'Paradise Chambre' in the long-vanished Tudor house at Appuldurcombe on the Isle of Wight in 1566.[143] At Wressle, it seems clear, the choice of the name clearly reflected the fact that this was both a private room and the highest status room in the whole castle. Sometimes referred to as 'My Lord's Library', it was accessible only by a spiral staircase from the leads and via an almost equally private 'Lady's Chamber', one of very few female spaces in an overwhelmingly male castle. As is clear from the Household Ordinances, even the most private rooms at Wressle were liable to be crowded with attendants, and Paradise was one of very few rooms where the Earl of Northumberland could rely on being genuinely alone. It was, in every sense, the most exclusive room in the castle.[144]

Leland's description is difficult to unpick, but comparison with plans drawn up in about 1600 helps to clarify matters a little. The 'closet in the middle of 8. Squares' was in fact a bandstand-like octagonal box, some 9 feet across (fig. 50). By 1574 the woodwork was painted green and white. The eight desks 'ledgid to set books on' were inside the Closet, which was entered through a door on its western side, facing onto a fireplace. The books themselves appear to have been kept in boxes or coffers. These were slotted into position above the ledged desks. Ordinarily boxes and desks alike were at head height or above, apparently attached to the roof of the Closet, but when required any or all of them could be lowered down into position. The desks and associated books would then have been at chest height, and the books would then presumably have been perused from a standing position.[145]

It is clear that the configuration of the room was unusually complicated, and it was evidently this that attracted Leland's attention. It is difficult to be sure, but his wording implies that the wooden structure in the Wressle Paradise was less a bookcase than a mechanised receptacle into which coffers which already contained books could be slotted. If this is so, it would support the idea that the Earl of Northumberland's books migrated with him from residence to residence, since there were remarkably similar Studies in at least two other

Percy houses.[146] At Leconfield Manor, according to Leland, there was 'a little studying chaumber ther called Paradice'. This contained 'the geneaologie of the Percys', presumably in the form either of some kind of wall hanging or of painted decorations, since we know that the walls of several of the principal apartments at both Leconfield and Wressle were decorated with verses composed by John Lydgate and John Skelton.[147] (The Northumberland Household Book suggests that there were in fact two Libraries at Leconfield, one for the duke and the other for the duchess.[148]) Far

[50] Isometric reconstruction by Peter Brears of the Wressle Chapel Tower with the Paradise Study

to the south at Petworth, there was a similar room located above a small chamber abutting the Great Chamber. In 1574 this was described as

> *a Studye, wherein is a chimney and two windows … About the same Studie is frames of wainskott for boxes and settles for writings; in the midst of which Studdie is a round counting house of wainscot with a round table in yt the counting house having deskes and seats round about it.*

The 1512 Northumberland Household Book provides further clues about the operation not just of the Earl of Northumberland's private Studies, but of related matters of administration, education and record keeping. Both Leconfield and Wressle

[51] A miniature from Lady Eleanor Percy's fifteenth-century Book of Hours (Powis Castle)

had 'Evidens Houses … wher all his Lordshippis Evidences and other Wrytyngs perteynynge his Lordships Lands doith remayne', with a keeper in charge of them 'charged with the delyvray of my said Lordis Evidences owt and for recyvynge of them in again'.[149] The Paradises (sometimes referred to simply as 'Lyberary' or 'My Lordes Lybrarye') were in the charge of a Groom of the Chamber. He was responsible for keeping the library fires, for which there was a special allocation of fuel both for summer and winter, as well as for the fires in the Earl of Northumberland's Jewel House, and in the 'Houses in the Garden and outher places where my Lord shall syt aboute his Books'. The arrangement provides further confirmation that books and reading were associated with peace and privacy, which were to be had either in private Studies high up at roof level, or in detached pleasure houses out in the gardens as found at both Leconfield and Wressle.[150]

All this would be remarkable enough, but we also know a good deal about the books owned by the Percys in the later Middle Ages. Twenty-four manuscripts which were in Percy ownership before the mid-sixteenth century can be identified with reasonable certainty, along with another six which may have been.[151] They are extremely varied, and now widely scattered. In the 1360s Henry, 3rd Lord Percy, borrowed a Latin Bible and a Life of St Sylvester from the Carmelites of Hulne, near Alnwick, and this interest in Latin religious texts and devotional books persisted down the generations.[152] The fourteenth-century Percy Hours, now in the British Library, contains early family obits, while another manuscript, a fifteenth-century Book of Hours (fig. 51), was 'brought from Petworthe' to Powis Castle on the marriage of Lady Eleanor Percy in the reign of Queen Elizabeth I.[153] A Wycliffite Bible sold from Petworth in 1928 was long said to have belonged to Harry Hotspur (1364–1403), while a massive Latin Bible with historiated initials which went in the same sale had probably also passed by descent since the Middle Ages.[154] In addition to this, surviving books suggest that the 4th and 5th Earls of Northumberland were actively acquiring vernacular literature, including manuscripts of Chaucer and Lydgate.

CHAPTER THREE

'This scribbling age'

The Country House Library from the Reformation to the Civil War

The wisest hath said it, that much reading is a wearisomnes vnto the flesh.
Therefore in this scribbling age, wherein presses be oppressed with the number of books
without number, it may seeme a thing not meete any more to write.
George Widley, *The Doctrine of the Sabbath Handled*, 1604

I · READING THE EVIDENCE

Writing in his *Rules and Orders for the Government of the House of an Earle* (1621), the gentleman-poet Richard Brathwait (1588–1673) set out detailed suggestions on the arrangement, contents and use of libraries:

> *The Earle not … be sparing of his purse, but to have a fair Library, furnished with books both of Divinitye and Philosophy, Astrology, Cosmography, Law, Arte of Warr, Heraldry; but especially to be furnished with books Historicall, both concerning the Church, and also all Countryes and Commonwealthes, with Globes, Cards, and Mapps; and, as leasure will serve, to exercise himself in reading and perusing of them.*[1]

Brathwait's prescription stands in sharp contrast to the picture presented in the standard literature on country houses. The National Trust's 1987 guidebook for Blickling Hall was typical in claiming 'libraries were introduced into the layout of none of the great houses built before the Restoration', while Mark Girouard's *Life in the English Country House* (1978) made several assumptions which others have not questioned sufficiently closely. In particular his assertion that 'only a dozen or so members of the upper classes … are known to have owned more than a hundred books in the sixteenth century' deserves further scrutiny.[2] First, it implicitly measured Renaissance libraries against the country house libraries of the eighteenth and nineteenth centuries when in fact by sixteenth-century English standards a library of 100 books was a substantial

collection. In 1582 Cambridge University Library had just 451 books and manuscripts, while in 1589 Corpus Christi College, Oxford, had 379.[3] Secondly, Girouard's conclusions were derived from a pioneering index of book inventories published by Sears Jayne in 1956. Valuable as this data was, it is dangerous to draw too many conclusions about Elizabethan and Jacobean private libraries from the random sample of documents which happen to have survived. It would have been more accurate to observe that only a dozen or so individuals for whom full book lists survive owned more than a hundred books. In addition we have evidence of other kinds for well over a hundred gentry libraries from the period from 1560 to the 1640s, though not necessarily giving details of their size. It seems certain that other libraries have disappeared without trace.[4] The patchy nature of sources on early modern libraries is one of the subject's most frustrating aspects, and it can be unwise to draw excessively firm conclusions from them.

Inventories provide one of the principal sources for our understanding of early domestic libraries. Their use is not straightforward, and they need to be read alongside other evidence, including that provided by the thousands of extant books once in Elizabethan and Jacobean libraries. Household inventories were usually created as part of the process for granting probate on the goods and chattels of the dead. Under legislation first passed in 1529, the deceased's books were supposed to be listed alongside other chattels.[5] In practice books

[52] Full-length portrait of Sir Nathaniel Bacon (1585–1627) in his Closet, by Henry Pierce Bone (1585–1627) (Trinity College, Cambridge)

are frequently absent from inventories, and this tends to encourage the unwary to assume that there were none, even in houses which other lines of enquiry suggest contained libraries. In a memorable phrase in her study of the library of the Sidney family at Penshurst Place, the Canadian scholar Germaine Warkentin placed books in 'the dim class of personal chattels' which are often invisible in documentary sources.[6]

The 1601 inventory of Hardwick Hall is a case in point. Not a probate inventory, and compiled seven years before Bess of Hardwick died in 1608, it seems to show that one of the grandest women in Elizabethan England owned just six books ('my Ladies books viz: Calvin, upon Jobe, Covered with russet velvet, the resolution, Salomans proverbes, a booke of meditations, two other books Covered with black velvet').[7] In fact recent work has revealed there was a substantial library at Hardwick in Bess's lifetime, housed in the ground-floor apartments of her son William Cavendish, 1st Earl of Devonshire (1552–1626), though the room or rooms in which the books were kept had not yet been fitted up in 1601.[8] The five books named appear to have been set out on a dressing table in Bess's Bedchamber. At least three had textile covers. They were in fact display objects, similar to the royal books 'bound in velvet of different colours' which the German traveller Paul Hentzner had admired in the Royal Library at Whitehall in 1598 (fig. 53).[9] Their luxurious fabric covers were probably what ensured their inclusion in the inventory, as the appraisers were clearly preoccupied with textiles. Whether Bess owned further books is an open question, but there is no reason why these should not have been among the unlisted contents of the coffers and trunks within easy reach of the 'three Deskes Covered with lether' in her Bedchamber.[10] These desks may have resembled the lecterns found in institutional Libraries. More likely they were sloped table tops for writing, while 'the little deske to write one guilded' sounds like the 'riche writing boxe imbrodered with gold' that was at Wilton, the Earl of Pembroke's house, in 1561.[11]

In principle a married woman owned no property of her own. One solution was a well-drafted marriage settlement, but by custom a woman also retained limited rights over her paraphernalia, the goods and chattels which she brought to a marriage, and which she would require for an honourable widowhood.[12] Whether these included her books

was a matter for debate. When the Warwickshire gentleman Sir Simon Archer of Tanworth died in 1640, he left most of the books in the house to his male heirs, but his will specifically excepted the books in his wife's Closet 'and others accounted hers'.[13] Bess, on the other hand, had buried four husbands by 1601, and had been estranged from the last, the 6th Earl of Shrewsbury (1528–90), for the last ten years of their marriage. In 1572 Shrewsbury had conveyed the lands he held in right of his wife to her two sons by her second husband William Cavendish (d. 1557). Her legal status was consequently ambiguous and complex, but regardless of this there is no reason for her inventory to have included chattels which belonged either to her son William, or her granddaughter Arbella Stuart (1575–1615).[14] Unlike her grandmother, born into a family of Derbyshire gentry in about 1527, Arbella had received a solid humanist education. She is known to have kept books in her 'study chamber', complaining bitterly when she was temporarily deprived of them after she fell under suspicion of plotting an unauthorised marriage.[15]

Hardwick is not the only country house where there appear to have been no books, but where a little poking around uncovers intellectual interests which suggest otherwise. According to an inventory compiled in 1624, the spendthrift Sir William

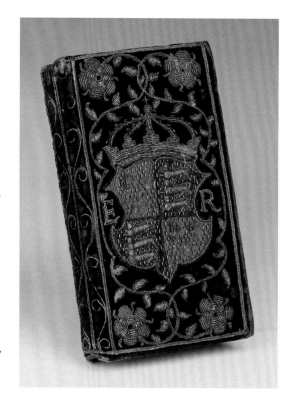

[53] Embroidered velvet binding on J. Udall, *Certaine Sermons*, London 1596 (Cambridge University Library). This is an example of the kind of textile binding known to have belonged to both the queen and Bess of Hardwick

Liber Sextus Decretalium.

[54] One of the fifteen law books formerly at Speke Hall, looted from the Edinburgh house of Cambuskenneth Abbey in 1544 (National Library of Scotland)

Norris of Speke Hall, Lancashire, had 'one map contayning the description of Jerusalem with a Latin book belonging to it' in his 'Little Parlour', but the fifteen massive law folios looted by his grandfather from the Edinburgh house of Cambuskenneth Abbey in 1544 and still in Speke in the eighteenth century are not mentioned (they are now in the National Library of Scotland; fig. 54). By 1624 the Speke estate was mired in debt, and since the chattels listed were to be placed in the hands of trustees, it could simply be that the Cambuskenneth books were not part of the arrangement.[16] At Worksop Manor in 1591, if the inventory is to be believed, the house contained no books, but hanging in the Gallery there were '24 mappes of sundrye partes'.[17] There were maps, too, in two rooms at Wollaton Hall in Nottinghamshire in 1601, but

though several books belonging to members of the Willoughby family survive today, the only hint of anything approaching a Library room in an inventory compiled in that year is the 'writing cubborde' in 'the east tower chamber upon the leades'.[18]

Even after several sales in the twentieth century, the library at Lacock Abbey still contains three books signed by Anne Sharington, stepdaughter of the William Sharington, who purchased the monastic buildings in 1540.[19] These include John Calvin's *Two and Twentie Sermons* (London, 1580), an early botanical book (fig. 55), as well as a law book published in 1579.[20] Anne was the daughter of the London alderman Robert Paget, and married Sharington's younger brother Henry (d. 1581). Her fine italic script shows that she, too, had received a fashionable humanist education. Anne's husband also owned books, some still at Lacock, but this is not apparent from the 1575 Lacock inventory, which again gives the impression of a house without books.[21] The autobiography written by Anne Sharington's daughter Grace Mildmay (1552–1620) tells a fuller story. Grace and her sisters grew up in a godly household, their education and spiritual development overseen by their governess, Mistress Hamblyn. In later life at her husband's house at Apethorpe in Northamptonshire, Grace was known as an accomplished musician, cook and confectioner, a well-informed practitioner of Galenic medicine, and a prolific writer who compiled some 2,000 pages of autobiography, spiritual reflections and medicinal notes. Grace had views on reading and education, recommending the Bible should be read 'continually every day', commending John Foxe's *Book of Martyrs*, chronicles and histories of England, statutes and laws, and exhorting her family that 'the wise and witting sentences of philosophers being heathen without the knowledge of God are worthy books to be used sometimes for recreation. For they exhort unto virtue and dehort from vice whereby the excellent gifts of God may be magnified in them.'

She took a dim view of contemporary English drama ('idle plays and all such unprofitable matter which pervert and carry the mind from all goodness') and urged that virtuous study was the proper path 'to prepare noblemen and gentlemen for worthy and great employments and make them wise'. Grace venerated her mother's memory, and her views were evidently formed during her childhood at Lacock. Anne Sharington had allowed her young daughters only four books, the Bible, the *Book of Martyrs*,

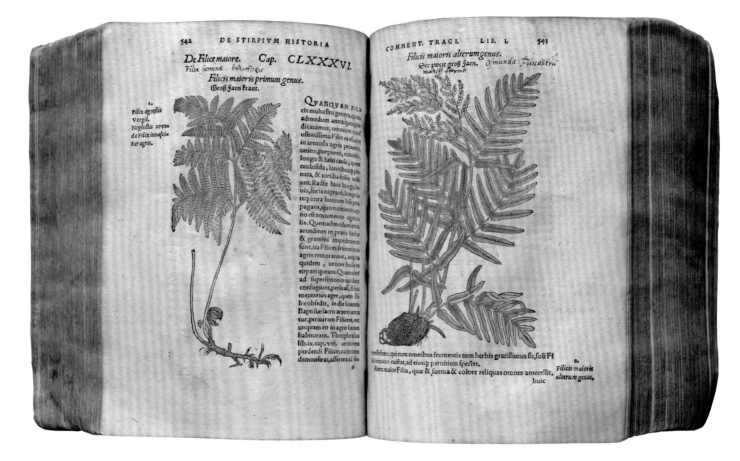

Thomas à Kempis's *Imitation of Christ* and the *Common Places* of the Calvinist theologian Heinrich Musculus (Mistress Hamblyn added the *Herbal* of the Duke of Somerset's physician William Turner, and a book on surgery by the Spaniard Johannes de Vigo). The inference from this is not that Lacock was a house without books, but that there were many. Lady Sharington and her husband simply believed that it was 'dangerous to suffer young people to read or study books wherein was good and evil mingled together'.[22]

One reason why houses like Lacock appear to have been bookless is because books as a category of object had evidently been excluded from the inventory process, probably because the functionaries charged with the task found it too time-consuming.[23] In other cases separate book inventories may once have existed which are no longer extant, or they may have been intended but never compiled. At Firle Place in Sussex an early owner kept his books in a series of cases (*classes* in Latin), but only the list of the 'prima classis' and part of the second survives.[24] In 1564 the Cornish gentlewoman Dame Elizabeth Arundell left 'all implements and household stuff in an inventory written by John Penhelege [the steward] … and also books and armour now remaining in his house of Lanherne'. The books and armour had to be specified in the will precisely because they had been excluded from the inventory.[25] In Somerset the botanist and gentleman-scholar Thomas Lyte (1568–1638) evidently owned a library at Lytes Cary, as 'all my librarye' was recorded in an inventory of the contents of the house, which, together with livestock, was valued at £480 19s. 6d. The inventory does not survive, and we only know of its existence because Lyte mentioned it in his commonplace book (see p. 229). This also contains lists of long-vanished 'rolls in the great wicker hamper in the closet' and 'writings in rolls in a square box', so it may be that Lyte's books were stored along with his evidences in his Closet.

When information on books exists in family papers, it can be frustratingly vague. In 1585 the Catholic traitor William Shelley kept his books 'in the Studye' at his house at Michelgrove in Sussex: valued at £1, they were recorded by the inventory-takers as 'Item – diverse sortes of boocks'.[26] At Henham Hall in Suffolk, in 1602, the appraisers noted the existence of 'certeyne bookes'

[55] Hieronymus Bock, *De Stirpium*, Strasbourg 1552 (Lacock Abbey)

in two Closets, one adjacent to the garden, and the other above a bakehouse. The second contained a square table and 'one old deske'.[27] In Ireland the scholarly Protestant planter Sir William Herbert (c.1553–93), an Oxford graduate and a native of Monmouthshire, had 102 books, recently arrived, at the castle at Castleisland, County Kerry, in 1590. The only ones mentioned by name were a 'great Geneva Bible' and a Book of Common Prayer, while the others went down as 'of sundry sortes great and little', with no attempt to assign a value, unlike the carefully enumerated lists of linen and plate.[28]

It is clear that appraisers were often baffled by books. The appraisers of the contents of a manor house in Elizabethan Bedfordshire sought advice from two local clergy.[29] Round about 1625 the servant William Palphrey set to work listing nearly 300 books which had belonged to his late master, the Norfolk gentleman Sir Nathaniel Bacon of Stiffkey, Norfolk (1549–1622; fig. 52), second son of Elizabeth I's Lord Keeper, Sir Nicholas Bacon (1510–79). Palphrey counted each volume with the same diligence which he devoted to the family accounts, but his inventory does not suggest any great understanding of what he was doing; occasionally he had trouble distinguishing between octavos and folios.[30]

[56] Two Wotton bindings, for *The Lamentacion of a Sinnere*, London 1548, and *Les Actes du Concile de Trent* [Geneva?], 1548. (Cambridge University Library)

Continental influences

The partial loss of inventories and other records has been matched by the almost total loss of early Library rooms. Large rooms like Great Halls and Long Galleries were easily adapted by later generations, but small and lavishly decorated private apartments were less easy to re-cast and have typically disappeared.[31]

In his 1624 paraphrase of Vitruvius, *The Elements of Architecture*, the diplomat and politician Sir Henry Wotton (1568–1639) admonished: 'Let all the principal chambers of Delight, All Studies and Libraries, be towards the East: For the Morning is a friend to the Muses.'[32] Wotton's knowledge of Vitruvius and his views on the orientation of Libraries is explained by his travels on the Continent and his long residence in Venice, where, with two short breaks, he served as James I's ambassador for nearly twenty years. But Sir Henry was also the younger son of one of the leading English bibliophiles of the previous generation, 'the English Grolier' Thomas Wotton (1521–87) of Boughton Malherbe in Kent. A zealous Protestant and, according to Izaak Walton, 'a gentleman excellently educated, and studious in all the *Liberall Arts*', Wotton travelled in France in his youth. He is best known for his exquisite gold-tooled bindings (fig. 56), the most elaborate of which were made in Paris.[33] This was a new taste in sixteenth-century England. One hundred and forty-three are known which belonged to Wotton or can be attributed to one of his binders, mostly on standard editions of Latin texts (he does not seem to have known Greek), though he also owned an especially beautiful copy of the first edition of Thomas More's *Utopia* (1516).[34] Some bear the Grolier-like tooled inscription 'Thomae Wottoni et Amicorum' ('the property of Thomas Wotton and his friends').

We can only guess where Wotton kept his books at Boughton, but Sir Walter Raleigh's Study at Durham House in London was, according to the antiquarian John Aubrey, in 'a little turret that looked into and over the Thames, and had the prospect which is as pleasant perhaps as any in the World'. Such a location, thought Aubrey, 'cheers the spirits' and 'I believe enlarges an ingeniose man's thoughts'.[35] A similar room survives at Raleigh's country retreat, Sherborne Castle in Dorset, where there is a panelled roof-top Study of about 1600.

Nothing is known of the configuration or use of either room, though we do know about the books Raleigh had while imprisoned between 1603 and 1616.[36] Towers had long been associated with Libraries and record keeping. Jacobean readers would have known of the example of Montaigne, who kept his books in a remote corner tower of the family chateau in Périgord. Montaigne's tower was a place of retreat, and this may also have been the case in England and Scotland. At Towneley Hall in Lancashire, there was a Library in the gate tower above the east wing, demolished in the 1730s. As early as the time of Richard Towneley VI (1566–1628), it contained up-to-date books on classical architecture.[37] The library at Cowdray Park in Sussex was kept on the first floor of the hexagonal kitchen tower, a less obviously safe place for books. According to a later commentator, this tower housed 'the rare black-letter books and curious manuscripts belonging to the Montague family'. By the time of the fire which gutted Cowdray in 1777, the tower Library had been superseded by another in the main body of the house, which contained 'the more useful or fashionable' books. These perished, but the ancient Library in the tower survived, only to succumb to neglect and decay in the nineteenth century. This is a sad loss, as the Cowdray library included the books of the last Catholic Archbishop of York, Nicholas Heath (1501–78), which were bequeathed to his co-religionist Anthony Browne, 1st Viscount Montagu (c.1528–92).

Libraries, Studies and Closets

The words 'library', 'study' and 'closet' are found in early documentary sources to describe rooms set aside for books and reading. All were clearly privileged spaces, but it is less clear what distinction contemporaries were attempting to draw in using one term over the others. Some historians have paid close attention to questions of gender, and the evidence sometimes bears this out.[38] At Corfe Castle in Dorset there was a Closet off Lady Bankes's room and a Study for her husband Sir John Bankes (1589–1644) off the Gallery.[39] In other cases too much theory may delude us into drawing unwarranted conclusions. Terms like Library, Study and Closet were used interchangeably. Later in the seventeenth century a wife wrote to a correspondent to explain that her husband had recently had a fire in his Study, while he, in another letter, told a friend that there had been

a fire in his Closet.[40] Sometimes social conventions could be subverted. Despite conventional prohibitions, between 1620 and 1644 the Closet of the Norfolk gentleman Sir Thomas Knyvett was regularly entered by his wife Katherine, whether he was away from the estate or not.[41] The antiquarian Sir Edward Dering of Surrenden, Kent, called his Study his 'Utopia', but was delighted when his wife visited, unbeknown to the servants.[42]

In 1659 the English translation of the *Orbis Sensualium Pictus* (The Visible World in Pictures) of Johann Amos Comenius (1592–1670) defined 'the *Study*' (fig. 57) as 'a place where a *Student*, a part from men, sitteth alone, addicted to his *Studies*, whilst he readeth *Books* … which being within his reach, he layeth open upon a *Desk* and picketh all the best things out of them to his own *Manual*.'[43] The Study, therefore, was not just a place of quiet, but contained the necessary equipment to allow the owner to make good use of its books. The wise student would work with a commonplace book at hand, filleting and abstracting the best nuggets as reading progressed.[44]

The least common word in contemporary sources is 'Library'. In 1588 at Belvoir Castle in Leicestershire, the Earl of Rutland's 'library over the chapel' was kept locked, but the castle also had at least one 'closet', as well as 'the counting-house'. In a grand house like Belvoir functions which might elsewhere have been combined had different rooms allocated to them.[45] At Thorndon Hall in Essex, the Catholic John, 1st Lord Petre (1549–1613),

[57] A contemporary view of 'the Study' from Comenius' *Orbis sensualium pictus*, Nuremberg 1679

spent money plastering and wainscoting a Study between 1586 and 1587. It, too, was kept locked, with 12d. spent on 'a new locke to my Studie' in 1597. This Study was located off the north side of the Long Gallery, but by 1639 a passageway on the east side of the house had become 'My Lords Library'. The books there were reckoned to be worth £35, and evidently space was running out – a common problem.[46] Another Elizabethan Catholic, the 1st Viscount Montague, also used the word 'Library' in his will (1592), though it is not clear whether it was at his main seat at Cowdray, at Battle Abbey or in his London town house, and equally unclear whether the word signified a room or a collection of books.[47] At Bramshill, the Hampshire seat of Sir Henry Wotton's friend Edward, Lord Zouche (1556–1625), 'the Librarie' was certainly a room. Its contents included 250 books, a pair of high chairs, a table covered with green cloth, an iron-bound chest 'and certaine mathematicall instruments'. If elsewhere 'Librarie' signified a storage place, at Bramshill it was evidently somewhere where books were used and read, a comfortable room with a fireplace and a lavishly appointed bed.[48] 'The library' in Arthur Coke's chamber at Bramsfield (Suffolk) contained the bulk of the books in the house, but there were also books in other, unspecified rooms; collectively they were valued at a substantial £86 15s., nearly four times the value of the furnishings in Coke's Parlour.[49] At Apethorpe the main collection of books in 1629 was in 'My Lord's Capanett Room', above the gateway in the north range. This contained 210 books, as well as sundry other furnishings, including an iron chest and 'one little Desk'. Some of the books remained at Apethorpe until the Mildmay library was sold in 1887. One of the most remarkable is an annotated 1545 Paris edition of Cicero's *De Philosophia*, owned by Sir Francis Walsingham (1530–90) during his Marian exile on the Continent and presented by him to his brother-in-law Sir Walter Mildmay (1520–89) on his return to England.[50]

Closets could be for reading, but were also for prayer and privacy. The preacher of the funeral oration for the Lady Frances Robartes (1584–1626), a pious Calvinist matron, characterised her 'closset' at Lanhydrock in Cornwall as a place of 'constant reading, hearing, meditating on the Word'.[51] The Yorkshire gentlewoman Margaret Hoby (c.1571–1633) prayed and read the scriptures in her Closet, though that does not necessarily mean

that her reading was a solitary or silent activity.[52] At the other end of the religious spectrum the staunchly Catholic Henry Somerset, 1st Marquess of Worcester (1577–1646), read devotional books in his Closet at Raglan Castle, weeping over them as he said his prayers and inviting his gentlemen to join him after dinner to share them.[53] At Knole the great heiress Lady Anne Clifford (1590–1676) habitually withdrew to her Closet in the reign of James I, where her gentlewomen read to her. In 1617 she noted that she had spent her time 'in the Closet & began to have Mr Sandy's Book read to me about the Government of the Turks'. Meanwhile her husband the 3rd Earl of Dorset (1589–1624) was 'sitting the most part of the Day reading in his Closet'. Some months later Lady Anne noted that she had gone to her husband's Closet, where she sat and read more of George Sandys's account of his travels in the Ottoman empire, as well as some Chaucer; a little later still she and her servants 'set up a great many of the Books that came out of the North in my Closet'.[54] Only about ten of Anne Clifford's books have come to light, but her mother Margaret Russell (1560–1616), her governess Anne Taylor and her tutor the poet and historian Samuel Daniel (1562–1619) saw to it that she was well educated. Having inherited her mother's books in 1616, Anne added more, assembling (in the words of one of her servants) 'a library stored with very choice books, which she read over, not cursorily, but with judgement and observation'. Lady Anne's Great Picture, commissioned in 1646 from the Flemish artist Jan van Belcamp (today in the Abbot Hall Art Gallery in Kendal), gives some indication of the richness of the Closet of a wealthy noblewoman, packed with books, portraits and other treasures.

Studies and Closets could also be used as places of business and concourse. The polymath Dr John Dee (1527–1608/9) was rich enough to own a fine Thameside retreat at Mortlake, where his Study was a hive of activity, with well-born and learned visitors coming and going, including on occasion the queen and her councillors. Alongside the 3,000 books, Dee's 'library room' (his words) was furnished with reading equipment such as tables and cases, and also had four 'appendixes' (again, the word is his own). The first was a collection of 'rare and exquisitely made instruments mathematicall', the second contained a cabinet of charters, seals and coats of arms, the third consisted of mirrors and other natural wonders, and the fourth comprised a collection of chemical and alchemical equipment housed in a laboratory attached to the Library. The books themselves were well read, over half the 500 extant containing underlining or marginal notes.[55]

Storage, fittings and furnishings

That Studies and Closets contained books does not necessarily imply that they had shelves, though some clearly did. At Everingham in Yorkshire in 1558 Sir Robert Constable had a 'flandres cheste' in his Study, and his books may have been inside it.[56] In 1580 Katherine Willoughby, Duchess of Suffolk (1519–80), a religious radical once in the inner circle of Queen Catherine Parr, kept her books in a chest.[57] When books were stored in chests, these could range from the plain and everyday through to objects of great grandeur, like the coffer which once belonged to the Willoughby de Brokes at Compton Verney, in Warwickshire.[58] At Esholt, a manor house in the West Riding, William Thomson's Study in 1612 contained a chest, a desk, a trunk, and 'boxe bookes [sic], & other implements'.[59] At Sherborne Park in Warwickshire in 1594, Henry Rogers kept 'a greate iron bounde chest to put in his evidence, his walnut deske' and 'all his books' together. If the books were not necessarily in the chest, the close connection between reading, writing and record keeping is implicit.[60]

Naturally, the more numerous the books, the more complex the fittings and furnishings were liable to be. If there were large numbers, shelving was needed and, as time went on, increasingly deployed. In 1604 George Widley, dedicating a wordy treatise to the soldier and theologian Charles Blount, 1st Earl of Devonshire (1563–1606), justified setting pen to paper by alluding to the Book of Ecclesiastes (12:12):

The wisest hath said, that much reading is a wearisomeness vnto the flesh. And therefore in this scribbling age, wherein presses be oppressed with the number of books withoute number, it may seeme a thing not meete any more to write, vnlesse for the sufficencie of the worke it might be in stead of all other writings, and so the reader might be eased on the labor of much reading.[61]

At the Archbishop's Palace at Canterbury in 1554 there was in a Study 'a longe press with iiij particons and v floures to set in bookes', suggesting a bookcase or cupboard four bays wide and five deep,

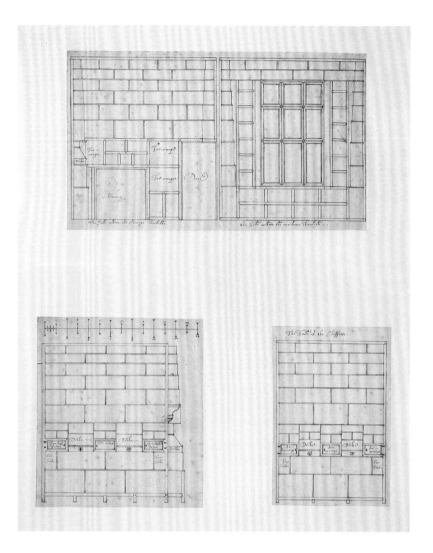

but whether the twenty compartments were shelves or pigeonholes, and whether the books sat flat or stood upright is unclear. (By way of comparison the 1517 portrait of Erasmus by Quentin Massys shows the great humanist in his Study, the books flat in pigeonholes, their titles written onto the lower edges.[62]) Another chamber in the Archbishop's Palace contained 'ij deskes to lay on bookes', and in the nearby 'lecture Chamber' there was 'a lecture to rede upon and a fourme'.[63] The complex fittings were dictated by the scale of the library of the disgraced Archbishop Cranmer. Two years later, at Stafford Castle, 341 books belonging to the 3rd Lord Stafford were kept in four cases in a Gallery, but were read in a nearby Study. They were listed in a catalogue compiled in that year and organised by size and subject: twenty-seven on civil law, seventeen on ecclesiastical law, thirty-five on grammar and poetry, fifty-one histories, thirty-six on astronomy and arithmetic, thirty-seven on rhetoric,

[58] Closet designs by Robert Smythson, c.1600 (British Architectural Library, RIBA, London)

oratory and philosophy, fifty-eight on medicine and surgery, sixty-four on theology and sixteen on miscellaneous subjects including cosmography, architecture, militaria and agriculture. Stafford's commonplace book suggests that they received substantial use; most were in Latin, but there were a few in English and other languages.[64] Stafford was a regular customer of two London booksellers, Mistress Burrell and William Riddell, encouraging them to procure books for him in Amsterdam.[65] He was also interested in antiquarian manuscripts. His library clearly evolved over time. In 1556 both books and their arrangement were different from those in 1537, and by 1566, on the death of his son Henry, 2nd Baron Stafford, layout and contents had changed again.[66] These glimpses into a sixteenth-century aristocratic Library are all the more interesting because Henry, Lord Stafford, was the grandson of the 4th Earl of Northumberland, the owner

and perhaps the creator of the Paradise Study at Wressle Castle.

Forty years later the diplomat Sir Henry Unton (c.1557–96) had a luxurious Study in his house at Wadley in Berkshire. Decorated with gilded hangings, it contained 'many books of diverse sortes, to the number of ccxx', again kept on shelves. Valued at £20, its contents were worth twice those in Unton's Great Chamber.[67] Wadley provides an interesting point of reference for the well-known designs (c.1600) by Robert Smythson (c.1535–1614) for a Closet (fig. 58). Smythson's elevations show the four walls shelved floor to ceiling, with fitted 'Deskes', cupboards for 'Loose Papers' and 'Incke'. The unusual staggered shelving (if shelving it is – it might be panelling) seems more reminiscent of coursed stone than of bookcases as we now know them. The design was presumably intended to be a combined Library and business room for a wealthy client.[68]

[59] Study at Holcombe Court, Devon

Hardly any rooms of this kind now survive. The most spectacular is at Holcombe Court in north Devon, where there is a richly carved and panelled chamber above the main gateway of the house (fig. 59). Variously dated between about 1570 and the second decade of the seventeenth century, it was probably constructed for Holcombe's late Elizabethan owner Richard Bluett (1544–1614). The room is remarkably like the Smythson designs, with three fitted shelves, and next to them two large cupboards, each containing two rectangular drawers and four squarish drawers of a kind familiar from institutional archives. Several of these bear traces of labels of various vintages from the seventeenth to the nineteenth centuries, describing the documents once lodged inside. The room is now

[60 A & B] *opposite*
The Kedermister
Library at Langley
Marish church

[61] *below*
Lady Anne Drury's
painted Closet (now
Christchurch Mansion,
Ipswich)

called the Muniment Room, and there can be little doubt that it housed the estate archive, but this was probably not its only purpose. The rich marquetry and carving, the iconography combining heraldry with flowers, scenes of harvesting, and references to the five senses, show that this was a high status room, its importance confirmed by the gatehouse location, with a view over the front of the house, and the direct link with the great chamber by a spacious spiral staircase. These points suggest that it was a Study, an exquisitely decorated chamber with a warming fire, where Richard Bluett and his son John (1603–34) withdrew to conduct business, to read and write, and to say their prayers.[69]

Indeed 'the Study' is precisely how the room was described in the earliest surviving Holcombe inventory (1700), and there is no reason to suppose that this was a new coinage.[70] Even without its original contents this room at Holcombe is a remarkable survival, a rustic northern European counterpart to magnificent Italian Renaissance *studioli* like that in the ducal palace at Urbino and its counterpart from Gubbio, since 1939 in the Metropolitan Museum of Art in New York.[71]

Another example, better known because it featured in Girouard's *Life in the English Country House*, is the Library (figs. 60a and b) added by the landowner Sir John Kedermister (d. 1631) to Langley Marish church in Buckinghamshire. Kedermister started to plan his Library in 1613, and the painted mannerist interior is, like the attached family pew, exceptionally lavish. Decoration like this can only have been replicated in the very grandest private houses. The Kedermister Library is a church Library, but nonetheless it may give some impression of what a Jacobean grandee's Study might have looked like. Unlike Holcombe, Langley Marish retains its original books, admittedly heavily repaired and no longer in their original arrangement. But there comparisons break down, as the books in the Kedermister Library were purchased by an agent acting for the founder, and did not come from his personal library.[72] With its shelved cupboards, the Kedermister Library illustrates one possible answer to the vexed question of storing books before the universal adoption of open wall shelving.

Another survivor, more lavish and now rather fragmentary, is the early seventeenth-century painted Closet of Lady Anne Drury (fig. 61), originally at Hawstead Place in Suffolk, but moved early on to Hardwick House, a manor house on the edge of Bury St Edmunds. The granddaughter of Sir Nicholas Bacon, Anne was married off to a wealthy county family, patrons of John Donne. In 1624 the Closet contained a table, a couple of carpets and a rug, a 'Couchbedd', bedding, chair and a couple of stools, as well as 'the Library' (contents unspecified).[73]

Further impressions can be gleaned from pictures, illustrations in books, and funerary monuments. One of the most impressive images comes from Scotland, a seventeenth-century portrait of Lord Rothes in his Library by George Jamesone.[74] In England the Great Picture of Lady

Anne Clifford (fig. 62) was designed to make a public statement about Lady Anne's lineage and learning, and if it cannot be read too literally, it captures a moment in time with great vividness. This is equally true of a series of Jacobean monuments which show the deceased with his books. At Canterbury Cathedral the monument to Dean John Boys (1571–1625), the younger son of a Kentish gentry family, depicts Boys sitting in his Study, with a reading lectern on an adjacent table, his books shelved upright and fore-edge outwards.[75] The tombs of Solicitor General Sir Henry Yelverton (1566–1629) of Easton Maudit, Northamptonshire, and the Buckinghamshire gentleman Francis Catesby (d. 1636) of Hardmead also feature books. They are depicted with less realism and are obviously primarily decorative in intent, but it is striking that even in the reign of Charles I a gentleman in his Library was shown with his books fore-edge outwards.[76]

For information on shelving practice we are largely reliant on the physical evidence of surviving books. The books which the courtier and diplomat Sir Arthur Throckmorton (c. 1557–1626) bequeathed to Magdalen College, Oxford, bear small paper fore-edge labels: an elegant refinement of the often elegantly bound books (fig. 63). Other owners appear to have kept their books fore-edge outwards and upright. This is true of a number of

books which belonged to Lord Burghley, with plain spines, ties and usually a fore-edge title written in ink just below the head of the book.[77] Since most Elizabethan libraries were dispersed long ago, and surviving books are widely scattered, it is difficult to form an opinion of whether Burghley's solution was the preferred one. A survey of books of armorial bookbindings in the National Art Library's Clements Collection suggests that few or no books from sixteenth-century English and Scottish aristocratic libraries have spine titles, while a few have fore-edge titles of one kind or another.[78] Many have no externally visible titles at all. Whether this is because they were always without titles or because labels like Arthur Throckmorton's have become detached is impossible to say. The first English binding with lettering on the spine for which we know the original owner was made for Sir Charles Somerset, a younger brother of the 1st Marquess of Worcester, when he left Eton in 1604.[79]

Unlike other book tombs, the stone books on the tomb of Sir Thomas Lucy III (1585–1640) have titles on the fore-edges (fig. 64). Sir Thomas was a learned Warwickshire gentleman,

the owner of Charlecote Park, a correspondent of Donne and a friend of Edward, Lord Herbert of Cherbury (1583–1648), with whom he visited Paris from 1608 to 1609.[80] The Lucy's was a godly household, associated with the circle of Lord Brooke of Warwick, Lord Saye and Sele, John Pym, and other critics of Charles I. Books were evidently important, and after his death his household preacher Thomas Dugard recalled that Sir Thomas had been 'accounted a living library'. Of his widow Dame Alice Lucy, physically infirm and confined to the house, a great reader, and the niece of Lord Chancellor Egerton, Dugard observed 'A great library had shee' (conceivably her late husband's, since she inherited a life interest in his chattels).[81] In contrast to the tomb books, the actual books on the shelves at Charlecote remain enigmatic. There

are plenty which look as if they could have been in the house since the sixteenth century, but the earliest catalogue dates from 1681, and only one book, a copy of Philippe Moreau's *Le Tableau des Armoiries de France* (Paris, 1609; fig. 65), can be unequivocally identified with Sir Thomas, because of its elegant gold-tooled binding with the initials 'T.L.' Other books also have fore-edge titles, and probably Sir Thomas Lucy's long-vanished Study was shelved just like his tomb. It may indeed have been arranged as it was in 1681, when the books were grouped by subject.[82]

Books in another sixteenth-century Warwickshire library, probably in a country house, were certainly kept on shelves. The existence of this collection can only be deduced from the distinctive shelf-marks written into a number of books in the

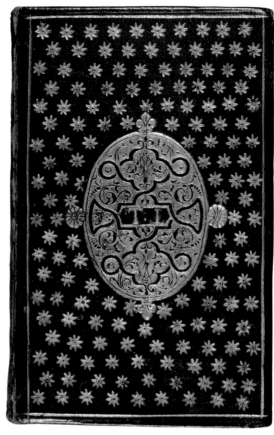

historic library of St Mary's Church, Warwick, now at Birmingham University. These refer to 'Chymney end', 'Low End', and 'Si:' (perhaps 'Sinister': the left-hand side), followed by the number of the shelf (for example 'Chym. e. 2 sh.'). The unknown owner – conceivably the scholar, poet and administrator Sir Fulke Greville, 1st Lord Brooke of Warwickshire (1554–1628), of Beauchamp Court and Warwick Castle – evidently had a Study with a fireplace and three substantial presses, with or without doors.[83]

Loseley Park

One of the best-documented sixteenth-century domestic libraries is that which belonged to the Surrey MP Sir William More (1520–1600) of Loseley Park, described in detail in two documents, one dating from 1556, and the other from 1600. The 1556 inventory describes the contents of the house just before Sir William rebuilt it in the 1560s. It includes a detailed enumeration of the contents of 'myne own closette', a richly furnished room, packed with books, furniture and useful articles of all kinds. The inventory begins with four maps, 'a little cronicle in frame', 'a p[er]petuall Kalender in a frame' and 'a lytlle' picture of 'Judythe', suggesting that the appraiser began with what was hanging on the walls. Then we move to the furniture, with 'a joined chayre of chesnut tree', 'a close cheyre of strawe', 'a deske of chesnut tree', 'a lyttle other deske to wryte on'. Next are writing implements and other items useful to the man of business: 'a standyshe [inkstand] of pewter', 'a globe', 'ij toche stones' (for identifying precious metals), 'a dust boxe of bone' (for smoothing parchment), 'a penne of bone to wryte wt', 'a Sele of many Seles', 'a penknyf'. Only then did the appraiser begin on the books. There were 125 of these, including a half dozen 'paper books', presumably commonplace or other writing books. About a dozen of the remainder are law books: 'all the Statuts of Henry theight', 'all the Statuts before', year books, 'Lytteltone tenures', 'a boke of p[re]cydents'. There are popular books of history and geography: 'munsters cosmografye', 'cronica cronicaru[m]', 'policronicon', 'ffabyans Cronicle'. There was a Bible, and New Testaments in English, French, Latin and Italian. Other books in Italian included 'ij bokes of machevels works', 'the Curtesan' (presumably Castiglione's *Il Cortegiano*), 'petrark' and 'Ovyd's epistiles'; there are also a few in French. Besides Ovid, classical writers were represented by Suetonius, Cicero, 'Cezar' and Juvenal. The relatively few items of native literature included 'Chausor' and 'Alexander's barkleys Eglog'. Practical matters were addressed by titles such as 'a boke of medsyns for horses', 'the glasse of helthe' and 'a boke against the Swette'. Light reading was perhaps represented by works like the four listed together as 'the Comentary of Ladys', 'for the apparell of women', 'the defense of good women' and 'a boke of women', and recreation by 'a boke of songs' and 'a lyttle ballet boke'. Overall the books seem to straddle two ages, with medieval favourites such as Hilton's 'Scala p[er]feccionis' and 'Lydgats proverbs', alongside best-sellers of the Renaissance like More's 'Utopea' and 'the prayse of follye' of Erasmus. That 'a wryten boke of p[ro]verbs' is the only book so described suggests, however, that all or most of the rest of the books were printed.[84]

If the 1556 inventory does not describe More's books with the precision deployed in the contemporary catalogue from Stafford Castle, it gives a vivid sense of their broader context. By contrast, in More's catalogue of about 1600 we have more information about the books, but less about their surroundings. The catalogue is arranged by subject, though this probably does not represent their physical organisation: had the books been stored as listed, very large volumes would have been placed next to small ones. Despite this, the categories in the 1600 Loseley catalogue give a good flavour of the library's contents, no less varied than it was in 1556:

> Lattyne bookes of dyvinytye [41]
> Other Latteyne bokes vz poets stories &c. [42–102]
> Italyon bookes [103–112]
> French bookes [113–119]
> Scripture bookes in Englishe [120–172]
> Cronicles [120–172]
> Treatisis stories and other Englishe bookes [180–255]
> Bookes of the lawe [256–76][85]

III · LIBRARIES AND THEIR OWNERS

Humanism, courtiers and service to the state

As the example of Sir William More shows, by the 1550s a Study, with books, as well as the maps, storage boxes and writing equipment associated with them, had become a badge of literacy, learning and civility, as recognisable in Renaissance Surrey as in Italy.[86] For the curious, the studious and the socially ambitious, cultural commentators spelt out what was involved, both in imported Latin books for the learned and in locally printed English paraphrases and translations. Thorough immersion in a Christianised version of the letters of antiquity provided the best possible means of equipping great men (and in a more circumscribed way, women) for the task of governing others. Elizabeth I's former tutor Roger Ascham, for example, recommended that 'the yougthe in England, specialle Ientlemen and namelie nobilitie, should be by good bringing up so grounded in judgement of learning' that when they were called to 'the execution of great affaires, in service of their Prince and countrie, they might be hable to use and to order all experiences, were they good were they bad, and that, according to the square rule, and line, of wisdom, learning and virtue'.[87] It was a radically different approach to that of a century earlier, but Ascham had no time for chivalric yarns like the *Morte d'Arthur*, which he dismissed as 'open mans slaughter and bold bawdrye'.[88] Instead the schoolboy should be taught 'cherefullie and plainliue' to put Cicero's letters into English, before being set to work to translate 'his own English into latine againe'. This sort of education required books, and Ascham's methodology suggested that 'the Grammer booke be ever in the Scholers hand', books which, both then and for centuries after, tended to end up in the family library.[89] In 1562, for example, Richard Bertie and his wife Katherine, Duchess of Suffolk, laid out 2s. for 'two gramer books for the children'; two years earlier they spent 20s. 6d. on school books, buying a copy of 'Eliotes dictionary' (12s.), four copies of Lily's *Latin Grammar* (4s.) and four of Aesop.[90]

Aristocratic boys were increasingly likely to go to university, and to train at the Inns of Court, but the fashion for a humanistic education could also extend to women. The three daughters of Edward VI's tutor Sir Anthony Cooke (1505/6–76), of Gidea Hall, Essex, were famous for their learning, each marrying into the heart of the Elizabethan establishment. Mildred Cooke's knowledge of Greek exceeded that of her husband Lord Burghley, and having inherited only three books from her father, she assembled an impressive library (some thirty volumes still exist inscribed by her, of which seventeen are at Hatfield).[91] Her sister Elizabeth married the diplomat and translator Sir Thomas Hoby (1530–66), while Anne Cooke married Lord

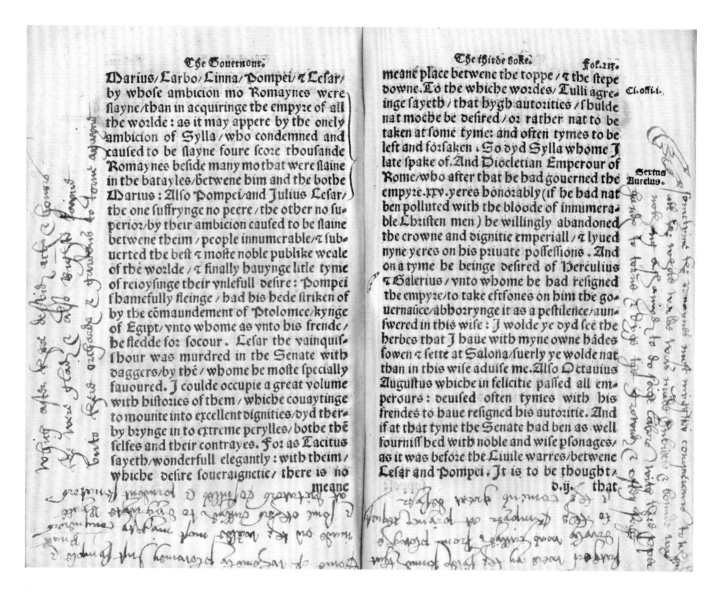

Keeper Sir Nicholas Bacon, was the mother of Francis Bacon and translated John Jewel's *Apology for the Church of England* (1564) from Latin into English. Her magnificently bound set of St Basil in Greek survives, a gift from her husband and a tangible memorial to her learning.[92]

One book which did impress Roger Ascham was Baldessare Castiglione's *Il Cortegiano*. First published in English in 1561 in a translation by Thomas Hoby, it was available earlier in imported editions in French and Italian (both owned by Sir William More).[93] Hoby's translation was found in many Elizabethan gentlemen's Studies, alongside similar manuals on conduct and courtly education.[94] Sir Francis Willoughby (1547–96), for example, had a copy of Sir Thomas Elyot's *The Boke named the Governour* (1531; fig. 66), the first published educational treatise in English, at

Wollaton Hall. Willoughby read it carefully, and his annotations in Latin and English include quotations and paraphrases from classical authors, as well as reminders to compare Elyot's text against passages in Virgil and Cicero.[95]

As Willoughby's elegant Italianate handwriting suggests, the Renaissance cult of studious leisure had found its way to Elizabethan England. But reading Cicero or Virgil could also serve practical purposes. In his essay 'Of Studies', Thomas Hoby's nephew Francis Bacon asserted that 'histories make men wise; poets witty; the mathematicks subtill, natural philosophy deepe; morall grave; logick and rhetoric able to contend'. Writing in 1578, Bacon's uncle Lord Burghley had taken a similar line, advising the young Sir John Harington (1561–1612) of Kelston to read Cicero for the Latin, Livy and Caesar for history – a subject 'exceeding fit for a

[66] Francis Willoughby's copy of *The Boke named the Governour*, 1531 (Nottingham University Library)

gentleman to understand' – and Aristotle and Plato for logic and philosophy.[96]

The success of Burghley's own career demonstrated how effective his prescription could be. His studies at St John's College, Cambridge, from 1535 to 1541 had not only provided him with a mastery of humanist scholarship in Latin and Greek, and a working knowledge of Italian, French and Spanish, but shaped his own views about the conduct of affairs. To prosper at court, to persuade at the council table, to analyse knotty problems, to exchange diplomatic letters with foreign princes – all these skills were dependent on a rigorous intellectual training founded on books. This is borne out in the career of Burghley's son Robert Cecil, 1st Earl of Salisbury (1563–1612). Educated at home by his mother and by tutors, James I's future minister was prescribed a curriculum that included the Latin classics, French, Italian and Spanish, as well as music, mathematics, cosmography, the Bible and Prayer Book. When Hatfield was completed in 1611, a portrait of Salisbury's father was hung in the Study there, a fitting memorial to a man who had set his family on the path to greatness, and done it through learning.[97]

Only a remnant of Burghley's library survived a great sale in 1687.[98] Of what remains, about 200 books are now at Hatfield (figs 67a, 67b, 67c).[99] Burghley owned many houses during the course of his life, but his books seem mostly to have been in London rather than at Theobalds or at Burghley.

[67] Books at Hatfield from Lord Burghley's collection

Certainly by 1615 the principal Cecil library was in Salisbury House in the Strand.[100] Its surviving parts are intriguing and include classical texts in the most up-to-date editions of Lord Burghley's youth, editions of the Fathers of the Church, and Reformed theology (Burghley acquired a copy of Philip Melanchthon's 1552 *Loci Praecipui Theologi* a year after its publication). Then there are presentation copies from clients and supplicants, some magnificently bound, one inscribed by the Protestant reformer Peter Martyr Vermigli (1499–1562). As interesting are the books of practical utility for a statesman, among them a spectacularly coloured copy of *Spiegel de Zeevaart*, a Dutch maritime atlas printed at Leiden by Christophe Plantin in 1584, and Plantin's 1580 edition of a treaty between Philip II and the Archduke Matthias: both interesting in the light of Burghley's handling of the Dutch revolt against the King of Spain.

Francis Bacon's views about the value of study reflected the experience of his own father, Sir Nicholas Bacon. The son of a Suffolk yeoman, Bacon progressed from grammar school to Cambridge, before embarking on a public career that culminated in his appointment as Lord Keeper in 1558. Details of his personal library are scanty. It may have been kept in his great house at Gorhambury in Hertfordshire, built between 1563 and 1568, with a Long Gallery added about 1574, a house for which very little documentation has survived. At any event a magnificent 'sunk panel'

armorial binding made for the Lord Keeper by the Huguenot binder Jean de Planche (active in London from about 1567 until the later 1570s) and Bacon's gift to Cambridge of 200 books, for which he had a special bookplate printed, suggest that he was a man thoroughly familiar with books and libraries.[101] This is reinforced by the *sententiae*, quotations from Seneca, Cicero and other Latin authors, painted onto the walls of the main rooms of his principal residence. Though they are mostly lost, a miniature version of those in the Long Gallery at Gorhambury was compiled for Bacon's friend Jane, Lady Lumley (1537–78), wife of the great book collector, in a manuscript still with Lumley's books in the British Library (fig. 68).[102]

Another Tudor scholar-statesman with an interest in books was the long-serving Secretary of State Sir William Petre (c.1505–72), a Catholic and a patron of William Byrd, who had risen to prominence as a tutor to the Boleyn family.[103] Petre's now incomplete accounts mention about thirty titles, plus other purchases without the names of the books. They include learned books from Continental Europe, medical works (Petre suffered from the stone), books for his children and the 1545

London edition of Froissart (costing 18s.). Petre was well placed to take advantage of diplomatic channels, receiving books from Nicholas Wotton in France in 1553, along with the ambassador's promise that more would follow 'when Paris is clear of the plague'. Some of his books, at least, were kept at his country house at Ingatestone, Essex, as a 'hogshead full of books' was carried there from London in 1552.[104]

Similar men did well in Scotland. Some 345 books from the library of the lawyer and administrator Thomas Hamilton, 1st Earl of Haddington (1563–1637) remained in the family until 1987, when they were purchased by the National Library of Scotland from Tyninghame House in East Lothian, an estate which Haddington had purchased in 1636. 'Tam o' the Cowgate' was an intimate of James VI and, as Clerk Register of the Privy Council, a key figure in the government of Scotland after the king's migration to London. His books, in Latin, English, French and Italian, are wide-ranging, covering mainly history, politics and political theory, with others on law, literature and practical subjects like agriculture and medicine. Like his English contemporary Lord Salisbury, and like many

[68] The *sententiae* of Sir Nicholas Bacon (British Library)

Scots of his day, Haddington studied in Paris, and about forty-five of his books appear to have been acquired there.

In England, too, the careers of two men with diplomatic connections underline the importance of foreign travel in the formation of libraries. Thirty-seven books have been identified from the library of Sir William Pickering (1516/17–75), a graduate of St John's College, Cambridge, and protégé of Lord Protector Northumberland. Some were bought while travelling in Italy, and others while Pickering was ambassador in Paris from 1551 to 1553. Pickering was proud of his library, leaving instructions on his death that it should not be 'spoiled nor dispersed' but should pass to his daughter's eventual husband (she married Thomas Wotton, whose taste in finely bound books closely resembled her father's).[105] Another scholar-administrator, Sir Thomas Smith (1513–77), resigned a professorship at Cambridge in 1547, becoming an MP and Clerk of the Privy Council. 'An universal and thorow-paced Scholar', Smith served as Secretary of State in the reign of Edward VI, and was ambassador in Paris from 1562 to 1566. He owned 'a most compleat Library', variously estimated at between 400 and 1,000 volumes, and partially assembled during his youthful studies in Padua and his diplomatic posting in France. Smith bequeathed his library to Queens' College, Cambridge, 'because', as he caustically observed of his family, 'I see that none of these which shall succeed me of long time are learned'. It was presumably kept at his house in Essex, Hill Hall, newly built in the latest classical style. The 1566 catalogue lists the books by subject: theology, civil law, history, philosophy, mathematics, medicine and surgery, grammar, and poetry. Smith's books were well read, and he was a great annotator, irritated at a lost book in 1572, 'because it was noted with my observations and notes'.

Longleat

If most sixteenth-century libraries have long since left the houses they were once in, parts of the early library from Longleat survive, embedded within the collection assembled by the Marquesses of Bath in succeeding centuries. This is remarkable enough, but the genesis of the Longleat collection predates the building of the present house by Sir John Thynne (c.1515–80), Steward to Protector Somerset. Thynne was the nephew of William Thynne (d.1546), a successful official of the royal

household, whose career began in the 1520s as Clerk of the Kitchen to Henry VIII. William Thynne had literary ambitions and (according to Anthony Wood) 'did make a search after all the works of Jeffrey Chaucer, the prince of our English poets' – publishing them in a two-volume edition dedicated to the king in 1532. His books were at Longleat by 1611; they include a significant proportion of the library's medieval manuscripts, as well as Caxton's translation of Boethius' *Consolation of Philosophy* (1478), used as printer's copy for Thynne's 1532 edition. Already in 1549 there were books in a 'Closett' at Longleat: a Bible, works by Chaucer, Gower and Froissart, Lydgate's Troy Book and sixteen printed bookes 'of sondary sortes'. In 1563 two French workmen were hired for work including decoration of the porch, panelling in the gallery and work on library bookcases. Then, in 1577, eighty-five printed books and manuscripts were recorded in a list of 'Sir John Thynne's bookes at Longleate'. Many of these books are still there, including a copy of Caxton's *Recuyell of the Historyes of Troye* (Bruges, 1473 or 1474), the first book printed in English. What is more, the figure of eighty-five books is likely to understate the true position. The crucial words are 'at Longleate', as there is evidence that Thynne's books and archives travelled from place to place with their owner.[106] Occasionally the wording in similar documents for other houses reminds us of the need for caution. In 1595, for example, a list was compiled of thirty-nine books belonging to the Yorkshire gentleman-soldier Sir William Fairfax (1531–97) 'remayning at Gilling'. It includes six books in Latin (mostly Bibles and a set of Augustine), fourteen in French (mostly translations of classical authors, as well as translations of Machiavelli and Boccaccio) and eighteen in English (including Chaucer, Froissart, Holinshed's Chronicle and 'A booke of hawkyn'). The phrase 'remayning at Gilling' implies that Fairfax also had books elsewhere, and not just at Gilling Castle.[107]

Libraries, religion and the Reformation

In 1533 John Leland had been given his commission to 'searche all the lybraryes of monasteryes and collegies', and if much of what Leland saw was soon lost, some private libraries benefited from the dispersal of monastic collections.[108] The Welshman John Prise (c.1502–55), a government official who worked for Thomas Cromwell, was patron of *Yn Lhyvr Hwnn* (1546), the first book printed in Welsh. He filled his library, in a country house fashioned out of the former monastery of St Guthlac outside Hereford, with the spoils of religious houses in the west of England. Forty-seven of his manuscripts ended up at Jesus College, Oxford, with another thirty manuscripts and thirty-one printed books at Hereford Cathedral.[109] Elsewhere, the Burdet family of Sonning netted books from nearby Reading Abbey, and the Yorkshire gentleman Sir Henry Savile of Banke (1568–1617) acquired others from Yorkshire houses, including Fountains and Rievaulx.[110]

By the later sixteenth and seventeenth centuries fine monastic manuscripts were liable to be snapped up by aristocratic collectors. The ninth-century Southampton Psalter, formerly at Dover Priory, was presented to St John's College, Cambridge, by the 4th Earl of Southampton in 1635, while the Luttrell Psalter belonged to Lord Howard of Naworth by the reign of James I.[111] At Lacock a small residue of the abbey library survived the Dissolution *in situ*, but elsewhere ancient manuscripts might be destroyed or cannibalised.[112] Fragments of the lost Ceolfrith Bible, a companion of the seventh-century Codex Amiatinus and one of the three earliest English Bibles, was found at Kingston Lacy, Dorset, as recently as 1982, wrapped round estate documents inherited from the Willoughbys of Wollaton.[113]

Catholic households continued to treasure pre-Reformation liturgical books. Sir Marmaduke Constable had two Psalters in the chapel of his manor house at Drax in the East Riding in 1575, though he also had an English Bible.[114] In Berkshire the owners of the Buckland estate retrieved the manuscript Missal which their ancestors had bought for the nearby church.[115] At Lyme Park the now unique Sarum Rite Missal, printed in Paris for Caxton in 1487 and perhaps originally in a Legh family chantry, also found its way to the house.[116] The magnificent choir book made for Arundel College in Sussex in about 1525 passed on the dissolution of the college to the 12th Earl of Arundel, and then into the Lumley Library.[117]

In Northamptonshire the recusant Sir Thomas Tresham (1534–1605) owned around 1,700 books by 1605 (a firm figure is elusive, the surviving catalogue consisting of two overlapping book lists).[118] The originator of a series of elaborate building projects, rife with religious symbolism, Tresham kept his books not at Lyveden New Bield, his unfinished summer house, but in the main family house, Rushton Hall, near Kettering. They subsequently passed to his son-in-law the 1st Earl of Cardigan (1578–1663), and many remain at Deene Park, one of the most remarkable early libraries in an English country house.[119] The possessions of another recusant, Edward Arundell of Lanherne (1539–86), included a clutch of interesting books, on a more modest scale than Tresham's, but clearly more typical. Many were in French, including translations of classical texts. There does not appear to have been a Library room at Lanherne, Arundell's books being divided between his Bedchamber ('Marcus Arelius in Frenche') and his Chamber ('David Psalters', 'the diall of Princes', 'the Hestorie of Italie', 'the life of Christe in Frenche', 'Plato in French', 'a frenche Dictionarie', 'a new testament in Lattine', 'the commentaries of Alphonsus Spanishe', 'Treasure of bookes of love in Frenche', 'a booke for the lute', 'Esopes fables in Lattine', 'a paraphrase of the psalms Frenche', 'another litell Frenche booke' and 'Summa Geographiae Frenche').[120]

At the other end of the religious spectrum Lucy, Countess of Bedford (1580–1627), fluent (according to John Florio) 'in Italian as in French as in Spanish, in all as in English', a collector of coins and recipient of numerous literary dedications, presented the library of her brother John, Lord Harington (1592–1614), to Sidney Sussex College, Cambridge, in 1617.[121] Her father-in-law Francis Russell, 2nd Earl of Bedford (1526/7–85), maternal grandfather to Lady Anne Clifford, had a library in his manor house at Chenies in Buckinghamshire. In 1584 there were 162 books in 221 volumes, including Protestant theology (Calvin, Beza, Zwingli and Jewel), as well as books on history politics, stored in a 'longe Trunck'.[122] There were limits to Bedford's interests, however, and when in 1566 a servant found a manuscript at Tavistock Abbey, which Bedford had acquired in 1540, the earl passed it to the bibliophile Archbishop Matthew Parker.

Books for the gentleman lawyer

One of the largest private libraries of the Jacobean era belonged to the judge, jurist and opposition politician Sir Edward Coke (1552–1634). Though many of his books are now at Holkham, the Norfolk seat of his descendants the Earls of Leicester, they seem to have been at Coke's house at Stoke Poges in Buckinghamshire at the time of his death. Coke's interest in his library is evident from his personal supervision of a 'Catalogue of All My Bookes Both Printed and Manuscripts', written on a parchment roll, 42 feet long, which he checked and signed off a section at a time. The 1,237 books were listed by subject, perhaps reflecting their arrangement in Coke's Study. A quarter were books of divinity, which included 'Popish Books' and 'Popish Manuscripts'. The other classes (all similarly subdivided) were 'Laws of England', 'Civill Lawe', 'Approved Histories', 'Philosophy', 'Rethoricke', 'Grammar', 'Lodgicke', 'Schoole Bookes', 'Science', 'Poetry', 'Dictionaries', 'Severall Sciences', 'Tracts and Discourses' and 'Antiquities & Rarities'. Many of Coke's books were in foreign languages, including a collection in Italian, inherited via his second wife, Burghley's granddaughter Elizabeth Cecil (1578–1646), from the library of her first

[69] Armorial stamp of the 12th Earl of Arundel from a Latin Bible, Venice 1544 (British Library)

husband's uncle Sir Christopher Hatton (1540–91). Edward Coke's engagement with his books reached back into his youth, and there is still at Holkham a copy of Horace which he annotated before 1567, when he was fifteen years old.[123]

Other country houses have in their libraries books which belonged to seventeenth-century lawyers. At Belton the core of the library consists of books that belonged to 'Old' Sir John Brownlow (1594–1679), trained in law and son of Richard Brownlow (1553–1638), the long-serving Chief Prothonotary (chief clerk) of the Court of Common Pleas. Thirty-six books can readily be identified as having belonged to Sir John, as well as a commonplace book; there are probably more on the shelves, unmarked and unidentifiable.[124] At Montacute in Somerset the lawyer Edward Phelips (c.1555–1614), Speaker of the House of Commons from 1604 to 1611, owned legal books, but also had a copy of Christopher Saxton's splendid 1579 atlas of the counties of England, as well as histories and classical texts.[125]

Sometimes studying law had unexpected benefits for the bookishly inclined. The Scottish gentleman-poet William Drummond (1585–1649) purchased 399 books during his legal studies in France between 1606 and 1608, a quarter of the final total of what grew to be an exceptional library, kept at Hawthornden Castle in Midlothian.[126] Drummond lived the life of a country gentleman, but a successful legal career could bring in money, and with it the wherewithal to indulge in expensive intellectual pursuits. The library of Thomas Egerton, 1st Viscount Brackley (1540?–1617), is a case in point. The illegitimate son of a Cheshire gentleman, Egerton invested his legal earnings buying land in the west of England, rose in the service of the Crown, and was ennobled and appointed Lord Chancellor in 1603. A noted patron (his second wife had close ties with Edmund Spenser), Egerton was the dedicatee of Bacon's *Advancement of Learning* (1605). The earliest written record of his library is a 'Catalogue of my Ladies Books at London', which lists more than 200 books and was compiled in 1627, a decade after his death. By the time of the Civil War at least part of the collection, by then in the hands of Egerton's son the 1st Earl of Bridgewater (1579–1649), was at Ashridge in Hertfordshire. Where Egerton originally kept his books is unclear but, like Coke's, they formed the nucleus of a great aristocratic library, a collection which remained in the hands of his descendants until sold to Henry E. Huntington for a million dollars in 1917.

Books for the 'Nobilitie'

Members of the ancient nobility also owned books. When she died in 1676, Lady Anne Clifford, proud of her lineage and her many castles, laid down that the books in each of her houses should remain *in situ*, as heirlooms.[127] Not all families were so fortunate, and it is likely that long-established aristocratic libraries vanished as a consequence of the political and religious instability of the era. Catastrophe engulfed the Howard Dukes of Norfolk in 1547, with the execution of the poet Henry Howard, Earl of Surrey (1517–47), the heir to the dukedom. Surrey's armorial stamp – along with a similar one used by his contemporary the 12th Earl of Arundel, the earliest non-royal English heraldic book stamp (fig. 69) – points to a now lost library, as does the survival of odd volumes, for example a manuscript history of Ireland which had once belonged to Surrey's grandfather the 2nd Duke of Norfolk (1443–1524).[128] Surrey's father the 3rd Duke escaped execution by the narrowest of margins in 1547, but his son the 4th Duke went to the block in turn in 1572.[129] No library survived these upheavals intact, though some books passed into the hands of other members of the extended Howard family. Other Howards certainly did own libraries. The 4th Duke's younger brother Henry Howard, 1st Earl of Northampton (1540–1614), rehabilitated in the reign of James I, had anti-quarian interests and was accounted a learned man. His library was sold after his death to his nephew the 'Collector' 14th Earl of Arundel (1585–1646) for the substantial sum of £529, only to be dispersed in the nineteenth century. Some of his surviving books are copiously annotated in his minute and elegant italic hand. Five commonplace books have also survived, one at Castle Howard, and the other four with the remnant of the library of another nephew, William, Lord Howard of Naworth, purchased in 1992 by Durham University Library.[130]

This Lord Howard (1563–1640) was the third son of the executed 4th Duke. Educated at St John's College, Cambridge, from the 1580s he became increasingly open in his Catholicism, perhaps influenced by his half-brother St Philip Howard (1557–95). Around the same time he started to associate with antiquaries and book collectors, including men

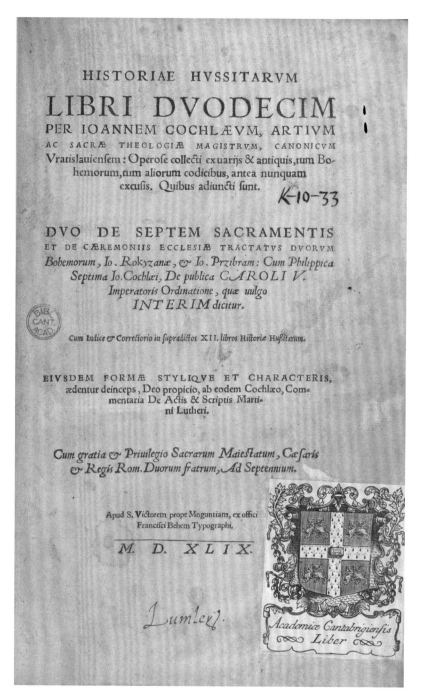

who had been in the circle of Archbishop Parker in the 1560s and 1570s. Howard clearly liked illuminated manuscripts and owned some extremely fine ones, including the Luttrell Psalter, possibly inherited from Howard or Arundel ancestors. Other books came from the family of his wife Elizabeth Dacre, including the cartulary of Lanercost Priory, less than a mile from Naworth Castle. He also bought manuscripts, acquiring eleven in 1589, twenty-six between 1587 and 1595, and owning 128 by the end of his life. Camden visited Naworth and described Howard as 'a singular lover of venerable antiquity and learned with all'. As with Northampton's, much of his library passed to his nephew, the 14th Earl of Arundel, though a rump of 282 books remained at Naworth until their sale to Durham University in 1992. Howard's interconnected Library room, bedchamber and chapel, in the so-called 'Lord William's Tower', escaped the fire which gutted the castle in 1844, but none retain their original furnishings.[131]

The Lumley Library

The largest private library of the period may have been that which belonged to the scholar-collector John, Lord Lumley, and which at the time of his death in 1609 contained over 2,600 books (fig. 70).[132] Lumley was a Catholic nobleman proud of his ancient lineage, and his books can only be understood in the context of his collections of portraits, antiquities and furniture. These are uniquely well known owing to the survival of a series of lavishly illustrated inventories, compiled in the last decades of his life.[133] Many of Lumley's possessions were kept at Lumley Castle, his ancestral seat in County Durham, but his library was at Nonsuch Palace in Surrey. The core was the collection of Lumley's father-in-law Henry Fitzalan, 12th Earl of Arundel (1512–80), another grandson of the 4th Earl of Northumberland, Lord Chamberlain to Henry VIII and Edward VI, and Lord Steward to Mary. Arundel had been instrumental in the Catholic queen's accession in 1553, and one of his rewards was the unfinished royal palace at Nonsuch (fig. 71), purchased for a bargain £485 13s. 4d. in 1556. At the time the palace housed the library confiscated from Archbishop Cranmer, consisting of more than 585 printed books and 70 manuscripts. To these books Arundel added a further 400 of his own, including former monastic manuscripts. His daughter and son-in-law joined

him in the summer of 1558, with both palace and library passing to Lumley on the earl's death in 1580.[134] Lumley retained ownership of Nonsuch until 1592, when the palace returned to the Crown, and remained as resident keeper until his death. The books stayed in place, and seem to have been given to James I's son Henry, Prince of Wales, just before Lumley's death, the childless collector taking it for granted that the library would remain *in situ* in royal ownership.[135]

Little is known of the purpose or use of the Lumley Library, and less about how and where it was kept at Nonsuch, a subject which has attracted surprisingly little interest. Demolished in the early 1680s, the palace was arranged around two large courtyards. The library may have been housed in or near the royal apartments on the first floor of the inner court, possibly in the vicinity of the palace's Long Gallery.[136] As subsequent difficulties fitting them into their new quarters at St James's Palace show, the books must have taken a considerable amount of space. Lumley's protégé Anthony Watson, Rector of nearby Cheam and later Bishop of Chichester, was deeply impressed, remarking in a Latin description of Nonsuch of about 1575: 'If Ptolemy could come back to life, he would die again of envy when he saw this library, with its books on the arts, philosophy, jurisprudence, medicine, mathematics, theology, history, and spheres, globes, bronze and paper instruments of all kinds.'[137]

We owe our knowledge of Lumley's books to a catalogue compiled in 1596 by Anthony Alcock, a clerk in Watson's household, which survives in a beautifully written transcript of 1609.[138] The books were arranged, on paper and perhaps also at Nonsuch, according to eight subject classes: 'Theologi', 'Historici', 'Artes Liberali et Philosophi', 'Medici', 'Legistae', 'Cosmographi et Geographi', 'Common Lawe Bookes' and 'Musici'. As these headings suggest, the majority were in Latin. The largest single class was theology, but the size of the history section surely reflects not just Lumley's antiquarian interests, but his fascination with pedigrees and portraits, a trait which provoked James VI and I to quip that he 'didna ken that Adam's ither name was Lumley' during an interminable guided tour of Lumley Castle in 1603.[139] Lumley seems to have been less interested in manuscripts, though his library included several extremely important ones, including the great ninth-century 'Royal Bible', and the eleventh-century Cnut Gospels, both from St Augustine's, Canterbury.[140] Nor did he display any particular interest in what are now called incunabula, of which he owned about a hundred. He routinely discarded older books in favour of newer editions, and his catalogue rarely includes imprint dates, the only printer ever noted being Aldus Manutius. The richness of the Lumley Library was in the range of texts it contained, not in editions, and to this extent Lumley cannot be called a bibliophile in the sense that the term came to assume later on.[141]

Books for the gentry

It is not clear whether there was any sense of dynastic pride in the books at Lyme Park, the great house of the Legh family in Cheshire, but the family was as conscious as Lumley of its ancient lineage. In 1590 Sir Peter Legh (1563–1636) wrote to his chaplain, Henry Sumner, asking for help in procuring books, including Scapula's edition of St Bernard, an edition of Aquinas, and 'two other mallengy' [melancholy] books, as well as a sermon for his 'two Brothers-in-law wch be now in the Country, for soe muche I promised theym'.[142] A generation later his son Francis Legh (1590–1643) sought help from his former tutor Ralph Richardson in procuring a history of the Council of Trent (presumably Paolo Sarpi's) as well as a copy of Raleigh's *History of the World*.[143] The Leghs' library, poorly documented but still partially extant at Lyme Park, was probably typical of the books found in a wealthy gentry house.

Another Cheshire gentleman, Sir Richard Brereton (c.1490–1558), had fifty-three books at his manor house near Middlewich. As well as sundry devotional books, books on the scriptures, law books and manuscripts of Piers Ploughman, there was Virgil; several chronicles and histories (Polydore Vergil, the Alexander Romance); 'a boke of jest'; works on hunting and hawking, physic, astronomy and natural philosophy; *Manipulus Curatorum* (a handbook for parish priests); the Latin dictionary *Ortus Vocabulorum*; and the thirteenth-century *Chanson de geste Huon of Bordeaux*. Some of these books were clearly printed, but many were presumably manuscripts, and could easily have been in the Brereton family for some time.[144]

Some gentry libraries were focused on specific interests. The botanist Henry Lyte was, according to Anthony Wood, 'a most excellent scholar in several sorts of learning'. He inherited the library

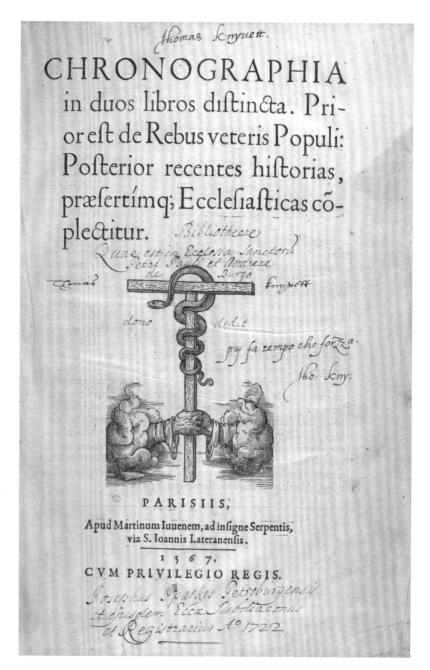

[72] A book from Thomas Knyvett's library: Gilbert Genebrard, *Chronographia in duos libros distincta*, Paris 1567 (Cambridge University Library)

at Lytes Carey from his father Thomas, travelled on the Continent and translated the *Cruydenboeck* of Rembert Dodoens into English, publishing it as *A Niewe Herball* in 1578. According to John Aubrey, he had 'a pretty good collection of plants for that age' and presumably bought botanical books, too. (His copy of a French edition of the *Cruydenboeck* is in the British Library, copiously annotated in his neat hand and inscribed 'Henry Lyte taught me to speake English'.[145]) Other families had more predictable interests. A list of 'My bokes of historie' (1597) survives from Place, the house of the Treffry family at Fowey in Cornwall. It includes classical works like Tacitus and Herodotus (perhaps translations), works in English (Hollingshead's and Hall's *Chronicle*, as well an English translation of the historian Guicciardini), the chronicles of Froissart and Philippe de Comines, as well as books by Boccaccio and Chaucer, More's *Utopia* and Spenser's then new *Faerie Queen*. Though the list clearly describes no more than a part of a larger library, it is interesting that the owner was apparently making catalogues of books by subject.[146]

Other country gentlemen bought books on a much grander scale. Sir Arthur Throckmorton (c.1557–1626), the Protestant cousin of the senior Catholic branch of the family, was the son of Sir Nicholas Throckmorton, ambassador in Paris from 1559 to 1564. He travelled extensively in Continental Europe, purchasing books of religious controversy, both Catholic and Protestant.[147] More books were bought on his return to England, and throughout the rest of his life.[148] At Magdalen College, Oxford, 221 titles survive from the library once kept in the Study of his great house at Paulerspury in Northamptonshire (fig. 63).[149] Marked with Throckmorton's 'ATM' monogram, they give a good flavour of the appearance of his library, though not necessarily of its intellectual range, as Sir Arthur left his English volumes to his widow. Throckmorton owned several splendid and expensive books, including the Plantin Polyglot Bible, a *Nuremberg Chronicle* (1493), the works of Luther in six folio volumes and Herberstein's finely illustrated *Rerum Moscoviticarum Commentarii* (Basel, 1556). In addition to five books by Tycho Brahe, the many French and Italian books included the 1541 edition of Castiglione, Bodin's *Six Livres de la République* (1577), a 1584 Venetian edition of Ariosto's *Orlando Furioso* and Continental Protestant books.

The library of the Norfolk gentleman Sir Thomas Knyvett (c.1539–1618), of Ashwellthorpe near Wymondham (much of which is now in Cambridge University Library), is especially interesting (fig. 72). Though not particularly wealthy, Knyvett was well connected, the father-in-law of Sir Nathaniel Bacon of Stiffkey, son-in-law of Elizabeth's Comptroller of the Household, distantly related to the Howards, and the grandfather of Henry Peacham, whose remarks on libraries in his *Compleat Gentleman* (1634) probably reflected his memories of Ashwellthorpe. During the course of a long life Knyvett assembled a library of about 1,400 printed books and seventy manuscripts,

valued at his death at a substantial £700.[150] At the beginning of his career many of the books bought were standard works, including classical texts and books on geography and antiquities, but by the 1570s Knyvett was becoming a serious collector, not only of books but also of medals and pictures. Year on year he added a succession of important and unusual books to his shelves, including works on anatomy and medicine, Indagine's *Introductiones in Chiromantium* (Strasbourg, 1522) – on palmistry – and two major architectural books, Alberti's *Architettura* (Florence, 1550), and a first edition of Palladio (1570). He was attracted to illustrated books, owning a copy of De Bry's *India Orientalis* (Frankfurt, 1598), and while many of his books were printed in his own lifetime, some were older. About three-quarters of the entire collection was in Latin, but Knyvett was also familiar with modern languages, travelling abroad in 1570–71 'for the increase of his experience, and knowledge of forrayne languages'.[151] At Ashwellthorpe the books, bought locally and ordered from London, were used by an appreciative circle of friends, and Knyvett occasionally noted details of his own reading in them. Though not ostentatiously bound, the collection was evidently well housed, and Knyvett, in addition to his coins, owned a pair of globes by Mercator, clearly associated with the library and borrowed by a grateful neighbour in the early 1590s.[152]

The ownership of a library or of books did not necessarily imply learning. Another Norfolk gentleman, Sir Edward Paston (1550–1630), had a large library in his house, Appleton Hall, notable for its printed and manuscript music.[153] At Hengrave Hall, the Suffolk seat of the recently deceased Sir Thomas Kytson, the 'chamber where ye musicyons playe' contained in 1603 'two lewting books covered with lether', as well as a further fifty-two music books, including part books, English songs, dances, part-songs and five books containing 'one sette of Italian fa-laes'. There was also 'one great booke wh[ich] came from Cadis', a piece of loot from the Earl of Essex's raid in 1596.[154] In Essex the Petres kept musical part books 'in the little cupboard in ye Drawing Roome': they included Byrd's *Gradualia* and *Sacrae Cantiones*.[155]

Readers like Grace Mildmay would have objected to such Popish books, but other houses contained books which would have attracted equal disapprobation. A cache of early popular literature was discovered in the attics of Lamport Hall in Northamptonshire in 1867, presumably evicted from the principal rooms of the house when a new Library was built in the eighteenth century.[156] Also in the Midlands Frances Wolfreston (c.1607–77) spent her married life at the still-extant manor house at Statfold, near Tamworth. Nearly a hundred of her books are known, many scarce English literary works of the sixteenth and seventeenth centuries, including works by Donne and Marlowe, as well as ten Shakespeare quartos, the leisure reading of a literate but not learned country gentlewoman.[157]

Display and the notion of the library

In his funeral poem for the Earl of Devonshire (1606), Lady Anne Clifford's tutor Samuel Daniel heaped praise on the dead earl's learning, contrasting it with those who bought books for show, 'thou hadst not books as many have / For ostentation but for use'.[158]

A handful of collectors of this period clothed their books in ostentatiously fine bindings, but this was not common. The best known were Sir Thomas Wotton and Elizabeth's favourite Robert Dudley, 1st Earl of Leicester (1532–88). Unlike Wotton, Leicester, the second Englishman to commission a sizeable number of gold-tooled bindings, patronised English binding shops (fig. 73). He seems to have begun his library in the early 1560s, though there is little evidence as to which of his many houses his books were kept in. They may have been in London, and certainly there was a chest of books valued at £5 'in ffrench, lattyn, Italian and Dutche' in the Wardrobe at Leicester House in the Strand in 1590.[159] Leicester's surviving books, of which there are a little over eighty, are generally standard editions of classical texts, the Fathers, and contemporary scholarship (only one is in English), all with armorial bindings.[160]

If fine bindings were embellished with arms they proclaimed lineage and ownership, in a code which contemporaries were used to reading. Leicester's books were generally of considerable grandeur, but other armorial bindings were more modest.[161] Sir George Carew, 1st Earl of Totnes (1555–1629), a long-serving government official in Ireland, liked his books painted with his arms in their correct colours. Most owners preferred gold, applied with a brass stamp like that in the British Museum which once belonged to Christopher Hatton,

[73] A Robert Dudley binding on a copy of the Aldine Aristotle (1495–98) (Lambeth Palace Library).

1st Baron Hatton (1605?–70), of Kirby Hall in Northamptonshire.[162] Altogether over fifty armorial stamps are known with the arms of members of English and Scottish owners active before 1603, and more from the period down to the Civil War.[163] Individual bindings hint at now scattered libraries, though when stamps survive on just a handful of copies it is difficult to be sure. A single seventeenth-century armorial binding survives at Wallington, in Northumberland (fig. 74). There are good reasons to assume that it was once in the Trevelyans' original home, Nettlecombe Court in Somerset. But since no other example of the stamp is known, we cannot be too confident about this. Some armorial stamps were made to be applied to presentation copies. Francis Bacon's stamp, for example, was used both on books which he gave away and on books from his own library, while there are a number of surviving copies of Edward, Lord Herbert's *De Veritate* (1648) in presentation bindings which incorporate the author's crest. In other cases we know that armorial stamps were made for institutional libraries, to commemorate benefactors.[164]

It is a moot point whether fine and armorial bindings were linked with the development of Library rooms as places of display.[165] Armorials clearly carry overtones of family pride and dynastic continuity, which in this context imply a self-conscious awareness of the notion, for want of a better word, of 'libraryness'. This is equally true of armorial bookplates, engraved and pasted inside books, but in Britain and Ireland very rare indeed until the later seventeenth century. The earliest British bookplates were made for Sir Nicholas Bacon's 1574 gift of books to Cambridge University Library, while one of the earliest personal examples is the bookplate of Sir Thomas Tresham.[166] These, along with other refinements like shelf-marks, are arguably markers that we are crossing the Rubicon, from the library as a pile of books in a closet or bedchamber to the library as something more

long-term or even permanent. However, the range of possible expressions is wide, and it is best not to draw too rigid conclusions.

When it comes to display, it seems clear that more qualification is necessary. Surviving aristocratic bindings with gold tooling and armorials do suggest a certain taste for show in aristocratic libraries (they would have looked especially good in candlelight), but many other books were quite plain, even when they came from grand libraries. Sir Thomas Knyvett owned only one fine binding at Ashwellthorpe, a pocket-sized edition of the Psalms published in Antwerp by Christophe Plantin in 1564, bound by the MacDurnan Gospels binder, and probably a gift.[167] And since early libraries seem generally to have been kept in private apartments, they would in any case have been unseen except by owners and their intimates. Presumably the books in rooms like Sir Henry Unton's Study at Wadley were, like his gilded hangings, there primarily for the owner's delectation, and as much about affirming his elevated status to himself and his household than about trumpeting it to the outside world.

In 1605 the civil servant and Cecil client Sir Walter Cope (d. 1614) built himself a great country house, Cope House (later renamed Holland House), in the village of Kensington, just to the west of London. He owned a fine collection of medieval manuscripts, at least 215 in number, though his motives for collecting them are less than clear. There is no obvious sign that Cope was particularly a scholar, but his house contained a notable collection of pictures and curiosities, visited by Queen Elizabeth, James I, and Christian IV of Denmark, and this is probably the key to the conundrum. Cope was active at much the same time that members of the aristocracy first started to assemble large collections of antiquities, a practice commended by Henry Peacham in 1634.[168] Like his visitors, Cope was a virtuoso, a gentleman collector who had read his Castiglione, knew about Italy and liked to make a display of his scholarly interests. With him, and them, we start to move into another world.[169]

[74] A seventeenth-century Trevelyan armorial stamp (Wallington Hall)

CHAPTER FOUR

'Your own admirable library'

Book Collecting and the Country House from Elizabeth I to the Eighteenth Century

You are now in the midst of that you with so much reason delight in, your own admirable library.
William Stratford to Edward Harley, 2nd Earl of Oxford, 1722

I · THE VIRTUOSO LIBRARY

The Arundel Library and the advent of collecting

Writing later in the seventeenth century, John Evelyn acclaimed Thomas Howard, 14th Earl of Arundel (1585–1648), as 'the father of vertu in England, the great Maecenas of all politer arts'.[1] The concept of *virtù*, today somewhat esoteric, would have been clear enough to Arundel and the emerging collectors of his generation. More than just moral virtue, *virtù* encompassed the full gamut of courtly accomplishments set out by Castiglione in *The Courtier*. The virtuoso was a man of culture, interested in the natural world, immersed in the arts and letters of antiquity, a collector of pictures, drawings, sculpture and inscriptions, of coins and antiquities, and, of course, of books.[2] The word was first used in English in *The Compleat Gentleman* of Henry Peacham, Sir Thomas Knyvett's grandson, and tutor to Arundel's sons.[3] Arundel – who but for the attainder of his grandfather in 1572 would have been Duke of Norfolk – came from a family with a long-standing interest in books and libraries. John, Lord Lumley, was his grandmother's brother-in-law; Lumley's father-in-law the 12th Earl of Arundel, his great-grandfather; and William, Lord Howard of Naworth, his uncle. The Collector Earl was married to the heiress Alethea Talbot (1585–1654), a collector in her own right, the granddaughter of Bess of Hardwick and daughter of Bess's stepson the 7th Earl of Shrewsbury. The descendant of the premier dukes and earls of England, Arundel in his youth had been part of the court of Henry, Prince of Wales, and numbered among his friends the great manuscript collector

Sir Robert Cotton (1570/1–1631). He was a central figure in the short-lived but brilliant court culture of Charles I, a patron of Inigo Jones, an art collector, the owner of the Arundel Marbles, and the object of suspicion for his family's Catholic leanings, his Popish pictures and his liking for Italy, where he died in exile in Padua in 1646.[4]

Arundel's library was partly founded on the books of his ancestors, together with the library of his uncle the 1st Earl of Northampton, which he purchased for £529 in 1615. But the most important part of the collection was the library of the humanist and bibliophile Willibald Pirckheimer (1470–1530), which Arundel bought from his descendants while passing through Nuremberg in 1636. Pirckheimer had been the friend and patron of Albrecht Dürer, and Dürer illuminated many of his books and designed his bookplates. Some of Pirckheimer's books in turn came from the famed Renaissance library of the Hungarian king Matthias Corvinus (1443–90), of which the German collector had acquired about a third after the Ottoman conquest of Buda in 1541.

In his lifetime the Collector Earl's books (fig. 76) were kept at Arundel House, in the care of his librarian the German-Dutch philologist Francis Junius (1591–1677), but as a result of their subsequent history they have been far less studied than his other collections. At the suggestion of John Evelyn, the books were given by Arundel's grandson the 5th Duke of Norfolk (1627–77) to the Royal Society in 1667, after grumblings that the young

[75] Anthony van Dyck, *Henry Percy, 9th Earl of Northumberland* (detail) (Petworth House)

duke's priests had been plundering the library.[5] The Society subsequently mixed up the 3,287 Arundel books with the rest of its library in breach of the deed of gift, sold Arundel's manuscripts to the British Museum between 1830 and 1832, and compounded the offence by selling most of the printed books in 1873 and 1925. The 1873 victims included an illuminated copy of the first edition of Augustine's *De Civitate Dei*, printed in Subiaco in 1467, with the Dürer bookplate, purchased from Quaritch by William Morris for £60 and now in the Huntington Library. Many more Arundel books remain untraced, and even the estimated 10 per cent of the books still at the Royal Society are difficult to locate, being poorly catalogued and often rebound with resulting loss of provenance evidence.[6] It is a catastrophic tale, but the Collector Earl's library set the scene for the great aristocratic book collectors of the late seventeenth and early eighteenth centuries.[7]

The motives of these collectors varied, but they were united in seriousness of purpose and persistence of effort.[8] The recovery of a real or imagined national past, joy in classical scholarship, delight in membership of a pan-European network of scholar-collectors, and a sense of the workings of divine providence manifested in the connections between print, Protestantism and emerging national greatness, all played a part. For many there was an obvious pleasure in the act of collecting and ordering books, a simple enough motive often obscured today in a welter of psychobabble which overlooks the fact that for those who can afford it, collecting was and is highly enjoyable. The emergence of this style of collecting also coincided with the early development of bibliography as an intellectual discipline, and the emergence of a new sort of book expert to help the aspiring collector navigate the ever-growing sea of books.[9] Despite, or perhaps because of, the hiatus of the Civil War, contacts with Continental Europe, with the flourishing book trade of the United Provinces and with aristocratic collecting in Paris became ever more important. New ways of doing business crossed the North Sea, and new approaches to running a library, the Channel. By the 1730s it was London, rather than Paris or Amsterdam, which was increasingly seen as the hub of the international trade in antiquarian books, as British collectors first vied with, and then exceeded, their Continental European competitors.

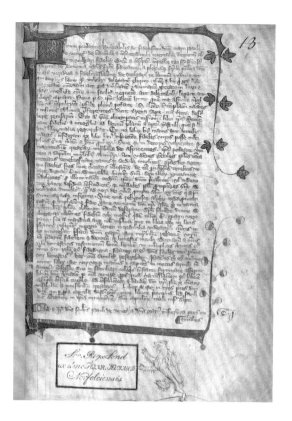

[76] Marco Polo's *Conditionibus et consuetudinibus orientalium regionum*, 1400–50, from the Arundel collection (British Library)

The Wizard Earl

Like Arundel, Henry Percy, 9th Earl of Northumberland (1564–1632; fig. 75) came from the highest tier of the ancient nobility, and his position in Elizabethan and Jacobean England was equally precarious. His sister Eleanor Percy was sufficiently staunch in her allegiance to the Catholic faith to take a Book of Hours with her to Powis Castle on her marriage, and his father the 8th Earl of Northumberland (1532–85) was twice imprisoned in the Tower for plots relating to Mary, Queen of Scots, being found dead there in June 1585, a jury returning a verdict of suicide.[10] The 9th Earl, traditionally known for his scientific interests as 'the Wizard Earl', was accused of complicity in the Gunpowder Plot and was like his father imprisoned in the Tower, spending seventeen years there until his release in 1621, as well as receiving a fine of £30,000. Like Arundel, the Wizard Earl was a virtuoso, and owned a magnificent library, but there comparisons break down. Unlike the lost 'Bibliotheca Norfolciana', the Wizard Earl's library is not only substantially intact (despite the sale of 172 books and manuscripts in 1928) but still *in situ* at Petworth. This library has also been intensively studied, mostly by the Durham scholar Gordon Batho (1930–2013), who published extensively on the Wizard Earl in the 1950s and 1960s. Batho continually revised his ideas during the course of a long and productive life, and died before his final thoughts on the library could be set in order and published. Nonetheless, his studies provide the basis for a far more detailed discussion than is usually possible.

The Wizard Earl certainly had books at Syon House in Middlesex, as his accounts for the period 1600 to 1602 record the expenditure of £1 5s. on 'sorting, titling and cataloguing of your Lordship's books at Syon'. Eight years later, when the earl was in the Tower, a further 28s. was paid for board and wages for the bookbinders who spent a month at Syon 'stamping of books'. Like Raleigh, the earl kept books with him in the Tower, where his suite included a Study, a Library, a Great Chamber, Withdrawing Room and two Dining Rooms, and throughout his imprisonment he continued to spend about £50 a year on books. Though a substantial sum, this was well within his means, as his annual income doubled to £12,000 during the same period.[11] On his release, Petworth replaced Syon as Northumberland's principal residence, and most of his books seem to have been there at the time of his death in 1632.[12]

A panelled Library had been fitted up at Petworth in 1595–6, a successor to the Paradise Study which had existed there a century or more earlier. If, as appears to be the case, the room described as 'the Library' in the 1632 inventory was the same room described as the Gallery in a slightly earlier document, then at the time of his death most of the Wizard Earl's books were in a Long Gallery, 130 feet long, 17½ feet wide and 12 feet high.[13] This room contained fifty-two 'chests of bookes of all sorts', with books sufficient to fill a further twelve chests besides.[14] If Batho's estimate that the Wizard Earl owned between 1,250 and 2,000 books is correct, this suggests an average of twenty to thirty books per chest, assuming that each contained roughly the same proportion of small and large books.[15] Chests seem old-fashioned for a large library in the 1630s, but we cannot rule out that the library was arranged in coffers as it might have been a century earlier. There are certainly coffers of the right date at Petworth, though not very many.[16] Another possibility is that the chests of books were in transit at the time of his death, though this does not square with the room at Petworth being clearly labelled 'the

Library', or with its obviously rich and ordered furnishings. The architectural historian Susie West, drawing parallels from Renaissance Italy, and noting the presence of a new-fangled glazed press ('one cupboard of cipresse open, but closed with glasse') in the Wizard Earl's Closet, has speculated that the Petworth library chests may actually have been wall or below-desk cupboards, rather than coffers.[17] This seems plausible, and West's observation that the 1632 appraiser was evidently puzzled by the glazed bookcase in the Closet is telling, explaining as it does why he might have reached for the familiar word 'chest' on encountering unfamiliar fittings in the Library.

Though no contemporary catalogue of the Wizard Earl's books survives, the arrangement of his library can be partially deduced from the numbers written onto the title pages of his books. These consist of two separate numbers, the first running from one to at least ninety-five, and the second from one to eight. The first element appears to represent a bookcase and the second its shelves, but this does not correlate with the fifty-two chests of the 1632 inventory. In any case ninety-five or more bookcases would have housed far more books than the Wizard Earl owned, and it is difficult to see how so many could have fitted against the walls of a Library room 130 feet long, especially as the room was also hung with pictures. On the assumption that Gordon Batho was right in associating the numbers with the Wizard Earl, and that they relate to the library at Petworth, one hypothesis is that each of the appraiser's 'chests' was in fact a wooden cupboard or press. Some of these may have been single presses, but most were double presses consisting of two compartments, set either side-by-side or back-to-back, each half-cupboard with its own number. Unglazed wooden doors can be presumed, as cupboards with glazed doors or presses with open shelves would not have been described as 'chests' by the appraiser. The chests would only have been moveable when empty (if then), as each half cupboard contained seven or eight shelves of books, with folios at the bottom, and smaller format books at the top. The arrangement by size indicates that the books were shelved upright, and the titles written in ink on the spines show that they were shelved spine-outwards.

Like the Lumley Library, the Wizard Earl's was arranged by subject, but only portions of the arrangement can now be reconstructed. Shelf 6/7, a high shelf, contained octavos about the New World, shelf 10/2 (one up from the bottom) housed folios on mathematics, and shelves 91/1 and 91/2 had large-format books by and about Aristotle. Some of the presses were dominated by books on a single subject. We do not know what was on the bottom shelf of press 8, but the second, third and fourth shelves were filled with books on architecture.[18] Judging by the size of the books in them, the presses are likely to have been no more than about 6 feet high; they may have included some sort of desk or ledge at waist height, though this is no more than conjecture.

Besides its books, the Petworth Library also contained four globes, one of them described as 'one very large globe, white, not perfited [completed]', perhaps the terrestrial globe made by the Lambeth instrument-maker Emery Molyneux in 1592, one of a group of terrestrial and celestial globes he put on sale in that year. These were the first globes to be made in England; examples were purchased by Thomas Bodley and the Warden and Fellows of All Souls, but the one still at Petworth, more than 2 feet in diameter, is the only one of the first batch to have survived (fig. 77).[19] A cupboard in the Library also contained scientific instruments, perhaps those which the Wizard Earl had once kept in the Tower. Another of his instruments, an Italian armillary sphere of about 1580, was presented to the Bodleian Library in 1601; it gives some indication of the magnificence of the contents of the cupboard.[20] The Petworth Library was richly furnished, its other contents including four tables, a bedstead and three dozen wainscot stools. There were seventy-eight pictures, including twelve portraits of Turks, twenty-four Roman emperors (bought in 1586 for £24), twelve pictures of the labours of Hercules, pictures of St Lawrence and the Maccabees, and others 'of all other sorts'. Unsurprisingly, the contents of the room, including the books, were valuable, appraised at £581 3s., more than twice the figure for any other room at Petworth, and a substantial proportion of the total probate valuation of £6,432 12s. 8d. However, although it had a fire and curtains, and a 'table with a foulding frame' (probably a table with a folding reading stand), the Library was not the only room associated with books at Petworth. The Wizard Earl also had forty-four vellum-bound folios, thirty-three pamphlets, 'mappes & other writinges' in a Study or Closet next to his bedchamber.[21]

[77] The Molyneux Globe made in 1592, in the North Gallery at Petworth House

Batho identified 826 books which belonged to the Wizard Earl: 371 at Petworth, 145 at Alnwick, 36 elsewhere and the rest known from documentary sources but not yet located. They were mostly learned books in Latin, but Northumberland was also familiar with French and Italian, and had a smattering of other languages. This is reflected in his advice to his son that the purpose of travel was 'not to learn apish gestures or fashions of attires' but to pick up languages 'that hereafter at your leisure you may discourse with them that are dead' – though surprisingly he thought that Greek was 'but loss of time'.[22] If the library does not suggest the pursuit of old books for their own sake, the Wizard Earl did own a copy of Conrad Gesner's *Bibliotheca Universalis* (Zurich, 1554–5), a key book in the development of bibliography. Surviving books suggest that the subject matter of the collection was rich and varied. As well as the major classical texts and commentaries on them, it included histories and chronicles, English and Continental atlases, books on travels and exploration, an impressive selection of books on architecture and related subjects like fortification. There were books of prints, books on mathematics and theology, and a number of important earlier scientific works, ranging from Paracelsus to Andreas Vesalius's *Vivae Imagines Partium* (Antwerp, 1566), Johannes Kepler's *Astronomia Nova* (Prague, 1609), the *Exoticarum Libri* X of the botanist Carolus Clusius (1605), Basilius Besler's *Hortus Eystettensis*

(1613) and Tycho Brahe's *Astronomiae Instauratae Mechanica* (Nuremberg, 1602). Sixty-nine books have manuscript annotations in Northumberland's own hand, but there is evidence that the books were used by others as well.[23] The Wizard Earl's copy of Jan van der Straet's *Equile Joannis Austriaci Caroli v. Imp. F.* (1578), a fine illustrated quarto on the horses of Don John of Austria, was signed by his steward Sir Edward Francis. Other clients included the mathematician and astronomer Thomas Harriot (1560–1621), who carried out his observations from the earl's house at Syon, and the geographer Robert Hues (1553–1632).[24] Another of the Wizard Earl's circle of savants, the mathematician Walter Warner (1550–1636), had specific responsibility for Northumberland's books, and was paid an annual retainer of £20.[25]

Three seventeenth-century libraries

The philosopher Thomas Hobbes (1588–1679; fig. 78) played a similar role to Warner at Hardwick Hall. Like the Wizard Earl and many other grand folk, members of the Cavendish family retained gentlemen servants, distinguished by the use of the title 'Mr' in accounts.[26] These included resident chaplains and tutors. Hobbes, the descendant of a family of Wiltshire clothiers, first arrived in 1608, when he was appointed as tutor to Bess of Hardwick's grandson William Cavendish, 2nd Earl of Devonshire (c.1590–1628). Hobbes accompanied his charge on a Grand Tour to Rome and Venice from 1613 to 1614. The two men were close in age and Hobbes remained as secretary and companion until Devonshire's premature death in 1628. After a break he then returned as tutor to the earl's children in 1630, travelling on the Continent with the 3rd Earl of Devonshire (1617–84) in the 1630s, before leaving with him for Paris on the outbreak of the Civil War. Hobbes remained a Cavendish retainer to the end of his life, dying at Hardwick in 1679, at the age of ninety-two.[27] Though there are relatively few books in the house today, Hardwick Hall housed the main Cavendish library for much of the seventeenth century, probably until about the 1690s, when the centre of gravity was shifting to Chatsworth.[28] Hobbes was much involved with this library, compiling a catalogue in 1628, with additions continuing until about 1635, by which time it contained about 2,000 books.[29] The shelf-marks in the 1628 catalogue (giving press or cupboard, shelf,

[78] Portrait of Thomas Hobbes, 1676, in the Long Gallery at Hardwick Hall

and position on the shelf) show that by then there was already a modern-style Library room of some sort at Hardwick, either in Bess's new building or in the adjacent Old Hall, and that things had moved on since the 1st Earl of Devonshire's books had been installed at Hardwick in the first decade of the seventeenth century. A further refit, or even a new room, followed at Hardwick Old Hall between 1657 and 1659.[30] 'I have heard him say', recalled John Aubrey, 'that at his lord's house in the country there was a good library, and books enough for him.'[31] Hobbes did not spend all of his time in Derbyshire, but this new Library appears to have been intended mostly for him, though the 3rd Earl of Devonshire was also something of a virtuoso, a learned man and a friend of John Evelyn. The room had shelves and wainscoting coated in 'oyle colour', and there were nine large wooden frames for displaying maps, provided with 'pullies each with two wheels … speeding pulling down to peruse them'.[32] Its construction necessitated a new catalogue, compiled under Hobbes's supervision by his amanuensis James Wheldon, a task for which Wheldon was paid £1 on 26 December 1657.[33]

Another Jacobean grandee, William, 4th Lord Paget (1572–1629), kept an equally substantial library at his manor house at West Drayton in Middlesex. The collection, partially inherited from his father, is gone, but a catalogue compiled in 1617 by Paget's chaplain John Hassall (1571–1654) survives.[34] It reveals that Paget owned about 1,550 books, arranged by subject (in order: theology, law, history, philosophy, medicine and chemistry, mathematics, vocabulary and grammar, rhetoric, miscellanies, poetry, militaria, logic, letters). They ranged from the five-volume Plantin Polyglot Bible to pamphlets asserting James VI's claim to the crown of England, works by Francis Bacon and Jean Bodin, an English translation of Charles Estienne's *Maison rustique*, and an unidentifiable book on mulberry trees. As at Petworth, learned books in Latin predominated, but there were also books in English and other modern languages, Catholic and Protestant books, books on witchcraft, Luther, histories ancient and modern, travel books, books on mathematics, optics and trigonometry, as well as Oronce Finé's *De Solaribus Horologijs & Quadrantibus*, on sundials.[35]

Not all aristocrats were bookish. When the future 1st Duke of Newcastle went up to Cambridge in the reign of James I, his tutors

complained that they 'could not persuade him to read or study much, he taking more delight in sports'.[36] But later in life he and his chaplain Dr Payne carried out chemical experiments at Bolsover Castle, and corresponded with Thomas Hobbes. Hobbes searched London for a copy of Galileo for him and Newcastle tried to entice the philosopher to move to Welbeck, Nottinghamshire, permanently in 1636. At the same time, as governor to the future Charles II, Newcastle told his young charge 'I confess I would rather you have study things than words'.[37]

Scotland, Wales and Ireland

If our view of private libraries in medieval and Renaissance Scotland is often hazy, by the seventeenth century the picture has become clearer. The historian and courtier Sir Robert Gordon, a younger son of the 12th Earl of Sutherland, kept an impressive library in his house at Gordonstoun in Morayshire, where he lived in retirement in the 1640s, doing his best to avoid taking sides between Covenanter relations and his former master Charles I.[38] A beautifully written inventory (fig. 79) of the possessions of the 1st Earl of Buccleuch (d.1633), compiled in 1634, lists 948 books (299 in Latin, 237 in Italian, 15 in Spanish, 326 in French and 71 in English). They included a 1550 edition of Vitruvius, a 1601 Palladio, a Mercator Atlas, French translations of standard Latin texts, and a copy of the 1602 Basel edition of Nicolaus Copernicus's *De Revolutionibus*.[39] The early seventeenth-century polygonal Library room at Ferniehirst Castle (fig. 80), one of several houses long associated with the Kerrs, Earls and Marquesses of Lothian, still survives.[40] Some of the books it once contained may have come to rest in the great libraries at Newbattle Abbey, near Edinburgh, and at Blickling, the family's English seat, which exchanged duplicates with Newbattle in the nineteenth century. The National Library of Scotland also holds substantial records of Lothian book collecting, reaching back to 1643.[41]

Among the most notable libraries in early modern Wales was that of Edward, Lord Herbert of Cherbury (1582/3–1648), older brother of the poet George Herbert. Herbert's books seem to have been divided between London and Wales, with the Welsh portion kept in the Library constructed for him when he rebuilt Montgomery Castle between 1622 and 1625. Little is known about the deployment of the books in the castle, but they

[80] A late nineteenth-century illustration of the seventeenth-century Library at Ferniehirst Castle

LIBRARY FERNIEHURST

FIG. 617.—Ferniehurst Castle. Ceiling of Library.

DETAIL OF BRACKET

clearly occupied a substantial room. From their publication dates it seems clear that the collection was installed shortly after the building project. Unlike the London library, which continued to grow through the 1630s, few books were added at Montgomery after 1628. A large number of books, apparently from London, were bequeathed to Jesus College, Oxford, but the books from Montgomery seem to have been recovered by the family after the destruction of the castle in 1649, entering the collection of the Earls of Powis at Powis Castle at some time between 1748 and 1819. About 250 books (overwhelmingly learned works in Latin) can be identified as having been at Montgomery before the Civil War, but after successive rounds of sales only fifty-nine are still at Powis.[42]

Another seventeenth-century Welsh landowner, Sir Owen Wynn of Gwydir (1592–1662), bought ninety-nine 'Chymick Bookes', mostly in Latin, from a London bookseller in 1629. Wynn was well educated and a younger son, but from his mid-thirties he seems to have lived mostly in an apartment at Gwydir Castle in Snowdonia, managing the family interests for his elder brother, whom he succeeded in 1649. The chemical and alchemical books and manuscripts seem to have been connected with lead mines and other mineral rights on the Wynns' extensive Welsh estates, but Sir Owen's literary interests went further. In the 1650s he had regular dealings with 'Coussen Ellis', a London bookseller. Sadly his library, partly inherited from his forebears, does not survive, but a memorial to his learning, which in seventeenth-century Wales did not just mean Latin and Greek, is the *Dictionarium Duplex* (1632) of Dr John Davies of Mallwyd (c.1567–1644), the publication of which he sponsored.[43]

In Ireland far less survives, the result of successive rounds of armed conflict in the early modern period, and of library sales and the destruction of archives in the twentieth. A remnant of the library of the 1st Viscount Claneboye from Killyleagh Castle, County Down, can be found at nearby Castle Ward, where the books went by inheritance in 1707 (fig. 81). Claneboye was a learned man, a graduate of the University of St Andrews who kept a public Latin school in late Elizabethan Dublin. The school was a cover for Claneboye's activities as confidential agent of James VI of Scotland in the Irish capital, but the scholarship was real. Claneboye's pupils included the future Archbishop

Ussher, and the Castle Ward library includes learned books from the great presses of continental Europe, including classical texts and a massive set of Cardinal Baronius.[44]

The library of the soldier Edward Conway, 2nd Viscount Conway (1594–1655), was on an altogether grander scale. Conway's books were divided between various houses in England and Ireland, but a catalogue now in Armagh lists about 9,900 titles, a huge collection, which appears to have been kept in his principal Ulster house, Lisnagarvey, County Antrim, burned in the Irish rising in 1641. This catalogue alone is enough to establish him as one of the most avid bibliophiles of the period.[45]

II · LIBRARIES AND THE CIVIL WAR

Sequestration and destruction

The Civil War brought a major hiatus in the history of the country house library, and the dislocation it caused is an important factor in the paucity of the evidence for early libraries and their contents. No record survives, for example, of a library of any sort at Wardour Castle, a medieval castle-palace lavishly updated in the 1570s. This may be because there was none. Equally it may be because the mine detonated in a garderobe chute during the recapture of the castle by the 3rd Lord Arundell in March 1644 simultaneously destroyed books, a Library interior and all the documentary evidence that might have shown both existed.[46] Elsewhere we know that libraries were indeed destroyed, either deliberately or as a result of being caught in the crossfire in buildings which were fought over. The Harleys of Brampton Bryan in Herefordshire, for example, resented the loss of 'an extraordinary library of manuscript and printed books' in 1643.[47] In other cases they were broken up not by physical violence, but by Parliamentarian sequestrations, sometimes in the aftermath of fighting and sometimes as punishment for their owners backing the opposing side.

Libraries in castles, high-status residences which were also defensible, were especially vulnerable. The sixteenth-century library of Edward, Lord Stafford, may have been lost in the siege of the castle in 1643.[48] By then Stafford Castle was already much decayed, but Montgomery Castle was, like Wardour, a refined and up-to-date modern residence, its residential quarters barely twenty years old. Offering terms in 1644, the Parliamentarian

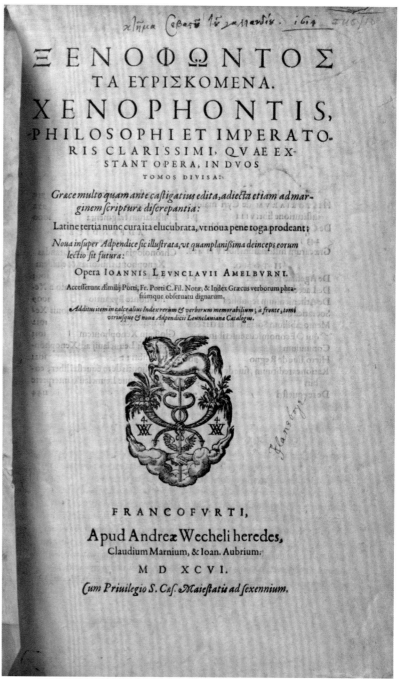

[81] A book from the library of Lord Claneboye: Xenophon, *Quae exstant opera*, Frankfurt 1596 (Castle Ward)

commander promised that all 'household stuff, books, trunks and writings' belonging to Edward, Lord Herbert of Cherbury, would be inventoried and returned if the castle surrendered. Herbert was doing his best to remain neutral, and the undertaking appears to have been honoured, though the castle itself was slighted in 1649.[49] There was clearly a library, probably a substantial one, in the great castle at Raglan in south Wales. Trading words with Charles I, its owner, the Catholic 1st Marquess of Worcester (1577–1646) quoted Aristotle to the king. Asked whether he knew Aristotle by heart, he replied testily 'if your Majesty please to get it by heart, I will lend you my book', an offer which Charles accepted.[50] Further evidence for a library survives in the form of a sixteenth-century French architectural book, Hugues Sambin's *La Diversite des Termes* (Dijon, 1572), subsequently owned by the architectural historian Sir Howard Colvin (1919–2007). Not only does the title page carry the signature of William Somerset, 3rd Earl of Worcester (d. 1589), who visited Paris in 1573, but illustrations in the book, marked in ink with large crosses, correspond exactly to designs executed for him at Raglan.[51] Nineteenth- and twentieth-century guidebooks to Raglan Castle tended to claim that the castle library was destroyed during or after the siege. This may be a pious fiction as the episode is not mentioned in contemporary sources, but without further evidence what actually happened may never be known.[52]

Elsewhere, Royalist propagandists seized on attacks on libraries as an affront to law, religion and common decency. Writing in the newsbook *Mercurius Rusticus*, Bruno Ryves (who had earlier taken refuge with Lord Arundell at Wardour) denounced Parliamentarian troops for attacking the house of the Royalist Sir Richard Mynshull at Bourton in Buckinghamshire, where 'they break open the Library, and the place where he kept his Evidence', and seized 'Bills, Bords, Deeds, Evidences, Writings and Books'.[53] At another Welsh castle, Chirk, a library was caught up in the sack of the castle in 1659, when the former Parliamentarian commander Sir Thomas Myddelton (1586–1666) changed sides too early. The Myddeltons lost all the

[82] Corfe Castle

many books they had purchased in the preceding decades, attempted to recover them after the Restoration, but eventually had to replace their library with books purchased from the estate of Robert Lloyd, a local clergyman who had supervised the publication of the 1630 Welsh Bible.[54]

In other cases the fate of country house libraries was less a matter of random destruction than of targeted punishment and income generation. This was organised by county Committees for Sequestrations, under the supervision of a Parliamentary Committee for Sequestrations and the Committee for Compounding with Delinquents, both established in 1643.[55] In January 1644, for example, two Parliamentarian officers ordered their subordinate Lieutenant Coleman 'to bring away all sort books in the library or study or any other place of Kirby House to Rockingham for the publick'. When John Evelyn visited Kirby in 1651, he described it as 'a very noble house'. It is likely that they found rich pickings on Lord Hatton's shelves, as several wonderful early manuscripts from his collection subsequently found their way into the Bodleian, but in December 1646 Hatton (1605–70) was obliged to compound, paying an eventual fine of £3,226.[56] At Corfe Castle (fig. 82) in Dorset, Parliamentarian troops under Colonel Bingham seized the contents of the castle, including books and papers 'at ye value of 1300l, all new and good' after its capture in 1646. The books were subsequently granted to the lawyer Sir John Maynard (1604–90), who was authorised to take possession of them wherever he could find them. We know nothing more about them, but the contents of Corfe as a whole were clearly of some magnificence, and the Bankes family tried hard to get its possessions back after the Restoration.[57] The library of Edward, Lord Conway, was divided between several locations, but the London portion was sequestered in 1644. The confiscated books, over 4,700 in total, were valued at £200, by far the largest group of books seized by the London Committee for Sequestrations. Conway bought the books back in 1647, and they eventually passed by descent to the Marquesses of Hastings, before being dispersed in 1868.[58]

Problems were greatly exacerbated when owners were, like the Marquess of Worcester, Catholics. In Parliamentarian Norfolk the library at Oxburgh Hall, the seat of the Catholic Bedingfelds, was sequestrated.[59] At Deene Park, where the library included books which previously belonged to Sir Thomas Tresham, the 1st Earl of Cardigan complained that 'his whole library was unjustly taken away', while at Coughton Court in 1642 an eyewitness described how 'many popish books' (possibly liturgical books as some were large and printed on parchment) were burned or hurled into the moat by Parliamentarian troops.[60] At Basing House the rabble-rousing preacher Hugh Peters (1598–1660) boasted that Parliamentarian forces had found 'Popish books many'.[61] It is unclear whether these were liturgical books found in the Marquess of Winchester's chapel, or Latin books from Continental Europe of a kind that could be found in any learned library of the period. Ordinary troops would probably not have been able to tell the difference, but the educated may have found opportunities in the turmoil. After the Restoration Thomas Ross, the recently appointed

Keeper of the Royal Library, visited the Tower with the antiquarian Elias Ashmole to interrogate Hugh Peter, accused of plundering books from the Royal Library. Probably others managed similar sleights of hand which ultimately went undetected.[62]

Some owners took precautions. On the eve of the Civil War the Wizard Earl's son-in-law, the 2nd Earl of Leicester (1595–1677), ordered that in the event of 'danger extraordinary' in London, his evidences should be shifted from his Study at Leicester House to his country seat at Penshurst. If necessary, his books, too, were to be carefully packed 'so that the raine come not', with Leicester adding 'let the housekeeper at Penshurst have order to set them in some roome apart, that they may be all brought to London againe, when it shall please God to send us peace and quietness.'[63] Similar measures appear to have been put in place by the family of the late Lord Chancellor Ellesmere, whose

[83] An annotated book at Kingston Lacy from the Bankes brothers' Grand Tour during the Civil War

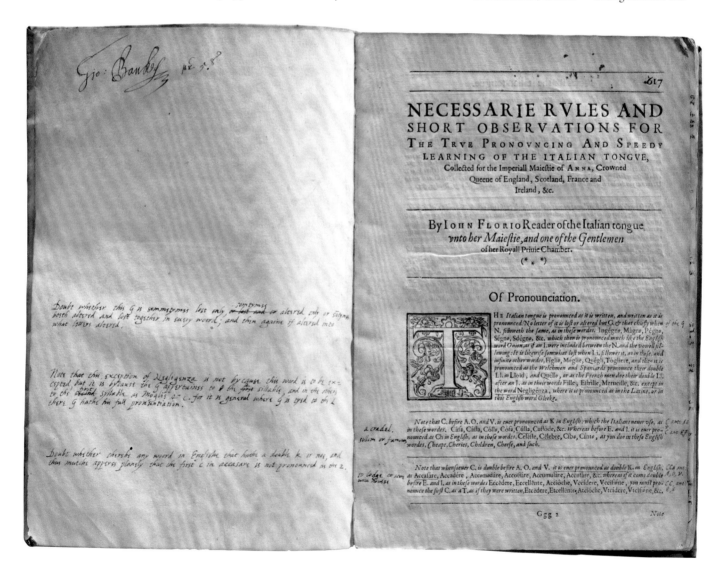

books were apparently hidden at Ashridge, the family estate in Hertfordshire.[64] Others, not so fortunate, lost their possessions, but managed to get them back, albeit at some cost. The goods and chattels of Sir Peter Osborne (1584/5–1653), of Chicksands Priory in Bedfordshire, were sequestered in April 1643 in retaliation for his holding Castle Cornet in Guernsey for the king. The war lost, Osborne paid his delinquency fine in May 1649, and when he made his will in February 1650, he specified that the library at Chicksands was to remain in place and be regarded as an heirloom.[65]

Royalist exiles

Some Royalists used enforced exile on the Continent to collect books, and after 1660 brought back not just new libraries, but new approaches to book collecting. Foreign book buying tends to be associated mostly with exiled Anglican clergy like Michael Honywood (1596–1681), who fled to Leiden in 1643, assembled a large library there and returned as Dean of Lincoln in 1660, eventually commissioning Wren to build a magnificent new cathedral Library to house his books.[66] In fact many members of the gentry and aristocracy spent time abroad in the 1640s and 1650s, and some brought books back with them. The Bankes family of Corfe and Kingston Lacy provide a striking example. After the loss of Corfe Castle, Ralph Bankes (?1631–77) and his brothers William and Jerome embarked on an extended Grand Tour of the Continent in 1648 and 1649. Their progress around France and Italy can be tracked on the shelves of Kingston Lacy, the great house built for them by the gentleman-architect Sir Roger Pratt from 1663, with many books carefully inscribed with their place and date of purchase, sometimes with the purchaser's name translated into the language of the book or the country where it was acquired (fig. 83). The books themselves, now shelved in a nineteenth-century room on the site of Sir Ralph's seventeenth-century Study, are a mix of contemporary English publications, learned books in Latin, and French and Italian books. They include books on architecture, hydraulics, cactuses and coins, as well as travel guides, maps and much else besides. The Bankes brothers evidently made good use of them, as some are annotated, and Sir Ralph's three commonplace books remain with the books they summarise and describe. It appears from the 'Catalogus Librorum' written into one of

these that the Study had thirty-seven shelves, about half of them double-banked, the books arranged in six classes: (1) History, policy medals and travels; (2) Mixed learning; (3) Poetry; (4) Law; (5) Divinity; (6) Mathematics. With about 1,800 titles, Sir Ralph Bankes's library was a substantial one, though probably only about half of the books remain at Kingston Lacy today.[67]

Aftermath

Three important aristocratic libraries passed into institutional hands in the years immediately after the Restoration. One was the Arundel House collection, given to the Royal Society in 1667 with the sad consequences already described. Another was the collection of the former royal commander William Seymour, 2nd Duke of Somerset (1587–1660), who had married Lady Arbella Stuart as long ago as 1610. Somerset's main seat was at Great Bedwyn in Wiltshire, and since he lived mostly on his estates during the Interregnum it is likely that his library, of about 1,000 books, came from there. After his death it was bequeathed to the Dean and Chapter of Lichfield by his second wife Lady Frances Devereux (1599–1674), to replace a library destroyed in the siege of the cathedral close in 1646.[68] The library of the Nottinghamshire Royalist Henry Pierrepont, 1st Marquess of Dorchester (1607–80), an enthusiastic bibliophile and botanist, also found its way into institutional hands, in this case the Royal College of Physicians, to replace a collection destroyed by the Great Fire in 1666.[69]

Another legacy of the period was the taste for collecting Civil War pamphlets, which can be found in considerable numbers in many libraries. Sometimes these belonged to contemporaries who had been active participants in the events under discussion, a notable example being the pamphlets owned by the Cornish Parliamentarian leader John Robartes, 1st Earl of Radnor (1606–85), at Lanhydrock. The subject continued to fascinate later collectors, especially those who felt they had a stake in the history. The Lincolnshire baronet Sir Richard Ellys (1682–1742), whose library, now at Blickling, includes hundreds of Civil War tracts, was the great-grandson of John Hampden (c.1595–1643), of ship money fame. Even in the early nineteenth century the reactionary Squarson William Robert Hay (1761–1839), whose 300-volume pamphlet collection is now at Nostell Priory, clearly saw connections between the Civil War and contemporary debates about political reform and Catholic emancipation, all strongly represented in his collection.

III · THE RESTORATION LIBRARY

Learning to collect

As in other cultural fields, the great changes which occurred in book collecting after 1660 were connected, above all else, with new and renewed contacts with France, Italy and the Netherlands. The Scot, Sir John Lauder, Lord Fountainhall (1646–1722), travelling in France in 1665, spent lavishly on books, packing his trophies up in a box in July 1666 to send them home via Dieppe, and expressing aggravation in his diaries at having to pay duty on them.[70] By 1687 an English guidebook to the French capital was extolling the glories of great private libraries like the Colbert and de Thou collections, praising the splendid rooms in which they were kept, the richness of their holdings, and the learning and industry of the scholar-librarians who oversaw them.[71]

As early as 1644 John Evelyn saw and admired the Duke of Orléans's library in the Palais de Luxembourg in Paris.[72] Travelling on to Italy, Evelyn visited the Laurentian library in Florence, and the Vatican Library, where he admired the great gallery where many of the books were kept, noted the way that the collection was 'all shut up in Presses of Wainscot and not expos'd on shelves', and saw the Bibliotheca Palatina, looted from Heidelberg in 1622. All in all he was deeply impressed, commenting in his diary: 'I hardly believe any Prince in Europ is able to show a more compleatly furnish'd Library.'[73]

Fluent in French and thoroughly conversant with French fashions, Evelyn published an English translation of Gabriel Naudé's 1627 treatise *Avis pour dresser une bibliothèque* in 1661.[74] Naudé (1600–53) was successively librarian to Henri de Mesme, President of the Paris Parlement, to Cardinal Barberini in Rome and to Cardinal Mazarin, and has long been seen as a key figure in the development of librarianship. It is a moot point how influential his text actually was in British country houses. In more than 150 libraries the National Trust has only one early edition (the 1645 French edition), at Belton. This was once owned by the bibliomaniac Thomas Frognall Dibdin

(1776–1847) and cannot have been in Lincolnshire in the seventeenth century, though Sir Ralph Bankes had Evelyn's translation at Kingston Lacy, now gone.[75]

Like many other Scots of his day, Lord Fountainhall also spent time in Leiden, matriculating there in 1666, and the Netherlands was another key influence on book collecting. There had been public book auctions in the Netherlands since at least 1593, but the first such auction in London occurred only in 1676, with the sale of the collection of the recently deceased Dr Lazarus Seaman, Master of Peterhouse, and former Chaplain to the 10th Earl of Northumberland. Formal sales with printed catalogues followed in Oxford and Cambridge (both 1686), in Edinburgh (1690), Dublin (1695), and various provincial towns. Despite doubts expressed about the morality of auctions, the enthusiasm of the Restoration collectors is evident in the number of aristocratic sales in London in the late seventeenth century. These included the libraries of the 4th Lord Brooke of Beauchamp Court (1678), the 2nd Earl of Bristol (1679) and the Duke of Lauderdale (1690–92; fig. 84), as well as the numerous sales of humbler folk whose books subsequently found their way onto aristocratic shelves.[76] The library of the Irish Protestant politician Arthur Annesley (1614–86) was sold in St Paul's Churchyard in October 1686.

[84] Peter Lely, *John Maitland, Duke of Lauderdale, in Garter Robes, c.*1672 (Ham House)

Ennobled in 1661 as Earl of Anglesey as a reward for furthering the Restoration of Charles II, for over thirty years Annesley pursued books that were 'rare and choice in all sorts of learning'. Corresponding with scholars all over Europe, he used his network to acquire 'rare and curious books'.[77]

Of course the whole point about the emerging taste in books was that it encouraged prospective purchasers to be choosy. In 1677 Evelyn inspected the Earl of Bristol's library at Wimbledon House with Lord Treasurer Danby, but recommended Danby, who was purchasing the house, not to buy the books, warning him 'it was a very broken Collection, consisting much in books of Judicial Astrologie, Romances, &c trifles'.[78] On the other hand, sometimes it was necessary to follow Naudé's advice and acquire whole libraries for the sake of especially desirable books. When it was sold in 1686, potential purchasers of books from the library of the Earl of Anglesey were informed in the auctioneer's preface that Anglesey had 'purchased many Libraries for the sake of some choice and valuable Books that he was not furnished wish'.[79]

The Duke of Lauderdale

Born in the reign of James VI, John Maitland, 1st Duke of Lauderdale (1616–82), was a key figure in Scottish politics during the Civil War and, after being imprisoned for a decade from 1651, became the unchallenged ruler of Charles II's northern kingdom after the Restoration. When Evelyn visited Ham House in 1678, he thought it 'inferior to few of the best villas in Italy itself; the house furnished like a great Prince's'.[80] Lauderdale was a learned man, described by Thomas Hearne as 'in his Younger Days one of the best Scholars of any Gentlemen in these Parts', and teased by other members of the Privy Council, who passed Latin treatises across the table for him to translate at sight.[81] Writing many years later, the Whig Bishop Gilbert Burnet, another Scot but no friend of Lauderdale, was caustic in his characterisation of the duke, but respectful in his assessment of his abilities:

he made but an ill appearance, his hair red, his tongue too big for his mouth, and his whole manner rough and boisterous, and very unfit for Court. His temper was intolerable, for he was haughty beyond all expression to all who had expectances from him, but abject where himself had any; and so violently

passionate that he often-times, upon slight occasions, ran himself into fits like madness. His learning was considerable, for he not only understood Latin, in which he was a master, but Greek and Hebrew; had read a great deal of divinity, almost all historians both ancient and modern; and having besides an extraordinary memory was furnished with a copious but very unpolished way of expression.[82]

Lauderdale's Scottish forebears had been noticeably bookish, and already in 1643 he was comparing notes on book collecting with another Scottish nobleman, the 1st Earl of Balcarres (1618–59), and ordering books from Paris, a city where he had met Hugo Grotius and the great book collector Jean de Cordes (1570–1642) in his youth. Other correspondence suggests that Lauderdale was familiar with the workings of the London antiquarian book trade, and he continued to buy books in great numbers during his imprisonment at Windsor in the 1650s.[83]

A key figure in the Lauderdale circle was George Hickes (1642–1715), his chaplain from 1676. Born in humble circumstances, Hickes travelled widely in France and later in life became a non-juring bishop and a pioneering Anglo-Saxonist, attracted to the study of the northern languages in the hope of demonstrating the continuity of the Church of England with the earliest period of English Christianity.[84] Hickes provides the link between Lauderdale and later collectors like Edward Harley, and his influence was felt in antiquarian circles well into the eighteenth century. According to Hearne, who knew him well, Hickes learned Hebrew 'to discourse' with Lauderdale 'in rabbinical learning', while his biographer Hilkiah Bedford recalled: 'The Duke had a very good Library, & I have often heard the Dr say, that he blessed God for the great benefit he had received from thence, & from the Duke's learned conversation.'[85]

The contents of Lauderdale's libraries are now known only from the four sale catalogues printed after his death. The first of these (14 May 1690) was of books in French, Italian and Spanish, 'in fine condition and magnificently bound' according to the catalogue. Many were quite recent, though there was an edition of *Les Prophéties de Merlin* printed in 1485. The English books went at a second sale beginning on 27 May 1690, with many works on history and geography, almanacs, a Shakespeare First Folio (1623) and a number of books apparently bought for their age, including one printed by

Wynkyn de Worde in 1495. Again, the catalogue was at pains to emphasise the splendour of the bindings, the presence of large-paper copies, and the desirability of especially luxurious items like a coloured copy of Christopher Saxton's *Atlas* (1574). The last two sales (26 March 1691 and 25 January 1692) comprised books in a range of languages: pamphlets, learned books, editions of the Bible, chronicles, histories and manuscripts, including nine 'in the Persian language'; the 1691 sale at least was salted with books from other sources, a common problem in interpreting sale catalogues of private libraries of the period.[86]

Lauderdale's famous Library room at Ham (see fig. 226) (1674) replaced an earlier Old Library, on the first floor in the now vanished south-west re-entrant turret and entered through a doorway on the east wall of the Gallery. This room was dismantled in 1673, when workmen were paid 'for helping to Loade his Graces Books'. Its replacement was still attached to the Gallery, much as it might have been in Italy, but was shifted to the west side, where it formed part of the duke's 'fine apartment'. With cedar panelling and joinery, some of its shelves appear to have been reused from its predecessor, but a fitted 'Seder table and drawers, in my Lords Librairie' were new. These cost £12, a substantial sum when set against the £16 13s. 8d. which Henry Harlow the joiner charged 'ffor 572 ft of shelves, with Cedar mouldings about them'.[87] The Ham library can only be understood in relationship to books in Lauderdale's other houses, including Thirlestane Castle in Scotland, his apartments at Court, a town house in Aldersgate Street and his country retreat at Highgate. In London, already in 1670 the duchess was complaining about the number and weight of the books on the upper floors at Highgate, demanding of her husband that 'you wold caus carei your bouks down to the roums below … or els it will fal down this winter'.[88] In the event, however, the Lauderdale library was the victim not of physical but of financial collapse, sold in 1690–92 to pay off the duke's debts by his widow.

Old wine in new bottles

Unsurprisingly the Restoration resulted in a house-building boom. Cassiobury in Hertfordshire was designed by Hugh May for Arthur Capell, 1st Earl of Essex (1631–83), whose wife Elizabeth Percy, brought up at Petworth, was the granddaughter of the Wizard Earl. Evelyn, visiting the house, was enthusiastic, remarking: 'The Library is large, & very nobly furnish'd, & all the books richly bound & gilded: no *Manuscripts*, except of the *Parliament Rolls*, and Journals, which his Lordship assured me cost him 500 transcribing and binding.'[89] House and library are both gone, and Essex committed suicide after being implicated in the Rye House Plot, but we know a little about the contents of the shelves from the sale catalogues compiled in 1922.[90] Fragments of the 'excellent Carving of *Gibbons*, especially the chimney piece of his Library' admired by Evelyn are now in the Library of Castle Hill, Ipswich, Massachusetts, and the great staircase from Cassiobury can be seen in the Metropolitan Museum of Art in New York.

Visiting Euston Hall, the recently rebuilt Suffolk seat of the minister Henry Bennet, 1st Earl of Arlington (1618–85), Evelyn was again impressed with the Library, which he described as 'full of excellent books'.[91] Elsewhere more modest owners kept books in the traditional Studies and Closets. For his own Study at Ryston Hall in Norfolk Sir Roger Pratt designed a room 10 foot by 16 foot, the books shelved together in a 10-foot square bookcase, with room for about 400 folio volumes.[92] However, there were clearly more large Library rooms in the seventeenth century than many published narratives, fixated with Ham House, have implied. At Penshurst by the middle of the seventeenth century there were more than 4,200 books, housed primarily in a splendidly furnished room with fireplace, cupboards and wall shelving. The library, which was largely the collection of the long-lived and well-read Robert Sidney, 2nd Earl of Leicester (1595–1677), survived until 1743, when the books were sold by the 7th Earl of Leicester to the predatory bookseller Thomas Osborne (*c*.1704–67), better known for his sale of the Harleian Library.[93]

At Longleat the heroic age of the library began with the arrival of Sir Thomas Thynne, 1st Viscount Weymouth (*c*.1640–1714), a staunch Tory who inherited the house following the assassination of his Whig cousin Thomas Thynne in 1682. The Old Library at Longleat (fig. 85), an L-shaped room on the top floor, closely resembles a college Library, perhaps unsurprisingly as Weymouth had studied at Christ Church, Oxford. Clearly buying books as much for their bibliographical significance as for their texts, Weymouth was interested in what they had to say about the history of printing. In 1706 he purchased a collection of seventy incunables from

[85] The Old Library at Longleat, c.1949

Venice, which was still a fairly novel interest in 1706, the term 'incunabula' having been coined by the German bibliophile Bernard von Mallinckrodt (1591–1664) in his 1638 pamphlet *De Ortu et Progressu Artis Typographicae* ('On the Rise and Progress of the Typographic Art').[94] Weymouth was innovative not just in his choice of books, but in the management of his library. His bookplate dates from 1704, and he spent money on 'lettering' spines: 995 were done in 1693, at a cost of 12s. a hundred – a task which would have been faced by any aristocratic collectors whose ancestors had once kept their books fore-edge outwards. The 'great turn-round' of the seventeenth century, which saw books almost universally placed spine-out and upright, remains a largely unknown phenomenon outside the narrow world of the rare books specialist, but one which would have had a profound impact on the appearance of Libraries of all kinds.

The Old Library at Longleat is especially associated with the saintly Thomas Ken (1637–1711), a friend of Weymouth's from his Christ Church days who took refuge there when he was deprived of the Bishopric of Bath and Wells in 1691, and bequeathed any books from his own collection

not present in the library to Weymouth in gratitude.[95] A similar arrangement prevailed north of the border, at Slains Castle in Aberdeenshire, where James Drummond, Bishop of Brechin, took refuge with the staunchly Episcopalian 12th Earl of Erroll (d.1704) after the Revolution in 1689, and bequeathed his collection of sixteenth- and seventeenth-century learned books to his hosts by way of thanks.[96]

Other Libraries contained fashionable scientific kit. Susceptible to loss or damage, only rarely does it survive *in situ*. At Blickling in 1700 a collection of mathematical instruments and globes was valued at £36, a significant sum set against the £115 attached to the modest seventeenth-century library of the Hobart family.[97] These, like the books kept with them, are long gone. Elsewhere libraries could be associated with museums or cabinets of curiosities. The most famous collection in a private house in Britain was perhaps that of the town house of Sir Thomas Browne (1605–82) in Norwich, described by Evelyn as 'a Paradise and Cabinet of rarities', but Robert Paston, 1st Earl of Yarmouth (1631–1683), also had a Cabinet of Curiosities at nearby Oxnead Hall, set around the walls of a 'closset', containing boxes, figurines and other treasures in shell, crystal and amber.[98] These are memorably depicted in the painting *The Paston Treasure*, now in the Castle Museum in Norwich.[99] There was a fine library at Oxnead, sold in 1734, rich in books on astrology, alchemy and magic, and some connection seems likely between it and James Fraser (1645–1731), a Scots book dealer with many aristocratic clients, esteemed by Evelyn, who was tutor to Yarmouth's children by 1682.[100] At Burghley House Celia Fiennes (1662–1741) saw a Closet with 'a greate deale of worke under glass and a glass-case full of all sorts of curyosities of amber stone, curall and a world of fine things', while Evelyn viewed Queen Mary's 'rare Cabinets & China Collection' at Whitehall in 1693, where he saw amber, statues and cabinets, gold plate and silver filigree, all apparently kept close by her Library, 'in which were many Bookes in English, French, Dutch, or all sorts'.[101]

Museums of this kind were clearly uncommon. They have perhaps received disproportionate attention from those reluctant to accept that libraries in Restoration Britain were primarily about books rather than ostrich eggs and coral.[102] Much of what we know of them is derived from traveller's diaries, and this raises an interesting historiographical issue. Not once does Celia Fiennes mention a library, and this is true of most travel diaries of the period. It is clear from contemporary descriptions of visits to institutional libraries that important books and manuscripts were shown only to the informed, and that ordinary visitors had to make do with a swift guided tour of the curiosities. Visiting Oxford in 1710, the Frankfurt scholar Zacharias Conrad von Uffenbach (1683–1734) looked down his nose at fellow countrymen content to be fobbed off by tourist fripperies, grumbled about librarians grasping for tips and made a thorough nuisance of himself pestering to see manuscripts, with varying degrees of success.[103] It is unlikely that tourists were received any differently in private aristocratic libraries of the period, though Uffenbach in London conversed with delight with Sir Hans Sloane, viewing the great collectors's rarities in his house in Chelsea, and taking coffee with him.[104]

IV · THE HEROIC COLLECTOR

Collectors and their critics

By the end of the seventeenth century grand book collecting had become very fashionable. Writing in his *English Historical Library*, the bookish bishop William Nicolson (1655–1727) wrote of 'the laudable Emulation which is daily increasing amongst the Nobility of England, vying with one another in the Curiosities and other rich Furniture of their respective Libraries'.[105] These libraries were much used by scholars, and were potentially more accessible than the public collections of the day.[106] Writing to Speaker Onslow about her father's manuscripts in 1753, Edward Harley's daughter the Duchess of Portland (1715–85), herself no mean collector, explained: 'My grandfather and father collected them for the use of the publick; while my father lived, he freely permitted every man to have access to them.'[107] Fifteen years earlier, in 1738, the antiquarian Maurice Johnson (1688–1755) had applauded the Lincolnshire baronet and collector Sir Richard Ellys (1682–1742) for throwing open the great library in his London town house to scholars. 'The learned Owner not only uses & understands his Treasures but freely allows the full use of them even to his Friends own houses,' he wrote.[108] The fact that many of the greatest libraries of the period were initially kept in London is significant. As early as 1684 the future archbishop Thomas Tenison discussed with Evelyn a scheme for a new library at St Martin in the Fields, a parish notoriously packed with under-employed private chaplains and other hangers-on. Evelyn thoroughly approved of the idea, as it would keep them out of 'Taverns or Coffè-houses'.[109] There were few alternatives for the studious at that time. The ancient Royal Library was in a state of decay, the victim of a devastating fire in 1731. George I and George II both had fine private libraries in Hanover, but the best royal library in England was the collection of George II's consort Caroline of Ansbach (1683–1737). Kent's Palladian Library building for Queen Caroline was completed only a month before her premature death in 1737, but her staff remained in place, and her library, by then larger than the Old Royal Library, came to be seen as the principal royal collection. But there was no English equivalent of the royal library in Paris, and private libraries to some extent filled the gap, much as Sir Robert Cotton's library had in the reign of James I.[110]

Not everyone approved. Writing in 1748, seven years after Harley's death, the 4th Earl of Chesterfield (1694–1774) denounced book collectors in a characteristically self-important letter of advice addressed to his son:

Buy good books, and read them; the best books are the commonest, and the last editions are always the best, if the editors are not blockheads; for they may profit of the former. But take care not to understand editions and title-pages too well. It always smells of pedantry and not always of learning. What curious books I have, they are indeed but few, shall be at your service … Beware of the Bibliomania.[111]

Despite Chesterfield's protestations, the 744 books in the library at Chesterfield House included many early and rare imprints, some inherited and all eventually categorised as heirlooms in Chesterfield's own will. Of the six editions of Aristotle on his shelves, five were printed in the sixteenth century, the earliest in 1543. Other books, readily available in more modern editions, included two sixteenth-century Venetian editions of Tasso's *Orlando Furioso* (1584 and 1587), and the first edition of Palladio, printed in 1570.[112] Either in London, or at Bretby Hall in Derbyshire, Chesterfield also owned a gold-tooled binding made for Thomas Wotton in about 1551, as well as a finely illuminated early sixteenth-century French Breviary, the former now in the British Library and the latter in New York.[113] Chesterfield was a staunch supporter of the Hanoverian succession, and his strictures were overlaid with a measure of politics, as many of the antiquarian book collectors were Tories, non-jurors or suspect Jacobites, and their librarians and favoured cultural advisers often also non-jurors, Scots or Huguenots, scholarly men shut off from profitable public employment by politics, nationality or religion.[114] They were closely associated with the flowering of antiquarian studies in the early eighteenth century, an activity often associated with those whom Chesterfield and his ilk regarded as politically suspect.[115]

Joseph Addison's lampoon of 'Tom Folio', the London collector, antiquarian and non-juror Thomas Rawlinson (1681–1725), 'a broker in learning, employed to get together good editions and stock the libraries of great men' who had 'a greater esteem for Aldus and Elzevir, than for Virgil or Horace', lays bare the divide between the collectors and their critics.[116] Rawlinson's friend and fellow non-juror the bibliographer Thomas Hearne (1678–1734) was robust in his response. Critics of the book collectors were

buffoons and persons of very shallow learning … Mr Rawlinson understood the titles and editions of

books better than any man I ever knew (for he had a great memory), but besides this, he was a great reader, and had read abundantly of the best writers, ancient and modern, throughout, and was entirely the master of the learning contained in them.[117]

In another case, criticism was less a matter of ideology than of personal pique. Horace Walpole not only inveighed against his father's enemies, the Harleys (of which more shortly), but dismissed Sir Richard Ellys as 'a rich childless baronet' who 'pretended to learning on the credit of a very expensive library'. Walpole's characteristically waspish criticism, quoted whenever Ellys's library is mentioned, needs to be set in context. Ellys was an unpredictable figure, a religious enthusiast whose vote could not be relied on in the House of Commons, but the marginal notes in his books suggest that his scholarship was real. However, there was another reason for the Walpole family to dislike him, as the Prime Minister's brother Horatio (1678–1757) had hoped to be Ellys's heir. Instead he was passed over in favour of another set of distant cousins, the Hobarts of Blickling, who inherited Ellys's library, his houses and his Lincolnshire estates in 1742.[118]

Not all book collectors were great landowners, but many certainly were. The 2nd Duke of Devonshire (1672–1729), a great collector, was the owner of Chatsworth and Hardwick in Derbyshire, and of great estates in Ireland. The 8th Earl of Pembroke (1656–1733; fig. 86) was master of Wilton, and dedicatee of Locke's *An Essay Concerning Human Understanding*, while the 3rd Earl of Sunderland (1675–1722) was a Whig politician who had married the daughter of the Duke of Marlborough in 1700, an alliance which eventually brought his descendants Blenheim. Others were new men, like Lord Chancellor Macclesfield (1666–1732), born in humble circumstances in Staffordshire, and Lord Chancellor Hardwicke (1690–1764), a Dover attorney's son who bought Wimpole when Harley ran out of money, and assembled a great library of his own on the empty shelves. Elsewhere others imitated and emulated the great collectors on a smaller scale. The Norfolk squire Sir Andrew Fountaine of Narford Hall (1676–1753) was a friend of Macclesfield and Devonshire, and a man with antiquarian and bibliographical interests.[119] Like other collectors, Fountaine, 'a very worthy gentleman', liked to keep an eye on potential rivals, and as a young man was eager to meet Harley, an introduction effected by George Hickes in 1707.[120]

In north Wales Robert Myddleton (1678–1733) collected early books at Chirk Castle, consulted James Gibbs about a new Library, and sought advice from Harley's librarian on its furnishing and arrangement.[121] Gibbs's Library at Chirk, if it was ever built, has gone, but some of the books bought by Myddleton and his younger brother John still remain at Chirk, typically in elegant eighteenth-century bindings like Harley's.

These libraries all differed from one another, but they tended to have certain features in common. Typically their owners pursued manuscripts, incunabula and, especially, classical *editiones principes*, regarded as honorary manuscripts. Full details of books printed by the great sixteenth-century scholar-printers such as Aldus Manutius in Venice or the Estiennes in Paris and Geneva were often entered in library catalogues, even when other books were described more briefly. Like Tom Folio, owners and their advisers understood, as Lord Chesterfield did not, that texts might differ from one edition to another, and even from one copy to another. They also grasped that books were themselves historical artefacts. The best editions were not invariably the most recent ones, and even when they were, they were not necessarily the most interesting.[122]

The Harleian Library

The greatest private library in early Hanoverian England was unquestionably that owned by Edward Harley, 2nd Earl of Oxford (1689–1741), eldest son of Queen Anne's disgraced chief minister Robert Harley (1661–1724; fig. 87). After his father's imprisonment, Harley rejected Hanoverian court culture with its fashionable artists and Palladian architects, and instead created his own counter-culture, centred around his two great estates, Welbeck and Wimpole, and his London town house in Dover Street, Piccadilly. He was the friend and patron of Jonathan Swift and Alexander Pope, and his circle included the poet-diplomat Matthew Prior (1664–1721), the architect James Gibbs (1682–1745), the antiquary and engraver George Vertue (1684–1756) and the musician Thomas Tudway (c.1656–1756). By the time of his death, Harley had worked his way through £400,000, confessing to his wife in 1728 that his financial straits were 'in very great measure due to my own Folly'. He took over his father's library

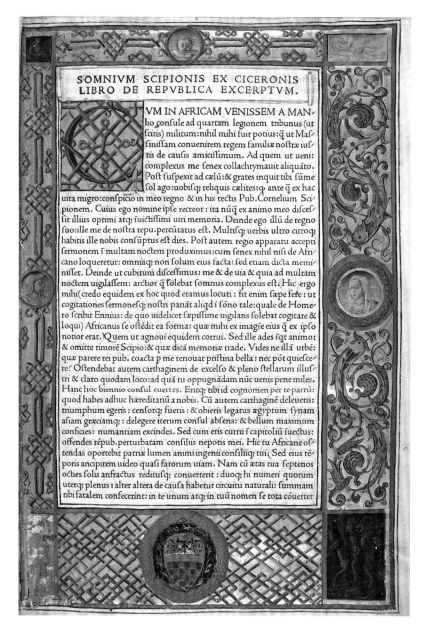

[86] A book from the Pembroke library: Macrobius, *In Somnium Scipionis*, Venice 1472 (Trinity College, Cambridge)

when fresh out of Christ Church, and under the guidance of his librarian Humfrey Wanley (fig. 88) it expanded enormously.[123] Writing in 1731 to thank Harley for a gift of wine and chocolate, a sympathetic correspondent enthused: 'I congratulate you upon the new accession of manuscripts to your Library, which without such an addition is already beyond any private library we have in England … Yet your Lordship will never have enough, though the world thinks otherwise.'[124]

Harley's collection was divided between his town house at 34 Dover Street, which by 1742 contained 150 presses filled with manuscripts and books, and Wimpole (fig. 89), where James Gibbs built a great Library room to house Harley's printed books.

later that during the building project 'the books are all in heaps upon the Ground, & some Waggons Loads are here to be sent down & added to them, so that the great Work of putting all in Order, will not begin suddenly'. Even this was not enough, and Harley's former tutor shortly after commiserated with him that 'your new library was so calculated so much short of your stock of books as not to be able to hold half of them'.[126]

The twelve-volume classed catalogue of printed books at Wimpole gives a good indication of the level of scholarship which underlaid the assembly of the Harleian Library.[127] It lists books on every conceivable subject, elegantly described, with full transcriptions of their title pages, cross-references to books in the catalogue of Harley's London library, and regular references to bibliographies and their inadequacies. Of a 1479 edition of Eusebius it notes: 'This Edition not taken Notice of by Any Author whatsoever, and as for Orlandi he doth not spell the Printers Name right, Nor Mr. Maittaire, not Le Caille, for they all follow One Another, like Pack-horses'.[128] Arrangements for binding were equally fastidious. Detailed bills survive, and early on Harley patronised the Oxford binder Richard Sedgeley.[129] Later a binder's shop was fitted up in the house at Dover Street, so precious manuscripts need not leave the house, but could be worked on there. Another favoured binder, Christopher Chapman, paid extended visits to Wimpole.[130]

[87] Portrait of Harley, with vignette of the interior of the Harleian Library (Society of Antiquaries, London)

[88] Thomas Hill, *Humfrey Wanley*, 1711. This portrait shows him holding open his *Book of Specimens* in which he has copied a page from an early Greek Gospel; the text is in the shape of a cross (Society of Antiquaries, London)

The exact size of the collection is open to debate, but it seems to have ended up at around 7,639 manuscripts, over 14,000 rolls, charters and legal documents, 50,000 printed books, 41,000 prints, and an extraordinary 350,000 pamphlets.[125] At Wimpole the first Library was fitted up by 1716, Harley writing to Wanley in that year that 'you will be wanted at Wimpole, now the room for my books is finished, to put them up and catalogue', and by September of that year there were already 12,000 books in the house, arranged in twenty-seven presses of up to fifteen shelves each. This rapidly proved inadequate, and further building work in 1719 added what Wanley called in June of that year 'Five large Rooms for a Library', adding a week

The Harleian books were well used by scholars, including the antiquarians William Stukeley (1687–1765) and Thomas Tanner (1674–1735), and the classicist Richard Bentley (1662–1742). But ultimately Harley's extravagance proved his undoing, and in 1740 he was obliged to sell Wimpole to his rival Hardwicke for £86,740, retiring to Dover Street and dying there eighteen months later. The collections, tragically, were gradually sold off. Antiquities, coins and medals went in March 1742. Later in the same year the printed books were purchased by Thomas Osborne for a knock-down £13,000, less than Harley had spent on binding them. Osborne progressively dispersed them by catalogue, with the bibliographical drudgery done by Harley's impecunious former literary secretary William Oldys (1696–1751) and by Samuel Johnson, who came to loathe the ruthlessly business-like bookseller.[131] Apart from a few remnants now at Welbeck, the Harleian manuscripts, one of the foundation collections of the British Museum and sold to the nation for a miserly £10,000, are the only extant part of the great collection.[132] One of the most stupendous collections of printed books ever assembled was scattered to the four winds.

Scotland, Wales and Ireland

In Scotland Andrew Fletcher of Saltoun (1653–1716), a campaigner against the Union with England and a pupil of the Whig bishop Gilbert Burnet (1643–1715), started collecting around 1675. By the end of his life he had assembled a substantial humanist library of about 6,000 books, one of the largest in Britain. A large proportion, about 4,800, were published before 1675, establishing Fletcher as a serious collector of old books. He spent large parts of his life away from Scotland, in London, at university in Paris and the Netherlands, and in exile in the Netherlands and Spain, and bought books in all of them. His collection included forty-eight incunables, eight first editions of Galileo, twelve first editions of Kepler, a first edition of More's *Utopia* (1516), De Bry's *America*, the Eliot 'Indian Bible' (1663) and about 100 Aldines, books from the press of the great Venetian humanist printer Aldo Manuzio (1449–1515), some of them rare. The books appear to have been kept at Saltoun Castle, in East Lothian, where a new Library room was added in 1779. The collection survived into the

[89] The Library at Wimpole Hall

twentieth century, but was sold at auction in 1966 and 1967 and dispersed.[133] Another Scottish library, that of the 3rd Marquess of Lothian (1690–1767), survives at Newbattle Abbey. Like his forebears, Lothian was a great collector: his most magnificent book, perhaps the early fourteenth-century Tickhill Psalter (see fig. 211), was sold in 1932 and is now in the New York Public Library.[134]

Just outside Edinburgh a new Library was added by the lawyer Sir David Dalrymple (c.1665–1721) to the existing villa at Newhailes in about 1722. The room (see fig. 163) is large, and though it was on the ground floor (unusual in Scotland at the time), it was raised above a vaulted brick basement to protect the books from damp, a wise precaution so near the North Sea. It had adjustable wall shelving and was well lit, with tall east-facing windows, but had a snug Study attached, for privacy and cold days.[135] Unlike Fletcher's, the collection was more concerned with contemporary scholarship rather than the pursuit of early imprints.[136] Another Scottish library, that collected by another gentleman-lawyer Sir George Gordon (1637–1720), 1st Earl of Aberdeen and Lord Chancellor of Scotland (another former student at Leiden), is partially extant at Haddo House in Aberdeenshire. It once included many early books, including manuscripts and the 1465 Fust and Schöffer edition of Cicero's *De Officiis*, though many of the grandest are long gone.[137]

Libraries of self-consciously rare books were less common in Ireland, where gentry families appear to have assembled solid libraries of useful everyday books rather than chasing early books and manuscripts. One notable exception, a late one, was that assembled by Denis Daly of Dunsandle (1747–91) in County Galway, who collected classical authors in the best available editions.[138] Earlier, the English lawyer Henry Bathurst owned Irish manuscripts at Old Park, near Kinsale, in County Cork. They were presumably once the property of a suppressed monastery or a dispossessed Irish Catholic owner, and their very availability reflected the turbulent history of seventeenth-century Ireland. Bathurst bequeathed them to his brother Ralph, Master of Trinity College, Oxford, in 1675, but if the manuscripts ever made it to England, their whereabouts are now unknown.[139]

Across the water Sir Thomas Mostyn (1651–92) assembled one of the finest collections of manuscripts ever made in Wales. At the time of his death the library at Gloddaeth, his house near Llandudno, contained 116 manuscript books, twenty-six or so in Welsh, a collection which remained intact there until its eventual transfer to Mostyn Hall, in Flintshire, where a new Library room was created to house books brought together from the family's seven Welsh houses in 1842.[140] The family's second great bibliophile, Sir Thomas's grandson, Sir Thomas Mostyn, 4th Baronet (1704–58), commissioned a catalogue of books and manuscripts at Mostyn Hall at some point between 1727 and 1733, and in about 1730 acquired a collection of mostly French and Italian illuminated manuscripts which had belonged to Dr Thomas Hobart, the Grand Tour 'bear leader' of another great manuscript collector, the 1st Earl of Leicester (1697–1759).[141] The Welsh manuscripts were an important part of the Gloddaith and Mostyn libraries, but the non-Welsh material was as spectacular. They are now scattered as the result of sales in 1920 and 1974, but a fourteenth-century illuminated Life of the Black Prince, now in Senate House Library in London, gives an idea of the splendour of the collection.[142] The printed books were no less magnificent, a fully fledged learned library similar to those assembled by English collectors, figures like Harley.[143] Like other bibliophiles of the era, the first Sir Thomas Mostyn was attracted to bibliographical trophies and curiosities: an especially beautiful Grolier binding bought from the Duke of Lauderdale's library in 1689, sold in turn in 1974, is now in the Getty Library at Wormsley.[144]

Several other important early Welsh libraries have, like Mostyn, been dispersed, but one extremely important collection has fared better. The library of the gentleman antiquarian Robert Vaughan (1592?–1667), rich in early Welsh manuscripts, was assembled at Hengwrt (fig. 90), an ancient manor house near Dolgellau in Meirionnydd. Vaughan's family squabbled over the collection after his death, and in 1676 Sir Thomas Mostyn heard from a sympathetic friend that he had secured a promise of a 'catalogue of the books in the study' at Hengwrt, with the assurance that 'noe booke there shall be sold or disposed of without my knowledge'.[145] In the event the books, of extraordinary significance, remained at Hengwrt for another 150 years, before finding their way to Peniarth near Tywyn in the middle of the nineteenth century, and finally to the new National Library of Wales in 1909.[146] As early as 1658 a catalogue of books at Hengwrt listed some 165 manuscripts; though the working language of

HENGWST.

J. Ingleby   *Delin 1793.*

Seat of S.ᵗ Rob.ᵗˢ Howell Vaughan.

[90] The manor house at Hengwrt, Meirionnydd

the catalogue was English, its grandiloquent Latin title explained that it was compiled by the antiquarian and manuscript collector William Maurice (d.1680), a 'Philobritannus', with the intention of preserving information about the manuscripts for the benefit of posterity.[147]

Holkham

Holkham (fig. 91), in Norfolk, is known above all else for its manuscripts, once 770 in number, mostly medieval, substantially collected by the 1st Earl of Leicester. Mostly purchased on Coke's grand tour in France and Italy between 1712 and 1718 under the guidance of Dr Thomas Hobart, they included western, Hebrew and important Greek manuscripts. Most of these manuscripts were stripped of their bindings for transport back to England, and remained unbound until the early nineteenth century, though four Romanesque treasure bindings survived intact, to be bought by the Morgan Library in 1927.[148] The printed books, which survive better, were described by the Victorian bibliophile Beriah Botfield in 1860–61. Botfield worked systematically through Bibles and liturgical books, beginning with the 1459 Psalter published by Gutenberg's successors Fust and Schöffer, before

moving onto sundry early incunables on vellum and a fine collection of Aldines. At that point, faced with the sheer size of the library, he seems to have given up, observing simply: 'This noble Library is very rich in works of Divinity, and on Civil and Canon Law; but enough has been said to show its value and extent.'[149]

The collection was housed in rooms of equal splendour. In 1765 the traveller Mrs Lybbe Powys was full of admiration:

> The gallery is painted a dead white, with ornaments of gildings; at each end is an octagon, the one fitted up as a library, the other with busts, bronze, and curiosities too numerous to mention … In the fourth wing is the eating-room, drawing room, library, bed-chambers, dressing-rooms, constantly used by Lord and Lady Leicester themselves.[150]

This remains substantially true, with the suite of three Library rooms at Holkham occupying about half the floor area of the Family Wing. Two, known as the Manuscript Library and the Classical Library, date from the nineteenth century, but the main Long Library, designed by William Kent, 54 by 18 feet and filling the whole of the west front of the wing, is still much as it was when Mrs Lybbe Powys visited.

Binding and bookplates

Many of the books in the Long Library at Holkham were bound by Jean Roubiquet, a French binder living in London, who spent nineteen weeks in the house in 1742, and '44 weeks and five days Binding Books' in 1748 (fig. 92). These visits were evidently part of a large-scale campaign, and thereafter Roubiquet's bill was generally of the order of £2 or £3 a quarter, enough to keep things ticking over.[151] Presumably part of an integrated approach to interior design at Holkham, where the house was begun in 1734, such a project was fairly uncommon. There had been a similar rebinding campaign at Hatfield, where in 1712 Joseph Pomfrett was paid the substantial sum of £146 for rebinding books, a project which clearly went hand in hand with the reorganisation of the library and the compilation of a new catalogue.[152] At Ditchley in Oxfordshire the Earl of Lichfield went one further, as the Library Closet in 1743 contained 'Apparatus for Printing & Bookbinding'. The apparatus was perhaps a small press for printing shelf-marks to go on the spines, but pre-printed sheets of alpha-numeric labels

could be bought from stationers, designed to allow
even semi-literate servants to put the books back
in their proper place.[153] Another refinement, not
confined to collectors but obviously liable to attract
them, was the bookplate. Bookplates were little
used in England down to the end of the seventeenth century, though David Loggan (1634–92)
sent 200 bookplates and the copper as 'a small
Niewe Yaers gieft' in 1676 to Sir Thomas Isham
of Lamport, explaining 'it is werry much used a
mongst persons of Quality to past ther Cotes of
Armes before ther Bookes in sted of Wreithing
their names'. The London engraver William Jackson
produced over 600 plates between 1695 and 1715,
and seems to have engraved plates in advance before
offering them speculatively to potential customers.
His eventual clients included roughly 100 members
of the nobility, including 14 dukes, over 60
baronets, and more than 250 country gentry.[154]

[91] Interior of the
Library at Holkham
Hall

[92] Bookbindings by
Jean Roubiquet from
Holkham

[93] Shirburn Castle in 1900

Macclesfield had acquired Shirburn in 1716, and his library survived his impeachment for financial irregularities.[156] He bought extensively on the antiquarian market, and his library, like others of the period, included many books from the library of the French administrator and bibliophile Nicolas-Joseph Foucault (1643–1721).[157] Ironically, the twenty-first-century dispersal of the books resulted in a far more detailed dissection of the contents of the shelves than has yet occurred for similar libraries which remain extant, and the Shirburn Castle sale catalogues together form one of the most accessible descriptions of the library of a wealthy eighteenth-century scholar-collector. The shelves at Shirburn housed a collection of such richness as to defy easy summary (fig. 94). Some treasures, like the Caxtons, a Christopher Saxton *Atlas* (1574), a fine copy of Besler's *Hortus Eystettensis* (1613) and a Complutensian Polyglot Bible (1514), were not unexpected, but the library also proved rich in more recondite publications, such as a first edition of the Bible in Finnish (1642). There were notable scientific books, including Copernicus's *De Revolutionibus* (Nuremberg, 1543) annotated by the Oxford astronomer and orientalist John Greaves (1602–52), and a copy of Newton's *Principia* presented by the author to the Welsh mathematician William Jones (*c.*1675–1749). Jones had spent much of his time at Shirburn,

Two Lord Chancellors

Despite a brief write-up by Edward Edwards in 1864, one of the most spectacular connoisseur's libraries of the early eighteenth century, that of Thomas Parker, 1st Earl of Macclesfield, remained essentially unknown until it was offered for sale in London between 2004 and 2008.[155] Macclesfield (1666–1732) was a self-made lawyer and a successful Whig politician, who served as Lord Chancellor from 1718 to 1725. As befitted the library of a Fellow of the Royal Society, the collection at Shirburn Castle, Oxfordshire (fig. 93), was rich in scientific books (about 3,200 separate items when sold); it also included many of Isaac Newton's papers.

[94] Shirburn Castle, the South Library, before the sale of the books between 2004 and 2008. This room housed many of the library's famed scientific books.

eventually bequeathing the 15,000 books in his own library to the 2nd Earl of Macclesfield (c.1697–1764).[158] Another book remarkable for its provenance was the copy of Henry Wotton's *Elements of Architecture* (1624), given by its author to Christopher Wren Sr. (1589–1658), the father of the architect. One final surprise when the collection came up for sale was the so-called Macclesfield Psalter, a small but spectacular East Anglian manuscript of about 1330, which had earlier belonged to Lumley's protégé Anthony Watson, Bishop of Chichester.[159]

Another Lord Chancellor, Philip Yorke, 1st Earl of Hardwicke (1690–1764), had a double association with Shirburn. In his youth a pupil of William Jones, the young Yorke was later tutor to Macclesfield's children and benefited greatly from his support and patronage.[160] Like Macclesfield, Hardwicke owned medieval manuscripts, one of which, a fifteenth-century manuscript of Augustine in French, is now in the Wren Library at Trinity College, Cambridge.[161] However, despite a sale of manuscripts and incunabula in 1791, much of Lord Hardwicke's library is still extant, the books housed in the magnificent Library built for Harley's printed books at Wimpole. Though not so splendid as Harley's nor even Macclesfield's, Hardwicke's library at Wimpole is impressive, the books wide-ranging and often elegantly bound, with a rich array of learned Renaissance books, books on law, politics, travel and history, as well as some especially grand architectural volumes. Hardwicke evidently believed in absorbing whole libraries as Naudé had recommended. His shelves include books from the collection of the physician and traveller Edward Browne (1644–1708), son of Sir Thomas Browne of *Hydriotaphia* fame, as well as a portion of the library of his wife's uncle, the Whig jurist John, Lord Somers (1651–1716), another Lord Chancellor and a leading bibliophile of the previous generation.[162]

Dynastic contexts

In the final analysis rare books could, as at Wimpole in 1742 and again in 1791, be turned into hard cash. Unsurprisingly, therefore, committed collectors frequently took steps to ensure that their cherished libraries remained together, usually by means of the law of entail. Viscount Weymouth's brother-in-law Sir Robert Worsley (1669–1747) was typical in directing that the contents of his house at Appuldurcombe on the Isle of Wight, which included the library he had inherited from his brother the botanist Henry Worsley, should remain in the house as heirlooms, held in trust by successive owners for the use of their successors.[163] This was particularly important if a house and title were likely to pass to distant relatives. A little later, the elderly 9th Duke of Norfolk (1685–1777), without direct heirs, saw to it that the contents of his houses were set out in meticulous detail in a massive parchment inventory. Clearly designed to control the second cousin who was to succeed to the title, it not only specified that the ducal chattels were to be treated as heirlooms, but laid down that they should not be moved from one house to another. The inventory included a list of the books in the three ducal libraries at Norfolk House in London, Worksop Manor in Nottinghamshire and Arundel Castle in Sussex.[164]

Dynastic pride of another kind was implicit in privately printed catalogues of private libraries. The earliest English example was the *Catalogus Bibliothecae Kingstonianae* (1727; fig. 232), a catalogue of the library of the Dukes of Kingston, at Thoresby Hall in Nottinghamshire, which was issued in just twenty copies.[165] Such catalogues were common in the eighteenth and nineteenth centuries; other eighteenth-century examples include the 1771 Osterley Park catalogue, and a magnificently illustrated description and catalogue of the library of the connoisseur and wealthy plantation owner Ralph Willett (1719–95) at Merly in Dorset. Willett was interested in typography, and had read two papers to the Society of Antiquaries in which he asserted, at a time when this was not universally accepted, that Mainz was the birthplace of printing. He had added a Library wing to Merly in 1772, decorated with lavish plasterwork depicting the progress of knowledge and designed to accommodate a collection of over 8,000 books, including over eighty incunables, seven Caxtons and four block books (books printed in the fifteenth century using woodblocks, not with moveable type), as well as prints and drawings.[166]

Willett was childless, and his collection did not long survive him. This was a prospect which also had to be faced in great houses inhabited ex officio by Bishops of the Established Church, who could not assume that either their houses or their incomes would pass to their heirs. In Ireland the bookish Bishop of Clogher John Stearne

(1660–1745) owned a magnificent library, the rarer books of which he bequeathed to Marsh's Library in Dublin.[167] The library of another Ulster bishop, Thomas Percy (1729–1811), author of *Reliques of Ancient English Poetry* (1765), was sold en bloc to the Irish nabob Lord Caledon in 1812 and shifted to Caledon House, County Tyrone. Percy's successor as bishop was 'anxious for their speedy removal', since he wanted to turn the episcopal Library into a nursery.[168] In England George III's former chaplain Richard Hurd (1720–1808), who became Bishop of Worcester in 1781, left his library of some 2,050 books in trust for the use of his successors. The books were installed in a splendid Neoclassical Long Gallery at Hartlebury Castle, designed for Hurd by the local architect James Smith in 1782. They remain *in situ*, having survived a series of potentially mortal threats, the room, its original furnishings and the books together forming a library ensemble the equal of any secular house of the era.[169]

Occasionally libraries could be alienated in ways which were not only spectacular, but positively insulting. The great library of the Jacobite 4th Earl of Orrery (1676–1731), like Macclesfield's rich in scientific books, was bequeathed in a fit of pique not to Orrery's son but to Christ Church, Oxford, where Orrery had been a favourite pupil of Dean Henry Aldrich (1647–1710). Orrery's son and heir had to be content with his father's books on the history and constitution of England, and was forced to endure the stinging rebuke in his father's will that he had never displayed 'Inclination for the Entertainment or Knowledge which Study and Learning afford'. The Orrery library was a town library, kept not in the main family house at Marston in Somerset, still less on the ancestral estates in Ireland, but in three rooms in Orrery's London house, near to Ellys, Sunderland, and to Harley in Dover Street.[170]

Coda

The death of Harley in 1742 marked the end of an era. Despite the occasional enthusiast, it was more than half a century before grand book collecting again occupied centre-stage as a favoured leisure activity for the aristocratic elite. By then the world had moved on from the political and religious controversies which had dominated the reigns of Queen Anne and the first two Georges. Harley's books had been scattered, and so had the great

libraries assembled by metropolitan collectors like Richard Mead (see p. 209) and the Rawlinsons. But for the most part the grandees' libraries survived, sometimes in the houses where they had been assembled in London, sometimes shifted to the country, protected by dynastic pride, family entails, and the thriving economy of an increasingly industrialised imperial power. The books assembled by the 2nd Duke of Devonshire would form the core of the great library at Chatsworth, Leicester's remained in Palladian splendour at Holkham, Lothian's at Newbattle, Macclesfield's at Shirburn, and Hardwicke's (admittedly somewhat depleted) at Wimpole.

By the last decade of the eighteenth century the 2nd Earl of Buckinghamshire, whose family had inherited the great library of Sir Richard Ellys in 1742, was making a will. Faced with a potential inheritance dispute with the children of his father's second wife, Buckinghamshire was forced to contemplate the disagreeable possibility that the 10,000 books in the Long Gallery at Blickling might not belong to him, and to consider the future of the room when his favourite daughter Caroline Harbord (née Hobart), Lady Suffield (1767–1850), came into her inheritance. The dismantling of the Gallery, expensively fitted up as a Library in the 1740s, was not to be contemplated, but Ellys's books, magnificent though they were, did not greatly attract. Buckinghamshire set aside money so that they might be bought from the family of his half-brother, who was to succeed to the title but not to the Hobart family estates in Norfolk. Failing this, replacement books were to be secured, and Buckinghamshire set his executors the clear brief that 'the Books to be so purchased shall be of the most general use and as well for Information as Entertainment and that no high prices be paid for such Books as derive particular Merit only from being scarce or finely bound'.[171] The earl was lining up with those who were sceptical of the merits of Grolier bindings, Saxon manuscripts, Renaissance editions of Aristotle, and books printed by Caxton. Ironically a combination of changing tastes and the vast number of early books released onto the market by French Revolutionary confiscations and by monastic secularisations right across Europe was about to render his apparently sensible approach completely outdated. 'Bibliomania', on a scale beyond anything Lord Chesterfield could ever have imagined, was in the air.

CHAPTER FIVE

'A Great Number of Usefull Books'

Ordinary Books and Ordinary Libraries from the Late Seventeenth to the Early Nineteenth Centuries

Library. A Great Number of Usefull Books.
Inventory of Dunham Massey, Cheshire, *c.*1758

I · NUMBERS, DEPLOYMENT AND ACQUISITION

Housing the ordinary

Visiting Kedleston in 1766, the 1st Duchess of Northumberland (1716–76) sniffed around the Library recently built for the 1st Lord Scarsdale by Robert Adam, and noted in her diary that it was 'furnished with Book Cases fill'd with well chosen entertaining & instructive rather than Curious Books'.[1] Earlier, on a bibliographical tour of England in 1721, Edward Harley had looked with interest at manuscripts in Lincoln Cathedral but, visiting Carlisle, merely glanced at the 'very useful books' of divinity in the altogether humbler cathedral library there.[2] At Dunham Massey, faced with a room full of ordinary modern books, an appraiser in 1758 noted that the Library there contained 'a great number of usefull books'.[3] (fig. 96)

For most country house owners, the family library was not a place for incunables and medieval manuscripts, but a repository of everyday reading matter. Its size might vary, according to the tastes of successive owners, the grandeur of the house and the depths of their pockets. Books, purchased new or second-hand, or inherited from friends and relations, could include a few grand treasures, and their housing could vary from the humdrum and the improvised through to up-to-date set-piece interiors, perhaps, like Kedleston, with magnificent furniture. In most houses the Library was a place where books accumulated rather than were collected. From the seventeenth to the twentieth centuries, the unremarkable, dowdy, stolid and nondescript formed an important component of many libraries, easily overlooked, but as worthy of interest as the erudite or spectacular.

The period from the lapse of the Licensing Act in 1695 to the introduction of steam-powered printing in 1814 saw a huge expansion of the book trade, in London and in major provincial centres, and the penetration of print into every aspect of life.[4] Libraries in country houses expanded, too, but their size varied, reflective of the fact that 'useful books' could attract anyone from the humblest country squire to the grandest peer of the realm. The Sussex gentleman Thomas Frewen (1691–1767) owned 1,747 volumes at Brickwall, his house near Rye, mostly recent and representing a quarter of the total value of everything in the house.[5] At Mersham Le Hatch in Kent the Knatchbulls had 892 books in 1755, but Sir Richard Myddelton of Chirk had about 1,300 in 1704.[6] In Worcestershire Richard Vernon (1615–79) wrote the titles of 159 of 'my books' into a printed almanac for 1663, but in 1708 his son the gentleman-lawyer Thomas Vernon (1654–1721) had 123 in the still-extant 'Studdy Adjoyning to the Gallery' at Hanbury Hall.[7] The Warwickshire gentleman Edward Ferrers (1739–60) had just thirty-eight books at Baddesley Clinton, though, as elsewhere, his probate inventory may not give us the full picture.[8] By contrast, his much wealthier neighbour at Stoneleigh, Edward, 5th Lord Leigh (1742–86) had over 1,000, mostly purchased by Leigh himself and some very grand indeed, though mainly printed since the late seventeenth century. Since Stoneleigh was the largest house in Warwickshire, and Baddesley an ancient moated manor house, the contrast needs

[95] John Gerard's *The Herball or General Historie of Plantes*, London 1633, entry for balsam mint with a pressed specimen inserted (Springhill, County Londonderry)

‡ 5 *Mentha spicata altera*.
Balsam Mint.

foure square, and the floures grow in eares or spokie tufts, like those of the second. ‡

¶ *The Place.*

Most vse to set Mints in Gardens almost euery where.

¶ *The Time.*

Mints do floure and flourish in Sommer, in Winter the roots onely remaine: being once set they continue long, and remaine sure and fast in the ground.

¶ *The Names.*

Mint is called in Greeke μίνθη and μίνθα: the sweet smell saith *Pliny* in his 19.booke *cap*.8. hath changed the name among the Græcians when as otherwise it should be called *Mintha*, from whence our old writers haue deriued the name: for ἡδύς signifieth sweet, and ὀσμή smel: The Apothecaries, Italians, and French men, do keepe the Latine name *Mentha*. the Spaniards do call it *Yerua buena*, and *Ortelana*: in High Dutch, Muntz: in Low Dutch, Munte: in English, Mint.

The first Mint is called in High Dutch, Diement: in Low Dutch, Bruyn heylighe: he that would translate it into Latin, must call it *Sacra nigricans*, or the holy blackish mint: in English, browne Mint, or red Mint.

The second is also called in High Dutch Krausz diement, krausz muntz, and krausz balsam: that is to say, *Mentha cruciata*: in French, *Beaume crespu*: in English, Crosse-Mint, or curled Mint.

The third is called of diuers *Mentha Sarracenica*, *Mentha Romana*: it is called in High Dutch Balsam muntz, Onser frawen muntz, Spitzer muntz, Spitzer balsam: it may be called *Mentha angustifolia*: that is to say, Mint with the narrow leafe: and in English, Speare Mint, common garden Mint, our Ladies Mint, browne Mint, and Macrell Mint.

The fourth is called in High Dutch Hertzkraut, as though it were to bee named *Cardiaca*, or *Cardiaca Mentha*: in English, Hart-woort, or Heart-mint ‡ This is the *Sisymbrium satiuum* of *Matthiolus*, and *Mentha hortensis altera* of *Gesner*: the Italians call it *Sisembrio domestico*, and *Balsamita*; the Germanes, Katzenbalsam. ‡

¶ *The Temperature.*

Mint is hot and drie in the third degree. It is saith *Galen*, somewhat bitter and harsh, and it is inferiour to Calamint. The smell of Mint, saith *Pliny* doth stir vp the minde, and the taste a greedy desire to meat.

¶ *The Vertues.*

Mint is maruellous wholesome for the stomacke, it staieth the Hicket, parbraking, and scowring in the Cholerike passion, if it be taken with the iuice of a soure pomegranate. A

It stoppeth the casting vp of bloud, being giuen with water and vineger, as Galen telleth. B

And in broth saith *Pliny*, it staieth the floures, and is singular good against that is to C say, that Mint which is described in the first place. For it is found by experience that many haue had this kinde of flux staied by the continuall vse of this onely Mint: the same applied to the forehead, or to the temples, as *Pliny* teacheth, doth take away the headache.

It is good against watering eies, and all manner of breakings out in the head, against the in- D firmities of the fundament, it is a sure remedie for childrens sore heads.

It is poured into the eares with honie water. It is taken inwardly against Scolopenders, Beare- E wormes, Sea-scorpions and serpents.

It is applied with salt to the bitings of mad dogs. It will not suffer milke to cruddle in the sto- F macke (*Pliny* addeth to wax soure.) therefore it is put in Milke that is drunke for feare that those who haue drunke thereof should be strangled.

It is thought, that by the same vertue it is an enemy to generation, by ouerthickning the seed. G

little explanation.[9] In Derbyshire in 1805 the Wrights of Eyam, a family on the lower rungs of the gentry, had 159 books, almost all in English (these included 'Eighty old volumes', worth only a few pence each), but in Westmorland by about 1750 the fiercely independent Brownes, a dynasty of prosperous Lakeland yeomen, had 142 at Townend, a large farmhouse on the edge of Troutbeck (fig. 97).[10] Across the water in Ireland, there were about 500 books in the library at Hillsborough Castle in 1771, though these included sixty-two volumes of pamphlets.[11] In 1742 the Morayshire baronet Sir Robert Gordon of Gordonstoun (1696–1772) had about 3,000 books, not counting pamphlets. Since these were valued at just £50

by an Edinburgh bookseller in 1771, Gordon was evidently one of many who had inherited books from his predecessors.[12]

Well into the eighteenth century books were more likely to be in Studies or Closets than formally designated Libraries. As in the seventeenth century, some commentators have attempted to draw sharp distinctions between the three, but again it is probably a mistake to assume on fixed meanings, or to draw too many conclusions about why the term 'Library' came to be preferred. The word 'library' could refer to a group of books, but it could also be a room. At Nettlecombe Court in Somerset in 1689 'the Library of books' belonging to Lady Mary Trevelyan was worth £40, but the

[96] The Library at Dunham Massey

[97] Three books at Townend with fore-edge titles

books themselves were in Sir George Trevelyan's 'Closett'.[13] On the other hand at Newbattle Abbey in 1719, the bulk of the books were 'in the Liberary Room'.[14] At Gordon Castle in Morayshire in 1728, there was a 'bigg Library' and a 'little Library', with some 1,800 books. The 'little Library' may indeed have been a room referred to elsewhere as the

[98] A free-standing bookcase, closely resembling those made for Samuel Pepys, perhaps once kept in William Blathwayt's Library at Dyrham Park, and at the time of writing, in the Great Hall at Dyrham.

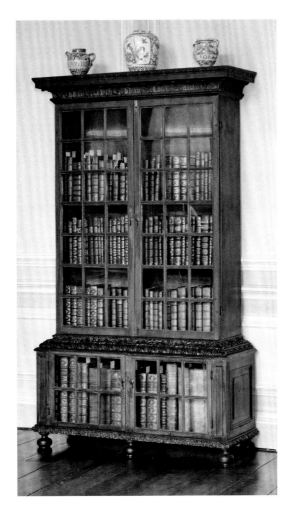

duke's Closet.[15] At Dyrham Park in 1711 William Blathwayt's books were in 'the Library', a small but richly furnished room, still extant but long empty (fig. 98).[16]

By contrast, in 1689 Sir John Borlase of Bockmore kept thirty-four books in his Closet at Bockmore in Buckinghamshire, while at Ashford in Somerset there were 220 books in 'ye Closett over ye Oriall' in the late seventeenth century.[17] In Ireland the 1684 inventory of Kilkenny Castle suggests that two Closets and at least two other rooms in the castle round tower contained shelving, but most of the Duke of Ormonde's books were in his Closet, where the appraisers noted 'Shelves & books which his Grace hath an account of'.[18]

It is a moot point whether Ormonde himself would have described this room as a Closet or Study, but most inventory-takers used the word Study. Drawing primarily on examples from Norfolk country houses, Susie West has posited 'a long seventeenth century' of Studies, encompassing a hierarchy of spaces from a simple panelled rectangular room, one bay wide, through to two-bay square versions, the latter ultimately developing into the species of richly fitted-out architectural interiors surviving at Houghton in Norfolk, and at Dunham Massey in Cheshire.[19] Very few early Studies have survived, but some were evidently lavishly appointed. At Osterley Park in 1668 the Study of the retired Civil War general Sir William Waller (c.1597–1668) contained 'one Table and Carpett, a rest with drawers, three little Cabinetts, a Chair and a Stoole, and Shelves about the roome and other odd things'. The books themselves were valued at £90.[20] At another West Country house, Trewithen in Cornwall, Thomas Hawkins's Study in 1768 had 923 books, valued at £118 17s. 7d., as well as a pair of globes and a microscope.[21] At the House of the Binns, near Edinburgh, General Tam Dalyell (1615–85) had a 'little studie in the dyningroume'. This was not a room but a large cupboard set into the thickness of the wall, still visible. It housed boxes, cabinets and drawers, containing weights and measures, scientific instruments, the general's military commissions, several pairs of spectacles, two telescopes, a pair of spurs, sets of house keys, writing equipment, tobacco jars, a silver brush and a 'multiplieing instrument'. Next door, in Dalyell's Chamber, were two more presses with a similar miscellany of curiosities, as well as 'a little iron studdie fixed in the North window' and 'a little iron studdie behind the door', both these evidently pieces of furniture. In addition the Chamber housed the general's books, described thus by the appraiser: 'Round about the said roume is locked shelfs wherin is his hail bibliothick conforme to the catalogue therein lying conforme to the alphabet that his therein written.'[22] Unfortunately this catalogue seems not to survive, and there are few books of the era on the shelves, but Dalyell's library may have been sizeable, since the contents of his Chamber, including books, were valued at £220.[23]

The location of Closets and Studies varied, but books were often in close proximity to bedchambers. In 1644 at Shardeloes, Buckinghamshire, Sir William Drake's 'Studdy', with 'two old boxes & divers old bookes and papers', was adjacent to his Bedchamber. There were more books, as well as instruments, 'for surveying' in the room above.[24] At Dunham and Houghton the Libraries were both next to the owner's bedroom. At Castle Howard no Library is apparent in John Vanbrugh's plans as published in *Vitruvius Britannicus*, but recent research has established that in the earliest phase of the house's history the 3rd Earl of Carlisle (*c*.1669–1738) kept books in a Library in his private suite of rooms. This was subsequently supplemented by a more public book room, the Grand Cabinet, destroyed in the 1750s.[25] At Ditchley Park, the Oxfordshire seat of the Earls of Lichfield, Mrs Lybbe Powys noted that 'the bed-chambers are very good, and on that floor an excellent library'. This room contained a wheel chair, 'the greatest treasure to a gouty or sick person'.[26] There was a similar 'Gouty Chair with leather Seat on Large brass Castors' at The Vyne in Hampshire in 1754, kept in an interconnecting 'Study and Closet Adjoyning', alongside 150 books.[27]

Other locations were, however, possible. At Calke Abbey, home of a wealthy family of Derbyshire squires, as late as 1741 the books were not concentrated together in one room. Some were in Sir John Harpur's Study, plain but comfortable, with a fire, chairs, 'a large deal bookcase', a spinet and 'two globes with leathern cases'. Others were in a pair of walnut bookcases in the adjacent Red Drawing Room, and by 1748 there were 399 books in all.[28] At Nannau in Snowdonia such few books as were in the house in 1768 were in bookcases in the adjacent Large and Small Parlours, and the former also had a 'Reading Table'.[29] At Dunster Castle in 1741 'the closett under the Great Staircase'

housed more than 300 books.[30] At Chicheley Hall the Buckinghamshire baronet Sir John Chester (1666–1726) had an unusual Library in a new house designed by Francis Smith of Warwick (1672–1738). The books in the room, situated on the third floor and now empty, were concealed behind hinged panelling installed by a local joiner from 1724 to 1725.[31] Upper-floor Libraries or Studies were not uncommon in seventeenth-century England – it seems likely that the long-vanished Book Room at Charlecote may have been on an upper floor – and in Scotland the 'skied' Library, a place of retirement in traditionally very vertical houses, survived into the eighteenth century. In Somerset the late Francis Luttrell had a 'Study on the Leades' at Dunster Castle in 1693, while at Englefield House in Berkshire in 1741 there was an 'old Library' with globes and 'sundry shelves' on an upper floor, but the centre of things had moved downstairs to 'the new Library', more fashionably furnished and hung with prints of horses.[32]

Well into the eighteenth century, books were usually kept on fitted shelves set into the panelled walls of the Study or Closet, potentially invisible in inventories.[33] At Castle Durrow, County Laois, an estate carpenter was ordered to install a pair of bookcases in 1748, presumably fittings.[34] However from about 1720, freestanding bookcases, not unknown earlier, became increasingly common. The most famous early examples were the glazed bookcases made for Samuel Pepys, which closely resemble a pair at Dyrham, where William Blathwayt (1649–1717) owned two 'Glazed Presses' originally made for his uncle, Pepys's colleague Thomas Povey (1613/14–1705).[35] These were less innovative than is sometimes imagined, as there was a glazed bookcase in the Wizard Earl's Closet at Petworth as early as 1632.[36] Certainly, by the middle of the eighteenth century bookcases were common. At Dromana in County Waterford, Lord Grandison's Library had three glazed bookcases, perhaps imported from England in the 1730s, while at Calke Abbey, Derbyshire, in 1741 one of the two 'walnuttre' bookcases was again glazed.[37]

In many houses books continued to be kept alongside personal and estate papers. In 1684 the Welsh grandee Lord Herbert wrote to apologise for a delay in answering a letter, explaining that a fire in his Library at Powis Castle had 'burnt within an inch of a shelf of books', and evidently particularly perturbed because he also kept his 'writings' there.[38]

In her history of the Willoughby family (1702) Cassandra Willoughby often mentions the existence of family papers 'in the Library at Wollaton'.[39] In 1701 another Nottinghamshire grandee, the Duke of Newcastle, kept estate papers in the Library at Welbeck, as did the Earl of Cardigan at Deene Park in 1726.[40] The precise purpose of the panelled seventeenth-century Cedar Closet at Tredegar (Monmouthshire) is unclear. It may have been a Muniment Room, but if it housed books, these had gone by 1826, when its drawers and cupboards contained family papers, as well as medals, coins and maps.[41] In Ireland, at Dromoland Castle in County Clare, Sir Edward O'Brien's Closet in 1753 included a 'Mahogany Alphabet with … Glass Door', evidently some sort of filing system.[42]

Acquiring the ordinary

All of these rooms contained books, and each one had to be acquired somewhere. One possibility was at auction, which presented rich pickings for collectors in pursuit of rarities, but were also potentially of interest to those with more modest aspirations. In 1724, for example, the Morayshire laird James Brodie picked up a copy of Algernon Sidney's *Discourses Concerning Government* (1698), still in the library at Brodie Castle, at 'the Auction of my lord Roseberry's Books'. Others went shopping in person. In 1731 the 5th Earl of Orrery (1707–62), with houses at Marston (Somerset) and Caledon (County Tyrone), wrote with amusement to a friend about the Bath bookseller James Leake, 'a most extraordinary Person' and 'the Prince of all the coxcomical Fraternity of Booksellers'. Despite 'not having any Learning himself', Leake was conscious of social niceties, treated members of the aristocracy as his social equals and graded visitors to his shop by rank, so that 'he speaks not to a Marquis whilst a Duke is in the Room'.[43] Thirty years later, Edward, Lord Leigh, was well known in fashionable West End bookshops, browsing the stock, pocketbook in hand, and running accounts with several.[44]

Those unable to visit shops in person could deploy agents. The Parliamentarian Sir Thomas Myddelton (1586–1666) used a favourite servant, Benjamin Cupper, to buy books for Chirk Castle both before the Civil War and to replace them after the sack of the castle in 1659. Cupper was a trusted retainer, and books were one responsibility among many.[45] More informal arrangements could

also prevail. In 1770 an Irish clergyman, Benjamin Domville, was poking around the bookshops of Bath on behalf of Sir William Lee of Hartwell, Buckinghamshire. Failing to find the books Lee had asked for, he reported that only one bookseller had ever heard of them, but warned against him, as he was 'remarkably dear'.[46] Others were obliged to haggle for themselves. The Northamptonshire squire Henry Purefoy (1697–1762) corresponded with the bookseller James Paine in nearby Brackley. In 1747 he attempted to negotiate trade-ins of 'severall old Books' for new ones, complaining that a volume of Terence was 'so badly bound I don't care to let it have a place in my study', while in March 1749 he was grumbling that Paine, having been asked to supply a book called *The Disadvantages of the Married State*, which Purefoy had seen mentioned in an advertisement, instead sent *A Serious Proposall for Promoting Marriage*. Purefoy was displeased, acidly observing, 'Your Behaviour to mee in this affair really puts me in mind of the Confusion of Languages at Babell,' but the mistake was his own fault as he had quoted the title from memory, garbling it in the process.[47] The episode serves as a reminder of the importance of advertisements and reviews. If bound sets of newspapers are now uncommon on country house shelves (though Picton Castle in Pembrokeshire has a long run of the *London Gazette*, starting in 1745), periodicals like the *Gentleman's Magazine*, issued monthly from 1731, are ubiquitous. As at Brodie Castle, sets of the *Gentleman's Magazine*, *Fraser's Magazine*, the *Annual Register* and several others are typical. For periodicals, as with other books, owners not content with publishers' paper wrappers had to commission suitable bindings. In 1735, for example, Henry Purefoy wrote to a Brackley schoolmaster who did a sideline in bookbinding: 'I send by ye bearer fifteen of the Gentleman's Magazine … I desire you'l bind 'em in calf against next Wensday.' To avoid mistakes, he added, 'Voll. 5. 1735 must be done on the back when bound', though other customers preferred to pencil the correct title on a blank leaf. A regular customer, Purefoy also stated: 'As to the colour of ye Leather it must be a speckled brown in the same colour the Salmon's history is bound in.'[48] Elsewhere, other gentry and aristocratic families also patronised local binders. The 9th Earl of Exeter was not only responsible for the current Library room at Burghley, but had many of his books bound in nearby Stamford.[49]

The Derbyshire squire Sir William Boothby (1637–1707), of Ashbourne Hall, was fussy about bindings. His letter books provide one of the most vivid sources we have for gentry book buying. In 1683, for example, he wrote to complain that books bound for him in plain calf were 'very deare'. When books were damaged after a parcel broke open, Boothby demanded rebinding, on another occasion whingeing to a binder that 'yr Books open very ill, so that it is troublesome reading'. He liked his books with gilt backs, but resented paying for small formats to be gilded, complaining when the gold came off or his armorial was stamped crooked on the covers.[50]

While focused on contemporary publications rather than early printing, Boothby was a true bibliophile, writing to a friend in 1685 that his books were 'the great joy of my life'. Between 1676 and 1689 he fired off letters to London and provincial booksellers, ordering or enquiring about hundreds of books, covering every possible area of interest.[51] His favourite booksellers were Richard Chiswell (1639–1711), in St Paul's Churchyard, and the Lichfield bookseller Michael Johnson (1656–1731).[52] Boothby received books on approval, returning those which he did not like. It is clear from surviving bills among family papers elsewhere that this was not uncommon. In the early 1760s the London bookshops frequented by Lord Leigh unhesitatingly rectified errors, offered credit, accepted orders by post, forwarded books by waggon and billed at convenient intervals. Some even sent unsolicited books, based on Leigh's previous purchases.[53] At Castle Howard the 3rd Earl of Carlisle made use of provincial and London booksellers. When books were ordered from London they were despatched to York by mail coach, to be picked up by servants.[54] Unsurprisingly, however, many shopped locally. At Toft Hall, in Cheshire, the notebook into which the library catalogue was written was supplied by a Knutsford bookseller, stationer and bookbinder called Green. Green presumably supplied books, and may even have compiled the catalogue, as the Kendal bookseller Thomas Ashburner did at Flatt Hall in Cumberland in 1756.[55] In country houses the length and breadth of Britain and Ireland, even when other sources are lacking, booksellers' and binders' tickets in books remain to give an impression of who was buying where. A now very rare 1763 directory of carriage designs at Calke Abbey,

for example, was either purchased or bound in nearby Ashby-de-la-Zouch, while at Lacock there are books with tickets from Bristol.[56] In Scotland and Ireland books often came from Edinburgh and Dublin, but provincial buying was also possible. One of the Balfours of Townley Hall, County Louth, for example, picked up a 1732 edition of Shaftesbury's *Characteristicks* in nearby Drogheda in May 1747.[57]

Another option was to buy by subscription, common by the 1720s and 1730s.[58] The mere sight of long lists of aristocratic names set out by rank in the front of expensive new books must have encouraged a competitive streak in many. Publications which involved substantial investment, with numerous engravings, or requiring very large quantities of expensive paper, were especially liable to be touted to subscribers. In grander country houses architectural books and other illustrated works fell into that category. Music, which required a large number of engraved plates and was aimed at a niche market, could be issued to subscribers, either as an act of local patriotism (a local composer publishing for a mostly local audience) or because the project was large and expensive. A signed subscriber's receipt for William Boyce's anthology of *Cathedral Music* (1760–73, fig. 99) survives among Lord Leigh's papers, for example.[59] Those with shallower pockets could pick up second-hand books of all kinds, as well as stock discarded by book clubs and subscription libraries. This is probably what is

[99] The signed receipt from William Boyce for Lord Leigh's copy of Boyce's *Cathedral Music*, 1763 (Shakespeare Birthplace Trust, Stratford)

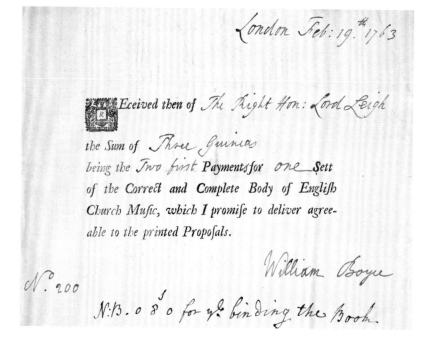

London Feb: 19th 1763

Received then of *The Right Hon: Lord Leigh* the Sum of *Three Guineas* being the *Two first* Payments for *one* Sett of the Correct and Complete Body of English Church Music, which I promise to deliver agreeable to the printed Proposals.

William Boyce

Nº 200

N:B. 0 8 0 for ye binding the Book.

Tab. II.

ANANAS aculeatus,
fructu ovato, carne albida
Plumerii, Tournef. Inst. p. 650.
Plum. Cat. Spec. p. 20.

[100] Christoph
Jakob Trew and
Georg Dionysius
Ehret, *Plantae Selectae*,
Augsburg 1750–73
(Saltram Park)

meant by 'For books bought at the society's sale in
St Albans 2 16 o' in the accounts of the Bacons of
Gorhambury in October 1787.[60]

Even in quite modest libraries the proportion
of books printed overseas was potentially considerable. In part this reflected the long-standing
British habit of importing learned books from
Continental Europe, especially when books on
eighteenth-century shelves had been inherited
from earlier generations. But books could also be
bought abroad. In the spring of 1662 two sons of
the 1st Earl of Orrery purchased books in England
en route for the Continent. These included scholarly
books, as well as devotional works by the Anglican
divines Richard Allestree and Henry Hammond.

Moving on to France, they picked up more, including
an edition of Martial, a French 'Poetical Dictionarie',
maps and 'comedies' in Protestant Saumur, and a
couple of play books in Paris.[61] As the eighteenth
century progressed, increased foreign travel and
especially the much studied phenomenon of the
Grand Tour naturally had an effect on library
shelves. An exploration of many ancestral libraries
turns up guidebooks from Italy, polite literature in
French, plate books from both countries and, less
frequently, books from central Europe. The copy
at Goodwood of J. B. Fischer von Erlach's *Entwurf
einer historischen Architectur* (1721), an unusual book
in England, may be a souvenir of the 2nd Duke of
Richmond's Grand Tour in 1721, for example.[62] Not
all books which look as if they were bought abroad
actually were. Some of the many Italian books at
Belton, often still in their original paper covers,
clearly were, and Sir John Brownlow returned from
his Grand Tour of 1710–11 with fluent Italian and
a taste for Italian books.[63] On the other hand the
architectural amateur Samuel Waring, who travelled
abroad shortly before inheriting Waringstown,
County Down, in 1703, stocked up on guidebooks
before setting out.[64] Foreign books were available
from ordinary shops and from specialist dealers like
Paul Vaillant in London, who billed Lord Leigh to
the tune of £182 16s. in 1764.[65]

The question of fine illustrated books also serves
as a reminder that 'useful' books were not necessarily cheap. At Saltram House the grandest books
in the Parkers' library include copies of Trew and
Ehret's *Plantae Selectae* (1750–73, fig. 100), and the
second edition of Mark Catesby's *Natural History
of Carolina* (1754, fig. 101). At Kedleston there are
fine copies of luxury books, like William Hamilton's
Campi Phlegraei (1776) and the companion volume
on Hamilton's collection of Greek vases (1766–7),
which clearly appealed to the 1st Lord Scarsdale
more than the early books added to the Kedleston
library by his successors. Lord Leigh also owned
Plantae Selectae and the Catesby, but his most expensive purchase was the Comte de Caylus's *Receuil
de Peintures Antiques* (Paris, 1757), an account of
antique Roman wall paintings issued in twenty-five
copies, exquisitely coloured with forensic accuracy
and beautifully bound by Antoine-Michel Padeloup.
It cost £48 10s., a modest-enough sum compared to
what the next generation of bibliomaniacs would
spend on competitive buying of incunabula, but a
substantial amount nonetheless.[66]

Libraries were not necessarily acquired by purchase, and in many houses many books were inherited from earlier generations. At Gunby Hall in Lincolnshire, the history of the books can be tracked through successive generations of ownership marks, including the 1704 bookplate of Margaret Massingberd. By 1781 Henry Massingberd of Gunby was using a letterpress book label, with a space left in each for a running number to be inserted giving the book's position on the shelves (the sequence runs to over 700). Elsewhere large blocks of books could be inherited not just from father to son, or even mother to daughter, but by marriage, from younger siblings or from childless relatives. At Charlecote, when a clerical younger brother, Dr William Lucy (d.1723), inherited in 1721, he brought his own books with him, pasted his bookplate into many already on the shelves and apparently reorganised the library (fig.102).[67] At Tatton Park Samuel Egerton (1711–80) inherited art, money and books from his uncle Samuel Hill in 1758, many bought in Venice and Rome, the start of a process which saw the Tatton library transformed from a mundane assembly of useful books to a treasure house of collectables.[68] At Nostell in Yorkshire, books belonging to members of the Winn family dating back to the seventeenth century are unsurprising, but the library also includes books from related families such as the Ropers, as well as decidedly workaday books brought from Switzerland by Sabine d'Hervart (1734–98), who married Sir Rowland Winn, 5th Baronet (1739–85) in 1761. At Springhill in County Londonderry the library benefited from the merger of two families, the Lenoxes, Derry merchants, and the

Conynghams, county gentry. But at least a hundred of the books on the shelves today once belonged to the wealthy William Stewart, Earl of Blessington (1709–69), and his wife Eleanor, Countess of Blessington (c.1712–74). The couple's only son had died at the age of nineteen in 1754, and when Lady Blessington died, she left many of the books from Blessington House, County Wicklow, to her goddaughter Harriet Molesworth (1745–1812). Harriet in turn married the County Tyrone landowner John Staples (1736–1820), leaving the books to her daughter, Charlotte Melosina Staples (1786–1847), who became chatelaine of Springhill in 1819. This line of inheritance, from godmother to

[101] Mark Catesby, *The Natural History of Carolina, Florida, and the Bahama Islands*, London 1754 (Saltram Park)

[102] Engraved bookplate of Dr William Lucy at Charlecote

goddaughter to daughter, was unusual, but similarly unusual arrangements brought books to other libraries as well.[69]

These libraries within libraries are only discoverable when books have survived *in situ*, and every early catalogue or inventory potentially conceals similar stories now lost beyond recovery. Even when libraries survive, the evidence is not always easy to read. Hundreds of books at Lacock Abbey bear the signature of William Davenport Talbot (1764–1800), the fall-out from some now forgotten farrago about inheritance or debts, as many had been in the house for a century or more at the time that the signing campaign took place in 1788. At Belton and Tatton, as elsewhere, bookplates, inserted retrospectively or pasted on top of earlier ownership marks, clearly provide an at-best unreliable indication of who really owned what.[70] In Cornwall Juliana St Aubyn, *née* Vinnicombe, first the mistress and eventually the wife of the Sir John St Aubyn of Clowance (1758–1839), signed her name in as many as she could lay her hands on, recording her husband's gift of the volume to her. In this case the attempt was evidently successful, resulting in the transfer of the books from Clowance to St Michael's Mount when the family inheritance was divided on Sir John's death.

Then, as now, books made good presents. Sometimes they marked signal moments in the recipient's life, for example at Charlecote, where Mary Elizabeth Lucy (1803–90) received a pair of elegant Gothic 'cathedral bindings' from her mother as a wedding present in 1823. At Ditchley Mrs Lybbe Powys was shown 'a fine book of plants painted exceedingly well', a gift from Lord Bute to Lord Lichfield.[71] A copy of Vanvitelli's *Dichiarazione dei Disegni del Reale Palazzo di Caserta* (Naples, 1756) at Ickworth – a favourite Spanish diplomatic gift – was presented by Charles III of Spain to the British ambassador the 2nd Earl of Bristol (1721–75) in Madrid in 1760.[72] More typically the earl's mother Molly Lepel (1700–68), wife of the courtier John, Lord Hervey, was the recipient of the finely bound dedication copy of *The Scripture-Doctrine, of the Existence and Attributes of God* (Cambridge, 1750), written by her chaplain Thomas Knowles (1723–1802).[73]

Potential patrons continued to be favoured with or embarrassed by presentation copies. The Restoration poet Elkanah Settle (1648–1724) made a speciality of honorific verses dedicated to potential aristocratic patrons, to whom he forwarded specially bound copies with the recipient's arms, if necessary retrieving the gift and trying elsewhere if he was not adequately remunerated. Unsurprisingly Settle bindings are not uncommon on country house shelves, with examples at Chatsworth, Lanhydrock, Blickling, Belton and (formerly) Stoneleigh Abbey, among others.[74]

II · ENTERTAINMENT AND INSTRUCTION

As the Duchess of Northumberland had noted in 1766, useful books could be both 'Entertaining and Instructive'. Writing in a conduct manual first published in 1731, the schoolmaster John Clarke (1687–1743) admonished his betters: 'Study serves … a double purpose of Life, for the Support and Directory of Virtue, as also for Diversion and Amusement.'[75] The purpose of books was to inform and to amuse, to pass the tedium of idle hours, and to offer readers profitable advice on material advancement, as well as the conduct of their duties as Christians, landowners, politicians, magistrates and cultural arbiters. Up to a point books inoculated their owners against rustic indolence, and for those in remote houses provided a substitute for company when no other was available.[76] Books of this kind, ubiquitous on the shelves of country squires, aristocratic women or grand men of affairs, could also be found alongside the curious books which dominated the libraries of the learned.

Music was an obvious source of entertainment, and printed and manuscript scores can be found in many libraries. At Boughton House a collection of mostly eighteenth-century music, perhaps brought to Northamptonshire from other Buccleuch houses, includes contemporary editions of works by Handel, Purcell and J. C. Bach, as well as sixteenth-century part books and music by Lassus and Palestrina, pointers to an interest in 'antient' music that went beyond the currently fashionable.[77] Some of the extensive collection of music in the library at Burghley may have arrived in the seventeenth century, but most was bought by the 9th Earl of Exeter (1725–93), a Patron of the Handel Commemoration of 1784, who retained a musical 'agent', Benjamin Christian, to procure and maintain instruments and act as a copyist.[78] At Belton, which, like Burghley, had a household chapel with music, a similar but smaller collection can be found, while Calke Abbey has scores by the Lichfield composer John Alcock (fig. 103), as well as a military march commissioned from Haydn for the Derbyshire Yeomanry by Sir John Harpur. This turned out to be an expensive business (24 guineas), but as Sir John's mother pointed out, 'there is no bargaining with such eminent Composers'.[79] At Springhill there are concert and oratorio programmes from London and Dublin, generally signed by Lady Blessington, as well as a 1675 manual on playing the viol, while at Kedleston there is organ music by Handel and John Stanley, presumably played on the Snetzler organ in the nearby Music Room. The library at Stoneleigh Abbey included string, keyboard and vocal music. Lord Leigh also owned a set of string instruments, and presumably players were brought in to play them.[80]

Most libraries contained lighter reading matter of all kinds, mostly in English, but also in French and other modern languages. Those who read it ran the risk of censure from smug contemporaries. In a manual of advice to his son, the 1st Earl of Warrington (1652–94), owner of Dunham Massey, chided that 'to read a *Play* or Romance now and then for diversion, may do no hurt; but he that spends most of his time in such Books, will be able to give a very ill account of it', while John Clarke, while disclaiming much knowledge of plays, warned that they were 'generally very indiscreetly and foolishly writ'.[81] On the other hand a contemporary biographer was disparaging about the Scottish judge Robert Dundas (1713–87) of Arniston, scoffing that he 'had or pretended to have great contempt for belles lettres and polite literature'.[82] Whether approved or not, printed drama found a market. At Longleat the library largely went to sleep on the death of Lord Weymouth in 1714, but when the future 1st Marquess of Bath (1734–96) married Lady Elisabeth Cavendish Bentinck in 1759, she added a collection of fashionable plays to the shelves, smartly bound, with her cipher on the spines.[83] Similar plays are to be found at Goodwood, while the now dispersed library at Blaenpant in Cardiganshire, sold in 1920, was noted for its large collection of Restoration drama.[84] Earlier the 10th Earl of Northumberland (1602–68) was probably the original owner of a remarkable set of Jacobean play quartos, now one of the great treasures of Petworth.[85] Despite their Northumberland livery bindings, these were clearly bought for reading and not seen as collectables, as

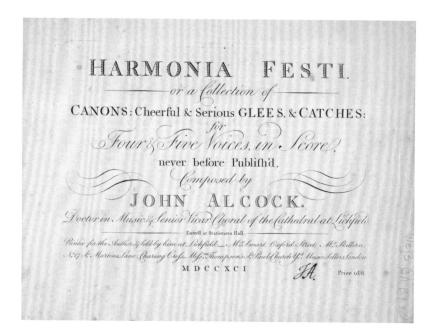

[103] Title page of *Harmonia Festi, or A Collection of Canons: Cheerful & Serious Glees, and Catches* composed by John Alcock, Lichfield 1791 (Calke Abbey)

they would have been a century and a half later. At Temple Newsam in 1669 'Playes' were stored alongside 'Paper Bookes' and may themselves have been unbound. From the eighteenth century novels became increasingly ubiquitous, found in great numbers in houses such as Saltram, Calke, Dunham Massey, Lacock, Scotney, Picton and Tullynally Castle, the home of the Pakenham family, in Ireland.

Sermons were simultaneously a literary genre, read for pleasure, and a practical tool for the care of the immortal soul. Sometimes they were bound together in sets, as at Castle Ward or Charlecote, and sometimes left unbound. At Dunham both categories are found. However popular, sermons were ultimately neither more nor less than the preacher's exposition of the word of God, which in practice meant the Authorised Version of the Bible, by the Restoration period virtually the only new edition of the text available in English.[86] Sir William Boothby, a religious man, noted in 1677 that he had just 'finished reading over the whole *Bible*', adding 'oh how great doth my soule delight in it, I find more pleasure in reading it than in any Booke besides', though in fact he evidently gained a good deal of pleasure in reading religious and theological works of all kinds.[87] Occasionally specific copies of the Bible themselves assumed the status of sacred objects, either because family lore was written into them, or for weightier and more solemn reasons. The so-called 'Juxon Bible', supposedly given on the scaffold by Charles I to Bishop

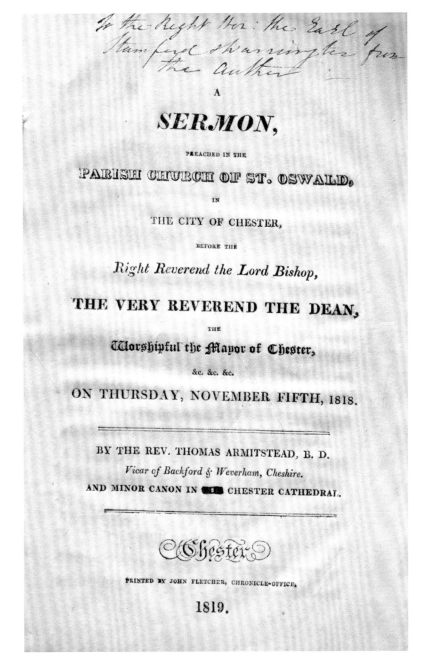

[104] Title page of Thomas Armitstead, *A Sermon, Preached in the Parish Church of St. Oswald, in the City of Chester, before the Right Reverend the Lord Bishop, the Very Reverend the Dean, the Worshipful the Mayor of Chester, &c. &c. &c. on Thursday, November fifth, 1818*, Chester 1819, (Dunham Massey)

Juxon, has long been one of the most admired treasures of Chastleton. Probably an ordinary Chapel Royal book, it was transmuted by wishful thinking into a sacred relic; the traditional story has been embroidered since the mid-nineteenth century, and similar claims have been made for at least five other Bibles elsewhere.[88]

In most houses public devotions would have been taken for granted, perhaps led by the owner, while at Dunham Massey the library still contains multiple copies of conduct manuals, clearly destined for servants (fig. 104). At Chevening in 1753 there were 'Books for Servants', perhaps in the Servants Hall: a Bible and a *Whole Duty of Man*, and originally an *Art of Cookery* and a *Present for an Apprentice*, both subsequently lost, moved or discarded.[89] At Felbrigg in Norfolk, Katherine Windham set about listing her books in the late seventeenth century. These included works on gardening, physic and cookery, but also manuals of piety by Restoration divines like Richard Allestree, Isaac Barrow and Jeremy Taylor, full of advice on how to live (and die) well.[90] Ubiquitous in libraries of the period, at least in England, these books provided the framework within which the devout interpreted the Scriptures in a specifically Anglican context. Such books made good presents and might be finely bound to mark moments of celebration. More rarely, especially down to the late seventeenth century, personal religious books were also found in exquisitely decorated textile bindings made for or by aristocratic women. An example at Chatsworth on a small-format metrical Psalter (1637) may have belonged to Christian, Countess of Devonshire (1595–1675); a similar embroidered binding at Saltram is now detached from its book.[91] In Catholic houses like Chillington Hall (Staffordshire) there were finely bound 'Mass Books in best Marochino', as well as other books – for example a Spanish dictionary – which hint at a different perspective on the world.[92] The origins of this world view are explicit at Burton Constable, where the great library of the Constables is full of evidence of the personal and educational connections between English Catholics and schools and colleges in France and the Austrian Netherlands. Elsewhere, Catholic families like the Thockmortons of Buckland and Coughton treasured medieval manuscripts inherited from better times.[93] At Harvington Hall in Worcestershire there was from the seventeenth century a library 'ad usum cleri', selected by a century and a half of priest-librarians to aid the Catholic missions.[94]

In Ireland the penal laws bit deeper. At Springhill one of the Lenox-Conynghams' more unexpected possessions was a satchel containing the papers of Fr John Fottrell, Provincial of the Irish Dominicans, arrested in 1739 and hauled before George Butle Conyngham (d. 1765), a reminder of the role which landowners played as magistrates and enforcers of government edicts.[95] The Conynghams' own devotional and theological books have a distinctively Presbyterian tinge, unsurprisingly for a family of Scots descent, suspected of being occasional conformists. Similar books are also found in Scotland, though in some Scottish libraries, among them Brodie Castle in Morayshire and Castle Fraser in Aberdeenshire, the owners' Episcopalian sympathies are clear.

In common with other Irish Protestant land-owners, at Springhill successive family members soldiered on the Continent. Unsurprisingly the library contains a number of books on military matters, including cavalry tactics and the care of horses. The subject had particular resonance in Ireland, where the penal code disqualified Catholics from owning a mount worth more than £10, but books on related matters were common elsewhere.[96] At Erddig in Wales, among many other useful books the library includes Philip Yorke's copy of *A Practical Treatise on Farriery*, written by William Griffths, a groom at Wynnstay (the nearby house of the Williams-Wynns), and published in Wrexham in 1784.[97] Earlier, before and during the Civil War numerous books were published in English on military matters as diverse as gunnery and the ransoming of prisoners.[98] One of the most striking books at Dyrham is one of William Blathwayt's two copies of Jean Errard's *La Fortification demonstrée* (Paris, 1619–22), with an

additional diagram and text added to explain the workings of a cannon. Another is Herman Hugo's *Le Siège de la Ville de Breda*, the French-language version of his account of the conquest of the city by Spanish troops under Ambrogio Spinola, published at the Antwerp Officina Plantiniana in 1631. These, along with diplomatic manuals, law books, maps, dictionaries and other useful tools of the ministerial trade, give a remarkably vivid sense of the interplay between Blathwayt's cultural and scientific interests, and his busy career as a military and colonial administrator. At the tail end of the period, the library at Goodwood includes a *Treatise on Bayonet Practice* (1791), with coloured illustrations, addressed to the Duke of Richmond as Master-General of Ordinance by one Anthony Gordon.

Despite social prohibitions, members of the aristocracy and gentry were involved in business, as estate owners, manufacturers and lawyers. Books offered advice on all these, and more. Several Irish houses contain books on the linen trade, but occasionally the proceeds of industry catapulted self-made men into the ranks of the landed.[99] The master potter Josiah Wedgwood (1730–95), for example, had by 1772 designed about a hundred vases with motifs derived from illustrations in

[105] Title page of Samuel Hayes, *A Practical Treatise on Planting: and the Management of Woods and Coppices*, Dublin 1794 (Florence Court, County Fermanagh)

[106] Plate from the Florence Court copy of *A Practical Treatise on Planting*, showing how to transplant a tree

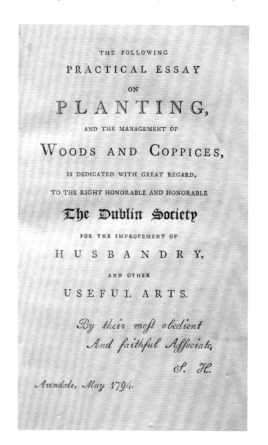

THE

Complete House-keeper,

A N D

PROFESSED COOK.

C A L C U L A T E D

For the greater Eafe and Affiftance of Ladies,
Houfe-keepers, Cooks, &c. &c.

Containing upwards of

SEVEN HUNDRED practical and approved RECEIPTS,
under the following Heads:

I. Rules for Marketing.

II. Boiling, Roafting, and Broil-
ing Flefh, Fifh, and Fowls;
and for making Soups and Sau-
ces of all Kinds.

III. Making made Difhes of all
Sorts, Puddings, Pies, Cakes,
Fritters, &c.

IV. Pickling, Preferving, and
making Wines in the beft Manner and Tafte.

V. Potting and Collaring: Af-
pikes in Jellies; favoury
Cakes, Blamonge, Ice Creams
and other Creams, Whips,
Jellies, &c.

VI. Bills of Fare for every Month
in the Year; with a cor-
rect Lift of every Thing in
Seafon for every Month;
illuftrated with two elegant
Copper-plates of a Firft and
Second Courfe for a genteel
Table.

By M A R Y   S M I T H,

Late Houfe-keeper to Sir Walter Blackett, Bart. and formerly
in the Service of the Right Hon. Lord Anfon, Sir Tho. Sebright,
Bart. and other Families of Diftinction, as Houfe-keeper and
Cook.

N E W C A S T L E:

Printed by T. SLACK, for the Author. 1772.

[107] Title page of Mary Smith, *The Complete House-Keeper, and Professed Cook*, Newcastle 1772 (Wallington Hall)

books of engravings, and the business became so successful that it eventually allowed him to build his own country house, Etruria Hall.[100] Business of all kinds also required practical tools like ready reckoners, and a copy of John Thomson's *Universal Calculator* (Edinburgh, 1784) was evidently in use at Brodie Castle in 1814. Similar books can be found in many libraries, for example at Lacock, while at Erddig a 1704 edition of Wingate's *Arithmetick*,

bought in 1706, was used to convert Flemish ells into square yards when ordering tapestries.[101]

The fortunes of the Yorkes of Erddig, who owned the estate from 1733 to 1973, were originally founded on the career of the London lawyer John Meller (1665–1733), who purchased the estate in 1716 and whose law books are still in the house today. At another Welsh house, Picton, there are many eighteenth-century legal books, the property of Sir Erasmus Philipps (c.1700–43), while Dunham Massey has a large set of statutes, which belonged to a younger brother. Sets of Irish statutes are common in the few surviving Irish libraries, a useful tool for legislators, but also a mark of Irish Protestant patriotism. They were also to be found in English houses where there were Irish connections, such as Goodwood. And many houses contain self-help books on the law, including, especially, books containing advice for Justices of the Peace.

Knowledge of the law was helpful when managing estates. At Ickworth there is a copy of the 1655 edition of Gervase Markham's *Hungers Prevention, or the Whole Art of Fowling by Water and Land*, which includes a woodcut of a duck decoy in operation, while Markham's books were evidently read with interest at Townend and remain on grander shelves at Kedleston and Scotney.[102] At Shugborough (Staffordshire), where the 1st Viscount Anson (1767–1818), the son-in-law of Coke of Norfolk (1754–1842), created a model farm, a number of volumes on agricultural economy survived a bankruptcy sale in 1842. Across the water the Royal Dublin Society, founded in 1731, actively promoted the study of farming and estate improvement, publishing books found on the shelves of the landed proprietors who were its members, as at Florence Court in County Fermanagh (figs. 105 and 106).[103] Books on domestic economy, and especially on cookery, survive less well, perhaps because they never made it to the Library shelves. The subject was of interest at Townend, while at Gunby and Dunham Massey there are manuscript cookery books, containing recipes for such delights as lemon pudding.[104] At Wallington, in Northumberland, the Trevelyans' cook Mary Smith published a distillation of domestic wisdom, *The Complete House-Keeper, and Professed Cook*, in 1772 (fig.107).[105]

Food and health were linked, and advice on both was available in print. At Erddig an eighteenth-century reader evidently had concerns about

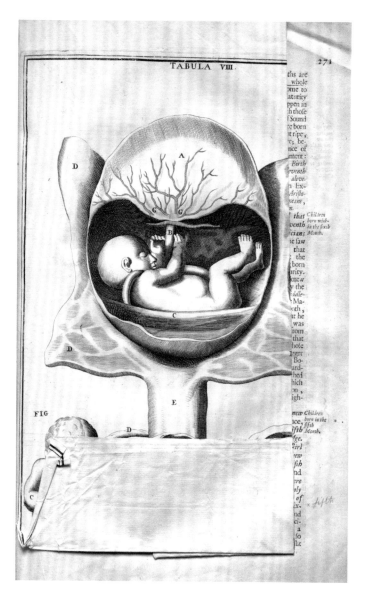

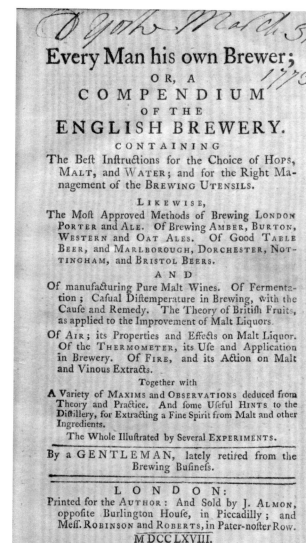

childbirth, as there is a copy of the 1689 English version of Diemerbroeck's *Anatomy of Human Bodies* with underlining on pages 271–2, the section dealing with premature birth (fig. 108).[106] At Dunham a copy of a 1703 anatomy manual certainly belonged to a woman, the heiress Lady Mary Booth (1704–72).[107] At Nostell the Swiss-born Sabine Winn was concerned about her health, creating her own dispensary and accumulating medical books of all kinds.[108] An otherwise inexplicable book on impotence, together with other medical books once on Lord Leigh's shelves at Stoneleigh, may explain why a young nobleman had evidently decided in his early twenties that he was unlikely to father an heir and that his library would go to his Oxford college, where the book remains.[109] Less commonly, houses contain books

owned by those who were themselves medical practitioners. Obstetrics books which belonged to Sir Richard Croft (1762–1818), who oversaw Princess Charlotte's fatal lying-in in 1817, are today at Croft Castle in Herefordshire.[110]

More enjoyably, gardening was a favourite pastime for many. In 1727 John, Lord Hervey, wrote to his lover Stephen Fox at Redlynch, offering to lend gardening books, opining: 'I should think Switzer's Compleat Gardner, Hubbard upon Agriculture, and Hales upon Vegetation would not be unwelcome.'[111] The owners of Erddig, and many others, bought *The Compleat Gard'ner* (1693, fig. 110), Evelyn's translation of *Instruction pour les jardins fruitiers et potagers* by Louis XIV's gardener Jean-Baptiste de la Quintinie (1626–88), attractively illustrated and replete with advice

[108] Plate VII in Isbrand van Diemerbroeck, *The Anatomy of Human Bodies*, London 1689 (Erddig)

[109] Title page of *Every Man his own Brewer*, London 1768 (Erddig)

on design, plantsmanship, pruning and so on, while Evelyn's own book on forestry was equally successful. A couple of generations later, Philip Miller's *Gardener's Dictionary* (1724), too, was overwhelmingly popular. Both Sir William Fownes at Woodstock, County Kilkenny, in 1735 and Richard Edgeworth at Edgeworthstown in 1734 had a copy, while at Nanhorron near Pwllheli a copy of the 1736 edition is marked up with planting in the garden.[112] Walled gardens produced fruit, which could be eaten, but was also used for cider, and John Philipps's poem *Cyder* (1708), written in imitation of Virgil's Georgics, can be found on the shelves at Scotney Castle in Kent, as well as at Stourhead and at Calke Abbey – though John Worlidge's *Vinetum Britannicum* (1676), also at Scotney, provided more useful information. At Erddig the 1768 small-format *Every Man his own Brewer* originally belonged not to a man, but to the owner's mother, Dorothy Yorke (d.1787), who acquired it in March 1773 (fig.109).[113]

For many, architecture was a more appealing pastime than brewing. Colen Campbell's *Vitruvius Britannicus* (1715–71) was the most popular book of all (fig.111), preserved in some twenty-eight copies (in various permutations) in the collections of the National Trust, as well as in many other houses including Goodwood, and once in many libraries now dispersed or despoiled, including Harewood (sold in 1965) and Buckland (now in the RIBA library), the Throckmortons' house in Berkshire.[114] With its large plates, it provided an overview of the progress of classical architecture in Britain, admittedly slanted towards the Palladianism of the Whig oligarchs. Plate books could be directly connected with the design of houses, particularly if the owner dabbled in architecture. The classical front of the Janus-faced Irish house Castle Ward, almost certainly a home-made effort by the owner, Bernard Ward, 1st Viscount Bangor (1719–81), was derived from a design in Abraham Swan's *Collection of Designs in Architecture* (1757), still in the library.[115]

[110] Double page from Evelyn's translation of Jean-Baptiste de la Quintinie, *The Compleat Gard'ner*, London 1693 (Erddig)

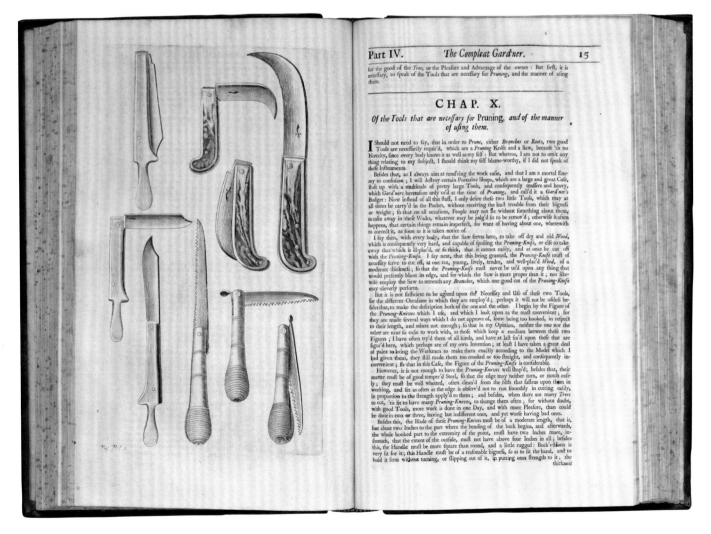

Books were directly linked with building projects elsewhere, too, whether in the form of presentation copies from architects, or books acquired by architects to inform or enthuse their clients. Lord Leigh's copy of the 1759 *Ruins of Athens* was ordered direct from the publisher Robert Sayer by Leigh's architect Timothy Lightholer in 1764.[116] At Kedleston there are finely bound copies of Robert Adam's *Ruins of the Palace of the Emperor Diocletian at Spalatro* (1764) and George Richardson's *Book of Ceilings* (1776), both probably presentation copies, while the superbly bound copy of Stuart and Revett's *Antiquities of Athens* now in the Getty collection at Wormsley (the binding almost certainly designed by James 'Athenian' Stuart) was once in the library of the 1st Earl Camden (1714–94).[117]

The architecturally adventurous cast the net wider. William Blathwayt, once resident in the Netherlands, owned Dutch architectural books, a few of which are still at Dyrham, and both Leigh and Lord Scarsdale owned many French and Italian books. Italian texts were also available in English for those who could not read the originals. The now partially dispersed library at Lyme Park still includes a volume of Giacomo Leoni's *Architecture of Leon Battista Alberti* (1726), appropriate since Leoni worked at Lyme for the Leghs.[118] In Ireland Sir Thomas Vesey of Abbeyleix in County Laois, also a bishop of the Church of Ireland, was a great builder, a former pupil of Henry Aldrich at Christ Church, Oxford, who retained enough of an interest in Aldrich's favourite subject of architecture to purchase a volume of Palladio from a Dublin bookseller in 1707.[119] Contemporary large-format architectural books of other kinds were popular in both Britain and Ireland, including works by Gibbs and later Adam, Stuart and Revett's *Antiquities of Athens* (1762), or the two massive plate books by Robert Wood on the buildings of Palmyra (1753) and Baalbek (1757), all volumes which provide access to information about the latest designs, or about far-away buildings which enthusiasts could not visit in person. These books were expensive, but occasionally an interest in architecture tipped over into the pursuit of early, rare and collectable books. At Kedleston Lord Scarsdale had a 1524 Italian edition of Vitruvius, finely illustrated with woodcuts, while Lord Leigh had a first edition of Palladio (1570) at Stoneleigh. Other books, cheaper and more mundane, but eminently practical,

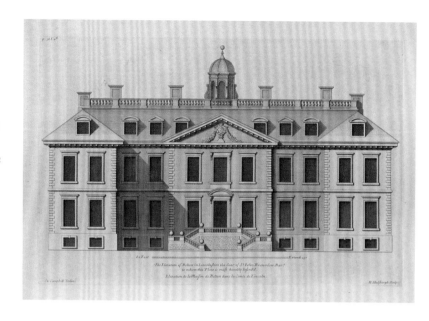

included pattern books on subjects as diverse as chimneys, Chinese buildings and the Gothick.

Travel books, too, might range from the practical, ordinary and everyday – practical guides for Grand Tourists at Tatton Park and Belton, for example, or the cathedral guidebooks of the York publisher Thomas Gent (1693–1778) at Nostell Priory – through to books of extreme grandeur. Topographical and perspective views, such as Kip and Knyff's *Britannia Illustrata* (1707, fig. 112), with views of houses, were popular, but so, too, were county histories, beginning with Dugdale and Plot in the seventeenth century, sometimes perhaps collected as much for their illustrations as their texts. Books from abroad were far from unknown, describing everything from individual buildings through to the contents of royal and princely collections. Maps could range from magnificent seventeenth-century Dutch atlases – generally the preserve of serious collectors like Sir Richard Ellys, though Lord Warrington at Dunham Massey had a fine set of Blaeu's *Atlas Maior* – through to county atlases or the best-selling itinerary books of John Ogilby (1600–76) and his successors, a suitable size and shape to slip into the pocket. Grander publications, like the superb perspective views of Paris created by Louis Bretez and issued in 1739, could reflect an interest in far-away or, in the case of Paris, not-so-far-away places but might also bear witness to foreign travels. Lord Leigh's many travel and architectural books, for example, appear to have been either a preparation for or alternative to the foreign travel which had to be abandoned when

[111] Belton House, as depicted in Colen Campbell's *Vitruvius Britannicus*, 1715–71

the protagonist was placed in the care of the mad-doctor Dr Willis.[120]

Writing in the late seventeenth century, the 1st Earl of Warrington had advised his son 'next to a knowledge in the Law; History is very necessary, and especially of our own Country', enjoining his children to read the lives of famous men, for example by Plutarch and Grotius, and even Machiavelli.[121] English translations of Plutarch are on many shelves – there is an edition of 1683 at Gunby, for example – while the nearby great house at Belton has dozens of seventeenth- and eighteenth-century county histories, typically attractively illustrated, a genre of publication clearly aimed at wealthy owners of private libraries.[122] For those who wished to look further afield, the works of the French Jesuit René Rapin de Thoyras (1621–87),

a determined classical humanist unimpressed by moderns like Copernicus, Descartes and Galileo, are ubiquitous in English libraries.[123] Almost equally common, the massive illustrated volumes of Bernard de Montfaucon's *Antiquité Expliqué* (1719, published in English in 1722) provided a compendious guide to the world of classical antiquity, while later histories by David Hume, Tobias Smollett and Edward Gibbon, as well as biographies, memoirs, and antiquarian texts of all kinds, were all popular, and perhaps especially welcome if of local interest. Chirk Castle, for example, has a pair of smart illustrated octavos on the cathedrals at Llandaff (1718/19) and St David's (1716) by antiquarian M P Browne Willis (1682–1760). Thomas Rymer's *Foedera* (1704–13), an immense sixteen-volume edition of treaties and alliances was on an altogether grander scale, and

[112] Johannes Kip and Leonard Knyff, *Britannia Illustrata*, London 1707; plate of Erddig, at Erddig, Wrexham

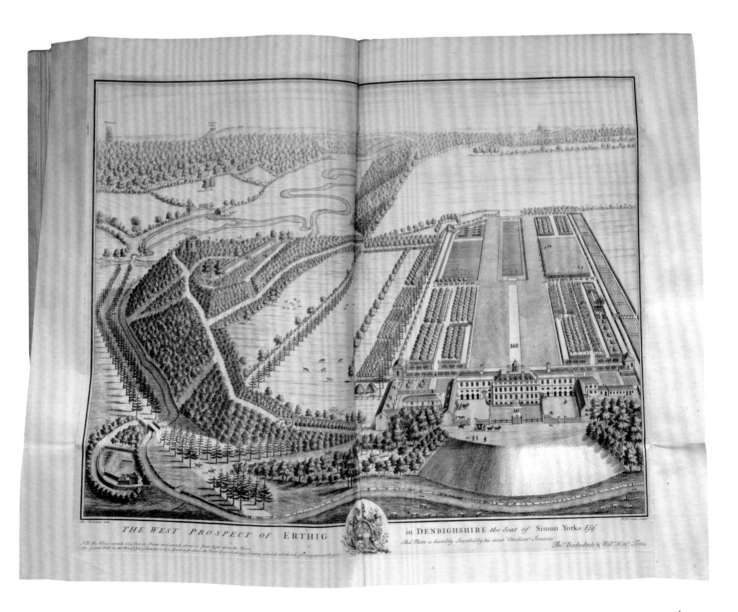

THE WEST PROSPECT OF ERTHIG in DENBIGHSHIRE the Seat of Simon Yorke Esq.

there are sets at Belton, Saltram and Wimpole, for example, as well formerly at Stoneleigh.

For those with a taste for more contentious events, Clarendon's *History of the Rebellion and Civil Wars in England* (1702), and William Dugdale's *Short View of the Late Troubles of England* (1675) both provided a comprehensive retrospective view of the upheavals of the mid-seventeenth century. On either side of the year 1700 families like the Massingberds, and others, were equally engaged by more recent histories. At Gunby, a strongly Protestant house, hagiographies of Good King Billy (William of Orange) stand alongside anti-Popish polemic and histories of the recent wars with France. Elsewhere, others were interested in the histories of their own families. In Ireland Protestant landlords, conscious of their status as interlopers, displayed a particular interest in commissioning manuscript pedigrees and family histories.[124] The 2nd Duke of Montagu (1690–1749) acquired the late fifteenth-century 'Writhe's Garter Book', now at Boughton, which in part commemorated his own ancestors.[125] The library of another ancient family, the Leghs of Lyme, still contains several early heraldic manuscripts, and an interest in lineage naturally shaded into the subject of heraldry. Books like John Guillim's *Display of Heraldrie*, first issued in 1610 and regularly reprinted, were common. Sometimes they might be coloured, as at Charlecote, an elegant but useful refinement. John Weever's *Ancient Funerall Monuments* (1631; there are nine copies in National Trust houses, including Baddesley Clinton, Dunham Massey and Erddig) continued to fascinate, as did numerous peerages and genealogical guides, constantly reprinted and updated.

Libraries often figured prominently in the education of the young. When no longer required, text books could be liable for disposal, as perhaps at Canons Teign in Devon, where in 1701 there was a trunk containing 'Seventeen old broken School Books and Pamphlets not worth 6d'.[126] Elsewhere, the forces of inertia could intervene. At Lacock, and at Attingham Park in Shropshire, similar books survive in libraries subsequently partially dispersed, presumably because they were of limited interest to later collectors. At Lamport the scholarly Sir Justinian Isham (1611–75) took a particularly close interest in the education of his sons. The family tutor Richard Richardson, vicar of nearby Brixworth, was an important influence, frequently mentioned in the Latin diary kept by the young Thomas Isham at the behest of his father.[127] Sent on a Grand Tour of the north of England with their Huguenot tutor M. de Blainville in 1703, the two sons of William Blathwayt were set to work reading the historian William Camden on a rainy September afternoon in Cambridge, and made to write to their father in French. The younger son, too, evidently knew some Greek.[128] Ashe Windham (1672–1749), owner of Felbrigg, travelled on the Continent from 1693 to 1696, forming a life-long attachment to his Scottish tutor and bear leader Patrick St Clair (1659–1755), who settled at Felbrigg, becoming tutor to Windham's children. Spending the rest of his life there, he became a trusted confidant, assisted in the management of the estate and kept up his scholarship by reading prolifically in his patron's rapidly expanding library.[129] At Catholic Oxburgh, again in Norfolk, the steward and tutor Thomas Marwood (d.1718) left his books to the Bedingfeld family. Though few now remain, many were still on the shelves in 1909.[130]

Classical texts were of course as apt for adults as for children, to be read in translation by those who needed to or in the original for those who could, and as likely to be read in contemporary editions as in ancient versions prized by book collectors. At Auchinleck in south-east Scotland, Dr Johnson was shown the great classical library which belonged to Boswell's father.[131] In 1749, on the other hand, Lord Chesterfield acknowledged the continuing importance of the classics but added a rider:

> *Greek, Latin and ancient history are ornamental in the opinion of the world and pleasing in one's own closet. The title, too, of a good scholar makes a figure among the other titles of a man of quality … but in the common course of life, whether in pleasures or in business, modern languages and modern history, are the necessary parts of knowledge.*[132]

The importance of modern languages had long been acknowledged. In 1650, for example, the 5th Lord Paget (1609–78) was buying books from 'Monsieur', the French tutor 'that doth teach my sonne to write'.[133] For all this, foreign language material, while common, was not found everywhere. The eighteenth-century library at Picton, for example, is almost entirely in English. Elsewhere, French books, whether published in France, or the product of the less censored presses of the Netherlands, were noticeably popular. At Springhill, for example, the library has large quantities of polite literature and belles-lettres in French, most of which once belonged to the well-read Staples family, of nearby Lissane (there are also a handful in Irish, just as Welsh libraries generally contain an infinitesimally small number of Welsh books). Similar French books can be found in many other gentry houses, though not always in such quantities. At Ickworth, a much grander reader, Molly Lepel, owned numerous French books of the most sophisticated and up-to-date kind.[134] By comparison with French, books in other tongues were rarer. Italian books were popular in some quarters, often as at Belton the consequence of travel. Spanish books were rarer, and other languages, including German, Dutch and Nordic languages, much rarer still, reflecting in part the dominance of French and Latin in court and learned circles in those countries, and the unfamiliarity of their languages.[135] Only when special circumstances prevailed were they generally found in any numbers. William Blathwayt, who had lived in the United Provinces and knew Dutch, had books in Dutch, some of which remain at Dyrham.

Many libraries clearly teemed with more everyday books. When they survive, they are now often rare, the kind of books traditionally neglected by research libraries. Both Calke Abbey and Dunham Massey have books about rat catching, while several houses not otherwise loaded with books about science and mathematics contain instruction manuals for globes or microscopes, objects which might well have been kept in the Study alongside the books. At Felbrigg Thomas Wyndham had bought a penny almanac as early as 1615, but later examples are ubiquitous.[136] Goodwood, for example, has a large set printed from the 1730s to the 1750s, and there are similar books at Belton and at Castle Ward. Crime narratives on the shelves ranged from low-life narratives through to descriptions of the fate of the Jacobite rebels in 1715 and 1745. Felbrigg, for instance, has a pamphlet printed in 1750, recounting the lives and deaths of Gabriel Tomkyns, Thomas Munns and John Hall, all highwaymen; Belton, the printed articles of impeachment of the rebel lords in 1716; and Ickworth, pamphlets about the 1745 rebellion as well as a bound set of five about the fate of the unfortunate Admiral Byng (1757). Pamphlets, generally, were popular. There were

large numbers, unbound, at Boconnoc in Cornwall in 1807.[137] Among extant libraries, houses like Belton, Kingston Lacy, Castle Ward, Nostell Priory, Felbrigg, Ickworth and Blickling all contain considerable numbers of pamphlets, some bound as collections, and others still in wrappers as issued. Sometimes, as at Nostell and Blickling, this was the result of retrospective collecting of Civil War pamphlets, but at Kingston Lacy and Lanhydrock there is Civil War material bought by readers who were contemporary with the events under discussion. The library at Felbrigg is rich in ephemeral eighteenth-century publications of all kinds, while that of the Herveys of Ickworth, a family of courtiers and politicians, has many eighteenth-century political pamphlets. The intellectually agile Molly Lepel evidently found these of absorbing interest, going to great lengths to identify anonymous authors, and noting them on endpapers.[138] At Dunham Massey there is a remarkable collection of mostly unbound pamphlets, from the eighteenth and very early nineteenth centuries. Covering topics as miscellaneous as false teeth, life-saving and the cultivation of pineapples, it forms an important component of the 'Great Number of Usefull Books' noted in 1758. Apparently mundane, like the rest of the library at Dunham, and others like it, they provide a series of sometimes startling insights into the everyday life and preoccupations of a great house.

CHAPTER SIX

'A *spacious* Room'

Library Architecture and Fittings from the Restoration to Queen Victoria

*The Library is a spacious Room, the Books disposed
in neat Cases, and an antique Busto over every Case.*
John Macky, Althorp, 1723

I · OUT OF THE CLOSET

The Library as set-piece interior

Country house owners had been building special
rooms for their books since at least the fifteenth
century, but only later did the Library as a grand
architectural statement become common. For
some, the modest Studies and Closets of an earlier
era developed naturally into similarly pocket-sized
rooms, associated into the eighteenth century
with bedchambers and private quarters. The Duke
of Lauderdale's Library (1672) at Ham House is
well known, but the room built in the 1720s or
1730s for the 2nd Earl of Warrington at Dunham
Massey is better preserved (fig. 114).[1] Another
fitted Library, of about 1680, survives at Denham
Place in Buckinghamshire, contemporary with
Roger North's published belief that 'nothing is
more useful than closets, cupboards and presses,
for the laying of books, swords, cloaks and other
things, which may be of quotidian use'.[2] As the
Dunham catalogue and the physical fabric of
the room show, the Library there was repeatedly reconfigured in a series of ways difficult to
pin down, the details of which perhaps scarcely
matter.[3] The crucial point is that over time it and
rooms like it frequently proved inadequate for
the needs of an eighteenth-century aristocratic
household. At Belton the 1st Viscount Tyrconnel's
Study (fig. 115), originally a School Room, but
in use as a Library by 1737, is a vastly enlarged
version of its seventeenth-century prototypes. It,
too, ultimately proved inadequate. Before long,
books started to colonise other parts of the house.

A new ground-floor Library was installed by Jeffry
Wyatville (1766–1840) in the early nineteenth
century, and its bookcases were moved to the floor
above when the first-floor Great Dining Room was
converted into a Library in 1876.[4] At Dunham as
early as 1758 surplus books had overflowed into the
Front Gallery.[5]

At Traquair, in the Scottish Borders, the
third-floor Library (fig. 116) is about the same size
as Dunham, and as at Belton, the bookcases are
decorated with classical busts: not sculptures but
figures painted onto a heavily coved cornice. The
classical authors and heroes serve as shelf-marks
for the bookcases beneath, just as they did in the
Cottonian Library. Once dated about 1700, in
its current form the Traquair Library is clearly
later than that. The current consensus, that the
room was fitted out no earlier than the middle
of the eighteenth century and modified later, is
corroborated by the books.[6] A surviving shelf-list,
in the same hand as the shelf-marks written into
each volume, suggests that their current configuration could be as late as the 1770s, though there
are earlier ownership marks in many, notably the
bookplate of the 4th Earl of Traquair (1659–1741),
dated 1708. The room was repainted in 1823 by
James West, an Edinburgh house-painter, and
the question of whether West was repainting an
existing scheme or introducing one of his own can
now be definitively answered: the shelf-marks show
that it was the former.[7]

[113] Arthur Devis
(1712–87), *Sir Roger
Newdigate (1719–1806)
in the Library at Arbury*

The Libraries at Traquair and Dunham were both, for their date, rather archaic. But even in the seventeenth century, books were not always kept in overgrown Studies. Writing in 1984, Gervase Jackson-Stops remarked that it was surprising that it took so long for the Library to emerge as a room in its own right, and John Cornforth took a similar tack in 2004.[8] In fact some country houses included grandiose book-rooms long before the eighteenth century. Susie West's dissection of Penshurst Place has shown that the seventeenth-century Earls of Leicester kept their books in a magnificent first-floor room, placed above an open loggia looking down onto the President's Court.[9] There seems to have been a similar room at Old Gorhambury House, while at Petworth and at Longleat books occupied large and splendidly appointed rooms in the later seventeenth century, both still extant.[10] At Petworth the Old Library is a large rectangular chamber, built on top of the medieval Chapel, at the east end of the north wing. This was the first part of the house to be remodelled under the 'Proud' Duke of Somerset (1662–1748), the Scots

visitor John Macky in 1723 observing 'he hath pull'd down the old House, all except the Chappel and Library'. Presumably because the plans involved the destruction of the previous Library, it was thought prudent to provide a new home for the books before demolition proceeded.[11] Though subsequently refitted, the bones of the Old Library have remained little altered since the 1680s. At Longleat the L-shaped top-floor Library (see fig. 85) closely resembles contemporary college Libraries, though it was new-fangled enough for the shelves to be set along the walls, rather than in bays projecting into the room.[12] At Althorp, the country seat of the 3rd Earl of Sunderland, Macky again saw a fine Library, 'a spacious Room, the Books disposed in neat Cases, and an antique Busto over each Case', though he reckoned that Sunderland's town Library in Piccadilly far outstripped it.[13]

More self-consciously architectural interiors became increasingly common from the 1720s and 1730s. At the most fundamental level, eighteenth- or early nineteenth-century owners had two possible paradigms when it came to thinking about Library

[114] The Library at Dunham Massey

[115] The Study
at Belton

[116] The Library
at Traquair

rooms. On the one hand, there was the classical inheritance from Greece and Rome. On the other, increasingly, there was the Gothic. The first was, in the view of its proponents, sophisticated, progressive and on the side of liberty. The other, easily characterised by critics as obscurantist and monkish, was, for supporters, patriotic, national and visibly British. While in practice such distinctions could be hard to maintain, one was implicitly Whiggish and the other Tory. Several of the most magnificent classical Libraries of the early Georgian period were built for powerful Whig oligarchs, while one of the earliest and most impressive of the earlier Gothick Libraries was built for Sir Roger Newdigate of Arbury (1719–1806), a closet Jacobite. It appears to have been a conversion of a pilastered Library of the 1730s, perhaps designed by Francis Smith of Warwick.[14]

The location of the Library

Whatever the style, architects and patrons first had to decide where in the house the Library should go. Sometimes their solution is far from clear in published plans, with books like Colen Campbell's *Vitruvius Britannicus* (1715–71) sometimes giving away little, even in houses like Castle Howard which we know from other sources contained Libraries.[15]

Vitruvius himself had little to say about Libraries, though he did comment on orientation, advising:

> Cubicula and Libraries should face east, for the morning light makes them serviceable, and furthermore the books in libraries will not rot. For in Libraries that face south and west, the books are spoiled by worms and moisture, as the oncoming moist winds give rise to such things and nurture them, while as they pour forth their moist breath they corrupt the scrolls by discolouring them.[16]

The reference to scrolls and climate immediately exposes the fundamental problems inherent in relying on an architectural treatise from the Mediterranean world of antiquity, especially in the very different climate of northern Europe, in an age when most books were printed, and where the codex had displaced the roll nearly 1,500 years earlier. On the other hand Vitruvian strictures on the location of Libraries clearly made some sort of sense in the oligarchic world of Augustan England:

> For the most prominent citizens, those who should carry out their duties to the citizenry by holding honorific titles and magistracies, vestibules should be constructed that are lofty and lordly … In addition to these, there should be libraries, picture galleries, and basilicas, outfitted in a manner not dissimilar to the magnificence of public works, for in the homes of these people, often enough, both public deliberations and private judgements and arbitrations are carried out.[17]

Despite this, Libraries in private rooms on upper floors, well away from damp, continued to be popular. At Chatsworth the Old Library was, according to *Vitruvius Britannicus*, a small room in 'his Grace's proper apartment' on the second floor (fig. 117), the floor above the State Apartments. It contained 'a Collection of the most valuable Authors'.[18] The interior, presumably by William Talman (1650–1719), contained 'Open Bookcases' with a 'Gilt foliage cornice' and 'shelves, Pillasters, drawers on Plinths', 'the upper part Painted black the lower part white'.[19] At Cannons, demolished in 1747, the spectacularly corrupt James Brydges, 1st Duke of Chandos (1673–1744), regarded his Library as his private den. There was a standing rule that it was not to be 'shewn to any person whatever', though Chandos's guests might be summoned to it to be received in audience.[20] In Scotland the 'skied' Library was a characteristic feature of many Scottish houses, including William Adam's Arniston (1726) with one of the more sophisticated and elegant rooms of its kind.[21] Further south at West Wycombe, a markedly Italianate villa built for the rakish dilettante Sir Francis Dashwood (1708–81), the Library was placed above the Saloon and immediately behind the pedimented central bays of the north front. A room of some splendour, probably from the 1750s, its first-floor location meant that it was well away from the main public rooms on the ground floor, and it commanded fine views onto the park.[22]

More conventionally, Palladian and Neoclassical architects tended to place the Library on the principal floor of the main block of the house. At Moor Park in Hertfordshire, attributed to Sir James Thornhill (1675/6–1734) and Giacomo Leoni (1686–1746), the Library, a comparatively small room, was on the garden front, next to the Saloon.[23] Later, at Basildon Park, John Carr of York (1723–1807) placed the Library in the main block in

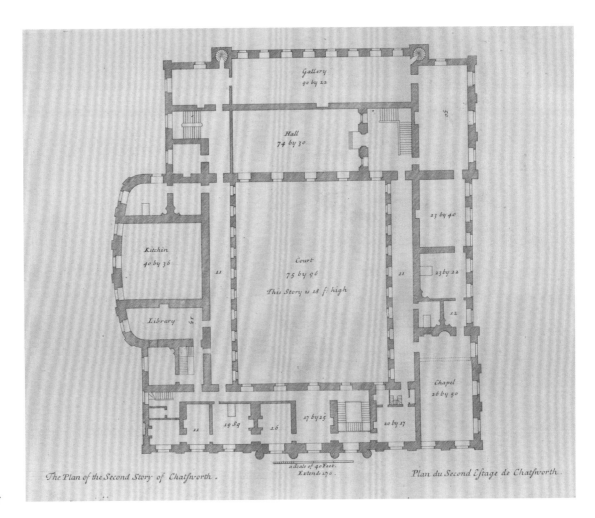

The Plan of the Second Story of Chatsworth.   a Scale of 40 Feet.   Plan du Second Estage de Chatsworth.
Extends 170.

Gallery
90 by 22

Hall
74 by 30.

Kitchin
40 by 36

Court
75 by 96

This Story is 18 f. high

Library

Chapel
26 by 50

[117] Plan of the second floor of Chatsworth from *Vitruvius Britannicus*, showing the original position of the Library

1776, just off the main Hall, as did Samuel Wyatt at Doddington in Cheshire (1777–98), Robert Adam at Harewood (1766) and Henry Holland at Berrington Hall in Herefordshire (1778–81).[24] At Fonthill Splendens, a house subjected to constant alterations, Alderman Beckford's Library was on the ground floor of the main block, but at the back of the house, separated from the main Hall by an ante-room, though with a connecting door through to the principal Bedchamber. Later, and on a much smaller scale, at Llanerchaeron in Cardiganshire, the ground floor of John Nash's model villa (1794) had just four principal rooms, one of them a Library, a typical plan for a house of its size and date.[25]

Another possibility was to put the Library in a side wing. At Buckland, in Berkshire, rebuilt by John Wood the Younger (1728–82) in 1757, the Library was in an octagonal east pavilion, 40 feet in diameter, linked to the house by a 60-foot corridor, balancing a Catholic chapel in the opposite wing.[26] At Compton Verney, in Warwickshire,

the Willoughby de Brokes' Library was in the left hand of the two projecting wings of the entrance front, facing across onto the main portico, but slightly detached from the main block of the house, with a an octagonal Study beyond.[27] At Wimpole James Gibbs designed a projecting Library at the north-west corner of the house for Edward Harley, an exceptionally ambitious building for an exceptional library and now much altered, though at Kirtlington Park (1742–8) in Oxfordshire the architect John Sanderson put the Library on the main front, just off the Hall, as Gibbs had done at Kelmarsh Hall (1728).[28] At Attingham Park in Shropshire (1783–85) the 'Outer Library', a magnificent Neoclassical pavilion designed by architect George Steuart (c.1735–1806), was in the west wing (fig. 118), linked to the main part of the house by an open loggia or via a circuitous route through service quarters.[29] A similar solution was also proposed in several variants at Duff House in Aberdeenshire, where the projected wings were never built, and at Nostell Priory in Yorkshire and Kedleston in

[118] The West or Outer Library Pavilion and colonnade at Attingham Park, designed by George Steuart

Derbyshire, where, again, the grandiose plans had to be scaled back.[30] The habit of placing the Library in a detached block, accessed via a link corridor, continued into the nineteenth century. At Castle Leslie in County Monaghan, a rather forbidding Italianate house built by the Belfast architect W. H. Lynn (1829–1915) in the 1870s, the interconnected Library and Billiard Room are reached by a long walk through a Conservatory and along a Long Gallery – perhaps less a matter of peace and quiet for study than of segregating after-dinner male roistering from more civilised parts of the castle.[31]

II · THE CLASSICAL LIBRARY

The Palladian Library

When it came to designing a Library, the architects of the Palladian revival of the early eighteenth century had little to go on, bar two brief remarks in Vitruvius and Palladio's reconstruction of a Vitruvian villa, the latter readily available to English connoisseurs in a range of early editions, as well as modern versions by Isaac Ware (1738; purportedly more accurate) and Giacomo Leoni (1721; certainly more elegant, with fine engravings by Bernard Picart).[32] Clients and architects studied these texts avidly. Lord Burlington, for example, had picked up a copy of the 1601 edition of Palladio

in Vicenza in 1719, and by 1737 had laid hands on Inigo Jones's own copy of the 1567 edition.[33] At Lyme Park, where Peter Legh XII (1669–1744) employed Leoni, a Venetian, to remodel the house as an Italianate *palazzo*, the much depleted library still contains Legh's copy of his architect's 1726 English edition of Alberti.[34] Elsewhere, subscription lists and the great wealth of architectural books in extant libraries tell their own story. Subscribers to William Kent's 1727 edition of Inigo Jones, for example, included ninety-seven members of the aristocracy, numerous gentry and rival architects like Gibbs and Nicholas Hawksmoor. Another key text, Robert Castell's *Villas of the Ancients Illustrated* (1728), was dedicated to Kent's patron Burlington, and again attracted many well-born subscribers. Imaginatively illustrated with plans supplied by Castell, it included descriptions of Roman villas by antique authors, including Pliny the Younger, whose villa at Laurentinum was held up as the model (fig. 119).[35] It even included advice on Libraries, as Pliny had referred to 'a cubiculum, that jets out in an Ellyptick Form, from which gradually at all its Windows it receives the whole Course of the Sun: It has in its Walls Repositories after the Manner of Libraries, containing Books, rather for Amusement, than Study.'[36]

Patrons and clients could also refer to compendia on more recent buildings, notably the

Palladian manifesto *Vitruvius Britannicus*. It is no coincidence that the appearance of this and books like it, combined with the burgeoning prosperity of the recently united Kingdom of Great Britain, resulted in a country house building spree by those who could afford it. Three of the grandest and most innovative domestic Library interiors of the 1720s were in great houses in Norfolk. At Raynham Hall, the home of Sir Robert Walpole's brother-in-law the 2nd Viscount Townshend (1674–1738), a new Library was installed in the late 1720s, with oak panelling and tall bookcases set flush into the walls. The work of William Kent (1685–1748) and Thomas Ripley (1682–1758), it cost £221. Books were transferred into it from the old Library in 1727.[37] At Houghton, Walpole's own great house,

[119] Plan of the first floor of Pliny's villa at Laurentinum from Robert Castell's *Villas of the Ancients Illustrated*, 1728

Kent again designed the almost contemporary fitted Library (*c.*1725–8; fig.120), a small panelled room like Raynham in some ways and quite similar to Dunham and Ham, but with self-consciously architectural, arched bookcases modelled on Venetian windows, open pilasters filled with books, and library tables and desks to match.[38] The extant Library which Kent designed for Thomas Coke, the future Earl of Leicester, at Holkham, equally grand and somewhat larger, was completed in about 1740. Another Library, which Horace Walpole thought 'delightful', was designed by Kent for General James Dormer (1679–1741) at Rousham Hall in Oxfordshire. A double-height 'great room', it was dismantled in 1764, just four years after Walpole had admired it.[39] A further point of comparison is

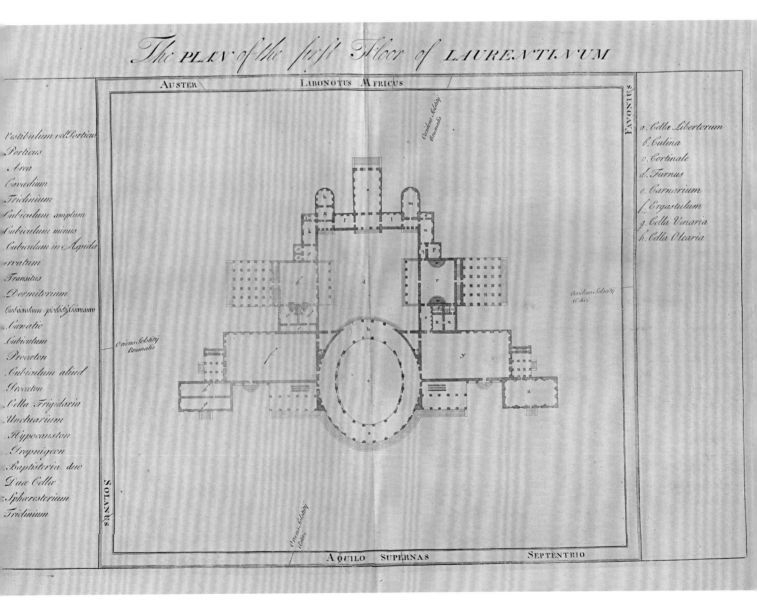

The PLAN of the first Floor of LAURENTINUM

provided by Kent's unexecuted designs of 1736 for
a Library for Queen Caroline at St James's Palace,
published in 1737 – a grandly Roman vision, with
strongly architectural bookcases and a spectacular
painted ceiling.[40] Another Library design which
never made it beyond the drawing board, by the
Irish architect Edward Lovett Pearce (1699–1733),
was for a grand Palladian Library at Stillorgan
House in County Dublin.[41]

Many of these Libraries rather resembled
designs for a fitted-up Library (fig. 121) by the
Huguenot designer, engraver and architect Daniel
Marot (1661–1752), published in The Hague
in 1703. Marot's book is now rare, and did not
circulate as widely as is sometimes supposed,
though it was clearly known to James Gibbs
(1682–1743), a Catholic Scot, who worked for the
Harleys and whose copy is now in the Bodleian.[42]
As at Houghton, the published Marot designs,
depicting the Library which Marot had installed
for William III at Het Loo in 1697, included open
pilasters filled with books.[43] The same conceit is

[121] Marot's design,
1703, for the Library at
Het Loo, Apeldoorn,
Netherlands

also found in other English Libraries of the period,
including at Badminton (fitted out about 1690, but
later reworked by Wyatville) and Christ Church,
Oxford, where the Harleys' former chaplain
William Stratford (c.1672–1729) was a key figure
in the protracted evolution of the new Library,
though the woodwork probably did not go in until
1752.[44] Rooms like these, based on the classical
orders, with pilasters, columns and pediments,
and bookcases based on arches, or even Venetian
windows, were new in early Georgian Britain. Even
by comparison to astylar interiors like the Libraries
at Dunham and Ham (where classical proportions
are implied, but not overtly articulated by columns
and pilasters), Libraries like those at Houghton
were highly innovative.

Several of the finest surviving Palladian Library
interiors are in Scotland. One of the earliest is
the High Library at Arniston, Midlothian (1726),
designed by William Adam (1689–1748) and exquisitely illustrated in his *Vitruvius Scoticus* (fig. 122).[45]
Placed in a third-floor attic above the entrance

Bibliotheque inuentée et grauée par D. Marot auec preuillige des Etats generaux des prouuces Vnie et d'hollande et West Frisse.

front, the Arniston Library is a sophisticated classical interior, its monumental glazed presses set between Ionic pilasters and surmounted by busts. Though its contents are extant, they were unfortunately shifted to a new ground-floor Library in 1868, and Adam's presses now house the family porcelain collection. Many of the Arniston books are elegantly bound, and when they were still *in situ*, William Adam's Library must have looked splendid indeed. In its original form decorated in white and gold, the Library was refitted to house more books in 1756, when it was redecorated to its current scheme.[46]

Close at hand and just outside Edinburgh, the great Library at Newhailes, built for Sir David Dalrymple (1665–1721), is on an even grander scale. An aristocratic lawyer who twice served as Lord Advocate, Dalrymple had purchased the estate in 1709, and with it a pioneering Palladian villa built by the previous owner, the architect James Smith (c.1645–1731). Between 1718 and 1721 Dalrymple expanded this house, adding a massive new Library pavilion, with an Ionic order of pilasters, designed by an unknown architect. Nearly as large as the original house, it was subsequently matched by a balancing pavilion on the other side of the main block. A skied Library was clearly impossible in the circumstances, and Dalrymple's Library was on the *piano nobile*, but placed on top of a vaulted basement. The link building joining it to the main block housed the Library Closet, complete with fireplace, necessary in the Scottish climate, especially since the Library was so vast as to make effective heating impossible.[47] Its cavernous interior is relatively simple, a sober room devoted to scholarship, the adjustable shelves rising from floor to ceiling, clearly intended to house as many books as possible in the available space.

Many houses gained new or reworked Libraries in the middle decades of the eighteenth century. At Apethorpe in Northamptonshire, the north range of the main courtyard was rebuilt as a Library in the 1740s.[48] At another Midland house, Lamport in Northamptonshire, built originally by John Webb (1611–72), a new Library room was added to a house by Francis Smith of Warwick in 1732, partly to house books inherited by Sir Justinian Isham, 5th Baronet (1687–1737), from his father-in-law, the grandson of John Hacket (1592–1670), former Bishop of Lichfield and Coventry. Of the original fittings only the fireplace remains, the two-storey

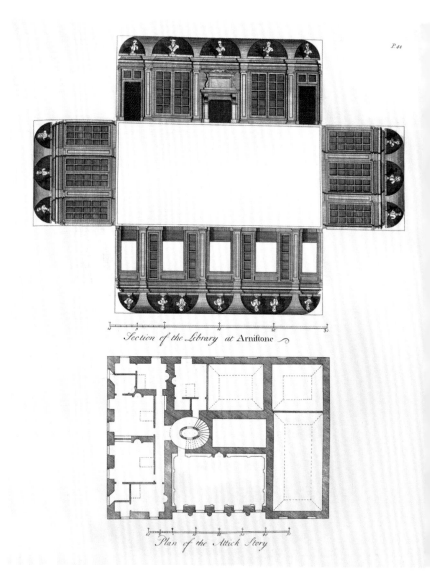

Section of the Library at Arniſtone

Plan of the Attick Story

[122] The Library at Arniston from William Adam's *Vitruvius Scoticus*, 1812

fitted bookcases designed by Henry Hakewill (1771–1830) and most of the present furnishings having been installed only in 1819.[49]

Increasingly, a safely Palladian Library, with open wall shelving and library busts, was a standard feature of the houses of the unadventurous or the cautiously conventional. At Petworth the so-called White Library (fig. 123), converted from an under-used ground-floor room in the State Apartment, was designed by Matthew Brettingham (1699–1769). Working in tandem with the seventeenth-century Old Library upstairs, its twenty-three elegant presses were surmounted by plaster busts after the antique, probably cast from moulds which Brettingham had recently obtained in Rome.[50] Visiting some decades later, the German traveller Prince Hermann von Pückler-Muskau (1785–1871) noted that it housed the more modern books in

Hamilton (1731–1803) were painted onto the dado cupboards by the Academician Charles Reuben Riley (1752–1798), who also worked for the bibliomaniac Ralph Willett (1719–95) in his Library at Merly in Dorset.[51]

In humbler houses or in older houses converted and modified, the architectural challenges were rather different. At Picton Castle in Pembrokeshire the books collected by the cultured Sir Erasmus Philipps (d. 1743) and his brother Sir John (d. 1764) are still housed in a beautiful interior from the 1750s, with glazed bookcases separated by fluted Ionic pilasters and shelves concealed inside them, the whole deftly fitted into a round medieval tower (fig. 124).[52] At another Welsh house, Fonmon Castle, the Library was created by the Bristol architect Thomas Paty in 1766–7: an elegant first-floor gallery punched through a twelfth-century keep, with fine Rococo ceilings by Paty's plasterer Thomas Stocking.[53]

Elsewhere, Long Galleries often ended up as Libraries. At Burton Constable, in East Yorkshire, the thirteen glazed elm bookcases in the Jacobean Long Gallery date from about 1742 and house the library of the Catholic antiquarian William Constable (1721–91; see fig. 14). By 1775 there were already some 9,600 books at Burton Constable.[54] At Drayton House, in Northamptonshire, the Library is in a Gallery high up in the house, while at Chequers Sir John Russell converted the Long Gallery into a Library in about 1780. At Sudbury Hall in Derbyshire and Lanhydrock in Cornwall, by the nineteenth century earlier Long Galleries had again been colonised by books.[55] At Blenheim Hawksmoor's Long Gallery had turned into a Library by 1749, when the town library of the 3rd Earl of Sunderland was shifted to Oxfordshire.[56] At Blickling an equally spectacular library, that of the great collector Sir Richard Ellys, was installed in the Jacobean Long Gallery by 1745 (both the Blickling and the Blenheim libraries are discussed in more detail in Chapter 10). At Syon House, with Robert Adam's spectacular transformation of the Long Gallery (1763; fig. 125), it is the architecture which unsurprisingly tends to attract attention. Adam's reworking of an awkward space, 136 feet long but only 14 feet wide, is a masterly achievement, but the room was, of course, designed as a Library, and though the main collection of the Dukes of Northumberland has long been at Alnwick, the Gallery at Syon

the house, and the older ones were still upstairs, a suggestion only partially true, now as then. Not far away, at Goodwood, there is a similar Library, again designed by Brettingham, filled substantially with the modern books of the day, since the eighteenth-century Dukes of Richmond had few early books to match the books inherited from the Wizard Earl at Petworth. Originally described as 'the Great Room' and later as the 'Large Library', the room has a fashionable Palladian ribbed ceiling, and bookcases and other refinements were added by George III's architect Sir William Chambers (1723–96) in the aftermath of the death of the 2nd Duke of Richmond in 1757. There was subsequent work by James Wyatt (1746–1813). Then, between 1772 and 1775 antique figures based on Greek vases in the famous collection of the diplomat Sir William

is still shelved end to end with Northumberland books. At Montacute, by contrast, the former Great Chamber, rather than the Long Gallery, became a Library (which it was by 1791), while at Burghley House books displaced by a building project by Capability Brown found their way to the Great Hall, where they still are.[57]

The Neoclassical Library

By the late 1750s the conventional Palladianism of early Georgian England was already passé for sophisticates, a fact abundantly clear from the success of Robert Adam in shunting aside older men like Brettingham and James Paine (1717–89) at Kedleston and Nostell.

   With its 'mosaic' ceiling, based on recurring motifs inspired by Roman pavements, and a massive Doric door case (a sober, masculine, order, in contrast to the more festive Music Room and Drawing Room), the Library at Kedleston is an unusually splendid room. Nonetheless as a Library the room is not without its problems. As illustrated in volume four of *Vitruvius Britannicus*, Kedleston was to have had four projecting pavilions, each joined to the main block by a curved quadrant, a plan derived from Palladio's proposals for the Villa Mocenigo (fig. 126). Library accommodation was to have been split between the present room on the south front and the adjacent south-east quadrant. In the event Sir Nathaniel Curzon, 1st Lord Scarsdale (1726–1804), decided that this was unaffordable, and the two southern pavilions were abandoned, reducing the space for books by half and leaving a Library with too many doors and windows for long runs of shelving. Adam was obliged to fit in seven small glazed bookcases, elegant but impractical, and housing an absurdly small number of books for such an enormous house. By 1830 the Library was already thought inadequate, and the two redundant doorways on the east wall were turned into makeshift bookcases. Adam's earlier designs for a large tripartite bookcase along the entire length of that wall, now in the Soane Museum, would clearly have provided a more satisfactory solution.[58]

At Nostell, where the house as designed by James Paine was also to have had four wings, the interconnected Library suite and chaplain's apartment were originally intended to be in the projected north-west wing.[59] By 1766 Adam had taken control, and a Library was placed on the west front of the main block, carefully contrived to achieve a symmetrical arrangement and to provide maximum shelving space for an already extensive collection. Typically enough, it rapidly proved inadequate, and a large proportion of the books at Nostell today are in the adjacent Billiard Room, fitted up to accommodate the constantly growing collection of the house's nineteenth-century owner, Charles Winn (1795–1874). Next door in the Library, other refinements included a fitted medal cabinet (fig. 127) by Thomas Chippendale (1718–79), and an oval painting of *Minerva Presenting the Arts of Painting, Sculpture and Architecture to Britannia* by Adam's decorative painter Antonio Zucchi (1726–95), placed over the fireplace after Sir Rowland Winn, 5th Baronet (1739–85), had decided that Adam's proposal for shelving was too risky. Brightly

painted, the Library's original colour scheme was replaced by a grained scheme by the decorator Thomas Ward around 1823, but some impression of the room in Adam's day can be gleaned from Hugh Douglas Hamilton's portrait of Sir Rowland and Lady Winn (fig. 128), with the couple in an imaginatively enlarged version of the space.[60]

Nostell was by no means the only Adam Library where self-consciously Neoclassical iconography was successfully blended with a dose of patriotism. It can be seen at Osterley, while in the Old Library at Harewood (1768) Minerva and her owl again feature prominently.[61] At Mellerstain in the Scottish borders, the Library (1770) included roundels of Minerva, flanked by representations of teaching and learning, and the ceiling was based on unexecuted designs made by Adam for Lord Bute for his English seat, Luton Hoo.[62] Nonetheless, despite Adam's well-known control of almost every aspect of his interiors, at Nostell, Kedleston and elsewhere this did not usually extend to the books themselves, which generally seem simply to have been transferred from earlier Libraries. Only at Audley End – with large numbers of books in characteristic quarter-leather bindings (marbled paper covers and matching spines with distinctive hatched gold tooling in a chequerboard pattern) – does it seem that there was much connection between binding and interior design. Ironically most of these books are now in the neo-Jacobean Library of the 3rd Lord Braybrooke (1783–1858) which superseded Adam's Library in the nineteenth century.

[126] Kedleston Hall, from Colen Campbell's *Vitruvius Britannicus*, 1715–71

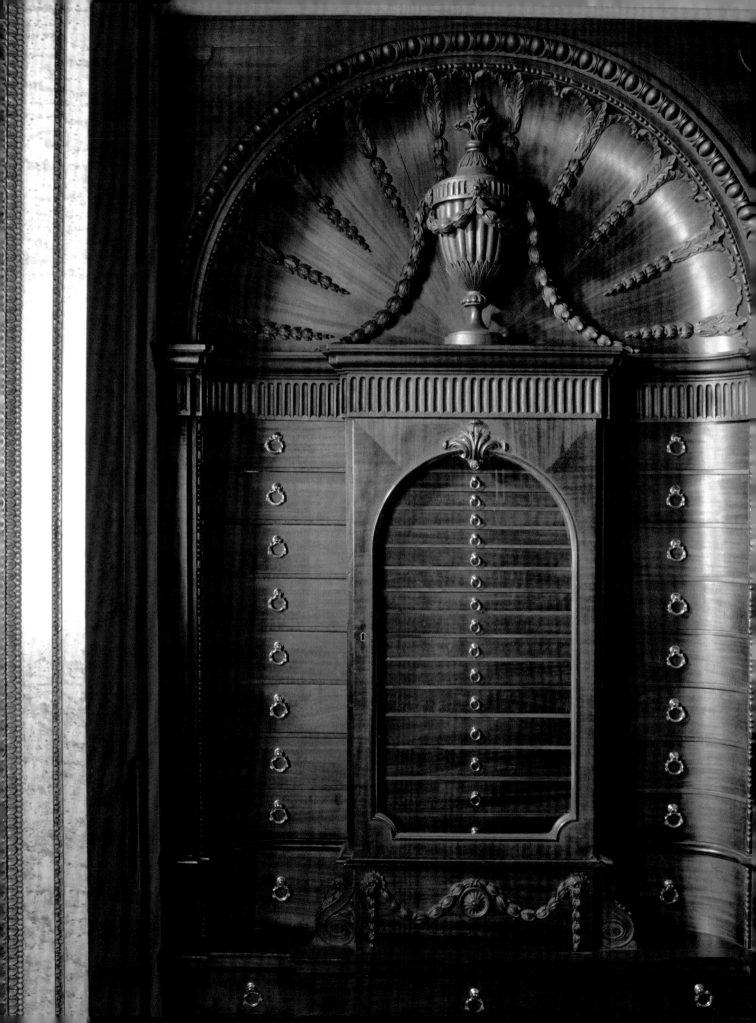

[127] The Chippendale medal cabinet (1767–8) at Nostell Priory

[128] Hugh Douglas Hamilton, *Sir Rowland Winn and his Wife Sabine Louise d'Hervart*, 1767, in the Library at Nostell Priory

Library was installed by 1770, when a visitor remarked that 'it is fitted up like a snuff box' and noted that 'there are more books than I thought'.[64] It swiftly fell victim to the Parkers' desire for a larger Dining Room. Under the joint direction of the estate carpenter and a builder from the nearby naval dockyard at Plymouth, the bookcases were removed, Adam's Library became a Dining Room (still with its Library iconography), and what had been the Eating Room was fitted up as a replacement.[65]

The work of Adam's imitators and rivals sometimes fared as badly. At Woburn a Library designed by Sir William Chambers and completed in 1770 was gutted by the 5th Duke of Bedford just eighteen years later and replaced by a more up-to-date interior by the Francophile architect Henry Holland (1745–1806).[66] This does not survive, but Holland's Library at Althorp (1787) does, though devoid of its once magnificent books. It incorporates bookcases projecting into the room at right angles, providing more shelf space and in the process producing a more compartmentalised room.[67] At Berrington Hall in Herefordshire, Holland's smaller but refined Neoclassical Library (1778–81) also survives, with ceiling medallions of writers from Chaucer to Pope, and neo-Palladian pedimented bookcases, now again bereft of the books they were designed to house.[68]

It was not just at Audley End that Adam's Libraries did not wear well. At both Saltram, and Newby in the North Riding of Yorkshire, Adam interiors were rejigged a generation or so later. At Newby Hall a Dining Room was converted into a Library for the 3rd Lord Grantham (1786–1833) in 1807. All seems consonant and handsome, but Zucchi's ceiling panel of Bacchus and Ariadne gives the game away.[63] At Saltram Adam's original

[129] The Library at Castle Coole, County Fermanagh

[130] The Library
at Felbrigg Hall

By contrast, both library books and Library
room survive at Castle Coole (fig. 129), James
Wyatt's masterpiece in County Fermanagh, where
the plain painted bookcases were knocked up to
the architect's designs by twelve joiners in just three
months in 1797.[69] Earlier in his career James Wyatt
had remodelled Adam's bookcases at Shardeloes
in Buckinghamshire for William Drake (1747–95)
in 1775, introducing plain continuous rectangular
bookcases and painted grisailles by the Italian
painter Biagio Rebecca (1731–1808) above them.[70]
Only a little earlier, the 5th Lord Leigh, a rich young
Oxford graduate recently come into his inheritance,
devised several schemes for Stoneleigh Abbey.
Though contemporaries could only have guessed
at it, Leigh was about to be committed for lunacy,
but his papers include plans for an enormous new
Library wing at Stoneleigh, with a principal Library
room 90 feet long, three reading rooms and a
'Musæum'. There are also sketches in his own hand
for the complete remodelling of Stoneleigh, some in
conventional classical taste, but others in a radical
and alternative style – the Gothic.[71]

III · THE GOTHICK LIBRARY

Visiting York Minster in 1792, Lord Torrington,
an indefatigable traveller, admired the medieval
Chapter House, musing in his diary: 'Whenever
I build a library, it shall be from the model of
a Chapter House.'[72] Once an exotic taste, by
the 1790s it was a sentiment shared by many of
Torrington's contemporaries.

Though Horace Walpole's Library at Strawberry
Hill (1754; see fig. 183) is better known, the first
Gothic Library in Britain was probably 'Merlin's
Cave', a *cottage orné* built in Richmond Park for
Queen Caroline and designed by Kent in 1735.[73]
A couple of decades later, at Felbrigg in Norfolk,
a large room above the Great Hall (possibly the
original Jacobean Great Chamber) was fitted out by
James Paine in 1753, with pinnacled bookcases with
restrained Gothick ornament, and a sober ribbed
plaster ceiling. Clearly designed to fit with the
existing house, the Felbrigg Library (fig. 130) was
part and parcel of the reworking of the entire house
for William Windham II (1717–61).[74] Another
splendid first-floor Gothic Library is that at Arbury

Hall (1754–1761), built by William Hiorn for the Warwickshire landowner, scholar and collector Sir Roger Newdigate. Arbury was constructed on the site of a former Augustinian priory, which perhaps explains the choice of style; the portrait of Newdigate by Arthur Devis (1712–87; fig. 113), still at Arbury, remains among the most compelling images of an eighteenth-century grandee in his Library.[75] Similar rooms of about the same date can be seen at Milton Manor in Berkshire (now devoid of its books) and at Sherborne Castle in Dorset, a Jacobean house, where the collection is extant, housed in an elegant room with fitted ogival Gothic bookcases created for the 6th Lord Digby by the master carpenter William Ride in 1757–8.[76]

At Arundel and Alnwick, two long-neglected ducal castles, owners set about remedying the neglect of centuries, and in both cases this involved a large new Library in the Gothic taste. At Arundel the particularly splendid Perpendicular Gothic Library (fig. 131) was built for the antiquarian-minded 11th Duke of Norfolk (1746–1815). Inspired by St George's, Windsor, it was begun in 1801 and

sumptuously refurnished by G. J. Morant for a visit from Queen Victoria in 1846. One of the few of the 11th Duke's interiors to escape later remodelling, with its galleries it conveniently housed a large number of books in a relatively constricted space.[77] A contemporary account of the duke's celebration of the 600th anniversary of Magna Carta in 1815 was full of admiration, explaining that the collection was mostly 'of the present Duke's forming, his Grace's ancestors having left him few books', and adding that 'the receptacles for the books are also of his Grace's taste, and have been very lately finished'.[78] By contrast, the earlier but now vanished Adam Library at Alnwick was swept away by the 4th Duke of Northumberland (1792–1865) and replaced by a sumptuous Italian Renaissance interior, a collaboration between Anthony Salvin (1799–1881) and a team of imported Italian designers.[79] A Regency guidebook published in 1818 had drawn the attention of visitors to Adam's Library, 'a very fine room, in the form of a parallelogram, properly fitted up for books, and ornamented with stucco-work in a very rich gothic style'.[80]

[131] The Library at Arundel Castle

At least one visitor agreed, admiring the 'four cases ornamented in the Gothic Stile', 'well filled with books on various Branches of polite and useful literature', and by the 1780s the Alnwick Library had also acquired an Egyptian mummy and two American flags captured during the Revolution.[81] However, opinions were not universally enthusiastic. In 1792 the tourist James Plumptre (who should have known a thing or two about Libraries, as his father had organised the collection at Wimpole for Lord Hardwicke) reckoned it the finest room in the house, though generally he was unimpressed with Alnwick, commenting: 'I must own the *light* gothic ornaments made in *plaister*, and painted in *gay* colours, seemed to be trumpery, and to ill accord with the massy, rich and sombre appearance of the outside.'[82]

One of the great treasures of the Alnwick library is the Book of Hours of Lady Margaret Beaufort,

made in Paris in about 1500 and purchased by the 1st Duchess of Northumberland in 1773.[83] However, the connection between Gothic books and a Gothic room was more explicit in the Gothic Library at Stowe (fig. 132), designed by Sir John Soane (1753–1837) for George Nugent-Temple-Grenville, 1st Marquess of Buckingham (1753–1813), between 1805 and 1807. Stowe already had a large classical Library, but Soane's new interior, originally designated the 'Saxon Room', was built to house the great collection of manuscripts which Buckingham purchased from the executors of the antiquarian Thomas Astle (1735–1803). Astle's will had offered the manuscripts for just £500, in acknowledgement of earlier Grenville patronage. Within a short time they had been joined by the collection of Irish manuscripts assembled by the aristocratic Irish Catholic antiquarian Charles O'Conor of Ballinagare (1710–91), which came to Stowe in 1799

[132] The Gothic Library at Stowe

[133] *opposite above* A bookcase in Ralph Willett's Library at Merly, 1785

[134] *opposite below* Francis Nicholson, *Sir Richard Colt Hoare in the Library at Stourhead, c.1808–13*

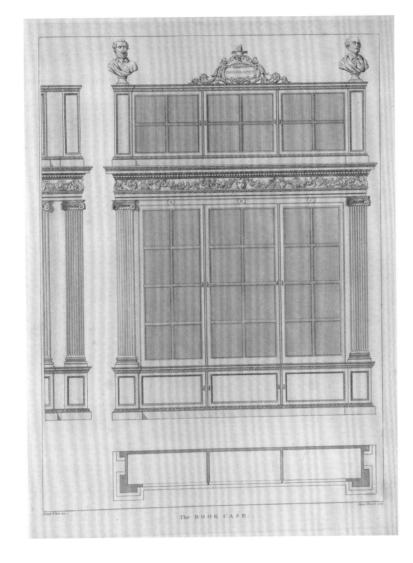

The BOOK CASE.

with his grandson Dr Charles O'Conor (1764–1828), librarian to the Marquess of Buckingham and Chaplain to his Catholic Marchioness.[84] A little-known masterpiece, long used as the private Study of the Headmaster of Stowe School, the details of the Gothic Library were based on Soane's study of the Henry VII Chapel at Westminster, and the room was decorated with 179 shields of various branches of the Grenville, Temples, Nugents and Chandoses.[85]

IV · FROM THE REGENCY TO QUEEN VICTORIA

By the 1790s, architects and clients contemplating a Library were faced with a bewildering and increasingly eclectic choice of styles. In Wiltshire Beckford's Fonthill Abbey (see fig.147), designed by James Wyatt, an architect willing to turn his hand to most things, included a lavishly appointed Library decorated in black and gold.[86] In neighbouring Dorset at Merly House, Ralph Willett (1719–95), like Beckford the son of a West Indies nabob, commissioned a large and magnificent Neoclassical Library, 84 by 26 feet. No longer extant, it was richly decorated with plasterwork reliefs depicting 'the Rise and Progress of Knowledge'. Willett's superlative collection of early books was stowed in a set of glazed mahogany bookcases, which covered almost all the available wall space, each 'enriched with a compleat Ionick Order' (fig.133). These were topped with busts, and 'between the Busts, on each Book-case' was 'an ornamental Scroll on which is written the kind of Books contained in the Case'.[87] The whole was commemorated in a privately printed plate book issued in 1785 – a spectacular piece of eighteenth-century vanity publishing, in which Willett rhapsodised about his decorative scheme, which included representations of Zoroaster, Moses, Mohammed and Christ, as well as King Alfred, Confucius, personifications of the arts and sciences, and repre-sentations of Athens in its prime and in ruins.[88] The antiquarian and archaeologist Sir Richard Colt Hoare (1758–1838) kept his books in a large barrel-vaulted room at Stourhead (fig.134), again in Wiltshire. Tacked onto the south side of a Palladian villa originally designed by Colen Campbell, and balanced by a Picture Gallery in the opposite north wing, it housed Colt Hoare's encyclopaedic topo-graphical library, dispersed in 1883. The room, with floor-to-ceiling shelving recessed into the walls, may have been designed by Colt Hoare himself. Certainly, unlike many architect-designed interiors, it is an exceptionally elegant solution to the perennial problem of housing a very large number of books in an efficient and accessible way. Among its most remarkable features are the two lunettes under the vault, the one at the north end filled with canvasses after Raphael's *Parnassus* by the local artist Samuel Woodforde (1763–1817), a Colt Hoare protégé, and at the south end a painted-glass version of Raphael's *School of Athens* by Francis Eginton (1737–1805). Both made perfect sense in a Library, and Colt Hoare was probably aware that the Raphael's frescos were in what had once been Julius II's private Library in the Vatican.[89]

In Ireland two houses in County Tyrone contain especially magnificent Regency Libraries. Unlike Stourhead, both were the work of established architects. At Caledon the Library by John Nash (1752–1835) is one of his grandest surviving rooms outside Buckingham Palace, with a top-lit coffered dome, Corinthian columns of porphyry scagliola and huge bookcases, some eight or nine shelves high, set into the walls.[90] These once contained one of the finest private libraries in Ireland, the collection of Thomas Percy, Bishop of Dromore (1729–1811), author of the best-selling *Reliques of Ancient English Poetry* (1765).[91] At Baronscourt in the same county, there are two Libraries by Sir Richard Morrison (1767–1849) and his son William Vitruvius Morrison (1794–1838): the so-called White Library, a fine Soanian interior with a pendentive vaulted ceiling, and the main Library, spectacularly redecorated by the interior designer David Hicks in the 1970s.[92] At another house with Irish connections, Ickworth, in Suffolk, the extraordinary ground plan of a gigantic domed rotunda linked to two rectangular wings by enormously extended curved quadrants was down to the foibles of the eccentric 'Earl-Bishop' Frederick Hervey, 4th Earl of Bristol and Bishop of Derry (1730–1803), and its semi-circular Library is one of the grandest rooms in the house, occupying about a third of the ground floor of the rotunda. If the Library at Stourhead illustrates how to house as many books as possible with the greatest possible elegance, the Library fitted up at Ickworth for the earl-bishop's son the 1st Marquess of Bristol (1769–1859) illustrates how to accommodate the smallest possible number into the largest possible space. Perhaps because of its 30-foot-high ceilings (supposedly insisted on by the earl-bishop because

they helped his asthma), the four huge rosewood bookcases supplied by Banting, France and Co. in 1829 almost recede into the background, and the room is dominated by pictures and furniture, as it was probably always intended to. Fortunately, given the magnificence of the Herveys' books, there was plenty of scope for bookcases elsewhere in the house.[93]

Elsewhere, space was more often at a premium. At Goodwood the 'Small Library' had originally served the ante-room to the adjacent Library, but shelved floor to ceiling, with a cast-iron gallery and spiral staircase to provide access to the higher shelves, it became what was, in effect, a Regency proto-bookstack, elegant, but primarily about storage.[94] There is an equally precarious gallery at Hatfield, inserted in 1875 into a room originally fitted up in 1782.[95] At Nostell, by contrast, if a similar gantry was ever considered in the Billiard Room, it was never installed, and in the 1870s a second tier was added to original Gillow bookcases, taking them right up to the ceiling, and making them inconveniently high.[96] The quest for space is illustrated most graphically at Calke Abbey, where the shelving of the sober Regency Library designed by William Wilkins climbed ever higher, becoming dangerously ramshackle and precarious.

Elsewhere, others preferred Gothic. At Lowther Castle, designed for the 1st Earl of Lonsdale (1757–1844) by Robert Smirke (1780–1867), the Library, like the Saloon and Dining Room, was adorned with Perpendicular plasterwork by the Anglo-Italian Francis Bernasconi (1762–1841), a suitably grandiose home for a collection which survived until the 1950s.[97] At Eaton Hall in Cheshire there was a Gothic Library 140 feet long, with a vaulted octagonal tower room. An 1824 guidebook acclaimed its 'immense massive clustered stone pillars', with 'rich gothic foliated ornaments'.[98] By 1821 the two-storey fan-vaulted Gothick Hall built for the widowed Countess of Oxford at Welbeck (1751) had been fitted up with spectacular ogival bookcases, which survived until the 1860s.[99]

All of these interiors were conceived on a grand scale, but by comparison the still-extant Library at Penrhyn Castle in North Wales was not just gargantuan, but exotically and astonishingly opulent (fig. 135). Built for the slate millionaires the Dawkins-Pennants and designed by the castle's architect Thomas Hopper (1776–1856), like the rest of Penrhyn the Library is an extraordinary essay in the neo-Norman style. The library furniture, again designed by Hopper, is in matching style, with massive carved bookcases modelled on Romanesque shrine cupboards.[100] Hopper designed a similarly implausible Norman interior (see fig. 212) for the Library at Gosford Castle in County Armagh, but was equally happy in other styles and was also responsible for an unusually refined Neoclassical Library at Melford Hall in Suffolk, fitted out with elegant grille-fronted bookcases and divided in two by a pair of Ionic columns.[101]

Many of the Libraries created in nineteenth-century Ireland have, unlike Gosford, entirely disappeared and are now known only from old photographs. Some of the rare exceptions include Glin Castle in County Galway (long devoid of books) and Castle Ward in County Down (still with them), both with plain, early nineteenth-century bookcases with heavy metal grilles, a feature apparently especially popular in Ireland.[102] At Mount Bellew, County Galway, for example, similar grilles were apparently so heavy that the contents of the library, once one of the finest in

Ireland, can have been barely visible at all.[103] By contrast at Borris Castle in County Carlow, the double-height Library, in a faintly Italianate style, is on an upper floor at the head of the main staircase, one of the principal rooms in the house, again with fine wooden bookcases, but this time glazed.[104]

Another possible solution was the neo-Elizabethan Library, particularly popular in houses with a genuine Elizabethan or Jacobean pedigree. At Oxburgh in Norfolk a genuinely ancient house was reworked and re-evoked by J. C. Buckler (1793–1894). Buckler converted the existing Library into a kitchen, and created a large neo-Elizabethan Library in the West Range. Complete with fitted bookcases and Gothic wallpaper, the room survives well, but most of the original books are gone.[105] At Aston Hall the Great Dining Room was fitted up as a Library by James Wyatt in 1824, with bookcases, library steps and other furnishings to match, designed by Richard Bridges.[106] All this is gone, but at Audley End a similar Library for the 3rd Lord Braybrooke survives along with its contents, while at Scotney Castle in Kent Salvin's neo-Elizabethan Library is especially well preserved and again

[135] The Library at Penrhyn Castle

retains its original books and furnishings. The even more spectacular Library at Charlecote (fig. 136) was built for George Hammond Lucy (1789–1845) and his Welsh wife Mary Elizabeth Lucy, and houses books that have been in the house since the sixteenth and seventeenth centuries, as well as some extremely grand purchases from William Pickering. With Kenilworth Castle, the subject of one of Scott's popular works (published in 1821), close by, it was clearly intended to feel like walking into a Walter Scott novel. Alongside the magnificent carved bookcases, the stained glass and heraldic carpet designed by Thomas Willement (1786–1871), and the Tudor portraits, some of the most splendid contents include a set of ebony chairs, sold to the Lucys as having belonged to Robert Dudley at Kenilworth, though in fact late seventeenth-century Goanese work.[107]

V · THE GARDEN LIBRARY

One of the more *recherché* oddities of Library design comes in the form of the garden or summer Library. Typically built for Enlightenment patrons in the second half of the eighteenth century, two of the most striking examples are in Ireland. The so-called Mussenden Temple (fig. 137) at Downhill in County Londonderry was built for the earl-bishop by the Cork architect Michael Shanahan (*c.*1731–1811). A domed rotunda perched on the edge of cliff overlooking the Atlantic, a few hundred yards away from nearby Downhill Palace, like Ickworth it reflects the strange preoccupation with round buildings characteristic of one of the eighteenth-century's more eccentric patrons. The palace itself also contained a Library, destroyed by fire in 1851, but the Temple – based on the Temple of Vesta at Tivoli and on Bramante's Tempietto at S. Pietro in Montorio in Rome – was built as a summer Library and certainly contained books in 1803.[108] A brass inscription round the base of the dome once bore a quotation from the Epicurean philosopher Lucretius (*c.*94–55 BC):

Suave mari magno turbantibus aequora
Ventis e terra alterius magnum spectare laborem

Meaning something like 'it is pleasant to watch from the land the mighty struggle of another in a sea swollen by rushing winds', the earl-bishop is likely to have revelled in the ambiguity of the quotation. Reading the inscription, only a practised classical scholar was liable to realise that Lucretius

went on to explain that the wise man should not revel in the travails of others, but needed to gaze down on the troubles of the world with an appropriate degree of detachment.

Elsewhere in Ireland, less bizarrely situated but equally refined, the Marino Casino, now in suburban Dublin, is a diminutive Neoclassical summer house that was designed by Sir William Chambers for the earl-bishop's enemy the 1st Earl of Charlemont (1728–99). The Casino, too, contained a library, though as at Downhill it was always intended to be a subordinate collection, a place of retreat from the cares of the world. Well to the north of Dublin, at Castle Ward, the eighteenth-century Temple at Castle Ward was pronounced in the 1770s to be 'sweetly calculated for reading and medication', a place to which the studious might withdraw with a well-chosen book from Lord Bangor's well-stocked library.[109] Though there is no evidence that it ever housed books, this fleeting remark poses tantalising questions about

[136] The Library at Charlecote Park

[137] The Mussenden Temple, County Londonderry

the use of other eighteenth-century garden buildings, as well as hinting at the mindset which had.

Elsewhere, at Stevenstone in north Devon, there survives an elegant garden pavilion of about 1710 to 1720. Probably originally a banqueting house but later converted into a Library, the two-storey façade has a giant order of Corinthian pilasters. The long-vanished books were housed on the upper floor, above an open loggia.[110] Another English library belonged to the gentleman-architect Sanderson Miller (1716–80). An early proponent of the Gothic Revival, Miller sighed over Sir Roger Newdigate's Gothic fantasies at Arbury, rhapsodising in the privacy of his diary:

> My House! 'tis true a Small and old one
> Yet now 'tis warm tho' once a cold one.
> My Study holds three hundred volumes
> And yet I sigh for Gothic Collums
> Such as Sr. Roger Learned Knight of Taste
> At Arbury so well has plac'd.[111]

In fact his library, at Radway, was far from negligible. His diaries show that Miller, a native of Warwickshire, read almost daily, keeping his main collection in his country house, The Grange, and a smaller antiquarian and topographical library at nearby Egge Cottage, a thatched *cottage orné*.[112]

VI · FITTINGS AND FURNISHINGS

By the eighteenth century the most obviously essential component of any Library was the bookcase. Only occasionally were these free-standing pieces of furniture, though sometimes grand architectural bookcases which look like fixtures were in fact fittings which could, with difficulty, be moved. In earlier Library interiors shelving was usually part and parcel of the panelled interiors that contained it. Later it was likely to be recessed into the walls, providing space for large numbers of books, but without intruding into the footprint of the room. The mechanics of shelving is a subject which has hardly been examined, though one which anyone working in a Library can hardly fail to engage with. Shelves could be fixed or adjustable, the latter offering obvious advantages for anyone trying to fit books of different sizes into the available space. When shelves were moveable, a range of options was available to support them, including wooden grooves set at regular intervals into the inside of each bookcases, wooden pegs which could be moved from one pre-bored hole to another, or metal fittings.

Made of various sorts of wood, luxe or everyday, and polished, left exposed or painted, country house bookshelves are ubiquitous articles, constantly in view, but rarely thought about in any very conscious way. Easily reworked by estate carpenters, their history is often difficult to unpick. Unsurprisingly taken for granted, such apparently quotidian items have rarely or never been subject to the level of forensic investigation which would be required to untangle their often obviously complex history. At Dunham Massey, for example, close examination of the fitted shelving in the Library reveals that it was been subjected to a bewildering range of modifications since it was first made in the reign of George II.

Bookshelves needed to meet certain practical needs. The most obvious was that each shelf had to be strong enough to take the weight of the books without bowing. In fact, it is striking how many country house shelves have caused inconvenience to generations of owners by being quite simply too weak for the task in hand. Traditionally books tended to be arranged with the large volumes at the bottom of each press and smaller ones higher up. When this is not so, there usually are specific reasons for it. At Erddig, for example, there is a long run of law folios on the upper shelves of the Library (which dates from the 1770s) – a perverse arrangement explained by the fact that, when the Edwardian daughters of the house rearranged the books, they placed those least likely to be used highest up.[113]

High shelves require ladders, and these ranged from humble objects made by estate carpenters – there is an especially alarming example at Florence Court, in County Fermanagh – through to magnificent pieces by master craftsmen.[114] The nature of the ladders begs the question of who would use them: were they primarily for servants or did owners expect to retrieve books for themselves? At Wimpole there is a pulpit-like set of steps (fig. 138) made to designs by Henry Keene (1726–76). This and the similar set at Ham House may have been crafted by Peter Hasert, who made library furniture for Harley in the 1720s. With their solid handrails and built-in lecterns, both seem to have been intended primarily for the owner, though help would have been needed to move them.[115] At Stourhead Thomas Chippendale the Younger (1749–1822) supplied a massive set of steps (fig. 2) for Sir Richard Colt Hoare, part of a suite of splendid and highly original furniture, decorated with Egyptian and Greek motifs.[116] An admiring visitor noted in 1824 that Colt Hoare could 'put his hand on the minutest book at a moment's notice', presumably by climbing up these steps to get

them.[117] Earlier, Chippendale's father had supplied a set of folding library steps at Nostell (fig. 139). These lift out of a stool, an elegant and practical solution in a fairly small room.[118] A similar level of delight in mechanical ingenuity is evident in metamorphic library chairs (there is one at Saltram), as illustrated in Ackermann's *Repository of Arts*, suitable for sitting on, and for folding open and climbing up.[119]

As with architecture, clients looking for library furniture could refer to published guides. The third edition of Chippendale's *Director* (1762) includes designs for library bookcases and library tables (probably an invention of the 1730s), though this is a book found on library shelves less frequently than is sometimes imagined.[120] Many houses still contain especially magnificent library furniture, for example at Nostell, where the Library was fitted out by Chippendale the Elder with a superb suite of furniture commissioned by Sir Rowland Winn. The large library writing table, acclaimed as Chippendale's finest piece of mahogany furniture, was finished by the end of 1766, by then curiously old-fashioned, but the set also includes a more up-to-date drawing table, metamorphic stool and a set of lyre-backed chairs.[121] At Osterley the equally grandiose Adam interior was supplied with marquetry furniture by the London cabinet-maker John Linnell in 1768–9. The desk was described

[138] A corner of the Library at Wimpole, with steps designed by Henry Keene

in the 1782 Osterley inventory as 'a large curious inlaid Library Table covered with green Cloth richly ornamented with Or Molee with Drawers Doors locks and keys'; the tables, too, had serge covers.[122] More homespun solutions were also possible, copying existing models or published designs. The library bookcases at Kedleston (1765), for example, were made locally, modelled on a bookcase in Lady Curzon's Dressing Room in the family pavilion, itself made in London by Linnell and designed by Adam in 1760.[123] Slightly earlier, the designs for a pair of exotic padauk-wood bookcases at Powderham Castle (Devon) seem to have been inspired by published engravings. Made by John Channon (1711–79) in 1740 and no longer in the first-floor Library for which they were intended, they are spectacularly decorated with gilded carving and brass inlay, pieces without parallel in English furniture of the period.[124]

Gothic equivalents were available for those who required them, for example at Felbrigg, where a Gothic library desk was supplied by George Church in 1756, while at Wilton there is pair of fine Perpendicular Gothic library tables, designed by James Wyatt to match his remodelling of the interior.[125] At Penrhyn Thomas Hopper designed Norman furniture to go with Norman bookcases.[126] Odder still, a Gothic breakfront bookcase, now

[139] Metamorphic library stool at Nostell Priory by Thomas Chippendale the Elder, with rectangular padded horsehair seat and panelled sides enclosing a stepladder on panelled square feet

at Nostell, but originally one of four supplied by Chippendale for the Winns' London townhouse, was by 1805 in use as a bird cage.[127]

In complete contrast, Lewis Wyatt's Library was the largest room at Tatton Park in Cheshire, magnificently but conventionally furnished for Wilbraham Egerton (1781–1856), its satinwood bookcases supplied by Gillows of Lancaster in 1811–12 at a cost of £840.[128] At much the same time a large apsidal Library was fitted up at Paxton House in Berwickshire by the Edinburgh cabinet-maker William Trotter (1772–1833). Trotter supplied bookcases *à deux corps*, the upper storey glazed for books, and the lower, with solid wooden doors concealing two decks of shelving, suitable for storing large volumes flat, but also providing a suitably solid base for the superstructure. Similar arrangements can be seen in many houses, including Osterley, Kedleston, Saltram and Attingham. By contrast, many of the designs labelled 'library bookcase' in Chippendale's *Director* are for glazed bookcases more suited to town houses than a great house in the country. Occasionally bookcases could migrate from one to the other, as at Melford Hall in Suffolk, and at Nostell.[129]

If Libraries were primarily about books, they often contained collectables of other sorts. One of the most beautiful features of the Nostell Library is the fitted coin cabinet supplied by Chippendale (see fig. 127), its interior, protected from light damage, still pristine. Its contents appear to have survived into the 1960s, and similar collections have generally fared badly in other houses as well, though occasionally the numismatics books that once accompanied the coins remain, as at Nostell. Harley's coin collection, dispersed after his death, was on a sufficiently grand scale to require a separate sale catalogue.[130] At Tatton, too, the library is rich in books about coins, but unlike Nostell a number of coins and medals remain, and this is also the case at Ickworth.[131]

Scientific instruments survive rather better and were, like coins, often associated with Libraries, as in earlier times. At Ham there are two globes supplied by the London cartographer John Senex (1678–1740), still in their now rare leather covers, replacements for a pair in the Long Gallery in 1679.[132] Often purchased as a pair (terrestrial and celestial), globes were easily broken, and were also liable to be discarded when out of date. At Dunham Massey the Library contains a

telescope, an armillary sphere and a magnificent orrery (fig.140), supplied by the instrument maker Thomas Wright (d.1767).[133] The orrery, in a protective glass case, has an oil lamp and clockwork mechanism, which made it possible not only to demonstrate the workings of the solar system, but to stage eclipses – an experiment memorably depicted by the painter Joseph Wright of Derby (1734–97) in his *Philosopher Lecturing on the Orrery* (c.1766).[134] The Dunham instruments have a particular resonance because the adjacent shelves still contain the original instruction manuals, notably Joseph Harris's *Description and Use of the Globes, and the Orrery*, printed for Wright in 1731 (fig.141).[135] As well as globes, Regency Libraries occasionally have pull-down maps, either of the estate or of the wider world, attached to rollers mounted on bookcases: examples survive at Calke Abbey, and at Sheringham Park in Norfolk. At Burton Constable the scientifically minded William Constable owned experimental electrical 'machines' in the 1750s, as well as optical and chemical equipment and a herbarium, while at Stoneleigh the Lord Leigh – who had paid extra for scientific demonstrations while at Oxford – owned a substantial array of scientific kit, including a 'lectrifying apparatus'.[136] In Ireland the contents of the Library at Hillsborough Castle in 1881 included two reflecting telescopes, a microscope, '2 Electrical Bottles' and a sundial, while at Hanbury Hall in 1790 there was 'an air pump'.[137]

Libraries could also contain more unexpected treasures. At Houghton in 1745 there was 'a Box

with a model of Gibraltar mountain', while at Hughenden in 1847, as well as the orrery and a telescope which had belonged to the late owner John Norris, there was 'an excellent model' of Wyatt's Radcliffe Observatory in Oxford.[138] The Library at Arundel still contains Viking and medieval antiquities, while at Attingham Park in Shropshire the 'Outer Library' served as a museum as well as a place for books. One of the more spectacular objects was 'a large model of Vesuvius' made by 'the late eminent traveller Dr Clarke', the Cambridge don Edward Daniel Clarke (1769–1822), the Berwicks' former Grand Tour bear leader.[139] All these represented a continuation of the Library's traditional function as a repository for curiosities, more explicit still at Dunham Massey, where Grinling Gibbons's virtuoso carving of Tintoretto's *Crucifixion* was first recorded over the library fireplace in 1758.[140] One of the most famous objects at Chatsworth, a lime-wood carving of a cravat often attributed to Gibbons, was similarly once in the Old Library at Chatsworth. In 1811 this room also housed scientific instruments, guns, swords and scabbards, 'Sundry Specimens of Minerals' and '2 Tables of Specimens of Stratas of Derbyshire'.[141] At Lyme Park the Library contains a Greek stele of about 350 BC, brought from Athens by Thomas Legh (1792–1857), an extraordinary and striking monument of the Grand Tour, while at Charlecote in the 1830s the Lucys placed Greek vases on top of the bookcases, a strange choice in a neo-Elizabethan interior. For others, modern copies had to do, as at Osterley, where there were 'Ten

[140] Detail of an orrery supplied by Thomas Wright (Dunham Massey)

[141] Joseph Harris's *Description and Use of the Globes, and the Orrery*, 1731 (Dunham Massey)

Elegant Wedgewood Etruscan Vases' in the Library in 1782.[142]

Busts have long been associated with Libraries, and when these were not classical heroes, they might be British worthies. Hagley Hall is typical, with busts of Spenser, Shakespeare, Dryden and Milton by Peter Scheemakers, a favourite combination. These stand in the broken pediments of the bookcases, and had once belonged to Alexander Pope and then to Frederick, Prince of Wales.[143] By contrast, at Gorhambury in Hertfordshire, a Palladian pile built by Sir Robert Taylor (1714–88) between 1777 and 1784, the bookcases in the very classical Library were adorned with sixteenth-century terracotta busts of their then owners the Bacons and brought, like many of the books, from the nearby Tudor house.[144] More usually, when Libraries housed family portraits, this meant pictures rather than sculpture.[145] At Kingston Lacy on the upper walls of the early nineteenth-century Library, various members of the Bankes family hang alongside four seventeenth-century Italian paintings of the Fathers of the Church, and blowsy Restoration beauties. At Calke Abbey the Library portraits were of horses rather than people, while at Melford it was ships, a memorial to the lucrative naval career of Vice-Admiral Sir Hyde Parker (1739–1807). At Hagley Jonathan Richardson's portrait of Pope and his dog Bounce hangs over the fireplace, but more commonly, as at Felbrigg, Shugborough, Houghton and elsewhere, tall bookshelves left no space for pictures.

VII · THE LIBRARY AS GALLERY: OR, THE ROAD TO BIBLIOMANIA

Few owners saw the Library as the obvious place for serious pictures, even if they had them, though at Narford Sir Andrew Fountaine had added a Library block to his Norfolk house on his return from his second Grand Tour in 1717, containing a gallery-like space housing books, portraits of great men, and objects of *virtù*.[146] From the second half of the eighteenth century there was increasingly a vogue for installing libraries in gallery-like rooms. At Croome Court, for example, Adam submitted an ambitious scheme in 1761 'for finishing the Gallery in the Manner of a Library'. In the event the scheme was rejected and Lord Coventry instead commissioned Adam to remodel an existing Library, installing a 'Sett of Large Mahogany Bookcases', their design adapted from the earlier proposals for the Gallery. The importance of this room to Coventry is underlined by the three-quarter-length portrait of him with his books, by Allan Ramsay (1764), originally placed over the chimneypiece.[147] At Sledmere the great vaulted Library designed by Joseph Rose (1745–99) for the Yorkshire baronet Sir Christopher Sykes (1749–1801) again has more than a whiff of a Gallery to it (fig.142), though the common misconception that rooms like this were intended primarily for indoor walking and for the display of paintings is in this case particularly absurd, as it once housed one of the finest private libraries in Britain.[148]

The Sledmere Library is a room of great magnificence. So, too, was Ralph Willett's vanished Library at Merly. At Chatsworth, where an existing Long Gallery was transformed into a Library by Wyatville for the 6th Duke of Devonshire (1790–1858), the architecture and fittings are if anything even more grandiose. All this hints at something new, and the sheer scale and splendour of these Library interiors is enough to alert us to the fact that we are entering another world.[149] By the 1790s really serious book collecting was once again becoming a key preoccupation for many grandees, in a way which it had been not since the Harleys. Over the next couple of decades the fashion spread far and wide. For some, book collecting became less a preoccupation than an obsession. We have arrived at the era of bibliomania.

[142] Thomas Moulton, *The Library at Sledmere*, in the 1790s

CHAPTER SEVEN

Bibliomania

The Book Craze of the Late Eighteenth and Early Nineteenth Centuries, and its Afterlife

Thomas Frognall Dibdin, *Bibliomania;
or Book-Madness* (London, 1809)

I · THE BOOK DISEASE

The Roxburghe sale

The early nineteenth-century cult of bibliomania was a bizarre episode, but one with long-lasting consequences. It culminated in the famous sale of the library of the 3rd Duke of Roxburghe (1740–1804), conducted by the auctioneer Robert Harding Evans (1777–1857), which took place in the dining room of Roxburghe's house in St James's Square in June 1812 (fig.144).[1] By then the duke had been dead for the best part of a decade. Contemporary gossip believed him to have been a shy and retiring man who had turned to book collecting having been disappointed in love.[2] Antiquarian book prices had climbed to unprecedented levels over the previous twenty years, but spectators nonetheless gaped as assorted aristocratic collectors and their agents pushed the bidding ever higher, and Roxburghe's books sold one after another for astonishing prices.[3] The fifteen Caxtons attracted special attention, and were pursued with particular determination by the 2nd Earl Spencer (1758–1834), well known as the greatest British book collector of the age.[4] The climactic moment was reached with the sale of the so-called 'Valdarfer Boccaccio' (fig.145), Roxburghe's copy of the *editio princeps* of the *Decameron* printed in Venice by Christoph Valdarfer in 1471, a copy then believed to be unique.[5] It was touted by Spencer's librarian the Revd Thomas Frognall Dibdin (1776–1847) (fig.148) with slovenly (but characteristic) illogicality as 'the very scarcest book that existed', and was apparently once coveted by Sunderland and Harley, making expectations high. Those present were not disappointed by the spectacle which followed.[6]

It was well known that the chief competitors were likely to be Spencer, the Marquess of Blandford (1766–1840) and the twenty-two-year-old 6th Duke of Devonshire (1790–1858), who had succeeded to the ducal title less than a year before. Dibdin could not resist describing the competition in terms of a chivalric tournament, and his account is full of talk of champions, battle axes, blows and skirmishes. More disturbingly in the context of the times (the Roxburghe sale occurred just a few days before Napoleon's *Grande Armée* marched into Russia), Dibdin's account is also packed with references to generals, guns and the effusion of blood. After the initial forays of the lesser contenders, the field was left open to the big three, and 'the champions named stood gallantly up to each other resolving not to flinch from a trial of their respective strengths'. Events then took a dramatic turn, as described by Dibdin:

'A thousand guineas' were bid by Earl Spencer – to which the Marquis [Blandford] added 'ten'. You might have heard a pin drop. All eyes were turned – all breathing well nigh stopped … every sword was put home within its scabbard – and not a piece of steel was seen to move or glitter save that which each of these champions brandished in his valorous hand. See, see! – they parry, they lunge, they hit: yet their strength is undiminished, and no thought of yielding is entertained by either … 'Two thousand Pounds are offered by the Marquis' … Then it was the Earl Spencer, as a prudent general, began to think of an useless effusion and expenditure of

[143] Detail of Henry Meyer, *George, 2nd Earl Spencer*, mezzotint published in 1812

ammunition – seeing that his adversary was as resolute and 'fresh' as at the onset. For a quarter of a minute he paused: when my Lord Althorp [Spencer's son] advanced one step forward, as if to supply his father with another spear for the purpose of renewing the contest. His countenance was marked by a fixed determination to gain the prize – if prudence in its most commanding form, and with a frown of unusual intensity of expression, had not bade him desist. The father and son for a few seconds converse apart; and the biddings are resumed. 'Two thousand two hundred and fifty pounds', said Lord Spencer! The spectators are now absolutely electrified. The Marquis quietly add his usual 'ten' ... and there is AN END OF THE CONTEST! *Mr Evans, ere his hammer fell, made a deep pause – and indeed, as if by something præternatural, the ebony instrument itself seemed to be charmed or suspended 'in mid air.' However, at length down dropped the hammer.*[7]

Sceptics scoffed when news of the sale emerged, *The Times* concluding that it was a 'lamentably erroneous way of indicating the love of learning, to give immense prices for rare or old editions.'[8] Even Dibdin, perhaps reflecting the disappointment of his patron Spencer, was prepared to admit that 'the expectations formed of the probable price for which it would be sold, were excessive; yet not so excessive as the price itself turned out to be.'[9]

Even allowing for the tendency of the ignorant to misunderstand the scholarly value of early editions, it is difficult not to sympathise. Examined today in Manchester, the Valdarfer Boccaccio is an unremarkable-looking book in a gaudy gold-tooled binding by Charles Lewis. It seems an unlikely object of fixation, even allowing for the fact that we now know, as Blandford and Spencer did not, that other copies existed (today in Paris, London, and Milan – not all of them complete). Blandford's successful bid of £2,260 was by the standards of the day a gigantic sum of money. Three months after the Roxburghe Sale, Jane Austen sold the copyright of *Pride and Prejudice* for £110, and Mr Darcy had an income of £10,000 a year.[10] The morning after the sale, advertisements in *The Times* included one for a second-hand pianoforte (24 guineas) and another for the lease on a twenty-bedroom coffee house in the City of London (annual rent: £1,900).[11] But ironically Earl Spencer was to have the last laugh. When the finances of

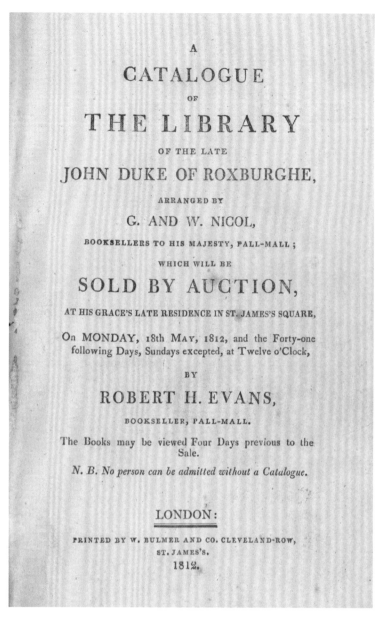

the perennially extravagant Blandford collapsed in
1819, the earl was able to secure the Boccaccio for
£918, less than half what Blandford had paid for it
in 1812.[12] The bubble had burst.

Origins of a malady

Not all bibliomaniacs lived in country houses,
and only a small proportion of early nineteenth-
century country houses contained bibliomaniac
libraries. Several of the leading collectors lived
very different lives. The reclusive Richard Heber
(1773–1833), who was present at the Roxburghe
Sale, was the son of a clergyman. Though a
landed proprietor and an MP, Heber was born
and died in London. His vast library was divided
between at least eight locations, and he spent a
large part of his life on the Continent, probably to
escape rumours of homosexuality.[13] Nonetheless,
as Dibdin put it, the book disease had almost
uniformly confined its attacks to the *male* sex, and
among these to people in the higher and middling
classes of society, while the artificer, labourer,
and peasant have escaped wholly uninjured. It
has raged chiefly in palaces, castles, halls, and gay
mansions; and those things, which in general are
supposed not to be inimical to health, such as
cleanliness, spaciousness, and splendor, are often so

many inducements towards the introduction and
propagation of the BIBLIOMANIA![14]

For the first time since Sunderland and
Harley, serious collecting of rare and ancient
books had become one of the favourite pursuits
of the aristocracy and gentry. Many of Dibdin's
'champions' were drawn from a narrow circle of
interrelated aristocratic collectors. Earl Spencer
was the Duke of Devonshire's maternal uncle,
while Blandford, who would succeed to Blenheim
as 5th Duke of Marlborough in 1817, was Spencer's
distant cousin, resident at White Knights, an
extravagantly appointed country seat on the site
of what is now the main campus of the University
of Reading.[15] Other bibliomaniacs included the
Yorkshire baronet Sir Mark Masterman Sykes
(1771–1823), Sir John Thorold (1734–1815) and
his son Sir John Hayford Thorold (1773–1831) of
Syston Park in Lincolnshire, who commissioned
a grandiose new Library from the architect Lewis
Vulliamy (1822–24).[16] Several decades earlier,
George III had been easily the most bibliophilic
of the Hanoverian kings, collecting useful modern
books, but also books pursued for their age and
rarity.[17] Lower down the social ladder, the influence of Bibliomania spread wider. Few landowners
were prepared to spend a substantial part of their
annual income on incunables. But many country
house libraries of the period contain at least a
whiff of bibliomania, from a fine copy of the
Nuremberg Chronicle (1493) from the dispersed
monastic library of St Emmeram in Regensburg
(Saltram Park) through to the illuminated
manuscripts, Aldines and books printed by the
Venetian Gabriele Giolito de' Ferrari (c.1508–78)
and collected by Sykes's brother-in-law Wilbraham
Egerton (1781–1856) at Tatton Park.[18] In Regency
Britain rare books were primarily the preserve of
rich aristocratic collectors and were in ready supply,
including trophies from the private libraries of
previous generations of British collectors, as well
as books from private and ecclesiastical libraries
in Continental Europe, tipped onto the market as
a result of post-Revolutionary wars, confiscations
and secularisations. The jewelled Romanesque
treasure bindings from Weingarten, purchased
in 1818 by the 1st Earl of Leicester following the
secularisation of the abbey in 1802, were merely
the most spectacular of thousands of books
with a similar history (fig. 146).[19] Public collections lagged far behind. In 1811 Joseph Planta,

Principal Librarian (i.e. Director) of the British Museum, lamented the state of its collection of printed books, which he claimed had improved little since the museum's foundation in 1753, while in 1812 the Bodleian's total expenditure on books was just £261, a tenth of what Blandford had paid for the Valdarfer Boccaccio.[20] The contrast with Napoleonic France, where high culture was inextricably associated with national glory, is instructive. At exactly the same time as the aristocratic collectors of a still-*ancien régime* Britain were spending huge sums indulging their own collecting instincts, books and other cultural artefacts, often looted from public, national and private collections all over Europe, were pouring into the Louvre and the Bibliothèque nationale in Paris.[21] In the United Kingdom – in Great Britain if not necessarily in Ireland – the nationalistic desire to possess and hoard for the nation was, by contrast, readily assimilated into a long-standing aristocratic and oligarchic tradition. The situation was the opposite in France, with its long history of centralised monarchical patronage.

How do we explain this? In the first place the lack of a home-grown revolution, and the easy identification of revolutionary aspirations with the national enemy, made it possible for many to associate national stability and prosperity with the continuation of the traditional social order. The bibliomaniac passion for Caxton and for early English books fitted very readily with this. It is notable, too, that many of the greatest bibliomaniacs – including Earl Spencer and the Duke of Devonshire – belonged to Whig dynasties which had long flaunted their own power and wealth, while ostentatiously proclaiming their commitment to liberty. Then there was the fact that Regency England was rich and, despite the fluctuations of the economic cycle, growing richer. Several of the bibliomaniac collectors were very rich indeed. The Sykes's Sledmere estate was booming as a result of enclosures and agricultural improvements in the rich farmland of the East Riding of Yorkshire.[22] Spencer and Devonshire both owned vast estates, and were by any standards extremely wealthy. William Beckford (1760–1834) owed his immense

[147] Projected design for Fonthill Abbey by James Wyatt and (?) J. M. W. Turner (Yale Center for British Art, New Haven)

fortune to West Indian sugar plantations worked by enslaved Africans.[23] The bibliomaniac library of the 2nd Earl of Powis (1785–1848) at Powis Castle, replete with incunabula, Aldines and manuscripts, was founded on a family fortune which owed much to the 'conquistador' activities of Powis's grandfather Clive of India.[24] At the same time bibliomaniac collectors were not immune to profligacy and stupidity: if anything, sometimes rather the reverse. It was not unusual for vast collections to be built on mountains of debt, without any regard for their true cost, both economic and human. This was certainly the case with Blandford, but was equally true of the much wealthier 6th Duke of Devonshire, whose legacy to Chatsworth was not just the stupendous library and art collection, but also long-term structural debts which even his vast estates could not sustain and which his successors struggled to clear. Inheriting in 1811, between 1812 and 1815 Devonshire had already overspent on his current account to the extent of £270,000.[25] Seen in this light, the new duke's addiction to building

and collecting had more in common with the notorious gambling habit of his mother, Georgiana, than either he or Georgiana's brother Earl Spencer might have wished to acknowledge. Even Beckford overreached himself and, though retaining his library, was forced to abandon his fantasy Gothic palace, Fonthill Abbey, in 1822 (fig. 147). Similarly, many of Masterman Sykes's books were sold soon after his death.[26] Spencer's library, by contrast, survived at Althorp for sixty years, a source of family pride, but also a collection with more than a hint of folly hanging over it.[27]

As with all bubbles, the bibliomaniacs were operating in a context where it seemed that it would never burst. The period between 1788, when Spencer started collecting, and 1812, when prices reached their peak, had seen a huge and apparently inexorable rise in the monetary value of old books. The Duke of Roxburghe's copy of Caxton's 1476 *Recuyell of the Historyes of Troye* was bought for £5 in 1794, but cost Spencer £116 at the 1812 sale. More striking still, when Spencer had purchased the 2,000 books which comprised the library of the Hungarian aristocrat Károly Reviczky (1737–93) in 1790, the entire collection, acquired by a downpayment followed by an annual pension, had cost £2,500. Even allowing for the fact that Reviczky, then imperial ambassador in London, lived only another three years, this was just £240 more than Blandford later paid for the Valdarfer Boccaccio in 1812. Spencer and his competitors evidently believed that the trend would continue indefinitely. For those who cared about the stability of the family finances, buying books was assumed to be a safe bet.[28]

Dibdin and Bibliomania

Bibliomania is inextricably associated with the name of Thomas Frognall Dibdin (fig. 148), born in Calcutta, a graduate of St John's College Oxford, failed lawyer and (from 1804) a clergyman of the Church of England. Dibdin's career as the public bookman par excellence began with his *Introduction to the Knowledge of Rare and Valuable Editions of the Greek and Latin Classics* (1802), which brought him to the attention of the reading public and of Earl Spencer, who became his lifelong friend. His patronage helped launch Dibdin's career as the author of a pair of best-selling 'bibliographical romances': *Bibliomania* (1809) and its sequel *The Bibliographical Decameron* (1817), as well as a never-completed new edition of Joseph Ames's

[148] The Revd. Thomas Frognall Dibdin (1776–1847), the high priest of Bibliomania

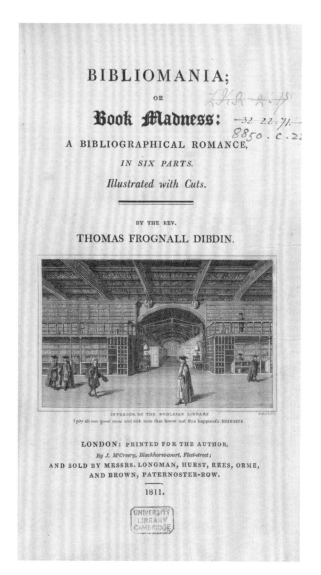

Typographical Antiquities (1810).[29] Dibdin's later works capitalised on his earlier successes, with two large-scale travel books – *A Bibliographical, Antiquarian and Picturesque Tour in France and Germany* (1821) and *A Bibliographical, Antiquarian and Picturesque Tour in the Northern Counties of England, and in Scotland* (1838) – as well as *The Library Companion, or the Young Man's Guide and Old Man's Comfort in the Choice of a Library* (1824) and *Reminiscences of a Literary Life* (1836).[30] Another late work, *Bibliophobia, or Remarks on the Present Depression in the State of Literature and the Book Trade* (1832), discussed with disapprobation the eclipse of the fashionable bibliomania of the earlier part of Dibdin's career.[31] As librarian and bibliographical fixer to Earl Spencer, he was also the custodian of the finest private library in Europe.[32] Zealous in pursuit of his friend's

interest, he also took full advantage of this by publishing two detailed accounts of the Spencer collection, then not fully accessible to the wider public: his *Bibliotheca Spenceriana* (1814–15) and *Aedes Althorpianae* (1822) describe both the finest books and the building in which most of them were kept.[33]

'Bibliomania' was in fact a coinage lifted by Dibdin from a satirical poem by the Scots physician John Ferriar (1761–1815), published in 1809. It also had French antecedents. In his 1802 *Dictionnaire raisonné de Bibliologie* the French librarian Étienne Gabriel Peignot (1767–1849) had explained: 'La *bibliomanie* est le fureur de posséder des livres, non pas tant pour s'instruire que pour les avoir et pour en repaître sa vue [Bibliomania is the overwhelming compulsion to own books, not so much as to inform oneself as to

[149] The title page of the second edition of Dibdin's *Bibliomania*, London 1811

[150] Camille Silvy, *Alexander William Crawford Lindsay, 25th Earl of Crawford*, 1863

possess them and feast one's eyes on them].'[34] The bibliomaniac was interested above all in editions, and bindings, either old or fine. These interests were, in essence, a disease of the mind, a futile, absurd and ultimately self-destructive obsession. The opening lines of Ferriar's poem had spoken of the 'wild desires' and 'restless torments' of 'the hapless man, who feels the book-disease', and most bibliomaniacs were, not unexpectedly, men. There were, however, certain exceptions. The Yorkshire collector Frances Richardson Currer (1785–1861) owned a magnificent library at Eshton Hall. Her books were lodged in a splendid neo-Elizabethan Drawing Room there, and her two privately printed catalogues (1820 and 1833) suggest that she coveted her books quite as much as any male bibliomaniac. So splendid was Miss Currer's library that it was said that Richard Heber intended to marry her for the books.[35]

The original 1809 edition of Dibdin's *Bibliomania* was little more than a pamphlet, a slender octavo of just eighty-seven pages. It was so successful that there followed a massively enlarged 1811 edition (782 pages), which was to all intents and purposes a new book (fig. 149).[36] Based on Izaak Walton's *Compleat Angler*, *Bibliomania* was Dibdin's attempt to make a fashionable but potentially dry subject appealing, attractive and – ultimately – saleable.[37] Cast in the light of a Socratic dialogue between the callow young Lysander and the learned Philemon (Dibdin himself), with a large cast of pseudonymous characters, it attempted to summarise, in admittedly discursive style, everything that the aspiring collector might need to know.[38] Dibdin's rambling prose, gothic exclamations and enormous parenthetical footnotes, have for two hundred years been adored by some and regarded by others to be barely readable. But his books were popular, as the number of copies still on country house shelves shows. They set the agenda and reflected the times.

When it comes to explaining why bibliomania exercised the appeal that it did, it is too easy to stray into pseudo-psychology. While occasionally entertaining, this is also ultimately futile. Whether a passing fad, a psycho-social disorder, an addiction or just another manifestation of aristocratic excess, bibliomania in all its various manifestations was a remarkably widespread phenomenon. The truly obsessive bibliomaniacs were small in number, but aspects of their approach to collecting remain influential two hundred years on. And if reactions

to bibliomania have generally ranged from sceptical to hostile, it is clear that the activities of the bibliomaniacs are too easily dismissed as ignorant trophy collecting carried out by the very rich and very idle. Lord Spencer, for example, clearly knew how to collate an early printed book, while a list of the Aldines in the *Bibliotheca Spenceriana*, written in his own hand, suggests a more than superficial understanding of the collection.[39] A similar impression emerges from Masterman Sykes's catalogues of books at Sledmere.[40] Writing in 1910, the 26th Earl of Crawford (1847–1913) stressed that his father the 25th Earl of Crawford (1812–80; fig. 150), one of the great Victorian scholar-collectors, was not 'satisfied with the mere possession' of books, but that 'what he bought, he read and absorbed, thus blessed with a wonderful memory, acquiring an encyclopædic knowledge, constantly increasing and never forgotten'.[41] Even the profligate Lord Blandford may be too easily dismissed as an extravagant dupe. The composition of his long-dispersed library and Blandford's correspondence with other collectors together suggest a more subtle and nuanced interaction between collector and collected than has traditionally been assumed.[42] Finally there is the simple fact that bibliomania resulted in the survival of books, perhaps ephemeral, implausible or simply grubby and unprepossessing, which are now greatly valued, but which might not have survived at all if the bibliomaniacs had not, for reasons of their own, decided to take a fancy to them.

The anatomy of bibliomania

Dibdin listed eight principal symptoms of bibliomania. Ostensibly a light-hearted skit on the foibles of his contemporaries, like many skits before and since, it also served as an incitement for others and a manual of instruction for those keen to join the party but not quite sure what to do. Many parts of Dibdin's diagnosis are immediately recognisable to any modern collector, highlighting themes and enthusiasms still readily spotted in any bookseller's catalogue: 'There is, first, a passion for *Large Paper Copies*; secondly, for *Uncut Copies*; thirdly, for *Illustrated Copies*; fourthly, for *Unique Copies*; fifthly, for *Copies Printed upon Vellum*; sixthly for *First Editions*; seventhly, for *True Editions*; and eighthly, for *Books* printed in the *Black-Letter*.' Dibdin also drew attention to books for private distribution, to private press books, to the desirability of condemned or suppressed books, to the bibliomaniac desire to collect all editions of a given work, and to amass unusually large and voluminous books.[43] Not all of these are tastes prevalent in contemporary bibliophilia, but many are tropes immediately recognisable today.

Not everyone was impressed by the Dibdinian approach to book collecting. The clerical author – likely, one imagines, to have read *Bibliomania* – of an 1841 guide to Belvoir Castle, the Leicestershire seat of the Dukes of Rutland, greatly admired the many early books and manuscripts in the ducal library there. But he was also at pains to make clear that *he* admired them for their intrinsic value, and not for 'the fictitious value which certain bibliomaniacs attached to tall folios, morocco and crimson velvet bindings, &c'.[44] If his hostility was not entirely focused on traits actually admired by Dibdin, it does at least illustrate that anti-biblio-mania, or at least the appearance of it, remained in some circles as potent a force as bibliomania itself.

Analysis of published catalogues suggests that at least one of Dibdin's highlighted symptoms was entirely correct. In 1828 the Flemish librarian Joseph Basile Bernard Van Praet (1754–1837), a member of staff at the Bibliothèque du Roi (later the Bibliothèque nationale) in Paris, published comparative statistics about the incidence of books on vellum in the principal European libraries. The results are startling, with 108 at Althorp, 30 at Blenheim, 27 at Chatsworth, but proportionately far smaller numbers in much bigger institutional libraries (50 each in the British Museum and the Imperial Library in Vienna, 40 in the Bibliothèque de l'Arsenal in Paris, 34 in the Royal Library in Copenhagen, and 30 in the Vatican). Even the Bibliothèque nationale, with an estimated 1,467 books on vellum, fell far behind the great English collections as a proportion of the total collection.[45]

Another feature of Bibliomaniac libraries, all too evident to modern commentators with different tastes, was the tendency to rebind books, one which few British collectors of the early nineteenth century manage to resist. Dibdin indeed cautioned against rebinding Elzevirs in limp vellum covers, but that was probably more for the sake of the margins as anything else. Large margins were a particular bibliomaniac enthusiasm, and binders were often accused of trimming copies too heavily.[46] Elsewhere his published works are full of enthusi-astic comments about the work of contemporary binders set loose on unassuming early books. This

was entirely typical of the period, with the Irish collector Lord Charlemont writing in 1786 to the Shakespearean scholar Edmond Malone (1741–1812) of some play quartos which he wished to have bound in morocco, 'as I would pay that compliment to every thing which had borne Shakespear's name'.[47] Then there was the bibliomaniac desire for 'clean' copies. In 1868, for example, Francis Bedford was paid £104 2s. 6d. for rebinding at Woburn, the details of his work carefully enumerated in his bill, including payment for washing out 'ink scrawlings' from the 1584 *Thesaurus Linguae Romanae et Britanniae*, an activity calculated to make today's historians of reading wince.[48] As early as the 1790s sodium hypochlorite (household bleach) was coming into common use to make old books fit for the luxury market by making their pages look white, bright and new.[49]

Althorp

The greatest bibliomaniac library of all was the Spencer collection at Althorp. Well tutored in the classics in his youth, and a youthful Grand Tourist, Earl Spencer's intellectual interests were evident from an early age. Despite the association with Dibdin, it was Spencer (fig. 143) himself who conceived the idea of collecting books on a stupen-dous scale. A Whig politician and landowner, he devoted the last three decades of his life to it, and his library of some 40,000 volumes remains essentially intact, though sold to the widow of the Manchester cotton magnate John Rylands in 1892 for £210,000. Based on the ancestral library from Althorp, it was augmented by the purchase of 2,000 books from Count Reviczky in 1790, and by many subsequent additions, including the library of the Italian Count Cassano in 1819.[50]

Spencer seems to have started collecting in about 1788, and his initial enthusiasm was for English black-letter printing.[51] A four-volume classed cata-logue compiled in 1792 suggests that by then Althorp already contained a large library of over 8,000 titles, meticulously arranged in seven main classes, each one subdivided as necessary, with class VII (history) having no fewer than twelve subdivisions.[52] Subsequent additions can be mapped out from a profusion of catalogues and lists, from working documents to a beautifully written and exquisitely bound catalogue of incunabula, which, as the absence of pressmarks and the Grolieresque binding shows, was clearly intended to be a bibliographical monument in its own right, rather than a simple finding aid.[53] Spencer bought incunabula, especially Caxtons, black-letter books, block books and other rarities, pursuing them with voracious enthusiasm.

At Althorp Spencer's books were deployed in five apartments on the ground floor of the house: the Long Library (fig. 151), the Raphael Library, the Billiard Library, the Marlborough Library and the Gothic Library. The Gothic Library was demolished after the sale of the books to Mrs Rylands, but the other former Library interiors survive, though only one remains in use as a Library. Quantities of shelving, ladders and other surplus library kit remained at Althorp until sold in 2010, ghostly reminders of lost glories.[54] In their original form, each Library room was shelved floor to ceiling, and their collective length ran to about 220 feet. Henry Holland's Long Library, still

extant, was the largest, painted white, to complement the colours of the bindings, and lit by five large windows. As recently as the late 1790s it had still housed the whole of the Spencer collection, but the library had expanded so prodigiously since then that the books had overflowed beyond it. The Long Library had once been wholly occupied by 'early printed volumes', but by 1822 it contained 'a selection of volumes, in all classes of literature, which are distinguished for their rarity and condition, and for the beauty of their bindings'.[55] Other books, including some of the finest incunabula, long remained in the Library at Spencer House in London and were transferred to Althorp only in the last years of Earl Spencer's life.[56]

The Raphael Library, a much smaller room, stood at right angles to the Long Library, and was

[151] The Long Library at Althorp, prior to the sale of the books to Manchester in 1892

named after the Raphael Holy Family which hung over the fireplace.[57] In it was shelved the 'mass of History, Poetry, &c' admired by a visitor in 1870.[58] Then there was the Billiard Library, 'so called, from a billiard table being placed in the middle', which housed books on history and poetry, as well as two portraits by Reynolds. In the Gallery above, on 'tier upon tier of shelves', were 'scores if not hundreds of quarto volumes' of Civil War pamphlets. Beyond was the Marlborough Library (converted from a bedchamber in 1816), which contained books on 'Voyages and Travels and History, as well as a portrait of the great Duke [of Marlborough], an ancestor'.[59]

These four rooms together formed what Dibdin called 'the *old* suite of apartments devoted to the Library', but a fifth, the so-called 'Gothic Library' attached to the main block of the house by a corridor hung with pictures, was added in 1820 to accommodate the ever-growing number of books. Well lit with plate-glass windows, it included a gallery, 6 feet wide, which ran round all four sides, 'as neat in appearance as it is admirable in contrivance: no space being lost for the reception of books'. This was reached by means of a spiral staircase, and since it was furnished with chairs and tables it was, said Dibdin, the perfect place for 'the studious to steal away from the animated discussions carried on below'. A further refinement was an Elizabethan-style alcove at the eastern end of the room, fitted with sliding-glass doors which could be closed, providing readers with a warm refuge in extremely cold weather. Unlike the other rooms, the Gothic Library contained only one picture, a copy by Henry Raeburn of an early portrait of the poet Edmund Spenser. According to Dibdin, it had 'a character peculiarly BOOKISH – and such as we might suppose to belong to a well-endowed monastery'. By 1822 it contained 'what may be called the finer copies, and especially those upon *large paper*', a concentration, boasted Dibdin, which exceeded the great libraries of Paris and Vienna. Finally, there was overflow shelving, in the Althorp Picture Gallery, 115 feet long, to accommodate books for which there was no room in the Library below.[60]

The Roxburghe Club

If Spencer, Devonshire and Blandford were the three central figures of the Roxburghe sale, they were by no means the only buyers, and the sale also spawned a rather curious by-product, the Roxburghe Club, an outfit which two centuries

Aedes Althorpianae;

OR

AN ACCOUNT OF THE MANSION,

BOOKS, AND PICTURES,

AT ALTHORP;

THE RESIDENCE OF

GEORGE JOHN EARL SPENCER, K. G.

TO WHICH IS ADDED

A SUPPLEMENT TO THE BIBLIOTHECA SPENCERIANA.

BY THE REV.

THOMAS FROGNALL DIBDIN, F.R.S. S.A.

LIBRARIAN TO HIS LORDSHIP.

LONDON:

PRINTED BY W. NICOL, SUCCESSOR TO W. BULMER AND CO.

Shakspeare Press,

AND SOLD BY PAYNE AND FOSS, LONGMAN, HURST AND CO. J. AND A. ARCH, R. H. EVANS, R. TRIPHOOK, AND JOHN MAJOR.

1822.

later continues to occupy a prominent place in the world of aristocratic bibliophilia.[61] Founded at a dinner held on 16 June 1812, the club has remained a mix of active book collectors, scholars, librarians and aristocratic owners of inherited collections. Its members continue to meet for dinner on 17 June, the anniversary of the sale of the Valdarfer Bocaccio, and it has published over 300 books, typically unpublished documents or reprints of rare published texts. In the early days the emphasis was, in true bibliomaniac taste, on reprints of English black-letter books, but later, facsimiles and scholarly editions of manuscripts became more prominent. The precise composition of the membership has naturally varied over time, and though the number of great hereditary libraries has dwindled, in 2015 members of the Roxburghe Club still included the Earl of Derby, the Marquess of Cholmondeley and the Duke of Buccleuch.

[152] Title page of Dibdin's *Aedes Althorpianae*, London 1822

Reactions to the Roxburghe Club have not always been entirely positive. As long ago as 1855 the bibliophile Robert Curzon (1810–73) complained that 'they have the folly to elect no end of great magnificos'. In consequence, he opined, the club had no real *esprit de corps*. Ostensibly about books, in reality its members, selected primarily for their rank, 'neither know nor care anything about the matter'. What was more, the club's 'stupid dinner' – gastronomy has always been part of the offer – was 'over-priced, at £4–19–6'.[62] Curzon's send-up of the Roxburghe Club hit the nail on the head. Was it really about books and collecting or primarily about rank and social status? Was it a champion of scholarship or a bastion of self-referential snobbery? The honest answer is that at different points of its two-hundred-year history it has been both, but with recent publications including an edition (2010) of the inventory of John, Lord Lumley, and a spectacular facsimile (2000) of the 'Great Book' of the recusant Thomas Trevilian (a manuscript sold from Petworth in 1928; figs. 153 and 154), its contribution to scholarship is not lightly dismissed.

Sources, sufferers and competitors

How and where did the Dibdinian bibliomaniacs find their books? One obvious source was from sales, but another way forward was to cultivate a close relationship with a favoured dealer. Beckford, for example, was a daily visitor to the bookshop of Henry Bohn (1796–1884) whenever he was in London. In the 1830s William Pickering supplied fine books, old and new, to stock a new Elizabethan-style Library built onto the back of Charlecote, while Payne and Foss worked for Lord Vernon at Sudbury in Derbyshire.[63]

At a more rarefied level, the only way to proceed might be to open discreet negotiations with existing owners of especially desirable books. In 1813, for example, Dibdin wrote to Spencer, observing, 'I despair of getting any more Caxtons except by private Contract', though in fact his fears proved in vain, as others subsequently appeared at auction.[64] In the same year Spencer successfully acquired fourteen early printed books from the library of Lincoln Cathedral for £525, having already secured three Caxtons – the 1475 *Game and Playe of Chess*, *The History of Jason* (*c*.1477) and *Raynart the Fox* (1481) from the Dean and Chapter three years earlier.[65]

[153, 154] The Great Book of Thomas Trevilian (1616), originally in the library at Petworth, now in the Getty collection at Wormsley and published in facsimile for the Roxburghe Club in 2000.

Experts like Dibdin were well placed to broker these sort of arrangements, and indeed he worked for others as well as Spencer, for example Sir Mark Masterman Sykes.[66] Despite the 1824 sale of 2,690 books from Sledmere by a successor more interested in hunting than incunabula, a remnant of Sykes's collection survives there, augmented in the middle of the nineteenth century.[67] The nucleus of the Sledmere library had been acquired by Sykes's father, but the bulk of the books, characterised in the 1824 sale catalogue as 'literary treasures at once instructive and curious, delightful, and magnificent', came in between 1801 and 1823.[68] Among other books, Sykes's copy of the Gutenberg Bible, now in the Morgan Library, had once belonged to Mazarin, while a beautiful illuminated copy of the Sweynheym and Pannartz edition of Livy, published in Rome in 1469, subsequently passed into the Grenville collection, now in the British Library. Bought for £903 in 1815, it sold for just £472 10s. in 1824, a price which had dropped to £262 by the next time it changed hands, in 1827 – a striking instance of book deflation in the years after the collapse of the Bibliomania cult.[69]

Another, earlier bibliomaniac, the Dorset squire Ralph Willett kept his library at Merly, a house better known for its interior (see p. 151). Like Roxburghe, and in common with other collectors of the pre-Spencer era, it was undeniably impressive, but only a small proportion of the books consisted of incunables, manuscripts and the like. A remarkably high proportion of the books as described in the catalogue printed for Willett in 1790 were printed in the seventeenth and eighteenth centuries. Dispersed by Leigh & Sotheby in 1813, the Merly library made £13,000, and provided rich pickings for Spencer, whose bids at the sale were placed by Dibdin.[70]

The flamboyantly proto-Romantic tastes of William Beckford were evident as early as 1780. Beckford's books, like the rest of his collection, owed much to his travels on the Continent, which he visited repeatedly in pursuit of novelty and to escape from scandal. Resident in Paris during the Revolution, he took advantage of the situation to buy books from French aristocratic collections. These included illuminated manuscripts, books in fine bindings and books with famous provenances. By 1822 he had some 800 medieval manuscripts at Fonthill Abbey, where the bulk of the library was housed in a space he named St Michael's Gallery, with particularly coveted books stowed in a cabinet in the collector's own sitting room. Beckford's library

escaped sale when he abandoned Fonthill in the same year. After his death it was inherited by his daughter Susan, passing via her to the Dukes of Hamilton, and remaining *in situ* at Hamilton Palace until sold in 1882 (a small remnant of the Beckford Library remains at Brodick Castle, a former subsidiary Hamilton residence on the Isle of Arran). Like other collectors of the day, Beckford liked his books expensively rebound, employing Samuel Kalthoeber from 1787 to 1804 and Charles Lewis from 1826 to 1836. By the time of his death he owned some 9,837 books, a collection then valued by Bohn at £30,000. Bought anonymously using agents, as well as from Bohn himself, Beckford's libraries, at Lansdowne Crescent and in the eccentric tower-retreat he created for himself above Bath, were cared for in the latter years of his life with obsessive fastidiousness: temperature and humidity were monitored and controlled, and direct sunlight and smut from oil lamps rigorously excluded. All these traits were adopted with equal enthusiasm by twentieth-century conservators, though unlike them, Beckford also liked to annotate books, his comments by turns malicious and entertaining.[71]

If recent analysis casts doubt on the traditional view of the Marquess of Blandford as a bibliomaniac dupe, after his succession to the Marlborough dukedom he eked out his later years in dismal retirement in a corner of Blenheim Palace. The money had run out, and by the time of his death Lord Spencer's former rival was worth just £12,000.[72] At Attingham in Shropshire the spendthrift Thomas Noel Hill, 2nd Baron Berwick (1784–1832), as prone to excess as Beckford, spent as lavishly on books as he did on architecture and art collecting.[73] A printed catalogue of his library was issued in 1809, but more books were added subsequently, and a better guide to the collection in its final form is provided by the sale catalogues which appeared after Berwick's eventual and inevitable bankruptcy. These suggest a rather second-hand understanding of what the most sophisticated collectors were attempting, and illustrate rather well how slippery was the slope which led from collecting to simple consumption. Nonetheless the Attingham library contained fine things, including a beautiful fifteenth-century manuscript of Josephus made for Edward IV (fig. 155), typical of the ultra-luxe late Gothic illuminated manuscripts favoured by English collectors of the era, and not unlike manuscripts owned by Beckford, or indeed

[155] Detail of the Soane Josephus manuscript, originally made for Edward IV (Sir John Soane's Museum)

octagonal Library room designed by John Nash. Library and mansion burned in a catastrophic fire in 1807 but, undaunted, Johnes started again.[76]

Another Midland landowner, George Venables-Vernon, 5th Lord Vernon (1803–66), was equally determined in pursuit of his chosen quarry, which was, in particular, Dante. Much of his library, from Sudbury Hall, Derbyshire, was subsequently dispersed (parts of it became the core of the Holford collection at Dorchester House), but, as surviving books as well as his catalogues show, his taste extended well beyond his chosen field.[77] In its heyday the Sudbury library included a gold-tooled Jacobean centrepiece binding now in the Getty collection at Wormsley, a fifteenth-century Breviary which subsequently ended up in Cardiff Public Library, a Gutenberg Bible, and Shakespeare folios – a row of trophies which, while it does not give a full picture of a very large and complex library, does at least reflect the grandeur of Vernon's bibliomaniac aspirations.[78] Nineteenth-century photographs show the interior of the seventeenth-century Long Gallery at Sudbury shelved end to end, though the final remnants of the bookcases were removed when the interior was redecorated by John Fowler for the National Trust.[79] Some 60 miles away, in south Lincolnshire, Vernon's younger contemporary Sir John Thorold (1734–1815) of Syston assembled a vast library rich in early printing, with many books printed on vellum or large paper, and books of famous provenance. All were ultimately housed in a gargantuan Library designed for his successor Sir John Hayford Thorold by Lewis Vulliamy between 1822 and 1824, a room with three linked compartments, a dome and a gallery.[80]

Sometimes, as with the Thorolds, an enthusiasm for books and manuscripts spanned the generations, as was true to an even greater extent with successive Earls of Crawford and Balcarres. This Scottish family, whose main English seat was Haigh Hall, just outside Wigan, had fingers in many cultural pies: the 28th Earl of Crawford (1900–75), for example, was a long-serving and extremely influential Chairman of the National Trust.[81] In the early nineteenth century the family already owned what the 26th Earl (1847–1913) later characterised as 'a good general country gentleman's library of a useful character', partly based on the ancient family library from Balcarres in Fife. The future 25th Earl of Crawford (1812–80, fig. 150) started collecting as a schoolboy in 1826, inherited money in 1834 and,

by Blandford, who owned the Bedford Hours. The Attingham Josephus was bought by Sir John Soane and remains with his library.[74] Others, as enthusiastic as Blandford and Berwick but wiser, recognised that it was sometimes necessary for even the most committed book collector to draw in his horns, with Spencer writing rather apologetically to Dibdin in 1813 that the impending marriage of his daughter to Lord Lyttelton obliged him to exercise some economy in his book buying.[75] But others encountered misfortune more telling than a temporary brake on collecting. The wealthy Shropshire squire Thomas Johnes (1748–1816) inherited the estate at Hafod in Ceredigion in 1780. Operating a private press, translating chivalric chronicles and collecting works of art, he also assembled a great library, including Welsh manuscripts, housed in an 'much under the influence of Bibliomania', set about acquiring a great library in a thoroughgoing and systematic way. Starting with standard works, by the 1860s he had moved onto the pursuit of rarities, though wary of buying for rarity's sake alone and approaching the subject with a certain caution and moderation. By then 'books came pouring in, on all subjects from all parts of the world: far quicker indeed than it was possible to shelve them: room after room had its walls covered and old portraits in the passages were hung in bedrooms and replaced by books'. Nonetheless Crawford only bought in subject areas that interested him: there were few books on mathematics, astronomy and chemistry in his library, for example. It was left to his son to fill some of these gaps, as well as to set about collecting rare books with a new gusto, a pursuit more expensive and difficult in the 1880s and 1890s than it had been earlier, despite the good offices of Quaritch.[82] In addition to the library at Haigh, from 1846 the Crawfords also had a house at Dunecht in Aberdeenshire, where G. E. Street built an extension with a Library and chapel, completed in 1881.[83]

The Crawfords were not unusual in being expansionist bibliomaniacs who were able to build great collections around already existing dynastic libraries. At Charlecote an ancient library assembled at least as far back as the early seventeenth century was enriched by expensive purchases from the London publisher and bookseller William Pickering (1796–1854), essentially books which George Hammond Lucy (1789–1845) and his heiress wife Mary Elizabeth Lucy (1803–89) thought should have been owned by the family's Tudor ancestors. In practice this meant buying books listed in the 1681 Charlecote catalogue but subsequently alienated, as well as other books – notably a Shakespeare Second Folio (1632), a second quarto of *The Merry Wives of Windsor* (1619; fig. 156) and an important Machiavelli manuscript – which a Warwickshire landowner felt sure his ancestors should have owned, even though, in fact, they had not.[84] There was also a good deal of rebinding, often done by the ubiquitous Charles Lewis, though other books escaped and remain much as they must have been 400 years ago.[85] At Longleat, similarly, the 2nd Marquess of Bath (1765–1837) bought large numbers of books between 1800 and 1815, as well as spending over £200 on rebinding ancestral books.[86] A more overt bibliomaniac, the 2nd Earl of Powis, was also able

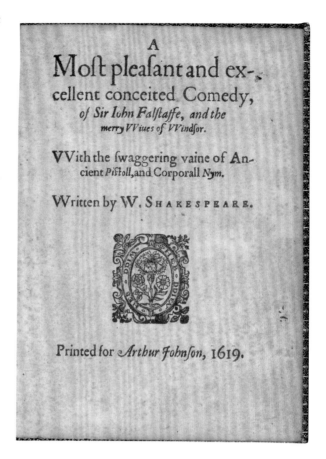

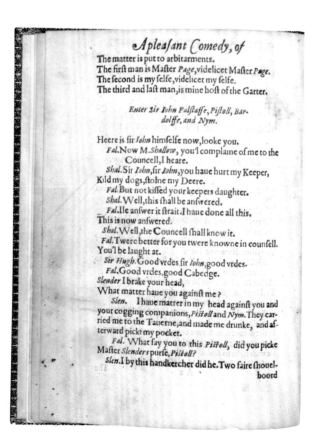

[156] Two pages from William Shakespeare, *A Most Pleasant and Excellent Conceited Comedy, of Sir Iohn Falstaffe, and The Merry Wives of Windsor*, London 16[..] (Charlecote Park)

to build on an inherited ancestral collection at Powis Castle, including books which had belonged to Edward, Lord Herbert of Cherbury, in the seventeenth century. Ironically the early segments of the collection, though by no means complete, now survive much better than the nineteenth-century bibliomaniac additions, a large proportion of which were progressively dispersed in a long series of twentieth-century sales.

The 4th Earl of Ashburnham (1797–1878) provides a more extreme case, and on an altogether vaster scale. Inheriting a fairly ordinary ancestral library at Ashburnham Place, near Brighton, from his mid-forties, he set about adding to it in spectacular style, funding further purchases from the sale of pictures in 1850.[87] The despotic and overbearing owner of an ancient estate, Ashburnham was irrationally jealous of his books and manuscripts, notoriously dismissing the Historical Manuscripts Commission (established in 1869) as 'a society of ruffians who tamper with title-deeds'.[88] Embarrassingly he was also the purchaser in 1847 of some 1,923 manuscripts stolen from the Bibliothèque nationale and other French libraries, books which he obdurately refused to return.[89] The whole sordid affair, tinged with Francophobia and an aristocratic contempt for the government of Napoleon III, was resolved only after his death. More salubrious Ashburnham purchases included the Stowe and the Barrois collections, both acquired in 1849, when the earl's manuscript buying (he eventually amassed some 3,600, at a cost of about £22,000) was at its height. Even then the acquisition of the Duke of Buckingham's manuscripts from Stowe, many originally the property of Thomas Astle, Keeper of the Records at the Tower, was tainted by Ashburnham's rather indecent determination to ensure that he got them rather than the British Museum (which ultimately secured them in 1883, with the exception of the famous Irish manuscripts from Stowe, which went to the Royal Irish Academy in Dublin).[90]

Chatsworth

At Chatsworth (fig. 157), too, the family's greatest book collector, the bibliomaniac 6th Duke of Devonshire, was able to build on an existing inheritance. The maternal nephew of Lord Spencer and descendant of a line of earlier book-collecting dukes, Devonshire had both books and profligacy in the blood. Having played a leading role in the

Roxburghe sale in 1812, he went on to become one of the dominant book collectors of the age, and was the dedicatee of Dibdin's *Bibliographical Decameron* in 1827.

As well as acquiring the library of the architect Earl of Burlington at Chiswick and various lesser collections on succeeding to the dukedom in 1811, Devonshire became the owner of three major libraries. One of these had once belonged to his recently deceased kinsman, the scientist Henry Cavendish (1731–1810), whose books had been kept in London.[91] The other two were the existing libraries at Chatsworth and at Devonshire House, of which the London library seems to have been considerably more grandiose. The 1813 Chatsworth catalogue, originally in three volumes but by then only a partial survivor covering titles from T to Z, suggests a library which on the death of the 5th Duke consisted substantially of fairly ordinary seventeenth- and eighteenth-century books. By contrast, the companion volume for Devonshire House reveals that many of the earlier books, including incunabula, Aldines, the first four Shakespeare folios and nineteen Caxtons were then there.[92] The basis for bibliomania was already very much in evidence, and to these the young duke swiftly added the library of the bibliomaniac Thomas Dampier (1748–1812), Bishop of Ely, bought from Dampier's widow for just £10,000 and swiftly transferred to Chatsworth.[93]

As the 6th Duke explained in his privately printed *Handbook to Chatsworth and Hardwick*, he decided early in his career to bring together books from these four libraries at Chatsworth.[94] There they were principally deployed in the ground-floor Lower Library (traditionally the duke's private den) and in a new Library carved out of the existing Baroque Great Gallery by the Prince Regent's architect Sir Jeffry Wyatville (1766–1840), and apparently complete by March 1818. The room's extraordinarily lavish furnishings included a set of Siberian jasper vases, a gift from the Tsar of Russia.[95] Despite its magnificence, from the beginning it was not big enough, and a gallery, accessed via a hidden stair, was introduced in 1835, while in the meantime acquisitions of books continued apace.[96] These included the Kemble play collection, purchased from the actor John Philip Kemble (1757–1823) for £2,000 in 1821. Initially kept at Chatsworth, the 6th Duke subsequently transferred his collection of early English plays to London 'for

the sake of reference by living authors'.[97] It remained in the Devonshire collection until sold, along with the Shakespeare folios and Caxtons to Henry E. Huntington.[98]

Nonetheless, and despite twentieth-century sales, the Chatsworth library remains substantially intact and, unlike the Spencer collection, still in the house and in the rooms designed to house it. Undeniably impressive, it also provokes more ambiguous responses. Not to put too fine a point on it, many bibliomaniac books now seem rather boring, and despite the splendour of the setting, this is often true at Chatsworth. Almost all of the surviving Devonshire incunables, washed and rebound for the 6th Duke, as well as thousands of other books are, to current tastes, profoundly unappealing copies. The same is true of many of the Spencer books in Manchester, and of thousands of books once in the now dispersed bibliomaniac libraries in houses like Syston, Sudbury and Powis Castle.

There was a reason – or at least a cultural context – for all of this. Bibliomaniac libraries were intended to be deployed in rooms like the Long Library at Althorp or the Library at Chatsworth. In these sorts of spaces the patinated but battered copies now admired by librarians and collectors would have seemed impossibly uncouth to a wealthy Regency grandee. Shabby volumes of play quartos or ancient bindings from monastic libraries simply did not fit in such a setting. Admittedly some collectors, including Earl Spencer, did occasionally take a sympathetic interest in the history of the books which passed through their hands, and sometimes went out of their way to preserve early bindings when these were judged to be attractive and interesting. Nonetheless for most collectors, Spencer included, rebinding was more usual than repair, and the bright and shiny bindings of master craftsmen like Charles Lewis were de rigueur.[99] The fortunate visitor to Chatsworth, or to the strong rooms of the

[157] The Library at Chatsworth

John Rylands Library, cannot fail to be impressed. At the same time it is undeniably a relief and a rare surprise, just occasionally, to find a seventeenth-century book in limp vellum wrappers among all the crushed morocco.

II · THE AFTERLIFE OF BIBLIOMANIA

Bibliomania enjoyed a long afterlife, and its collecting habits continued to influence the evolution of libraries in country houses into the later nineteenth and twentieth centuries. At Drum Castle in Aberdeenshire, the library assembled by successive members of the Irvine family includes fine, clean copies of Renaissance and later books, in obvious Dibdinian taste – a library quite unlike those in neighbouring Scottish houses like Castle Fraser and Brodie Castle.[100] Further south, at Madresfield Court in Worcestershire, the collection was substantially the creation of the High Churchman Frederick Lygon, 6th Earl Beauchamp (1830–91) elected to the Roxburghe Club in 1867, with books of ecclesiastical interest, illuminated manuscripts and above all the fourteenth-century *Liber Regalis*, a text on coronations once in the library at Westminster Abbey (he presented a facsimile to the Roxburghe Club in 1870). It is now MS. 38 at Westminster Abbey, while the equally splendid Madresfield Hours, a fourteenth-century English manuscript still in its original chemise binding, was sold to Sir Paul Getty of Wormsley in 1994. Other medieval books remain in the house.[101] The Liberal Prime Minister the 5th Earl of Rosebery (1847–1929) was another Roxburghite and president of the club from 1908 until his death. He presented 7,000 books from his collections to the National Library of Scotland in 1928, and others were bestowed elsewhere: a fifteenth-century Flemish manuscript of the Golden Legend of Jacobus de Voragine, for example, was given to Glasgow University Library in the same year.[102] Rosebery's books were divided between his many houses, in England at Mentmore in Buckinghamshire and in London, and in Surrey at The Durdans, at Dalmeny House on the shores of the Forth and at nearby Barnbougle Castle, which he rebuilt essentially as a Library, though with some limited living accommodation. His libraries included a collection of about 300 books relating to Mary, Queen of Scots, as well as pamphlets and broadsides on Scottish history. Contrary to the popular view of the aristocratic book collector,

Rosebery was as enthusiastic a reader as he was a bibliophile.[103]

Like Rosebery's, the libraries of the 3rd Marquess of Bute (1847–1900) were scattered across a large number of town and country houses in England, Wales and Scotland, the vast patrimony of an ancient family grown stupendously wealthy on the proceeds of industry. These collections have now to a large extent become concentrated at the Butes' ancestral home, Mount Stuart, on the Isle of Bute, where already in 1896 the library was large enough for a catalogue of six stout volumes.[104] Bute's collecting also illustrates how a combination of wealth and space could allow bibliomania to branch out beyond incunabula and manuscripts. As well as the main libraries at Mount Stewart and in Cardiff Castle, there were Civil War tracts and Scottish books and manuscripts in his Edinburgh house in Charlotte Square, and early learned books, including a remnant of the library of the 2nd Marquess of Bute from Luton Hoo, at Garrison, an eighteenth-century house on the Isle of Cumbrae, as well as a large collection of books in Gaelic, Irish and Manx once owned by the Celtic scholar Donald Maclean.[105]

Bibliomaniac libraries of any kind did not flourish to the same extent in Ireland, a country beset with instability, poverty and – catastrophically – famine. The library of the short-lived Denys Daly (1747–91), an Irish Protestant and politician, and owner of Dunsandle, County Galway, was perhaps the most grandiose private library ever assembled in the west of Ireland. When it was sold in Dublin in 1792, the authors of the sale catalogue appealed, probably largely in vain, to Irish patriots, that Daly's books should not leave Ireland, asserting that 'it would have been … disgraceful to the literary character of their Countrymen, if such a Library as this were carried out of the Kingdom'. A visibly bibliomaniac collection, it included the copy of Caxton's 1483 edition of Gower's *Confessio Amantis* which ended up in the Roxburghe collection, the future Grenville copy of the Shakespeare First Folio, illuminated manuscripts, classical *editiones principes*, and a host of fine books, though only one manuscript in Irish. Daly reckoned he had spent some £2,300 on his books (when sold they fetched £3,876 14s. 4½d.).[106]

Libraries could express an owner's enthusiasms or plain eccentricities in a range of other ways. At Welbeck, in Nottinghamshire, an estate which had once belonged to John Cavendish-Scott Bentinck, the 5th Duke of Portland (1800–79), nicknamed the 'Burrowing Duke', has become notorious for the enormous network of tunnels which he created under the house. The complex included a vast Library, partly underground, the work of the local architect Charles Neale.[107] At Elton Hall, near Peterborough, a great if late bibliomaniac library of about 12,000 books was assembled by the bibliophile 5th Earl of Carysfort (1836–1909) and housed in a suite of rooms designed in the 1860s by Henry Ashton, a pupil of Sir Robert Smirke. In true bibliomaniac style, many of the earlier books were rebound, a fact very evident to the visitor walking along the shelves, though nineteen books 'of the highest importance', including a Gutenberg Bible, were sold in 1923.[108] At Parham in Sussex, Robert Curzon collected armour and Gothic objets d'art as well as books.[109] A visitor in 1871 admired the 'Durer prints, first editions of Shakespeare & the Bible: gems and thumb-screws: Hebrew scrolls … locks of King Charles' hair and armour of every country'.[110]

Ultimately, however, the influence of Bibliomania went beyond the private domain and infected public collecting. At Wigan Public Library, for example, the Borough Librarian Henry Tennyson Folkard (1850–1916) was clearly influenced by Lord Crawford. Folkard assembled what was almost a bibliomaniac library funded by the rate-payers, a collection of early books for the use of the citizens of what was then a thriving industrial town, and progressively dispersed since 1978.[111] The Wigan sales illustrate the general withdrawal of British public libraries from the business of collecting rare books in the later twentieth century. This was the opposite of the situation a century before, when expanding municipal libraries, as well as the libraries of newly founded learned societies and red-brick universities, had all vied with one another to collect the treasures of the past. In parallel the great national libraries of late Victorian England aimed at universality with increased conviction, both at the British Museum and in the longer-established university libraries of Oxford and Cambridge, where reforming librarians like E. W. B. Nicholson (1849–1912) and Henry Bradshaw (1831–86) had altogether greater ambitions than their predecessors. A generation later saw the creation of new national libraries for Scotland and Wales, the former created out of the

ancient Advocates' Library; in Ireland the process had started earlier, and the implicitly green-hued National Library existed alongside the great library of the historically Protestant Trinity College.

All of these institutional libraries to varying extents drew inspiration, as well as some of their most prized books and manuscripts, from the private libraries of Regency bibliomaniacs. This is illustrated most graphically by the sale of the Spencer Collection to Mrs Rylands. Originally conceived as an endowed private foundation (it was absorbed by the University of Manchester only in 1972), the Rylands Library (fig.158) was the closest British equivalent of American libraries like the Huntington Library (1919) in San Marino, California, and New York's Morgan Library (1924). In the United States of America, as in Britain, there was often a fine line between private collecting for ultimate public benefit, and private collecting which subsequently found its way into public hands. In both cases, and on both sides of the Atlantic, the influence of bibliomania was long lasting and profound in its consequences. The eighty-two copies of the Shakespeare First Folio bought by the oil magnate Henry Clay Folger (1857–1930) and now in the Folger Shakespeare Library (1932) easily attract ridicule, but they have had profound consequences for Shakespearean scholarship. Something in the region of seventy of all the extant copies of the First Folio were once in British country houses, many in bibliomaniac-type collections, and given the complexity of the subject and the tendency for copies to move around, the actual figure may well be higher.[112] The same is true of other trophies, from the treasure bindings of Weingarten, bought from Holkham by J. P. Morgan, to the Gutenberg Bible at Cambridge, used as printer's copy for an edition published in Strasbourg in 1469 and long in the library at Hopetoun House near Edinburgh.[113] How and why were these transfers possible? The answer lies in a series of profound economic and political changes which were already underway by the time the Spencer books were bought by Mrs Rylands in 1892. The crucial and interlinked point is that the libraries of the Regency bibliomaniacs were not just a source of inspiration for newer collections, both public and private, they were also the source of many of the books.

[158] The historic reading room at the John Rylands Library, Manchester

CHAPTER EIGHT

The Country House Librarian

Bibliomania required, or at least implied, a librarian, except in those circumstances where collectors felt that they themselves had the time, interest and expertise to take on the role for themselves. Some owners were confident that they did, but others were more doubtful. At Chatsworth, for example, the 6th Duke of Devonshire, though a graduate of Trinity College, Cambridge, was self-conscious of his lack of learning, writing to his librarian the Shakespearean scholar and notorious forger John Payne Collier (1789–1883): 'I am not worthy of my own collection, I am sorry to say; and I want you, as far as you can, to make me worthy of it by informing my ignorance.'[1] Nonetheless his papers include detailed notes outlining what would now be called a job description for a librarian, while Payne Collier was paid a handsome £200 a year.[2] The well-bred bachelor duke enjoyed at best an uneasy relationship with his self-made librarian, whom he thought 'simple and vulgar'. But at Stowe the 1st Duke of Buckingham (1776–1839) had a closer and more affectionate friendship with the learned Dr Charles O'Conor (1764–1828), a Catholic priest, but also a member of an ancient and aristocratic Irish family, whose grandfather the antiquarian Charles O'Conor (1710–91) had once owned many of the famed Irish manuscripts. Going down to Soane's Gothic Library in 1827 to take his leave of O'Conor for the last time, Buckingham was deeply moved to find that his 'old friend', a man with a history of mental illness and by then apparently senile, was struggling to pack for his final journey back to Ireland, and was upset when

the librarian displayed no signs of emotion as his employer kissed his forehead.[3] Similarly close relations existed between Humfrey Wanley and his employers. Wanley was assiduous in deploying his bibliographical and palaeographical skills on Lord Oxford's behalf, recording his day-to-day activities in a diary which he kept from 1715 to 1726, a document which provides some of the most vivid descriptions we have of an acquisitive eighteenth-century librarian at work. He was also delighted when he received in return signs of the family's affection and approbation, as in 1722, when Lady Oxford presented him with 'a fine & large Silver Tea-Kettle, Lamp & Plate, & a neat Wooden Stand', to add to the silver tea-pot she had already given him. 'I shall never cease from praying Almighty God to Bless Her & all this Noble Family with all Blessings Temporal & Eternal', he noted in his diary.[4]

Sometimes librarians might be less compliant figures. At Bowood, Wiltshire, the radically minded Swiss pastor Pierre-Étienne-Louis Dumont (1759–1829) in 1786 succeeded the chemist and political radical Joseph Priestley (1733–1804) as librarian to the 1st Marquess of Lansdowne (1737–1805), Prime Minister from 1782 to 1783, when he was ousted from office after securing peace with America. There, as part of the radical 'Bowood Circle', Dumont first came into contact with Jeremy Bentham, whose work he edited and promoted in both Britain and France.[5] By 1854, when the antiquary John Britton (1771–1857) made extensive use of the Bowood library, the librarian was a

[159] Printed broadsheet by Bernard Lintot (1675–1736), designed to be cut down to produce spine labels (Record Office for Leicester, Leicestershire and Rutland)

An Alphabetical list of Numbers for the better regulating Gentlemens Libraries Contriv'd in such a manner that any Servant who knows his Letters may keep the Books in Order

A 1 2 3 4 5 6 7 8 9 10 11 12 13 14 15 16 17 18 19 20 21 22 23 24 25 26 27 28 29 30 31 32 33 34 35 36 37 38 39 40 41 42 43 44 45 46 47 48 49 50

B 1 2 3 4 5 6 7 8 9 10 11 12 13 14 15 16 17 18 19 20 21 22 23 24 25 26 27 28 29 30 31 32 33 34 35 36 37 38 39 40 41 42 43 44 45 46 47 48 49 50

C 1 2 3 4 5 6 7 8 9 10 11 12 13 14 15 16 17 18 19 20 21 22 23 24 25 26 27 28 29 30 31 32 33 34 35 36 37 38 39 40 41 42 43 44 45 46 47 48 49 50

D 1 2 3 4 5 6 7 8 9 10 11 12 13 14 15 16 17 18 19 20 21 22 23 24 25 26 27 28 29 30 31 32 33 34 35 36 37 38 39 40 41 42 43 44 45 46 47 48 49 50

E 1 2 3 4 5 6 7 8 9 10 11 12 13 14 15 16 17 18 19 20 21 22 23 24 25 26 27 28 29 30 31 32 33 34 35 36 37 38 39 40 41 42 43 44 45 46 47 48 49 50

F 1 2 3 4 5 6 7 8 9 10 11 12 13 14 15 16 17 18 19 20 21 22 23 24 25 26 27 28 29 30 31 32 33 34 35 36 37 38 39 40 41 42 43 44 45 46 47 48 49 50

G 1 2 3 4 5 6 7 8 9 10 11 12 13 14 15 16 17 18 19 20 21 22 23 24 25 26 27 28 29 30 31 32 33 34 35 36 37 38 39 40 41 42 43 44 45 46 47 48 49 50

H 1 2 3 4 5 6 7 8 9 10 11 12 13 14 15 16 17 18 19 20 21 22 23 24 25 26 27 28 29 30 31 32 33 34 35 36 37 38 39 40 41 42 43 44 45 46 47 48 49 50

I 1 2 3 4 5 6 7 8 9 10 11 12 13 14 15 16 17 18 19 20 21 22 23 24 25 26 27 28 29 30 31 32 33 34 35 36 37 38 39 40 41 42 43 44 45 46 47 48 49 50

K 1 2 3 4 5 6 7 8 9 10 11 12 13 14 15 16 17 18 19 20 21 22 23 24 25 26 27 28 29 30 31 32 33 34 35 36 37 38 39 40 41 42 43 44 45 46 47 48 49 50

L 1 2 3 4 5 6 7 8 9 10 11 12 13 14 15 16 17 18 19 20 21 22 23 24 25 26 27 28 29 30 31 32 33 34 35 36 37 38 39 40 41 42 43 44 45 46 47 48 49 50

M 1 2 3 4 5 6 7 8 9 10 11 12 13 14 15 16 17 18 19 20 21 22 23 24 25 26 27 28 29 30 31 32 33 34 35 36 37 38 39 40 41 42 43 44 45 46 47 48 49 50

N 1 2 3 4 5 6 7 8 9 10 11 12 13 14 15 16 17 18 19 20 21 22 23 24 25 26 27 28 29 30 31 32 33 34 35 36 37 38 39 40 41 42 43 44 45 46 47 48 49 50

O 1 2 3 4 5 6 7 8 9 10 11 12 13 14 15 16 17 18 19 20 21 22 23 24 25 26 27 28 29 30 31 32 33 34 35 36 37 38 39 40 41 42 43 44 45 46 47 48 49 50

P 1 2 3 4 5 6 7 8 9 10 11 12 13 14 15 16 17 18 19 20 21 22 23 24 25 26 27 28 29 30 31 32 33 34 35 36 37 38 39 40 41 42 43 44 45 46 47 48 49 50

Q 1 2 3 4 5 6 7 8 9 10 11 12 13 14 15 16 17 18 19 20 21 22 23 24 25 26 27 28 29 30 31 32 33 34 35 36 37 38 39 40 41 42 43 44 45 46 47 48 49 50

R 1 2 3 4 5 6 7 8 9 10 11 12 13 14 15 16 17 18 19 20 21 22 23 24 25 26 27 28 29 30 31 32 33 34 35 36 37 38 39 40 41 42 43 44 45 46 47 48 49 50

S 1 2 3 4 5 6 7 8 9 10 11 12 13 14 15 16 17 18 19 20 21 22 23 24 25 26 27 28 29 30 31 32 33 34 35 36 37 38 39 40 41 42 43 44 45 46 47 48 49 50

T 1 2 3 4 5 6 7 8 9 10 11 12 13 14 15 16 17 18 19 20 21 22 23 24 25 26 27 28 29 30 31 32 33 34 35 36 37 38 39 40 41 42 43 44 45 46 47 48 49 50

U 1 2 3 4 5 6 7 8 9 10 11 12 13 14 15 16 17 18 19 20 21 22 23 24 25 26 27 28 29 30 31 32 33 34 35 36 37 38 39 40 41 42 43 44 45 46 47 48 49 50

W 1 2 3 4 5 6 7 8 9 10 11 12 13 14 15 16 17 18 19 20 21 22 23 24 25 26 27 28 29 30 31 32 33 34 35 36 37 38 39 40 41 42 43 44 45 46 47 48 49 50

X 1 2 3 4 5 6 7 8 9 10 11 12 13 14 15 16 17 18 19 20 21 22 23 24 25 26 27 28 29 30 31 32 33 34 35 36 37 38 39 40 41 42 43 44 45 46 47 48 49 50

Y 1 2 3 4 5 6 7 8 9 10 11 12 13 14 15 16 17 18 19 20 21 22 23 24 25 26 27 28 29 30 31 32 33 34 35 36 37 38 39 40 41 42 43 44 45 46 47 48 49 50

Z 1 2 3 4 5 6 7 8 9 10 11 12 13 14 15 16 17 18 19 20 21 22 23 24 25 26 27 28 29 30 31 32 33 34 35 36 37 38 39 40 41 42 43 44 45 46 47 48 49 50

& 1 2 3 4 5 6 7 8 9 10 11 12 13 14 15 16 17 18 19 20 21 22 23 24 25 26 27 28 29 30 31 32 33 34 35 36 37 38 39 40 41 42 43 44 45 46 47 48 49 50

Vol. I	Vol. V	Vol. IX	Vol. XIII	Vol. XVII
Vol. II	Vol. VI	Vol. X	Vol. XIV	Vol. XVIII
Vol. III	Vol. VII	Vol. XI	Vol. XV	Vol. XIX
Vol. IV	Vol. VIII	Vol. XII	Vol. XVI	Vol. XX

The Large Capitals denote the Shelf, the small Capital and number to be cut off, pasted on the backs of the Books on the Shelf A B C &c.

Printed for Bernard Lintot

'Mr Matthews'.[6] At the opposite end of England, at Holkham, the Liverpool historian, banker and collector William Roscoe (1753–1831) in 1814 offered to prepare a catalogue of the great collection of medieval manuscripts. It was subsequently revised and rewritten by Frederic Madden (1801–73), the future Keeper of Manuscripts at the British Museum, but as costs rose, the catalogue was never published, though twenty-five proof copies of the intended illustrations were issued (fig. 160).[7] Roscoe, a pioneering enthusiast for early Italian painting, was an appropriate choice for the Holkham library, which was rich in Italian manuscripts, but foreign librarians like Dumont also appealed. Better known for his association with Dibdin, Lord Spencer had earlier retained the Italian Tommaso de Ocheda (1757–1831), a graduate of Bologna and Pavia who had previously worked in Amsterdam and was employed by Spencer for twenty-eight years until his retirement in 1818. Interestingly, while Dibdin haggled with dealers and auctioneers or negotiated purchases with other collectors, de Ocheda's duties included compiling a long series of catalogues (cribbed by Dibdin without due acknowledgement), preventing the ordering of duplicates – a key task in any great library – as well as sorting good from inferior copies, and making sure that reading copies of useful books were available as required in any of Spencer's four houses.[8]

Later in the nineteenth century at Chatsworth, the 7th Duke of Devonshire employed Sir James (Giacomo) Lacaita (1813–95), like Sir Antony Panizzi an anglicised Italian émigré, to catalogue his uncle's great library, a task he performed rather badly, visiting during the summer months when the family were away – though the four large volumes describing its contents, published in 1879, remain the best guide to the Chatsworth collection.[9] In the generation following, Lord Bute retained a series of learned librarians: in 1896 this was R. F. R. Conder, but by 1909 Dr Walter de Gray Birch (1842–1924), a Cambridge graduate, a Fellow of the Society of Antiquaries and recently retired after thirty-eight years in the Department of Manuscripts at the British Museum, had taken over.[10] At Wallington in the 1850s, Walter Calverley Trevelyan (1797–1879) and his learned wife Pauline, well read but certainly not bibliophiles or bibliomaniacs, retained David Wooster (1824?–88), the former curator of the Ipswich Museum, as librarian. He had first come to Northumberland to sort the

Trevelyans' private museum. Gauche and awkward, not a servant but not quite the social equal of the Trevelyans and their sophisticated pre-Raphaelite entourage, Wooster haunted the Library, answered bibliographical queries, caused embarrassment at the breakfast table and compiled a large-scale slip catalogue of the books, similar to the one he had already produced at Ipswich.[11] This catalogue, along with countless others, simply underlines the extent to which nineteenth-century private libraries were liable to be accessible to a surprisingly wide audience (see pp. 229–31).

Elsewhere, others relied on the more traditional approach of engaging a local clergyman to care for their books. At Althorp in 1870, the Rector of nearby Brington, F. J. Ponsonby, was Lord Spencer's honorary librarian, while at nearby Deene Park in

[160] Proofs of the illustrations for William Roscoe's projected catalogue of Holkham's medieval manuscripts

the 1830s it was the the clergyman and topographer John Harwood Hill (1809–86).[12] A trusted family retainer, Hill, it was reported, 'lives among the books, and loves his labour'.[13] At Blickling in the early nineteenth century the librarian was the Reverend Mr Churchill, who received Dibdin; later the role was taken on by a local gentleman-scholar, Mr Bulwer, who corresponded with the owner, the 8th Marquess of Lothian (1832–70), on terms of easy equality. Bulwer was one of two Lothian librarians, as the great collection in the family's Scottish house, Newbattle Abbey, was in the care of an Edinburgh bookseller, a typical arrangement. A similarly gentlemanly relationship existed at Wimpole, where Lord Hardwicke's library was in the care of the Revd Dr Robert Plumptre (1723–88), Rector of Wimpole and President of Queens' College, Cambridge.[14] In Scotland, too, Archibald Anderson, the Duke of Gordon's resident librarian at Gordon Castle in Morayshire, was sure enough of his status in the ducal household to send a long lesson of pompous advice to the duke, then a schoolboy at Eton, in 1760, pointedly reminding the young man that he had 'had the Honour not only to know but also to have been generously used by Yr· Grace's three last Predecessors'.[15] Anderson was still ensconced in the castle a dozen years later, in 1772, when the duke corresponded with his factor about the need to move the old man from his accustomed room, a subject to be approached with some circumspection, the duke observing that 'if the old man should have an objection to do it I don't think I should like to force him', but adding that the room would need to be cleaned, as he believed it had not 'been washed these 40 years'.[16] By contrast, Richard Salter, who looked after the books at Badminton, emerges in his diary (1848–52) as more of a clerk and a book cleaner than a gentleman-librarian.[17]

Until the twentieth century librarians were unlikely to be women, but Lord Derby's librarian at Knowsley in the 1950s was a Miss Dorothy Povey, and the librarian at Longleat in the 1970s was a Miss Betty Austin.[18] Another atypical figure, Francis Needham (1900–71), was 6 feet 7 inches tall and began his career as an assistant in the Bodleian. He then moved to Welbeck as librarian to the Duke of Portland in 1930, stayed on for thirteen years before going onto a part-time retainer in 1943, was briefly Clerk of the Records to the House of Lords in 1946 and succeeded A. R. C. Grant as librarian to the Duke of Wellington in 1948.[19] Needham's

predecessor at Welbeck, Richard Goulding, who came from a family of printers and booksellers in Louth, was librarian there for twenty-seven years from 1902 to 1929 and was sufficiently esteemed to get a memorial plaque in the house after his death.[20] At Chatsworth the librarian Francis Thompson, equally respected, not only contrived emergency plans for the future of the great house as a public museum in the post-war era but also cared for the collection and organised exhibitions for the girls of Penrhos College, evacuated there during the Second World War.[21]

In some libraries the owner himself acted, at least in some measure, as his own librarian. Beckford, a voracious reader, was reportedly able to pounce on any book like a bird of prey, even though his books were essentially unordered.[22] In a more systematic way, successive Earls of Crawford in effect acted as their own librarians, studying bibliographical reference books, formulating desiderata lists, corresponding with booksellers, musing over a classification scheme and even compiling a massive slip catalogue, pasted up between 1862 and 1865. All these pursuits were continued into the 1880s and beyond. Nonetheless between 1891 and 1910, no fewer than eleven staff (ten men and one woman) worked in the Crawfords' Library – the Bibliotheca Lindesiana – as librarians, assistant librarians and assistants.[23] In mid-nineteenth-century Warwickshire the massive two-volume slip catalogue (1867) of the library at Ettington Park appears to have been compiled by the owner, the antiquarian E. P. Shirley; a third of the collection, rich in topographical books, had been assembled by Shirley himself, a third by his father and a third by his ancestors.[24]

Another route was to bring in the trade. In the second half of the eighteenth century the Chester bookseller Broster and Son advertised that they organised libraries 'alphabetically and according to Subjects, upon an entire new plan which has been universally approved of', a claim which others booksellers would no doubt have repeated.[25] The John Edward Martin who billed Lord Brownlow for £107 in 1847 'for arranging the library at Belton' and compiling the catalogue, as well as for work in the family town house in London, was presumably also a member of the trade.[26] At Wilton in 1811, the catalogue was done by 'Mr Payne', of Payne and Foss, and at Arbury in Warwickshire in 1835 by a bookseller from nearby Nuneaton, one

E.W. Short.[27] The 1856–57 catalogue of Chevening was done by a member of staff from Hatchard's. At £70 1s. 6d. this was considerably cheaper than the Belton project, probably because it was created by cutting up existing catalogues and then pasting up the slips, to produce a single consolidated catalogue.[28] This catalogue was in turn the basis of the one printed in 1865.[29] Elsewhere, catalogues were on slips from the beginning, for example the massive late nineteenth-century slip catalogue of the books at Duff House in Banffshire.[30] At Goodwood the librarian William Hayley Mason, a bookseller from nearby Chichester, compiled a catalogue published in 1838.[31] Friendly relations with the trade could pay dividends in other ways, as in 1764 when the London bookseller Thomas Osborne (1704?–67) wrote to Sir William Lee of Hartwell in Buckinghamshire, informing him that he had come across four volumes of Don Quixote with Lee's bookplate inside them, and wondered whether these ought to be returned.[32]

Another route was to seek guidance from a member of staff from an established library. At Trelissick in Cornwall in 1884, the owner Mrs Davies Gilbert consulted W. H. Allnutt (1849–1903), of the Bodleian, who had been brought in by Lord Clifden at nearby Lanhydrock to work on the library there in 1878.[33] The Welds of Lulworth retained Robert Harrison of the London Library to catalogue their books in 1867.[34] At Patshull in Staffordshire, a catalogue by the booksellers T. and W. Boone, revised and expanded by the British Museum's Cyril Davenport (1848–1941) in 1884, was replaced by another catalogue in about 1910 by C. Kenelley of the London Library.[35] In 1901 Sir Thomas Acland of Killerton consulted A. R. Atkinson of the Devon & Exeter Institute, who charged 10 guineas, but passed the task of compiling a catalogue on to a local schoolmaster, one E. G. Mardon. Acland wanted his books arranged alphabetically, but Atkinson pushed for a subject arrangement, which went wrong, obliging him to write an apologetic letter to Sir Thomas in which he said, 'I am sorry Mardon has made such a mess of the classification', adding rather lamely: 'When I spoke this morning about Mr Mardon's want of knowledge I only meant of course technical knowledge, which he cannot be expected to possess, being untrained in library work.'[36] Similar failings occurred elsewhere, for example in the 1832 catalogue of the library at Swynnerton, a Catholic house in Staffordshire, where the compiler clearly had great problems with the reversed Cs (a typographical convention used to create the Roman numerals 'm' and 'd') in the imprint dates of many Renaissance books.[37]

The tasks carried out by librarians varied considerably from place to place. At the most basic level, books ideally needed to be numbered so that they could be placed correctly on the shelves and retrieved via the catalogue when required. A memorandum in a library catalogue of 1767 from Waldershare, the North family house near Dover, explained the working method, as common now as then: 'The Great Letter denotes the Book Case, the figures on the left side the Shelves, and those on the right side the Number of Volumes.'[38] Innumerable libraries still contain books with spine labels, either handwritten or (commonly) printed, and the chance survival of a printed broadsheet (fig. 159) from a house in Leicestershire reveals how this was done. Produced for the London bookseller Bernard Lintot (1675–1736), the broadsheet contains a matrix of letters and numbers, designed to be razored into its component pieces and pasted onto the spines of books. The instructions explain: 'The large Capital denotes the Shelf. The Small Capital and number to be cut off and past'd on the backs of the Books on the Shelf A.B.C. &c.'[39] But in other libraries, shelf-marks might be written onto flyleaves rather than on labels pasted onto the spines, and in many cases books were not numbered at all. In the grandest libraries the librarian might deal with external visitors, as at Blickling in 1819, when the librarian Mr Churchill received the classical scholar Edmund Henry Barker, but made it clear that manuscripts from the library might not be borrowed, or in 1895, when A. E. Bullen (representing the Duke of Buccleuch, but a member of staff at the London booksellers Lawrence and Bullen) was robust in his response to an enquirer who wished to write an article about the ducal libraries, advising a colleague: 'This man … is not in any sense a scholar or a bibliophile. He is a hack of very mean quality … If he returns to the attack, refer him to me.'[40] Librarians might also be asked to advise on what subsequent generations would describe as strategic decisions. In 1851 another librarian working for the Buccleuchs, David Laing, of the Signet Library in Edinburgh, was asked to investigate whether the ducal collections in the various Buccleuch houses should be amalgamated 'to form one large library'. He recommended against the idea, but the episode illustrates another area where librarians might be active: in considering or implementing proposals for fundamental changes in the way that libraries were organised or run.[41] At Knole between 1806 and 1824, someone was checking books in the library, noting moves to London and keeping a record of missing books: the librarian as administrator and manager of cultural property.[42]

In many libraries librarians compiled catalogues, then, as now, a task which took far longer and was far more complicated than those in charge had expected. The authorship of extant catalogues is not now always clear, but as two large and well-organised classed catalogues (catalogues arranged by subject) of the library of the Dukes of Kingston at Thoresby Hall, Nottinghamshire, show, even when anonymous they could be the work of people who knew what they were doing.[43] At Chirk Castle as early as 1704, the meticulously laid-out catalogue was clearly the work of a serious scholar whose work now provides a remarkably vivid insight into the arrangement and organisation of a long-vanished Library room.[44] Many libraries, at least the larger or better organised, had two catalogues: a shelf-list, enumerating the books in the order in which they stood on the shelves (which may well have been loosely by subject), and an alphabetical catalogue or at least an author index to go with with it.[45] Printed catalogues were not uncommon by the nineteenth century, but more unusual earlier: the first English printed catalogue of a private library was that of the 1st Duke of Kingston (1665–1726), produced in 1726 (fig. 232).[46] Another early example of a printed country house catalogue comes from Osterley, where the *Catalogus Librorum in Bibliothecae Osterleiensi* (1771) was compiled by Handel's librettist the lexicographer Thomas Morell (1703–84).[47] Many libraries also had some sort of subject index, usually in manuscript, but later not infrequently printed, especially in the nineteenth century, as at Weston Park, Staffordshire, in 1887.[48] But librarians could also end up doing their own thing. At Lanhydrock W. H. Allnutt not only compiled a catalogue and extracted binding fragments (now split between the Bodleian and Harvard), but also clearly spent a good deal of time doing his own research – much as he did at the Bodleian, which sacked him in 1896 for doing private work in work time.[49]

Library posts could be lucrative and were certainly desirable perches, whether for established members of the book trade, gentleman amateurs, local clergy or indigent private scholars. When the 5th Duke of Buccleuch's librarian died of a stroke in London in 1836, no fewer than sixteen potential applicants immediately wrote to offer their services as a replacement. Many were, of course, booksellers. One was French, and others were Scots, one of whom stressed his poverty and his nationality in pushing his claim. Another candidate was a German, and four more, including a twenty-eight-year-old minister of the Kirk, an impecunious Cambridge MA and an unemployed Doctor of Divinity, had no very obvious qualifications for the job beyond an evidently shared belief that it sounded like an agreeable sinecure. Others had long-standing involvement with aristocratic libraries, including a bookseller who had supplied the Duke of Bedford and the Marquess of Abercorn with books, a London bookseller who had worked for Lord Salisbury, and another who had worked for Lord Bradford, the Duke of Wellington and the Marquess of Bute, and had recently been engaged as Librarian to the Duke of Bedford.[50] But elsewhere it is clear that similarly productive relationships were brokered via established firms, as when a 'J. G. Jennings', of Primrose Hill, was recommended to the Ulster magnate the Marquess of Dufferin and Ava by Quaritch, for whom he had once worked.[51]

CHAPTER NINE

'A *very pretty and comfortable room*'

The Library and Country House Life in the Eighteenth and Nineteenth Centuries

The new Library will be finished this week and all the books up the next.
I do assure you it will be a very pretty and comfortable room.
Anne Robinson, Saltram Park, New Year's Eve, 1780

I · THE SOCIAL LIBRARY

The Library as sitting room

Visiting in the late 1820s, the German traveller Prince von Pückler-Muskau (1785–1871) was very taken with English country house life. He wrote admiringly of its relaxed tone, and especially of 'the ban on all the most burdensome ceremonies' which remained de rigeur at home in Saxony. The Library was the hub of this alluringly informal way of living, the place where guests went to read and to write letters. It also offered other opportunities, which the prince, a well-known philanderer, was not slow to observe:

> *Here you also arrange rendezvous, general as with particular persons, in which you are entirely unconstrained. Often you have the chance to chat for hours at a stretch with the young ladies, who are always literary-minded. Many a marriage, or seduction of the already married, is woven between the Corpus Juris on one side and Bouffler's works on the other, while the novel of the moment lies between as a means of communication.*[1]

A couple of decades earlier, in 1809, a young lady visiting Wimpole was altogether more innocent in her intentions, but equally explicit in drawing a connection between books, Library and friendship, enthusing:

> *I have been here a month with people that I love, in a comfortable family-circle, surrounded by every comfort and every luxury of life, and sitting in a Library – such a Library! As would*
> *Make those read now, who never read before;*
> *And those who always read, now read more.*[2]

The Library as sitting room was a subject which much interested country house historians from the second half of the twentieth century. Writing in *Country Life* in 2001, John Cornforth explored the issue in an article in which he argued that the practice, while often associated with the Regency, actually reached back into the first half of the eighteenth century.[3] 'Libraries have always been more than just repositories of books', observed the furniture historian Clive Wainwright (1942–99) in a much-quoted article which examined in detail almost every aspect of libraries – as social spaces, repositories for antiquities and of works of art – except the obvious, as places for the storage and use of books, a subject which he, in common with Cornforth, largely ignored.[4] This mode of analysis is clearly overdue for revision, and an approach is needed which successfully manages to look at the history of libraries as social spaces without editing out the books.

Whether owned by bibliomaniac collectors or by ordinary country squires, country house Libraries of the later eighteenth and nineteenth centuries were typically comfortable sitting rooms and family rooms, where sociable activities, including the private and collective use of books, could be pursued. They could also serve as places of assembly and display, where finely bound books were deployed in grand spaces which were in some measure public. As rooms, they could be about collecting, conspicuous expenditure, private enthusiasms, dynastic pride – but equally about the

[161] The Adam Great Room at Kenwood House

provision in private houses of the sort of pleasures otherwise to be enjoyed in theatres, coffee houses, assembly rooms, bookshops and, by the early nineteenth century, in public libraries of all kinds. Often it was a complex mix of several or even all of these.

To serve its purpose, the Library needed to be suitably furnished. At Ampthill House in Bedfordshire, the Library was already in the eighteenth century furnished with 'two walnut tree elbow chairs on castors cover'd with scarlet cloath', as well as 'a walnut tree writing table on castors with drawers', sundry other chairs, and 'a stove compleat and an iron back to the chimney'.[5] This was typical of the period, and inventories, such as that compiled for Darley Abbey in Derbyshire in 1808, often give a general impression of the Library as a comfortable and richly upholstered space.[6] At Holkham in 1760, the Earl of Leicester's Library, designed by William Kent, and already the repository for a series of marvellous treasures, was already fitted out with a suite of settees and a large array of chairs.[7] Later, the very bookish Gothic Library at Althorp had tables, chairs and sofas 'of every comfortable and commodious form', liberally scattered throughout the room. When Lord Spencer was entertaining, it was used as an evening Drawing Room, into which dinner guests retired at the end of formal meals.[8] On at least one occasion, when a turkey pie was served in it, the Long Library was even used for eating.[9] On more informal family occasions, the nearby Marlborough Library, a much smaller room, served a similar purpose when the family dined alone.[10] The accent was on comfort, as Anne Robinson, daughter of the 1st Lord Grantham explained to her nephew Frederick (the future Prime Minister Lord Goderich), writing from Saltram Park on New Year's Eve, 1780. 'The new Library will be finished this week,' she enthused. 'I do assure you it will be a very pretty and comfortable room.'[11] In the event the books did not go onto the shelves until 22 January 1781, but when Frederick visited later that year he was suitably impressed, writing in turn to another correspondent: 'The New Library is comfortable & the room is improved.' A little later, in November 1781, Anne Robinson was still harping on about the subject, writing home: 'I have taken to set in the library you cannot immagine what a comfortable room it is.'[12]

A decade later, John Byng, 5th Viscount Torrington (1743–1813), a great traveller but often a grumpy one, visited Trentham, the Marquess of Stafford's house, in 1792. Complaining as usual and unimpressed with what he found here, he concurred with Anne Robinson and other contemporaries that the crucial point about a Library was that it should be comfortable, and the Trentham Library was wanting in this regard:

> At Trentham House, there are no comforts, nor is the Library fitted up as it should be! A Library is the first of rooms! What stores of paper, pens, wax, ink standishes, albums, good writing tables, should furnish a Library. People spend fortunes, and waste great estates, without ever having passed one hour in a comfortable room, or in a good bed.[13]

The same ideal – of comfort – is expressed very powerfully in one of the most compelling visual impressions we have of a country house Library of the early nineteenth century. In 1815 the antiquarian John Britton (1771–1857) published a spectacularly illustrated description of the great house of the Earls of Essex, at Cassiobury in Hertfordshire. As depicted in A. C. Pugin's splendid aquatint (fig.162), the Great Library at Cassiobury was not just magnificent, but was also a place for quiet study and letter-writing, and a place of relaxation, with comfortable chairs and sofas, and the family dogs at play.[14] The slightly later catalogue of the library suggests that reality was not very far removed from this, as the contents of the shelves were not antiquarian books for the delectation of the bibliomaniac, but useful practical books of all kinds, including county histories, books of antiquities and travels, and novels, including a nice set of the works of Jane Austen: *Pride and Prejudice* (1818), *Mansfield Park* (1814), *Emma* (1816) and *Northanger Abbey* (1818), alongside many others.[15] Visiting Cassiobury in 1826, Prince von Pückler-Muskau was suitably impressed, noting that the Library there served 'as the main salon for company' and admiring 'two little cabinets leading into the garden, both filled with rare objects'.[16] Like the rather similar Library built by Lewis Wyatt (1777–1853) for the Egertons at Tatton Park, the Library at Cassiobury was at the upper end of the range of possibilities, but in its combination of a fashionable interior, entertaining books and comfortable furniture, in its aspirations, it was typical of the era. On a more modest scale in 1813, the Highland gentlewoman Jane Grant (1775–1852), who had according to her daughter 'long wished for a little more comfort around her',

[162] The Great Library at Cassiobury Park by A. C. Pugin, from John Britton, *The History and Description … of Cassiobury Park*, 1837 (coloured copy, Belton House)

refitted the Drawing Room at Rothiemurchus, the family house in the Cairngorms, as a Library. An elegant room stocked with books which had 'accumulated quite beyond the study shelves', it was comfortably furnished, the bookcases which entirely surrounded the room made from fir on the estate, artfully varnished to look like satinwood.[17]

These developments can usefully be set in the context of the breakdown from the middle of the eighteenth century of the traditional, sequentially arranged State Apartment, to be replaced with configurations of rooms based on circuits rather than enfilades, more suited to fashionable styles of entertaining. The circulating plan worked equally well in modest villas as in grand houses,

such as at Llanerchaeron, an elegant but fairly small house built by John Nash for a family of Welsh squires, where the Library was one of four principal rooms, along with the Drawing Room, Breakfast Room and Dining Room.[18] And when houses were designed with entertaining in mind, increasingly they were equipped with rooms set aside for particular purposes, such as Music Rooms and Libraries, or even for particular times of day, like Morning Rooms. For obvious enough reasons in an age of candlelight, Libraries, too, tended to be thought of as daytime rooms.[19] While they could be used for receiving company, in practice they functioned as favourite wet-day rooms, when inclement weather made outdoor pursuits unappealing. At Coleshill in Berkshire, the Library was furnished by 1833 as a sitting room, but it also had two backgammon sets and two chess sets.[20] The Library at Tatton still has its chess men, while rather earlier, Mrs Lybbe Powys, visiting Middleton Park in Oxfordshire, found a 'a good collection of books' in the Library, alongside 'every other kind of amusement, as billiard and other tables'.[21]

Sometimes existing Library rooms could be modified, either structurally, or at least in their use, to meet changing fashions. At Newhailes the great Palladian Library (fig. 163) was by the early nineteenth century being used as a Drawing Room, at least in summer. It also served as a Dining Room for very large parties, as well as a venue for balls.[22] By the late 1870s the Library at Wollaton, the home of books which had been in the house since Tudor times, was crowded with furniture, including, again, a billiard table.[23] At Lanhydrock Victorian photographs show the Jacobean Long Gallery (fig. 164) filled with comfortable clutter, the subject of scorn for Lord Esher (1881–1963), the National Trust's chairman, who in 1953 complained that 'a greater collection of junk could hardly be seen anywhere'.[24] The Library at Hinchingbrooke, Huntingdonshire, as photographed in about 1890 (fig. 165), was, if anything, even more congested, while the monumental neo-Norman Library at Penrhyn and Colt Holt's Regency Library at Stourhead were both by end of the nineteenth century crammed with comfortable armchairs and enormous pot plants.[25]

The Library as a space for entertaining reached its apotheosis in the 'Great Room'. At Kenwood, Adam's 'Great Room' (1770; fig. 161) was 'intended', as the architect explained in print, 'both for a library and for receiving company', with semi-circular recesses for the books and the rectangular central part for the company.[26] Nonetheless its library functions should not be underplayed. Visiting Scone Palace in 1838, Dibdin was dismayed not to find more books, as the bulk of Lord Mansfield's books were at Kenwood.[27] At Syon House, too, Adam's Long Gallery-cum-Library was a place to receive polite company.[28] On a more modest scale the elegant Library at Fonmon Castle in South Wales, designed by the Bristol architect Thomas Paty in the 1760s and punched through the first floor of a medieval keep, seems to have been intended from the beginning as a formal reception room.[29] In 1838 Dibdin, visiting Kinfauns Castle in Perthshire, enthused about the great Library

[163] Newhailes Library around 1930, before removal of the books

recently built for the 14th Lord Gray (1765–1842) by Robert Smirke (1780–1867) and again clearly intended to be one of the principal reception rooms in the castle:

You proceed into the Library after the dining room; which is forty feet long, by twenty-seven and a half wide, and nineteen feet high: a noble room in all respects – and wisely made a receiving room … Immediately connected with the library are two drawing-rooms – with a bay window, at right angles, on entering, twenty-nine feet long – the ceiling all continuing of the same height.[30]

Later, at Arundel Castle, the importance of the Library as a ceremonial room was underlined by the opulent refurnishing of the Regency Gothic Library for a visit by Queen Victoria in 1846.[31] At Highclere Castle (Hampshire) its location in the centre of the east front and its great size make it clear that the architect Sir Charles Barry (1795–1860) and his client the 3rd Earl of Carnarvon (1800–49) saw the Library as one of the principal apartments in the castle.[32] Later still, at Flintham Hall in Nottinghamshire, remodelled by the local architect Thomas Chambers Hine (1813–99) for Thomas Blackborne Thoroton Hildyard (1821–88)

[164] The Library at
Lanhydrock, Cornwall,
in the late nineteenth
century

[165] The Library at
Hinchinbrooke House,
Huntingdonshire,
around 1890

between 1852 and 1857, the suite of Library rooms dominates the house. Consisting of a 'Little Library' and a galleried and two-storey Great Library, and with its books and the characteristic furniture, upholstery and chandeliers of the mid-nineteenth century still in place, Flintham's remains one of the most remarkable and evocative of all Victorian country house Libraries. The impact is only increased by the attached 40-foot-high conservatory, clearly inspired by the Crystal Palace.[33]

Enforced sociability did not suit everyone, with Pückler-Muskau, visiting an unnamed house in 1828, complaining that:

> Country life here is in some respects too social for my tastes. If, for instance, you want to read, you go to the library where you are seldom alone; if you have letters to write, you sit at a great common writing table, and they are then put in a box with holes and taken to the post by a servant. To do all this in your own room is not usual, and therefore surprises and annoys people.[34]

A slightly different picture emerges in Robert Kerr's *The Gentleman's House* (1865), a handbook for architects, where Kerr, though again emphasising that the Library was about more than books and study, nonetheless mentions 'the family collection; and the bookcases in which this is accommodated form the chief furniture of the apartment'. But he then explained: 'It is primarily a sort of Morning-room for gentlemen rather than anything else. Their correspondence is done here, their reading, and, in some measure, their lounging – and the Billiard-room, for instance is not infrequently attached to it. At the same time, the ladies are not exactly excluded.' Kerr emphasised that a Library should be easily accessible to the principal living rooms of the house, but also detached enough to be quiet and secluded, with decoration inclining towards the sober, and well (though not too well) lit. It needed to be properly ventilated to prevent books becoming musty, and it also needed a good fireplace for the winter.[35] When libraries were very grand, and where outside readers were expected, the scale of the Library room needed to reflect that, perhaps carried up to two storeys, with galleries, as at Flintham, and perhaps equipped with a Library Closet, which might well be used as the librarian's room.[36] When grander still, a suite of Libraries was more apt to a domestic building rather than one massive room, as again at Flintham and at

Highclere. Where necessary, these Libraries might be equipped with transverse bookcases arranged in collegiate style, and they would certainly need to be adequately lit and possibly embellished with 'artistic or scientific collections' – a typical combination in a Victorian ducal mansion.[37]

Whatever the level of grandeur, issues of practicality had to be addressed. At Wrest Park, where another of Anne Robinson's nephews, the 2nd Earl de Grey (1781–1859), insisted on a resolutely Frenchified Library to suit an equally Frenchified house, practical matters nonetheless impinged. The Library – 50 feet long – was provided with two fireplaces to see that it was warm, and, as originally planned, the adjacent Ante-Library was intended to contain a billiard table.[38] As Kerr observed, lighting was important, and as the nineteenth century progressed, new technologies offered new possibilities. At Cragside Lord Armstrong introduced electric light in the 1890s, but further north the four spectacular chandeliers in the enormous neo-Georgian Library at Haddo House in Aberdeenshire allowed for the use of the room late into the evening, whether for entertaining or for reading.

During the nineteenth century there was a definite tendency for books to invade the entire house, reflective of the extent to which, in the age of the steam-driven press, mass-produced publications permeated every aspect of life. Once confined to Libraries and Studies, books, now increasingly in publisher's cloth rather than in bespoke leather bindings, spread far and wide, spilling over into Billiard Rooms, Boudoirs, Morning Rooms, Nurseries and corridors. In many houses, by the early twentieth century, books were carefully set out in guest bedrooms to amuse visitors. At Mount Stewart in the 1920s, the society hostess Lady Londonderry (1878–1959) put a good deal of thought into this, and the same was true elsewhere.[39] This profusion of printed matter is today often difficult to grasp, especially in show houses purged of Victorian clutter in the post-war era. Many National Trust houses, for example, were subject to Georgianising campaigns by well-meaning curators between the 1940s and the early 1980s. Some of these houses still have large numbers of nineteenth- and early twentieth-century books stashed away in attics and stores, books once central to the social and mental fabric of the Victorian and Edwardian country house.[40]

[166] J. M. W. Turner,
*The Old Library at
Petworth*, 1827
(Tate Britain)

Elsewhere, as at Tatton Park, books remain in many of the principal rooms, once a common pattern in many houses. At Hackwood Park in Hampshire, for example, in 1828 there were large numbers of books in the North and South Libraries, the Saloon and the Study.[41] At Wynnstay in 1846 the 9,080 volumes in the library of Sir Watkin Williams Wynn (1820–85) were divided between ten different rooms (as set out in the catalogue, the Breakfast Room, Library, Drawing Room, Passage & Ante Room, Billiard Room, Study, Miss Wynn's Sitting Room, the Audit Bed Chamber, Passageway and 'Mr Herbert Wynn's Room'). At Haddo in Scotland, Erddig in Wales and Baronscourt in Ireland, books remain all over the house, rather than being tightly corralled in a single Library room. At Welbeck in 1893 the books in the ducal collection were split between fourteen different rooms, and this did not include outlying spaces like the Estate Office, where the presence of books can probably be assumed.[42]

Occasionally the use of the Library as a social space might spill over into more personal activities. The newly married Lionel and Victoria Sackville-West in 1890 embarked on the physical side of their union with such gusto that Victoria felt impelled to

note the venues chosen in her private diary – they included the marital bed, the new bride's private Sitting Room, a black rug and, more surprisingly, the Library at Knole.[43] More oddly still, in 1704 the Cornish gentleman Sir James Tillie (1645–1713) set out in his will that his executors should eschew 'the Pompous Solempnity of a Funerall', instructing instead that his body should be placed in a specially made oak chair, which was to be set 'in One of the Little Rooms near Pentillie Library' until it was time for his burial.[44] At Calke Abbey in 1830, the pious and high-minded Sir George Crewe (1795–1844) waited up all night in the Library, the second largest apartment in a large house, while the family *accoucheur* Mr Godwin supervised the difficult birth of his daughter Elizabeth Jane.[45] More unexpectedly the library table at Canons Ashby was, according to a housemaid who worked in the house between 1929 and 1931, the implausible venue for an emergency operation on the owner, Sir Arthur Dryden (1852–1938), an elderly semi-invalid.[46] By contrast at Petworth, the rakish connoisseur the 3rd Earl of Egremont (1751–1837) turned over the seventeenth-century Old Library at Petworth to his his protégé J. M. W. Turner, who used it as a Studio on his many visits to the house (fig.166).[47]

Books and the social library

All this talk of spaces, sociability and interiors is apt to imply that the books were of not more than secondary importance, but the evidence suggests otherwise. The sheer number of printed catalogues issued in the later eighteenth and nineteenth centuries, often describing libraries of no obvious interest to external scholars and evidently intended for the use of family and friends, is testament in itself to the fact that books and the sharing of books were important components of the social library. The 1842 catalogue of the books at Leigh Park, the Hampshire seat of the Earls of Portsmouth, is typical, describing a library consisting overwhelmingly of novels, school books, navy lists and similarly mundane publications, including even 'Macadam on Roads'. Typically for the genre, the Leigh Park catalogue now seems to survive only in a single copy in the family archives – a warning that similar catalogues are often not traceable, even in the age of electronic library catalogues, by looking at the holdings of great research libraries, but lurk, potentially unseen, elsewhere.[48]

Catalogues and surviving nineteenth-century libraries reveal an extraordinary array of printed matter. At Calke Abbey, for example, books inherited from eighteenth-century forebears and magnificent Victorian colour-plate books sit alongside devotional books and sermons, literary periodicals, books on natural history, agricultural improvement and mathematics, as well as innumerable works of history, topography and belles-lettres, volumes in English, French, Latin, Greek and occasionally German, Italian and Spanish, political tracts, printed and manuscript music, and even books on rat-catching and the purchase of carriages. A similar mix can be seen in many other libraries, for example at Castle Fraser, a library split since 1982 between the house and the National Library of Scotland, but rich in practical and educational books of all kinds including those on history, religion, geography, travel and medicine, as well as school books and others quite explicitly destined for the children.[49]

Even the act of recording what was on the shelves could become sociable activity or at least one to be kept in the family. At Bramshill (Hampshire) in 1898 Ada Beatrice Cope (1878–1953) compiled a catalogue of the library, based on a slip catalogue created by her grandfather Sir William Cope (1811–92), 'hoping that

some enterprising Cope of the Future will have it printed' (they didn't). A century earlier, in 1783, Boswell's sister Margaret (1738?–89) had catalogued the books at Auchinleck, the family house in Ayrshire.[50] In similar vein, in 1824 Sir Henry Fitzherbert (1783–1858) of Tissington Hall in Derbyshire, then ensconced on the Isle of Wight, received a letter from Lady Fitzherbert, who had evidently stayed at home, to let him him know that

> Selena, Mad^elle· and myself have been very busy indeed & done what we think I what I hope you will think a very good job. We have taken down and aired & wiped all the Books in the Study, and made a list so you be able to find your books for we have arranged I am sure as you will like them, & any of them would have been totally ruined if they had not been aired. They were going mouldy.[51]

How useful Lady Fitzherbert's list actually was is open to question, but probably the slender inventory of the books at Sulham House in Berkshire, compiled in a marble paper notebook in 1831, arranged by subject, and the titles copied down from the spines of the books, had a similar history.[52] The same is true of catalogues compiled for the library at Kenmure Castle in south-west Scotland (1820), the library of Sir Hugh Williams at Bodelwyddan in north Wales (1859), and many similar documents describing in sketchy detail modest libraries of what were then ordinary modern books.[53] At Felbrigg in 1793, the Lukin sisters, Mary and Kitty, were entrusted with the reorganisation of the books by the owner, their uncle William Windham (1750–1810), who noted with approval:

> Mary and Kitty began the putting of the library to rights. They have performed a task which was very necessary, and which had been so neglected that it is difficult to say to what period it might have been deferred. The comfort of having the books in the state to which they are already brought, I feel very sensitively.

Windham also taught classics to the two sisters, asking them to read passages out loud to him at breakfast and at dinner.[54]

It is striking from her letter how anxious Lady Fitzherbert was to assure her husband that he would not be incommoded by female intervention in the Library at Tissington. The same trait emerges equally clearly in the well-known housekeeping manual compiled by the Kentish gentlewoman Susanna Whatman (1753–1814), of Vintners near Maidstone. Giving guidance to her servants in around 1787, Mrs Whatman was emphatic in her ruling that 'the Books are not to be meddled with, but they may be dusted as far as a wing of a goose will go'. This steer was based on past experience, as her husband, a successful paper manufacturer, had been extraordinarily angry when a well-meaning housemaid had taken down library busts and books so that they could be dusted. But Whatman was also concerned about the potential for light damage to her husband's precious books, admonishing: 'The sun comes into the Library very early. The window on that side of the bow must have the blind let down.'[55] Books were liable to be damaged, not only by sunlight but also by careless handling or by pests whose presence was easily attributed to a slovenly approach to housekeeping. A little earlier, a Bedfordshire gentleman wrote to a retainer with the laconic but important warning: 'Care should be taken y^t mice do not gnaw ye Books.'[56] But such rulings were not always effective. The Library at Lacock still contains a book with covers made of medieval manuscript waste, partially eaten by rodents at an unknown date, but clearly before the middle of the seventeenth century.[57]

The Library as tourist attraction

By the nineteenth century many country houses had long been open to polite tourists, though whether visitors got to see the Library was another matter. At Croome Park in Worcestershire they did, as the guidebook published in 1824 shows. It noted that the Library was 'open to public inspection' and described it as 'plainly but appropriately furnished', before adding that 'it contains a collection of books, not large, but choice'.[58] But as often as not, it is clear that casual tourists were not permitted to view Libraries, something which remains true in some privately owned country houses to this day. Visiting Belvoir Castle in 1789, Lord Torrington found mistakes in the guided tour irritating and was contemptuous about the castle and the taste of its owners, ending a litany of complaints by observing: 'The Library (if any in this not-read family) was locked up.'[59] Torrington made a point of asking after Libraries, a question which could cause consternation or at least a terse response from guides, again something not

unknown today. Visiting Raby Castle in 1792, he enquired of the housekeeper and was briskly told, 'Yes, one upstairs, kept locked', but two years earlier at Apethorpe, persistence paid off, Torrington noting that 'at my desire I was shown the library, a good room'.[60]

Sociable reading

The fact that Libraries were not accessible to visitors did not necessarily imply that they were in any way lacking in magnificence, even when comfort was also accorded a high priority. At Charlecote, for example, the Elizabethan Revival Library, added to the house between 1830 and 1837 and designed by Charles S. Smith, a pupil of Wyatville, was and remains a room of great splendour. Beautifully fitted out with richly carved Elizabethan-style bookcases, it contains flock wallpaper, heraldic stained glass and an armorial carpet designed by Thomas Willement (1786–1871), and its shelves are packed with a fascinating mixture of everyday reading, grand nineteenth-century collecting and books inherited from the sixteenth and seventeenth centuries. The writer William Howitt (1792–1879) viewed it with approval in 1840, commending the hospitality of the owners George Hammond Lucy (1789–1845) and Mary Elizabeth Lucy (1803–90), and admiring the collection of portraits, as well as the furniture, a mix of new pieces and antiques, which included 'eight fine ebony chairs inlaid with ivory, two cabinets, and a couch of the same, said to have been brought from Kenilworth, and to have been a present of Queen Elizabeth to Leicester' (they are, in fact, from Batavia or Goa and date from the seventeenth century).[61] Similarly grandiose Libraries survive at Audley End, the creation of the antiquarian-minded 3rd Lord Braybrooke (1783–1858), and at Scotney, where the Library, designed by Salvin, remained in use as the principal living room into the early years of the twentieth century. At Audley End, when the American visitor Mrs Bancroft stayed, she noted that while she enjoyed looking over 'curious illuminated missals' after breakfast and a tour of the house, the other ladies present sat in the Library and occupied themselves with their embroidery.[62]

From this it was only a short step conceptually to Humphry Repton's well-known designs for 'a modern living-room', in effect a Library, in his *Fragments on the Theory and Practice of Landscape Gardening* (1816) – a species of room seen to perfection in the still-extant 'larger room, to contain books, instruments, tables, and every thing requisite to modern comfort and costume' built by his son John Adey Repton (1775–1860) for a Norfolk gentry couple, Abbot and Charlotte Upcher, at Sheringham Park.[63] The text accompanying the plate in *Fragments* spelled out the form and function of the Sitting Room Library in admirable detail but terrible verse:

A MODERN LIVING-ROOM
No more the Cedar-Parlour's formal gloom
With dullness chills, 'tis now the Living Room;
Where Guests, to whim, or taste, or fancy true,
Scatter'd in groups, their different plans pursue.
Here Politicians eagerly relate
The last day's news, or the last night's debate,
And there a Lover's conquer'd by Check-mate.
Here books of poetry and books of prints
Furnish aspiring Artists with new hints;
Flow'rs, landscapes, figures, cram'd in one portfolio
There blend discordant tints to form an olio.
While discords twanging from the half-tun'd harp,
Make dullness cheerful, changing flat to sharp.
Here, 'midst exotic plants, the curious maid
Of Greek and Latin seems no more afraid.
There lounging Beaux and Belles enjoy their folly,
Nor less enjoying learned melancholy.
Silent midst crowds, the Doctor here looks big,
Wrap'd in his own importance and his wig.[64]

Similar 'Living Rooms' can be seen in many smaller Regency houses, for example John Adey Repton's Library at Barningham Hall, also in Norfolk, and at Wassand Hall, a neat brick villa in East Yorkshire, designed by Thomas Cundy the Elder (1765–1825) and built between 1813 and 1815.[65]

Rooms like this underline the fact that reading was not necessarily either private or solitary. George III's consort Queen Charlotte, for example, employed 'readers' in French and German, and she also expected the novelist Fanny Burney (1752–1840), a member of her household, to read to her in English. Much of their work was presumably done at Frogmore, the Queen's Trianon at Windsor, where she kept her library, a collection at least partly assembled with the educational needs of her children in mind.[66] Public reading of one sort or another was clearly commonplace in the houses of the aristocracy and gentry as well, sometimes possibly in conjunction with other worthwhile and improving activities.

The idea that women, even if bookishly inclined, should deploy their time on useful handicrafts, was deeply ingrained. Shared reading, too, was for many an ideal to be aspired to, especially if the person doing the reading was a parent or, particularly, a father or other male relative. The two combined well, and contemporary commentators recommended them. Writing in her enormously popular *Domestic Duties* (1825), a manual of conduct and domestic economy for young married ladies, Frances Byerley Parkes (1785–1842), a great-niece of Josiah Wedgwood, advised:

Needlework, the reading aloud some amusing publication, or occasionally playing at chess and backgammon, may serve to give a pleasant variety to the evening's occupation of the different members of the family circle. Nothing delights the female part of a family so much as the reading aloud some volume of interest by one of the party, whilst the others are employed in light or elegant needlework. In this manner a knowledge of polite literature may be acquired, without any sacrifice of more important duties. Even books of a deeper and more permanent character, which few have the taste or inclination to pursue when alone, are often listened to with great pleasure and much profit, when read aloud in such a circle … Besides the information and gratification which listening to works thus read aloud to a family circle this custom contributes, materially, to a never-failing flow of conversation, and sharpens our wit by the opportunities it offers, or displaying our critical acuteness, both in pointing out the beauties and in detesting the defects of the work under perusal. It is a species of winter evening employment I strongly recommend you to encourage.[67]

In fact it is clear that many contemporaries needed no encouragement. In 1813, for example, the seventeen year-old Elizabeth Grant of Rothiemurchus (1797–1885) sat with her mother and sister on spring evenings, 'reading and working', and mending household linen while getting through novels, books by Maria Edgeworth and Oliver Goldsmith, and *The Spectator*.[68] A century later, Lady Gregory (1852–1932) of Coole Park, County Galway, recalled how childhood evenings at her family home, Roxborough, County Galway, had been dominated by family reading, not by talk, and that she, the youngest girl, was 'glad enough to be seen and not heard'.[69] Recalling her long life in old age, she contrasted her youthful experiences with 'journals and wireless and the peck of profitless talk which is part of ones daily provender', an important reminder of the impact of mass communications on long-established libraries deep in the country, a subject which has been little considered.[70] But the experience for girls and women was not necessarily so positive. Unlike Lady Gregory, another grande dame, Queen Mary's confidante Mabell, Countess of Airlie (1866–1956), in old age recalled with irritation a Victorian childhood dominated by moralising Evangelical books and tracts, an annoyingly painful contrast to the solid education given to her brothers, but denied to her.[71]

Reading, whether private and in silence or public and out loud, was of necessity an activity which took place in the context not just of what was available in the family but of reading matter to be had from other sources, in particular from local circulating libraries. In 1842, for example, the recently widowed Lady Prinn (1797–1888) of

Charlton Park, near Cheltenham wrote to the local circulating library of Messrs Saunders & Ottley to ask for a copy of the prospectus setting out their terms and conditions, the sort of enquiry which must have been commonplace.[72] In altogether sterner vein at Ballykilbeg House in County Down, the staunchly Protestant mid-nineteenth-century proprietor Barclay Johnston ran a lending library, which loaned books out for a fortnight, was open from 4.00pm to 6.00pm on Saturdays and charged a quarterly subscription of 3d. Johnston also sponsored a newsletter, *The Ballykilbeg Newspaper*, which was, like the library, strongly polemical and sectarian in tone.[73] Elsewhere gentry libraries and gentry book clubs might themselves function as something closely approaching a formally constituted lending library (see p. 231).

From public and shared reading it was only a short step to full-blown entertainments, and even theatricals. At Calke the library still contains not

[167] J. M. W. Turner, *The White Library at Petworth, c.*1828 (Tate Britain)

only locally printed music from nearby Lichfield but also eighteenth-century printed plays, some marked up for performance – fascinating in a house whose misanthropic owner Sir Henry Harpur (1763–1819) had married a lady's maid and avoided company, but nonetheless enjoyed amateur dramatics.[74] In 1793, for example, a pair of neighbours went 'to the Calk theatricals', where they were amused to see Sir Henry 'coaxing his gouty legs into harlequin agility' when performing.[75] At Tyntesfield a century later the Library was itself the preferred venue for amateur dramatics, apparently held in the great Gothic bay window at the far end of the room.[76]

Like plays and reading, music could be pursued in private, but could also be a matter of public performance. Whether or not Libraries were the chosen venue, they were at the very least often the place where score and part books were kept. In 1801, for example, the Library of the 5th Earl of Abingdon (1784–1854) at Wytham, just outside Oxford, housed a 'Large quantity of printed Musick', as well as a 'Small quantity of D° written'.[77] At Tatton Park the Music Room is one of the most magnificent rooms in the house. Placed right next to the equally magnificent Library, it still houses the many volumes of finely bound music which once belonged to Elizabeth Sykes (1777–1853), the sister of the bibliomaniac Sir Mark Masterman Sykes who married Wilbraham Egerton (1781–1856) of Tatton in 1806. The Tatton music collection (and 'collection' is not too strong a word) is especially fascinating because it was by a female amateur musician and clearly an exceptionally skilled one. While it contains marked-up copies of contemporary music, it also includes the sort of 'Ancient Music' more often associated with male connoisseurs and professionals, notably a volume of scores of music by Henry Purcell. Copied by the Oxford composer and Professor of Music, Philip Hayes (1738–97), this was once owned by the Handel scholar Samuel Arnold (1740–1802), one of Purcell's successors as Organist of Westminster Abbey, and it includes a now unique score of Purcell's Ode 'The Noise of Foreign Wars'.[78] But despite the musicological interest of this otherwise lost work, the ultimate significance of the Tatton music collection now clearly lies in the very rich evidence which it contains of musical life in a great Regency house, as well as details of the performance practices of Elizabeth Sykes and her circle.

A rather similar collection, of over 2,000 titles, survives at Castle Fraser, as at Tatton originally the property of a woman, Eliza Fraser (1734–1814).[79] The music collection of the 9th Earl of Exeter (1725–93) at Burghley again reflects an interest in early music and practical music making both at Burghley and in the earl's London house – a mix equally discernible at another Lincolnshire house, Belton, and at Boughton.[80] A musical monument of another kind, Turner's 1827 painting *Music in the White Library*, shows the principal Library at Petworth in use as the venue for musical entertainments – though the artist also painted the same room in use for a whole range of social occasions, as various as a visit from the vicar through to animated female conversation (fig. 167).[81]

II · THE GENTLEMAN-SCHOLAR

Despite the lures of field sports, muscular Christianity and imperial derring-do, many nineteenth-century landowners were clearly actively and enthusiastically engaged with their books. For some, indeed, they were among their most central preoccupations. To some extent this emerges from documentary sources: the diaries of the 15th Earl of Derby (1826–93), for example, are replete with references to books and reading.[82] As often, however, this is something which emerges most clearly from the contents of the extant libraries. Many country house shelves are still packed with books, often visibly quite well read, reflective of the enthusiasms and interests of 150 years of gentleman- (and more rarely lady-) antiquarians, theologians, philologists and amateur scientists. Though the majority of his books were sold in 1885, a remnant of the great topographical library of the antiquarian baronet Sir Richard Colt Hoare (1758–1838) survives in the great room which he created for it at Stourhead. The splendour of the collection and its comprehensive and indeed encyclopaedic nature are most evident in the classed catalogue published in 1840, in which the books were enumerated county by county: clearly Colt Hoare's intention was neither more nor less than the comprehensive and systematic coverage of the history and antiquities of every corner of his native land. The dispersed topographical library seems all the more impressive when it is remembered that Colt Hoare also collected books about Italy, presenting his Italian library of some 1,740 books to the British Museum in 1825 and 1828.[83] Not far

[168] Plate in John Stevens, *The History of the Antient Abbeys*, London 1722–3, a book from the library of Charles Talbot (Lacock Abbey)

A SOUTH WEST PROSPECT OF THE CHURCH OF RADFORD, BY WORKSOP.

away, at Lacock Abbey, a good part of the more modest but still impressive antiquarian library of Lacock's penultimate private owner Charles Talbot (1842–1916), fascinated above all by the history and antiquities of the abbey, remains in the house (fig. 168). Talbot's father, William Henry Fox Talbot (1800–77) was a Cambridge-educated classical scholar. Despite some surviving books on optics, unsurprisingly his classical textbooks survive much better than those reflective of his pioneering photographic career, mostly sold during the course of the twentieth century.[84] Disraeli's library at Hughenden, though including political books and books inherited from Dizzy's bibliomaniac father Isaac D'Israeli (1766–1848), also houses the Prime Minister's copies of his own novels, as well as annotated Latin books, a reminder that he was a more-than-competent classical scholar. By way of contrast, at Chartwell, Churchill's library, though no longer fully intact, contains few books in Latin, but many more reflective of his literary and political career, including a copy of the first English edition of Hitler's *Mein Kampf* (1924) and the Prime Minister's own copy of his 'Finest Hour' speech.[85]

More modest in every way, the eccentric Northamptonshire antiquarian, Sir Henry Dryden (1818–99), like Colt Hoare an amateur archaeologist, again assembled a library of books reflective of his intense interest in history, ecclesiology and medieval architecture. Like Colt Hoare's, much of this library was subsequently dispersed, not in the 1880s but in the 1980s. Another Midland landowner, Charles Holbech (1816–1901), Archdeacon of Coventry from 1873 to 1887, was the original owner of many of the more interesting books in the small but attractive Library at Farnborough Hall, where Holbech was simultaneously the parson and the squire.[86] Not far away, at Ettington Park, E. P. Shirley, parodied by Disraeli in *Lothair* as Mr Ardenne, 'a man of ancient pedigree himself, who knew everybody else's, which was not always pleasant', mostly collected books in pursuit of his antiquarian interests – principally genealogy and local history. But he also had a second library at his Irish house, Lough Fea, in County Monaghan, 'an almost perfect collection of Irish books', some of which eventually ended up in the National Library of Ireland in Dublin.[87] A rather similar

library of Irish books (in English, not Irish) once existed at Adare Manor, a Gothic extravaganza in County Limerick built by the 2nd Earl of Dunraven (1782–1850).[88] Elsewhere in Ireland, Henry John Beresford Clements (1869–1940), a scholar and bibliophile, inherited the estates in Kildare and Leitrim of his distant kinsman the assassinated 3rd Earl of Leitrim (1806–78), one of Victorian Ireland's most unpopular landlords, who had disinherited many of his closer relatives. Succeeding in 1904, he is now known principally for his great collection of armorial bookbindings, bequeathed to the Victoria and Albert Museum, though other antiquarian books were still at Killadoon, in County Kildare, in 2009.[89] Another divisive figure, William Willoughby Cole, 3rd Earl of Enniskillen (1807–86), of Florence Court,

County Fermanagh, had two great passions: fossils and the Orange Order. But despite his vehement Unionism and his fierce opposition to Irish Home Rule, Lord Enniskillen's books also suggest an informed and enthusiastic interest in the history, topography, archaeology and history of Ireland.[90] In a rather similar vein, but a couple of generations later, the library of another arch-Unionist family, the Vane-Tempest-Stewarts, Marquesses of Londonderry, at Mount Stewart, County Down, contains an if anything even more intriguing mix of Orange and Green, with early twentieth-century books on imperial politics sitting alongside Celtic revival books, books on aircraft production (the 7th Marquess of Londonderry was Air Minister between 1931 and 1935, accused by some of an excessively accommodating approach to Hitler) and

[169] The Library at Madresfield Court, remodelled in 1902–5 by C. R. Ashbee

presentation copies from Yeats and Sean O'Casey – inscribed to Edith, Marchioness of Londonderry, the leading political hostess of the inter-war era.[91]

National sympathies also seem implicit with Charles Kemeys-Tynte, of Cefn Mabli (Glamorgan), an enthusiast for the Welsh language and, according to an obituary published in 1891, 'a most cultured man who spent a great portion of his time in the splendid library he had gathered, and published for private circulation two or three volumes of verse'.[92] Another great Victorian library, the working collection of the antiquarian and Egyptologist Sir John Gardner Wilkinson (1797–1875), has been at Calke since shortly after his death, but earlier was at his own house, Brynfield, on the Gower Peninsula, where he developed a deep interest in the history and archaeology of Wales.[93] At Llangibby Castle in Monmouthshire, the library was dominated by books on the history and antiquities of the archetypal border county collected by Major Alfred A. Williams. As a cataloguer put it in 1953, 'the special feature of the library is the concentration on books, pamphlets, manuscripts, prints, maps, etc., relating to the County of Monmouth', covering 'every aspect of local life, history, tradition, and literature'.[94] By contrast at Sizergh Castle in Westmorland, the focus was on family rather than county: the substantial library of mostly twentieth-century books includes long runs of *Victoria County Histories*, published editions of medieval primary sources and other materials used by Henry Hornyold-Strickland (1890–1975) to write the history of his wife's family, the Stricklands, as well as an account of Lancashire MPs from 1290 to 1550.[95] The Stricklands were Catholics and fiercely proud of it, but elsewhere other religious sensibilities tipped in: at Madresfield in Worcestershire, the great Arts and Crafts Library created in 1902–5 by C. R. Ashbee (1863–1942; figs. 169 and 170) still houses a large quantity of Tractarian theology which once belonged to Frederick Lygon, 6th Earl Beauchamp (1830–91), an interest also much in evidence at Tyntesfield, where there are many books on theology, liturgy and (aptly) the Gothic Revival. Most impressively of all, at Wallington in Northumberland the library, despite a bookcase of books about Northumbrian history, addresses global rather than parochial or local themes. Among the thousands of well-read books (successive generations of Trevelyans liked to read and re-read with pencil in hand) are numerous volumes which belonged to the historian and classical scholar George Otto Trevelyan (1838–1928), the very broad-ranging additions of his son and daughter-in-law Sir Charles Philips Trevelyan (1870–1958) and Lady Trevelyan (the sister of Gertrude Bell), and at the heart of it all the roughly 470 books, many richly annotated, from the library of Thomas Babington Macaulay (1800–59).[96] Few books seem to summarise the world of private scholarship more impressively than Macaulay's copy of the 1696 Oxford edition of Thucydides, richly annotated in English, Latin and Greek, and a book cherished by the great historian's well-read descendants.[97] Such a level of scholarship was clearly exceptional, but perhaps rather less so than the popular assumption that aristocratic and gentry books sat unread on the shelves from one generation to the next might suggest.

[170] Detail of a bookcase in Madresfield Library, showing the Tree of Knowledge carved by Will Hart

CHAPTER TEN

Town and Country

The Relationship between Libraries in Country Houses, Town Houses and Suburban Villas

I · LIBRARIES IN THE TOWN HOUSE

Libraries in London

Visiting London in 1712, the Irish antiquarian Samuel Molyneux (1689–1728), penned a series of letters to his uncle back in Dublin, describing some of the things he had seen in the metropolis. A graduate of Trinity College, and soon to be private secretary to the future George II, the Irishman did not impress everyone. The Oxford antiquarian Thomas Hearne, perennially hostile to Whigs, thought Molyneux's knowledge 'only superficial', based 'only upon Conversation with Gentlemen, and not from study'. Elsewhere, his reception was kinder, and aided by letters of introduction (one from Sir Andrew Fountaine), Molyneux successfully penetrated into the private apartments of several wealthy collectors.[1] He was especially taken with the collection of the poet and Privy Councillor Charles Montagu, 1st Lord Halifax (1661–1715), then in the political wilderness, but shortly to become First Lord of the Treasury under George I:

> He has three noble large rooms in one apartment perfectly well furnished with some original Pictures and many copies of the best hands, which are well worth seeing, but that which deserves a more distinct regard is his Cabinet in which are several true ancient Roman and Grecian Bustes … I believe at least 20 or 30 … among these in this Gallery are his books which are a very valueable Collection of the most Curious, distinguished into Classes according to the Sciences and the Shelves so contriv'd that every two contiguous apartments are joyn'd at the forepart, in the middle by two Hinges

> so that you can shut 'em up about carry away the Books without disturbing any one which is very convenient in case of Fire, Over the Shelves are hung several original Portraits of Ingenious Men of England, principally Poets, so that in the whole and in his manner of shewing them, which has been allways been extreamly obligeing I think I have never met with any thing yet so completely satisfactory in its kind as this.

Aside from the busts and the shelves, the most remarkable thing about Molyneux's account is that Halifax's library was not in a country house, but in the middle of London, in a 'very convenient and very handsome house' carved out of the ancient Palace of Westminster.[2] It was one of many aristocratic libraries in the capital. The most famous, only yards away, was 'the celebrated Library of ancient manuscripts' of Sir Robert Cotton (1571–1631), admired in the 1720s by the Scots traveller, John Macky, who described 'Fourteen Wainscot Presses, each mark'd with a Busto of a Caesar'.[3] Across the centuries, as the centre of gravity shifted, private libraries could also be found in the City of London, in Renaissance town palaces along the Strand, in St James's and the West End, and in suburban villas in places like Highgate or Twickenham, country villages swallowed up by the metropolis.

By 1520 there were already about seventy-five aristocratic residences in London.[4] These houses dominated the London townscape, as their successors would into the twentieth century.

[171] Johan Zoffany, *Charles Townley's Library, No. 7 Park Street, Westminster*, 1781–3, showing Townley seated right with his friends and statues (Townley Hall Art Gallery and Museum, Burnley)

Even in Tudor times town houses could be of considerable size, sometimes exceeding the grandest country houses.[5] Unsurprisingly they often contained books. In the reign of Henry VII, Robert Morton, a kinsman of Archbishop Morton, had liturgical books (essential for saying mass) both in London and at his country house at Standen, in Hertfordshire.[6] In 1539 the country house of the Catholic martyr Sir Adrian Fortescue also contained liturgical books, but there was a 'Study Chamber' in his lodgings at Blackfriars.[7] At Northumberland House (fig. 172), built originally for the collector Henry Howard, 1st Earl of Northampton (1540–1614), there were two Library rooms in 1614, both lavishly furnished, as well as a Study. The 'Lower Library' was on the river front, at the south-east corner of the ground floor, next to the Great Hall. Stairs in an attached corner turret led up to the 'Lower Wardrobe' in the middle floor, and then up to the 'Upper Library' on the top floor, with a bay window looking onto the 318-foot formal garden and beyond to the Thames. A doorway from the Upper Library gave access to a roof terrace.[8]

Near by, the principal library of the Cecils, more powerful than Northampton, was kept at Salisbury House, reconstructed between 1611 and 1613. This contained a comprehensive collection of books, arranged by subject and described in catalogues compiled in 1615, 1637 and 1647.[9] A room of some grandeur, the Library at Salisbury House was the venue for a 'showe' attended by James I in 1608, when £51 11s. was spent preparing the room for royal use. As well as new curtains, this covered seven days' work by Lord Salisbury's binder Thomas Herbert, who was paid for 'bynding, covering and stringing of bookes'. Pictures, genealogical tables and hanging maps of Ireland and Venice were coloured or procured, and two 'great books' of maps and fortifications acquired. Money also found its way to the 'actors and devisors of the showe', who included Inigo Jones and Ben Jonson. Evidently well pleased, shortly afterwards Lord Salisbury celebrated his success by spending £8 17s. 6d. buying books.[10]

Intriguingly the Library at Devonshire House (fig. 173) was used for similar purposes more than

[172] Canaletto, *Northumberland House*, 1752, showing the house at the western end of the Strand (demolished 1874)

200 years later, in 1851, when Dickens staged a benefit performance in the presence of Queen Victoria.[11] By then most of the 6th Duke of Devonshire's grandest books were at Chatsworth, though earlier the principal library seems to have been in London. Eighteenth-century visitors to Devonshire House were overwhelmed by its grandeur, but in 1766 a visitor to Chatsworth had complained it had 'very little in it that can attract the eye of the Connoisseur'. As late as 1798 books, prints and pictures in Piccadilly were valued at £13,311 but their equivalents in Derbyshire at just £3,428.[12]

By 1939 only four London town palaces were still in family occupation, and by the twenty-first century just one, Apsley House, survived with its original contents, though in state ownership since 1947.[13] The Library (fig. 174), too, survived, in the private quarters of the Dukes of Wellington and unseen by visitors. Other ducal residences once housed Libraries which were similarly private sanctums. The 8th Duke of Rutland (1852–1925), for example, forced himself to spend each

morning working in the Library of his town house in Piccadilly, only emerging for his daily constitutional when the clock struck noon.[14] The altogether grander library of the Earls of Ellesmere survived at Bridgewater House (fig. 175), their Italianate *palazzo* in Westminster, until the books were sold to Henry E. Huntington in 1917. Transferred to London from Ashridge in 1802 by the canal-building 3rd Duke of Bridgewater (1736–1803), despite rebinding orchestrated by the ducal librarian Henry John Todd, the core of the collection was still that assembled by Lord Chancellor Egerton in the reign of James I.[15] In the first half of the twentieth century, the Library (fig. 176) at Londonderry House was used for the glittering political entertaining of the 7th Marquess of Londonderry (1878–1949) and his wife Edith. The house survived until sold for demolition in 1962. By then some of the books were at Mount Stewart in Ireland, where they remain, along with George Stubbs's *Hambletonian*, which had once hung in the Library at Londonderry House.[16] Chesterfield House in Mayfair, the home of another fine library, was demolished in 1934.[17]

[173] The Library at Devonshire House, demolished in 1927

Whether families kept their books in town or country was dependent on practicality as well as personal preference. Michael Ward (1683–1759), a Justice of the King's Bench in early Georgian Dublin, is likely to have kept his legal books in his chambers on Ormonde Quay, rather than at Castle Ward, where they now are.[18] A sixteenth-century judge, Sir William Westone (c.1546–94), Chief Justice of the Common Pleas in Ireland, had a Bible and some law books in his Dublin 'Studdy', while the 3rd Earl of Hardwicke (1757–1834), Lord Lieutenant of Ireland from 1801 to 1806, had his main library at Wimpole, but kept a large collection of pamphlets in London.[19] The 1st Earl of Mansfield (1705–93), Lord Chief Justice under George III, inherited Scone Palace in Scotland, bought Kenwood as a suburban retreat in 1754, but kept a splendid library in his house in Bloomsbury

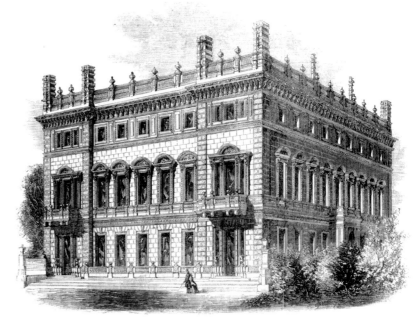

Square, burned in the Gordon riots in 1780.[20] Ministers, too, needed to be in London, and most of the books of the 1st Lord Stanhope (c.1673–1721), First Lord of the Treasury, were in his house in Pall Mall, and not at Chevening, where it appears there were only three shelves of books. Stanhope's library, of 953 titles, included many sixteenth- and seventeenth-century learned books from Continental Europe. His many Spanish books, bought in Madrid when his father was ambassador in the 1690s, and by Stanhope himself while British Commander-in-Chief during the War of the Spanish Succession, were more unusual.[21]

Those with houses near the capital might well keep their libraries in the country. By the eighteenth century the Cecils were no longer at the centre of affairs, and the bulk of their books were certainly at Hatfield by 1712.[22] Some decades earlier, Evelyn had admired books at Cassiobury, the great house of the Earls of Essex (just north-west of London), and at Euston Hall (somewhat further away, but hardly remote).[23] But those whose power base was further away might opt for London. In 1700 the Duke of Ormonde had books in 'Three Glass Booke Cases for the 3 Corners of ye Roome' in a private Closet in his house in St James's Square, a room placed between his Dressing Room and 'Supping Roome'.[24] At Monymusk in Aberdeenshire, it appears there was no Library, perhaps because Sir Archibald Grant (1696–1770) was an M P generally resident in London, returning to Scotland only after his expulsion from the Commons for fraud.[25] In 1742 the principal library of the recently deceased 8th Earl of Thomond (1688–1741), a substantial collection of new and nearly new books (1,118 titles, as well as pamphlets and unbound plays), was in his house in Dover Street in Piccadilly, rather than in Ireland, or at Shortgrove, his English house.[26] A little later Thomond's fellow countryman the diplomat Lord Macartney (1737–1806) kept a fine library at his town house in Curzon Street, rich in contemporary books of all kinds, organised by subject and divided between an Upper and Lower Library.[27] But there also seems to have been a library at Lissanoure Castle, the family house in County Antrim.[28] The 3rd Duke of Argyll (1682–1761), a grandson of the Duchess of Lauderdale, was so well known for his literary interests that contemporaries dubbed his London house 'the library'. A powerful Whig politician descended from a long line of Presbyterians, Argyll had interests that veered towards polite

secular scholarship, and he kept his principal collection of books at Luton Hoo.[29] Another Scot, Lord John Murray, had libraries in London, Perth and his Perthshire house, Huntingtower Castle, in 1762.[30]

Despite difficulties of transport, books could be moved around.[31] In the 1650s the Sackvilles shuffled books back and forth between Knole and Dorset House, their town house in Salisbury Court, off Fleet Street, destroyed in the Great Fire of 1666.[32] In 1815 Lord Bristol shifted seven packing cases of books from St James's Square to Ickworth, but the town house already had about 1,185 books in the mid-1780s, so more may have stayed in London. Over time the centrifugal pull of the capital lessened. With the advent of turnpikes and later of railways, regular travel back and forth between town and country became a more realistic prospect, leading eventually to the phenomenon of the country house weekend. By the middle of the nineteenth century owners could move back and forward with relative ease, rendering ancestral libraries in the country accessible, especially if there was a librarian in residence to answer queries and forward books. In addition, London offered an ever-greater choice of institutional libraries. Circulating libraries, libraries in clubs, in the House of Lords and the House of Commons, the London Library (founded in 1841) and the vast resources of the British Museum between them offered a range of options which had not been open to earlier generations.

Many owners had libraries in both town and country: the Berwicks at Attingham and in Portman Square in the later eighteenth century, or the Londonderrys at Londonderry House in London (see fig.176), Wynyard in County Durham and Mount Stewart in the nineteenth century.[33] The 3rd Duke of Richmond (1735–1806) went one further, in 1763 owning a small library of 115 books at the Chateau d'Aubigny in France, inherited from his French great-grandmother Louise de Kérouaille (1649–1734). Almost all were in French, though these included translations of Inigo Jones and of Philip Miller's best-selling *Gardener's Dictionary* (1731).[34] The eighteenth-century Dukes of Norfolk had libraries at Worksop Manor in Nottinghamshire, recently rebuilt by James Paine (1717–80), at Arundel Castle and at Norfolk House in St James's Square. While it is difficult to be dogmatic about this, from the second half

[174] *opposite*
The Library at Apsley House (photographed between 1880 and 1905)

[175] *opposite below*
Bridgewater House

of the eighteenth century there is a sense that
the centre of gravity was gradually shifting to the
country. In 1777 the Norfolks' main library was
clearly at Norfolk House. That at Worksop, while
not negligible, was secondary, while at Arundel the
library was a modest collection clearly intended
primarily for the resident Catholic priest, located
close to his rooms and to the castle chapel.[35] There
was still a substantial library at Norfolk House
in the nineteenth century, but by the time the
town house was abandoned in 1938 it had gone:
the ducal books had long since been concentrated
at Arundel.[36] In the reign of George II, Thanet
House, the London residence of the Coke Earls of
Leicester in Bloomsbury, had both a Library and an
'Upper Library', both richly furnished, but 'bound
books' from them were 'sent in Aprill 1760 by Sea'
to Holkham.[37] The library of the Tory politician
William, Lord Huntingtower (1766–1833) was
shifted to Buckminster when the London house

was sold in 1835. A substantial collection, the books
were valued at £630 by Sotheby's.[38] Sometimes
external circumstances might intervene. The 1st
Earl of Normanton (1736–1809), from 1801 also
the Protestant Archbishop of Dublin, had 2,597
volumes in his house on St Stephen's Green. In 1811
these were packed up, some to remain in Ireland,
some for London, and others sent to Somerley, the
English house in Hampshire.[39] With the loss of its
Parliament in 1801, the Irish capital was less alluring
than it had been.

For really serious seventeenth- and eighteenth-
century collectors, London was a better place for a
library than a country house. Book collecting was a
competitive pursuit, but library visiting could also
be an agreeable sociable activity, with large numbers
of private libraries concentrated in the capital. The
diaries of the antiquarian bishop William Nicolson
(1655–1727) are full of bibliographical gossip,
including notes of visits to aristocratic and clerical

libraries in London. These involved Harley's, as well as 'the choice Library' of the future Archbishop of Canterbury, William Wake (1657–1737), which Nicolson found 'plentifully furnished with the best Editions of Fathers, Councils, Historians Ecclesiastical'. Nicolson also visited the huge library of another clerical bibliophile John Moore (1646–1714), Bishop of Ely (presented to Cambridge University Library by George I), and admired Sir Andrew Fountaine's 'most valuable Collections of Medals and Coins'.[40]

Even when collectors owned a country house, it made sense to keep their bibliophilic trophies in proximity to the centre of the book trade, and to the great libraries of clerics and of wealthy professional men like the physicians Sir Hans Sloane (1660–1753) and Dr Richard Mead (1673–1754).[41] Mead kept his 10,000 books in a Library built by James Gibbs in the garden of a house in Great Ormonde Street, an example followed by the 3rd Earl of Sunderland (1675–1722), with a specially designed Library built onto the back of his town house.[42] Most of the printed books in the Harleian Library were at Wimpole, but Edward Harley's cherished manuscripts – the items most likely

to attract visitors – were in his house in Dover Street, in Piccadilly.[43] The library of Sir Richard Ellys, founded on early printed books more than manuscripts, was in Ellys's house just round the corner in Bolton Street, rather than in his country house in Lincolnshire.[44] Later, the Catholic connoisseur Charles Townley (1737–1805) kept his books and his antique marbles not at Towneley Hall in Lancashire, but in his house at Park Street, Westminster, designed by Samuel Wyatt (1737–1807). He was painted in the Library there by Zoffany in 1782 (fig. 171), surrounded by statues and friends.[45] The bulk of the 30,000 volumes owned by Townley's contemporary, the Scottish bibliomaniac the 3rd Duke of Roxburghe (1740–1804), were also in London, at 13 St James's Square.[46] The very fact is a reminder that some of Roxburghe's rivals were not landed proprietors, but wealthy London collectors like C. M. Cracherode (1730–99), of 32 Queen Anne's Gate, and Charles Grenville (1755–1846), who reversed his decision to bequeath his 16,000 books to his profligate nephew the 2nd Duke of Buckingham (1797–1861) – just in time to avoid their being swept up in the 1848 Stowe bankruptcy.[47] The duke was furious, denouncing

[177] The Library at Chesterfield House in 1922

the ingratitude of the British Museum, destined
to receive them, and complaining that his uncle
had put 'the use and advantage of a few librarians'
above 'those of your own name and family'.[48] Even
in the late nineteenth century the long-established
tradition of keeping fine books in London was not
entirely dead. The wealthy connoisseur Robert
Stayner Holford (1808–92) kept his illuminated
manuscripts and early printed books – many
purchased from the library of the 5th Lord Vernon
at Sudbury Hall – at Dorchester House in Park
Lane (fig.178), rather than at Westonbirt, his
equally palatial mansion in Gloucestershire. They
remained there until dispersed between 1924 and
1928.[49]

Libraries in London could be modest domestic
interiors, but sometimes they were of considerable
size and grandeur. One of the finest was the lofty
apsidal Library at Lansdowne House in Berkeley
Square, a splendid Neoclassical room designed by
the London architect George Dance the Younger
(1741–1825), built between 1788 and 1791 and
remodelled as a Picture Gallery two decades later.[50]
The Library at Chesterfield House was one of
the most magnificent rooms in the house: Lord
Chesterfield, indeed, reckoned it the finest room
in England (fig.177). Its more unusual contents
included 'a large Win Dial with a Mahogany
case', but the 794 books, mostly dating from the
seventeenth and eighteenth centuries, were more
conventional.[51] They were deployed in bookcases

decorated with busts, but the cornice of the room
was inscribed in huge letters with a quotation from
Horace:

> *Nunc veterum libris, nunc somno, et inertibus horis*
> *Ducere sollicatae jucunda oblivia vitae.*[52]

Another Library, at Spencer House, was designed
by John Vardy, a disciple of William Kent, and
begun in 1756. It was, as Arthur Young noted, 30
feet by 25, and handsomely fitted out. It was soon
found inadequate, and was remodelled and enlarged
by Henry Holland for Lord Spencer in the 1780s.[53]
At Shelburne House the design and purpose of the
Library gradually evolved. Adam initially advised
that the room should be 'for private business', but
in 1789 his client, Lord Shelburne, a great collector,
brought in the Italian Joseph Bonomi (1739–1808)
to create a new Library, described by Gavin
Hamilton as 'the finest room in England'.[54]

Libraries in provincial town houses and in Dublin

Town houses were not necessarily in capital cities.
Many gentry families kept a house in the local
county town, and these, too, might contain libraries.
The 1663 probate inventory of the seventeenth-
century Worcestershire squire Henry Townshend
included 'severall bookes of all sorrtes att Elmely,
and att Worcester'.[55] Another Midland gentleman,
Michael Biddulph (d.1657) had a 'study chamber' in
his house at Elmhurst, Staffordshire, but his books,
valued at £20, were divided between the country
and his house in Lichfield.[56] Later, books were often
taken to spas or resort towns, usually temporarily,
but sometimes on a more permanent basis. The
6th Duke of Devonshire had a library at Compton
Place, his seaside house in Eastbourne.[57] William
Beckford kept books in Beckford Tower above Bath
(a 'Small Library' and an 'Etruscan Library' on the
first floor), as well as in the splendidly appointed
Library of his house at 19 Lansdown Crescent,
later occupied by the diarist James Lees-Milne
(1908–97).[58] Hundreds of miles north, in Orkney,
part of the small eighteenth-century library of
the Baikie family (about 487 titles) survives in
Tankerness House, the family's former town house
in Kirkwall, the islands' capital, where local lairds
traditionally spent the long Orcadian winters. The
surviving books evidently belonged to Robert Baikie
(d.1817), the seventh Baikie of Tankerness, and are
mostly later eighteenth-century works of fiction,

history, drama and belles-lettres.[59] Grander families might retain a town house in places like York or Shrewsbury, important regional centres with their own thriving social scene, but the Brownlows of Belton had a house in nearby Grantham. Grantham House stands next to the great church of St Wulfram and had its own library, as several hundred books with the bookplate of 'Lord Brownlow's Grantham House' are now at Belton. Like the Brownlows, the Herveys of Ickworth were keen to maintain their interest in nearby Bury St

Edmunds, and long kept a house there. Whether any of the many books at Ickworth today were once in the Bury town house is a matter of conjecture, but some probably were.[60] The presence on the shelves at Belton of a pair of engraved Psalm books for Grantham Parish Church (1756 and 1792) and at Ickworth of an equally rare guide to the Bury Botanical Garden (1822) is a reminder of the importance of local networks. Many houses of the era contained – and sometimes still contain – similar and equally rare locally printed books.[61]

[180] The Library at Shugborough

One of the grandest town Libraries of all was in Dublin. Completed in the early 1770s, the Library at Charlemont House (fig. 179), on the once fashionable north side, was built for James Caulfield, 1st Earl of Charlemont (1728–9), a former Grand Tourist, a great collector and a leading figure in Irish politics. Charlemont likened his Library, designed by Sir William Chambers, to a favourite mistress. Located in a rectangular pavilion in the garden of Charlemont House, it was linked to the house by a long passageway. The visitor passed through a square vestibule half way along the link passage, before climbing a short flight of stairs, and proceeding to the top-lit 'Venus Library'. To the left in a niche stood a full-size copy of the Venus de' Medici by the English sculptor Joseph Wilton (1722–1803). To the right, a monumental pedimented doorway led into the main Library, the shelves punctuated by giant Corinthian pilasters and lit from above by windows punched through the vault. Beyond were two smaller rooms, one for pictures and antiquities, and the other, facing across the garden and back to the house, for Charlemont's medal cabinet, a magnificent object since 1984 in London. When Charlemont was away, this suite of rooms was supervised by his friend Andrew Caldwell, who kept an eye on the building and dealt with booksellers, though he cavilled in 1773 when Charlemont demanded he supervise the dusting of the medal room, observing that 'the Work Men were there ten days and made such Dirt that if

anything the Room is rather not so well as before'. Visitors were admitted to Charlemont House, but again Caldwell was inclined to grumble, whining about 'this stupid Town' and complaining that the common herd was disrupting his own enjoyment of the Library: 'I don't mix with the World but as often as I can I retire to a certain Bibliotheque where I am always delighted; but some how or other I am continually found out and intruded upon.'

Ultimately even this grandiose construction proved inadequate, and in 1788 Charlemont added a third Library, dedicated to the memory of the recently deceased Whig Prime Minister Lord Rockingham (1730–82) and designed by Chambers's pupil James Gandon (1743–1823). But unfortunately all three Libraries were effectively destroyed when Charlemont House was converted into an art gallery from 1929.[62] Charlemont's was not the only Dublin town house with a Library. One of the grandest was in the mighty town *palazzo* of Ireland's premier dukes, now the home of the Irish legislature. Designs for a Library at Leinster House were submitted by the German-born Richard Cassels (1690–1751) about 1745, but the room as executed was the work of the Englishman Isaac Ware (1704–68), a protégé of Lord Burlington and author of a best-selling translation of Palladio (1738), who drew inspiration from published designs by William Kent for pedimented bookcases at Burlington House in London.[63]

Libraries at Shugborough and Lichfield House compared

When grandees had libraries in town and country, it can be difficult to form any very clear sense of how one collection related to another. Many London town houses have entirely disappeared, and even when they survive, Library rooms have often been destroyed. Their contents have almost without exception been dispersed. When documentary evidence remains in the form of inventories, catalogues and photographs, a direct comparison may still not be possible because evidence for town and country does not coincide by date. The two libraries of the Earls of Lichfield – at Shugborough in Staffordshire and at Lichfield House in St James's Square – as a pair form a comparatively unusual exception. The London collection is long gone, and only a small proportion of the original books remain in Staffordshire, but both Library rooms survive. We also have a detailed picture of

[181] The Library at Lichfield House from the May 1910 *Architectural Review*

both libraries as they were in 1842, for the simple reason that the 1st Earl of Lichfield (1795–1854), a spendthrift Whig politician, went bankrupt. This resulted in the sale of the contents of both houses in consecutive weeks by the flamboyant London auctioneer George Robins (1777–1847), the pickings described in detail in a pair of sale catalogues which survive in marked-up copies in the family archive.[64]

The family of the Earls of Lichfield only achieved any real eminence with Admiral George Anson (1697–1762), who successfully circumnavigated the globe between 1740 and 1744. His armed expedition was intended to undermine Spanish rule in the New World and underpinned Britain's growing naval hegemony. It earned its commander vast sums of prize money, which allowed the admiral's elder brother Thomas, a son-in-law of Lord Chancellor Hardwicke, to remodel the family seat at Shugborough.[65] The Library there (fig. 180), attributed to the architect, astronomer and landscape gardener Thomas Wright (1711–86), is an intriguing and beautiful room, completed in 1748.[66] Just 40 feet long, as seen in photographs it looks bigger than it is, a monumental Rococo hall reduced to a diminutive dolls' house scale. When Thomas Anson's sister-in-law Lady Grey saw it, she thought it 'exceedingly odd and pretty', an impression perhaps based partly on the exquisite plasterwork by Francesco Vassalli.[67]

At the time of the 1842 sale the Library at Shugborough was richly furnished with chairs, tables, well-stuffed sofas and bronze-mounted vases, introduced in the Regency period, as earlier the room had been much sparser. Other contents included globes, a Broadwood grand piano and a caricature screen, as well as, more unexpectedly, 'a stuffed monkey, representing a Cobbler, in case, with glazed front'.[68] In London the equivalent Library at Lichfield House, 15 St James's Square (fig. 181), was furnished with a suite of elegant French or Frenchified furniture, including a 'Grecian couch', bronze candelabra and a 'red tortoiseshell and Buhl library table', which sold for 19 guineas.[69] It was one of the principal apartments of the exceptionally fine Neoclassical town house built for Thomas Anson by James 'Athenian' Stuart (1713–88) and in use by 1768. The Library at Lichfield House, located like Lord Charlemont's at the rear of the house, was the result of remodelling by Samuel Wyatt (1737–1807) in the 1790s, when two previously separate rooms were knocked together, the

dividing wall replaced by a screen of columns and pilasters in verd-antique scagliola.[70]

Books in both town and country had much in common, with large numbers of valuable seventeenth- and eighteenth-century works and a few earlier ones (mostly at Shugborough) including some eminently collectable sixteenth-century books, among them a 1549 *Book of Common Prayer*, John Bale's *Illustrium Maioris Britanniae* (1548) and a small collection of Aldines. At the country house sale at Shugborough books occupied the first three days of the fourteen-day sale and made £1,456 11d., with another £256 16s. 'bought in' (rather less than 10 per cent of the entire sale). In London the whole sale made a more modest £8,239 6s. 1d., a clear indication of the relative size and and grandeur of the two houses and their contents. A striking feature of the Shugborough library was a large collection of architectural books and prints, which included twenty-three volumes of Piranesi (lot

[182] The Library at Ham House in 1920, prior to the sale of the books collected by the 4th earl of Dysart (1708–1770)

653), Athenian Stuart's annotated copy of Antoine Desgodetz's *Les Edifice antiques de Rome* of 1682 (lot 658), books which had belonged to Mead and Jean-Baptiste Colbert, sundry predictable but expensive English and French books, and a 1762 Chippendale's *Director* (lot 696). These impressed George Robins sufficiently to merit a special section in the sale catalogue. In comparison the smaller library in London, though not without grander books, was more focused on polite literature and leisure reading, ranging from French Enlightenment books through to history, printed Parliamentary proceedings, periodicals and even a twenty-part set of *Nicholas Nickleby*. More surprisingly there was also a published description of Stephenson's 'Patent Loco-motive Engine' (1838).

Another key difference between the two libraries is that, when disaster struck, the books in London were sold in their totality, whereas a small but distinguished part of the Shugborough collection was bought in by the family. These books largely remain at Shugborough, where the battered remnants of the library were reconfigured for the 2nd Earl of Lichfield in 1855 by the London book-seller J. H. Boone – a mix of salvaged books from the eighteenth-century library and others of more recent date, attractive and useful, but evidently bought partly to fill the shelves.[71]

II · THE SUBURBAN LIBRARY

Libraries in villas

Libraries could also be found in houses which were neither in town, nor really in the country. Travelling from Richmond to London, Defoe in his *Tour through the Whole Island of Britain* noted 'the river sides are full of villages, and those villages so full of beautiful buildings, charming gardens, and rich habitations of gentlemen of quality than nothing in the world can imitate it'.[72] A little later the poet Robert Lloyd (1733–64) poked fun at the emerging commuter belt around London:

> Some three or four miles out of town
> (An hourly ride will bring you down)
> He fixes on his choice abode,
> Not half a furlong from the road;
> And so convenient does it lay,
> The stages pass it every day:
> And then so snug, so mighty pretty,
> To have a house so near the city![73]

Houses 'near the city' were not new. In the 1630s Alethea, Countess of Arundel, had built a suburban villa, or *casino*, Tart Hall, in the open countryside west of St James's Park. Intended primarily as a pleasure house for the display of art, it did not obviously contain a library, though that is not impossible.[74] Suburban houses near London ranged from small residential homes to pleasure houses pure and simple, as well as subsidiary country estates within a short carriage drive of the metropolis. Ham House, which housed the Lauderdale library in the seventeenth century and the library assembled by the Earls of Dysart in the eighteenth (fig. 182), in some ways combined elements of all three. Writing in 1904, the historian of book collecting William Younger Fletcher (1830–1913) beautifully captured the flavour of the Dysart collection before its dispersal in 1938:

> This little room is perhaps the smallest of the libraries of Europe, and yet in proportion to its size it contains books of greater value than any other. The Library is lighted by two small windows, which are generally kept closely shuttered, so that neither light not the heat of the sun may injure the books. In the centre of the room is one great table, upon which are laid some of the folios and large books. There is a quaint set of oaken steps with a most convenient seat at the top with a shelf attached, so that the reader may rest a volume upon the shelf and enjoy it at leisure.
>
> All around on the closely filled shelves are the books, some bound in brown or crimson, and glowing with gold, some covered with white vellum or with parchment. There is not a modern book to be seen, nothing breaks the harmony; all speak of a bygone age, of an antique world. Here are the choice productions of the earliest presses, the editiones principes of the great classics, the books of the earliest dramatists, all the volumes which the book-collectors of a past age loved to acquire, and which a great nobleman who valued books delighted to have in his library. Here they rest, fitting memorials of the luxury of Grolier, of the affection of the Maioli, or the book-loving tastes of Henry, Prince of Wales, the short-lived youth on whom Ham was settled in 1610.[75]

Scarcely a mile away, another important library, that assembled by Lord Chancellor Clarendon, was destroyed by a fire at Petersham Lodge in October 1721.[76] At Syon, the Thames-side estate of the Earls and Dukes of Northumberland near

Isleworth, there had been an important library in
the time of the Wizard Earl of Northumberland in
the seventeenth century, and later, when Petworth
had passed sideways by inheritance and family
attention had shifted back to Alnwick, Syon House
still retained a substantial library. A large number
of books remain on site, housed in the magnificent
interior converted from a Long Gallery by Robert
Adam in 1763.[77] Upstream, but on the same
side of the river, George II's mistress Henrietta
Howard, Countess of Suffolk (c.1688–1767), had
a library of some 900 volumes at Marble Hill
House, her Palladian villa near Twickenham. Lady
Suffolk was the sister of John Hobart, 1st Earl
of Buckinghamshire (1693–1756), the owner of
Blickling. Her library at Marble Hill was a British
equivalent of the libraries of the French royal

mistresses (like her, often well-read and influential cultural figures as well as royal companions
and concubines) – a collection probably more
usefully compared with the dispersed and largely
unexplored private libraries of members of the
Hanoverian dynasty, rather than with libraries in
ordinary private houses.[78] Lady Suffolk's friend
Horace Walpole (1717–97) created a large and now
much better-known library at Strawberry Hill.
The Library at Strawberry Hill of 1754 (fig.183),
its bookcases designed by John Chute (1701–76) of
The Vyne and based on a Gothic tomb illustrated
in Dugdale's *Old St Paul's* (1658), is well known,
its original contents investigated and published
in meticulous detail in 1969.[79] A remarkably high
proportion of Walpole's library of 7,300 volumes
of 'curious books', sold in 1842, was reassembled

by the American collector Wilmarth 'Lefty' Lewis (1895–1979), the basis of the Lewis Walpole Library at Farmington, Connecticut.[80] Rich in classics and belles-lettres, despite Walpole's interest in provenance and his 'Glass Closet' of precious books, the Strawberry Hill library was essentially a working, reading library, arranged by subject and quite different in content and conception from the libraries assembled by the scholar-collectors of the late seventeenth and early eighteenth century.

Another riverside villa which once housed an important library was Chiswick House, designed by the 3rd Earl of Burlington and completed in 1729. 'Too small to inhabit, and too large to hang on one's watch', sniffed the courtier John, Lord Hervey (1696–1743), and indeed in its original form the villa was never intended to be lived in: the family apartments were in the adjacent great house, later remodelled and eventually demolished in 1956.[81] But it is often forgotten that, as well as works of art, the villa also housed Burlington's library, which occupied (after 1733) three interconnecting private rooms on the garden side of the ground floor, filled with books and drawings which had earlier been at Burlington House.[82] Still in place in 1869 but subsequently transferred to Chatsworth, the 1,318 titles on shelves at Chiswick are recorded in detail in the still-extant 1742 catalogue. Many remain in the Devonshire collection, as well as the four Kentian bookcases which once housed them.[83]

[184] The Library at Osterley Park in 1926

Osterley

The great house at Osterley was built for the financier Sir Thomas Gresham in the 1570s, but the current Library room (fig. 184), like the Syon Long Gallery, was the work of Robert Adam, part of his spectacular remodelling of the house for the banker Sir Francis Child (1735–63). Strongly architectural in character, Adam's Library is on the north side of the house, on the principal floor, and was completed in 1766, when Child was dead and his brother Robert had taken over. With its pedimented bookcases and Ionic pilasters, as Eileen Harris has noted, the Osterley Library resembles a classical temple turned inside out. Inset paintings set into the walls form an integral part of the scheme. The work of Adam's favourite decorative artist Antonio Zucchi, their subjects include *Britannia Encouraging and Rewarding Arts and Sciences* and *Virgil Reading his Works to Augustus and Octavia*, an iconography completely consonant with the splendid Neoclassical interior and the magnificent furniture by Linnell, including eight lyre-backed chairs, a pair of library tables and a large pedestal desk decorated with emblems of architecture, sculpture, painting and music.[84]

Despite the magnificence of the interiors, in the eighteenth century Osterley was as famous for books as for architecture. Based on the collection of the wealthy antiquarian Bryan Fairfax the Younger (1676–1749), the Osterley library was a rare example of an already existing collection purchased en bloc for a country house, just as Naudé had recommended a century earlier. Despite being offered for public sale in 1756, in the event the Fairfax library was sold intact before it could go to auction: Child paid £2,000 for it.[85] His family continued to take their books seriously, and a catalogue was published in 1771, a fairly early date for a printed catalogue of a private collection.[86] Issued in just twenty-five copies, the *Catalogus Librorum in Bibliotheca Osterleiensi* was the work of the classical scholar the Revd Dr Thomas Morell (1703–1784), a resident of nearby Turnham Green, an intimate of William Hogarth, from 1768 full-time secretary to the Society of Antiquaries and better known as the librettist of Handel's *Judas Maccabaeus* (1747).[87] Morell arranged the Osterley books in ten classes, his Latin headings reflective of both the contents of the shelves and the world view of an eighteenth-century savant:

1. *Theologia. Biblia; Aliique libri, sacri et historici.*

2. *Historia et antiquitates.*

3. *Historia, Itineraria, &c. Philosophia, Geographia, Architectura, Sculptura, Pictura, Numismata.*

4. *Scientiae et artes variae, continuatae.*

5. *Scientiae et Artium Variarum, Continuatio; cum libris miscellaneis, Hist. et Poet. –*

6. *Humaniorum Literae classici; aliique scriptores Graeci*

7. *Lexigraphi et Grammatici.*

8. *Classici, aliique scriptores Latini.*

9. *Libri Miscellanei.*

10. *Libri Miscellanei.*

Since the 1771 Osterley catalogue is in fact a printed shelf-list, it reveals not only what was in the collection, but the physical arrangement of the library, including the contents of the 'Presses' underneath each bay of shelving, a typical feature of English Libraries of the period. Though well supplied with comparatively recent publications, including many English books, the Osterley library was equally rich in early Continental printing. There were many incunables, incorporating at least fifteen Caxtons, as well as a beautifully illuminated copy of the 1462 Mainz Bible, printed on vellum by Gutenberg's successors Fust and Schöffer, and now in Cambridge University Library.[88] Other treasures included manuscripts, print albums, fine architectural books and a collection of printed ballads. As well as 2,130 books there were also volumes not described in detail in the catalogue.

Osterley illustrates more than most places the need to look at interiors and books together, since the books which the room was designed to house related to their physical setting as surely as the various elements of the decorative scheme were intended to mesh together. As originally conceived, the Osterley Library was nothing less than an extremely grand eighteenth-century *Gesamtkunstwerk*, an integrated work of art destroyed by the sale of the books in 1885. Some of most desirable were previously in the Harleian Library.[89] The Fairfax-Child copy of Caxton's *Recuyell of the Historyes of Troye* (Bruges, *c.*1473–4), the first book printed in English, belonged to Harley, was bought by Fairfax from Thomas Osborne, spent more than a century at Osterley and has been in the Morgan Library in New York since

1908.[90] Morgan's copies of Caxton's 1477 *Dictes or Sayengis of the Philosophres*, the 1478 Caxton Christine de Pizan, the 1481 *Mirrour of the World*, the 1485 *Morte d'Arthur* and the 1490 Virgil all have a similar history.[91] Books like these, together with the room and the Morell catalogue, are indicative of the grandeur of the Childs' aspirations and the depths of their pockets. This is true in a different way of another Child book, not an antiquarian trophy, but an exceptionally ambitious contemporary publication, William Hayes's *Portraits of Rare and Curious Birds*, a beautiful but bibliographically complex hand-coloured plate book of the exotic birds in the financiers' private aviary at Osterley, issued between 1794 and 1800.[92] By then the birds themselves had gone, dispersed after the death of Sarah Child in 1793.[93]

III · LIBRARIES MOVED FROM TOWN TO COUNTRY

Moving house

One historical phenomenon which would benefit from more study is the extent to which books from town libraries subsequently ended up in the country. The extant evidence rarely permits much beyond cautious conjecture, town books migrating to ancestral shelves more-or-less unnoticed during the course of the nineteenth and twentieth centuries. In other cases we know that libraries assembled in London and carefully deployed in specially designed accommodation were subsequently shifted to country houses, sometimes by choice and sometimes because of accidents of inheritance. Among the most spectacular instances are the libraries of the 3rd Earl of Sunderland, moved to Blenheim by his son and dispersed in 1882, and the still-extant library of Sir Richard Ellys, since the 1740s at Blickling. In both cases major libraries assembled with skill, purpose and discrimination by sophisticated metropolitan collectors effectively went to sleep in the country, ignored by successive generations of aristocratic owners who had played no part in their assembly and displayed only a limited understanding of what they had inherited.

The Sunderland Library certainly impressed Evelyn, who saw it in 1695, noting in his diary: 'Dined at the Earl of Sunderland … My Lord shewed me his incomparable Library now againe improved by many books.'[94] Like other collectors of his generation, Sunderland, a powerful Whig

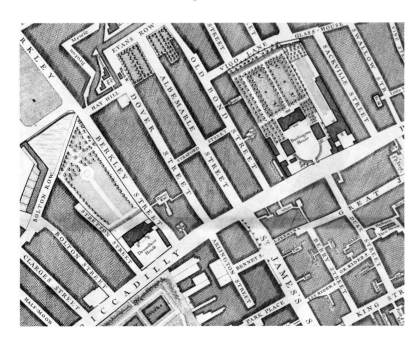

politician, educated at Leiden and undeniably studious, kept his library in London, latterly at Sunderland House just opposite St James's, Piccadilly, which he purchased in 1710. However, his marriage to Anne Churchill, daughter of the great Duke of Marlborough, resulted ultimately in the couple's son succeeding as 3rd Duke of Marlborough in 1733, and this led to the transfer of the books to Blenheim, where they were by 1749.[95] Sunderland was a serious bibliophile, his collecting fuelled by a lucrative political career. His library contained an almost complete sequence of first editions and early editions of the major classical texts, over 160 early Bibles, Americana, tracts, early English books and thousands of early Renaissance books. At the time of his premature death the collection, acclaimed as one of the finest private libraries in Europe, consisted of nearly 21,000 books, many of the earlier ones printed on vellum.[96] Based on the library of the Dutch classical scholar Hadrian Beverland (c.1651–1716), which the twenty-year-old Sunderland had purchased for £200 in 1693, it was housed in a purpose-built home built onto the back of Sunderland House between 1719 and 1722.[97] This is clearly visible in John Rocque's 1746 street map of London (fig.185).[98] It greatly impressed John Macky, who, while admiring the Library in Sunderland's country seat at Althorp, thought his town Library 'one of the greatest Curiosities in London for a Learned Traveller', acclaiming it as

[185] Part of John Rocque's 1746 map of London, Westminster and Southwark from Dunham Massey Library, showing the location of aristocratic town houses in the West End. Among others, as well as the library in Devonshire House, the Harley's London base was in Dover Street; Sir Richard Ellys's library was probably in Bolton Street; and the 150-foot library extension reaching into the garden on the back of Sunderland House can be clearly seen just to the west of Sackville Street.

the finest in Europe, both for the Disposition of the Appartments, as of the Books: the Rooms divided into Five Appartments, are full 150 Foot long, with two Stories of Windows, and a Gallery runs round the whole of the Second Story, for the taking down Books. No nobleman in any Nation hath taken greater care to make his Collection compleat, nor does he spare any cost for the most valuable and rare Books.[99]

Once at Blenheim, the books were placed in the Long Gallery, a room fitted up as a Picture Gallery in the 1720s and then converted into a Library to accommodate them. The Gallery, one of the largest rooms in any house in England, proved a far less suitable home for the books than their purpose-built accommodation in London. Sunderland had kept his books in fashionably up-to-date wall shelving, fourteen tiers high.[100] At Blenheim, too, the books were placed along the walls in richly carved bookcases, but those on the 200-foot east wall were exposed to direct sunlight, while the cases placed in blocked window apertures at either end of the Gallery proved prone to damp.[101] Visitors in 1789 were invited by their guidebook to admire 'the grand SUNDERLAND collection of books, comprising upwards of twenty thousand volumes, in various languages arts, and sciences; all arranged in commodious cases with latticed doors', but in reality the library was going to sleep.[102] When a printed catalogue was prepared in 1872, its editors George Parker and W. H. Bliss, both on the staff of the Bodleian, were furious that the duke refused them access to the books, insisting that they were simply revising an existing handwritten catalogue compiled by the former Blenheim librarian Vaughan Thomas (1775–1858), a High Church Oxford antiquarian and ecclesiastical pluralist, whose work they derided as incomplete and inaccurate.[103] As their note in the Bodleian's copy shows, the 1872 Blenheim catalogue was widely recognised for what it was, not a working catalogue for a living library cherished by the 7th Duke of Marlborough, but a botched reissue of a never very good home-made catalogue, the first stage of a campaign designed to end the Marlboroughs' financial problems by selling the long-unwanted books in the Long Library.[104]

A library moved from Piccadilly to Norfolk

A similar history is discernible at Blickling, where the library of Sir Richard Ellys (1682–1742; fig.186) still fills the Jacobean Long Gallery in the former home of Ellys's distant cousin, the 1st Earl of Buckinghamshire. Despite the splendour of his library, Ellys remains an enigmatic figure, a wealthy Lincolnshire baronet whose papers were destroyed in a house fire in 1834, an accomplished classical scholar and a Dissenter, who was the chief financial backer of the London congregation led by the Nonconformist divine Dr Edmund Calamy (1671–1732). A great landowner whose principal residence was Nocton Hall near Lincoln, Ellys also owned a town house in Bolton Street, Piccadilly, as well as Place Hall, a suburban villa south of the then-village of Ealing, which he purchased in 1729.[105] He inherited a library of about 1,200 books from his father in 1727, and two hundred of these were swiftly despatched from Nocton to London, where it seems that Ellys kept his most cherished books.[106] Space was evidently a problem, and we know that there were major building works at Bolton Street in the last five years of Ellys's life, resulting in the eventual transformation of the single plot occupied by his first wife's family since 1713 into a large mansion created by knocking five adjacent houses together.[107] Though it has long since left London, the library, only slightly dented by a sale in 1932, is of the utmost magnificence, packed with fine books, some grandiose, but others suggestive of a subtle and understated interest in the curious and the rare, and a keen appreciation of bibliographical niceties.[108]

Ellys's partner in his great enterprise was his librarian Dr John Mitchell (c.1685–1751), 'a learned physician' and a Scot, though the collector also took advice from the bibliographer Michael Maittaire (1668–1747). He was also a respected member and patron of the Spalding Gentlemen's Society, and was surrounded by a coterie of dependents and admirers.[109] These included his chaplain Andrew Gifford (1700–84), a numismatist, Fellow of the Society of Antiquaries and from 1757 an Assistant Librarian at the newly founded British Museum. A serious collector in his own right, Gifford bequeathed his library to the Bristol Baptist College, his greatest treasure one of only two known copies of the 1526 Tyndale New Testament, a book which had once belonged to Harley and was purchased by the British Library in 1995.[110] As a staunch Calvinist, Ellys, like his chaplain, was evidently interested in the connections between the progress of Protestantism and

[186] Missing portrait by Thomas Frye (1710–1762) of Sir Richard Ellys, original owner of the core of the library now at Blickling Hall (whereabouts unknown)

the spread of printing, and the Reformation-era books at Blickling are predictably outstanding, ranging from an exquisitely illuminated copy of the 1519 Erasmus Greek New Testament through to the Ferrara Ladino Old Testament of 1553.[111] Other books in a similar vein include two copies of the 1535 Coverdale Bible, sundry sixteenth-century English books and the 1517 Complutensian Polyglot Bible, a landmark in biblical scholarship which had formerly belonged to the family of the scholar-printer Frans Raphelengius (1539–97), who had supervised the printing of the Antwerp Polyglot (1568–73) for Plantin.[112] The continuing potency of this distinctive religious tradition is evident in the interest which Ellys, MP for Boston in Lincolnshire, displayed for the Protestant inhabitants of New England, whom he 'esteemed a manly people', according to a note by Thomas Holls in his copy of Ellys's *Fortuita Sacra*, a philological treatise on the Creeds.[113] Among other high points of the collection are his copy of the 'Eliot Indian Bible' of 1663, the first Bible printed in British North America and a book which miraculously escaped sale in 1932, as well as the copy of the 1723 Harvard library catalogue sent to 'R. Ellys Esq.ʳ', clearly being considered as a potential benefactor.[114] Indeed, Ellys's interest in America was sufficiently well known that it seems that New England's first university was eyeing up his collection, a transfer which fortunately never came to pass, as Harvard Library burned to the ground in 1764.[115]

Back in England, Ellys's bibliographical reference books, his collection of marked-up sale catalogues, the library catalogues compiled by Mitchell, and the tersely learned notes written into many of the books still tell their own tale. Few of Ellys's books contain contemporary marginal notes. On the other hand Maittaire writes that 'the author was very exact, and was at immense pains' in the Blickling copy of Andrew Maunsell's *First Part of the Catalogue of English Printed Books* (1595) – the first English bibliography – and that 'these are the first Greek Types that ever were used in France, as Mr Maittaire assured me', in a compilation of Greek texts printed in Paris in 1512, which indicates engagement with books far removed from clichés about conspicuous consumption, still less from the lofty generalisations of Lord Chesterfield.[116] Mitchell, too, emerges from the Blickling books and from scraps of surviving correspondence as an industrious and learned man, his characteristic 'M' written into many of Ellys's books to show that he had catalogued them, and his medical training standing him in good stead in Ellys's household, as the great collector spent his last year as a chronic invalid, 'his limbs tormented by a terrible gout'.[117] Like Ellys, Mitchell was a fully paid-up member of a still-vibrant international Protestant network, a man who first came to his master's attention through an appeal for the support of distressed Livonian Protestants.[118]

But Ellys, as well as being a theologian, religious enthusiast and landowner, was also a sophisticated collector and a classical scholar. Educated in his youth by his father's chaplain Joseph Farrow (1652?–92), a Nonconformist graduate of Magdalene College, Cambridge, and friend of John Locke, he found his way to the Netherlands after travels on the Continent. Although he entered neither university, he appears to have been educated at Leiden and Utrecht, key intellectual centres. He was a pupil of the German philologist Ludolf Kuster (1670–1716), who reckoned his command of Greek the equal of anyone's in Europe.[119] His many early books include incunabula and several thousand sixteenth-century books. Books from the libraries and cabinets of great Continental collectors from the Medicis to sixteenth-century French collectors like Claude de Laubespine and Grolier (four bindings, including the only surviving velvet binding) mark him out to be as enthusiastic a disciple of the humanist tradition as any Renaissance princeling.[120] Many of these books had, of course, been collectable for a long time by the 1730s, and Ellys's shelves contained books from many great libraries, including the dispersed Colbert collection, the library of Naudé's friend Jean de Cordes (1570–1642), the Uilenbroeck library (sold in Amsterdam in 1729), as well as volumes which had belonged to English collectors like Thomas Rawlinson and John Bridges (sold in 1726), who had themselves bought from earlier Continental libraries. Books also came from a myriad of other sources, now coming to light as the books are properly examined for the first time since the eighteenth century. Collectively a compelling witness to the increasing centrality of London to the international trade in rare books, Ellys also acquired books from his home county of Lincolnshire, including two Anglo-Saxon manuscripts, purchased from the Lincoln antiquarian William Pownall (1692–1735) in 1725.[121] He also retained agents at many of the great continental sales of the era. If some were clearly professional bookmen, others included the bibliophile Robert Hampden-Trevor (1706–83), British Ambassador in The Hague from 1739 to 1741, a distant relation and, like Buckinghamshire and Horatio Walpole (1678–1757), an aspiring claimant to Ellys's libraries and his estates, as the collector was childless.[122]

The ultimate purpose of Ellys's library remains enigmatic. Unlike dynastic libraries in other great houses, the books at Blickling contain little explicit evidence of use. There is certainly no sense, as at nearby Felbrigg Hall, of a great library interacting over several centuries with the owners of the surrounding estate who had assembled it. Aside from the editions themselves, the interest of the individual copies derives from the bibliographical notes added by Ellys and Mitchell, and the evidence of their previous history. One interpretation of this would be that Ellys was more interested in collecting than reading. This is not wholly implausible but is deflated by the fact that he bought contemporary books of all kinds, in great numbers, and did not confine himself to publications which were already two hundred or more years old. The contemporary books in Ellys's library range from pamphlets through to a magnificent set of the *cabinet du roi*, describing the court and collections of the Kings of France, and suggest a wider engagement with current events than one might have expected. Another interpretation, perhaps more

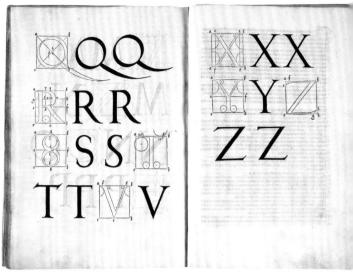

plausible in the light of his evident scholarship and industry, is that Ellys's library was a work still in progress at the time of his death in 1742, when he was sixty years old. There was clearly a degree of scrabbling around to find a future for Ellys's books as death approached, and as it became ever more obvious that the great collector would never father an heir. The gossip mill asserted he intended to leave his books to a Dissenting academy, or that it would go to America, while meanwhile the competitor claimants circled like vultures.[123] Thomas Hollis, at least, had heard all of these rumours, and also suggested that, had Ellys lived just a decade longer, the books would have gone to the British Museum on its foundation in 1753.[124] In reality Ellys, having inherited the family estates in 1727, had barely a decade and a half to devote his family's ample resources to books, leaving little time either for their intensive use or even to work out how, in the long term, they might best be housed or employed. Maurice Johnson, the founder of the Spalding Gentlemen's Society, was in no doubt as to Ellys's plans. Writing in 1738, he noted not only that Ellys had recently enlarged 'his Noble Library', but that further enlargements were in progress and that, when they were finished, the Library was 'to become the general rendezvous of all his Reading friends', adding 'and indeed the learned Owner not only uses & understands his Treasures but freely allows the full use of them even to his Friends own houses'.[125]

On Ellys's death his books were swiftly transferred to Norfolk, an operation probably organised by John Mitchell, his last service to the library which he had done so much to create. The move itself was no mean feat and cost over £150, which included £55 1s. 3d. for packing cases and £62 14s. 5d. for carriage, presumably by road (one wonders whether those involved were aware of the catastrophe which had recently befallen the library of Bishop Thomas Tanner, transported from Norwich to Oxford by barge in 1731, which had to be dried out on the Bodleian leads after toppling into the water).[126] Though Blickling already had a Library room, the scale of the Ellys collection was such that it must have been obvious that something altogether larger was required. As at Blenheim, the choice fell on the Long Gallery ('an extraordinary good gallery' thought an appraiser in 1756), built in the reign of James I, the largest room in the house, and only recently fitted up as a Picture Gallery.[127] The recently painted full-length portraits of 'Norfolk Worthies' were evicted, finding their way to the neighbouring staircase hall, and the Gallery was fitted in a slightly dated Palladian style (see fig. 4), with bookcases, with painted grisailles of classical subjects by Francis Hayman (1708–76), lining the walls. A bust of Ellys by Peter Scheemakers presided over it all, like a tutelary deity, surrounded by a galaxy of supporting luminaries:

Apollo	Plato	Pope	Vitruvius
Diana	Socrates	Shakespeare	Carracalla
Homer	Democritus	Milton	Venus
Seneca	Aristotle	Dryden	Niobe daughter
Horace	Hypocrates	Newton	Vestal Virgin
Cicero	Agathocles	Inigo Jones	Antinous
Virgil	Demosthenes	Palladio	Jupiter[128]

[187] Double page in Gabriel Martin, *Catalogus librorum bibliothecae illustrissimi viri Caroli Henrici Comitis de Hoym, olim Regis Poloniae Augusti II. Apud Regem Christianissimum Legati Extraordinarii*, Paris 1738, from the Ellys collection (Blickling Hall)

[188] Double page in Albrecht Dürer, *Vnderweysung der Messung, mit dem Zirckel vn[d] Richtscheyt, in Linien, ebnen vnnd gantzen Corporen*, Nuremberg 1525 (Blickling Hall)

A visitor in 1745 was impressed, enthusing at the sight of

> *a very beautifull Library 132 × 20 × 18. & a rich Cieling, a charming Chimneypiece design'd by Ld. Burlington. Sr Rich'd Ellis who left the Book's his Busto is plac'd between the broken parts of a pediment which turn into 2 scrolls, & from the middle Point of each one to the other hangs a garland neatly executed in white marble quite detach'd only pendant at each end. Over the Books are Heads of most famous Poets, Homer &c stand in a window.*[129]

The overall effect of this scheme, now lost, must have been overwhelming. Yet despite its grandeur, the Gallery, with two exposed outside walls, is a difficult environment for books, prone to fluctuations of temperature and humidity, illustrative as at Blenheim of the problems inherent in unbookish people lodging large numbers of books in spaces never intended for them. As if that were not enough, Ellys's books swiftly became the subject of a protracted family tussle. On the death of the 2nd Earl of Buckinghamshire in 1793 Blickling passed to his daughter Caroline, Lady Suffield, but in default of a direct male heir the title and the former Ellys estates in Lincolnshire went to the dead earl's half-brother George Hobart (1731–1804). By then Hobart already owned the Ellys library, which he had inherited from his mother Elizabeth Bristow (d.1762), who herself inherited it, along with other personal possessions, on the death of her husband the 1st Earl in 1756.[130] For almost fifty years, therefore, Blickling and its great library belonged to different members of the same family, an obviously precarious situation, resolved only in 1802, when the elderly 3rd Earl of Buckinghamshire accepted an offer of £2,500 for the books. The 2nd Earl of Buckinghamshire had evidently regarded the Ellys library as a thoroughgoing nuisance. Taking it for granted that it was likely to be removed by his half-brother, he set aside money in his will to buy another library to replace it, enjoining that any books purchased should be 'of most general use and as well for Information as Entertainment', and ordering – echoing Lord Chesterfield – 'that no high prices be paid for such Books as derive particular Merit only from being scarce or finely bound'.[131]

Only for a brief period in the nineteenth century did the Blickling library receive the attention and respect which its riches deserved. In Lady Suffield's time the collection had two capable and learned librarians. The first, the Revd Mr Joseph Churchill, was also Lady Suffield's chaplain, and entertained Dibdin when he visited Blickling. The second, James Bulwer (1794–1879), was a member of a well-known Norfolk clerical dynasty, and a founder member of the Norfolk and Norwich Archaeological Society. Both men answered public enquiries and made the Blickling library available to scholars, and both evidently had a solid understanding of the books and manuscripts in their care.[132] Bulwer went on to work for Lady Suffield's nephew and successor, the short-lived 8th Marquess of Lothian (1832–70), overseeing the 1858 refit of the Long Gallery by the Dublin architect Benjamin Woodward (1816–61), which involved muscular Gothic bookcases with carvings by the O'Shea brothers, a massive thirteenth-century-style fireplace and spectacular pre-Raphaelite murals by John Hungerford Pollen (1820–1902).[133] Lothian also laid plans for a proper printed catalogue of his two great libraries, at Blickling and at Newbattle, but with his early death the project was abandoned and thereafter the books slumbered.[134] From 1870 to 1930 Blickling functioned first as a dower house and then as a place of refuge for the mentally disabled 10th Marquess, before being inherited by a cousin, whose only real impact on the library was the sale of books and manuscripts in 1932, and his decision to bequeath the house and its contents to the National Trust. After decades of paying lip service to the great library, only in the 1990s did the Trust finally start to get to grips with it in earnest.

[189] Detail from a page in Peter Langtoft, Verse Chronicle, fourteenth century (Blickling Hall)

CHAPTER ELEVEN

Reading and Borrowing
Using the Library

I · BOUGHT BY THE YARD?

'Did anyone read them?' My own experience was that this was the single most commonly asked question by visitors to National Trust libraries. What gradually became more intriguing was not that so many country house visitors were convinced that no one could ever have read the books on the shelves, but that an appreciable number were reluctant to discard the idea even when presented with evidence that it was untrue. A variant, often heard on tours in private houses, involves owners and volunteer guides proudly asserting that the books on their own shelves were read, but claiming that this made their library particularly special because books in other houses were not.

The 'bought by the yard' myth is a pervasive one, endlessly repeated in newspaper articles, blogs and works of fiction. So commonplace has it become that it regularly slips into guidebooks, the scripts of guided tours and even into articles in peer-reviewed journals. Dickens wrote about it in *Hard Times*, and Tom Sharpe in *Porterhouse Blue*, while in the eighteenth century Alexander Pope was derisive about book collectors, writing with scorn in his *Epistle to the Earl of Burlington*:

> *His Study! With what Authors is it stor'd?*
> *In Books, not Authors, curious is my Lord;*
> *To all their dated Backs he turns you round,*
> *These Aldus printed, those Du Suëil has bound.*
> *Lo some are Vellom, and the rest as good*
> *For all his Lordship knows, they are but Wood.*[1]

The unread library provides the perfect symbol of decadence and stupidity, brilliantly satirised by the columnist Flann O'Brien in the send-up 'Buchhandlung' in the *Irish Times* column 'Cruiskeen Lawn', with proposals for 'a professional book-handler, a person who will maul the books of illiterate, but wealthy, upstarts so that the books will look as if they have been read and re-read by their owners'.[2] In reality, while wealthy collectors from Harley to Huntington certainly acquired pre-existing libraries, there is little evidence for the bulk buying of books to fill shelves. I have never seen a bill for the purchasing of books by the yard or by any other unit of measurement, though certainly nineteenth-century architectural treatises make it clear that the houses of the newly rich required a Library. That is not to say that all country house owners always esteemed their libraries equally, especially if books had been inherited from previous generations. The story that, when Lord Salisbury, visiting Chatsworth in the late nineteenth century, asked how one got into the Library gallery, a puzzled Duke of Devonshire replied 'damned if I know' may be apocryphal. It may also mask a deeper truth.[3] Elsewhere, in all generations there were inevitably some who remained resolutely uninterested in libraries and their contents. Writing from Brussels in 1760, the tutor of the 2nd Earl of Massereene (1743–1805) gloomily informed his charge's mother that the young Irish nobleman 'never opens a book except to read aloud to me or hear me read'.[4]

[190] Detail of the front cover of the library catalogue from Appuldurcombe (1777), Isle of Wight (Lincolnshire Archives)

CATALOGUE OF THE LIBRARY OF SIR RICHARD WORSLEY, BAR.T OF APPULDURCOMBE PARK, ISLE OF WIGHT.

1777.

_____

NOTE, NO PERSON TO TAKE A BOOK OUT OF THIS LIBRARY, WITHOUT LEAVING THEIR NAME AND DATE ON PAPER, IN THE PLACE OF IT.

Nonetheless my own view, based on two decades poking around country house books, is that the 'bought by the yard' myth could very helpfully be laid to rest. At the very least we need to face the fact that book buying as overtly conspicuous consumption was the exception rather than the norm. This is abundantly apparent from examining books in large numbers of libraries of all periods, where, for the most part, the physical evidence of the books themselves indicates fairly clearly that many, and in some libraries most, were read. Collections like Dr Worth's Library in Dublin – the time-capsule collection of an eighteenth-century physician still absolutely pristine because for two hundred years the books were locked undisturbed in their presses in the city's main teaching hospital – are rarely found in country houses.

II · COUNTRY HOUSE READING

The history of reading has been a growth area in recent humanities scholarship. Unsurprisingly, when dealing with such a fugitive activity, it is not straightforward. Underlying it lurk complex questions about what reading is, and what we and our ancestors do or did when casting an eye over apparently arbitrary marks impressed on pieces of paper. Historically the relationship between reading and writing is less than straightforward, as well as between reading silently and reading out loud, either privately or as a social activity, the latter, unsurprisingly, popular in country houses.[5] Then there is the question of mechanics: the practical realities of reading by candlelight, of taking notes with pen and ink. In a nutshell it is too easy to assume that we know what reading is, and how, where and when it was done.

Anyone wanting to understand the economics underlying the functioning of a landed estate can analyse rent rolls, and read bills and receipts, before placing the resulting statistics in context and drawing conclusions from them. A historian of upholstery can use documentary evidence in a similar way. All can, if they wish, place their findings within their preferred theoretical framework. By contrast, reading was an activity which often proceeded in a way which has left no evidence, or evidence hard to read or interpret.

The most obvious way to tell if a book has been read is to see whether it contains handwritten notes, or at least try to gauge whether it appears to have been extensively handled. Flann O'Brien's

book-maulers offered a special *traitement superbe*, charging £32 7s. 6d. for particularly brutal handling, followed by 'suitable passages in not less than fifty per cent of the books to be underlined in good-quality red ink and an appropriate phrase … inserted in the margin'. Real book owners, on the other hand, may or may not have marked their books, but whether they did could be determined by a range of historical factors. My own impression, unsupported by rafts of statistical data, is that in most libraries, many and sometimes most books contain evidence of reading or at least of human interaction. But to a large extent whether people wrote in the margins of books was determined not just by personal preference, but by fashion. The earlier a book, the more likely it is to contain marginal notes, as readers across early modern Europe were taught to annotate their books (fig. 191).[6] Later, these assumptions were gradually turned on their head. Many of the incunabula in the Spencer Collection are crisp and pristine, like the books of other grand early nineteenth-century collectors, washed of 'imperfections', and often rebound, in pursuit of the bibliomaniacal ideal of 'the clean copy'. Of course very few nineteenth-century collectors would have been 'reading' incunables or illuminated manuscripts, which were collected fundamentally as antiquarian objects and works of art. But over time the cult of the clean copy reached more recent books. A fair number of eighteenth- and particularly nineteenth-century country house books are entirely 'clean'. This could indicate that they were not read, but in other cases it seems likely that it is because their owners had absorbed the message that it was wrong to write in books. Speaking not long before her death, the long-lived Lady Mairi Bury (1921–2009), youngest daughter of the 6th Marquess of Londonderry, was puzzled that anyone should have expected her parents' books at Mount Stewart in County Down to contain marginal notes. Her parents had taught her not to write in books – it was disrespectful to the book, and to future readers. This did not mean that the Londonderrys did not read. Lady Mairi was clear that they did, and other evidence bears out that she was right, but the evidence of their reading is not to be found in the books.[7] If marginal notes in other libraries, especially earlier ones, provide clear evidence of reading, the comparative absence of notes at Mount Stewart and other houses like it certainly cannot be taken as clear evidence of non-reading.

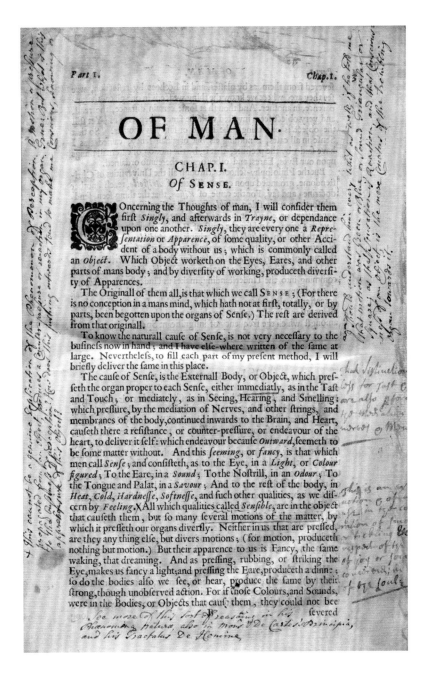

[191] Extract from Thomas Hobbes, *Leviathan*, London 1651, with notes in the hand of an early owner, David Conyngham (Springhill)

Marks on books may be difficult to interpret. No one examining books from Macaulay's library at Wallington in Northumberland could doubt that the historian read his books, and his often pungent comments leave little doubt as to what he thought of what he was reading.[8] At Ickworth, on the other hand, the 1st Earl of Bristol (1665–1751) liked to read with a pencil in hand, leaving cryptic marks in the margins. Even when spotted, they reveal little of the reader's mental processes, though they do give an indication of which passages interested Lord Bristol. Similar marks can be found in Horace Walpole's books, formerly at Strawberry

Hill, tangible evidence of reading from a man who declared: 'I love nothing so much as writing notes in my books.' A cross and an asterisk marked passages of unusual interest, while an exclamation mark signified scorn.[9] At Panshanger, Mary, Countess Cooper (1685–1724), a Lady of the Bedchamber to the well-read Queen Caroline of Ansbach, was a great annotator, a fact noted in the nineteenth century but no longer possible to investigate in detail, as the house, in Hertfordshire, was demolished in the early 1950s and the library dispersed.[10] Elsewhere, researchers face loss of evidence of a different kind. At Erddig it was customary in the eighteenth century for notes to be written not in the margins, but on slips of papers inserted into the books. These were removed by volunteers acting for the National Trust in the 1970s and placed in a separate file where, detached from the books to which they referred, they are now of limited use to anyone interested in reading. If the Erddig habit was replicated elsewhere, then it is likely similar paper slips have been removed elsewhere and perhaps discarded.

In other cases we know from specific notes on title pages and endpapers about instances of reading. In a copy of John Selden's *Titles of Honor* (1631) now at Yale, Lady Anne Clifford noted: 'I beegane to overloke this Booke the 18 of February and I did make an end of reding, or over loking itt all over the first of Marche following 1638.'[11] Similar notes can be found in country house books of all periods. At Wallington, the home of the famously and self-consciously intellectual Trevelyans, large numbers of books have reading dates pencilled into them, and favoured books were read again and again.[12] A little later, the self-educated 1st Lord Fairhaven (1896–1966), better known for bindings and colour-plate books, but clearly an autodidact, was assiduous in writing reading dates into his 'ordinary' books at Anglesey Abbey, near Cambridge.[13]

Drawing conclusions about reading from wear and tear is more problematic. Faced with the second edition of *Pride and Prejudice* at Saltram, it is difficult to resist the conclusion that Jane Austen's most famous novel was especially esteemed there, since it is in particularly poor condition. This is inherently problematic, because there are all sorts of reasons why books might be in poorer condition than their neighbours, ranging from faults in their materials and construction through to accidental damage in modern times. We may be on safer ground with entire libraries. At Wallington conservators working on the books have noted the library as a whole is in poorer condition than would be expected from a collection of comparatively recent books.[14] Since this correlates precisely with the evidence of reading inside them, the correct inference, clearly, is that the books are fragile because they were intensively used.

In the absence of notes in the margins, documentary sources can provide useful insights into the use of libraries. Commonplace books, when they survive, are among the most remarkable. Sixteenth- and seventeenth-century readers were taught to read pen in hand. According to Roger North, it was the 'constant practice' of the 1st Lord Guilford (1637–85) 'to commonplace as he read', because 'the looking over a commonplace book on any occasion gave him a sort of survey of what he had read about ... which refreshed them somewhat in his memory'.[15] As late as 1793, Elizabeth Sykes of Sledmere was noting in her own commonplace book: 'Young Persons should have always at hand a *Common Place Book*, for keeping in remembrance observations in reading, reflecting, conversing, travelling.' Presumably taking dictation from her governess, she continued:

> First it keeps the attention awake, in order that
>   nothing of importance may escape ... A person
>   who reads merely for amusement gives little
>   attention ... But let a Common Place Book be in
>   view: attention is on the stretch to find matter, &
>   impressions are made that the memory retains.
> Next the judgment is in constant exercise, in order to
>   distinguish what particulars deserve remembrance.
> Third. Perseverance in this practice brings on a habit
>   of expressing our thoughts readily, & distinctly.
> Fourth. A facility of writing quickly currently
>   is acquired.
> And in the last place: it fills up the time pleasantly,
>   and makes activity habitual.[16]

Earlier commonplace book examples are not unusual; the 1st Earl of Northampton's, formerly at Naworth Castle, and Sir Francis Willoughby's, from Wollaton, both went with libraries now dispersed. Willoughby (1547–96) took notes from chronicles by Stowe, Hall, Holinshed and Polydore Virgil, as well as from Palladio. The impression of studious activity is reinforced by marginal notes in surviving books at Nottingham University.[17] His descendant the naturalist Francis Willoughby (1635–72) was equally industrious, his reading recorded in a massive

commonplace book, while the commonplace books of Rachel, Lady Fane, compiled between 1623 and 1633, include notes on sermons, on Latin grammar and vocabulary, notes on theological and devotional books, recipes, and abstracts of Seneca, written in English.[18] The 1st Earl of Warrington's commonplace book, now at Enville Hall in Staffordshire, provides insights into the use of his library at Dunham Massey, even more useful because Warrington's published advice to his son includes observations on reading.[19] The working notes of the 1st Duchess of Beaufort (1630–1715) show beyond doubt that she read extensively around her collection of natural history books, still at Badminton, an antidote to melancholy, from which she, like Robert Burton, sought refuge in books.[20]

Those who commented on their reading in letters and diaries were by definition uncommon readers, but sources exist from all periods which reveal how books were read. The range of experiences is potentially so varied that it could only adequately be captured in an online database, but a few examples provide food for thought. In 1731 the 5th Earl of Orrery wrote to a friend of the pleasures of a retired life, adding: 'My Books, My Horse and my Family are sufficient Entertainment.' Twenty years later, writing from the family's Irish house, Caledon, his wife wrote to the earl of how she filled time with letter-writing and outdoor pursuits, 'and when it grows dark we read, worke, play till tea-time, then read, work and play till nine'.[21] A little earlier, the daughter of Francis Willoughby recalled that it was the great naturalist's 'constant Custome to Study very hard from ye time he Rise, till eleven a Clock in ye Morning', before dining and then, unless there was company, returning to his books.[22] In 1788 William Windham of Felbrigg noted in his diary that he had read 'some portion of different French books' on a visit to nearby Costessey Hall. Two hundred years later the Yorkshire baronet Sir Marcus Worsley (1925–2012), of Hovingham Hall, revelled in Victorian novels and modern political biographies, ignoring his wife's protests that he really ought to take more interest in contemporary fiction.[23] In the late nineteenth century the Marchioness of Salisbury 'read voraciously all sorts and kinds of books' each evening at Hatfield.[24] In the 1770s the Scottish gentleman-lawyer John Erskine of Cambo kept a meticulous register of his reading, ploughing through 135 books between 1774 and 1781, peaking in 1780, when he got through thirty-two. Mostly in English, his varied

diet included Dr Burney's *Travels in Germany*, a
translation of Ariosto's *Orlando Furioso*, Sir William
Hamilton's recent description of the eruption of
Vesuvius, Gibbon's *Decline and Fall*, Hogarth's
Analysis of Beauty, Hume's *Essays*, and bestsellers
like Robertson's *History of America* and the *Sermons*
of the Scottish Enlightenment preacher Hugh
Blair (1718–1800).[25] In the mid-eighteenth century
William Constable read extensively in the library at
Burton Constable, taking notes as he did. Among his
reading, in both English and French, were works by
Bolingbroke, Voltaire, Buffon, Boerhaave and Francis
Willoughby, as well as Hook's *Micrographia* and
Burke's *Philosophical Enquiry into the Origin of our
Ideas of the Sublime and Beautiful*.[26] Somewhat earlier,
the 8th Earl of Pembroke (1656–1733) was acclaimed
by Defoe as 'a man of learning, and reading, beyond
most men of his lordship's high rank'.[27]

Reading could be a sociable activity. In the seventeenth century Lady Anne Clifford was frequently
read to by others, while at Calke towards the end
of the eighteenth century, the library contained
contemporary plays, the dramatis personae marked
up with the names of the members of the household
who read each part.[28] A little later, in the late 1820s,
Prince von Pückler-Muskau visited Cobham Hall
in Kent and noted: 'Yesterday after dinner we all sat
(nine persons) at least a couple of hours together in
the library, reading, – each, of course, I mean, in his

own book, – without a single word being spoken.'[29]
Sometimes readers read in ways which defied convention. Lady Mary Wortley Montagu (1689–1762)
covertly educated herself in her father's Library at
Thoresby Hall in Nottinghamshire, studying Latin
when 'everyone thought I was reading nothing but
romances', while Molly Lepel (fig. 192) of Ickworth
knew Latin, but was careful to conceal her learning.[30]

III · THE USE OF LIBRARIES BY OUTSIDERS

It is easy to underestimate the extent to which
outsiders used country house books. The library
at Arniston still has a copy of Arnot's *History of
Edinburgh*, read by Boswell while waiting to be
received, and in many houses guests might well find
their way to the library. The Somerset clergyman
John Skinner, visiting Stourhead in 1819, 'spent a
couple of hours in the library before breakfast',
something which was repeated on subsequent
visits.[31] Travelling round the Scottish Highlands
with Boswell, Dr Johnson, too, was conducted to the
library by several of his hosts, an alarming experience
as the English visitor cast an appraising eye over their
books.[32] Signs in several houses, enjoining browsers
to put books back in their proper place, show that
good behaviour could not be taken for granted:
there are nineteenth-century examples at Clandon in
Surrey, at Eastnor Castle in Herefordshire and a later
one at Mount Stewart. Another, perhaps earlier, is
preserved out of sight at Blickling. At Wallington the
Trevelyans' very literary house guests may have been
better behaved, but their librarian, David Wooster
(1824?–88), according to Augustus Hare 'always on
hand to find anything you want', presumably helped
to maintain order.[33] By contrast, when Dibdin, a
tourist rather than a guest, asked to take down books
at Castle Howard, he was firmly told: 'It is strictly
interdicted – unless there be an order from My Lord.'
When he protested that Lord Carlisle had granted
him permission, the housekeeper asked to see the
letter, which Dibdin was unable to produce.[34]

From browsing the shelves, it was only a short step
to informal loans. A note in the late seventeenth-
century catalogue of Petworth reveals that Daniel
Marot borrowed a copy of Montaigne from the
library, the only record that he was at Petworth.[35] In
Wales the antiquarian Thomas Pennant (1726–98)
borrowed copies of Nehemiah Grew's 1681 catalogue of the collections of the Royal Society and
Walter Charleton's *Exercitationes de Differentiis &*

Nominibus Animalium (1677) from the Mostyn library in 1757.[36] In Ireland Swift made use of the library at Castle Dobbs, in County Antrim, while at Felbrigg Humphry Repton and his wife borrowed books in 1782 and 1783, and were evidently familiar with the library, its arrangement and contents.[37] Country house borrowers were not necessarily figures of any special eminence. A certain Mrs Pallant borrowed a 1741 edition of Foxe's *Book of Martyrs* from Boxted Hall in Suffolk in May 1850, for example, while in 1790 a M. de Villedeuil, presumably a royalist refugee, borrowed some twenty-five books, many in French, at Burton Constable.[38]

The motivation for borrowing books varied, but often boiled down to the fact that prospective borrowers wanted certain books, and owners were prepared to lend them. At Sledmere an early twentieth-century correspondent wrote to Mark Sykes asking to borrow a couple of books on the French Revolution, explaining that he was out of money, and couldn't afford to buy them for himself.[39] Elsewhere, patronage and *noblesse oblige* played a role. The young A. L. Rowse (1903–97), a working-class Cornish boy, was shown over the library of the nearby big house by its elderly owner, a reward for winning a scholarship to the local secondary school.[40] At Felbrigg John Ketton lent books and papers to George Edwards (1850–1933), a once illiterate farmhand who went on to become General Secretary of the Agricultural Labourers' Union and a Labour MP.[41] In the more unstable environment of early twentieth-century Ireland, the radical nationalist poet Francis Ledwidge (1887–1917), the son of a farm labourer, was given the run of the library at Dunsany Castle in County Meath.[42]

Instances like these were the last gasp of a tradition which had endured for hundreds of years. In seventeenth-century Lancashire the mathematician Sir Jonas Moore (1617–79), a man of humble birth, read widely in the library of the Shuttleworth family, of nearby Gawthorpe Hall.[43] At Blenheim the 3rd Duke of Marlborough provided the classical scholar Jacob Bryant (1717–1804) with a house and allowed him unrestricted use of the library.[44] Elsewhere, particularly fine libraries attracted even those who themselves owned many books. The 1686 sale catalogue of the London library of the 1st Earl of Anglesey (1614–86) noted that 'many Persons of Honour … (tho' possessed of very great Libraries of their own) had frequent recourse to this for the perusal of many [books] out of the ordinary Road

of Learning.'[45] This was clearly true in other learned libraries of the period. In 1566 Archbishop Parker had thanked William Cecil for the loan of a manuscript in Cecil's library, 'in the riches whereof … I reioice as moche as thei wer in myn owne', while a century later some forty-one books were borrowed from the library at Salisbury House between 1637 and 1665.[46] Archbishop Ussher consulted a manuscript 'among my Lord of Pembroke's books', while in sixteenth-century Cornwall the historian Richard Carew borrowed a scientific treatise from the library of Sir Francis Godolphin (*c*.1534–1608) at Godolphin House, translated it from Italian to English, and returned it with thanks.[47] Books were clearly being loaned from Knole in the middle of the seventeenth century, a fact noted in garbled form in the library catalogue.[48] Rather later at Portledge, the north Devon gentleman Richard Coffin (1622–99) lent books to fifteen borrowers in 1684, their names now difficult to decipher after being crossed out in the library catalogue when they were returned.[49]

Sometimes the process could go wrong. In late seventeenth-century Scotland, for example, the Countess of Perth wrote to Anna, Countess of Eglinton, 'to plede peardon' for having kept a couple of books for so long.[50] To guard against this, in the mid-eighteenth century the owner of the small library at Panmure (Angus) demanded a deposit before letting books out.[51] Others were sterner, and at Blickling in the nineteenth century the rule was that scholars wishing to see books and manuscripts might consult them on site, but could not take them away.[52] By contrast, in 1850 a former subordinate at the War Office wrote to the Duke of Richmond, asking whether his son might have access to the library at Goodwood while stationed in nearby Chichester. The duke assented and agreed that the young man could take books back to his barracks, so long as he left a list of what he had borrowed.[53] Not all were so liberal, the Bedfordshire gentleman Richard How II (1727–1801) ruling that books might not be taken out of his library, with a single favoured exception, 'Miss Johnson', who was enjoined 'to write ye Title of ye Books on a Slip of paper & put in ye place whence ye Books are taken'.[54] A similar rule was enforced in Sir Richard Worsley's library at Appuldurcombe on the Isle of White, where the cover of the 1777 catalogue (fig. 190) carried the gold-blocked instruction: 'NOTE, NO PERSON TO TAKE A BOOK OUT OF THIS LIBRARY, WITHOUT LEAVING THEIR NAME AND DATE ON PAPER, IN THE PLACE OF IT.'[55]

IV · THE COUNTRY HOUSE LIBRARY AS LENDING LIBRARY

From slips of paper on the shelves it was only a short step to a borrowers' register – a situation which went beyond ad hoc loans and saw a library starting to function as something approaching a public lending library. Several surviving borrowers' registers run for many decades: at Dalkeith Palace in Scotland from 1795 to 1832, at Wilton from 1772 to 1826, and at Abbeyleix in Ireland from 1815 to 1916 (the 3rd Lady de Vesci was a younger daughter of the 11th Earl of Pembroke, of Wilton).[56] More typically, formalised arrangements often petered out, though whether that was because borrowing ceased or because the system broke down when no one was bothering to enforce it is less than clear. At another Irish house, Edgeworthstown, a projected borrowers' register (1848) at the back of the library catalogue contains only five names.[57] Even at Abbeyleix the majority of the 576 loans were clustered thickly between 1815 and 1838, with only five loans between then and 1863, and regular borrowing again down to the mid-1870s. Loans typically ran for several months, and the books borrowed were varied. The de Vescis expected borrowers to sign their books in and out, and judging by their names they were mostly Protestant gentlefolk. Formally shelf-marked books from the main collection were popular, but there was also a 'novel shelf' for current light reading, which may or may not have made it into the main run of the library.[58]

Borrowing appears to have been especially common in Scotland, either because of wider literacy or perhaps because of lack of other opportunities to obtain books. At Glamis, where the borrowers' register runs from 1740 to 1754, it is clear that borrowers included any respectable folk who asked, including friends, relations, factors, lawyers, ministers and tenants.[59] At Cullen House in Banffshire the antiquarian William Robertson (1740–1803), who was factor to Lord Findlater from 1766 to 1777, made extensive use of his employer's fine library.[60] Not far away, at Brodie Castle, a borrowers' register runs from 1780 to 1827, but the earlier pages have been torn out, presumably when books were returned, indicative in itself of the potential for evidence to vanish. Nonetheless even in its incomplete state it provides evidence of 300 to 400 loans from the castle library, sometimes of single volumes, and sometimes of larger clutches of books. Some of the borrowers came from a considerable distance away, and they included professional folk, women and members of neighbouring gentry families.[61]

When it came to servants' reading, there was a fine line between paternalism and social (and religious) control. In the reign of Charles II, the pious Lady Warwick not only scattered 'good books in all the common rooms and places of attendance', but expected them to be read.[62] Two centuries later there was a boxed servants' library at Felbrigg, bought from the Society for Promoting Christian Knowledge.[63] Grander servants' libraries existed in many houses, among them Blickling, Hatfield and Disraeli's Hughenden.[64] More are likely to have vanished without trace. At Charlecote the housekeeper, Mrs Philippa Hayes, a respectable widow described by a friend as 'a great Book worm', had the run of the library in the 1770s.[65] At Erddig at about the same time, a similarly trusted retainer, the lady's maid Betty Ratcliffe, had access to the library.[66]

At Tyntesfield the borrowers' register (fig. 233) was supervised by the chaplain, John Bacon Medley, who had also compiled a printed catalogue (another signal that a library was intended for wider use) and probably arranged the books by subject on the shelves. It, too, was intensively used for a short period, before petering out, perhaps on Medley's departure.[67] At Calke Abbey the relationship between the house library and the 'Calke Lending Library' – known only from a single copy of an early nineteenth-century handbill (fig. 1) – remains unclear. The lending library charged borrowers a penny a month and allowed just one loan at a time, to be collected at 3pm on each Thursday. It may have been elsewhere on the estate, but possibly it was a mechanism to allow tenants to borrow from the library in the Abbey.[68] How far down the social spectrum use extended must remain a matter for conjecture, but the characteristic inscription 'Calke Abbey Library', often written transversely across the title page, has a distinctly institutional flavour, more like a public library stamp than a personal ownership inscription. The Calke Lending Library raises many intriguing questions. The most important of these is one to which, as yet, there is no conclusive answer, namely whether the recoverable examples of lending and borrowing were exceptional, or whether the scraps of evidence that we have imply the existence of a phenomenon so widespread that only rarely did anyone bother to record it?

CHAPTER TWELVE

The Nouveaux Riches

New Money and New Libraries in the Nineteenth and Twentieth Centuries

I · THE INDUSTRIAL BOOM

The coming of new money

Joseph Nash's *Mansions of England in the Olden Times* was published in four tall slender volumes between 1839 and 1849. Taking advantage of the new technology of lithography, the author, a pupil of the architectural draftsman A. C. Pugin (1762–1832), offered his subscribers the sort of warm Romantic glow calculated to appeal to a public obsessed with the novels of Sir Walter Scott. Nash's stroke of genius was to populate picturesque views 'glowing with the genial warmth of baronial hospitality' with equally picturesque people: jousting at Compton Wynyates, Cavaliers and Roundheads at Aston Hall, or Henry VIII arriving at Hever. *The Mansions of England* was a tremendous success, and one MP claimed in the Commons that it had sparked off a tourist boom.[1] Like many traditions, 'Merrie England' was a recent invention. Every mellow manor house had started out raw and new, and for every country gentleman who could trace his ancestry back to the Norman Conquest, there were others whose forebears had been social climbing Elizabethan lawyers or grasping East India Company nabobs. Over many centuries whenever an old county family ran out of heirs or went down in the world, new money appeared, bought up the estates and took their place.

Nonetheless the fruits of industry and the loot of empire meant that the process gathered pace in the nineteenth century. Victorian Britain dominated the global economy, and London was the world centre of the financial markets and the hub of the international telegraph network. British entrepreneurs built railways, invented new industrial processes and exported consumer products to the corners of the globe. The first modern industrial cities sprang up in Birmingham and Manchester, and the north of England boomed. Dundee had jute magnates, and Belfast produced linen; ships were built on the Clyde and the Tyne, and coal was mined in Wales, the Midlands and Yorkshire. The British empire coloured the map pink, and colonial administrators ran their fiefdoms with an eye on the well-being of the Mother Country, opening up new markets to British goods and exploiting apparently inexhaustible sources of raw materials. Capital generated in an earlier era by slaves and sugar, from agricultural improvement and from the pioneering efforts of eighteenth-century industrialists, was already available to invest in the imperial project.

The consequences for the country house were profound. Long-established aristocratic dynasties did well out of the boom. The Butes, the Fitzwilliams of Wentworth Woodhouse and the Londonderrys were leading coal owners. This was reflected in the grandeur of their houses. But many nouveau-riche factory owners, financiers, South African diamond magnates or successful brewers decided that they, too, needed a slice of the country house cake. New money gobbled up estates and houses with a voracious appetite, and also built completely new houses, ranging from modest suburban villas for wealthy but practical men, through to gargantuan piles, crammed with treasures and set in acres of parkland. The alarmed,

[193] Detail of the ground plan of Tyntesfield, 1866

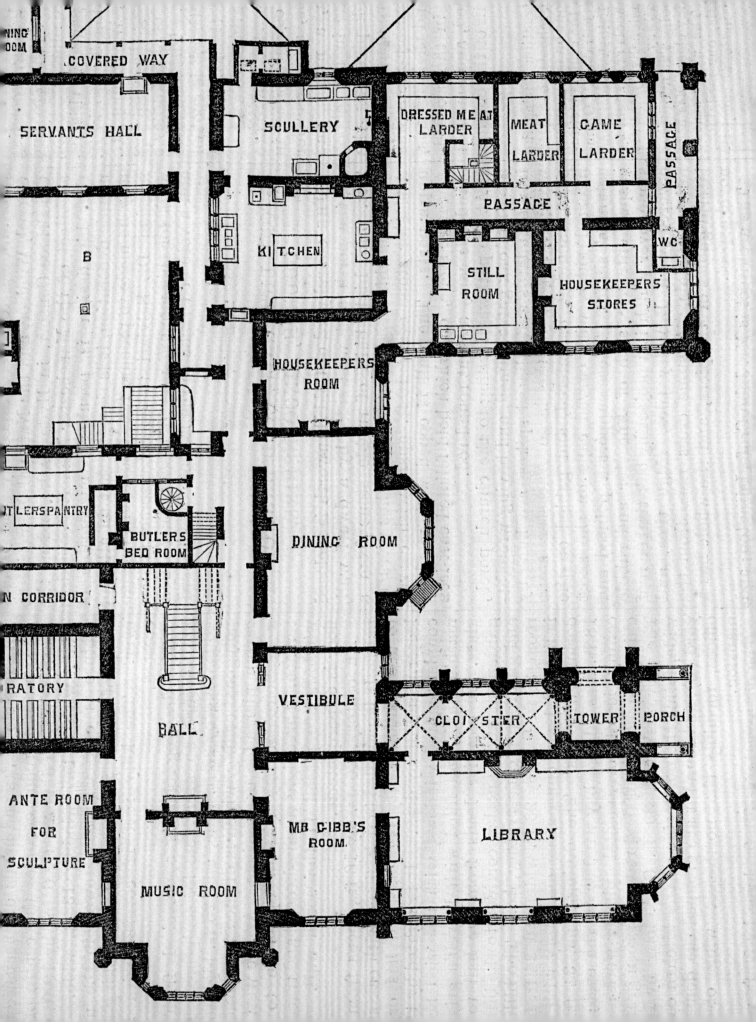

DINING ROOM

COVERED WAY

SERVANTS HALL

SCULLERY

DRESSED MEAT LARDER

MEAT LARDER

GAME LARDER

PASSAGE

B

KITCHEN

PASSAGE

WC

STILL ROOM

HOUSEKEEPERS STORES

HOUSEKEEPERS ROOM

BUTLERS PANTRY

BUTLERS BED ROOM

DINING ROOM

CORRIDOR

ORATORY

VESTIBULE

CLOISTER

TOWER

PORCH

HALL

ANTE ROOM

FOR

SCULPTURE

MR GIBB'S ROOM.

LIBRARY

MUSIC ROOM

the snobbish and the plain anti-Semitic could only wrinkle their noses in disgust. By the reign of Edward VII men and women whose great-grand-parents had mended shoes or eked out a cautious living in the ghettos of Continental Europe were becoming fully integrated into the elite, welcomed at court, fêted as cultural arbiters, or active in politics. Country houses were an important part of this, providing a venue where the new elite could entertain the old on increasingly equal terms, in a society where social and political prestige had traditionally been tied to the ownership of land. Wealthy or not, the new plutocrats needed the security of a great house and its surrounding acres to underpin their entry into the elite. Unlike her son and grandson, Queen Victoria generally resisted her Prime Ministers' attempts to persuade her to ennoble industrialists, but from Edwardian times a judicious combination of wealth, lifestyle and some suitably conspicuous public service could smooth the path to the ermine.[2] The weekend country house party became part of the established way of things, facilitated by the expansion of the railway network.[3]

Railways also allowed the self-made millionaire to set up permanently in the country, safe in the knowledge that the works or the family bank were only a short train ride away. The Newcastle arms manufacturer Sir William Armstrong (1810–1900; from 1887 Lord Armstrong) had first built himself a country retreat, Cragside, in Upper Coquetdale in 1863.[4] Only with the decision to build a railway linking the city to north Northumberland in 1870 did he take up full-time residence there. Armstrong was typical in becoming deeply attached to his country house, enlarged for him by the up-and-coming architect Richard Norman Shaw between 1869 and 1884.[5] Useful as it was for entertaining potential clients, or even royalty, Cragside provided a haven from the noise and pollution of a Victorian industrial city, and Armstrong suffered from respiratory problems. Another attraction, again typical, was that Cragside had been built to Armstrong's personal specification. Like many plutocrat houses, it was a new build. When Baron Ferdinand de Rothschild (1839–98) bought the Waddesdon estate from the impecunious Duke of Marlborough in 1874, there was no house on the site, and he was not even particularly attracted to the location, though it was convenient because there were trains from nearby Aylesbury back to London. He had

been looking for a substantial estate for some time and nothing else had come on the market.[6]

The parvenu's Library

The nouveau-riche country house was invariably provided with a Library, but in each case the motivation in having such a room, and indeed the form it took, varied considerably. For some it was evidently a matter of convention: the Library was an essential and necessary part of a gentleman's residence, a room which visitors would expect to find and which no *arriviste* could do without. For those who were unsure, published advice was not lacking, the architect Robert Kerr pronouncing in 1864 that the Library was 'primarily a sort of Morning-room for gentlemen rather than anything else. Their correspondence is done there, their reading, and, in some measure, their lounging; – and the Billiard-room, for instance, is not infrequently attached to it.'[7] Traditionally there has been a tendency to assume that libraries were created in country houses to make a parade of the owner's learning, a commonplace which clearly needs some refinement, as the sets of novels or runs of the *Racing Calendar* which figure quite prominently in many Victorian houses were hardly calculated to do that. For others, libraries were part and parcel of entertaining guests, or were esteemed, at least in part, because they were useful. But sometimes they went beyond practical utility, when a combination of intellectual curiosity, acquisitiveness and enormous wealth tipped the nouveau-riche country house owner into full-blown bibliomania.

Though not very large, the Library at Cragside (fig. 194) was still the largest room in the house at the time of its completion in 1872. With its low bookcases, Morris glass and oriental porcelain, its library functions are not immediately very prominent, and as the abundance of seating suggests, it was in part a comfortable room for the family and their guests.[8] However, it would certainly be a mistake to assume that it was not also a place for books and reading, as read the books certainly were, especially by house guests on wet days.[9] At 20 feet by 33 feet, the room was large enough to be plunged in gloom when the weather closed in, and lighting was taken very seriously. Shaw had originally intended oil lamps, but Armstrong – inventor, hydraulics expert and armaments manufacturer *extraordinaire* – preferred to light his Library using Joseph Swan's filament

light bulbs, one of the first rooms anywhere to take advantage of electricity. As Armstrong himself explained, eight lamps were required to provide the necessary light levels: 'Four are clustered in one globe of ground glass, suspended from the ceiling in the recess, and the remainder are placed, singly and in globes, in various parts of the room, upon vases of enamelled copper set on a base.'[10] By contrast, the books themselves are predictable and unremarkable, though also far more numerous than at first sight, as, in common with many Victorian country houses, printed matter overflows far beyond the Library, which contains only about 650 books, considerably fewer than are present in several other rooms, including a Study and a room now known as the Japanese Room, but originally Lord Armstrong's Business Room. The picture is further confused because books appear to have left Cragside since the nineteenth century. Armstrong acquired a second residence at Bamburgh Castle in the last years of his life, and it is clear that books moved from one to the other until Cragside's acquisition by the National Trust in 1977. This fluidity was quite typical of similar libraries. Books migrated easily from one plutocrat house to another, and from one room to another. At Cragside it is striking how few books there are on science, engineering and mathematics – precisely those one would expect to see on the shelves of one of Victorian Britain's most renowned industrialists.

Another library where it seems clear that we are only getting part of the picture is that of the socialite Maggie Greville (1863–1942; fig. 195) at Polesden Lacey in Surrey.[11] The illegitimate daughter of the Edinburgh brewing magnate William McEwen (1827–1913), Mrs Greville obtained and swiftly lost a presentably anaemic husband, pushed her way into the raffish Marlborough House set and established herself as one of Edwardian London's most prominent society hostesses. She bought Polesden, convenient for London, as her country base in 1906, almost immediately bringing in Mewès and Davis, who had recently finished the Ritz Hotel, to transform it into a house fit for royalty. For the next thirty years Mrs Greville's acid tongue reigned supreme over a relentless sequence of weekend house parties, political salons and entertainments, helped along by a superb wine cellar and some of the best food in England. At the first cocktail party, in 1936, there were between 300 and 400 guests, but Maggie

Greville's greatest coup was in 1923, when Polesden hosted the honeymoon of the Duke and Duchess of York (later George VI and Queen Elizabeth). Harold Nicolson, who accepted Mrs Greville's hospitality but detested her flirtation with the Nazis, called her 'a fat slug filled with venom', while Cecil Beaton thought her 'a galumphing, greedy, snobbish old toad'. The sumptuous Library at Polesden (fig. 196) can only be understood in the context of Mrs Greville's entertaining, and remains much as she left it, though without the Pye television set that was there in 1943. It would clearly be going too far to suggest that the many books reflect her personal interests, and Mrs Greville had no particular intellectual pretensions ('my dear, I know I am not an educated woman'). But while there is nothing of extraordinary grandeur on the shelves, and certainly nothing to match Mrs Greville's splendid pictures, many of the Polesden books are attractive, and it seems likely that she took advice from the London trade. In part, the books were bought in to enhance the overall *mise-en-scène*, but they were also evidently intended for the convenience and amusement of Mrs Greville's house guests. A number are rather enigmatically inscribed 'Polesden Lacey Club Library 1915', and

[195] Alice Hughes, *Mrs Greville in fancy dress as 'Mary Seton' at the Devonshire House ball*, 1897

this and the opulence of the Library room, with its
luxurious and carefully arranged furniture, give the
game away. In many ways Mrs Greville's library is
more like a club library than the personal collection
of a single individual (as at Cragside the picture is
confused because books may have been disposed
of after the National Trust took over in 1943). Just
as she would have provided her guests with the
finest wines and the best cigars, so, too, her books
– from leather-bound sets to fine colour-plate
books and a large paper copy of the first edition of
Beckford's *Vathek* (1786) – were selected to delight
and impress.

The Library in the nouveau-riche holiday house

In Ireland another brewing dynasty, the
Guinnesses, collected houses and libraries. One of
the more modest was Muckross House in County
Kerry, purchased by Arthur Edward Guinness in
1895. Bought as a holiday home and often rented
out for shooting and fishing, it was sold to the
American William Bowers Bourn in 1911. Muckross
still retains its original interconnecting Library and
Drawing Room, the oak shelves filled with books
of the period. Also in Ireland Glenveagh Castle,
a castellated shooting lodge in County Donegal,
belonged from 1937 to 1981 to the American

millionaire connoisseur Henry McIlhenny (1910–86).[12] Again, very much a holiday home, the books which it contained were (and still are) modest, focusing especially on McIlhenny's favourite subjects of art and antiques. Details of the books owned by *Country Life* founder Edward Hudson (1854–1936) at Lindisfarne Castle are scanty, and there are none in the castle today. Nonetheless there evidently was a library of some sort in his Northumbrian holiday retreat, possibly quite small. Hudson owned two other Lutyens houses, but a separate bookplate was printed specifically for books at Lindisfarne. In Scotland Kinloch Castle, on the Hebridean island of Rùm, was another substantial holiday home, built in 1900 for Sir George Bullough (1870–1939), the son of the self-made Lancashire cotton millionaire John Bullough (1837–91). Bullough senior was an aggressive philistine, writing forcefully to the *Accrington Gazette* in 1887 to denounce proposals for a free public library as an unnecessary burden on the ratepayers. By contrast, his son George was an extravagant

and eccentric playboy. Some of the legends – the steam yachts, wild parties and the heated ponds for turtles and alligators – are essentially true. Others, including the story that the Kinloch library was stocked with a vast collection of pornography, are unfortunately myths.[13] However, there certainly is a substantial library there, of about 2,000 books, surprisingly varied, ranging from contemporary politics, the Boer War, English and French novels, travel books and penny dreadfuls. More oddly, the castle also contains over 400 copies of the three-volume *Letters and Speeches* of John Bullough (Manchester, 1892), which weigh down shelves all over the building.[14]

Industrialists and Prime Ministers

Despite a more sober reputation, the small library at Fyvie Castle in Aberdeenshire, though mostly populated with moderately smart copies of moderately ordinary books, does contain one rather racy surprise. Presumably the Fyvie copy of Richard Payne Knight's *Account of the Remains of*

the Worship of Priapus (London, 1786) – an illustrated and undeniably amusing mixture of learned antiquarianism, Enlightenment religious scepticism and barely suppressed hilarity – belonged to the Scottish-American industrialist Alexander Forbes-Leith (1847–1925), 1st Baron Leith of Fyvie, who purchased the castle in 1889. Regrettably the book, with its notorious engraved frontispiece showing the wax ex-votos of 'St Cosmo's Big Toe' failed to make it into an exhibition of art treasures from Fyvie, held in Edinburgh in 1985 to celebrate the National Trust for Scotland's acquisition of the castle the previous year.[15]

By contrast, John Rylands's library was a middle-brow mix of piety and practicality. The son of a draper from St Helens, Manchester's first multi-millionaire lived from 1857 at Longford Hall, an Italianate mansion which he had built in the nearby village of Stretford. The house was unpretentious, and the library, of some 1,808 volumes, could hardly have been less like the library which Mrs Rylands later founded in her husband's memory. Entirely devoid of antique or rare books, it included volumes of light reading (Dickens and Walter Scott) but also many religious books, as Rylands was a devout Congregationalist. In addition to biblical commentaries, there were volumes of apologetics: J. R. Beard's *Religion of Jesus Christ Defended from the Assaults of Owenism* (1839) is striking, since the utopian socialist reformer Robert Owen (1771–1858) had once been a mill manager in Manchester and was elected to the radical-tinged Manchester Literary and Philosophical Society in 1798. Other books, like a *Boy's own Book of Boats* (1868) seem somewhat more unexpected, while *Scott's Practical Cotton Spinner, and Manufacturer* (Preston, 1840) and *Etiquette for Gentlemen* (1854) provoke interesting and perhaps rather moving reflections on the life story of a self-made man.[16]

If John Rylands was content with a comfortably sensible residence, other Victorian millionaires were more ambitious. Some houses were built on a heroic scale, and a few were monuments of the most bloated giganticism. The Droitwich 'Salt King' John

Corbett (1817–1901), for example, commissioned Chateau Impney, a huge Second Empire mansion, from the Parisian architect Auguste Tronquois. Built between 1873 and 1885, it included a large Library in French Renaissance style, housing a working library of 8,000 books, which subsequently went to Birmingham University Library.[17] Earlier at Penrhyn Castle in north Wales, the Prince Regent's architect Thomas Hopper (1776–1856) had built an equally enormous residence for George Hay Dawkins-Pennant (1764–1840), who had inherited the estate and a large fortune from his second cousin Richard Pennant. The neo-Norman castle, a huge building of brooding Wagnerian grandeur, naturally included a Library (fig.197), an opulent room inspired by the zigzag splendour of Tickencote church in Rutland. Even the bookcases, castellated structures with heavy brass grilles, are Norman, with carved library furniture to match. A number of the grandest books were sold in the early 1950s, but many others remain. Nevertheless, the odd plate book notwithstanding, the collection has more than a whiff of solid, useful practicality to it. The Dawkins-Pennants became famed for their magnificent art collection, but their shelves housed a good gentleman's library of the early nineteenth century (with some earlier inheritances) rather than rows of incunables and medieval manuscripts.[18]

One of the Penrhyn pictures, Henry Hawkins's *Penrhyn Slate Quarry* (1832; fig.198), also acts as an important reminder that the castle and its treasures were funded by the labour of thousands of Welsh slate miners and, earlier, of enslaved Africans on the family sugar plantations in the West Indies.[19]

With their books by John Henry Newman and other Oxford Movement figures, the Dawkins-Pennants' books hint at a particular form of High Toryism very different from the robust populism of Benjamin Disraeli (1804–81), whose library remains substantially intact at Hughenden Manor in Buckinghamshire. Though Dizzy's books are no longer in the room which housed them in his lifetime (fig.199), and 175 of them were sold in 1937, enough survives to give a compelling flavour of the interests of the Victorian era's most implausible Prime Minister.[20] Disraeli's purchase of the Hughenden estate in 1848 was in itself indicative of the importance of a country house to a self-made politician. But the books could not be more unlike those in many industrialists' houses. They include a rump of the bibliomaniac library inherited from Dizzy's father the author Isaac D'Israeli (1766–1848). The contents of the shelves comprise seventeenth-century English books, a finely illuminated incunable, classical texts, books on politics and imperial adventures, as well as

[199] Benjamin Disraeli in his Library at Hughenden in 1881

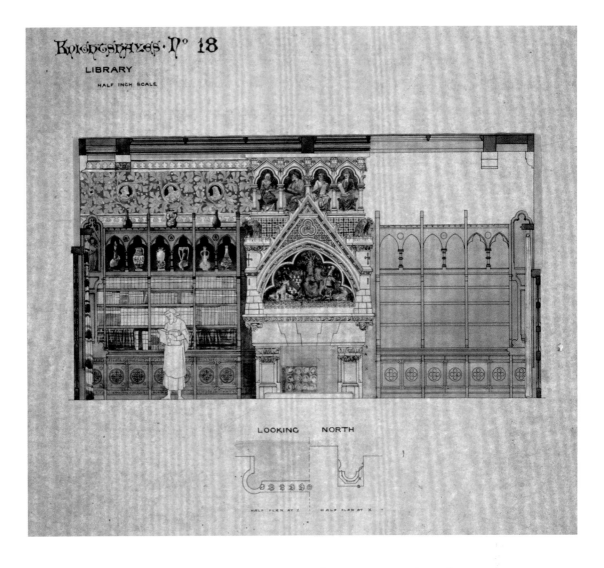

The Victorian Gothic Library

maps from the Congress of Berlin in 1878, marked up in red crayon. There is also the spectacular photographically illustrated *History of the Imperial Assembly at Delhi* of 1877, a gift from Lord Lytton, showing the proclamation of Disraeli's 'Faery' as Empress of India, as well as Disraeli's copies of his own novels.[21] Not surprisingly, Disraeli's library was eclipsed by the much larger library assembled by William Ewart Gladstone (1808–98), who had some 30,000 books in his country retreat at Hawarden in Flintshire.[22] Nonetheless the perennially self-dramatising Disraeli has to be taken seriously when he declared: 'I have a particular passion for books and trees. I like to look at them. When I come down to Hughenden I pass the first week in sauntering about my park and examining all the trees, and then I saunter in the library and survey the books.'[23]

The Gothic Library at Tyntesfield (fig. 201), near Bristol, is strikingly redolent of the age of Gladstone and Disraeli, though in fact the books only reached their current arrangement in 1896, when the library was rearranged by the family chaplain John Bacon Medley (1831–1907), and there have been further changes to the shelves and especially the furnishings since then. The great room was designed by the Bristol architect John Norton (1823–1904), a pupil of Benjamin Ferrey, for the merchant prince William Gibbs (1790–1875), whose family had made a fortune importing guano from South America, an essential raw material for the manufacture of the fertilisers needed to feed a fast-growing industrial population.[24] Gibbs's son Anthony was sent to Exeter College in Oxford, where George Gilbert Scott had recently built an equally magnificent Library (1856–7), while

William Gibbs himself was subsequently one of the chief financial backers of Keble College, Oxford.[25] At Tyntesfield this religious allegiance is clear not just from the architecture, but in the contents of the shelves, with numerous works by John Henry Newman and John Keble, classical Anglican theology of the seventeenth century, and books on church history. These sit alongside books on the Gothic Revival: A. W. N. Pugin's *Contrasts* (1841), his father's *Specimens of Gothic Architecture* (1825), and John Ruskin's *Stones of Venice* (1851–53) and *Seven Lamps of Architecture* (1849). Earlier works are thin on the ground, though there are some sixteenth- and seventeenth-century liturgical books, and a single late Gothic illuminated manuscript in a nineteenth-century silver repoussé binding, and there was a first edition of Richard Hakluyt's *Principal Navigations* (sold before the National Trust took over in 2002). None of this should be taken to imply any backwards-looking obscurantism. As a working Victorian library, Tyntesfield could hardly be bettered; rich in novels (Charlotte M. Yonge was a regular visitor), history, travel, topography, folklore and much else, neither did it shy away from controversial books like Darwin's *Origin of Species*.

Similar libraries still exist elsewhere, in various states of preservation. At Knightshayes Court in Devon, a Library room designed by William Burges (fig. 200) is devoid of most of its original books, and is now in part a twentieth-century recreation of a toned-down interior designed by John Diblee Crace in 1879, the house's owner, the lace manufacturer Sir John Heathcoat Amory, having decided that Burges's fantastical original designs were too extravagant.[26] The books from Burges's even more extravagant Library for the Marquess of Bute at Cardiff Castle are now at Mount Stuart, on the Isle of Bute, the home of one of the most magnificent private libraries in Britain. By contrast, and also in Wales, J. L. Pearson's Gothic Library for the High Church banker Robert Raikes (1818–1901) at Treberfydd (1851), in the Brecon Beacons, survives better, and with Raikes's books.[27] But if the modest little Treberfydd Library was a rather monastic retreat from the world, Norton's great room at Tyntesfield was very much a public space. Amateur theatricals were held in the bay window, and if William Gibbs's Study was just behind a disguised

[201] The Library at Tyntesfield

'jib door', the Library was evidently very much open to all.[28] The reorganisation carried through by the resident chaplain in 1896 was thorough and businesslike, and in itself points up the extent to which the Tyntesfield Library was intended to be used. Carefully arranged for easy access, each bay of shelving has an ivory subject label, and there is a printed catalogue, presumably for distribution to friends and family. There was even a formal loans register, maintained until 1911, with books carefully checked in and out.[29]

II · THE NOUVEAU-RICHE COLLECTOR AND THE COUNTRY HOUSE

The Quaritch customer

By the second half of the nineteenth century the Gibbses of Tyntesfield had largely withdrawn from the day-to-day affairs of the family business. The baton passed to their cousin, Henry Hucks Gibbs (1819–1907), 1st Lord Aldenham (fig. 202), senior partner from 1875 but a dominant figure in the firm as early as the 1850s.[30] His ascendancy coincided with a stratospheric rise in profits, but Henry Hucks was unwilling to accept the rustic catalepsy of life as a landed proprietor, which he feared would 'make my life an idle one'. Nonetheless he owned two country seats, at Clifton Hampden in Oxfordshire and at Aldenham in Hertfordshire. It was at Aldenham (now a school) and at his London house in Regent's Park that he kept his library. Like Tyntesfield this contained contemporary publications, but there were also many early books. Typographical facsimiles of early books, including Shakespeare quartos, the 1496 Book of St Albans and several Caxtons, sat alongside the original editions of the 1482 Polychronicon and the 1483 Golden Legend.[31] A similar mixture of old and new is evident in the copy of Gibbs's own Game of Ombre (1878), which he sent to Tyntesfield, beautifully bound in a neo-Grolieresque binding by Joseph Zaehnsdorf.[32] Already in 1888, he had a fine collection of manuscript and printed Bibles and Books of Hours, the Bibles including examples in multiple languages, a Complutensian Polyglot, and a 1535 Coverdale Bible, one of several Bibles bought from the Quaker entrepreneur and collector Francis Fry (1803–86), whose library formed the basis of the collection of the British and Foreign Bible Society.[33] Other trophies incorporated a

[202] Henry Hucks Gibbs, 1st Lord Aldenham

first edition of Beckford's Vathek (1786), on large paper, a Nuremberg Chronicle, a Shakespeare First Folio, the thirteenth-century 'Windmill Psalter' (fig. 203) and twenty-two early books by or about Charles I, an appropriate interest for a High Church Anglican.

Gibbs bought many of his books from Bernard Quaritch Ltd, whose German-born founder set up in London in 1847. Quaritch's influence on nineteenth-century English book collecting was all-pervasive, and from the 1850s he dominated the sale rooms. The firm's seventeen-volume priced General Catalogue (1887–97), as well as its Dictionary of Book Collectors, underlined the symbiotic relationship between dealer and clients.[34] Not all of these clients were newly moneyed, and not all kept their libraries in country houses, but many were and did. As The Spectator put it in 1872, 'our millionaires are maniacs for collecting things'.[35] One of Quaritch's hungriest customers, the Quaker banker Lord Peckover (1830–1919), lived in Bank House in Wisbech, a magnificent Georgian town house at the front, looking onto the canalised river Nene, but at the back, with a large garden, almost like a country house. His dispersed library included typical bibliomaniacal trophies, as well as an astonishing collection of ancient biblical, liturgical and patristic manuscripts. The library of another

Quaritch customer, William Tyssen-Amsherst (1835–1909), at Didlington Hall in Norfolk, comprised three block books and 135 incunables, including the Gosford Castle Gutenberg Bible. Despite his landed background (he was brought up at Narford), Tyssen-Amsherst owed his fortune to property in Hackney inherited from his maternal grandmother, taking the title Lord Amherst of Hackney in 1892. His collection, however, had to be sold in 1909 to offset frauds perpetrated by the family solicitor, raising £32,592 at auction, though in addition seventeen Caxtons were sold privately to J. P. Morgan.[36] Other collectors with libraries included Samuel (1810–89) and Sydney Christie-Miller, of Britwell Court (fig. 204), just north of

in consilio impiorum: & in uia pec
catorum non stetit: & in cathedra pe
stilencie non sedit. Sed in lege domini uoluntas eius:
& in lege eius meditabit dic ac noctc.
Et erit tanquam lignum qd plan
tatum est secus decursus aquarum:

Slough, Buckinghamshire, and the Worcestershire sauce millionaire C. W. Dyson Perrins (1864–1958), of Davenham, in Worcester.[37] At Britwell Court the emphasis was on early printed books, and especially early British imprints, partly inherited from the bibliomaniac William Henry Miller (1789–1848) and described in great detail in a series of sale catalogues, as well as in a post-dispersal *Handlist* published by Quaritch in 1933.[38] This underlines the importance of relations between collectors and the trade, as well as the connection between private libraries and contemporary developments in bibliography (Pollard and Redgrave's *Short Title Catalogue* was first published in 1926). At Davenham, a mid-nineteenth-century house rebuilt after a fire in 1904, Dyson Perrins concentrated on illuminated manuscripts, mostly collected between 1900 and 1920, and again dispersed after his death.[39]

Waddesdon

One of the more astonishing libraries assembled in Victorian England is at Waddesdon Manor, the vast Renaissance chateau built for Baron Ferdinand de Rothschild (1839–98) by the French architect and collector Hippolyte Destailleur (1822–93). Baron Ferdinand belonged to the Viennese branch of the Rothschild family and settled in England in 1860, following family tradition and marrying his English cousin Evelina five years later.[40] His library of fine books was comparatively small (768 books, plus albums of bookplates, drawings and ephemera), lodged in the Morning Room (fig. 205) at Waddesdon, a later extension and the result of the baron's 'Projet du Bibliothèque' (1888). Despite the French terminology, this unusually opulent room is dominated by works of art rather than floor-to-ceiling shelving. The books are stored in a series of small but ornately decorated glazed cabinets, the emphasis on quality rather than quantity. Their contents were conceived as just one component of the wider collection, which includes pictures, fine furniture and objets d'art, often of astonishing magnificence. They were quite distinct from the modern books in Baron Ferdinand's various houses, acquired to be read.[41] In addition, most of the Morning Room books are in luxe or super-luxe bindings, the work of Derome, Padeloup and the other great *ateliers* of the *ancien régime* (fig. 206). Exquisite objects, the equal of Baron Ferdinand's equally marvellous porcelain and silver, they can really be appreciated only by handling the books – admittedly with all the care which the baron and his sister, author of Waddesdon's famously exacting housekeeping rules, would have demanded.

As a collector, Ferdinand was very much his own man. While his contemporaries pursued incunables and medieval manuscripts or chased first editions, the Baron's interests lay in graphic arts, fine books and, of course, bindings – above all from eighteenth-century France. Over seventy per cent of the Morning Room books were printed between 1700 and 1789, and about two-thirds are in French. Buying mostly in the period between about 1880 and his death in 1898, Baron Ferdinand was collecting at a period when, after the collapse of the Second Empire, antiquarian book prices were at historically low levels.[42] His books include works on travel, the theatre, social and courtly life, state occasions, crime and religious persecutions (reflective of the Rothschild's Jewish heritage), topography, architecture, calligraphy and typography, art and horses – many lavishly illustrated. He assembled his library late in life, at a time when, due to ill health, there was less grand entertaining at Waddesdon. Buying was at its most intense from about 1891, when the Morning Room was completed.[43] Typically for a Rothschild collector, few acquisitions records now survive, but between 1889 and 1898 it seems that the baron spent at least £7,687 17s. 12d. on books in London, and another £28,201 8s. in Paris.[44] Favourite dealers included Quaritch and the Pall Mall dealer John Pearson & Co. in London, and in Paris Morgand et Fatout, whose stock books suggest that they supplied more than a fifth of the whole collection, including virtually all the most important books and bindings.[45]

Apart from the extreme splendour of most of the individual copies, Baron Ferdinand's books display a very evident interest in provenance. Royal books include seventeen which belonged to Louis XIV, twenty or twenty-one to Louis XV, seven to Marie-Antoinette and six to Louis XVI, as well as fourteen from the library of Mme de Pompadour and four from Mme du Barry. There are books with the armorial stamps of at least twenty seventeenth- and fifty eighteenth-century French collectors, as well as an extraordinary array of super-luxury *ancien régime* bindings (and one, surely bought in a fit of black humour, which belonged to Dr Guillotin).

[204] Britwell Court in 1919

Another notable feature is the 1897 Waddesdon catalogue, reportedly published in just twelve copies, and correspondingly rare. Like many similar publications, it is not especially accurate but is notable for its twenty-one colour plates of bindings – an innovative use of new technology, and one which became increasingly common in grander sale catalogues as the twentieth century progressed.[46]

The twenty-six medieval manuscripts now at Waddesdon have a quite different history. They did not belong to Baron Ferdinand, who collected medieval manuscripts and bequeathed them to the British Museum, but to his French cousin Edmond de Rothschild (1845–1934), whose son James A. de Rothschild bequeathed Waddesdon to the National Trust in 1957. They form just a part of Baron Edmond's original collection, which also included Persian and Hebrew manuscripts, as well as numerous other categories of object.[47]

[205] The Morning Room at Waddesdon

More old wine in new bottles

Despite the French accent at Waddesdon, a surprising number of Baron Ferdinand's books came from British aristocratic libraries. There were twenty-six books from the Beckford collection, sold by the 12th Duke of Hamilton from 1882, six from Gosford Castle in County Armagh, as well as books from Apethorpe, Burton Constable, Strawberry Hill and Syston, while the Waddesdon copy of Loggan's *Oxonia Illustrata* (1675) came from Osterley.[48] The more conventional Amherst library at Didlington had the Osterley Caxtons and other books from the Harleian Library, as well as books from the Arundel and Sunderland collections, the libraries at Auchinleck, Narford and Newnham Paddox, a manuscript *Horae* once in the Lumley Library, and a fifteenth-century *Brut* manuscript from Dalkeith Palace in Scotland. Britwell Court

had books from the libraries of more than fifty titled collectors, as well as numerous members of the gentry.[49] Often the libraries of nouveau-riche collectors, packed with books only recently sold from long-established aristocratic libraries, survived only for a generation or two, a brief intermission before the books were sold again to American collectors like Huntington, Folger or Morgan. But for this to happen, large numbers of books needed to be finding their way onto the market, for reasons less dramatic but almost as alarming as the fate which overtook the French aristocracy after 1789. In both countries new collections were only possible because others were selling. And by the late nineteenth century books which had been on the shelves of British country houses for centuries were starting to come onto the market in great numbers.

[206] Bookbindings at Waddesdon

CHAPTER THIRTEEN

'Ravaged by body-snatchers'

The Dispersal of the Country House Library, from the Late Nineteenth Century

The empty shelves at Blenheim, Sledmere and Althorp gave me the ghastly gasp
as of coffins and vaults ravaged by body-snatchers.
Shane Leslie, *Long Shadows*, 1966

I · DECLINE AND FALL

The agricultural depression

By the mid-1880s the British empire was approaching its zenith, but this did not necessarily mean that all was well in the aristocratic garden. The previous decade had seen a protracted agricultural depression, which began in 1874 and had hit the countryside hard. As railways and refrigerated steam ships made it possible to shift agricultural products round the globe quickly and cheaply, this and the opening up of the American West meant that the European markets were flooded with cheap foodstuffs. Grain prices in Britain tumbled by about 50 per cent, and low prices continued into the late 1890s. This, as well as a run of bad harvests (in 1875, 1877, 1878 and 1879), led to a dramatic fall in the value of land, and a concomitant fall in the incomes of those who worked it and of those who owned it. In general landowners in the south and east, heavily dependent on grain, were most affected, while those in the north and west, where mixed agriculture predominated, escaped more lightly – but none were unaffected.[1]

In the decades after 1880 average aristocratic incomes fell by between one quarter and one third.[2] To take just one example, the 65,000-acre estates of the Dukes of Rutland were already operating at a loss by the early 1880s. By 1899 they were in debt to the tune of £234,000, with annual interest payments at over £10,000 per annum; by 1909 the debts had risen to £289,000.[3] In Scotland the 7th Earl of Aberdeen (1847–34), a marquess from 1916, had once owned 75,000 acres, with an annual rent roll of some £40,000. By 1920 the land-holdings

had shrunk to just 14,000 acres, and many other assets had had to be liquidated to meet ongoing expenditure.[4] At the same time the progressive widening of the franchise resulted in a noticeable loosening of the still-strong aristocratic grip on politics. The last Prime Ministers to sit in the Lords were the bibliophile 5th Earl of Rosebery (1847–1929), in office from 1894 to 1895, and the extremely patrician 3rd Marquess of Salisbury (1830–1903), owner of the great library at Hatfield. Thereafter, while peers and their relatives did not by any means disappear from the political process, their influence waned, and the advent of the secret ballot (1872) and the creation of county councils (1889) meant that landowners' dominance of their localities grew less strong than it had been. At the same time, as the nineteenth century progressed, other traditional sources of income became harder to come by. The great book collector Thomas Grenville (1755–1846), a grandson of the 1st Marquess of Buckingham, was candid that he had funded his book habit by the 'huge payment of a sinecure office', and this was in part one of his reasons for eventually bequeathing his library for public use to the British Museum.[5]

In Ireland from 1879 Charles Stewart Parnell's Land League challenged the very foundations of the traditional social order, deploying a campaign of intimidation and social ostracism which set in motion a train of events which within half a century would lead to the virtual extinction of the Irish landlord class. In England the rise of nouveau-riche families – bankers like the Rothschilds,

[207] Detail of the title page of the Sunderland library sale catalogue, 1881–3

BIBLIOTHECA SUNDERLANDIANA

SALE CATALOGUE

OF THE

TRULY IMPORTANT AND VERY EXTENSIVE

LIBRARY OF PRINTED BOOKS

KNOWN AS THE

SUNDERLAND OR BLENHEIM LIBRARY

COMPRISING A

REMARKABLE COLLECTION OF THE

GREEK AND ROMAN CLASSIC WRITERS

IN FIRST EARLY AND RARE EDITIONS.

A LARGE SERIES OF

𝕰𝖆𝖗𝖑𝖞 𝕻𝖗𝖎𝖓𝖙𝖊𝖉 𝕭𝖎𝖇𝖑𝖊𝖘 𝖆𝖓𝖉 𝕿𝖊𝖘𝖙𝖆𝖒𝖊𝖓𝖙𝖘

IN VARIOUS LANGUAGES.

𝕬 𝖋𝖊𝖜 𝖆𝖓𝖈𝖎𝖊𝖓𝖙 𝖆𝖓𝖉 𝖎𝖒𝖕𝖔𝖗𝖙𝖆𝖓𝖙 𝕸𝕾𝕾.

RARE EDITIONS of the GREAT ITALIAN WRITERS notably DANTE, BOCCACCIO, PETRARCH, and ARIOSTO. IMPORTANT BOOKS and TRACTS relating to AMERICA. EARLY AND RARE CHRONICLES in SPANISH, PORTUGUESE, ENGLISH and FRENCH. Important ENGLISH COUNTY HISTORIES. A very extensive collection of TRACTS RELATING to the POLITICAL and RELIGIOUS EVENTS in ENGLAND and FRANCE in the 15th and 16th Centuries. Many very uncommon POETICAL TRACTS in FRENCH, ITALIAN and SPANISH. COLLECTIONS of COUNCILS, LIVES of SAINTS, BOOKS on CANON and CIVIL LAW. FIRST EDITIONS of the WRITINGS of the chief FRENCH, ITALIAN and SPANISH POETS of the 16th and 17th Centuries.

ETC. ETC.

THE FIRST PORTION—TEN DAYS' SALE

arms manufacturers like Lord Armstrong or merchant princes like the Gibbses of Aldenham and Tyntesfield – exposed all too clearly that wealth and social status no longer automatically depended on the ownership of thousands of rolling acres. An elderly and increasingly cantankerous Queen Victoria resisted government demands for peerages for industrialists, but for those with eyes to see, the grandeur of great houses like Waddesdon and Cragside told their own story. By the twentieth century the world was fast changing, and as time went on it changed faster. Between 1900 and 2000 probably 1,700 British country houses – about a sixth of the total – were demolished.[6] Along with houses, families, too, faced rates of attrition, just as they had always done: 50 per cent of the families listed in *Burke's Landed Gentry* in 1863 had disappeared by 1914.[7]

Another significant factor in the progressive collapse of aristocratic finances was rising taxation, especially Estate Duty ('death duties'), introduced in 1894. Its impact was not initially very great, but grew as taxation got stiffer. By the 1930s, as Queen Mary's friend Lady Airlie later recalled in her memoirs, 'taxation was crippling many of the old landowning families', and many were being forced to retrench.[8] In 1928 the 9th Duke of Devonshire (1868–1938) had set up a limited company to hold the family properties, in an ultimately vain attempt to help minimise any future obligations.[9] The 9th Duke of Richmond (1904–89) was forced to abandon his ancestral inheritance in Scotland, selling his estates and the contents of Gordon Castle to pay two successive rounds of death duties, after two of his predecessors had died in the space of just eight years. In future the Richmonds would be based exclusively at Goodwood. During the immediate crisis period of the Second World War, death duties were levied at between 50 and 60 per cent, rising to 75 per cent by 1946.[10] But in addition, there was also the question of general taxation. As recently as the 1870s, Income Tax, introduced as an emergency measure during the Napoleonic wars, was levied at just 1 per cent, and there was serious talk of abolishing it entirely. Lloyd George's People's Budget (1909) included a new 'Super-Tax', which would have taken the top rate of tax to 7½ per cent on the highest incomes (fig. 208). It provoked uproar in the Lords, and a constitutional crisis. Nonetheless at the start of the First World War the standard rate of income tax stood at 6 per cent,

Reprinted from the "DAILY DISPATCH," October 21, 1909.

IN THE COILS.

ASQUITH : "Don't touch it, my lord, or you'll get bitten."
The Government's advice to the Lords to keep their hands off the Budget for fear of the consequences sounds somewhat ironical in view of the position of affairs.

a figure which had risen to 30 per cent by 1918, by which time the total tax revenue of government was about seventeen times what it had been in 1905.[11]

Aristocratic libraries had always been sold when occasion or finances demanded. In the late seventeenth century 'the main part of the library of that famous secretary, William Cecil, Lord Burghley' had been offered for sale in London in 1687, though in reality what was being sold was the library of the 1st Earl of Ailesbury (1626–85), who had inherited Burghley's manuscripts and possibly some of his printed books.[12] The 1st Duke of Lauderdale's books, from Ham House and probably from elsewhere, went in a series of sales in the 1690s, part of a desperate attempt by the widowed duchess to stave off bankruptcy.[13] Three decades later, in 1729, the Kentish gentleman Sir Edward Filmer (1683–1755) engaged in a protracted tussle with the London bookseller Charles Davis about the sale of books from the library of his country seat, East Sutton Place. Filmer was especially annoyed because Davis had paid just £20 for the books, but had been overheard boasting in nearby Rochester that he would make £100 profit on the transaction.[14] The sale of the Harleian Library was not the only dispersal of the 1740s, with the library of the spectacularly corrupt 1st Duke of

[208] *The Manchester Evening News'* view, 1909, of the People's Budget (Townend)

Chandos (1674–1744) sold after his death and his great palace at Cannons demolished between 1747 and 1748, while the library of 'Ancient and Modern Books Elegantly Bound' at Wanstead House was sold *in situ* in 1822, in some 827 lots.[15] The 3rd Earl of Hardwicke (1757–1834) sold books from Wimpole in 1792; one of the victims, a fifteenth-century manuscript of St Augustine, ended up not far away, in the Wren Library at Trinity College, Cambridge, but the rest are now widely scattered.[16] Later still the 2nd Lord Berwick of Attingham and the 1st Earl of Lichfield both went bankrupt, and the libraries were sold at Attingham and Shugborough, to be followed by the even more spectacular ducal bankruptcy sale at Stowe in 1848, where already in 1844 the 2nd Duke of Buckingham (1797–1861) was over £1 million in debt.[17] As Disraeli wrote to the Marchioness of Londonderry at the time, 'all the world is talking about Stowe'.[18]

From the 1880s, sales from country house libraries moved from being exceptional events with specific causes, to something that was routine and systemic, the consequence not of private calamities or personal stupidity, but of fundamental changes in the economic and political landscape. In addition, there was the inescapable fact, as A. N. L. Munby put it in 1974, that 'the loss of the Caxtons was … much less conspicuous than the loss of the Van Dycks or the Gainsboroughs'.[19] When cash was needed, books could be the answer, but for this to happen, for many owners, changes in legislation were required.

The Settled Land Act (1882)

The law of entail had evolved over many centuries into a system which effectively allowed the heads of landed families to declare certain lands and chattels inalienable. In parallel with the Roman Law system of *fideicommissum*, the entail protected a family patrimony from being whittled away in a single generation by a foolish or profligate heir, by turning the owner into a tenant for life, who held lands, houses and heirlooms in trust for his successor. A family's library was often among its entailed chattels. In 1711, for example, the will of the Welsh gentleman Robert Jones, of Fonmon Castle, gave his widow a life interest in most of his possessions, but decreed that his books should pass immediately to his eldest son and that 'ye s^d. books [are] not to be sold, disposed of, or diminished'.[20] A little later,

when the Devon heiress Elizabeth Harris of Hayne married in 1779, she brought a wide range of property with her to her new husband, and her family's books were enumerated in exhaustive detail in her marriage settlement.[21] The library at Cassiobury was entailed, the books tied to the ownership of the estate, under the terms of the will of the 5th Earl of Essex (1757–1839), a typical arrangement, replicated many times over elsewhere.[22]

By the 1880s, with many landowners feeling the pinch, making changes to the law of entail was an obvious way to help them out, and the Settled Land Act of 1882, introduced during Gladstone's second administration but conceived by Disraeli's former Lord Chancellor Lord Cairns (1819–85), was designed to do this.[23] Hitherto the only way to break entails had been by costly and time-consuming private legislation, and in 1882 there was an immediate precedent at hand in the form of the 1880 Blenheim Settled Estates Act. This had authorised the 7th Duke of Marlborough (1822–83) to break the family entail and bring in the London auction house Puttick and Simpson to sell the Sunderland Library (fig. 207; see pp. 218–19). The sales took place between 1881 and 1883, and were justified in the Act on the grounds that the books were deteriorating at Blenheim.[24] All this attracted criticism, with *The Times* urging that the library should be bought for the nation, suggesting a purchase price of £40,000 (the eventual sale in fact made £56,851).[25] But following the 1882 Act, private legislation was no longer needed to sell inherited books. Thereafter heirlooms of all kinds could be treated much like any other piece of private property and, subject to not very onerous conditions, could be sent to auction, provided that permission was first obtained from the Court of Chancery.[26]

This opened up all sorts of possibilities, from settling debts to repairing the roof. It also became possible to sell books which would previously have passed to a single male heir for the profit of several members of one family, including women. In 1890, for example, the two daughters of the Liberal politician the 7th Earl of Buckinghamshire (1860–1930) each received £75 as their share of the proceeds of the sale of the library at Great Hampden, in the Chilterns.[27] Sometimes, it is clear, the fashionable philistinism of imperial Britain helped ease any pangs which vendors may have felt. As the celebrity photographer Patrick Lichfield recalled in the 1980s, his grandfather the 4th Earl of Lichfield (1883–1960) had 'cared little for book-learning' and 'concentrated his attention' on country sports.[28] A couple of generations earlier, Lady Phyllis MacRae (1899–1990), a daughter of the 4th Marquess of Bristol, similarly recalled:

> I don't think people worried if their sons were bookish in those days, as long as they were hunting, shooting and fishing as well. You were allowed to be artistic, and you were allowed to have a knowledge of old things – objets d'art, things like architecture and anything else you chose to have – but you had to have some hunting, shooting and fishing as well.[29]

But other owners reacted with crossness to any idea of dispersals, with the 7th Earl of Stamford (1827–83), owner of two fine libraries, at Enville and Dunham Massey, writing to a kinsman: 'I have never had any intention of selling Dunham, & it is the last thing I should ever think of doing. The Books in the Library I consider of great value, & should be very sorry to part with any of them.'[30]

The great sales: from 1882 to 1939

Lord Stamford's scruples notwithstanding, the years after the Settled Land Act saw a series of spectacular sales. These liberated onto the market a run of country house libraries which, it must once have seemed, were destined to remain together for ever, providing rich pickings for a new species of collector. At Osterley the great library of Sir Robert Child (see pp. 217–18) was sold in 1885 (fig. 209).[31] The Thorold Library at Syston, one of the greatest of all the bibliomaniac collections, went in 1884, the relentless procession of spectacular trophies at the sale including *editiones principes* and a Gutenberg Bible (lot 284).[32] At Hamilton Palace, the largest house in Scotland, there were two Libraries. The first, a monumental apartment known as the Hamilton Library (fig. 210), was adjacent to the main Drawing Room and housed the inherited ducal collection. Another, the top-lit Beckford Library, was a T-shaped room which housed the books once owned by William Beckford and was, like the main Library, built for the 10th Duke of Hamilton (1767–1852), who had married the eccentric collector's daughter, Susan.[33] The books had been admired by Waagen in the 1850s, but were sold, along with much of the rest of the ducal collection, between 1882 and 1884; the sale of the Beckford collection alone raised £73,551, considerably more than the Sunderland collection

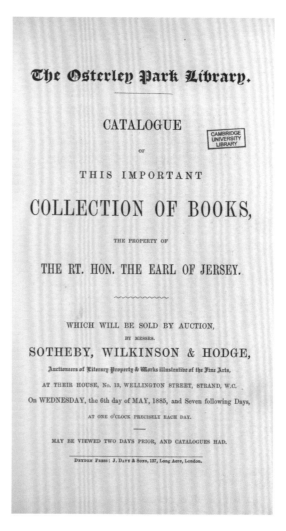

[209] The Osterley Park sale catalogue, 1885

at Blenheim'.[34] In Ireland the Achesons of Gosford Castle sold up in 1884. Shane Leslie (1885–1971), whose family owned the neighbouring Glaslough estate, but who himself turned Catholic and supported Home Rule, claimed that they had sold £120,000 worth of books to pay 'an Ascot debt of £10,000'.[35] Whether this was true is debatable, as Leslie had reasons of his own for being sceptical about his Unionist neighbours. A marked-up copy of the Puttick and Simpson sale catalogue suggests that the Gosford library went for £11,318 5s. 6d.[36] *The Times* noted that there were 'comparatively few rare books in the sale', before going on to mention a Shakespeare First Folio and the inevitable Gutenberg Bible, alongside hundreds of lesser books: as ever, the idea of what sorts of books were rare, valuable or desirable varied.[37]

On a smaller scale, the library of the Onslows of Clandon, many of the books annotated by Speaker Arthur Onslow (1691–1768), was sold in March 1885, and a good part of the library at

Burton Constable in June 1889, though there, unlike Clandon, many books escaped sale and are still in the house.[38] The marvellous early English books found in the attic at Lamport in 1867 did not long survive *in situ*, divided between the British Museum and the Britwell Court library (there was a large private sale to W. C. Christie Miller in 1893), with a public sale of mostly sixteenth- and seventeenth-century books in 1904.[39] Commenting on the state of the family finances in 1896, a sympathetic aunt noted that the Lamport entail had been broken to make provision for the owner's daughter, 'so it is to be hoped yet more precious Elizabethan relics in the shape of unique books in vellum will be discovered in the library'.[40]

Many other libraries followed. The Welsh collector John Cole Nicholl (1823–94), of Merthyr Mawr, had been forced to sell his cherished Dante collection because of falling rents (though he left over 20,000 books at the time of his death in 1894).[41] Those parts of the library of Lord Vernon not already sold to the stupendously wealthy Robert Stayner Holford (1808–92) went in 1918.[42] The rump of the library of the antiquarian Thomas Pennant from Downing, Flintshire, sold in 1913, and books went from Powis Castle, the first of a long series of sales that would continue into the 1960s.[43] Library sales continued right through the 1920s and 1930s, when the more spectacular victims included the library of the 4th Earl of Dysart (1708–70) at Ham House (1938) and the great library of the Dukes of Newcastle from Clumber Park in Nottinghamshire (1937–38).[44]

Some of the libraries sold were comparatively recent bibliomaniac collections, but others had survived intact for centuries. The library of the

[210] The Hamilton Library at Hamilton Palace, prior to its dispersal. The house was demolished in 1919

Phelips family of Montacute, sold in 1915 and 1916, must (to judge from the sale catalogue) have contained books which had been in the house since it was built in the reign of James I.[45] The same is true of books from Apethorpe (sold in 1887), some of which had clearly belonged to the Mildmays in the seventeenth century, and of repeated sales from Lacock, where the origins of the library reached back to monastic times, while the 1928 Petworth sale included books from the library of the Wizard Earl of Northumberland.[46] Owners did not always or necessarily have any very clear understanding of the nature and value of what they were selling, as Shane Leslie, recalling book-hunting expeditions in Ireland with the great Philadelphia dealer A.S.W. Rosenbach (1876–1952), noted in his memoirs.[47] Others took a robust commonsensical approach, like the redoubtable Matilda Talbot (1871–1958) at Lacock, who thought repairing the tenants' drains was more important than hoarding old books, and anyway did not much like the Library room at Lacock.[48] Her viewpoint was understandable in the context of the times, but with hindsight there can be little doubt that at Lacock, as often elsewhere, what was sold was of a historical interest out of any proportion to its relatively modest monetary value at the time.

Reactions to the dispersals varied, from those who disapproved of the sales to those who disapproved of the prices, a leader writer of the *Irish Times* commenting on the Syston sale, with all the self-confidence of the supremely ill informed, that 'these are times when fac-similes of Shakespeare quartos may be purchased for a trifling sum. Nearly all that is best worth reproducing in the original form has been reproduced, and the *editio princeps* has a wholly fictitious value'.[49] Remarkably, by contrast with occasional grumbles about literary 'treasures' exported to America, there is little sense that many at the time paused to consider what now seems painfully obvious: that the real loss was less the disposal of trophy books which had only been in libraries for a short time (and which generally ended up in safe homes elsewhere), but the breakup of ancient libraries whose books – at least with hindsight – collectively meant far more together than they did scattered.

Sometimes library sales caused family ructions. In 1883, for example, there was a spat between lawyers acting for Sir Henry Ainslie Hoare (1824–94), who owned Stourhead, and those representing the guardians of the heir, Henry Hugh Hoare (1865–1947), who had already established the principle that 20 per cent of any income generated by the cash product of any sales should go to the young heir. The sales were, as the surviving lawyers' paperwork shows, a direct response to the opportunities offered by the 1882 Act.[50] Short of cash, Henry Ainslie wished to sell the great topographical library assembled by his Regency predecessor Sir Richard Colt Hoare, described in the ensuing sale catalogue as 'probably the most choice collection of British Topography ever formed'.[51] The guardians, on the other hand, were determined to prevent the library from being 'denuded of all articles of value and interest', complaining that they had not had advance notice of the books for sale and demanding that some be struck out of the catalogue already issued by Sotheby's. Henry Ainslie's lawyers, alarmed at the prospect of further delay, explained that the cataloguing of the books had been 'a much more tedious and lengthy process than had been anticipated', that decisions had been left to Sotheby's and that, since it would now be impossible to withdraw anything from the sale, they proposed to buy in the books concerned. This solution seems eventually to have been adopted (many of the books on the shelves at Stourhead today were brought from another family house, Wavendon, in March 1895, though some clearly belonged to Colt Hoare), but the wrangle illustrates the potential for conflict – and also the practical difficulties which had to be faced – when libraries went for sale.[52] Prior to 1882 the Stourhead books could not have been sold, as they were entailed along with other Stourhead heirlooms under the will of Sir Richard Colt Hoare.[53] A similar case emerged at Blenheim, where the duke's younger brother Lord Randolph Churchill (1849–95) vehemently objected to the sale of the Sunderland Library, again occasioning a family row.[54]

The Lothian sale

The great house at Blickling was inherited by Philip Kerr (1882–1940), a Liberal politician and Lloyd George's former private secretary, in 1930. Succeeding a cousin as the 11th Marquess of Lothian, as well as the Norfolk estates, the new marquess also took over the Lothian estates and houses in Scotland, the largest of which, Newbattle Abbey, was nearly as grandiose as Blickling.[55] Faced with death duties and alarmed about the

future prospects for British agriculture, Lothian sought to plug the gap in the family finances by selling books from both. Instead of plumping for one of the London auction houses, the obvious choice, he decided, was to send them to America to be sold by a new arrival on the scene, American Art Association-Anderson Galleries, the result of a 1929 merger between two bitter rivals. The sale was held in New York in January 1932, a decision which attracted criticism at home.[56] In an account tending to the eulogistic, Lord Lothian's authorised biography (1960) laid heavy stress on his distress at the sales, his original intention to present the eighth-century Blickling Homilies to the British Museum, and his relief at the high prices which the books made in New York, where the two-day sale benefited from long-distance telephone bidding on an open line from Chicago. The reliability of some of these claims is now difficult to test, but there is little in Lothian's papers to suggest much engagement with the bibliographical treasures which he had inherited, while Shane Leslie, a great friend of Dr Rosenbach, and well versed in Anglo-American bibliographical transfers, was categorical that the Lothian sale was rigged. The principal victim, surprisingly, was not the Marquess of Lothian, but the piratical Philadelphia dealer. The aftermath of the Wall Street crash was not the ideal time to sell books to American collectors, though Lothian was pleased with the $410,545 (£102,225) which the sale made – a sum which passed immediately to the Treasury. On the other hand Britain's abandonment of the Gold Standard in September 1931 and the ensuing collapse of sterling meant that the proceeds, in dollars, were worth more than they would have been a few years earlier.[57] The success of the sale owed a good deal to the catalogue descriptions, by the Anglo-French bibliophile Seymour de Ricci (1881–1942), and to the fact that the catalogue was issued in two versions, one of them with colour illustrations, which were, by the standards of the day, extremely impressive. Despite some treasures from Blickling, the majority of the books seem to have come from Newbattle (fig. 211), and apart from the Caxtons and some other choice items, Sir Richard Ellys's great collection of early printed books (see pp. 219–23) was barely dented and remains on its shelves in Norfolk to this day.

Wartime and other emergencies

Unlike in other European countries, few libraries were directly destroyed in England, Scotland and Wales during the Second World War. One exception was Mount Edgcumbe in Devon, whose vulnerable location on Plymouth Sound led to the destruction of the house by bombs in 1941, the library apparently still *in situ*. Another victim was the library of Holland House, no longer in the country, but once a suburban retreat just outside London, which was bombed out in September 1940 (by then Lord Ilchester had already removed some of the most valuable books).[58] Elsewhere owners wisely took precautions against a threat which fortunately never came. At Firle Place in East Sussex, a house which would have been on the front line if Hitler had invaded, the 6th Viscount Gage (1895–1982) packed up thirteen treasures from the library on 21 June 1940 and sent them for safekeeping, noting in the inventory: 'I am removing certain of the most valuable things out of the house to Panshanger with the idea of not having all my eggs in one basket.' The chosen books included first editions of Boswell and *Tom Jones*, a Mercator *Atlas*, three medieval manuscripts and a Shakespeare Third Folio, which, together with six others, were collectively thought to be worth £1,025 – a substantial portion, in monetary terms, of the entire library, valued at £3,552 7s. in April 1939.[59]

If few houses were destroyed in the Second World War, many were requisitioned for official purposes, a process which may have helped the war effort, but seldom did the houses much good. If owners were lucky (or clever), requisitioning could be for fairly innocuous purposes, such as accommodating evacuated girls' schools (as at Chatsworth and Castle Howard) or housing evacuated national collections (Belvoir Castle and West Wycombe). At Gosford Castle the Library (fig. 212), whose contents had been sold in 1884, served as the home for papers evacuated to the safety of the Armagh countryside from the Public Record Office of Northern Ireland in Belfast.[60] Other houses were taken over directly by the military. The consequences for libraries varied from place to place, depending on the nature of the wartime intruders, the quality of the books, and the good sense of those left in charge of them. The Long Library at Blenheim, by then housing a large, finely bound and comparatively unimportant collection purchased between 1897 and 1900 by the 9th Duke of Marlborough as a replacement for the Sunderland Collection, was used as a dormitory for the boys of Malvern College.[61] It was not the first time that it had been taken over, as it had, like the Outer Library at Attingham, been used a military hospital during the First World War.[62] When the RAF took over Blickling, Lord Lothian's former secretary Muriel O'Sullivan did her best to keep the military out of the Long Gallery and the other state rooms, while at Warwick Castle in 1940 the Library was stacked to the gunwales with the contents of sixteen other rooms, though the library books seemed to have remained in place on the shelves.[63] Similar arrangements were put in place at Vale Royal, Lord Delamere's house in Cheshire, which from June 1940 was occupied by a sanatorium evacuated from Norfolk and where the Library, again, was pressed into service as a store and kept locked. At Arundel, too, the ducal collection was stored in the Library and the Dining Room.[64] At Dinton Park, Wiltshire, the Library was gravely affected. With the takeover by the US Army, the bookcases in the Library were, according to the folk memory, thoughtfully covered with tarpaulin, resulting in the appalling condition of many of the books today. At Gunby, in Lincolnshire, the survival of the eight-eenth-century house, threatened with demolition by the Air Ministry, was down not just to plans to present it to the National Trust but to the effective lobbying of its last private owner's husband, Field Marshal Sir Archibald Montgomery-Massingberd

(1871–1947), a former Chief of the Imperial General Staff. By then parts of the historic library had already been burned by the field marshal's batman, on his instructions, but the rest survived, a small collection of exceptional interest, together with Montgomery-Massingberd's own books on military tactics and related subjects.[65]

Fires were not, of course, unknown in country houses (at both Lanhydrock in 1881 and at Hatfield in 1835, books had had to be turfed out of the windows to save them from the flames), but condi-tions of total war could add a new twist.[66] At Castle Howard a large part of the house was gutted in an accidental fire in November 1940. As a sixth former from the girl's school which had recently moved into the house later recalled, she and many of her fellow pupils engaged in frantic efforts to rescue the 'priceless old books' by carrying them to safety in their school cloaks. The aftermath of the blaze saw books and objets d'art piled on the lawns, and with the house wrecked, many of the finest Castle Howard books were sent for sale in 1944, though many more still remain.[67] More generally neglect was clearly occasioned in many houses by lack of staff and the collapse of traditional housekeeping regimes. At Blickling, for example, a housemaid employed by Lord Lothian before the war could still remember decades later the marathon task

[212] The Library at Gosford Castle, County Armagh, in 1963

of cleaning the books in Long Gallery (the task took four people six weeks), but by 1945 the house was in the hands of the National Trust.[68] No staff existed who could have contemplated the pre-war cleaning regime, and it was years before the Trust was able to turn its attention to the business of dusting the books on a grand scale. This kind of situation often persisted even longer in Ireland, where money and staff were by the mid-twentieth century in short supply. Visitors to Lissadell, the Gore-Booth house in County Sligo, commented on the pervading smell of damp, as Aideen Gore-Booth, who lived alone in the house for twenty-two years until her death in 1994, struggled to do the work once done by armies of servants.[69]

Under the wire: private sales

Library sales were not necessarily either grand or packed with valuable books, or conducted by prestigious London auction houses.[70] In 1891, for example, the library of the late John Francis Buller (1818–90), of Morval, a Tudor manor house in east Cornwall, was sold in job lots by the Plymouth firm of Skardon and Sons, while ninety years later the historic library of the Dryden family from Canons Ashby, Northamptonshire, was sold in July 1980, along with the other contents of the house, by a local general auctioneer from nearby Brackley.[71] In 1967 the library from Bodysgallen – a Welsh house which had once housed a Shakespeare First Folio – was sold by the Llandudno auction house Blomfield & Co., while five years earlier the books at Stackpole Court in Pembrokeshire (the house demolished in 1963) were sold alongside the other contents of the house, again mostly in job lots.[72] In 1953 the executors of the late Lady Desborough sold the enormous library at Panshanger, in Hertfordshire, demolished a year later. The residue sale, held at the house in September of that year, included no fewer than 10,000 books, sold in a mere 427 lots, while at Vale Royal in Cheshire as many as sixty-two lots out of 278 were sold as a 'shelf of books', and another sixty-two lots as 'bundles of books'.[73] As late as 1962, a handbook on compiling inventories was advising 'in most houses the library contains little of value. The total value of the books barely justifies the time spent cataloguing, in fact they may have to be sold in lots of a dozen'.[74]

Elsewhere sales were even less systematic and certainly less easily traceable. The sale of books in 1932 from Frampton Court, Gloucester, to Bayntun's of Bath, for example, is not something easily recoverable via sale catalogues, but the victims were noted in a copy of the printed catalogue of the library (1884) now in the Bodleian Library.[75] Munby, writing in 1974, recalled his labours, sifting 'the grain from the chaff' while working for Sotheby's in the late 1930s, and reflected, with some evident surprise, how little regret he felt at the dispersal of the libraries which passed through his hands, collections which forty years later seemed to him remarkable in the 'layers of culture represented by any library which has been maintained for several generations'.[76] The true extent of sales from country houses was less visible than was in fact the case, as not untypically owners chose to sell discreetly, perhaps by private treaty or anonymously, 'the property of a gentleman'. In July 1964, for example, Sotheby's sold four sixteenth- and seventeenth-century books from the library at Wilton. There is no mention of either Wilton or the 16th Earl of Pembroke in the sale catalogue, but the provenance of lots 443, 457, 464 and 468 is clear from a marked-up copy in the family archive, a microcosm of a much bigger problem.[77]

The country house library and the book trade

One party's financial predicament was of course another's business opportunity. As early as May 1885, the London bookseller Charles Edmonds had posted a notice in *The Athenaeum*, touting his services as a cataloguer and investigator of 'old and unused libraries'. Just in case potential clients failed to get the point, he underlined his previous successes in rooting out 'Precious and Hitherto Unknown Books' at Lamport Hall, Lowther Castle and elsewhere, citing these examples as 'evidences of what Literary Treasures still awaited the skilled knowledge of the Expert'.[78] Sixty years later, in the immediate post-war period, the Cambridge booksellers Deighton, Bell & Co. circulated a note to country house owners in May 1946, a copy of which survives slipped inside a catalogue of the library at Thoresby Hall, Nottinghamshire, compiled in the same year:

> *Dear Sir (or Madam),*
> *If you have a library of books, or even a single volume which you believe to be valuable, the present is a very favourable time to sell, prices being higher than for many years past.*

We are prepared to purchase good books of all kinds, and from the large proportion of our offers which are accepted, we are satisfied that the prices we offer are exceptionally high.

In the case of large collections, a representative can usually attend and make a valuation, but for small lots it is usually sufficient to send a list, quoting especially the date of publication.

Should you have any books for disposal, we invite correspondence.[79]

Of course, in pursuing books from great houses, smaller booksellers faced formidable competition from established London firms such as Quaritch (founded in 1847) and Maggs Bros (1853), both with long-standing relationships with buyers and sellers. Many of the great country house sales of the late nineteenth century were dominated by Bernard Quaritch (1819–99), whose purchases made up more than half the total receipts at the Beckford sale. At the 1884 Syston sale he twice broke the record for the highest price ever paid for a printed book (£3,900 for a Gutenberg Bible followed by £4,950 for a 1459 Mainz Psalter), and he had earlier bought a significant proportion of the books sold from the Sunderland Library.[80] Quaritch greatly influenced many of the new collectors of the era, publishing *Contributions towards a Dictionary of English Book Collectors* (1892–1921), as well as

[213] Henry E. Huntington

his massive sixteen-volume *General Catalogue* (1887–92), to whet the appetite of the Harleys and the Spencers of the future.

The main London auction houses were locked in a symbiotic, if not necessarily always especially friendly, relationship with the dealers. Sotheby's, for example, first came to prominence with the career of John Sotheby (1740–1807), and by the late nineteenth century was an established part of the London book scene, at a time when the imperial capital was the great centre of the international trade in rare books.[81] The firm's relationship with its rival Christie's was mirrored by the rivalry between Maggs and Quaritch, while for periods in the late nineteenth and early twentieth centuries, other auction houses edged into the country house scene, with Puttick and Simpson netting several important sales, including those at Blenheim and Gosford Castle.

The extent to which country houses sales were fixed is, inevitably, a subject which is difficult to pin down and which many have understandably been reluctant to address. There can be little doubt that 'the Ring' (a covert arrangement, illegal since 1927, whereby members of the trade agree not to bid against one another at public auctions, and then meet privately to stage a second sale and divide the resulting profits) was often active. In one of the most notorious instances, the Lowther Castle sale of 1956, the operation became so brazen that it caused a furore in the press. The official auction fetched just £2,200, but two rounds of auctions at a nearby pub added no less than £16,000 to that total.[82] At the time the issue was widely evaded in the trade, but one author with inside knowledge candidly admitted that most of the great country house sales of the first half of the twentieth century 'had been totally dominated by the ring'.[83] If this is true, then not only had books been sold from great houses in vast numbers, but in many cases they were dishonestly sold at less than their real value.

Sales to America and further afield

Writing in 1855, the American commentator Luther Farnham (1816–97) had rather gloomily observed:

This country is sadly in want of books … In opulence, population, present and prospective, in the character of its institutions, and in the intelligence of the people, and in most that goes to make a great nation, this republic ranks as a first-rate

power … But what visitor crosses the sea to view our libraries? Who ever has ever heard of them abroad, except their diminutive size and meagre character?'[84]

It was certainly not a charge which could have been laid a century later, and successive purchases from European and especially British collections was the basis of this change. In a mirror image of the activities of the British bibliomaniacs in the Napoleonic period, by the late nineteenth century rich American collectors were buying books on a grand scale from long-established libraries in less prosperous lands. The oil magnate Henry Clay Folger (1857–1930), who became famous for his pursuit of Shakespeare First Folios, purchased the separate and self-contained Shakespeare collection from Warwick Castle en bloc in 1897.[85] Henry E. Huntington (1850–1927, fig. 213), then a recent entrant to the rare book market, bought Shakespeare and Caxtons from Chatsworth in 1914, before going on to secure the 4,400 books in the Bridgewater Library, a collection whose origins reached back to Lord Chancellor Egerton in the seventeenth century and which was sold in 1917 to pay death duties.[86] His library, transferred from New York to California in 1920, was conceived as a collection reflective of 'the history of the English-speaking peoples', and following his retirement in 1910, Huntington devoted the remaining seventeen years of his life to it.[87] European vendors took the hint, and a year after Huntington's death, Americana figured prominently among the 128 books and manuscripts sold from Petworth in 1928, clearly selected to tempt transatlantic collectors with dollars to spare.[88]

Sales to America were not always well received in Britain. As early as 1910, a correspondent to *The Athenaeum* had complained vehemently about the recent sale of official (or at least quasi-official) papers kept by the heirs of William Blathwayt at Dyrham Park. *The Times*, while regretting the sale of the Bridgewater Library to Huntington, conceded that the sale was necessary to 'meet the heavy burden of death duties' and that the books would be as well cared for in America as in England.[89] But even Shane Leslie, usually unsentimental about books crossing the Atlantic, felt that the eighth-century Blickling Homilies, a key text in the development of the English language, ought never to have been allowed to leave the country.[90]

Many lesser American collectors were able to take advantage of the flood of books from British country houses, as the briefest investigation of almost any US research collection swiftly reveals. Sometimes those who bought them had interests more recondite than the pursuit of obvious trophies. One obvious example was Wilmarth Sheldon Lewis (1895–1979), who spent a large part of his life pursuing books that had once belonged to Horace Walpole, bequeathing the Lewis Walpole Library at Farmington, Connecticut, to his alma mater Yale on his death. 'Lefty' Lewis reckoned that having started to collect Walpole books in 1924, he averaged one title a week for the rest of his career. One of the largest concentrations arrived in 1953 and 1954, a very favourable time in terms of exchange rates, with Lewis's purchases of books and manuscripts from the library of the 13th Earl of Derby (1775–1851), long at Knowsley Hall, Derby himself having been a major purchaser at the 1842 Strawberry Hill sale.[91] Books and manuscripts from country houses can be found without difficulty in almost every major American library, whether as whole collections or as individual volumes, either purchased piecemeal or subsequently received as gifts from the private libraries of donors. To quote a small number of examples more or less at random, the Houghton Library at Harvard has an album of seventy-two pieces of medieval manuscript waste extracted from bindings at Lanhydrock, as well as books from Wrest Park.[92] In addition to the Caxtons from Osterley and the treasure bindings from Holkham (see p. 163), the Morgan Library has the tenth-century Blickling Psalter and the early thirteenth-century Lothian Bible from Newbattle, as well as manuscripts from Helmingham. The Blickling Homilies are in the Scheide Collection, at Princeton since 1959, and bequeathed to the University by William H. Scheide (1914–2014), while the Clumber copy of Audubon's *Birds of America* (1827–38) is in the New York Historical Society.[93] Manuscript books from the Ashburnham collection are unsurprisingly ubiquitous, while the Canons Ashby Shakespeare First Folio, sold from the house in 1913 and re-sold in New York in 2001 for a record $5,600,000, is, in common with many other former country house books, in private hands in the US.[94] The number of possible examples, even at the highest level of the market, is huge, and at a slightly lower level, in both public and private hands, beyond any possible count or estimation. Occasionally their story was a strange one, as at Castle Hill, a 1929 mansion near Ipswich, Massachusetts, where in 1953 empty library shelves (themselves bought from Cassiobury) were stocked with 176 feet of books bought en masse from Killeen Castle, the seat of the Earls of Fingal in Ireland, at a knock-down price of $1 per foot.[95]

Nor was America the only possible destination. In 1963 the Cliffords of Chudleigh sold the library from Ugbrooke Park in Devon, which included about 6,430 printed books as well as nine medieval manuscripts, to the National Library of Australia in Canberra. The slightly unexpected choice of the vendor was presumably determined by the fact that the 13th Lord Clifford (1916–88), who had succeeded in 1957, had an Australian mother and had spent part of his youth in Australia.[96] By the 1980s books, following money as surely as they always had, not infrequently found their way to Japan, either to private collectors or into institutional libraries. The second largest concentration of Shakespeare First Folios after the Folger is now in Mesei University, Tokyo, acquired between 1975 and 1992, where there are now twelve copies, several of which were once in British country houses, including Hagley Hall in Worcestershire and Packington Hall in Warwickshire. How many humbler books have travelled so far must remain a matter of guesswork.

The post-war era

The Labour landslide of 1945 marked in every sense a new era, and one with momentous implications for country houses, their contents and those who owned them. With the United Kingdom bankrupt, and the new government desperate for money, new legislation was introduced to restrict the use of companies to avoid death duties payable on agricultural land, as the Devonshires discovered to their cost when the 10th Duke died unexpectedly in 1950, leaving his successor liable to 80 per cent tax on everything the House of Cavendish possessed. The total tax bill racked up to a then-astronomical £4.72 million, which immediately started to attract interest at a rate of £1,000 a day.[97] The Benedictional of St Æthelwold (see fig. 7) was one of the eight stellar objects at Chatsworth which the Treasury accepted as representing four-fifths of the monetary value of the collection.[98] A manuscript which Harvard's W. A. Jackson (1905–64),

on a 1938 fishing expedition round country house libraries, had acclaimed as 'the greatest MS. which now exists in private hands', it had been coveted by Humfrey Wanley but had passed to the 2nd Duke of Devonshire from the executors of Bishop Compton of London between 1713 and 1720.[99] Further books from the library went in 1981, sold along with Poussin's *Holy Family*, to raise the endowment for the newly founded Chatsworth House Trust, while the 11th Duke of Devonshire (1920–2004), writing towards the end of his life, was candid that the capital raised would probably one day 'have to be supplemented' by further sales from the collection.[100] This is, indeed, precisely what has happened.

Nonetheless in 1945 there was, quite apart from the economic situation, a sense on the part of many country house owners that the show was over, accepted with resignation by some, but also the subject of some protest. The heir to Wilton, for example, wrote to the Ministry of Works in 1942 to ask 'what is to happen to the large, old-fashioned and probably historic house? … Is it to be allowed to deteriorate, decay and fall into disrepair? … Is this good for the country, and how does it benefit the People?'[101] This loss of confidence affected country house libraries as much as anything else, with a widespread sense, still to some extent alive and well, that there was something slightly indecent in the very idea of great libraries in private hands. Writing in 2004, the 11th Duke of Devonshire admitted that he had always felt that the Benedictional of St Æthelwold was too important to be in private hands, a reasonable view, but certainly not one which would have been shared by his eighteenth-century predecessors.[102] Munby, in an essay on country house libraries published in 1974, took the view that books in private hands had generally not been used enough.[103]

Nonetheless by comparison with what was happening elsewhere in Europe, the assault on the landed class – and the destruction of their libraries – was limited in extent, but the results for many collections were still catastrophic.[104] At Oxburgh in Norfolk, where the 9th Baronet (1915–2011) inherited the estate but no money, the house came within an ace of destruction in 1950, and over 2,500 volumes from the library were dispersed in October 1951, though a smaller sale had already occurred in 1922.[105] Three years earlier, in the desperate year 1947, with the economy of the United Kingdom on

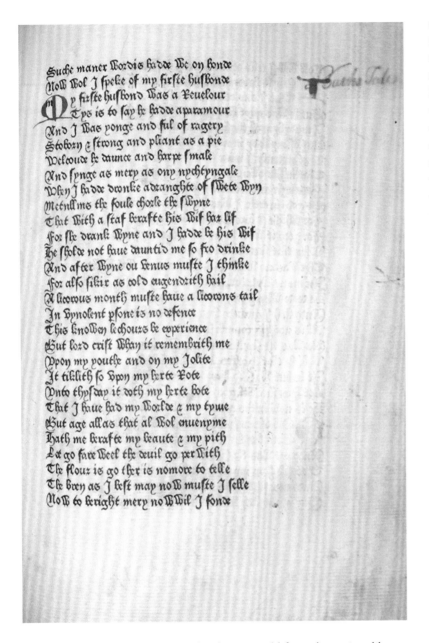

of Derby from Knowsley went between 1953 and 1954, and another great eighteenth-century library, that of the Earls of Malmesbury, from Hurn Court in Dorset in 1950.[109] All of these sales are easily lamented in hindsight, but there can be little doubt that at the time they were just one small part of a post-war consensus. At the time, complaints about demolished country houses were very much a minority interest. The British electorate in 1945 was clearly comfortable with the idea that the world which had existed until 1939 had had its day, and that vested interests and inherited wealth needed to be taken on to address a situation of national emergency, to fund a National Health Service and to allow for the emergence of a new world of public ownership, social welfare and nationalised industries.

Even when houses were taken over by public or charitable bodies, this did not necessarily mean that libraries remained intact. A fine collection of travel and colour-plate books, for example, were removed from Penrhyn Castle and sold in 1953, just after the National Trust had acquired the house in lieu of death duties in 1951, while a generation later, in 1971, the 4th Lord St Oswald (1916–84) sold his Shakespeare First Folio from Nostell Priory (it ended up in the Foreign Studies University in Kyoto).[110] Books sold in 1946 from Lyme Park, Cheshire, included a fair number of ordinary-enough eighteenth- and nineteenth-century books, books which with hindsight would have illuminated life in one of the great houses of northern England. The earlier ones, some of which may have been *in situ* since the sixteenth century, would have provided a foil for the unique 1487 Caxton, which survived to be purchased by the National Trust in 2008, having been in the hands of the Legh family since at least 1507.[111]

II · IRELAND: THE END OF THE OLD ORDER

If the middle years of the twentieth century saw huge changes for the owners of British houses, in Ireland things changed much more dramatically, and the story there was fundamentally different. By contrast with England and Scotland, the twentieth century saw the almost total eclipse of the old order in Ireland, certainly in the South and, to a slightly lesser degree, in Northern Ireland. Landowning families lost power and wealth, and above all their land. For the most part their great houses and

[215] The 1476–7 Caxton Chaucer from Wentworth Woodhouse, now in the Wormsley Library

its knees, books were sold from the ancient library at Naworth.[106] A year later there was a major sale from Wentworth Woodhouse, though other books remained and still remain in the family, if not necessarily in the house (a spectacular copy of the Caxton Chaucer of 1476–7 [fig. 215], which had once belonged to the 2nd Marquess of Rockingham (1730–82), was sold to Sir Paul Getty in July 1998).[107] It was presumably one of the books which Jackson had eyed covetously in 1938, frustrated that they could not be fetched out of their display case because Earl Fitzwilliam's Comptroller was away playing golf.[108] Elsewhere sales continued well beyond the immediate crisis period of the late 1940s. A large part of the library of the Earls their contents have vanished as well, to an extent which country house enthusiasts in Britain often find difficult to grasp. That is not to say that Irish country houses had not been subject to catastrophe at earlier periods in their history – the library at Castlecomer House, County Kilkenny, for example, was burned in the 1798 Rising – but the events of the late nineteenth and early twentieth centuries were on an altogether grander scale.[112]

Land had been one of the defining issues of nineteenth-century Irish politics, but by the time of the revolutionary era (1916–23) it was a problem which had in large measure already been solved. Embarrassed by the activities of the Land League from the 1870s, under pressure from Irish Nationalist MPs at Westminster and in at least some measure discomfited by the callous and inadequate response of an earlier generation to the horrors of the Great Famine, British officials, both Liberal and Conservative, increasingly turned their attention to the vexed question of Irish land ownership. The key event was the so-called Wyndham Land Act of 1903, named after George Wyndham (1863–1913), who was a Tory but also a great-grandson of the Irish Republican hero Lord Edward FitzGerald (1753–98) and, as Chief Secretary, the leading figure in the Dublin Castle administration from 1900 to 1905. The precise details of this and earlier reforms are not germane here, but essentially the Wyndham Act made it possible for tenant farmers to buy out their land-lords with state funding. It was not the first legislation of its kind, but it was the most far-reaching, and there was nothing comparable in Great Britain. The associated financial package was underwritten by the United Kingdom's National Debt, and was designed to be attractive both to buyers and sellers. The landlords received a 'Bonus' of 12 per cent from the government, while the tenants were offered the chance to buy on terms which they could afford.[113] As Shane Leslie put it: 'The Wyndham Land Act brought peace between landlord and tenant by bribing both.'[114] Despite the contemporary furore about Home Rule, the settlement largely worked. In the short term even the landlords did well out of it. In 1907 at Powerscourt, County Wicklow, not only did the house still have a library, but Lord Powerscourt had the money and the self-confidence to commission a new printed catalogue.[115] The land reform project continued on both sides of the border after Partition in 1922, in the new Free

State, at least, on terms which, if less sympathetic to the landowners than previously, were by no means so punitive as the land reforms in other European states which emerged after 1918. As far as the country house was concerned, the crucial point was that the former ruling class exchanged land for capital, the value of which, in the inflationary era following the First World War, was steadily eroded. Houses which had historically been financed by the agricultural rents of the surrounding estate became ever more impossible to maintain at a time when the value of investments was falling, while simultaneously running costs were increasing. At the same time, the national ethos of the new Irish state, if not necessarily actively hostile to the former landlords, was at least potentially unwelcome to them. An Ireland which overtly defined itself as Catholic and Gaelic was a country where the former Irish Protestant upper class needed to behave with a certain circumspection, and where they could no longer take it for granted that they would be at the centre of affairs. In many cases the process of decline was a gradual one, but as the older genera-tions died out, Irish big houses not untypically fell into decay, leading to their abandonment and demolition, and the sale of their contents, including hundreds of libraries.[116] In many cases these contents were scattered, lost or sold abroad.

Other houses and other libraries, far less gran-diose and far less magnificent, must have vanished if not without trace, then certainly without leaving much historical footprint. The £10 worth of books at Annaghmore, County Sligo, in 1939, are unlikely to have been in any way spectacular, and the fittings and furnishings of the Library there, collectively valued at just £37 5s., are unlikely to have been any more grandiose. Nonetheless both components will, in some way, have mirrored something of the lives of those who lived and worked in the house. Annaghmore House still survives, the seat of the Catholic O'Haras, but elsewhere in Ireland houses of similar status have vanished completely, along with their contents and the archives which would have once described them, and cumulatively the historic loss is considerable.[117]

Then there was the question of violence. This was important, but in statistical terms perhaps not so important as is sometimes imagined. It mostly occurred in two distinct phases: the latter part of Anglo-Irish war of 1916 to 1921, and the ensuing Civil War of 1922 to 1923, which saw armed conflict between the forces of the newly constituted Irish Free State and Republican irregulars hostile to the 1921 Treaty with Britain. The first major casualty, Summerhill, a magnificent Palladian mansion in County Meath, the seat of the Viscounts Langford, was burned in February 1920.[118] The motivation for burnings was mixed. Sometimes it was to prevent their use, or rumoured use, by the British Army or later by the opposing side in the Civil War, especially if the house was unoccupied at the time. Elsewhere burnings were carried out quite explicitly in retaliation for atrocities committed in other places (as when IRA forces burned Moydrum Castle, the home of Lord Castlemaine, in County Westmeath in July 1920), or as punishment for owners who were excessively outspoken or prominent on the wrong side of the debate (Senators of the Irish Free State, as quasi-hereditary members of the short-lived upper house of a bicameral legislature, were a particular target during the Civil War). In other cases burnings were primarily about agrarian disputes, with local people taking advantage of a period of social breakdown to drive out landlords or former landlords, or to settle long-standing grudges. In the twenty-six counties of the Free State, seventy-six houses were burned between January 1920 and July 1921, and 199 between January 1922 and May 1923, making a grand total of 175 – a large number of houses, certainly, but unevenly distributed and a small proportion of the total.[119] In the North, by comparison, activity was muted in the earlier period, though country house owners were unsurprisingly alarmed, often demanding and getting substantial police presence from the authorities. The peak of the burnings was later, in the summer of 1922, and country houses in the north and east of Ulster were as much at risk as those in the more vulnerable border areas. The principal victims included Shane's Castle, the ancestral seat of the eighty-three-year-old Lord O'Neill, and Antrim Castle, the seat of the Viscounts Massereene, though at Killyleagh Castle in County Down the raiders were seen off by determined gunfire from the battlements of the Plantation-era castle.[120] Another great house survived longer in Northern Ireland, but ultimately came to a terrible end, in a ghastly recapitulation of the Troubles of an earlier era. Tynan Abbey, County Armagh, barely a mile from the border, was torched in 1981. The bodies of its owner, Sir Norman Stronge (1894–1981), a former Speaker of the Commons

of Northern Ireland, and of his son Major James Stronge (1932–81), both shot through the head by the Provisional IRA, were left to be devoured by the flames, along with the family's ancestral books, in the Library of the great Regency Gothic house.[121]

In both North and South, there can be no doubt that the burnings resulted in the destruction of an appreciable number of books, though the details, unsurprisingly, can be difficult to substantiate. Of course the protagonists had no particular animus against either books or Libraries, except insofar as they represented the power and affluence of the landed interest: when books burned, it was simply because they were in the way. Sometimes they escaped, either because family and servants rescued them, or because the incendiaries, perhaps neighbours but certainly keen to make the point that they were soldiers, disciplined and correct, and not mere *banditti*, allowed them to be rescued before houses were torched. In July 1921 at Castle Bernard, County Cork, the castle burned, but the contents of the shelves were saved.[122] Some books, at least, evidently survived the destruction of Antrim Castle in 1922, as the career of the successful Belfast antiquarian bookseller Jack Gamble (d. 2015) was launched when he found a cache of inscribed Handel first editions which had once belonged to Handel's Irish patron, the 1st Earl of Massereene (1715–57), in an Antrim antique shop.[123] Elsewhere big house books might have a different fate. The County Clare landowner and soldier Col. George O'Callaghan-Westropp (1864–1944) suggested in his *Notes on the Defence of Irish Country Houses* – a pamphlet or broadside occasionally cited or mentioned in the secondary literature, but impossible to track down – that antique books made ideal barricades for doors and windows, useful for keeping out armed raiders.[124] And indeed in April 1916, twenty-two volumes of bound newspapers, 'a convenient way of making windows bullet-proof', were despatched to O'Callaghan-Westropp's house, Lismehane, County Clare, by Browne and Nolan.[125]

Nonetheless the eclipse of the big house was more often a matter of economics rather than incendiaries. In the period immediately after the Second World War (in most of Ireland 'The Emergency', as the twenty-six counties were neutral), the experience of great houses in Britain and Ireland was often remarkably similar. For many they were redundant relics of a bygone era. The great shift in attitude came later, with the gradual but from the 1950s increasingly widespread acceptance in Britain that country houses had a cultural and economic value, whether one sympathised with their owners or not. This attitude was certainly not mirrored in Ireland, where official and popular opinion tended to be resolutely sceptical about the legacy of an unlamented colonial past, a view which remains common even in the twenty-first century.

The library of the grandest family of all, the Dukes of Leinster, was sold on site at Carton House, County Kildare, over three days in June 1949, though there had already been an earlier sale in 1925 (fig. 216).[126] Just a few months after the Irish state had finally completed its progressive disengagement from the British sphere, the operation was understandably overseen by the Dublin auctioneers Allen and Townsend, rather than by a firm from London.[127] Many decades later the renowned Dublin bookseller Fred Hanna (1934–2011) recalled attending the sale with his father, leaving the demesne with their car so loaded with 'beautifully bound vellum books' that the vehicle sank low on its suspension and they had difficulty in getting it out through the park gates.[128]

The library at Coole Park, County Galway, survived until March 1972, when it fetched £37,536. Close by Yeats's house Thor Balee, Coole was associated more than anything else with Augusta, Lady Gregory (1852–1932), with Yeats and J. M. Synge, who was one of first directors of the Abbey Theatre and a key figure in the Celtic Revival. Many of Yeats's great poems were written at Coole, and Lady Gregory herself penned a description of the library there in her book *Coole*, printed by the Cuala Press in 1931, at a time when finances were especially tight and when she feared that she would not live there much longer.[129] As she herself explained, her late husband had given her a life interest in his family's library, a collection that she had cherished and read over many decades.

The loss of libraries in Ireland was often about the the loss of interiors as well as of books, now remembered, albeit in ghostly fashion, mostly in period photographs in the Irish Architectural Archive in Dublin, and occasionally online or in published form. Despite demolitions and burnings, here and there buildings survive, though not necessarily in their original form and still less with their original contents. At Ballyfin, County Offaly, the great house of the Coote baronets, occupied by

[216] The Library at Carton House, County Kildare, prior to the sale of the books in 1949

the Patrician Brothers between 1930 and 2001, was spectacularly restored for a Chicago couple between 2002 and 2010 and now functions as a super-luxury hotel. The Library, its original appearance recorded in nineteenth-century photographs and a watercolour, is among the most magnificent of the reconstructed interiors.[130] By contrast, Shelton Abbey, County Wicklow, a spectacular Regency mansion 45 miles from Dublin, includes a large and impressive Gothic Library, but the house was sold to the state in 1951 and has been used as an open prison since the early 1970s.[131]

Unlike interiors, books, once sold, become effectively irrecoverable, and library sales in Ireland have been inexorable. The house sale at Abbeyleix, County Laois, made IR£600,000 when the de Vescis sold up in 1995, with the remaining books from the family library sold in the same year by Mealy's of Castlecomer, an important firm in Ireland, at the Montrose Hotel in Dublin.[132] At Clonbrock, the County Galway seat of the Dillons, the 1976 house contents sale was conducted by Christie's and was held in a marquee. The house, for fifty-one years from 1925 the ever-more decayed home of the elderly Miss Ethel Dillon (1880–1978), was 'strictly out of bounds' during the sale and burned, accidentally, in 1994. The fine Regency library furniture from Clonbrock sold well, and the books 'produced some startling high prices', including £7,000 for a copy of 'Lewin on Birds' and £3,200 for an 'Edwards on Birds'.[133] This was by any standards a startling increase on the £195 paid for a copy of Edwards at a sale of books from Westport House, County Mayo, in 1955 when a large portion of the library of the Marquesses of Sligo was sold. There was another large sale from Westport by Mealy's in 1983.[134]

A few books remain *in situ* at Strokestown, County Roscommon, but others were sold in 1952 and, no doubt, at other times.[135] More remain at Caledon, County Tyrone, but there the library, much of which had once belonged to the scholar-bishop Thomas Percy (1729–1811), was the victim of a successful fishing expedition by Dr Rosenbach in 1928, accompanied by his friend Shane Leslie, who had been at Eton and Cambridge with the 5th Earl of Caledon (1885–1968). Rosenbach paid Caledon $29,280 (£6,000) for six printed books, including Percy's annotated Shakespeare First Folio, as well as a volume of six Shakespeare play quartos and Percy's manuscript glossary. Further books from Percy's library at Caledon were sold to Queen's University Belfast in 1969, a situation mirrored south of the border where Trinity College, Dublin, acquired part of the library from Townley Hall, County Louth.[136]

At Lissadell the library survived, though much depleted, into the twenty-first century, but was sold in 2003, Sir Josslyn and Lady Gore-Booth having decided that they felt unequal to the scale of what needed to be done to set the place on a sound footing. Despite demands that the place be taken on by the Irish state, plausible because of Lissadell's links with the Republican leader Countess Markievicz (1868–1927), first the contents and then the house went to private buyers. The new owners secured some of the books, and others went, but the house sale included works on polar exploration, the former floating library from the Gore-Booth yacht *Kara*, and an interesting array of eighteenth-, nineteenth- and early twentieth-century books.[137] These were clearly no more than a rump of the books once in the library at Lissadell. In 1963, for example, Jack Gamble, planning a visit to Sligo, wrote to Gabrielle and Aideen Gore-Booth at Lissadell to say that he had 'often wondered if you have done anything more about your books', and explained that he had considerable experience of dealing with books from Irish houses, 'having purchased some very large collections, privately and at auction'.[138]

By then the collection at Lissadell was already much diminished from its nineteenth-century heyday, a situation familiar all over Ireland, even in the minority of cases when houses still survived. It is a pattern which has continued into modern times, and seems set to continue, with the dispersal of the library at Mourne Park, County Down, part of the fall-out from a protracted family feud which landed the house's chatelaine in gaol in 2002, and the reported sale of Westport House and its remaining contents, announced in 2016.[139] With the exception of the libraries in the care of the National Trust in the North, and an ever-dwindling handful of libraries in private hands on both sides of the border, the history of the country house library in Ireland is one which seems almost to have run its course. For those with a taste for the counter-factual, the Irish story illustrates very graphically a turn of events which could, had history turned out differently, have come to pass in Great Britain.

CHAPTER FOURTEEN

The Body in the Library

Libraries and the Politics of Heritage in the Twentieth Century

*'Do you mean to tell me', demanded Colonel Bantry, 'that there's
a dead body in my library – my library?'*
Agatha Christie, *The Body in the Library*, 1942

I · LIBRARIES IN PRIVATE HANDS

Despite the advent of death duties in 1894, not all
country house owners started the twentieth century
in a cloud of gloom. In Ireland the ambitious or the
unwise used the capital accumulated from compulsory tenant buy-outs to start on a spending spree.
Others had additional and more reliable sources of
income. At Farmleigh in County Dublin, Edward
Arthur Guinness (ennobled in 1891) embarked
on a series of building projects throughout the
1880s and 1890s, funded from the brewing fortune
started by his grandfather. The house incorporated
a magnificent two-storey galleried Library, its
shelves now filled with marvellous Hibernica
created by Guinness's grandson, the 3rd Earl of
Iveagh (1937–92). In England in 1909, the 6th
Marquess of Anglesey (whose ancestors included a
Tudor Secretary of State and one of Wellington's
generals) commissioned a grandiose Tudorbethan
Library for his sixteenth-century house Beaudesert,
Staffordshire, a house demolished just twenty-six
years later.[1]

Perhaps inevitably the story of the country
house library in the twentieth century is mostly
about loss or dispersal, but that was only part of
it. The body in the Library at Agatha Christie's
Gossington Hall may well have been dead.
Elsewhere the body could take a long time to
expire. More than a century after commentators started talking about punitive taxation and
political oblivion, many landed families still had a
great library in their house at the dawn of the new
millennium, whether they took much notice of it

or not. In many twentieth-century country houses
the Library continued to play its traditional role
as the favoured sitting room and centre of family
life. When the National Trust's James Lees-Milne
(1908–97) visited Wallington during the Second
World War he was impressed and terrified by the
overt intellectualism of his left-wing hosts, the
Trevelyans. Subjected to a compulsory general
knowledge quiz by the formidable Lady Trevelyan,
he retreated from the Library with his tail between
his legs; unsurprisingly his wartime diaries make
no mention of the well-used and thoroughly annotated books kept there.[2] Three decades later, Lady
Victoria Leatham (b.1947), a well-known television
personality in the 1980s, used the Ante-Library at
Burghley as the nerve centre of the estate, while the
adjacent Library, 'with a fire crackling away in the
hearth', was the place for shooting teas and trustees'
meetings.[3] Forty-odd miles away at Althorp, Raine
Spencer (1929–2016), undaunted by the memory
of the 2nd Earl Spencer's books, had firm views
on the Library, 'a room for daytime, for wearing
corduroy trousers. Not just stately-home things,
but comfortable chairs and good reading lights,
a good lamp next to the card table, a place to put
down a cup of coffee.'[4] It was a view which, by the
latter years of the twentieth century, could be found
in the pages of interior design magazines from
Mayfair to Manhattan. As one country house chatelaine put it in 1995: 'Books are so much nicer than
wallpaper.'[5] The English country house Library
had style and class, which clients of the celebrity

[217] The Library at
Anglesey Abbey

interior designer John Fowler (1906–77) – and his imitators, on both sides of the Atlantic – could only covet and envy. At the same time the Library as sitting room, traditional though it was, could be fraught with difficulties for the unwary. When the National Trust took on the Library at Chirk Castle in 2004, many of the books, in the castle since the seventeenth century, were in a truly terrible state, the victims not of centuries of neglect, but of comfortable post-war central heating. Interviewed in 2012, the 12th Duke of Northumberland (b.1955) remembered with embarrassment an unfortunate student scrape – a forgotten keg of Christmas beer left in the Library at Alnwick, which exploded three weeks after its owner had returned to Oxford. 'I wasn't very popular', he recalled.[6]

Given the cachet of a well-stocked Library, those whose parents or grandparents had denuded ancestral shelves often refilled them. At Clandon, in Surrey, where the library of Speaker Arthur Onslow (1691–1768) had been sold in 1885, his descendants stocked the shelves with a mixture of useful modern books and bulky leather-bound 'set dressing' (fig. 218). If it seems unlikely that anyone ever opened the thirty-volume set of the French historian Adolphe Thiers (1797–1877), other books, like Frances and Merrill Mason's *Among the Nudists* (1932), raise all sorts of intriguing questions. A few miles away at Osterley, the 8th and 9th Earls of Jersey replaced the great library of the Childs, once rich in marvellous rarities, with a useful but elegant working library, now vanished

[218] The Library at Clandon Park prior to its destruction by fire in April 2015

in its turn, but recorded in a printed catalogue of 1926.[7] At Beaulieu in Hampshire the 3rd Lord Montagu (1926–2015) moved the Library and its contents from downstairs to an upstairs room to get it off the visitor route.[8] At Berrington Hall in Herefordshire the Cawleys, north-country cotton magnates who bought out the profligate Lord Rodney in 1901, restocked Henry Holland's elegant Neoclassical Library with a mixture of everyday modern books and handsome but decrepit eighteenth-century books in calf bindings. Some of these had once graced the shelves of Heaton Hall, the James Wyatt masterpiece just outside Manchester, purchased by the Manchester Corporation in 1906.[9] Not far from Berrington, at Croft Castle, the Crofts, who had sold up in 1746, returned in 1923. Getting into bed with the National Trust in 1957, the family – in the form of the Croft Castle Trustees – assembled a delightful small library, a mixture of inherited family books, and books old and new about Wales and the Marches, as well as books on the Picturesque.[10] By contrast, members of the Lewes family at Llanerchaeron replaced a historic library sold in 1918 with books of the most mundane kind: middle-brow volumes on field sports and mass-market women's fiction predominated.[11] Apparently unremarkable, a fair number of these books, evidently seen as beneath the notice of scholarly research libraries, missed legal deposit. By the time the National Trust took over in 1994, it was difficult to resist the conclusion that the Llanerchaeron library was an intriguing if perhaps comparatively minor social document.

At the opposite end of the spectrum several of the very grandest houses saw a curious mix of dislocation and continuity. In Norfolk the 5th Earl of Leicester (1908–76) at Holkham was forced to surrender some of his choicest books and manuscripts to the Bodleian in payment of death duties (fig. 219), a process somewhat eased by the fact that Bodley's own W. O. Hassall (1912–94) was also librarian at Holkham from 1937 to 1983.[12] More famously, when Andrew Cavendish succeeded as 11th Duke of Devonshire in 1950, he was faced with enormous death duties, and after the surrender of Hardwick Hall and various works of art to the Treasury, the Chatsworth library supplied a substantial part of the residue. But the duke was in parallel assembling a collection of his own, including botanical books and Hibernica, shelved in Chatsworth's nineteenth-century Lower Library, which he used as his private den.[13] Some of his book collecting acumen was no doubt connected with his ownership of Heywood Hill, Mayfair's booksellers to the gentry, at just exactly the period when antiquarian bookselling, traditionally a

[219] A fourteenth-century manuscript of Dante's *Divine Comedy* once at Holkham Hall (now Bodleian Library)

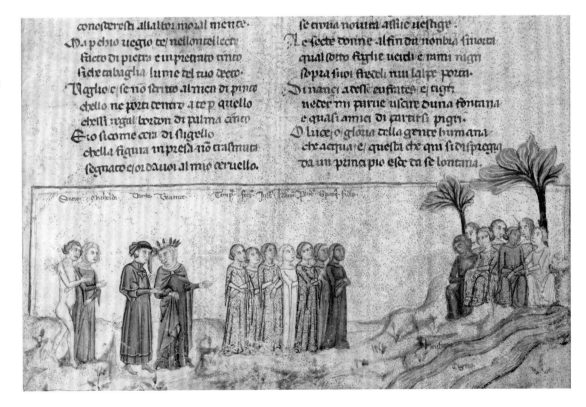

pursuit for bright working-class boys, was invaded by the children of the upper and upper middle classes.[14] Several of Devonshire's contemporaries shared his bibliophilic interests. At Hatfield the 6th Marquess of Salisbury (1916–2003) collected rare books, and published a fine account of the historic family library in 1967.[15] At Hovingham Hall in Yorkshire Sir Marcus Worsley (1925–2012) collected Penguin first editions, a taste shared – for Penguins, if not first editions – by the 6th Marquess of Exeter (1905–81), who shelved his paperback thrillers and art reference books on a massive run of Utility shelving in the Blue Drawing Room at Burghley.[16] Simon Howard of Castle Howard, building on the sensational success of Granada TV's *Brideshead Revisited* (1981), brought in the classically trained architect Julian Bicknell (b.1945) to design a completely new Library room (fig.220) in a house which, despite sales, already contained a generous collection of ancestral books.[17] A similar room, designed by Roderick Gradidge (1929–2000) and David Hicks (1929–98) and subsequently altered, was put in for the Heskeths at Easton Neston in 1964.[18] At Castle Howard Christopher Ridgeway, the librarian who

created the new library, went on to become curator of the collection, and an influential figure in country house studies. It was a modern reworking of the traditional country house librarian as cultural factotum. At Chatsworth Francis Thompson (d.1964) was held in some awe by the young Debo Devonshire: 'the very archetypal librarian, already old when I first knew him, white face and hands, a tonsure of yellow-white hair showing under black skull cap'.[19]

In other privately owned houses owners became curators. At Scotney Castle Christopher Hussey (1899–1970), long-standing architectural editor of *Country Life*, famously 'got' the Picturesque while looking out of the Library windows round about 1924.[20] As regards the books, his insights were reflected in what he added to the family library: modern working books on art and architecture alongside early guidebooks and books on landscape gardening. At Felbrigg in Norfolk, the scholar-squire Wyndham Ketton-Cremer (1906–69) not only cherished thousands of books he had inherited with the house, but filled gaps left by a sale in 1919, as well as buying large numbers of important modern books to underpin his own

[220] Julian Bicknell's Library at Castle Howard

[221] The Tower Room, Vita Sackville-West's Library at Sissinghurst

antiquarian studies. Since his scholarly cronies included the American Wilmarth 'Lefty' Lewis (1895–1979), creator of the Lewis Walpole Library at Farmington, Connecticut, these books include some interesting association copies.[21] By contrast at Dunham Massey in Cheshire, Roger Grey, 10th Earl of Stamford (1896–1976), a reclusive Christian socialist, filled his Study with worthy books on politics and international relations. Similarly the private shelves of the 11th Marquess of Lothian at Blickling were filled with books on the League of Nations, agricultural and tariff reform, and (again) international relations. In Ireland the library of the 7th Marquess of Londonderry at Mount Stewart, County Down, has a rather similar flavour, though there books inherited from eighteenth- and nineteenth-century forebears were

also augmented by books reflecting the interests of his wife Edith, which included gardening, the Celtic Revival and Irish private press books, many inscribed by Yeats, Shaw and O'Casey: an interesting encounter between Orange and Green in an arch-Unionist house. From the opposite end of the political spectrum, but at much the same time, Jim and Ruth Pennyman of Ormesby Hall, an eighteenth-century house on the outskirts of Middlesborough, bought left-leaning books for a famously left-leaning house. In north-west Wales, by contrast, the 7th Marquess of Anglesey (1922–2013) bought books on military history, which he used to write his acclaimed *History of the British Cavalry*. Henry Anglesey retained the ground-floor Library at Plas Newydd, with huge nineteenth-century glazed bookcases and

[222] The Long Library at Sissinghurst

spectacular views over the Menai Strait, when he handed over the house to the National Trust in 1976.

A couple of generations earlier, two more libraries – one assembled by a great imperial proconsul, and the other by the great poet-seer of the British empire – left a very definite mark on two very different houses. The erstwhile Viceroy of India, Lord Curzon (1859–1925), cherished and augmented the historic library at Kedleston: one of his more spectacular additions was a second copy of Robert Adam's 1764 *Ruins of the Palace of the Emperor Diocletian at Spalatro*, a gift from Prince Regent Paul of Yugoslavia (1893–1976). Curzon's personal library, unsurprisingly rich in books from and about India, is partially extant in a ground-floor room next to his Indian Museum. At Bateman's in Sussex, Rudyard Kipling's library is richer still in books from the Subcontinent; but understanding it is greatly complicated by the fact that some of his books – including incunabula and early editions on beekeeping – were borne off after his death by his daughter and son-in-law, to fill gaps on the shelves of the depleted but still-magnificent Library of the Earls of Hardwicke at Wimpole, just outside Cambridge.

Despite the constant flow of books out, the twentieth century also saw the creation of a surprisingly large number of new or partly new country house libraries. The books in the Long Gallery at Chequers, gifted with the house by Viscount Lee of Fareham (1868–1947) as an official residence for British Prime Ministers, were partly acquired by him with the house in 1909 and include manuscripts and incunabula; Lee himself added nineteenth-century first editions.[22] Not far away Dorneywood, a modest neo-Georgian mansion, has a small collection of exquisite English and Scottish fine bindings assembled by Sir Courtauld Thomson (1865–1954), whose father had invented the pneumatic tyre and who left the house and its contents to the National Trust, again as an official residence for a government minister. Within living memory his finest bindings were displayed in the French style inside his glazed bookcases, like plates on stands.[23]

At Kenwood in the early twentieth century there was another library besides that on the shelves of the great Adam Library – that of Grand Duke Michael Mikhailovich (1861–1961), a grandson of Tsar Nicholas I exiled for contracting a morganatic

marriage in 1891.[24] Unusual domestic arrangements also prevailed at Sissinghurst, where Vita Sackville-West (1892–1962) and her husband Harold Nicolson (1886–1968) created three Libraries – a joint library of (mostly) review copies in a Long Library (fig. 222) designed by Philip Tilden (1887–1956), and two private Studies, one in the South Cottage, for Harold, and the other, in an eyrie above the Gate Tower (fig. 221), for Vita. Packed with interesting twentieth-century books, often first editions with their original dust jackets, sometimes autographed and frequently annotated or with letters and reviews inserted into them, between them they contain nearly 9,000 titles. Aside from the conceit of three Libraries placed so apparently artlessly in a garden itself made up of a series of outdoor rooms, Sissinghurst itself became an important part of the late twentieth-century cult of the country house, Vita's consolation prize for the loss of Knole. The couple's son Nigel Nicolson (1917–2004) not only stoked this cult with *Portrait of a Marriage* (1973), a remarkably candid exposé of his parents' decidedly unconventional lives, but continued the family tradition as co-founder of Weidenfeld and Nicolson and as the guardian of his parents' literary legacy. In a modest way, with a garden retreat safe from the tourists (the place was given to the National Trust in 1967), and a house complete with its own library, Nicolson himself continued the tradition of the eighteenth-century garden Library.[25]

Not far away at Port Lympne, Tilden also designed an elegant octagonal Library for Sir Philip Sassoon (1888–1939).[26] He was a key player too, at Chartwell, where he created a Library and Study for Winston Churchill. Unoccupied during the Second World War, the house was central to Churchill's life in the 1930s, and again after 1945. The Library, though stripped of association copies and its more grandiose books by Randolph Churchill in the late 1960s, remains deeply evocative, with endless presentation copies on subjects ranging from budgerigars through to Churchill's own works in Hebrew, as well as a printed copy of his 'Finest Hour' speech. By contrast, the art historian Kenneth Clark (1903–83) created a new Library in the great hall of Saltwood Castle, again in Kent, which he had purchased in 1955. His son the politician and diarist Alan Clark (1928–99) wrote of the euphoria of sitting all alone on a July evening in the long hot summer of 1976, dressed only in a towel, revelling in a huge room which looked and felt like a college Library.[27]

To one extent or another, many of the new twentieth-century libraries unsurprisingly smacked more of accumulation and practical utility than bibliophilia. But there were exceptions. At Ascott (Buckinghamshire), Anthony de Rothschild (1887–1961) assembled a superlative library of private press books in the massive half-timbered mansion built for his father Leopold de Rothschild (1845–1917), a collection which, despite National Trust visitors from 1949, enjoyed a low public profile until it was looted by a former President of the Antiquarian Booksellers Association, who had been brought in to catalogue it (he was jailed for twenty-eight months in 2009).[28] Many miles to the north at Stobhall Castle (Perthshire), the 17th Earl of Perth (1907–2002), a member of the Roxburghe Club, put together a fine library of books at the family's ancestral seat, which he had reacquired in a derelict state in 1954. His particular enthusiasm was his Jacobite Collection, an appropriate choice as the Perth peerage had been in abeyance between 1715 and 1853 as a result of the 4th Earl's support for the Old Pretender. Other books included maps, atlases, travel books and a copy of Robert Thornton's *Temple of Flora* (1799–1807), dispersed by his family after his death.[29] An equally specialised library belonged to the 2nd Lord Wardington (1924–2005). Scion of a wealthy Quaker banking family, Wardington inherited a fine collection of Bibles and incunabula, but added magnificent maps and atlases. Narrowly escaping a fire at Wardington Manor (Oxfordshire), the books were again sold after his death. They included forty-six incunabula, mostly bibliomaniac copies in grand bindings, about half of them from the library of Sir John Thorold (1734–1815) at Syston Park in Lincolnshire.[30] In Ireland the Celtic Tiger boom (mid-1990s to mid-2000s) had an impact on Irish houses which few would have anticipated some decades earlier. A lavish refurbishment of Ballyfin, County Offaly, the former house of the Coote family, in institutional hands since 1923, naturally included work on the Library. Though some Coote family books returned, the emphasis was more on the Library as a room rather than the library as a collection of books.[31] By contrast, William Forwood (1927–2011), Managing Director of Guinness Mahon in Ireland, assembled a large library of nineteenth-century fiction, history, travel

and natural history at Woodstock, one of the largest Georgian houses in County Wicklow. Books and owner subsequently moved to Coity Mawr, a Welsh manor house in Radnorshire, where the Library was fitted up with specially made bookcases made from tropical hardwood specially imported from Vietnam.[32]

Connections with the trade were more overt with the library of the Foyles at Beeleigh Abbey in Essex. Occupying a magnificent medieval room, and funded from the proceeds of the famously eccentric West End bookshop, the library was assembled by William Foyle (1885–1963) and sold after the death of his daughter Christina in 1999. It ranged from incunabula and medieval manuscripts to Nelson autographs and iconic works of English literature. The Christie's sale in July 2000 made some £12.6m, then a record price for a European private library at auction.[33] The library of Major J. R. Abbey (1894–1969) was one that, with hindsight, many concluded had been destined from the beginning to be sold. Possessing what was not generally thought of as a country house library, Abbey lived from 1957 to 1967 at Redlynch House in Wiltshire. A series of lavish scholarly catalogues, published in his lifetime, served to emphasise the desirability of his library. Paid for by his father's brewing fortune, it included medieval manuscripts, private press books, fine bindings and marvellous colour-plate books, providing rich pickings for the next generation of collectors. The colour-plate books, in particular, broke new ground, opening up an area of interest previously despised by more sophisticated and fastidious collectors. There were eventually no fewer than 1,914 of them, a good haul for a man reputedly none too literate.[34]

Some of Abbey's most magnificent books found their way into the library of Sir Paul Getty (1932–2003) at Wormsley (fig. 223), in the Chilterns, a collection which became increasingly well known in the final years of the twentieth century. This was due partly to the welcome extended to specialist groups like the Bibliographical Society, partly to an exhibition held at the Morgan Library in New York in 1999 and partly to the publicity generated by Getty's last great coup as a collector, his purchase in April 2002 of the Shakespeare First Folio (see fig. 6) bequeathed to Oriel College, Oxford, by Lord Leigh in 1786. Like his eighteenth- and nineteenth-century precursors, Getty enjoyed close relations with a favoured bookseller, the great London firm

[223]
The Wormsley Library

of Maggs Bros, which provided much of the expertise underpinning the creation of perhaps the most magnificent country house library of the late twentieth century. Dedicated to the arts of the book, it included superlative medieval manuscripts, incunabula, illustrated books and fine bindings, ancient and modern. Another obvious parallel with the past was Getty's creation of a suitably grandiose receptacle for his books and manuscripts, a castellated extension to the main house, beautifully fitted out and provided with every refinement which modern conservation could offer. Getty had purchased Wormsley in 1984, partly because his books were outgrowing his house in Chelsea. The new Library wing (fig. 224), which included a Doric portico of knapped flint, was designed by Nicholas Johnston and furnished by the interior designer Chester Jones. At the back a battlemented toytown tower provides extra space for a librarian's office, while the galleried main room, top-lit, has Gothic bookcases in American oak, furniture by Wyatville and Philip Webb, and a clock and candlesticks made for Pugin by Hardman's.[35]

Other twentieth-century owners chose less conventional settings for their books, though the preferred solutions varied considerably. At Eaton Hall, Cheshire, the monster Gothic pile, built for the 1st Duke of Westminster (1825–99) by Alfred Waterhouse (1830–1905), was torn down in 1963. It replacement was a modernist building by the 5th Duke's brother-in-law John Dennys (remodelled in turn within twenty years), and a Library room, with fitted teak and cedar bookcases, featured prominently.[36] Elsewhere, more traditional solutions were often preferred. At Hinton Ampner in Hampshire, the aesthete Ralph Dutton (1898–1985) remodelled an unfashionable Victorian house as a foil for his collections. One of the high points was a lavish neo-Regency Library, designed by the aristocratic architect Gerry Wellesley (from 1943 the 7th Duke of Wellington) and, despite wartime restrictions, completed by 1945. This was totally destroyed by fire in 1960, but the reconstructed Library was essentially a reproduction of its predecessor.[37] If the books, paid for by insurance money, have often been taken for interior design, more careful examination reveals that they were purchased

[224] Wormsley Park, Buckinghamshire; the castellated flint building to the left is the Library wing

with some thought and care. Dutton's colour-plate books, in particular, are rather fine.[38] At Longleat a suite of stylistically rather similar Library rooms was fitted up by the French designer Stéphane Boudin (1888–1967), who also worked for Jackie Kennedy at the White House between 1961 and 1963. At Longleat his new interiors were conceived to house the magnificent library of the bibliomaniac Beriah Botfield (1807–63), which was inherited in the nineteenth century, moved to Longleat in the 1940s and subsequently depleted by sales in 1994 and 2002. The Library interior at Leeds Castle, Kent, for the American heiress Olive, Lady Baillie (1899–1974), was also Boudin's work.

At Anglesey Abbey Anglo-American oil money paid for another great library (fig. 217), ultimately less grandiose – and certainly less varied – than Wormsley, but with certain features in common. Huttleston Broughton, 1st Lord Fairhaven (1896–1966), was the American-born son of an English father and an American mother, co-heir to the Standard Oil fortune of his maternal grandfather the tycoon Henry H. Rogers (1840–1909). Moving to England in 1912, Huttleston received the peerage originally destined for his father in 1929, three years after he and his younger brother had set up in a decayed former Augustinian priory 7 miles outside Cambridge. Using his mother's millions, and certainly drawing on memories of the Gilded Age America of his youth, Huttleston, left in sole occupation on the marriage of his brother, set about transforming the house and filling it with treasures. His library was an important part of the overall project. Initial designs by the Sussex architects Wratten and Godfrey (who had recently built a neo-Georgian Library for Huttleston's fellow bachelor Sir Paul Latham in the north range of Herstmonceux Castle in Sussex) gave way to a large mirror-ended room by Sidney Parvin, the in-house architect of the Mayfair interior designers Turner Lord. Shelved floor to ceiling, Lord Fairhaven's Library provided space for a good seven or eight thousand volumes. Despite the sumptuous livery bindings, commissioned from the most expensive London firms, the upper shelves housed what was very much a working library of current books. By contrast, the book grilles below each bay of shelving provided secure storage space for sumptuous treasures: fine bindings, private press books, illustrated and colour-plate books, typically superb copies on large paper in the finest possible condition.

Fairhaven differed from Getty to the extent that his library was very much his own creation. Decades after his death, members of the London trade still recalled regular visits from the fastidious customer in kid gloves, but there was no favoured dealer in the background to take charge of purchases. The sometimes idiosyncratic tastes underlying both the library and other parts of his collection were very much Fairhaven's own. In its eclecticism and its implicit rejection of a canon of good taste based around the 'great' works of English and classical literature, Fairhaven's library was typical of its day. It was no coincidence that his lifetime coincided with the retreat of the humanistic curriculum which had lain at the heart of elite British education since the sixteenth century. The absence of medieval manuscripts and incunabula seems notable. With Fairhaven's bequest of Anglesey Abbey to the National Trust in 1966, the Trust acquired some of its most grandiose books, though it has to be said that initially some of its grandees were as uninterested in the library as they were dismissive of the Americanised millionaire chic of the house.[39]

II · THE NATIONALISED LIBRARY

The National Trust

Announcing his decision to give the Wallington estate to the National Trust in 1936, the Stalinist baronet Sir Charles Trevelyan (1870–1958) was explicit about his intentions. As a Socialist, he declared, he had no sense of attachment to private property (critics wondered therefore why the gift only took full effect on Sir Charles's death). Divesting himself of the great house and his surrounding estates was primarily a means of ensuring their long-term survival in a world which – as Sir Charles and many of his contemporaries assumed – had no further use for aristocrats and landlords, or for great houses and their contents. But it was also a desirable course of events in its own right, a step on the way to the creation in the United Kingdom of the egalitarian utopia which Sir Charles confidently believed was under construction in Soviet Russia. A well-known cartoon published in *Punch* in 1947 (fig. 225) expressed the prevailing view after the Labour landslide victory two years earlier, with a stern Victorian paterfamilias solemnly rebuking his spivvish son in the columned ancestral library: 'This is my last warning, Charles. If you do not mend your ways I shall leave the estate to you instead of to the National Trust.'[40]

Founded in 1895, for many decades the Trust was preoccupied almost exclusively with landscape and vernacular buildings. An initially tiny organisation, it would not have had the money to become involved in country houses, even if it had wanted to. Nonetheless, by the 1930s, public opinion was beginning to take an interest in the country house 'problem', and the sale from Blickling in 1932 of a clutch of spectacular books – including two extraordinary Anglo-Saxon manuscripts (both ended up in America) – was a key moment.[41] In 1934 Lord Lothian, probably influenced by Christopher Hussey and other well-informed string-pullers, gave the famous speech which led to the creation of the Trust's Country House Scheme. But it took the cataclysm of the Second World War and subsequent political developments for many houses to come into the Trust's possession. Blickling, which even after the 1932 sale still contained a stupendous library, was one of the first. Ultimately only the social dislocation of the times and penal levels of taxation made the developments of the post-war era possible. Between 1940 and the 1980s the National Trust – and to a lesser extent other public and charitable bodies – acquired dozens and dozens of great houses. The experience of the neighbouring Republic of Ireland, fully independent from 1949, set out an alternative path. With no direct equivalent of the National Trust, little money and very limited public sympathy for the former landowning class, great houses toppled like ninepins.

The story of the National Trust and the country house is too well known to warrant more detailed exploration here. The crucial point is that as a result of a series of historical coincidences the Trust became, unwittingly, the custodian of an extraordinary portfolio of historic libraries – a phenomenon unparalleled in any other European country. Some of these were acquired as gifts or bequests, but others were the result of huge tax bills and the allocation of houses and their contents via the Treasury (the public purse as donor, rather than the family). Circumstances varied widely from place to place. Collectively, however, the process amounted to a discreet and rather British form of nationalisation, a word which the Trust, understandably, would never have used in the

1940s and 1950s. The roll call of great libraries was, by any standards, remarkable – to pick out only the most notable: Blickling (1940), Wallington (1944), Gunby Hall (1944), Charlecote Park (1944), Stourhead (1946), Dorneywood (1947), Hughenden Manor (1947), Townend (1949), Castle Ward (1950), Attingham (1953), Ickworth (1956), Clandon (1956), Waddesdon (1957), Saltram (1957), Springhill (1957), Tatton Park (1960), Dyrham

Park (1961), Anglesey Abbey (1966), Shugborough (1966), Felbrigg (1969), Erddig (1973), Dunham Massey (1976), Wimpole (1976), Dunster Castle (1976), Baddesley Clinton (1980), The Argory (1980), Kingston Lacy (1981), Belton (1984), Calke Abbey (1985) and Kedleston (1987). In the early days of the Country House Scheme, the Trust commonly acquired houses, while all or some of their contents (including many libraries) remained in private ownership. In many cases these had to be secured later, sometimes via Acceptance in Lieu (AIL) inheritance-tax relief (introduced between 1953 and 1956), occasionally by gift and often by purchase, either with grant aid or, as the Trust itself grew, from its own resources.[42] The more notable instances included Lanhydrock (the house acquired in 1953, the books round about 1970); Petworth (the house acquired in 1947, a magnificent Chaucer manuscript and a set of Jacobean play quartos taken by the Treasury in 1957, but only transferred to the National Trust in 1990); Florence Court

[225] *Punch's* view of the country house crisis, 1947: 'This is my last warning, Charles. If you do not mend your ways I shall leave the estate to you instead of the National Trust.' The cartoonist 'Acanthus' was in fact the architect Frank Hoar (1907–1976). The setting is somewhat reminiscent of Kenwood House.

(a partial return in 2000 of a library removed to Scotland in 1973); Nostell Priory (1953 and 2002, with funding from the Heritage Lottery Fund); Penrhyn Castle (1951 and the books by AIL in 2002); Chirk Castle (1981 and 2004); Sissinghurst (1967 and 2007 via AIL); Lacock Abbey (1944 and 2010); and Mount Stewart (2014, though a portion of the library had been gifted with the house in 1978). Since the 1980s the acquisition of full-scale country houses has slowed considerably, but nonetheless both Chastleton (1991) and Tyntesfield (2002) came with fine libraries. The 7th Earl of Bradford no doubt spoke for many former owners in January 2000 when, writing in a sale catalogue about Weston Park in Staffordshire (not a Trust house, but a parallel case, as it had been owned by a charitable foundation backed by the National Heritage Memorial Fund since 1986), he remarked that 'although I retained ownership of the books … they remained in the house and out of my sight, and so in many ways the emotional attachment had already been severed'.[43]

Other National Trust Libraries, long despoiled of their original contents, presented more intractable problems. Some saw shelves restocked with books, at worst rows of rather dispiriting leather-bound school-prize books, and at best imported libraries of real quality and distinction, like that introduced into Ham House in 1991 (fig. 226). As early as April 1945 the Trust was appealing for seventeenth-century chattels for Montacute in *The Times*. In an interesting reflection of the times many of the books which eventually found their way onto the shelves there were transferred from Brockhampton Hall in Herefordshire, which the Trust had been given in 1946 and had decided not to show to the public.[44] Inevitably these ersatz libraries have provoked mixed reactions. Some, including sceptical cultural commentators and increasingly the Trust's own specialist staff, have questioned whether an organisation like the Trust should be peddling historical myths, or showing houses in a way not reflective of their appearance at any point of their history. The critics, nonetheless, have had to face up to the fundamental problem – and few have had any coherent answer – of what to do with yards of empty shelves in a show house when the original books have gone.

Initially, it has to be said, the Trust showed little interest in its libraries. Given the financial constraints of the post-war era, it hardly could have done, but it was much a matter of will as of wherewithal. Put rather simply, Trust aesthetes of the Lees-Milne era tended to be interested in classical architecture, pictures, porcelain and silver, but generally not in old books. When a

[226] The seventeenth-century Library at Ham House, set-dressed with books introduced in 1991 from the library of the Brighton collector Norman Norris

hopeful enquirer wrote asking about the books at Charlecote Park in 1944, he was fobbed off with the observation that the shelves contained nothing that could not be found in 'ordinary libraries'. Since the Charlecote library dated back to the sixteenth century and included magnificent additions bought from William Pickering in the nineteenth century, Lees-Milne and the Trust were skating on thin ice. He and his friend Eardley Knollys (1902–91) were equally cavalier at Stourhead in the late 1940s. Much of the vast library assembled there by the last chatelaine Alda, Lady Hoare, an aspiring 'soul' and an intimate of Thomas Hardy, was discarded in favour of neo-Georgian fantasies of what Colt Hoare's great Library should look like. Despite a series of reports commissioned from Lees-Milne's friend Robert Gathorne-Hardy (1902–73), the brother-in-law of the bookseller Heywood Hill (and well informed when it came to books, but better known in a less tolerant era for his 'flagrant and rackety homosexuality'), for many at the Trust the books were simply wallpaper.[45] Even at Blickling, where Gathorne-Hardy was thunderstruck by the splendour of the library, Lees-Milne, apparently after pressure from Nancy Astor, commissioned Lord Lothian's former private secretary to compile a catalogue, despite her sensible protests that she knew nothing about books. 'An expert librarian may be all very fine but I think you will do it much better,' he assured her in 1946, a decision which put back the Trust's conduct of its greatest library by fifty years.[46] As late as the 1960s, Knollys, by then the Trust's chief aesthete in south-west England, responded with truculence to a head office memo asking staff to take their libraries more seriously and pursue friendly relations with university libraries. The perceptive Martin Drury, Director General of the Trust from 1996 to 2001 but the new boy in the early 1970s, was struck by the prevailing belief that its libraries were an embarrassment. His boss Robin Fedden (1908–77) showed no interest in them beyond their role in 'dressing' shelves, in 1959 instructing that 'the leather-bound books' in the historic Library at Springhill in Northern Ireland should be 'properly arranged' and the others 'stored away or sold' (fortunately they were not).[47] Despite an exhibition at the National Book League in 1958 and a one-page article in the Trust magazine in 1978, for decades Trust publications ignored its books – easily the largest category of object in its

collections – right into the 1990s.[48] They were certainly not usually mentioned in guidebooks. The coffee-table book *Ancestral Houses* (1984) was typical. It contained descriptions by the Irish architectural historian Mark Bence-Jones (1930–2010) of a lengthy sequence of houses, some National Trust and others in private hands, and each including a paragraph devoted to architecture and collections. Of the sixty-one houses covered, only six libraries were mentioned (Blickling, Elton Hall, Holkham, Knebworth, Lamport and Stonor), and even then in a fairly cursory way. Since the other houses included several dozen with important books and seven (Alnwick, Belton, Charlecote, Chatsworth, Lanhydrock, Powderham and Saltram) with libraries of the first rank, the omission was, to say the least, unfortunate.[49]

Tellingly Drury himself never met the Trust's freelance Libraries Adviser, Cecil Clarabut, brought in with funding from the Pilgrim Trust in 1957 to compile a card catalogue of pre-1701 books (the rest were left to their own devices), a Sisyphean task carried forward according to a bibliographically rather shaky methodology. When Clarabut's successor Edward Miller (1914–80) arrived from the British Library in the 1970s, he was unimpressed by the muddled handwritten file cards (fig. 227) he had inherited, but his planned revisions were left unfinished when he retired on health grounds, to be succeeded by the 'eccentric and uproarious' John Fuggles (1949–2002; fig. 228), fresh from a junior post at the British Library. A corner of sorts had been turned, as Fuggles was appointed as a permanent full-time member of staff, with parity of status with the Trust's Adviser on Pictures and Sculpture and its Architectural Historian – a wise move for a dispersed library which already comprised over a quarter of a million books. The initiative was mostly down to Bobby Gore (1921–2010), the Trust's Historic Buildings Secretary, who had previously held the Pictures and Sculpture brief and was more aware than most of the scale and complexity of its constantly growing collections. With Fuggles the history of the Trust's libraries comes within living memory. Initially this engaging if occasionally waspish young man set about his duties with commendable energy, but things started to go wrong. The card catalogue went forward, but imperceptibly slowly. Right through the 1980s, new libraries were acquired with alarming regularity as Fuggles's battered

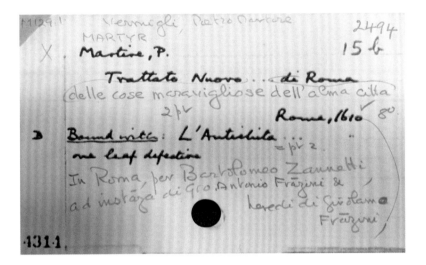

[227] A multi-layered entry from the National Trust's never-completed card catalogue of pre-1701 books

[228] John Fuggles (1949–2002), displaying the late seventh- or early eighth-century Ceolfrith fragment found at Kingston Lacy in 1982 by his colleague Nicholas Pickwoad

Morris Minor, packed with index cards and a miniaturised copy of the British Library catalogue, trundled round the country, its increasingly erratic driver overwhelmed by a torrent of print. Some of the problems were strictly professional. Fuggles was something of a young fogey, and like many librarians of his generation he had problems in coming to terms with the computer. Offers for the Trust to become involved in the new *Eighteenth-Century Short Title Catalogue* – an extraordinarily ambitious Anglo-American project to create an automated catalogue of the entire output of the

eighteenth-century British press – were firmly rebuffed. But gradually drink, depression and hypochondria started to take their toll, precipitating Fuggles's departure in 1991. He never worked again, dying aged fifty-three, after a long bibliomaniacal twilight exposed in affectionate posthumous tributes written by his friends. Fuggles was following in the footsteps of a long line of bibliophilic eccentrics. The rumour that he had died crushed under a bookcase was untrue, though it was the sort of story that Dibdin (or Fuggles himself) might have invented. In any case by the 1980s the National Trust had taken possession of so many libraries that the actions and foibles of its staff had become part of the story.[50]

The Trust's apparently voracious appetite for country houses did not go unremarked by critics, especially in the 1980s. But James Lees-Milne's magisterial put-down (1984) of the New Right philosopher Roger Scruton in the letter pages of *The Times* ('I had to read it twice to make sure it was not a joke') was telling. Lees-Milne had long since retired, and his misgivings about the Trust were well known. But he was swift to point out that it had never had a shopping list, and had simply stepped in when other options ran out. Many of its houses would have vanished without its involvement, their contents dispersed.[51] In reality, whatever the weaknesses of its approach to its books, most of the libraries which the National Trust acquired and then ignored between the 1940s and 1980s would not have survived at all but for its intervention. What is more, without the sophisticated approach to their conservation pioneered from the early 1980s by its conservation adviser Nicholas Pickwoad, an increasingly influential figure on both sides of the Atlantic, they would not have survived so well. Pickwoad's emerging philosophy that books were physical artefacts whose structures had much to tell about their past history was well made, and has become the established orthodoxy.[52]

A second turning point came with the arrival of Nicolas Barker, Head of Conservation at the British Library from 1976 to 1992. Editor of the *Book Collector* since 1965, Barker was a formidable published scholar, and his appointment as a part-time consultant at first looked like a return to the past. But he was shrewd enough to realise that the Morris Minor and the handwritten cards had had their day, that the Trust needed a team of qualified library cataloguers and that the only way forward was to embrace new technology and adopt electronic cataloguing in MARC format (Machine Readable Cataloguing), as serious research libraries had been doing for some years. He pushed for the appointment of an assistant who would work in close collaboration with the ESTC (*English Short Title Catalogue*) project team at the British Library. These efforts were supplemented by bringing in another senior professional Peter Hoare, recently retired as Librarian of Nottingham University and then working as General Editor of the *Cambridge History of Libraries in Britain and Ireland*. Hoare set to work with the Trust's second largest library, at Belton House, in Lincolnshire. Over the succeeding decade he produced impeccably crafted electronic descriptions of over 11,500 books, creating what became in effect the base file of the National Trust Union Catalogue, as many of the books at Belton also existed in copies in other houses. The old idea of working on pre-1701 books, old-fashioned thirty years before but absurd by the 1990s, was quietly dropped. Discoveries at Belton ranged from an unspotted incunable to *The Chameleon* (1894), a suppressed and rare landmark of gay literature, reinforcing the realisation that the Trust's libraries were packed with treasures of all kinds.[53] In tandem, Barker's contacts in America paid dividends. He, Martin Drury and Simon Jervis (Drury's successor as Historic Buildings Secretary, whose long association with the V&A and the Fitzwilliam Museum in Cambridge meant that he was used to dealing with libraries) became key figures in the Campaign for Country House Libraries run in the late 1990s by the Trust's American Affiliate, the Royal Oak Foundation. Finally, there was Barker's farewell contribution, a lavishly illustrated catalogue for the 'thank you' exhibition held at the Grolier Club in New York in 1999. Reviewers were enthralled, one remarking that he was 'astounded' by the unknown riches on the Trust's shelves.[54] With enough money to create two new posts and to provide spare cash for worthwhile projects in houses with important books and limited money, the Trust's libraries were gradually starting to come out of the closet.

Of subsequent developments the present author – brought in as Barker's full-time successor in 1999 – has been too closely involved to offer much comment. But the rescue of a series of libraries, the increasing prominence of the Trust's books (which represent more than a third of the total number of objects in its care) and above all the integration of 250,000 catalogue records into Copac, the United Kingdom national library catalogue, are themselves indicative that much has changed. A raft of publications have attempted to improve public understanding of libraries in British and Irish country houses, the National Trust's in particular. The purchase for £465,000 of the now unique 1487 Caxton Sarum Rite Missal (figs. 229 and 230) for Lyme Park (2008) was another milestone, made possible by major grants from the Art Fund and, especially, the Heritage Lottery Fund. Forty years earlier such a book would have been 'saved for the nation' with an export stop, but the chances of it remaining in a country house would have been remote. Like the Benedictional of St Æthelwold, it would have been borne off in triumph to a national collection, severing its five-hundred-year association with Lyme. The importance attached to the Lyme Missal remaining in its historic home was testament not just to a new regard for the claims of the regions, but to a growing appreciation of the interest of books in context, and perhaps also a vote of confidence in the National Trust's growing success in the management of its portfolio of accidentally acquired libraries. While the 1940s enquirer after Charlecote had been given the brush-off, a twenty-first-century researcher could, increasingly, investigate Trust libraries online and then send an email to arrange access.

Country house libraries in other institutional hands

The National Trust has had the lion's share of the attention in this analysis for the simple reason that with over 160 collections it owns far more libraries than any of its counterparts. In Scotland the entirely separate National Trust for Scotland also assembled a smaller but still substantial portfolio of libraries, with somewhere between 30,000 and 50,000 books (by comparison, the Trust in England, Wales and Northern Ireland has probably in excess of 300,000). The NTS, nonetheless, is the guardian of the most remarkable collections of rare books in Scotland, and a portfolio of historic libraries which is, in European terms, extraordinary and important. For a series of partly accidental reasons, the great bulk of the Trust's books are in houses in the north-east of Scotland. The largest library is at Haddo House

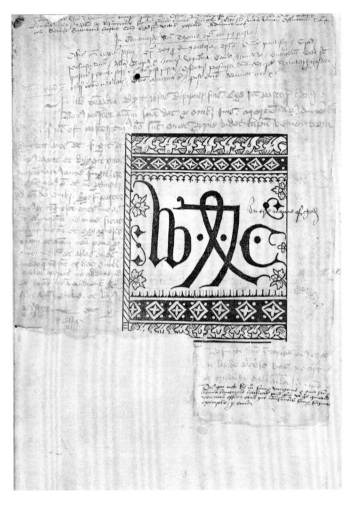

[229, 230] The Caxton Missal at Lyme Park

in Aberdeenshire, the ancestral home of the Marquesses of Aberdeen, but there are substantial libraries near by at Drum Castle and Castle Fraser, and another 60 miles to the north-west, at Brodie Castle in Morayshire. By contrast, the NTS's largest house, Culzean Castle in Ayrshire, has no library as such, while at Newhailes, just outside Edinburgh, the house came to the NTS in 1997, but the books had been removed to the National Library of Scotland a generation earlier, in 1976, in payment of death duties (fig. 231). The question of the Newhailes Library developed into a minor cause célèbre, the subject of a protracted tussle between the estate solicitor, local MPS, and the Historic Buildings Council for Scotland on the one hand and the National Library of Scotland on the other. The Historic Buildings Council asserted the value of the books *in situ* (or, probably more accurately, thought that the house looked better with them on the shelves). Leading the charge for the National Library, the Librarian, Denis Roberts (1927–90), was especially trenchant in his views, writing in a

memo to the Scottish office in August 1976 that 'books are not furniture, and a collection which has … been accepted as of pre-eminent national importance ought to be in a library where scholars can consult it' – and adding the peppery exclamation 'Money!' in the margin when his opponents suggested that the NLS should run Newhailes as an out-station.[55] The debate continued after the acquisition of the house by the National Trust for Scotland. Unspoken but probably at the back of several minds was the realisation that the NTS had no librarian and nothing really resembling a library catalogue. In the event, when the Trust ran into serious financial difficulties in 2009, one of the most trenchant criticisms of the ensuing commission of enquiry was that it had no proper register of its assets.[56] The criticism was understandable, but so far as the libraries went, the problem was not easily resolved by an organisation with limited resources and thousands of books, most of which would have required considerable expertise to document in a meaningful and useful way.

In Ireland the Office of Public Works – a public
body rather than a charity – had a smaller portfolio
of libraries than the National Trust for Scotland,
but despite financial stringencies was able to run
them to good effect. Several were comparatively
modest, including a small collection of imported fine
Irish bindings at Castletown, the twentieth-century
library at Ilnacullin (the island house of the Bryce
family in County Cork) and the small library at
Derrynane House, County Kerry, the former home
of Daniel O'Connell (1775–1847), which contains
O'Connell family books – though not the Liberator's
own library. The jewel in the library crown was at
Farmleigh, the suburban villa of the Guinnesses,
on the edge of Dublin's Phoenix Park. Following its
sale to the state in 1999, and the subsequent gift of
the books to the Trustees of Archbishop's Marsh's
Library, Marsh's Library placed the books on loan
with the OPW.

By contrast, the much larger English Heritage
had relatively few libraries and appeared to take
correspondingly little notice of them. A number of
the most notable were 'lost libraries' – houses where
a library formed an important part of the story, but
was no longer present. Chiswick House, for example,
was once dominated by Lord Burlington's library,
but the books had long been at Chatsworth. The
villa did, at least, still have a roof. Appuldurcombe
(Isle of Wight), Sutton Scarsdale (Derbyshire)
and Witley Court (Worcestershire) were all gutted
shells, though a catalogue survived for Witley
in Nottingham University Library, making the
intellectual reconstruction of the library at least a
possibility.[57] The most spectacular English Heritage
library by some way is at Audley End, a library
comparable in scale, complexity and quality to the
National Trust's finest collections.

Then there were books separated from their
houses but still recognisable as collections, not as
the result of gifts or bequests (as at Queens' College,
Cambridge, in the sixteenth century or Oriel in the
1780s), but by processes ultimately rather similar to
those which brought books to the National Trusts
and to state heritage bodies. Two of the most note-
worthy examples were in Ireland: Queen's University,
Belfast, in 1969 bought a substantial part of the great
library of Bishop Thomas Percy (1729–1811), which
had been at Caledon House, County Tyrone, since
1812;[58] and, south of the border, Trinity College,

[231] The Library at Newhailes, denuded of books

Dublin, acquired books from Townley Hall, County Louth, in 1960 (a generation or two later, its staff admitted that they might have taken the whole library, rather than selecting books from it).[59] The National Library of Ireland bought several hundred volumes from the Irish library at Lough Fea, County Monaghan, in 1924, and the National Library of Wales acquired 1,500 from the library of the Buckley family of Castell Gorfod, Carmarthenshire, in 1920.[60]

III · A FUTURE FOR THE PAST

As the new millennium approached, the changed economic and political climate which had developed in the United Kingdom since 1979 meant that fewer historic private libraries were dispersed than thirty or forty years earlier. The regular heritage crises of the 1970s and 1980s became less common, partly because of reduced taxation and partly because cannier private owners had assembled an armoury of survival tactics in the difficult post-war era. The wise took advantage of the United Kingdom's system of 'conditional exemption', whereby tax could be deferred on heritage assets, only needing to be paid if they were sold. This was separate from, but closely related to, the system of export stops first introduced in 1952. Since it was possible to defer multiple rounds of tax bills, owners with exempted chattels were liable to become progressively less likely to sell them, except to a 'Schedule 3' body (generally national collections, the two National Trusts, universities and other public bodies). The system carried with it a requirement for public access, in principle straightforward with works of art in houses open to the public, but problematic with books, archives and other portable artefacts requiring close study, and occasionally it attracted criticism.[61] Help was available from auction houses and dealers, which had became expert in the intricacies of the tax system. Sometimes things went further, with the creation of complex and overlapping networks of companies and trusts to own country houses and their contents, often set up and, to varying extents, ultimately controlled by their traditional owners. At Arundel, for example, the state rooms were handed over to a charitable trust on the death of the 16th Duke of Norfolk in 1975, and similar trusts followed at Burghley and Chatsworth.[62] Elsewhere trusts provided a way forward for houses where the family was extinct or for some

reason no longer involved: of these, Weston Park, Paxton House in Berwickshire and Lamport Hall in Northamptonshire were just three with fine libraries, though that at Weston was depleted by the sale in 2000 of eighty-six fine books, including a set of the *Description de l'Égypte* (1817–22; lot 17) and some expensive colour-plate books.[63]

The dramatic rise in prices was significant. Increasingly owners with a good library who needed cash raised it by selling a single item or a carefully selected group of books, rather than the entire collection. The victims of a 2002 sale from Longleat, for example, were sensibly chosen from books bequeathed by Beriah Botfield, which had only been there since the 1940s, rather than from books which had been in the house for centuries.[64] More recently the sale from Chatsworth in 2012 of a Raphael drawing and two illuminated Burgundian manuscripts bought at the Roxburghe sale in 1812 raised some £33m (over £29m for the Raphael and £3,849,250 for one of the two manuscripts: the other remained unsold). As the press release explained, the Devonshire collection contained another fourteen major drawings by Raphael.[65] Similarly while the Calke Abbey copy of Audubon's *Birds of America* had sold for just £890 in 1924, in 2010 the 2nd Lord Hesketh's copy of the same book made £7.4 million, while an imperfect copy of the Shakespeare First Folio made £1,497,250.[66]

When wholesale dispersals did occur, from the 1980s it was often for quite specific reasons. The sale of the contents of Tew Park, Oxfordshire (1987), which included a substantial nineteenth-century gentleman's library, was fundamentally the result of the long-term neglect of the entire estate, going back to the time when its administration had been taken over by the Public Trustee many decades earlier.[67] When Lord Hesketh sold up at Easton Neston in 2005, it was because of a strategic decision to rid himself of the ongoing liability of the house's enormous running costs. As far as the library went, the decision was surely made a little easier by the fact that parts of it had been acquired as recently as the 1950s.[68] The dispersal in thirteen great sales of the superb library of Lord Chancellor Macclesfield at Shirburn Castle in Oxfordshire (2004–2008) was the most spectacular in years. It was a house which had long had a reputation for oddity. Pevsner was refused admittance, and the V&A's Roy Strong was baffled on a tax-related visit in 1974 by the fleeting appearance of Lord Macclesfield 'in a plebeian cloth cap and overalls, carrying a cardboard box, for all the world like a removal man'.[69] The sale of the library was precipitated, as the tabloid newspapers gleefully reported, because the 9th Earl of Macclesfield, who owned the books, was faced with eviction from the castle as the result of a protracted feud with other family members, who collectively controlled the company which owned the Macclesfield estate.[70]

By contrast, from the 1950s and 1960s places like Chatsworth, Beaulieu and Longleat became heritage 'brands', which not only defined certain families in the public mind, but could be conspicuously successful from a financial perspective. Some commentators suggested that the focus on shared 'heritage' could be an elegant form of camouflage which allowed wealthy landowners to gloss over quite how rich they still were.[71] Nor was the area of finance the only one where specialist services were on offer. In the aftermath of the Florence floods of 1966, scientific conservation advanced in leaps and bounds. Increasingly private owners with inherited libraries could draw on advice from professional conservators. Adept at managing historic books *in situ* in a way which required different specialist skills from those deployed in environmentally controlled book stacks, conservators also developed tactics for managing and training conservation volunteers – essential, if well-meaning enthusiasts were not to do more harm than good. The work of NADFAS library volunteers (the National Association of Decorative and Fine Arts Society was founded in 1968, and from the 1970s its conservation teams became a common sight in country houses) was lauded by some, apparently enjoyed by those engaged with it, and occasionally viewed with a certain alarm by specialists.[72]

With a few notable exceptions, documentation lagged far behind conservation. Sir Hugo Boothby published a typescript catalogue of the eighteenth-century library at Fonmon Castle in 1969, in collaboration with nearby Cardiff University. Cheshire County Council followed suit in 1977 with a similar but larger record (not especially accurate) of the books at Tatton Park, which it ran on behalf of the National Trust, but these eminently sensible collaborative projects were few and far between.[73] There were few successors to the scholarly ledger and privately printed catalogues of the nineteenth century. A notable exception was at Longleat, under the effective leadership of its long-serving librarian

Kate Harris, where an ever-increasing part of the great library made its way onto an electronic catalogue the equal of anything going on in public collections. Many thousands of Longleat's early British books were even reported to the ESTC, a rare occurrence indeed in a private collection of this kind. By contrast many houses, even very grand ones, made do with auction-house valuations. At Chatsworth a marked-up copy of the printed catalogue compiled by Sir James Lacaita in 1879 remained in use, its utility compromised because post-war sales had not always been recorded in a very systematic way. In Scotland the National Library of Scotland was noticeably successful in maintaining contacts with the owners of private libraries. Elsewhere – and by contrast with museums and galleries – contacts between private libraries and the curators of the major public collections were often regrettably patchy, to the detriment of both. Only with advent of PhDs funded by the AHRC (Arts and Humanities Research Council) was there some improvement. Predictably one of the first to address a library-related topic was a fascinating joint project between the University of York, the Yorkshire Country House Partnership (founded in 1999) and the well-organised and resourceful curatorial department at Castle Howard.[74]

The introduction in Ireland and in parts of the United Kingdom of new legislation on weddings and civil partnerships added another ingredient to the mix. From the 1990s privately owned houses which had been open to the public for decades became increasingly difficult to get into on Saturdays. The country house Library became a favourite wedding venue, grandiose but free of possibly unwelcome religious associations. It was equally likely to be used for other sorts of corporate hospitality. These issues did not just come into play in houses in private occupation, but applied equally in popular country house hotels. All three of the Historic House Hotels given to the National Trust by the entrepreneur Richard Broyd in 2008 had Library rooms dressed with appropriate-looking leather-bound books, as did many others.

As the twentieth century drew to a close, sophisticated commentators became increasingly assertive about the importance of books as physical objects. As early as 1985 Roger Stoddard of the Houghton Library at Harvard published a large-format book called *Marks in Books, Illustrated and Explained*.[75] Lisa Jardine and Anthony Grafton's article (1990) on how the Elizabethan scholar Gabriel Harvey (c.1552/3–1631) read Livy was hugely influential and much cited.[76] At much the same time David Pearson published books on provenance research (1994) and bindings (2005) which were much admired, and had a great influence on his professional peers.[77] He developed many of the same themes in his best-selling *Books as History* in 2008. Declaredly aimed at opinion-formers as much as at specialists, Pearson asserted, with considerable conviction, that in the age of the digital book, the true value of old books was generally not for their printed texts. These were easily available in digital form. Their real significance was the material evidence which they provided about the operation of the book trade, the work of binders and, especially, the interests, activities and aspirations of earlier owners. He was equally assertive about the collective value of historic libraries, including those in country houses.[78] As the digital revolution proceeded apace, there was an increasing awareness from specialists, if not necessarily in the wider world, that books in country houses were often more interesting than books which had been in public collections for centuries: typically heavily repaired, rebound, washed or simply used to death.

At the same time in privately owned houses, libraries (along with other chattels) have become increasingly important, if not necessarily always the focus of much active attention. Owners whose parents and grandparents had succeeded in hanging onto the contents of their houses were in a happy position. In the United Kingdom, if not the Republic of Ireland, there were plenty. The vast sums of capital locked up in historic collections – including libraries – became the ultimate guarantor of the family fortunes and a painless way of generating ready cash when it was needed. In earlier generations aristocratic collectors had sometimes brought ruin on their families by their obsessive collecting. Their twenty-first-century counterparts might also spend money on books, but it was as likely to be on conservation and insurance as on collecting. For many owners, questions of access did not necessarily occupy centre stage. Some actively welcomed it, and others were obliged to do so by the tax authorities. Most owners who showed their houses to the public as a going concern were at least concerned to see that their visitors enjoyed themselves and came back. For them, as in houses owned by the National Trusts, the challenge is

not just to preserve their collections and ensure that they are sufficiently well documented to make research possible, but to make fragile historic libraries which were intended for the few visible, accessible and meaningful for the many. To that conundrum there have been many answers but, so far, few wholly successful solutions. What is most likely is that the future of country house libraries will take two parallel paths. Those in private hands will continue to evolve with the fortunes of their owners – some for good and some for ill – as they always have done. Meanwhile for those in public hands, or supported by quasi-public funding, the huge upsurge of interest in the social history of material culture along with scholarly advances in providing access to digital humanities means that the future potentially offers great opportunities, for research, understanding and survival.

[232] A page from the *Catalogus Bibliothecae Kingstonianae*, London [?1727], the first English private library catalogue, issued in twenty copies

KINGSTONIANA.

De Spiritu & Anima, & de Visitatione Infirmorum, cum aliis Opusculis. MS. CC 21.

ALBOH-AVICENNA.

Canon Medicinæ, Lat. per Ger. Cremonensem, cum Notis Costæi & Mongii; & cum additionibus Paulini Uticensis. ii Vol. *Ven.* 1595. M 13.

Vita ex Sorsano. Per N. Massam. Ibid.

De Ratione Medendi. Vide *Campegius.*

AVIGNON.

Letters from a Lady at Paris to a Lady at Avignon. 8º *Lond.* 1616. OO 20.

PIERRE D'AVITY.

Nouveau Theatre du Monde, continant les Estats, Empires, &c. 4º *Paris* 1613. U 26.

Et *Par.* 1661. Z 36.

Bannisement des Folles Amours. 8º *Lyon.* 1618. OO 190.

ABR. AURELIUS.

Epithalamium in Nuptias Friderici Principis & Elizabethæ Jac. Regis filiæ. 4º *Lond.* 1613.

D. AUSONIUS, *Burdigal.*

Vita & Opera. Ex Recognitione Jos. Scaligeri. 12º *Ludg. Bat.* 1595. OO 53. Trav. Libr.

AUSTRIA. Vide *Fridericus.*

Triga Pactorum & Conciliorum Austriacorum, ex Ordinum Bohemicorum Scripto. 4º — 1619.

JO. AUSTRIACUS. Vide *Paepp.*

De Memoria Artificiosa. 8º *Argent.* 1603. MM 132.

AUTHOR.

La Guerre des Autheurs anciens & modernes. 8º *A la Hay,* 1671. — EE 149.

AWBREY. Vide *Aubrey.*

A Pedigree of Awbrey of Wales, a Roll of Vellum. MS. II 178.

BALT. AYALA.

De Jure & Officiis Bellicis: Et Disciplina Militari. Libri iii. 8º *Ant.* 1597. OO 154.

GUL. AYLEWORTH.

Metaphysica Scholastica. *Col.* 1675. N 33.

MATTH. AYLEWORTH.

Trebellius. (Tragœdia sic dicta.) 12º *Lond.* 1674. N 198.

MART. AZPILCUETA.

Enchiridion Confessariorum & Pœnitentium. 8º *Ant.* 1589.

Reference Abbreviations

Alnwick
Alnwick Castle Archives

Arundel
Arundel Castle Archives

BAL
British Architectural Library,
RIBA, London

BL
British Library, London

Blickling
Blicking Hall (the National Trust)

BLRS
Bedfordshire and Luton Records
Service, Bedford

BnF
Bibliothèque nationale de France,
Paris

Bodley
Bodleian Library, Oxford

BRO
Berkshire Record Office, Reading

CALS
Cheshire Archives and Local
Studies, Chester

CBS
Centre for Buckinghamshire
Studies, Aylesbury

CHBB
*The Cambridge History of the Book
in Britain*, ed. D. F. Mackenzie,
D. K. McKitterick and I. R.
Willison, Cambridge 1998–2012

CHLBI
*The Cambridge History of Libraries
Britain and Ireland*, ed. Peter
Hoare, Cambridge 2006, 3 vols

CornRO
Cornwall Record Office, Truro

CUL
Cambridge University Library

DevRO
Devon Record Office, Exeter

DLB
Dictionary of Literary Biography,
vol. 213: *Pre-Nineteenth-Century
British Book Collectors and

Bibliographers, ed. William Baker
and Kenneth Womack, Detroit
1999

DRO
Derbyshire Record Office,
Matlock

EH
English Heritage

ERCRO
East Riding County Record
Office, Beverley

ERO
Essex Record Office, Colchester

ESRO
East Sussex Record Office
(The Keep), Brighton

ESTC
*English Short Title Catalogue
Online*: estc.bl.uk

EUL
Edinburgh University Library,
Edinburgh

Folger
Folger Shakespeare Library,
Washington, DC

GA
Gloucestershire Archives,
Gloucester

HALS
Hertfordshire Archives and
Local Studies, Hertford

Harvard
Harvard University, Houghton
Library, Cambridge, MA

Hatfield
Hatfield House Archives,
Hatfield

HHC
Hull History Centre, Hull

HL
Huntington Library, San Marino,
CA

HMC
Historical Manuscripts
Commission

HRO
Hampshire Record Office,
Winchester

JRULM
John Rylands University Library,
Manchester

KHLC
Kent History and Library Centre,
Maidstone

LA
Lincolnshire Archives, Lincoln

Lambeth
Lambeth Palace Library, London

MMBL
Neil Ker, *Medieval Manuscripts in
British Libraries*, Oxford 1969–83

NLI
National Library of Ireland,
Dublin

NLW
National Library of Wales,
Aberystwyth

NorthRO
Northamptonshire Record Office,
Northampton

NRO
Norfolk Record Office, Norwich

NRS
National Records of Scotland,
Edinburgh

NT
National Trust

NTS
National Trust for Scotland

NUL
Nottingham University Library

ODNB
*Oxford Dictionary of National
Biography*, online version, Oxford
2004: http://www.oxforddnb.
com

PML
Pierpont Morgan Library,
New York

PRONI
Public Record Office of
Northern Ireland, Belfast

SBRO
Shakespeare Birthplace Record
Office, Stratford

SHC
Surrey History Centre, Woking

SRO
Somerset Record Office, Taunton

StaffRO
Staffordshire Record Office,
Stafford

STC
Alfred W. Pollard, Gilbert R.
Redgrave et al., *A Short Title
Catalogue of Books Printed in
England, Scotland & Ireland and
of English Books Printed Abroad
1475–1640*, 2nd edn., London 1991

SuffRO
Suffolk Record Office, Bury St
Edmunds

TCD
Trinity College Library, Dublin

TNA
The National Archives, London

VAM
Victoria and Albert Museum,
London

WAAS
Worcestershire Archive and
Archaeology Service, Worcester

Wing
Donald Wing, *Wing Short-Title
Catalogue* [CD-Rom]: *Short-Title
Catalogue of Books Printed in
England, Scotland, Ireland, Wales
and British America and of English
Books Published in Other Countries*,
Cambridge 1996

WRO
Warwickshire County Record
Office, Warwick

WSHC
Wiltshire and Swindon History
Centre, Chippenham

WSRO
West Sussex Record Office,
Chichester

Notes

Introduction

1. Robert Donaldson, 'Traquair House Library', *Bulletin du Bibliophile*, iii (1984), pp. 321–5; Colin G. C. Tite, *The Manuscript Library of Sir Robert Cotton*, London 1994.

2. John G. Cochrane, *Catalogue of the Library at Abbotsford*, Edinburgh 1838; Martin Spevack, 'The Library at Hughenden Manor', *The Book Collector*, lix, 4 (Winter 2010), pp. 547–80.

3. *Catalogus Librorum A.C.D.A.* [i.e. Archibald Campbell, 3rd Duke of Argyll], Glasgow 1758, ESTC T28876.

4. Ralph Dutton, *Hinton Ampner: A Hampshire Manor*, London 1969, p. 94.

5. Mark Purcell, *The Big House Library in Ireland: Books in Ulster Country Houses*, Swindon 2011a, pp. 16–17.

6. No copy traced, but I am grateful to Gordon Wheeler (formerly of Queen's University Library, Belfast) for his description of a leaflet sold by Kenny's Bookshop, Galway (their List 42, part 1), *Notes on the Defence of Irish Country Houses*. The leaflet was dated (*c.*1900) by Kenny's, but Wheeler suggests, plausibly, that a date in the 1880s is more likely.

7. Sean O'Reilly, *Irish Houses and Gardens from the Archives of Country Life*, London 1998, p. 72.

8. WRO, CR229/193; William Reeves, *Catalogue of the Library at Lough Fea in Illustration of the History and Antiquities of Ireland*, London 1872; Shane Leslie, 'The Shirley Library at Lough Fea, Carrickmacross in Co. Monaghan, Ireland', *Book Collectors' Quarterly*, ii, 6 (1932), pp. 1–9.

9. Linda Levy Peck, 'Uncovering the Arundel Library at the Royal Society: Changing Meanings of Science and the Fate of the Norfolk Donation', *Notes and Records of the Royal Society*, lii (1998), pp. 3–24; Lichfield Cathedral Library, MS. 27, 'A Catalogue of her Grace ye Dutchess of Somersett's Great Library, Taken August MDCLXXI'.

10. Mark Purcell, '"A Lunatick of Unsound Mind": Edward, Lord Leigh (1742–86), and the Refounding of Oriel College Library', *Bodleian Library Record*, xvii, 3–4 (April–October 2001a), pp. 246–60; John Martin Robinson, *James Wyatt (1746–1813): Architect to George III*, New Haven and London 2012, pp. 206–8; H. George Fletcher (ed.), *The Wormsley Library: A Personal Selection by Sir Paul Getty*, 2nd edn., London 2007.

11. Anthony Lister, 'The Althorp Library of Second Earl Spencer, Now in the John Rylands University Library, Manchester, Its Formation and Growth', *Bulletin of the John Rylands University Library*, lxxi, 2 (1989), pp. 67–86 (p. 77).

12. A. N. L. Munby, 'The Acquisition of Manuscripts by Institutional Libraries', in A. N. L. Munby (ed.), *Essays and Papers*, London 1977, pp. 67–81.

13. PML MS. M.776; Princeton, Princeton University Library, MS. Scheide Library M71.

14. Merlin Waterson, *The National Trust: The First Hundred Years*, London 1994, pp. 102–08.

15. Giles Mandelbrote, 'The Library of the Duke of Lauderdale (1616–1682)', in Christopher Rowell (ed.), *Ham House: Four Hundred Years of Collecting and Patronage*, New Haven and London 2013, pp. 222–31 (p. 224).

16. Gervase Jackson-Stops, 'Most Learned Decoration', *Country Life*, 24 March 1988, pp. 120–23; Gervase Jackson-Stops, *The English Country House: A Grand Tour*, London 1984, pp. 198–211.

17. Gustav Waagen, *Treasures of Art in Great Britain*, London 1854.

18. Lawrence Stone, *The Crisis of the Aristocracy*, Oxford 1965, pp. 705–7, Appendix xxxvii, p. 794.

19. Lawrence Stone, 'The Revival of Narrative: Reflections on a New Old History', *Past and Present*, lxxxv (1979), pp. 3–24.

20. Illustrated in Douglas Smith, *Former People: The Last Days of the Russian Aristocracy*, London 2012, plate 14.

21. Breandan MacAodha, 'The Big House in Western Ireland', in Jacqueline Genet (ed.), *The Big House in Ireland: Reality and Representation*, Dingle 1992, pp. 19–29 (p. 25).

22. Augusta Gregory, *Coole*, Dublin 1931, pp. 1–2.

23. Giles Worsley, *England's Lost Houses*, London 2002, p. 7; Marcus Binney, *Lost Houses of Scotland*, London 2006, p. 8; Thomas Lloyd, *Lost Houses of Wales: A Survey of Country Houses in Wales Demolished since c.1900*, London 1989.

24. Dan Cruickshank, *The Country House Revealed*, London 2011.

25. Hugh Montgomery-Massingberd, *Great Houses of England and Wales*, London 1994, p. 189.

26. *Bibliotheca Sunderlandiana: Sale Catalogue of the … Library of Printed Books Known as the Sunderland or Blenheim Library*, Puttick and Simpson, London 1881–3.

27. Ian Gow, *Scotland's Lost Houses*, London 2006, pp. 27–33.

28. Charles Mynors, *Listed Buildings, Conservation Areas and Monuments*, London 2006, p. 11.

29. Giles Worsley, 'Beyond the Powerhouse: Understanding the Country House in the Twenty-First Century', *Historical Research*, lxxviii, 201 (August 2005), pp. 423–35 (p. 431).

30. Mark Purcell, 'The Country House Library Reassess'd: or, Did the "Country House Library" Ever Really Exist', *Library History*, xviii, 3 (November 2002), pp. 157–74.

31. Purcell 2011a, pp. 40–52.

32. Mark Purcell, 'The Library at Lanhydrock', *The Book Collector*, liv (2005), pp. 195–230.

Chapter One

1. Camillo Paderni, Extract of a Letter from Camillo Paderni Keeper of the Museum Herculaneum to Tho. Holles, Esq; Relating to the Late Discoveries at Herculaneum', *Philosophical Transactions*, xlviii, 1 (1754), pp. 821–5 (p. 823).

2. Christopher Parslow, *Rediscovering Antiquity: Karl Weber and the Excavation of Herculaneum, Pompeii, and Stabiae*, Cambridge 1995, pp. 103–4.

3. David Sider, *The Library of the Villa dei Papiri at Herculaneum*, Los Angeles 2005, pp. 60–64; Paul Roberts, *Life and Death in Pompeii and Herculaneum*, London 2013, pp. 77–8, 103–9; Parsley 1995, p. 78.

4. Roberts 2013, p. 109; Richard Gameson, 'From Vindolanda to Domesday: the Book in Britain from the Romans to the Normans', in Richard Gameson (ed.), *CHBB, vol. I: c.400–1100*, Cambridge 2011, pp. 1–9 (p. 2).

5. Andrea Palladio, *The Four Books of Andrea Palladio's Architecture*, London 1738, ESTC T40073, plate 29.

6. Raymond Irwin, *The English Library: Sources and History*, London 1966, p.89.

7. *Gesta Abbatum Monasterii Sancti Albani, a Thoma Walsingham, Regnante Ricardo Secundo, Ejusdem Ecclesiae Praecentore, Compilata*, 3 vols, London 1867–9, vol.I, pp.26–7.

8. Roger Tomlin, 'The Book in Roman Britain', in Richard Gameson (ed.), CHBB, vol.I: c.400–1100, Cambridge 2011, pp.375–88 (p.376).

9. Tomlin 2011, pp.378–81, 386–7; Cicero, *Ad Atticum*, 4.16.7; Martial, *Epigrams*, xi, 3.

10. Anthony A. Barrett, 'Knowledge of Literary Classics in Roman Britain', *Britannia*, ix (1978), pp.307–13 (pp.308–9); Richard de Kind, 'The Roman portraits from the Villa of Lullingstone: Pertinax and his Father P. Helvius Successus', in T. Ganschow and M. Steinhart (eds), *Otium: Festschrift für Volker Michael Strocka*, Remshalden 2005, pp.47–52.

11. Florence, Biblioteca Medicea-Laurenziana, MS. Am. I, fol. 5r; Christopher de Hamel, *A History of Illuminated Manuscripts*, 2nd edn., London 1994, pp.18–19.

12. Gameson 2011, pp.1–9; David Ganz, 'Anglo-Saxon England', in Elisabeth Leedham-Green and Teresa Webber (eds), CHLBI, vol.I: To 1640, Cambridge 2006, pp.91–108 (pp.91–2).

13. BL, Cotton Tiberius MS. A. ii; Lambeth, MS. 1370.

14. Scot McKendrick and Kathleen Doyle (eds), *Royal Illuminated Manuscripts: From King Athelstan to Henry VIII*, London 2011, p.103; Simon Keynes, 'King Athelstan's Books', in M. Lapidge and H. Gneuss, *Learning and Literature in Anglo-Saxon England: Studies Presented to Peter Clemoes on the Occasion of his Sixty-Fifth Birthday*, Cambridge 1985, pp.143–201.

15. M. T. Clanchy, *From Memory to Written Record*, 2nd edn., Oxford 1993, p.161.

16. Bodley, MS. Lat. liturg. fol. 5.

17. Clanchy 1993, p.155.

18. Christopher de Hamel, 'Books in Society', in Nigel Morgan and Rodney Thomson (eds), CHBB, vol.II: 1100–1400, Cambridge 2008, pp.3–23 (p.3).

19. The *Chanson* manuscript is Bodley, MS. Digby 23.

20. Clanchy 1993, p.216.

Chapter Two

1. Ralph Hanna and Thorlac Turville-Petre (eds), *The Wollaton Manuscripts: Texts, Owners and Readers*, Woodbridge 2010.

2. *Friends of the National Libraries: Annual Report* (1991), pp.17–19.

3. Quoted in Malcolm Wanklyn, 'Stratagems for Survival: Sir Robert and Sir Francis Throckmorton, 1640–1660', in Peter Marshall and Geoffrey Scott (eds), *Catholic Gentry in English Society: The Throckmortons of Coughton from Reformation to Emancipation*, Farnham 2009, pp.146–70 (p.148).

4. Susan Hagen Cavanaugh, *A Study of Books Privately Owned in England: 1300 to 1450*, Part I, Ann Arbor, Michigan: UMI Dissertation Services, 1980, p.9.

5. Richard F. Green, 'King Richard II's Books Revisited', *The Library*, xxxi (1976), pp.235–9 (p.235).

6. 'The Inventory of Juliana de Leybourne, Countess of Huntyngdon', *Archaeologia Cantiana*, i (1858), pp.1–8; Cambridge, Corpus Christi College, Parker Library, MS. 20; see Paul Binski and Stella Panayotova (eds), *The Cambridge Illuminations: Ten Centuries of Book Production in the Medieval West*, London 2005, no. 51 (pp.135–6).

7. Vincent J. Scattergood, 'Two Medieval Book Lists', *The Library*, 5th series, xxiii (1968), pp.236–9.

8. Nigel Morgan, 'Books for the Liturgy and Private Prayer', in Nigel Morgan and Rodney Thomson (eds), CHBB, vol.II: 1100–1400, Cambridge 2008, pp.291–316 (p.291).

9. Neil Ker, *Medieval Libraries of Great Britain: A List of Surviving Books*, 2nd edn., London 1964, p.xi.

10. Boethius, I pr. V. 15.

11. Richard Gameson, 'The Medieval Library (to. c. 1450)', in Elisabeth Leedham-Green and Teresa Webber (eds), CHLBI, vol.I: To 1640, Cambridge 2006, pp.13–50 (p.13); Kate Mertes, *The English Noble Household 1250–1600: Good Governance and Politic Rule*, Oxford 1988, pp.18–21; Kent Rawlinson, '"In Chapel, Oratory or Other Suitable Places in Their Houses": Religious Routines and the Residences of Greater Medieval Households', in Malcolm Airs and Paul Barnwell (eds), *The Medieval Great House*, Donington 2011, pp.171–99 (pp.186–9).

12. John Goodall, *The English Castle*, New Haven and London 2011, p.23.

13. Christopher de Hamel, 'Books in Society', in Nigel Morgan and Rodney Thomson (eds), CHBB, vol.II: 1100–1400, Cambridge 2008, pp.3–23.

14. Bodley, MS. Bodl. 264; Frances Williams, *Pleshey Castle, Essex (XII–XVI): Excavations in the Bailey. 1959–1963* (London: British Archaeological Reports, 48, 1977), pp.129–35.

15. W. J. Courtenay, 'Bury, Richard (1287–1345)', ODNB.

16. Richard de Bury, *The Philobiblon: With an Introduction by Archer Taylor*, Berkeley 1948.

17. W. Mark Ormrod, *Edward III*, New Haven and London 2011, p.12.

18. Nicholas Orme, 'The Education of the Courtier', in Vincent J. Scattergood and J. W. Sherborne, *English Court Culture in the Later Middle Ages*, London 1983, pp.63–85 (p.65).

19. Kathleen Doyle, 'The Old Royal Library: "A Greate Many Noble Manuscripts Yet Remaining"', in Scot McKendrick, John Lowden and Kathleen Doyle (eds), *Royal Manuscripts: The Genius of Illumination*, exh. cat., British Library, London 2011, pp.67–93 (pp.67–8); Clanchy 1993, p.82.

20. R. Weiss, 'The Private Collector and the Revival of Greek Learning', in Francis Wormald and Cyril E. Wright, *The English Library before 1700*, London 1958, pp.112–35 (p.114).

21. Courtenay 2004.

22. Clanchy 1993, p.161; Alec Reginald Myers (ed.), *The Household of Edward IV: The Black Book and the Ordinance of 1478*, Manchester 1959, p.118.

23. *The Regulation and Establishment of the Houshold [sic] of Henry Algernon Percy, the Fifth Earl of Northumberland, at his Castles of Wresill and Lekinfield in Yorkshire*, London 1770, ESTC T131520, pp.153–6, 323, 389–91; C. M. Woolgar, *The Great Household in Late Medieval England*, New Haven and London, 1999, p.182.

24. Jonathan Alexander and Paul Binski (eds), *Age of Chivalry: Art in Plantagenet England, 1200–1400*, exh. cat., Royal Academy of Arts, London 1987, pp.426–7.

25. Burnett Hillman Streeter, *The Chained Library: A Survey of Four Centuries in the Evolution of the English Library*, London 1931, pp.118–19.

26. De Bury 1948, p.48.

27. W. H. St John Hope, 'The Last Testament and Inventory of John de Veer, Thirteenth Earl of Oxford', *Archaeologia*, lxvi (1915), pp.275–348 (p.300); Anthony Emery, *Greater Medieval Houses of England and Wales*, Cambridge 2000, ii, pp.113–14.

28. J. Whitehead, 'An Inventory of the Goods and Chattels of Sir Richard Worsley of Appuldurcombe, A.D. 1566, *Papers and Proceedings of the Hampshire Field Club and Archaeological Society*, v (1904–6), pp.277–95.

29. BL, Add. MS. 5702, fols. 61v–68r.

30. Orme 1983, pp.63–5; I. Doyle, 'English Books in and Out of Court from Edward III to Henry VII', in Vincent J. Scattergood and

J. W. Sherborne, *English Court Culture in the Later Middle Ages*, London 1983, pp.163–81 (p.164).

31. Clanchy 1993, pp.15, 19, 227.

32. Clanchy 1993, p.225.

33. Eamon Duffy, *Marking the Hours: English People and their Prayers, 1240–1570*, New Haven and London 2006, p.69.

34. de Hamel 2008, pp.17–19.

35. CUL, MS. Dd.5.5; Binski and Panayotova 2005, pp.132–3.

36. BL, Royal MS. 19.D.ii; Jenny Stratford, *The Bedford Inventories: The Worldly Goods of John, Duke of Bedford, Regent of France (1389–1435)*, London 1993, p.95–6.

37. Nigel Morgan and Paul Binski, 'Private Devotion: Humility and Splendour', in Binski and Panayotova 2005, pp.163–9 (p.164); de Hamel 2008, p.15.

38. Duffy 2006, p.17.

39. Morgan and Binski 2005, p.163.

40. *The Pomander of Prayer*, London 1531, STC 25421.5, ESTC S4968; quoted in Andrew Taylor, 'Into his Secret Chamber: Reading and Privacy in Late Medieval England', in James Raven, Helen Small and Naomi Tadmor, *The Practice and Representation of Reading in England*, Cambridge 1996, pp.41–61 (p.42).

41. JRULM, EGR1/8/1/1 (Will of John Booth of Barton, 1422).

42. Belinda Jack, *The Woman Reader*, New Haven and London 2012, p.87.

43. Cambridge, Fitzwilliam Museum, MS. 242; Binski and Panayotova 2005, pp.192–3.

44. Andrew Clark (ed.), *Lincoln Diocese Documents, 1450–1544*, London 1914, p.48.

45. Rawlinson 2011, p.189

46. John Goodall, *Ashby de la Zouch Castle and Kirby Muxloe Castle*, 2nd edn., London 2011, p.6.

47. S. J. Gunn and P. G. Lindley, 'Charles Brandon's Westhorpe: an Early Tudor Courtyard House in Suffolk', *Archaeological Journal*, cxlv (1988), pp.272–89 (p.286).

48. BL, Royal MS. 2.A.xviii; Scot McKendrick (ed.), *Royal Manuscripts: The Genius of Imagination*, London 2011, pp.146–7; Janet Backhouse, 'Patronage and Commemoration in the Beaufort Hours', in K. Smith and C. Krinsky (eds), *Tributes to Lucy Freeman Sandler: Studies in Manuscript Illumination*, London 2007, pp.331–44.

49. BL, Add. MS. 42130.

50. H. George Fletcher (ed.), *The Wormsley Library: A Personal Selection by Sir Paul Getty*, London 1999, pp.26–7; Janet Backhouse, *The Madresfield Hours: A Fourteenth-Century Manuscript in the Library of Earl Beauchamp*, Oxford 1975.

51. NLS, MS. 21000; John Higgitt, *The Murthly Hours: Devotion, Literacy and Luxury in Paris, England and the Gaelic West*, London 2000, pp.5, 15, 24; Woolgar 1999, p.129.

52. Higgitt 2000, p.26.

53. Clanchy 1993, p.216.

54. Clanchy 1993, p.268.

55. Madelaine Blaess, 'L'Abbaye de Bordesley et les Livres de Guy de Beauchamp', *Romania*, lxxii (1957), pp.511–18; J. S. Hamilton, 'Guy de Beauchamp (c.1272–1315)', ODNB; online edn., January 2008.

56. Lucy Freeman Sandler, *The Lichtenthal Psalter and the Manuscript Patronage of the Bohun Family*, London 2004, pp.11–28 (material in the remainder of this section drawn from this source unless otherwise referenced).

57. BL, Egerton MS. 3277, fol. 32v.

58. McKendrick 2011, pp.368–9.

59. Bodley, MS. Douce 319; O. Pächt and J. J. Alexander, *Illuminated Manuscripts in the Bodleian Library*, Oxford 1966–73, ii, p.16.

60. Quoted in Taylor 1996, p.41.

61. Goodall 2011, p.23; Howard Colvin, *The History of the King's Works*, London 1963–82, ii, p.935.

62. BnF, ms. fr. 782, fol. 2v; illustrated in Christopher de Hamel, *A History of Illuminated Manuscripts*, 2nd edn., London 1994, p.165.

63. For what follows, see Stratford 1993, p.91–6, 119–23.

64. BL, Add. MS. 18850; McKendrick 2011, pp.398–9.

65. BnF, MS. fr. 403; Alexander and Binski 1987, pp.348–9.

66. Gilbert Ouy, 'Recherches sur la Librairie de Charles d'Orléans', *Comptes rendus de l'Académie des Inscriptions et belles Lettres* (1955), pp.272–88.

67. John Goodall, *God's House at Ewelme*, Aldershot 2001, pp.12–13, 79.

68. Goodall 2001, pp.282–7; the Caxton edition of *Les Quatre Fils* (1490), in English, is STC 1007, ESTC S110385.

69. BL, Cotton Nero MS. D.vi; McKendrick 2011, pp.352–3.

70. BL, Arundel MS. 38; Richard Marks and Paul Williamson, *Gothic Art for England, 1400–1547*, exh. cat., Victoria and Albert Museum, London 2003, p.182.

71. C. L. Kingsford, 'Two Forfeitures in the Year of Agincourt', *Archaeologia*, lxx (1920), pp.71–100 (pp.77, 82–3).

72. Benjamin G. Kohl, 'Tiptoft [Tibetot], John, First Earl of Worcester (1427–1470)', ODNB; online edn., September 2015; R. Weiss, 'The Library of John Tiptoft, Earl of Worcester', *Bodleian Quarterly Record*, viii (1935–8), pp.158–64; R. Mitchell, 'A Renaissance Library: the Collection of John Tiptoft, Earl of Worcester', *The Library*, xviii (1938), pp.72 8; for the current working list of Tiptoft manuscript, see the PDF files attached to the *Bonae Litterae*, the blog of Dr David Rundle of the University of Essex <http://bonaelitterae.wordpress.com/david-rundles-research-projects/tiptoft/>. The Lydgate manuscript is BL, Royal MS. 18.D.iv.

73. Bodley, MS. Bodl. 646, MS. Auct. F.I.13; MS. Arch. Seld. B. 50; Oxford, Jesus College, MS. 109.

74. David Rundle, 'Habits of Manuscript-Collecting: the Dispersals of the library of Humfrey, Duke of Gloucester', in James Raven, *Lost Libraries: The Destruction of Great Book Collections since Antiquity*, London 2004, pp.106–23 (pp.108–9, 114, 118).

75. Carole Rawcliffe, 'Somerset, John (d.1454)', ODNB; online edn., January 2008.

76. Goodall 2011, p.351; R. Weiss, *Humanism in England During the Fifteenth Century*, Oxford 1957, pp.61–2.

77. Bodley, MS. Duke Humfrey d. 1; David Rogers, *The Bodleian Library and its Treasures*, Henley 1991, no. 4.

78. Leiden, University Library, MS. Hebr. Scaliger 8; Los Angeles, Getty Museum, MS. Ludwig XV 4.

79. BL, Royal MS. 16.G.vi; McKendrick 2011, pp.384–5.

80. BL, Royal MS. 14.C.vii; McKendrick 2011, pp.338–9, 294–5.

81. de Hamel 2008, p.20.

82. HL, MS. EL.26.C.9; Herbert C. Schulz, *The Ellesmere Manuscript of Chaucer's Canterbury Tales*, San Marino, CA 1999.

83. John M. Manly and Edith Rickerts, *The Text of the Canterbury Tales: Studied on the Basis of All Known Manuscripts*, Chicago 1940, i, pp.617–18, 621–2.

84. Manly and Rickerts 1940, i, pp.410–14; MMBL, iv, p.179; F. Furnivall, *The Petworth MS. of Chaucer's Canterbury Tales*, London 1868–84.

85. *Catalogue of Exceedingly Rare and Valuable Americana, with Some Important English Books & Manuscripts, Largely from the Library of Henry Percy, 9th Earl of Northumberland (1564–1632) at Petworth House*, Sotheby's, London 23–24 April 1928, lot 76.

86. BL, Royal MS. 18 D.ii.

87. Cambridge, Trinity College, MS. O.5.2; Binski and Panayotova 2005, pp.280–81.

88. Bodley, MS. Eng. Poet. a. 1; P. Robinson, 'The Vernon Manuscript as a "Coucher Book"', in Derek Pearsall (ed.), *Studies in the Vernon*

Manuscript, Cambridge 1990, pp. 15–28 (pp. 17, 27–8); Thorlac Turville-Petre, 'The Relationship of the Vernon and Clopton Manuscripts', in Pearsall, *Studies in the Vernon Manuscript*, pp. 29–44 (p. 35). I can attest from personal experience quite how bulky the Vernon manuscript is, having had to move it as a junior member of staff at the Bodleian. See, too, I. Doyle's introduction to *The Vernon Manuscript: A Facsimile of Bodleian Library, Oxford, MS. Eng. poet. a. 1*, Cambridge 1987, pp. I, II, 14–15.

89. BL, Harley MS. 2253; Woolgar 1999, p. 179.

90. BL, Harley MS. 1706; Taylor 1996, pp. 52–5.

91. Dublin, Royal Irish Academy, MS. 23 E 29.

92. John Carey, Maire Herbert, James Knowles, *Travelled Tales: The Book of Lismore at University College, Cork*, Cork 2011, pp. 13–16, 22.

93. Richard Suggett, *Houses & History in the March of Wales: Radnorshire, 1400–1800*, Aberystwyth 2005, pp. 37–38.

94. MMBL, ii, pp. 1–2.

95. Bodley, MS. Arch. Seld. B. 24; R. J. Lyall, 'Books and Book Owners in Fifteenth-Century Scotland', in Jeremy Griffiths and Derek Pearsall, *Book Production and Publishing in Britain, 1375–1475*, Cambridge 2007, pp. 245–6; 250.

96. Cambridge, St John's College, MS. H.5; Binski and Panayotova 2005, p. 270.

97. BL, Royal MS. 19.B.xvii; McKendrick 2011, pp. 260–61; Jacobus de Voragine, *Thus Endeth the Legende Named in Latyn Legenda Aurea*, Westminster 1483, STC 24873, ESTC S541.

98. Quoted in George R. Keiser, 'Practical Books for the Gentleman', in Lotte Hellinga and J. B. Trapp (eds), CHBB, vol. III: *1400–1557*, Cambridge 1999, pp. 470–94 (p. 470); the original edition of 1486 is STC 3308, and De Worde's 1496 edition, STC 3309.

99. Caxton has been subject to intense study, and our understanding of his press has developed considerably since many earlier works were published. My comments here are based on material in *Catalogue of Books Printed in the xvth Century now in the British Museum* [British Library], London 1908–2006, ix. A commentary, drawing on this data and reflecting the current state of scholarship, can be found in Lotte Hellinga, *William Caxton and Early Printing in England*, London 2010, especially pp. 6–7, 33–4, 40–43, 52–3, 57–8, 60–61, 72, 98, 100–101.

100. Keiser 1999, pp. 471–6.

101. Bodley Arch G.d.16 – Christine de Pisan, *The Book of Fayttes of Arms and of Chyualrye*, London 1489, STC 7269, ESTC S106571; Alan Coates (ed.), *A Catalogue of Books Printed in the Fifteenth Century now in the Bodleian Library*, Oxford 2005, C-191(2); BM 15th cent., pp. 61–70.

102. Aisling Byrne, 'The Earls of Kildare and their Books at the End of the Middle Ages', *The Library*, 7th series, xiv, 2 (June 2013), pp. 129–53.

103. CCC, MS. 133; PML, MS. M.105; Bodley, MS. e Mus. I; BL, Egerton MS. 92; Byrne 2013, pp. 131–2.

104. Byrne 2013, p. 141.

105. Philadelphia Museum of Art, Philip S. Collins Collection, 1945/65/2; James Tanis and Jennifer A. Thompson, *Leaves of Gold: Manuscript Illuminations from Philadelphia Collections*, Philadelphia 2001, pp. 60–64.

106. BL, Add. MS. 54782.

107. BL, Royal MS. 18.D.vii; McKendrick 2011, pp. 246–7.

108. John Ridgard (ed.), 'Medieval Framlingham: Select Documents, 1270–1524', *Suffolk Records Society*, xxvii (1985) pp. 148–49.

109. *Bibliotheca Norfolciana: Sive Catalogue Libb. Manuscriptorum & Impressorum Omni Arte & Lingua, quos Illustriss. Principis Henricus Dux Norfolciae, &c. Regiae Societatis Londiniensi … Donavit*, London 1681, Wing N1230, ESTC R14407. I am grateful to John Martin Robinson, Librarian to the Duke of Norfolk, for his advice on the ducal collections.

110. Woolgar 1999, p. 176; BL, Add. MS. 50001; McKendrick 2011, pp. 154–5.

111. de Hamel 2008, p. 17.

112. Marshall and Scott, 2009, p. 7.

113. de Hamel 2008, p. 7.

114. BL, Sloane MS. 2027; Keiser 1999, p. 485; BL, Add. MS. 82949; Marks and Williamson 2003, pp. 302–3

115. BL, Sloane MS. 372; Keiser 1999, pp. 482–3;

116. Cambridge, MA, Harvard Law School, MS. 22; Seymour de Ricci, *Census of Medieval and Renaissance Manuscripts in the United States and Canada*, New York 1961, i, p. 1026.

117. S. West, 'The Development of Libraries in Norfolk Country Houses, 1660–1830', PhD Thesis, University of East Anglia, 2000, pp. 7, 135; see, too, BL, Add. MS. 41439, fol. 23v, a list of 21 books owned by Roger Townshend of Raynham.

118. R. Hanna and T. Turville-Petre, 'The History of a Family Collection', in Hanna and Turville-Petre 2010, pp. 3–19 (p. 4–7).

119. Philip Stell (ed.), *Probate Inventories of the York Diocese, 1350–1500*, York 2006, p. xx.

120. Mark Girouard, *Old Wardour Castle*, London 2012, p. 15.

121. A. D. K. Hawkyard, 'Thornbury Castle', *Transactions of the Bristol and Gloucestershire Archaeological Society*, xcv (1997), pp. 51–8 (p. 53).

122. Woolgar 1999, pp. 61, 68.

123. William Abel Pantin, 'Instructions for a Devout and Literate Layman', in

J. J. G. Alexander and M. T. Gibson (eds), *Medieval Learning and Literature: Essays Presented to Richard William Hunt*, Oxford 1976, pp. 398–422 (p. 406).

124. W. Clarke-Maxwell, 'An Inventory of the Contents of Markeaton Hall. Made by Vincent Mundy, Esq., in the Year 1545', *Journal of the Derbyshire Archaeological and Natural History Society*, li (1930), pp. 116–40 (pp. 118–20).

125. Gilles Corrozet, *Les Blasons domestiques*, Paris 1865, p. 33; Dora Thornton, *The Scholar in his Study: Ownership and Experience in Renaissance Italy*, New Haven and London 1997, p. 54.

126. Clarke-Maxwell 1930, pp. 121–2, 130, 138; JRULM, Crawford MS. 60.

127. Stafford, Staffordshire Record Office, D1810/f.117d (Indenture lease of Stafford Castle, with inventory, 1537).

128. John Darlington (ed.), *Stafford Castle: Survey, Excavation and Research, 1978–98*, Stafford 2001, i, pp. 60–61.

129. BL, Royal MS. 14.e.v; BL, Royal MS. 18.e.iv; J. W. Clark, *Libraries in the Medieval and Renaissance Periods*, Cambridge 1894, pp. 57–8.

130. Dominicus Mancinus, *Here Begynneth a Ryght Frutefull Treatyse, Intituled the Myrrour of Good Maners*, London 1518?, STC 17242, ESTC S103749; the Lincoln lectern is illustrated in Gameson 2006, p. 36.

131. Deborah Thorpe, 'Writing and Reading in the Circle of Sir John Fastolf (d.1459)', PhD Thesis, University of York, 2011, i, p. 277; Woolgar 1999, p. 65, 179.

132. Maria Hayward (ed.), *The 1542 Inventory of Whitehall: The Palace and its Keeper*, London 2004, p. 28.

133. Mark Purcell, 'Libraries at Lacock Abbey', in David Adshead (ed.), *National Trust Historic Houses & Collections Annual* (2012), pp. 36–43 (p. 39).

134. *The Paston Letters A.D. 1422–1509*, London 1900, iv, p 182.

135. Ibid., v, pp. 116–17.

136. J. Charles Cox, 'Norbury Manor House and the Troubles of the Fitzherberts', *Journal of the Derbyshire Archaeological and Natural History Society*, vii (January 1883), pp. 221–59 (p. 238).

137. Quoted in Gordon R. Batho (ed.), *The Household Papers of Henry Percy, Ninth Earl of Northumberland (1564–1632)*, London 1962, p. xxi.

138. Emery 2000, i, p. 292.

139. David Neave, 'Wressle Castle', *The Archaeological Journal*, cxli (1984), pp. 58–60.

140. R. W. Hoyle, 'Percy, Henry Algernon, Fifth Earl of Northumberland (1478–1527), ODNB; Peter Brears, 'Wressle Castle: Functions,

Fixtures and Furnishing for Henry Percy "The Magnificent", Fifth Earl of Northumberland, 1498–1527', *Archaeological Journal*, clxvii (2010), pp.55–114 (pp.56–7, 63).

141. John Leland, *Itinerary*, London 1906–10, i, p.53.

142. William B. Rye, *England as Seen by Foreigners in the Days of Elizabeth and James the First*, London 1865, p.134.

143. *Bramhall Hall*, Stockport 2001, p.22; Brears 2010, p.98.

144. Brears 2010, pp.79, 82–3.

145. Taylor 1996, p.42.

146. WSRO, PHA, 3538–47; illustrated in Brears 2010, p.59.

147. Leland 1906–10, i, p.46; Gerald Brenan, *A History of the House of Percy from the Earliest Times Down to the Present Century*, London 1902, i, pp.144–5, 268.

148. *The Regulation and Establishment of the Houshold [sic] of Henry Algernon Percy, the Fifth Earl of Northumberland*, p.378.

149. Ibid., pp.34–35, 100, 351.

150. Ibid., pp.99, 101, 365, 453.

151. A. S. G. Edwards, 'Books owned by Medieval Members of the Percy Family', in M. Villalobos Hennessy, *Tributes to Kathleen L. Scott: English Medieval Manuscripts: Readers, Makers and Illuminators*, London 2009.

152. A. Edwards 2009, pp.74–75.

153. BL, Harley MS. 1260; NT, Powis Castle, inv. 118034; MMBL, iv, pp.186–8; Edwards 2009, p.76.

154. A. Edwards 2009, p.75.

Chapter Three

1. *Miscellanea Antiqua Anglicana; or a Select Collection of Curious Tracts Illustrative of the History, Literature, Manners and Biography of the English Nation*, London 1816, ch. 8.

2. John Maddison et al., *Blickling Hall, Norfolk*, London 1987, p.50; Mark Girouard, *Life in the English Country House*, New Haven and London 1978, p.165.

3. Sears Jayne, *Library Catalogues of the English Renaissance*, Berkeley 1956, pp.77, 67.

4. Pamela Selwyn and David Selwyn, '"The Profession of a Gentleman": Books for the Gentry and the Nobility (c.1560 to 1640)', in Elisabeth Leedham-Green and Teresa Webber (eds), CHLBI, vol. I: *To 1640*, Cambridge 2006, pp.489–519 (p.489).

5. 21 Henry VIII, c.5.

6. Germaine Warkentin, 'The World and the Book at Penshurst: the Second Earl of Leicester (1595–1677) and His Library', *The Library*, 6th series, xx, 4 (December 1998), pp.325–46 (p.329).

7. Lindsay Boynton (ed.), *The Hardwick Hall Inventories of 1601*, London 1971, p.32.

8. Mark Purcell and Nicola Thwaite, 'Libraries at Hardwick', in David Adshead and David Taylor (eds), *Hardwick Hall: A Great Old Castle of Romance*, New Haven and London 2016, pp.177–91 (pp.178–82).

9. H. M. Nixon, *Sixteenth-Century Gold-Tooled Bookbindings in the Pierpont Morgan Library*, New York 1971, p.248.

10. Boynton 1971, p.32.

11. VAM, MS. L.30–1982 (Transcript of 'An Inventorie of All the Golde and Sylver Plate, Jewelles, Apparell and Warderobe Stuffe … Belonging to the Right Honorable William Earl of Pembroke', 1561).

12. John B. Saunders, *Words and Phrases Legally Defined: Lexis Nexis*, London 1969–86, x, pp.425–26.

13. SBRO, DR/37/2/BOX 90/30.

14. Philip Riden and Dudley Fowkes, *Hardwick: A Great House and its Estate*, Chichester 2009, pp.24, 32.

15. Purcell and Thwaite 2016, p.183.

16. I am grateful to Brian Hillyard for notes on these books.

17. Sheffield, Sheffield Archives, ACM/W/123.

18. P. Marshall, *Wollaton Hall: An Archaeological Survey*, Nottingham 1996.

19. M. Purcell, 'Libraries at Lacock Abbey', *National Trust Historic Houses & Collections Annual* (2012), pp.36–43.

20. This last, C. Barker, *An Abstract of all the Penal Statutes*, London 1579, ESTC S116378, STC 9285.5, is now Chippenham, Wiltshire and Swindon History Centre, WRO/2664/8.

21. T. Vernon, 'Inventory of Sir Henry Sharington: Contents of Lacock House, 1575', *Wiltshire Archaeological and Natural History Society Magazine*, lxiii (1968), pp.72–82.

22. L. Pollock, 'Grace Mildmay', ODNB; L. Pollock, *With Faith and Physick: The Life of a Tudor Gentlewoman, Lady Grace Mildmay, 1552–1620*, London 1993, pp.23–9.

23. R. Fehrenbach, 'Sir Roger Townshend's Books', in R. Fehrenbach and E. Leedham-Green, *Private Libraries in Renaissance England*, 2 vols, Binghamtown, NY 1992, i, pp.79–135, especially pp.80–82.

24. ESRO, SAS/G45/16, fol. 93v.

25. CORNRO, AR21/15/1.

26. H. Whitley, 'An Inventory of the Goods and Chattels of William Shelley of Michelgrove, 1585', *Sussex Archaeological Collections*, lv (1912), pp.284–98 (pp.288–9).

27. A. Suckling, *The History and Antiquities of the County of Suffolk*, London 1846–8, ii, p.357.

28. NLI, MS. 7861, fols. 166–74; published in K. O'Shea, 'A Castleisland Inventory, 1590', *Journal of the Kerry Archaeological and Historical Society*, xv–xvi (1982–83), pp.37–46; C. Morgan, 'Herbert, Sir William (c.1553–1593)', ODNB.

29. C. Freeman, 'Elizabethan Inventories', *Publications of the Bedfordshire Historical Record Society*, xxxii (1952), pp.92–156 (p.102).

30. R. Fehrenbach 1992, i, pp.80–81. The inventory is Folger, MS. L.d.776.

31. M. Howard, *The Early Tudor Country House*, London 1987, p.109.

32. H. Wotton, *The Elements of Architecture*, London 1624, STC 26011, ESTC S120324, p.8.

33. H. M. Nixon, *Twelve Books in Fine Bindings from the Library of J. W. Hely-Hutchinson*, Oxford 1953, pp.34–48; M. Foot, 'Thomas Wotton and His Binders', in M. Foot, *The Henry Davis Gift: A Collection of Bookbindings*, London 1978–2010, i, pp.139–55; H. Avray Tipping, *English Homes, Period II … Early Tudor*, London 1929, i, pp.213–29.

34. H. M. Nixon 1953, pp.36–48; H. George Fletcher (ed.), *The Wormsley Library: A Personal Selection by Sir Paul Getty*, London 1999, no. 29.

35. J. Aubrey, *Aubrey's Brief Lives: Edited from the Original Manuscript and with a Life of John Aubrey*, London 1972, p.254.

36. M. Girouard, *Elizabethan Architecture: Its Rise and Fall*, London 2009, p.65; for Raleigh's library see: W. Oakeshott, 'Sir Walter Raleigh's Library', *The Library*, 5th series, xxiii, 4 (December 1968), pp.285–327.

37. W. John and K. Smith, *An Architectural History of Towneley Hall, Burnley*, Nelson 2004, pp.35, 38, 40–41.

38. P. Collinson, A. Hunt and A. Walsham, 'Religious Publishing in England', CHBB, vol. IV: *1557–1695*, pp.29–66 (p.60).

39. V. Bankes, *A Dorset Heritage: The Story of Kingston Lacy*, London [1953], p.88.

40. N. Cooper, *Houses of the Gentry, 1480–1680*, New Haven and London 1999, p.254.

41. H. Brayman Hackel, *Reading Material in Early Modern England*, Cambridge 2009, p.43.

42. N. Krivatsy and L. Yeandle, 'Books of Sir Edward Dering of Kent, 1598–1644', in R. Fehrenbach and E. Leedham-Green, *Private Libraries in Renaissance England*, 2 vols, Binghamtown, NY 1992, i, p.145.

43. J. Comenius, *Orbis Sensualium Pictus*, Sydney 1967, p.200.

44. E. Leedham-Green and D. McKitterick, 'Ownership: Private and Public Libraries', CHBB, vol. IV: *1557–1695*, pp.323–35 (p.324).

45. *Historical Manuscripts Commission. Twelfth Report, Appendix, Part IV. The Manuscripts of His*

Grace the Duke of Rutland, G.C.B., Preserved at Belvoir Castle, London 1888, i, p. 264.

46. Jennifer C. Ward, Old Thorndon Hall, Chelmsford 1972, pp. 6, 8; Folger, MS. V.a.334 (Account Book of William Petre), November 1597 (microfilm at Essex Record Office, T/A 174/1).

47. WSRO, SAS-BA/67 (probate of the will of Anthony Browne, Lord Montague, 1592).

48. TNA, C108/187 (Inventory of Edward, Lord Zouche of Bramshill, 1634).

49. F. Steer, 'The Inventory of Arthur Coke of Bramfield', Proceedings of the Suffolk Institute of Archaeology & History, xxv (1951), pp. 264–87 (p. 281).

50. NorthRO, W(A)/6/V/1–2 (Westmorland Inventory, 1629); there is also a late seventeenth-century Apethorpe catalogue, BL, Add. MS. 34220; Catalogue of a Portion of the Valuable Library of a Nobleman, Sotheby's, London 13–15 July 1887: a marked-up copy is now Lincolnshire Record Office FANE/6/10/8/J/1, and unusually for the period the catalogue includes substantial details about early annotations and ownership inscriptions. Cicero, De Philosophia, Paris 1545, Beinecke Library, New Haven, Elizabethan Club, 276/1–2, illustrated in Other People's Books: Association Copies and the Stories they Tell, Chicago 2011, pp. 32–42.

51. Hannibal Gamon, The Praise of a Godly Woman, London 1627, STC 11458, ESTC S102888, p. x.

52. A. Cambers, 'Readers' Marks and Religious Practice: Margaret Hoby's Marginalia', in J. King (ed.), Tudor Books and Readers: Materiality and the Construction of Meaning, Cambridge 2010, pp. 211–31 (pp. 216–17).

53. T. Bayly, Worcesters Apophthegmes, London 1650, ESTC R204142, Wing W3535, pp. 63–4.

54. D. Clifford (ed.), The Diaries of Lady Anne Clifford, Stroud 1992, pp. 45, 54, 56.

55. W. Sherman, 'The Place of Reading in the English Renaissance: John Dee Revisited', in J. Raven, H. Small and N. Tadmor (eds), The Practice and Representation of Reading in England, Cambridge 1996, pp. 62–76 (pp. 64–6).

56. Hull, Hull History Centre, DDEV/X1/663 (Inventory of Sir Robert Constable of Everingham, 1558).

57. L. Stone, The Crisis of the Aristocracy, 1558 to 1641, Oxford 1965, p. 794.

58. Warwick, Warwickshire Museum Service, H13118 1/1966.

59. Leeds, West Yorkshire Archive Service, ACC 3491 (Inventory of William Thomson of Esholt, 1612).

60. Nottingham, Nottinghamshire DD/E/86/84.

61. G. Widley, The Doctrine of the Sabbath Handled in Foure Severall Bookes of Treatises, London 1604, ESTC S119957, STC 256110, A2; Stone 1965, p. 705.

62. Royal Collection, RCIN 405759.

63. TNA, E 154/2/39, fols. 80v, 81v; I am grateful to Alden Gregory for pointing me to this.

64. A. Anderson, 'The Books and Interests of Henry, Lord Stafford (1501–1563)', The Library, 5th series, xxi (1966), pp. 87–144 (p. 88); Stafford, Record Office, D(W)1721/1/10 (Library Catalogue of Henry, Lord Stafford, 1556); San Marino, CA, Huntington Library, HM 202 (Commonplace Book of Henry, Lord Stafford).

65. Anderson 1966, pp. 88–9.

66. Anderson 1966, p. 94.

67. J. Nichols, The Unton Inventories, Relating to Wadley and Faringdon, Co. Berks in the Years 1596 and 1620, London 1841, p. 3.

68. BAL, SC232/11/13.

69. C. Scott-Fox, Holcombe Court: A Bluett Family Tudor Mansion, Exeter [2012], pp. 17–18; B. Cherry and N. Pevsner, Devon: Buildings of England, 2nd edn., New Haven and London 1989, p. 490; Girouard 2009, p. 65.

70. SRO D/11/1/11.

71. The most spectacular extant examples include the exquisite intarsia-lined rooms made for the ducal palaces in Urbino and Gubbio in the 1470s, for which see D. Thornton, The Scholar in his Study, New Haven and London 1997, p. 8.

72. J. Francis, 'The Kedermister Library: an Account of its Origins and a Reconstruction of its Contents and Arrangement', Records of Buckinghamshire, xxxvi (1994), pp. 62–85 (pp. 62–3, 65); John Harris, 'A Rare and Precious Room: the Kedermister Library, Langley, Buckinghamshire', Country Life, 1 December 1977, pp. 1576–9.

73. H. Meakin, The Painted Closet of Lady Anne Drury, Farnham 2013, p. 2. Since 1924 the panels from Anne's Closet have been in Christchurch Mansion, once the home of the sixteenth-century Ipswich MP Edmund Withypoll (1510/13–82) and now the Fine and Decorative Arts department of the Ipswich town museum.

74. Private collection (Fife), but illustrated as the frontispiece to John, 5th Earl of Rothes, A Relation of Proceedings Concerning the Kirk of Scotland, from August 1637 to July 1638, Edinburgh 1830. I am grateful to David Taylor for drawing this picture to my attention.

75. W. Richardson, 'John Boys (bap. 1571, d. 1625)', ODNB; B. Bailey, N. Pevsner and B. Cherry, Northamptonshire: Buildings of England, New Haven and London 2013, pp. 247–8, plate 49.

76. N. Pevsner and E. Williamson with G. Brandwood, The Buildings of England: Buckinghamshire, Harmondsworth 1994, pp. 370–71.

77. For example, from Wollaton, but now Nottingham University Library, WLC/P/1, T. Elyot, The Boke Named the Governour, London 1531, ESTC S105376, STC 7635, and numerous examples still at Hatfield.

78. For an overview of the Clements Collection, see D. Pearson, Provenance Research in Book History, London 1994, pp. 111–12.

79. H. M. Nixon and M. Foot, The History of Decorated Bookbinding in England, 2nd edn. Oxford 1992, p. 52.

80. R. Cust, 'Lucy, Sir Thomas (1583–1640)', ODNB.

81. T. Dugard, Death and the Grave: or, a Sermon Preached at the Funeral of that Honorable and Virtuous Ladie, the Ladie Alice Lucie, London 1649, ESTC R6467, Wing D2453, p. 46; TNA, PROB 11/185/287 (Will of Sir Thomas Lucy of Charlecote, 1641); R. Cust, 'Alice, Lady Lucy (c.1594–1648)', ODNB.

82. WRO, L6/1095 (Catalogue of the Books at Charlecote House, 1681); severely damaged by damp, but a typescript transcript prior to this is WRO, Z/22, with a further copy in the files of the National Trust Libraries Curator. See, too, H. Summerson, 'The Lucys of Charlecote and their Library', National Trust Studies (1979), pp. 147–59.

83. Most of the 30 surviving books found their way into the library of St Mary's Church, Warwick, and are now in Birmingham University Library. See P. Morgan, 'A 16th-Century Warwickshire Library: A Problem of Provenance', Book Collector, xxii, 3 (Autumn 1973), pp. 337–55.

84. J. Evans, 'Extracts from the Private Account Book of Sir William More, of Loseley, in Surrey, in the time of Queen Mary and of Queen Elizabeth', Archaeologia, xxxvi, 2 (January 1855), pp. 284–310.

85. Folger, MS. L.b.550, fols. 2r–7r, 104–105v, 180r–181r.

86. Thornton 1997, p. 2.

87. R. Ascham, The Scholemaster, London 1934, p. 54.

88. Ascham 1934, p. 74.

89. Ascham 1934, p. 20.

90. Historical Manuscripts Commission, Report on the Manuscripts of the Earl of Ancaster, Preserved at Grimsthorpe, Dublin 1907, pp. 462, 468.

91. C. Boweden, 'Cecil [Cooke], Mildred, Lady Burghley (1526–1589)', ODNB.

92. H. M. Nixon 1971, no. 28.

93. Ascham 1934, pp. 60–61; B. Castiglione, *The Courtyer of Count Baldassar Castilio*, London 1561, ESTC S122029, STC 4778.

94. Selwyn and Selwyn 2006, pp. 491–2.

95. NUL, WLC/P/1. T. Elyot, *The Boke Named the Governour*, London 1531, STC 7635, ESTCS105376.

96. Stone 1965, p. 679.

97. P. Croft, 'Cecil, Robert, First Earl of Salisbury (1563–1612)', ODNB.

98. *Bibliotheca Illustris: Sive Catalogus Variorum Librorum in Quâvis Linguâ & Facultate Insignium Ornatissimae Bibliothecae Viri Cujusdam Praenobilis ac Honoratissimi Olim Defuncti*, [London] 1687, Wing A801A, ESTC R282. Though sold as 'the main part' of Burghley's library the true picture seems to have been more complicated: for discussion of this, see D. Huws, 'Sir Thomas Mostyn and the Mostyn Manuscripts', in J. Carley and C. Tite, *Books and Collectors, 1200–1700: Essays for Andrew Watson*, London 1996, pp. 451–72.

99. Selwyn and Selwyn 2006, p. 500.

100. W. MacCaffrey, 'Cecil, William, First Baron Burghley (1520/21–1598)', ODNB.

101. Lambeth, MS. 723, fols. 56r–v, 60v; R. Titler, 'Bacon, Sir Nicholas (1510–1579)', ODNB; Nixon and Foot 1992, p. 37.

102. E. McCutcheon (ed.), *Sir Nicholas Bacons's Great House Sententiae: The Latin Text, along with the First English Translation, and Introduction*, Honolulu 1977.

103. F. Emmison, *Tudor Secretary: Sir William Petre at Court and Home*, London 1961, p. 5.

104. Emmison 1961, pp. 220–21.

105. S. Doran, 'Pickering, Sir William (1516/17–75)', ODNB; I. Philip, 'Sir William Pickering and His Books', *Book Collector*, v, 3 (Autumn 1956), pp. 231–8 (pp. 233, 237).

106. J. Collins, *A Short Account of the Library at Longleat House*, London 1980, pp. 5–7; D. Burnett, *Longleat: The Story of an English House*, London 1978, pp. 32, 34; K. Harris, 'An Augustan Episode in the History of the Collections of Medieval Manuscripts at Longleat House', in A. Edwards, V. Gillespie and R. Hanna, *The English Medieval Book: Studies in Memory of Jeremy Griffiths*, London 2000, pp. 233–47 (p. 233). The 1577 catalogue is Longleat MS. 258.

107. E. Peacock (ed.), 'The Inventories made for Sir William and Sir Thomas Fairfax, Knights, of Walton, and of Gilling Castle, Yorkshire, in the Sixteenth & Seventeenth Centuries', *Archaeologia*, xlviii (1885), pp. 123–56 (pp. 152–3).

108. J. Carley, 'The Dispersal of the Monastic Spoils and the Salvaging of the Spoils', CHLBI, vol. I: To 1640, pp. 265–91 (p. 272).

109. N. Ker, 'Sir John Prise', *The Library*, 5th series, x, 1 (March 1955), pp. 1–24.

110. MMBL, pp. xii–xiii; A. Watson, *The Manuscripts of Sir Henry Savile of Banke*, London 1969.

111. Cambridge, St John's College, MS. C.9; P. Binski and S. Panayotova, *The Cambridge Illuminations: Ten Centuries of Book Production in the Medieval West*, London 2005, pp. 69–70.

112. Purcell 2012, pp. 37–9.

113. BL, MS. Loan 81 (on loan from the National Trust); Leslie Webster and Janet Backhouse (eds), *The Making of England: Anglo-Saxon Art and Culture*, London 1991, no. 87(b).

114. Hull, Hull Record Office, UDDEV/ X1/66/6

115. Bodley, MS. Don. b. 5.

116. Edward Potten and James Rothwell, '"The Ewe-Lamb" of Lyme Park Library: William Caxton's 1487 Missale ad Usum Sarum', *National Trust Historic Houses and Collections Annual* (2009), pp. 42–7 (p. 46).

117. Lambeth, MS.1; D. Skinner, *The Arundel Choirbook*, [London] 2003.

118. BL, Add. MS. 39,830.

119. N. Barker (ed.), *The Library of Thomas Tresham & Thomas Brudenell*, [London] 2006.

120. Cornro, AR 21/22, fols. 5v–6r (Inventory of Edward Arundell of Trebeliew and Lanherne).

121. K. Hearn, 'A Question of Judgement: Lucy Harington, Countess of Bedford, as Art Patron and Collector', in E. Chaney (ed.), *The Evolution of English Collecting: Receptions of Italian Art in the Tudor and Stuart Periods*, New Haven and London 2003, pp. 221–39 (pp. 222, 229).

122. M. St Clare Byrne and G. Scott Thomson, '"My Lord's Books": the Library of Francis, Second Earl of Bedford in 1584', *Review of English Studies*, VII, 28 (October 1931), pp. 385–405.

123. W. Hassall (ed.), *A Catalogue of the Library of Sir Edward Coke*, New Haven and London 1950, pp. xi–xii, xvi, xix–xx; S. West, 'The Development of Libraries in Norfolk Country Houses, 1660–1830', PhD Thesis, University of East Anglia, 2000, pp. 282–3.

124. P. Hoare, 'Belton House, Lincolnshire, MS. S.115.20: http://scriptorium.english.cam. ac.uk/resources/articles/pdf/hoare_Belton_ House_s.115.20_copy1.pdf.

125. SRO, DD/PH/249.

126. R. MacDonald, *The Library of Drummond of Hawthornden*, Edinburgh 1971, pp. 37–40.

127. TNA, PROB 11/350/410 (Will of Lady Anne Clifford, 1676).

128. < http://armorial.library.utoronto.ca/ stamps/HOW006_s1>; Bodley, MS. Laud. misc. 526.

129. See, for example, the richly decorated armorial binding made for him – one of the earlier non-royal armorial stamps used in England – now NAL CLE M11, N. Perotti, *Cornucopiae Latinae Linguae*, Basel 1536, with Surrey's autograph monogram on the front binder's leaf.

130. N. Barker, 'The Books of Henry Howard, Earl of Northampton', *Bodleian Library Record*, xviii, 2 (October 1990), pp. 375–81 (p. 375–6); R. Ovenden, 'The Libraries of the Antiquaries (c.1580–1640) and the Idea of a National Collection', CHLBI, vol. III, pp. 527–61 (p. 547).

131. D. Mathew, 'The Library at Naworth', in D. Woodruff (ed.), *For Hilaire Belloc: Essays in Honour of His 72nd Birthday*, London 1942, pp. 115–30; E. Rainey, 'The Library of Lord William Howard (1563–1640) from Naworth Castle', *Friends of the National Libraries Annual Report* (1992), pp. 20–22; D. Howard, *Lord Arundel and his Circle*, New Haven and London 1985, p. 12; R. Ovenden, 'The Libraries of the Antiquaries (c.1580–1640) and the Idea of a National Collection', CHLBI, vol. III, pp. 546–8; R. Ovenden and S. Handley, 'Howard, Lord William (1563–1640)', ODNB.

132. S. Jayne and F. Johnson, *The Lumley Catalogue: The Catalogue of 1609*, London 1956.

133. M. Evans (ed.), *Art Collecting and Lineage in the Elizabethan Age: The Lumley Inventory and Pedigree*, [London] 2010.

134. L. Gooch, *A Complete Pattern of Nobility: John, Lord Lumley (c.1534–1609)*, Rainton Bridge 2009, pp. 18–19; J. Lock, 'Fitzalan, Henry, Twelfth Earl of Arundel (1512–1580)', ODNB.

135. Gooch 2009, pp. 62–3.

136. M. Biddle, *Nonsuch Palace: The Material Culture of a Noble Restoration Household*, Oxford 2005, p. 54; J. Dent, *The Quest for Nonsuch*, London 1969, pp. 58–59, 104–5.

137. Trinity College, MS.R.7.22, printed in translation as A. West, 'Magnificae et Plane Regiae Domus Quae Vulgo Vocatur Nonesuch Brevis et Vera Descriptio', *Garden History*, xxvii, 1, (1999), pp. 168–78.

138. Cambridge, Trinity College, MS. O.4.38 (class catalogue of the Lumley Library, 1609), MS. R.14.24 (author index of the catalogue).

139. Jayne and Johnson 1956, pp. 15–16.

140. BL, Royal MS. I.D.ix; BL, Royal MS. I.E.vi.

141. Jayne and Johnson 1956, pp. 11, 26.

142. E. Newton, *The House of Lyme: From its Foundation to the End of the Eighteenth Century*, London 1917, pp. 68–9.

143. Newton 1917, p. 155.

144. G. Piccope, *Lancashire and Cheshire Wills and Inventories from the Ecclesiastical Court*,

Chester: The First Portion, Manchester 1854, pp.168–83 (pp.173–5).

145. H. Maxwell Lyte, *The Lytes of Lytescary*, Taunton 1895, p.44.

146. CornRO, TF/678.

147. P. Marshall, *Faith and Identity in a Warwickshire Family: The Throckmortons and the Reformation*, Stratford 2010, p.17.

148. A. L. Rowse, *Ralegh and the Throckmortons*, London, pp.61, 89, 91, 121, 196–7, 202–3, 278–80, 288–90.

149. TNA, PROB 11/149 (Will of Sir Arthur Throckmorton, 1623).

150. D. McKitterick, *The Library of Sir Thomas Knyvett of Ashwellthorpe, c.1539–1618*, Cambridge 1978, pp.2–3, 13, 22–3.

151. McKitterick 1978, pp.6–7, 11.

152. McKitterick 1978, pp.5, 11, 14.

153. P. Brett, 'Edward Paston … and His Musical Collection', *Transactions of the Cambridge Bibliographical Society*, IV (1964), pp.51–69.

154. J. Gage, *The History and Antiquities of Hengrave*, London 1822, pp.24–5.

155. Colchester, ERO, D/BP/E2/8.

156. S. de Ricci, *English Collectors of Books & Manuscripts (1530–1930) and their Marks of Ownership*, Cambridge 1930, p.27.

157. P. Morgan, 'Frances Wolfreston and "Hor Bouks": a Seventeenth-Century Woman Book-Collector', *The Library*, 6th series, xi, 3 (September 1989), pp.197–219 (pp.198–201).

158. Quoted in W. Sherman, *Used Books: Marking Readers in Renaissance England*, Philadelphia 2008, p.65.

159. C. Kingsford, 'Exeter House, formerly Leicester House and Exeter Inn', *Archaeologia*, lxxiii (1923), pp.1–54 (p.51).

160. P. Needham, *Twelve Centuries of Bookbindings, 400–1600*, New York 1979, pp.262–3.

161. For illustrations see the (otherwise unreliable) W. Moss, *Bindings from the Library of Robt. Dudley, Earl of Leicester, K.G.*, Sonning-on-Thames 1934.

162. London, British Museum, BM 1913/7-10-7.

163. http://armorial.library.utoronto.ca/

164. Pearson 1994, pp.97–115.

165. Selwyn and Selwyn 2006, p.229.

166. Pearson 1994, p.56. The dating of this "1585" bookplate is discussed by Brian North Lee, in his British Bookplates: a pictorial history (Newton Abbot: David & Charles, 1979), pp.22–23, with an illustration.

167. McKitterick 1978, p.6.

168. Henry Peacham, *Peacham's Compleat Gentleman, 1634*, Oxford 1906, p.III.

169. Andrew G. Watson, 'The Manuscript Collection of Sir Walter Cope (d.1614)', *Bodleian Library Record*, xii, 4 (April 1987) pp.262–97 (pp.263, 265–7).

Chapter Four

1. Quoted in J. Levine, *Between the Ancients and the Moderns: Baroque Culture in Restoration England*, New Haven and London 1999, p.6.

2. P. and D. Selwyn, "The Profession of a Gentleman': Books for the Gentry and the Nobility (c.1560 to 1640), CHLBI, vol. I: To 1640, pp.489–519 (p.489), pp.517–19.

3. Levine 1999, p.7.

4. R. Smuts, 'Howard, Thomas, fourteenth Earl of Arundel, fourth Earl of Surrey, and first Earl of Norfolk (1585–1646)', ODNB; D. Howarth, *Lord Arundel and his Circle*, New Haven and London 1985, pp.9–11, 23, 40, 121.

5. J. Evelyn, *The Diary of John Evelyn*, Oxford 1955, iv, p.144; J. Miller, 'Howard, Henry, Sixth Duke of Norfolk (1628–1684)', ODNB.

6. L. Levy Peck, 'Uncovering the Arundel Library at the Royal Society: Changing Meanings of Science and the Fate of the Norfolk Donation', *Notes & Records of the Royal Society*, lii, I (January 1998), pp.3–24.

7. S. van Romburgh, 'Junius [Du Jon], Franciscus (1591–1677)', ODNB; *Bibliotheca Norfolciana: Sive Catalogus Libb. Manuscriptorum & Impressorum in Omne Arte & Lingua, quos Illustriss. Princeps Henricus Dux Norfolciae, &c. Regiae Societati Londinensi … Donavit*, London 1681, Wing N1230, ESTC R14407.

8. The traditional account in S. de Ricci, *English Collectors of Books & Manuscripts (1530–1930) and their Marks of Ownership*, Cambridge 1930, pp.33–53, can helpfully be read in parallel with K. Jensen, *Revolution and the Antiquarian Book: Reshaping the Past, 1780–1815*, Cambridge 2011, which contains useful material on earlier book collecting as well.

9. N. Ramsay, 'English Book Collectors and the Salerooms in the Eighteenth Century', in R. Myers, M. Harris and G. Mandelbrote (eds), *Under the Hammer: Book Auctions since the Seventeenth Century*, New Castle, DE 2001, pp.89–110 (pp.91–5); T. Birrell, 'Books and Buyers in Seventeenth-Century English Auction Sales', in Myers et al. 2001, pp.51–64.

10. Powis Castle, inv. 1181034; C. Levin, 'Percy, Henry, Eighth Earl of Northumberland (c.1532–1585)', ODNB.

11. G. Batho, 'The Wizard Earl in the Tower', *History Today*, vi (1956), pp.344–51 (pp.345, 351).

12. G. Batho, 'The Percies at Petworth, 1574–1632', *Sussex Archaeological Collections*, xcv (1957), pp.1–27 (pp.12, 21–2).

13. G. Batho, 'Notes and Documents on Petworth House. 1574–1632', *Sussex Archaeology*, xcvi (1958), pp.108–34 (pp.110–11).

14. G. Batho (ed.), *The Household Papers of Henry Percy, Ninth Earl of Northumberland (1564–1632)*, London 1962, pp.112–30 (p.119).

15. Batho 1956, p.252.

16. For example Petworth House, inv. 485361.

17. S. West, 'Studies and Status Spaces in Seventeenth-Century Penshurst Place', *Transactions of the Cambridge Bibliographical Society*, xii (2002), pp.266–92 (p.271).

18. WSRO, MP/1840 (G. Batho, 'A Catalogue of the Books from the Library of the Ninth Earl of Northumberland at Petworth House, Sussex, First Draft').

19. H. Wallis, 'The First English Globe: A Recent Discovery', *Geographical Journal*, cxviii (1951), pp.275–90.

20. Oxford, Museum of the History of Science, inv. 70229.

21. Batho 1962 p.118–19.

22. Batho 1956, p.254; G. Batho, 'The Education of a Stuart Nobleman', *British Journal of Educational Studies*, v (1956–7), pp.131–43 (pp.135, 142).

23. Batho 1956, pp.259–60.

24. Batho 1962, p.xxi.

25. G. Batho, *Thomas Harriot and the Northumberland Household*, [Oxford] 1992, p.4.

26. P. Riden and D. Fowkes, *Hardwick: A Great House and its Estate*, Chichester 2009, pp.60–61.

27. N. Malcolm, 'Hobbes, Thomas' (1588–1679)', ODNB.

28. The shift is readily apparent from the large array of catalogues of both houses in the Chatsworth Archives.

29. Chatsworth, Hobbes MSS. E.I.A, illustrated and discussed in N. Barker, *The Devonshire Inheritance: Five Centuries of Collecting at Chatsworth*, Alexandria, VA 2003, p.95; see, too, J. Hamilton, 'Hobbes's Study and the Hardwick Library', *Journal of the History of Philosophy*, xvi (1978), pp.445–53.

30. N. Malcolm, *Aspects of Hobbes*, Oxford 2002, p.80

31. J. Aubrey, *Brief Lives*, Oxford 1898, i, pp.337–8.

32. Chatsworth, Brief Day Book, 1655–68; quoted in B. Cowell, 'Hardwick Hall in the Eighteenth Century', *Georgian Group Journal*, xvi (2008), pp.43–58 (p.43).

33. Chatsworth, Hardwick MS. 14; Barker 2003, p.95.

34. I. Atherton, 'Hassall, John (*bap.* 1571, d. 1654)', ODNB.

35. Paget's catalogue is BL, MS. Harley 3267; full transcript in A. Besson, 'Classification in Private Library Catalogues of the English Renaissance, 1500–1640', PhD Thesis, School of Library, Archive and Information Science, University College, London, November 1988, pp.376–467.

36. Quoted in A. Turberville, *A History of Welbeck Abbey and its Owners*, London 1938–9, i. p.44.

37. Turberville 1938–9, i, pp.52–4, 59–60.

38. D. Stevenson, 'Gordon, Sir Robert, of Gordonstoun, First Baronet (1580–1656)', ODNB.

39. NRS, GD224/935/22 ('Inventory of the Earle of Buccleuch his Books taken up 7. August 1634 at Newwork by My Lord Scottsstarvett').

40. D. McGibbon and T. Ross, *The Castellated and Domestic Architecture of Scotland from the Twelfth to the Eighteenth Century*, Edinburgh 1887–92, ii, p.159.

41. NLS, MSS 5818–28.

42. I am grateful to Dunstan Roberts for information on his investigation of the library of Edward, Lord Herbert of Cherbury.

43. O. Morris, *The 'Chymick Bookes' of Sir Owen Wynne of Gwydir: An Annotated Catalogue*, Cambridge 1997, pp.1–7; J. Gwynfor Jones, 'Wynn Family (*per. c.*1465–1678)', ODNB; J. Davies, *Antiquae Linguae Britannicae … Dictionarium Duplex*, London 1632, STC 6347, ESTC S12250; J. Gwynfor Jones, *The Wynn Family of Gwydir: Origins, Growth and Development, c.1490–1674*, Aberystwyth 1995, pp.171–2, 177–8.

44. M. Purcell, *The Big House Library in Ireland: Books in Ulster Country Houses*, Swindon 2011a, pp.21–6.

45. Armagh, Public Library, MS. g.III.15; H. Plomer, 'A Cavalier's Library', *The Library*, 2nd series, v (1905), pp.158–72; B. Boydell and M. Egan-Buffet, 'An Early Seventeenth-Century Library from Ulster: Books on Music in the Collection of Lord Edward Conway (1602–1655)', <http://eprints.maynoothuniversity. ie/372/1/03_Boydell-Buffet_An_Early_17c_ Library.pdf>, pp.30–31.

46. J. Scott-Warren, *Sir John Harington and the Book as Gift*, Oxford 2001, p.56.

47. Quoted in D. Adlam, *The Great Collector: Edward Harley, 2nd Earl of Oxford*, Welbeck 2013, p.8.

48. A. Anderson, 'The Books and Interests of Henry, Lord Stafford (1501–1563)', *The Library*, 5th series, xxi (1966), pp.87–144 (p.94).

49. W. Smith (ed), *Herbert Correspondence: The Sixteenth and Seventeenth Century Letters of the Herberts of Chirbury, Powis Castle and Dolguog, formerly at Powis Castle in Montgomery*, Cardiff 1963, p.115.

50. T. Bayly, *Worcesters Apophthegmes*, London 1650, ESTC R204142, Wing W3535, p.20.

51. H. Colvin, *Essays in English Architectural History*, New Haven and London 1999, p.116.

52. C. Heath, *Historical and Descriptive Accounts of the Ancient and Present of Ragland* [sic], Monmouth 1829, p.55; A. Clark, *Raglan Castle and the Civil War in Monmouthshire*, Chepstow 1953, p.62.

53. B. Reeves, *Mercurius Rusticus*, London 1685, ESTC R35156, Wing R2449, pp.37–9.

54. M. Purcell, 'National Trust Libraries in Wales', *National Trust Historic Houses & Collections Annual* (2011b), pp.12–19 (pp.14–15).

55. C. Firth and R. Rait (eds), *Acts and Ordinances of the Interregnum*, London 1911, i, pp.106–17, 254–60; the central records of the two committees are TNA, SP/20 (the administrative history is outlined in the introductory notes of the catalogue), and records of county committees are generally either in county archives or the British Library.

56. NorthRO, FH4841; R. Stater, 'Hatton, Christopher, First Baron Hatton (*bap.* 1605, *d.* 1670)', ODNB.

57. Y. Lewis, 'Sir Ralph Bankes (?1631–1677) and the Origins of the Library at Kingston Hall', *Library History*, xviii, 3 (November 2002), pp.215–23 (p.217).

58. I. Roy, 'The Libraries of Edward, 2nd Viscount Conway', *Bulletin of the Institute of Historical Research*, xli, 103 (May 1968), pp.35–47 (pp.43–5).

59. S. West, 'The Development of Libraries in Norfolk Country Houses, 1660–1830', PhD Thesis, University of East Anglia, 2000, p.88.

60. Quoted in *Deene Park, Northamptonshire*, Norwich 1988, p.17; M. Wanklyn, 'Stratagems for Survival: Sir Robert and Sir Francis Throckmorton, 1640–1660', in P. Marshall and G. Scott (eds), *Catholic Gentry in English Society: The Throckmortons of Coughton from Reformation to Emancipation*, Farnham 2009, pp.146–70 (p.148).

61. H. Peters, *The Full and Last Relationship of All Things Concerning Basing House*, London 1645, Wing P1702, ESTC R200323, p.2.

62. P. Lewin, 'Ross, Thomas (*bap.* 1620, *d.* 1675)', ODNB.

63. Historical Manuscripts Commission, *Report on the Manuscripts of the Right Honourable Viscount de L'Isle, V. C., Preserved at Penshurst Place, Kent*, London 1966, vi, P. 327.

64. S. Tabor, 'The Bridgewater Library', in W. Baker and K. Womack (ed.), *Pre-Nineteenth-Century British Book Collectors and Bibliographers*, Detroit 1999, pp.40–50.

65. J. Elzinga, 'Osborne, Peter (1521–1592)', ODNB.

66. N. Bennett, 'Honywood, Michael (1596–1681)', ODNB.

67. Lewis 2002, pp.217–20.

68. D. Smith, 'Seymour, William, First Marquess and Second Duke of Somerset (1587–1660)', ODNB; Lichfield, Lichfield Cathedral Library, MS. 60 ('A Catalogue of her Grace the Dutchess of Somersett's Great Library, taken August 1671').

69. London, Royal College of Physicians, RCP-LIBRID/SR/2000/81 ('Bibliotheca Marchionis Dorcestriae', 1664); P. Seddon, 'Pierrepont, Henry, Marquess of Dorchester (1607–1680)', ODNB; L.M. Payne & C. E. Newman, 'The history of the College library: the Dorchester Library', Journal of the Royal College of Physicians of London, vol. 4 (1969/70) no. 3, pp. 234–46.

70. *Journals of Sir John Lauder, Lord Fountainhall*, Edinburgh 1900, pp.155–63.

71. B. Germain, *A New Description of Paris*, London 1687, Wing B4440, ESTC R3651, pp.51–2.

72. S. West 2000, p.157; Evelyn 1955, ii, p.128.

73. Evelyn 1955, ii, pp.198, 301–2.

74. G. Naudé, *Instructions Concerning Erecting of a Library*, London 1661, Wing N247, ESTC R8116.

75. Lewis 2002, p.221.

76. D. Pearson, *Provenance Research in Book History*, London 1994, p.136; A. Coral and A. N. L. Munby, *British Book Sale Catalogues, 1676–1800*, London 1977.

77. *Bibliotheca Angleseiana, Sive Catalogus Variorum Librorum in Quavis Linguâ, & Facultate Insignium*, London 1682, ESTC R30816, Wing A3166, A2.

78. Evelyn 1955, iv, p.126.

79. *Bibliotheca Angleseiana* 1682, A2.

80. R. Hutton, 'Maitland, John, Duke of Lauderdale (1616–1682)', ODNB; Evelyn 1955, iv, p.144, 27 August 1678.

81. Mandelbrote 2013, p.224.

82. Quoted in *Ham House, Surrey*, London 1995, p.64.

83. Mandelbrote 2013, pp.222–4.

84. D. Douglas, *English Scholars*, London [1943], p.21; T. Harmsen, 'Hickes, George (1642–1715)', ODNB.

85. Quoted in Mandelbrote 2013, p.224.

86. Mandelbrote 2013, pp.225–7; *Bibliotheque de Feu* [sic] *Monseigneur de Lauderdale*, London 1690, ESTC R43356, Wing L607; *The English Part of the Library of the late Duke of Lauderdale*, London 1690, ESTC R43357, Wing L611; *Catalogus Variorum Liborurum. Sive*

Bibliotheca Instructissima Doctimissi Cujusdam Genorosi Nuperrime Defuncti. Cui Praefigitur Bibliorum Polyglotton D. Ducis Lauderdaliensis, London [1691], ESTC R43369, Wing L610; *Bibliotheca Instructissima ex Bibliothecis Duorum Doctissimorum Theologorum Londinen, Nuper Defunctorum, Compsita. Cui Adjicitur Bibliotheca Manuscripta Lauderdaliana, Sive Catalogus Librorum Manuscriptorum, … & Alii Variis Linguis Facultatibusque Insig. Nondum Impressi, a Bibliotheca Ducis Lauderdaliana,* London, 1692), ESTC R221235, Wing L605.

87. D. Adshead, 'Altered with Skill and Dexterity: the Caroline House', in Christopher Rowell (ed.), *Ham House: Four Hundred Years of Collecting and Patronage,* New Haven and London 2013, pp.95–113 (p.108).

88. Mandelbrote 2013, p.222.

89. Evelyn 1955, iv, pp 199–200.

90. *A Catalogue of Valuable and Splendid Books from the Cassiobury Park Library,* Hodgson, London 24 May 1922; *A Catalogue of Valuable and Rare Books from the Extensive and Interesting Cassiobury Park Library,* Hodgson, London 22 November 1922; *A Catalogue of Rare Books and Tracts Mostly from the 16th and 17th Centuries, Selected from the Extensive and Valuable Cassiobury Park Library,* Hodgson, London 30 November 1922.

91. Evelyn 1955, iv, p.121.

92. S. West 2000, p.157.

93. G. Warkentin, J. Black and W. Bowen, *The Library of the Sidneys of Penshurst Place, Circa 1665,* Toronto 2013, pp.1–42.

94. J. Collins, *A Short Account of the Library at Longleat House,* London 1980, p.16.

95. Collins 1980, pp.8–10; H. Lancaster, 'Thynne, Thomas, First Viscount Weymouth (*bap.* 1640, *d.* 1714)', ODNB.

96. J. Johnstone, *Notes on the Library of the Earl of Erroll, Slains Castle, Aberdeenshire,* Aberdeen 1917, pp.1–5.

97. TNA, PROB 4/19641 (Probate Inventory of Sir Henry Hobart, Bt., 1700).

98. A. MacGregor, 'The Cabinet of Curiosities in Seventeenth-Century Britain', in O. Impey and A. MacGregor, *The Origins of Museums: The Cabinet of Curiosities in Sixteenth and Seventeenth-Century Europe,* Oxford 1985, pp.155[?]–8, 157.

99. A. Moore, *Dutch and Flemish Painting in Norfolk: A History of Taste and Influence, Fashion and Collecting,* London 1988, pp.90–1.

100. J. Miller, 'Paston, Robert, First Earl of Yarmouth (1631–1683)', ODNB; B. Moffat, 'Fraser, James (1645–1731)', ODNB; *Catalogue of the Library of the Right Honourable the Earl of Yarmouth … Which Will be Sold … on Wednesday the Tenth of this Instant, April, 1734 … By Olive Payne,* s.n., London 1734, ESTC T81780.

101. *The Journeys of Celia Fiennes,* London 1983, p.133; Evelyn 1955, v, p.147.

102. See, for example, the discussion of libraries in P. Thornton, *Seventeenth-Century Interior Decoration in England, France and Holland,* New Haven and London 1978, pp.303–6.

103. Z. von Uffenbach, *Oxford in 1710,* Oxford 1928.

104. Z. von Uffenbach, *London in 1710,* London 1934, p.185.

105. W. Nicolson, *The English, Scotch and Irish Historical Libraries: Giving a Short View and Character of Most of Our Historians, Either in Print or Manuscript,* London 1736, ESTC T60243, p.xii.

106. R. Irwin, *The English Library: Sources and History,* London 1966, p.212.

107. Historical Manuscripts Commission, *Calendar of the Manuscripts of the Marquis of Bath Preserved at Longleat,* Dublin 1907, ii, p.183.

108. D. Honeybone and M. Honeybone (eds), *The Correspondence of the Spalding Gentleman's Society, 1710–1761,* Woodbridge 2010, p.116.

109. Evelyn 1955, iv, p.367.

110. E. Jay, 'Queen Caroline's Library and its European Contexts', *Book History,* ix (2006), pp.31–55 (pp.34–40).

111. Philip Dormer Stanhope, Earl of Chesterfield, *The Letters of Philip Dormer Stanhope, Earl of Chesterfield,* London 1893, i, p.330.

112. TNA C/112/186 ('A Catalogue of the Books at Chesterfield House Which Belonged to the Right Honble. Philip Dormer Earl of Chesterfield and which were Bequeathed by his Will as Heir Looms').

113. M. Foot, *The Henry Davis Gift: A Collection of Bookbindings,* London 1978–2010, iii, p.80 (Davis 393); S. de Ricci, *Census of Medieval and Renaissance Manuscripts in the United States and Canada,* New York 1961, ii, p.1366.

114. N. Ramsay, 'English Book Collectors and the Salerooms in the Eighteenth Century', in R. Myers, M. Harris and G. Mandelbrote, *Under the Hammer: Book Auctions Since the Seventeenth Century,* New Castle, DE 2001, pp.89–110 (pp.89–95).

115. S. Piggott, *William Stukeley: An Eighteenth-Century Antiquary,* London 1985, p.18.

116. *The Tatler,* clviii (13 April 1710), pp.150–53.

117. *Reliquae Hearnianae: the Remains of Thomas Hearne,* Oxford 1857, ii, p.569.

118. Charles Hanbury Williams, *The Works of the Right Honourable Sir Chas. Hanbury Williams,* London 1822, i, pp.47–50; M. Honeybone and

119. Y. Lewis, 'Ellys, Sir Richard, Third Baronet (1682–1742)', ODNB.

119. A. Moore, 'Fountaine, Sir Andrew (1676–1753)', ODNB.

120. Historical Manuscripts Commission, *The Manuscripts of His Grace the Duke of Portland, Preserved at Welbeck Abbey,* London 1897, iv, p.376.

121. Purcell 2011b, p.16.

122. Jensen 2011, p.70.

123. D. Stoker, 'Harley, Edward, Second Earl of Oxford and Mortimer (1689–1741)', ODNB.

124. Historical Manuscripts Commission 1897, vi, p.38.

125. C. Wright, 'Portrait of a Bibliophile VIII: Edward Harley, 2nd Earl of Oxford, 1689–1741', *Book Collector,* xi (1962), pp.158–74.

126. D. Adshead, *Wimpole: Architectural Drawings and Topographical Views,* [Swindon] 2007, pp.17–18.

127. Adshead 2007, p.17; BL, Add. MSS. 19746–57.

128. BL, Add. MSS. 19746, fol. 115r.

129. H. M. Nixon, 'Harleian Bindings', in *Studies in the Book Trade in Honour of Graham Pollard,* Oxford 1975, pp.153–94.

130. E. Potter, 'To Paul's Churchyard to Treat with a Bookbinder', in R. Myers and M. Harris (eds), *Property of a Gentleman: The Formation, Organisation and Dispersal of the Private Library, 1620–1920,* Winchester 1991, pp.25–41 (p.35).

131. O. Brack, 'Osborne, Thomas (*bap.* 1704?, *d.* 1767)', ODNB.

132. Stoker, 'Harley, Edward', ODNB.

133. P. Willems, *Bibliotheca Fletcheriana: or the Extraordinary Library of Andrew Fletcher of Saltoun,* Wassenaar 1999, pp.xi–xiii.

134. New York, New York Public Library, MS. Spencer 26.

135. H. Horrocks, *Newhailes,* Edinburgh 2004, p.22.

136. R. Betteridge, 'The Library of the Dalrymples of Newhailes', *Journal of the Edinburgh Bibliographical Society,* viii (2013), pp.33–71.

137. *Haddo House Library,* [Aberdeen c.1920], p.3.

138. P. Melvin, *Estates and Landed Society in Galway,* Dublin 2012, p.152.

139. T. Barnard, 'From Imperial Schatzkammer to the Giant's Causeway: Collecting in Eighteenth-Century Ireland', *Irish Architectural and Decorative Studies,* vi (2003), pp.141–61 (p.148).

140. D. Huws, 'Sir Thomas Mostyn and the Mostyn Manuscripts', in J. Carley and C. Tite, *Books and Collectors 1200–1700: Essays Presented*

to Andrew Watson, London 1997, pp. 451–72 (pp. 452–3); S. West 2000, p. 289.

141. Huws 1997, p. 454; *A Handlist of Manuscripts in the Library of the Earl of Leicester at Holkham Hall: Abstracted from the Catalogues of William Roscoe and Frederick Madden and annotated by Seymour de Ricci*, [London] 1932, p viii.

142. Sotheby's, 13 July 1920; Christie's, 24 October, 1974; London, Senate House Library, ULI MS. 1, illustrated in J. Alexander and P. Binski (eds), *Age of Chivalry: Art in Plantagenet England, 1200–1400*, London 1987, no. 623.

143. NLW, MS. 21244C (Catalogue of Mostyn and Gloddaith [1720]).

144. H. George Fletcher (ed.), *The Wormsley Library: A Personal Selection by Sir Paul Getty*, KBE, 2nd edn., London 2007, pp. 72–3.

145. MMBL, i, p. 21; Huws 2007, p. 456.

146. T. Nicholas, *Annals and Antiquities of the Counties and County Families of Wales*, London 1872, ii, pp. 652–3.

147. NLW, Peniarth MS. 537 ('Bibliothecae MS. Cambricorum Recensio', 1658); Dictionary of Welsh Biography, http://wbo.llgc.org.uk/en/s-MAUR-WIL-1680.html. For later Hengwrt catalogues, see NLW, Peniath MS. 533 ('A Catalogue of the Books and Manuscripts at Hengwrt', eighteenth century), and Peniarth MS. 534 ('Catalogue of the Hengwrt Manuscripts Arranged in the Year 1825 by Aneurin Owen').

148. *A Handlist of Manuscripts in the Library of the Earl of Leicester at Holkham Hall*, pp. vii–xii.

149. B. Botfield, 'The Holkham Library', *Miscellanies of the Philobiblon Society*, vi, 4 (1860–61), pp. 72–85.

150. C. Lybbe Powys, *Passages from the Diaries of Mrs Philip Lybbe Powys*, London 1899, p. 10.

151. Nixon and Foot 1992, pp. 85–6.

152. Hatfield, 'Act. of Binding, Gilding and Lettering the Earl of Salisbury's Books' [1712]; Hatfield, 'Catalogus Librorum tam Impressorum quam Manuscriptorum … Honorattissimi Nobilissimique Viri Dom: Domini Jacobi Comitis Salisburiae … in Magnificis Suis Aedibus apd. Hatfield Extantits' [1712] (both unreferenced).

153. T. Murdoch (ed.), *Noble Households: Eighteenth-Century Inventories of Great English Houses: A Tribute to John Cornforth*, Cambridge 2006, p. 156.

154. B. North Lee, 'Gentlemen and their Book-Plates', Myers and Harris 1991, pp. 43–76 (pp. 50–55).

155. E. Edwards, *Libraries and the Founders of Libraries*, London 1864, pp. 327–67.

156. P. Quarrie, 'The Scientific Library of the Earls of Macclesfield', *Notes & Records of the Royal Society*, xx (2006), pp. 5–24.

157. E. Edwards 1864, p. 338.

158. R. Wallis, 'Jones, William (c. 1675–1749)', ODNB.

159. Cambridge, Fitzwilliam Museum, MS. 1–2005; S. Panayotova, *The Macclesfield Psalter*, London 2008.

160. Wallis, 'Jones, William', ODNB; P. Quarrie, 'The Scientific Library of the Earls of Macclesfield', p. 13; P. Thomas, 'Yorke, Philip, First Earl of Hardwicke (1690–1764)', ODNB.

161. Cambridge, Trinity College Library, R.17.23; MMBL, ii, p. 264.

162. BL, Add. Ms 36, 116, fol. 172.

163. L. Boynton, *Appuldurcombe House, Isle of Wight*, London 1986, p. 15.

164. Arundel, IN/56.

165. *Catalogus Bibliothecae Kingstonianae* [London 1727?], ESTC T123378; A. Lister, 'Catalogus Bibliothecae Kingstonianae', *Book Collector*, xxxiii (1985), pp. 63–77.

166. R. Willett, *A Catalogue of the Books in the Library of Ralph Willett, Esq., at Merly, in the County of Dorset*, London [1790], ESTC T08827; *A Description of the Library at Merly* (1776); R. Willett, *A Description of the Library at Merly in the County of Dorset*, London 1785, ESTC T88028; M. Vaubert de Chantilly, 'Willett, Ralph (1719–1795)', ODNB.

167. T. Seccombe, 'Stearne, John (1660–1745)', ODNB.

168. PRONI, D2433/A/2/11/112 (Letter from the Revd S. Cupples to Lord Caledon, 16 August 1812).

169. C. Penney, 'A Bishop and His Books', *Book Collector*, lx, 3 (Autumn 2011), pp. 401–16.

170. O. Massey, 'Notes on the Orrery Collection (2)', *Christ Church Library Newsletter*, v, 1 (Michaelmas 2008), pp. 6–8; L. Smith, 'Boyle, Charles, Fourth Earl of Orrery (1674–1731)' ODNB; L. Smith, 'Boyle, John, Fifth Earl of Cork and Fifth Earl of Orrery (1707–1762)', ODNB.

171. NRO, MC 3/289, p. 23.

Chapter Five

1. Alnwick, DNP MS. 121/16, pp. 25–7 (Diaries of the 1st Duchess of Northumberland).

2. *Historic Manuscripts Commission. Report on the Manuscripts of His Grace the Duke of Portland Preserved at Welbeck Abbey*, London 1901, vi, pp. 189–90.

3. JLRUM, ER7/17/1 (Inventory of Dunham Massey, 1758).

4. J. Raven, 'The Book Trades', in I. Rivers (ed.), *Books and their Readers in Eighteenth-Century England*, London 2001, pp. 1–34 (p. 1).

5. ESRO, FRE/8071 ('An Inventory of the Household Furniture, Linen China, and Books, &c. Belonging to Thomas Frewen Esqr deceas'd: Taken at his late House call'd Brickwall', 1767).

6. KHLC, U951/E17 (Catalogue of the Library of Mersham Le Hatch, 1755); M. Purcell, 'National Trust Libraries in Wales', *National Trust Historic Houses & Collections Annual* (2011b), pp. 12–19 (p. 16).

7. WAAS, BA 7335/705/7/69/i/1 ('A Note of My Books taken 9ber 1663', written into a copy of *Rider's British Merlin*, 1663); BA 7335/40/iv ('A Catalogue of Books in the Studdy Adjoyning to the Gallery at Hanbury', 1708).

8. SBRO, DR3/402, fol. 4v.

9. M. Purcell, '"A Lunatick of Unsound Mind": Edward, Lord Leigh (1742–86) and the Refounding of Oriel College Library', *Bodleian Library Record*, xvii, 3–4 (April–October 2001a), pp. 246–60.

10. DRO, D5430/31/13 ('Valuation of the Real and Personal Estate of Mr J. F. Wright [deceas'd] of Eyam', 1805); M. Purcell, 'Books and Reading in Eighteenth-Century Westmorland: the Brownes of Townend', *Library History*, xvii, 2 (2001b), pp 91–106 (p. 98).

11. PRONI, D3561/B/2 ('A Catalogue of the Books in the Earl of Hillsborough's Library at Hillsborough, taken 18 Novr 1771').

12. NLS, MS. 3804 ('Catalogue of Books Belonging to Sir Robert Gordon of Gordonstoun, Baronet, 1743').

13. SRO, DD/WO/40/5/4 ('An Inventory of the Goods and Chattels of the Lady Mary Trevelyan', 1689).

14. NRS, GD40/8/442 (Inventory of Newbattle Abbey, 1719).

15. NRS, GD44/49/14 9 ('Catalogue of Books which Belonged to the deceased Alexander Duke of Gordon', 1728).

16. GA, E/255 ('An Inventory of the Goods and Furniture in Mr Blathwayts House at Dirham', 1716).

17. M. Reed (ed.), *Buckinghamshire Probate Inventories, 1661–1714*, Aylesbury 1988, p. 20; Taunton, Somerset Record Office, DD\SF/2514 ('A Catalogue of Books in ye Closett over ye· Oriall', late seventeenth century).

18. J. Fenlon, *Goods & Chattels: A Survey of Early Household Inventories in Ireland*, Dublin 2003, pp. 117–20.

19. S. West, 'An Architectural Typology for the Early Modern Country House Library, 1660–1720', *Library*, 7th series, xiv, 4 (2013a), pp. 441–64 (pp. 454–6).

20. M. Reed, 'Osterley Park in 1668: the Probate Inventory of Sir William Waller', *Transactions of the London and Middlesex Archaeological Society*, xlii (1991), pp. 115–29 (p. 119).

21. CornRo, J. 1691 (Inventory of Trewithen, 1768).

22. 'Inventory of the Plenishing of the House of The Binns at the date of the Death of General Thomas Dalyell', *Proceedings of the Society of Antiquaries of Scotland*, 5th series, x (1924), pp. 344–70 (pp. 354–5).

23. Ibid., p. 369.

24. CBS, D/DR/10/1 (Inventory of Sir William Drake at Shardeloes, 1644).

25. H. DeGroff, 'Textual Networks and the Country House: the 3rd Earl of Carlisle at Castle Howard', PhD Thesis, University of York, December 2012, pp. 43–4.

26. C. Lybbe Powys, *Passages from the Diaries of Mrs Philip Lybbe Powys*, London 1899, p. 199.

27. HRO, 31M57/645 ('An Inventory of the Houshold [sic] Furniture, Plate, Linen, China and Library of Books of Anthony Chute, Esq:ʳ', 1754).

28. M. Purcell and N. Thwaite, *The Libraries of Calke Abbey*, [London 2013], pp. 11–12.

29. Bangor, Bangor University Library, MS. 3616 ('An Inventory of the Household and Furniture at Nanney', 1768).

30. H. Maxwell Lyte, *A History of Dunster*, London 1909, ii, p. 369.

31. J. Lees-Milne, *English Country Houses: Baroque, 1685–1715*, London 1970, p. 234; N. Pevsner, E. Williamson with G. Brandford, *The Buildings of England: Buckinghamshire*, Harmondsworth 1994, p. 248.

32. TNA, PROB 4/3594 (Will of Francis Luttrell of Dunster Castle, 1693); BRO, D/3By/E2 (Inventory of Pawlet Wright of Englefield House, 1741).

33. S. West 2013a, p. 448.

34. T. Barnard, 'Learning, the Learned and Literacy in Ireland, *c.*1660–1760', in T. Barnard, D. Ó Cróinín and K. Sims, *'A Miracle of Learning'; Studies in Manuscripts and Irish Learning: Essays in Honour of William O'Sullivan*, Aldershot 1997, pp. 209–35.

35. GA, E/255 ('An Inventory of the Goods and Furniture in Mr Blathwayts House at Dirham', 1716); of the two bookcases on show at Dyham Park, NT 452939 is original and the companion NT 45940 a 1927 copy, replacing the second original, now VAM W.12–1927.

36. S. West, 'Studies and Status Spaces in Seventeenth-Century Penshurst Place', *Transactions of the Cambridge Bibliographical Society*, xii (2002), pp. 266–92 (p. 271).

37. Purcell and Thwaite 2013, p. 11.

38. W. Smith (ed.), *Herbert Correspondence: The Sixteenth and Seventeenth Century Letters of the Herberts of Chibury, Powis Castle and Dolguog*, Cardiff 1963, p. 306.

39. C. Willoughby, *The Continuation of the History of the Willoughby Family*, Eton 1958, p. 22.

40. *The Letters of Daniel Eaton to the Third Earl of Cardigan, 1725–1732*, Kettering 1971, p. 65; Nottingham, Nottingham University Library, Pw 2/478 and Pw 2/499 (letters from the 3rd Duke of Newcastle to his wife Margaret, April and June 1701).

41. NLW, AE5 3/4 ('Inventory of Deeds and Papers in Drawers in the Study, also of Cupboards, at Tredegar', 1826).

42. Fenlon 2003 pp. 117–20; NLI MS. 2791/16 (Designs for Bookcases at Dromoland Castle).

43. *The Orrery Papers*, London 1903, ii, p. 99.

44. Purcell 2001a, p. 253.

45. Purcell 2011b, p. 14.

46. CBS, D/LE/D3/24 (B. Domville to Sir William Lee, 1770).

47. G. Eland (ed.), *Purefoy Letters, 1735–1753*, London 1931, pp. 281–3.

48. Eland 1931, pp. 274–5

49. V. Leatham, *Burghley: The Life of a Great House*, London 1992, p. 203.

50. P. Beale, '"My Books are the Great Joy of My Life": Sir William Boothby, Seventeenth-Century Bibliophile', *Book Collector*, xlvi, 2 (1997), pp. 356–62.

51. Beale 1997, pp. 350–73.

52. Beale 1997, pp. 354–5.

53. Beale 1997, p. 360; Purcell 2001a, p. 253.

54. DeGroff 2012, pp. 65–6.

55. JRULM, Eng. MS. 1411 (Catalogue of the Library at Toft Hall, near Knutsford); Carlisle, Carlisle Archive Centre, DLONS/W/26G/27 ('A Catalogue of the Library of the Late Sʳ James Lowther. Bart. … Taken at Flatt Hall in Whitehaven', 1757).

56. NT, Calke Abbey, NT 318229, *The Nobleman and Gentleman's Director and Assistant in the True Choice of their Wheel-Carriages*, London 1763, ESTC T101566.

57. TCD, 190.r.62–64, A. Ashley Cooper, 3rd Earl of Shaftesbury, *Characteristicks of Men, Manners, Opinions, Times*, London 1732, ESTC T144565.

58. Beale 1997, pp. 354–5.

59. SBRO, DR/18/5/3989 (Receipt from William Boyce, 1763).

60. *Historical Manuscripts Commission, Report on the Manuscripts of the Earl of Verulam, Preserved at Gorhambury*, London 1906, p. 219.

61. NLI, Microfilm P. 7074 (Orrery Papers Folder 14).

62. I am grateful to James Peill for showing it to me, and for the suggestion.

63. A. Brundin and D. Roberts, 'Book-Buying and the Grand Tour: the Italian Books at Belton House in Lincolnshire', *The Library*, 7th series, xvi, 1 (March 2015), pp. 51–79.

64. T. Barnard, *Making the Grand Figure: Lives and Possessions in Ireland, 1641–1770*, New Haven and London 2004, p. 30.

65. Purcell 2001a, p. 253.

66. P. Mariette and A Caylus, *Recueil de Peintures Antiques*, Paris 1757; Purcell 2001a, pp. 253–4.

67. H. Summerson, 'The Lucys of Charlecote and their Library', *National Trust Studies* (1979), pp. 149–58 (pp. 152–3).

68. E. Potten, '"Bound in Vellum and Lettered": the Tatton Park Library', *National Trust Historic Houses & Collections Annual* (2013), pp. 4–11 (pp. 5–7).

69. M. Purcell, *The Big House Library: Books in Ulster Country Houses*, Swindon 2011a, pp. 54–60.

70. P. Hoare, 'The Perils of Provenance: Serial Ownership, Bookplates and Obfuscation at Belton House', *Library History*, xviii (2002), pp. 225–34.

71. Lybbe Powys 1899, p. 199.

72. I am grateful to Dr María Luisa López-Vidriero, Director of the Royal Library in Madrid, for her comments on this book.

73. T. Cooper, 'Knowles, Thomas (1723–1802)', ODNB.

74. N. Barker (ed.), *The Devonshire Inheritance: Five Centuries of Collecting at Chatsworth*, Alexandra, VA 2003, p. 115.

75. J. Clarke, *An Essay upon Study*, London 1731, ESTC T144041, p. 5.

76. Barnard 1997, p. 214.

77. R. Langley, 'The Music', in T. Murdoch (ed.), *Boughton House: The English Versailles*, London 1992, pp. 175–7.

78. G. Gifford (ed.), *A Descriptive Catalogue of the Music Collection at Burghley House*, Stamford, Aldershot 2002, pp. 1–56.

79. J. Haydn, *Two Marches Composed by J. Haydn M. D. for Sir Henry Harpur Bart.*, London 1794; Purcell and Thwaite 2013, pp. 13–14.

80. SBRO, DR18/4/43, inventory of Stoneleigh Abbey (1774).

81. H. Booth, *The Works of the Right Honourable Henry late L. Delamer*, London 1694, p. 126; Clarke 1731, p. x.

82. Arniston, F7, typescript copy of a 'Memoir of the Second President Dundas', transcribed

in 1896 from the original manuscript of 'Mr Fordyce MP'.

83. J. Collins, *A Short Account of the Library at Longleat House*, London 1980, p.23.

84. T. Lloyd, 'Country-House Libraries of the Eighteenth and Nineteenth Centuries', in P. Jones and E. Rees, *A Nation and its Books: A History of the Book in Wales*, Aberystwyth 1998, pp.135–46 (p.138).

85. E. Miller, 'A Collection of Elizabethan and Jacobean Plays at Petworth', *National Trust Studies* (1975), pp.62–4.

86. S. Mandelbrote, 'The English Bible and its Readers in the Eighteenth Century', in I. Rivers (ed.), *Books and Their Readers in Eighteenth-Century England: New Essays*, London 2001), pp.33–78 (p.37).

87. Quoted in Beale 1997, p.353.

88. M. Purcell, '"A Relic of King Charles the Martyr?": the Juxon Bible at Chastleton', *Apollo*, April 2000, pp.30–35.

89. KHLC, U1590/E13 (Inventory of Chevening, 1753).

90. R. Ketton-Cremer, *Felbrigg: The Story of a House*, London 1986, p.52.

91. Barker 2003, p.84.

92. WRO, CR1998/LCB/59 (Inventory of Chillington Hall, 1746).

93. G. Scott, 'The Throckmortons at Home and Abroad, 1680–1800', in P. Marshall and G. Scott (eds), *Catholic Gentry in English Society: The Throckmortons of Coughton from Reformation to Emancipation*, Farnham 2009, pp.171–211 (pp.175–6).

94. G. Pullen, 'The Harvington Library at Oscott', *Worcestershire Recusant*, i (April 1963), pp.18–20.

95. H. Fenning (ed.), *The Fottrell Papers, 1721–39*, Belfast 1980.

96. Purcell 2011a, p.48.

97. NT, Erddig, NT 307294: W. Griffiths, *A Practical Treatise on Farriery*, Wrexham 1784, ESTC N20539.

98. S. Porter, *The Blast of War: Destruction in the English Civil Wars*, Stroud 2011, pp.9–11.

99. Purcell 2011a, pp.47–8.

100. R. Reilly, 'Wedgwood, Josiah (1730–1795)', ODNB.

101. NT, Erddig, NT 3082105: E. Wingate, *Mr Wingate's Arithmetick*, London 1704, ESTC T86925; the tapestry calculations, subsequently detached from the book, are now Hawarden, Flintshire Record Office, D/E/3457.

102. NT, Ickworth, NT 3103161: G. Markham, *Hungers Prevention: or, the Whole Art of Fowling by Water and Land*, London 1655, Wing M657, ESTC R12445.

103. Barnard 2004, p.198.

104. N. Barker, *Treasures from the Libraries of National Trust Country Houses*, New York 1999, p.120.

105. NT, Wallington, NT 3066441: M. Smith, *The Complete House-Keeper, and Professed Cook*, Newcastle 1772, ESTC T92200.

106. NT, Erddig, NT 3008765: I. van Diemerbroeck, *The Anatomy of Human Bodies*, London 1689, Wing D1415, ESTC R15368.

107. NT, Dunham Massey, NT 3050057: P. Dionis, *The Anatomy of Humane Bodies Improv'd*, London 1703, ESTC R114735.

108. R. Larsen (ed.), *Maids & Mistresses: Celebrating 300 Years of Women and the Yorkshire Country House*, York 2004.

109. Oxford, Oriel College Library, G. Abbot, *The Case of Impotency as Debated in England*, London 1715, ESTC T76337. I am grateful to Louisiane Ferlier for pointing this book out to me.

110. J. Peel, 'Croft, Sir Richard, Sixth Baronet (1762–1818)', ODNB.

111. Quoted in J. Martin, *Wives and Daughters: Women and Children in the Georgian Country House*, London 2004, p.86.

112. Barnard 2004, p.209; Lloyd 1998, p.138.

113. NT, Erddig, NT 3081318: *Every Man his Own Brewer*, London 1768, ESTC T100687.

114. Barker 2003, p.116.

115. NT, Castle Ward, NT3016635: A. Swan, *A Collection of Designs in Architecture*, London 1757, ESTC T101999.

116. Purcell 2001a, p.252.

117. NT, Kedleston, NT 3002262: R. Adam, *Ruins of the Palace of the Emperor Diocletian at Spalatro*, London 1764, ESTC T46923, and NT 3082338, G. Richardson, *A Book of Ceilings*, London 1776, ESTC T90834; H. George Fletcher (ed.), *The Wormsley Library: A Personal Selection by Sir Paul Getty*, 2nd edn., London 2007, pp.150–51.

118. NT, Lyme Park, NT 3048754: L. Alberti, *The Architecture of Leon Battista Alberti*, London 1726, ESTC N65008.

119. Barnard 2004, p.51.

120. Purcell 2001a, *passim*.

121. Booth 1694, p.18.

122. K. O'Brien, 'The History Market in Eighteenth-Century England', in I. Rivers (ed.), *Books and their Readers in Eighteenth-Century England: New Essays*, London 2001, pp.105–33 (p.106).

123. At the time of writing, for example, the National Trust library catalogue contained more than 120 separate works by Rapin.

124. Barnard 1997, p.223.

125. N. Barker, 'Books and Manuscripts', in T. Murdoch (ed.), *Boughton House: The English Versailles*, London 1992, pp.170–73 (p.171).

126. SRO, DD/WHH/443 (Probate Inventory of William Helyer of Canons Teign, 1701).

127. T. Isham, *The Diary of Sir Thomas Isham of Lamport*, Farnborough 1971, pp.15–16.

128. N. Hardwick (ed.), *A Diary of the Journey through the North of England made by William and John Blathwayt of Dyrham Park in 1703*, [Bristol] 1972, pp.7, 9.

129. A. Moore, *Norfolk & the Grand Tour*, Norwich 1985, p.42; Ketton-Cremer 1986, pp.80ff.

130. S. West, 'The Development of Libraries in Norfolk Country Houses, 1660–1830', PhD Thesis, University of East Anglia, 2000, p.43.

131. James Boswell, *Boswell's Life of Johnson*, London 1851, p.391 (2 November 1773).

132. *Letters of Lord Chesterfield to Lord Huntingdon*, London 1923, p.2.

133. CBS, X728/1 (Account Book of the 5th Lord Paget, 1649–52), fols. 11c, 31r, etc.

134. For Ickworth see M. Purcell and J. Fishwick, 'The Library at Ickworth', *The Book Collector*, lxi, 3 (September 2012), pp.366–90.

135. Brundin and Roberts 2015.

136. Ketton-Cremer 1986, p.34.

137. CORNRO, AD/1335 ('Boconnoc Library Dec. 1807').

138. Hervey, Mary, *Letters of Mary Lepel, Lady Hervey*, London 1821, pp.18–19.

Chapter Six

1. J. Rothwell, 'Dedicated to Books', *National Trust Historic Houses and Collections Annual* (2010), pp.56–61.

2. H. Colvin and J. Newman (ed.), *Of Building: Roger North's Writings on Architecture*, Oxford 1981, p.138.

3. NT, Dunham Massey, NT 3048713 ('Catalogue of Books in the Library at Dunham', 1768); I am grateful to David Adshead and the late Nigel Seeley for looking over the room with me.

4. LINCSRO BNLW 2/2/6/8; NT, Belton Hall, NT 3023178 (Library Catalogue, 1847); A. Tinniswood, *Belton House, Lincolnshire*, London 2006, pp.16–17, 27.

5. Rothwell 2010, p.59.

6. R. Donaldson, 'Traquair House Library', *Bulletin du Bibliophile* (1984), pp.320–25; K. Cruft, J. Dunbar and R. Fawcett, *Borders: The Buildings of Scotland*, New Haven and London 2006, p.735, and my own examination of the books.

7. I. Gow, '"The Most Learned Drawing Room in Europe?": Newhailes and the Scottish

Classical Library', in D. Mays, M. Moss and M. Oglethorpe (eds), *Visions of Scotland's Past: Looking to the Future: Essays in Honour of John R. Hume*, East Linton 2000, pp. 81–96 (p. 82).

8. G. Jackson-Stops, *The English Country House: A Grand Tour*, London 1984, p. 198; J. Cornforth, *Early Georgian Interiors*, New Haven and London 2004, p. 68.

9. S. West, 'Studies and Status: Spaces for Books in Seventeenth-Century Penshurst Place, Kent', *Transactions of the Cambridge Bibliographical Society*, xii (2002), pp. 266–92.

10. E. McCutcheon (ed.), *Sir Nicholas Bacons's Great House Sententiae: The Latin Text, along with the First English Translation, and Introduction*, Honolulu 1977; C. Campbell et al., *Vitruvius Britannicus*, London 1715–71, ii, p. 3.

11. J. Macky, *A Journey through England, in Familiar Letters*, London 1723, ESTC T57749, p. 98.

12. J. Collins, *A Short Account of the Library at Longleat House*, London 1980.

13. Macky 1723, pp. 172–3.

14. Cornforth 2004, pp. 70–71.

15. H. DeGroff, 'Textual Networks and the Country House: the 3rd Earl of Carlisle at Castle Howard', PhD Thesis, University of York, December 2012, pp. 43–4.

16. Vitruvius Pollio, *Ten Books on Architecture*, Cambridge 1999, p. 80.

17. Vitruvius 1999, p. 81.

18. Campbell et al. 1715–71, i, p. 6, plate 73.

19. CHA, CH36/5/3 (Inventory of Chatsworth, 1811), p. 34.

20. S. Jenkins, '"An Inventory of His Grace the Duke of Chandos's Seat att Cannons Taken June the 19th 1725" by John Gilbert', *Walpole Society*, lxvii (2005), pp. 93–192 (p. 97).

21. W. Adam, *Vitruvius Scoticus: Being a Collection of Plans, Elevations, and Sections of Public Buildings, Noblemen's and Gentlemen's Houses in Scotland*, Edinburgh [1812?], plate 41; I. Gow, *The Scottish Interior*, Edinburgh 1992, p. 15.

22. Campbell et al. 1715–71, v, plate 47; N. Pevsner, E. Williamson with G. Brandwood, *The Buildings of England: Buckinghamshire*, Harmondsworth 1994, pp. 730–31.

23. C. Hussey, *English Country Houses: Early Georgian, 1715–1760*, London 1955a, pp. 43–4.

24. G. Richardson, *The New Vitruvius Britannicus*, London 1802, i, plates 13, 58; Campbell et al. 1715–71, v, plate 24; C. Hussey, *English Country Houses: Mid Georgian, 1760–1800*, London 1955b, pp. 61–9, 160–64, 184–93.

25. M. Mansbridge, *John Nash: A Complete Catalogue*, Oxford 1991, pp. 49–50.

26. Campbell et al. 1715–71, iv, plate 91; Hussey 1955a, pp. 204–7.

27. Campbell et al. 1715–71, v, plate 43.

28. Hussey 1955a, pp. 170–71; Cornforth 2004, pp. 69, 72.

29. Hussey 1955b, pp. 195–202.

30. Richardson 1802, ii, plate 26; Campbell et al. 1715–71, v, plate 14; Adam 1812, plate 147.

31. K. Mulligan, *South Ulster: The Counties of Armagh, Cavan and Monaghan: The Buildings of Ireland*, New Haven and London 2013, pp. 338–42.

32. A. Palladio, *The Four Books of Architecture … Literally Translated from the Original Italian by Isaac Ware*, London [1738?], ESTC N18580, book 2, plate 51; A. Palladio, *The Architecture of A. Palladio, in Four Books … Revis'd, Design'd and Publish'd by Giacomo Leoni*, London 1721, ESTC T22366, plate 53.

33. N. Barker, *The Devonshire Inheritance: Five Centuries of Collecting at Chatsworth*, Alexandria, VA 2003, nos 91–92.

34. C. Hartwell, M. Hyde, E. Hubbard and N. Pevsner, *Cheshire: The Buildings of England*, New Haven and London 2011, p. 440; NT, Lyme Park, NT 3048754: L. Alberti, *The Architecture of Leon Battista Alberti*, London 1726, ESTC N65008.

35. R. Castell, *The Villas of the Ancients Illustrated*, London 1728, ESTC T50805, p. 127.

36. Castell 1728, pp. 6–7.

37. S. West, 'The Development of Libraries in Norfolk Country Houses, 1660–1830', PhD Thesis, University of East Anglia, 2000, pp. 138, 143, 166.

38. S. Weber, 'Kent and the Georgian Baroque Style in Furniture: Domestic Commissions', in S. Weber (ed.), *William Kent: Designing Georgian Britain*, New Haven and London 2013, pp. 469–525 (p. 505).

39. Weber 2013, p. 508; J. Bryant, 'From "Gusto" to "Kentissime"; Kent's Designs for Country Houses, Villas and Lodges', in Weber 2013, pp. 183–241 (pp. 215–16).

40. London, Sir John Soane's Museum, SM vol. 147/197. Cat. 95; for the engraving see S. Brindle, 'Kent the Painter', in Weber 2013, pp. 111–49 (p. 135).

41. H. Colvin and M. Craig (eds), *Architectural Drawings in the Library at Elton Hall*, Oxford 1964, p. xlv, plate LXXVIII.

42. Bodley, Radcliffe d. 37, D. Marot, *Oeuvres du Sr. D. Marot, Architecte de Guillaume III. Roi de la Grande Bretagne, Contenant Plussieurs, Penssez utile aux Architectes, Peintres, Sculpteurs, Orfeures & Jardiniers, & Autres*, The Hague [1703], plate [7] ('Bibliotheque Inventée et Gravée par D. Marot'), with James Gibbs's bookplate. For

some of the problems of working with Marot's engravings, see also A. Bowett, 'The Engravings of Daniel Marot', *Furniture History*, xliii (2007), pp. 85–100.

43. A. Vliegenthart, *Het Loo Palace: Journal of a Restoration*, Appeldoorn 2002, pp. 197–9.

44. J. Cook and J. Mason (ed.), *The Building Accounts of Christ Church Library, 1716–1779*, Oxford 1988, pp. 3, 37–9.

45. Adam 1812, plate 41.

46. Gow 2000, p. 82; *Vitruvius Scoticus*, plate 41; Gow 1992, p. 15; P. Wiggston, 'A Grain of Truth', *Architectural Heritage: The Journal of the Architectural Heritage Society of Scotland*, xii (2001), pp. 13–26.

47. Gow 2000, pp. 84–8.

48. Pete Smith, 'Apethorpe Hall: Complexity and Interpretation', in Malcolm Airs and Paul Barnwell (eds), *The Medieval Great House*, Donington 2011, pp. 125–40 (p. 127).

49. G. Isham, *Lamport Hall: Past and Present*, Kettering 1985, pp. 8–9; B. Bailey, N. Pevsner and B. Cherry, *Northamptonshire: The Buildings of England*, New Haven and London 2013, p. 384; H. Hallam, 'Lamport Hall Revisited', *Book Collector*, xvi, 4 (Winter 1967), pp. 439–49 (p. 443).

50. C. Rowell, *Petworth: The People and the Place*, London 2012, p. 76; WSRO, PHA/6271 ('Catalogue of Ld. Egremont's Books in the New Library, Petworth' [c. 1770–1830]).

51. R. Baird, *Goodwood: Art and Architecture, Sport and Family*, London 2007, pp. 70–72, 80–81, 122–3.

52. T. Lloyd, 'Country-House Libraries of the Eighteenth and Nineteenth Centuries', in P. Jones and E. Rees, *A Nation and its Books: A History of the Book in Wales*, Aberystwyth 1998, pp. 135–46 (p. 137); T. Lloyd, J. Orbach and R. Scourfield, *Pembrokeshire: The Buildings of Wales*, New Haven and London 2004), p. 362.

53. J. Newman, *Glamorgan: The Buildings of Wales*, London 2004, pp. 350–51.

54. I. and E. Hall, *Burton Constable Hall: A Century of Patronage*, Hull 1991, pp. 72–4. Large parts of the collection survive, but 1,026 lots of books were sold in 1889, for which see *Catalogue of the Burton Constable Library of Printed Books, Collected Chiefly by William Constable, Esq.*, Sotheby, Wilkinson & Hodge, London 27–29 June 1889.

55. N. Major, *Chequers: The Prime Minister's Country House and its History*, London 1996, p. 45.

56. K. Swift, 'The Formation of the Library of Charles Spencer, 3rd Earl of Sunderland (1674–1722): a Study in the Antiquarian Book

Trade', D.Phil. Thesis, University of Oxford, 1987, p.23.

57. M. Rogers, *Montacute House, Somerset*, London 1991, p.65.

58. E. Harris, *The Genius of Robert Adam: His Interiors*, New Haven and London 2001, pp.29–31; L. Harris, *Robert Adam and Kedleston: The Making of a Neo-Classical Masterpiece*, London 1987, pp.11–12; Palladio 1738, plate 58.

59. Campbell et al. 1715–71, iv, plate 71.

60. Harris 2001, pp.198–200; NT, Nostell Priory, NT 960061.

61. G. Jackson-Stops, 'A British Parnassus: Mythology and the Country House', in G. Jackson-Stops (ed.), *The Fashioning and Functioning of the British Country House*, Washington 1989, pp.217–38 (pp.235–6); F. Sands, 'The Art of Collaboration: Antonio Zucchi at Nostell Priory', *Georgian Group Journal*, xix (2011), pp.106–19; M. Mauchline, *Harewood House*, Ashbourne 1992, pp.70–71.

62. *Mellerstain, Gordon, Berwickshire*, Derby 1980, p.3; Harris 2001, p.249.

63. *Newby Hall*, S.l. 1982, p.20

64. Harris 2001, pp.238–9.

65. Harris 2001, pp.240–41.

66. M. Snodin (ed.), *Sir William Chambers*, London 1996, p.165.

67. D. Stillman, *English Neo-Classical Architecture*, London 1988, i, pp.303–5.

68. A. Brooks and N. Pevsner, *Herefordshire: The Buildings of England*, New Haven and London 2012, p.103.

69. J. Martin Robinson, *James Wyatt: Architect to George III*, New Haven and London 2012, pp.20, 163.

70. Robinson 2012 p.43.

71. M. Purcell, '"A Lunatick of Unsound Mind": Edward, Lord Leigh (1742–86) and the Refounding of Oriel College Library', *Bodleian Library Record*, xvii, 3–4 (April–October 2001a), pp.246–60 (pp.252, 255).

72. J. Byng, Viscount Torrington, *The Torrington Diaries*, London 1934–8, iii, p.36.

73. W. Kent, *Some Designs of Mr. Inigo Jones and Mr. Wm. Kent*, [London] 1744, ESTC T116216, plate 32.

74. R. Ketton-Cremer, *Felbrigg: The Story of a House*, London 1986, pp.137, 142.

75. Hussey 1955b, pp.43–4.

76. A. Smith, *Sherborne Castle*, Shaftesbury 2011, p.12.

77. J. Martin Robinson, *Arundel Castle, the Seat of the Duke of Norfolk, E.M.: A History and Guide*, Chichester 2011, pp.160–68.

78. *The Courier*, 13 June 1815, quoted in J. Martin Robinson, *Arundel Castle, a Seat of the Duke*

of Norfolk, E.M.: A Short History and Guide, Chichester 1994, p.35.

79. N. Pevsner and I. Richmond, *Northumberland: The Buildings of England*, Harmondsworth 1992, pp.138–9; J. McDonald, *Alnwick Castle: Home of the Duke and Duchess of Northumberland*, London 2012, pp.67–72.

80. *Description of Alnwick Castle*, Alnwick 1818, p.17.

81. Quoted in Harris 2001, p.89.

82. J. Plumptre, *James Plumptre's Britain: The Journals of a Tourist in the 1790s*, London 1992, p.103.

83. R. Marks and P. Williamson, *Gothic: Art for England, 1400–1547*, London 2003, p.252.

84. M. McCarthy, 'Soane's "Saxon" Room at Stowe', *Journal of the Society of Architectural Historians*, xliv, 2 (May 1985), pp.129–46 (pp.129–31).

85. McCarthy 1985, p.141.

86. Robinson 2012, p.288.

87. R. Willett, *A Description of the Library at Merly*, [London? 1785?], ESTC T60831, p.5.

88. R. Willett, *A Description of the Library at Merly in the County of Dorset*, London 1785, ESTC T08828; T. Knox, '"A Mortifying Lesson to Human Vanity": Ralph Willett's Library at Merly House, Dorset', *Apollo*, July 2000, pp.38–45; *A Catalogue of the Books in the Library of Ralph Willett, Esq., at Merly*, s.n., London 1790, ESTC T88027; *A Catalogue of the Well Known and Celebrated Library of the late Ralph Willett, Esq.*, Leigh and Sotheby, London 6–23 December 1813).

89. K. Woodbridge, *Landscape and Antiquity: Aspects of English Culture at Stourhead, 1718 to 1838*, Oxford 1970, pp.149–53.

90. C. Hussey, 'Caledon, Co. Tyrone', *Country Life*, 27 February and 6 March 1937.

91. Purcell 2011a, p.9.

92. G. Jackson-Stops, 'Barons Court, Co. Tyrone', *Country Life*, 12, 19and 26 July 1979; *The Architecture of Richard Morris (1767–1849) and William Vitruvius Morrison (1794–1838)*, Dublin 1989, pp.23–8.

93. M. Purcell and J. Fishwick, 'The Library at Ickworth', *Book Collector*, lxi, 3 (Autumn 2012), pp.366–90 (pp.370–72); N. Strachey, *Ickworth, Suffolk*, London 1998, p.13.

94. Baird 2007, p.152.

95. *Hatfield House*, Ipswich 2011, p.30.

96. E. Potten, 'Beyond Bibliophilia: Contextualizing Private Libraries in the Nineteenth Century', *Library & Information History*, xxxi, 31, 2 (May 2015), pp.73–94 (p.86).

97. J. Martin Robinson, *A Guide to the Country Houses of the North West*, London 1991, p.280.

98. *The Eaton Tourists, or A "Colloquial Description" of the Hall, Grounds, Gardens, &c. at Eaton, the Seat of the Right Hon. Earl Grosvenor*, Chester 1824, pp.69–77.

99. P. Smith, 'Lady Oxford's Alterations at Welbeck Abbey, 1741–55', *Georgian Group Journal*, xi (2001), pp.133–68 (p.153–4).

100. J. Marsden, '"Far from Elegant, yet Exceedingly Curious": Neo-Norman Furnishings at Penrhyn', *Apollo*, April 1993, pp.263–70; M. Purcell, 'The Library at Penrhyn Castle', *Book Collector*, lix, 2 (Summer 2010), pp.241–50; M. Purcell, 'National Trust Libraries in Wales', *National Trust Historic Houses and Collections Annual* (2011b), pp.12–19 (p.19).

101. Purcell 2011a, pp.18–19; G. Jackson-Stops, 'Thomas Hooper at Melford and Erddig', *National Trust Studies* (1981), pp.69–83.

102. H. Montgomery-Massingberd, *Great Houses of Ireland*, London 1999, p.32.

103. Dublin, Irish Architectural Archive, s/4954/15 (photograph of the Library at Mount Bellew, County Galway, 1885).

104. E. Joyce, *Borris House, Co. Carlow, and Elite Regency Patronage*, Dublin 2013, pp.40–41.

105. A. Menuge, 'Antiquarian Romance: John Chessell Buckler at Oxburgh Hall', *National Trust Historic Houses and Collections Annual* (2007), pp.4–13.

106. V. Glenn, 'George Bullock, Richard Bridges and James Wyatt's Regency Furnishing Schemes', *Furniture History*, xv (1979), pp.54–67.

107. C. Wainwright, *The Romantic Interior: The British Collector at Home, 1750–1850*, New Haven and London 1989, pp.225–40.

108. Purcell 2011a, pp.66–73.

109. Purcell 2011a, p.72.

110. S. Horton, and K. Oakes, *The Landmark Trust Handbook,*, Maidenhead 2003, p.91.

111. S. Millar, *The Diaries of Sanderson Millar of Radway*, [Stratford-upon-Avon] 2005, p.411.

112. Millar 2005, p.7.

113. Hawarden, Flintshire Record Office, D/E/3435; D/303, vol.1, 6r.

114. NT, Florence Court, NT 630619.

115. F. Collard, 'A Design for Library Steps by Henry Keene', *Furniture History*, xxvi (1990), pp.34–8, cited in S. Jervis, 'The English Country House Library', in N. Barker, *Treasures from the Libraries of National Trust Country Houses*, New York 1999, pp.13–33 (p.26), which contains much useful material on library furniture.

116. Woodbridge 1970, p.260.

117. J. Skinner, *Journal of a Somerset Rector, 1803–1834*, Oxford 1884, p.258.

118. NT, Nostell Priory, NT 959724.

119. Jervis 1999, p.26.

120. T. Chippendale, *The Gentleman and Cabinet-Maker's Director: Being a Large Collection of the most Elegant and Useful Designs of Household Furniture, in the Most Fashionable Taste*, 3rd edn., London 1762, ESTC T102007, plates 77–101; Cornforth 2004, p.74.

121. Harris 2001, pp.200–201.

122. M. Tomalin, 'The 1782 Inventory of Osterley Park', *Furniture History*, xxii (1986), pp.107–35 (pp.108, 120).

123. Harris 2001, p.31.

124. VAM W.1A-1987; Cornforth 2004, p.70.

125. P. Leach, *James Paine*, London 1988, p.184; Robinson 2012, p.159.

126. Marsden 1993.

127. NT, Nostell Priory, NT 959711; C. Gilbert, *The Life and Work of Thomas Chippendale*, London 1978, i, pp.173–4. I am grateful to Roger Carr-Whitworth for this reference.

128. N. Goodison and J. Hardy, 'Gillows at Tatton Park', *Furniture History*, vi (1970), pp.1–39 (p.27).

129. Jackson-Stops 1981, p.74.

130. *A Catalogue of Greek, Roman and English Coins, Medallions and Medals, of the Right Honourable Edward Earl of Oxford, which will be Sold by Auction, by Mr Cock, at his House in the Great Piazza, Covent Garden, on Thursday March the 18th, 1741–2*, s.n [London] 1742, ESTC T30132.

131. I am grateful to Caroline Schofield for details of these.

132. NT, Ham House, NT 1139982.1–2; *Ham House, Surrey*, London 1995, p.30; E. Dekker, '"Uncommonly Handsome Globes"', in E. Dekker, *Globes at Greenwich: A Catalogue of Globes and Armillary Spheres in the National Maritime Museum, Greenwich*, Oxford 1999, pp.87–136 (pp.120–24).

133. NT, Dunham Massey, NT 931682, NT 931662, NT 931663,

134. J. Rothwell, *Dunham Massey, Cheshire*, London 2000, pp.32–3.

135. NT, Dunham Massey, NT 3050065: J. Harris, *The Description and Use of the Globes, and the Orrery*, London 1731, ESTC T113888.

136. Hall 1991, pp.25–33; Purcell 2001a, p.255.

137. PRONI, D3561/B/2 (Inventory of Books in the Library at Hillsborough House, 1771); *A Catalogue of the Entire Genuine Household Furniture and other Valuable Effects of the Hon. Henry Cecil, at Hanbury-Hall, in the County of Worcester*, I. Tymbs, Worcester [1790], not known to ESTC, but copy at WAAS, 7335/705/7/3/ii/3.

138. T. Murdoch (ed.), *Noble Households: Eighteenth-Century Inventories of Great English Houses*, Cambridge 2006, p.190; *Hughenden House, Bucks, Midway Between Oxford and London. A Catalogue of the Valuable Household Furniture, Rich China, and Glass, Fine Oil Paintings, Ancient Coins, Telescopes, Microscopes … Which will be Sold by Auction, without Reserve, by Alexander Davis, on Monday May 10th, 1847, and Five Following Days … by Order of the Executors of the Late John Norris, Esq.*, J. Blacket, Newbury [1847], pp.15–17.

139. Robinson 2011, pp.161–4; W. Otter, *The Life and Remains of Edward Daniel Clarke*, London 1825, i, p.125.

140. JLRUM, ER7/17/1 (Inventory of Dunham Massey, 1758).

141. CHA, CH36/5/3 (Inventory of Chatsworth, 1811), p.34.

142. Tomalin 1986, p.121.

143. G. Jackson-Stops, *Hagley Hall: Seat of the Viscount Cobham*, Derby 1982, p.2.

144. *Gorhambury: Historic Home of the Grimston Family*, Derby 1998, p.8.

145. F. Russell, 'The Hanging and Display of Pictures, 1700–1850', in Gervase Jackson-Stops, *The Fashioning and Functioning of the British Country House*, Washington 1989, pp.133–53 (p.135).

146. S. West, 'An Architectural Typology for the Early Modern Country House Library, 1660–1720', *The Library*, 7th series, xiv, 4 (2013a), pp.442–64 (pp.443–4); S. West, 'Life in the Library', in G. Perry, K. Retford, J. Vibert, and H. Lyons, *Placing Faces: The Portrait in the Country House in the Long Eighteenth Century*, Manchester 2013b, pp.63–95.

147. Harris 2001, p.41; WAAS, Box 28/F62/33.

148. Stillman 1988, i, p.307.

149. Jackson-Stops 1984, p.211.

Chapter Seven

1. T. F. Dibdin, *The Bibliographical Decameron; or Ten Days Pleasant Discourse upon Illuminated Manuscripts* (London 1817), iii, pp.45–69.

2. DLB, pp.196–206 (pp.196–7).

3. Dibdin 1817, iii, p.60.

4. Dibdin 1817, iii, p.53.

5. G. Boccaccio, *Decamerone*, Venice 1471, ISTC ib00725300; the Roxburghe/Blandford/Spencer copy is now JRULM 17659.

6. Dibdin 1817, iii, p.62.

7. Dibdin 1817, iii, pp.64–5.

8. *The Times*, 18 June 1812, p.2.

9. Dibdin 1817, iii, p.63.

10. M. Butler, 'Austen, Jane (1775–1817)', ODNB.

11. *The Times*, 18 June 1812, p.1.

12. *White Knights Library. Catalogue of that Distinguished and Celebrated Library, Containing Numerous Very Fine and Rare Specimens from the Presses of Caxton, Pyson, and Wynkyn de Worde &c.*, London 1819, lot 765.

13. A. Sherbo, 'Heber, Richard (1774–1833)', ODNB.

14. T. F. Dibdin, *The Bibliomania; or, Book-Madness; Containing Some Account of the History, Symptoms and Cure of this Fatal Disease. In an Epistle Addressed to Richard Heber, Esq.*, London 1809, pp.15–16.

15. B. Hoole, *A Descriptive Account of the Mansions and Gardens of White Knights … With Twenty-Three Engravings from Pictures … by T. C. Hofland*, London 1819)

16. M. Purcell, 'Thorold, Sir John, 9th Baronet (1734–1815)', ODNB.

17. J. Goldfinch, 'Royal Libraries in the King's Library', in K. Doyle and S. McKendrick, *1000 Years of Royal Books and Manuscripts*, London 2013, pp.213–36 (pp.213–19).

18. NT, Saltram Park, inv. NT3069418; B. Wagner, 'Libri Impressi Bibliothecae Sancti Emmerammi: the Incunable Collections of St Emmeram, Regensburg, and its Catalogue of 1501', in K. Jensen (ed.), *Incunabula and their Readers: Printing, Selling and Using Books in the Fifteenth Century*, London 2003, pp.179–277 (p.200).

19. They remained at Holkham until 1926; P. Needham, *Twelve Centuries of Bookbindings, 400–1600*, New York 1979, pp.33–45.

20. P. Harris, *A History of the British Museum Library, 1753–1973*, London 1998, p.34; W. Macray, *Annals of the Bodleian Library*, Oxford 1890, p.193.

21. K. Jensen, *Revolution and the Antiquarian Book: Reshaping the Past, 1780–1815*, Cambridge 2011, pp.5, 11–12.

22. J. Fairfax-Blakeborough, *Sykes of Sledmere: The Record of a Sporting Family and Famous Stud*, London 1929, pp.38–9.

23. V. Bemis, 'William Beckford', DLB, pp.21–30 (p.22).

24. S. de Ricci, *English Collectors of Books and Manuscripts (1530–1930) and their Marks of Ownership*, Cambridge 1930, p.115.

25. D. Cannadine, 'The Landowner as Millionaire: the Finances of the Dukes of Devonshire, c.1800–c.1926', *Agricultural History Review*, xxv (1977), pp.77–97 (pp.80–82).

26. V. Bemis, 'William Beckford', DLB, pp.21–30 (p.27); *Catalogue of the Splendid, Curious and Extensive Library of the Late Sir Mark Masterman Sykes*, London 1824.

27. C. Spencer, *Althorp: The Story of an English House*, London 1998, pp.85–8.

28. A. Lister, 'The Althorp Library of Second Earl Spencer, now in the John Rylands University

Library of Manchester: its Formation and Growth', *Bulletin of the John Rylands University Library of Manchester*, lxxi, 2 (Summer 1989), pp. 67–88 (pp. 68–9).

29. T. F. Dibdin 1809 and 1817; J. Ames, *Typographical Antiquities*, London 1810–19.

30. T. F. Dibdin, *A Bibliographical, Antiquarian and Picturesque Tour in France and Germany*, London 1821; T. F. Dibdin, *A Bibliographical, Antiquarian and Picturesque Tour in the Northern Counties of England and in Scotland*, London 1838; T. F. Dibdin, *The Library Companion, or the Young Man's Guide and Old Man's Comfort in the Choice of a Library*, [London] 1824; T. F. Dibdin, *Reminiscences of a Literary Life*, London 1836.

31. T. F. Dibdin, *Bibliophobia, or Remarks on the Present Depression in the State of Literature and the Book Trade*, London 1832.

32. J. Richardson, 'Dibdin, Thomas Frognall (1776–1847)', ODNB.

33. T. F. Dibdin, *Bibliotheca Spenceriana; or a Descriptive Catalogue of the Books Printed in the Fifteenth Century, and of Many Valuable First Editions, in the Library of George John, Earl Spencer*, London 1814–15; T. F. Dibdin, *Aedes Althorpianae; or an Account of the Mansion, Books, and Pictures, at Althorp*, London 1822.

34. E. Peignot, *Dictionnaire raisonné de Bibliologie*, Paris 1802, i, pp. 51–2.

35. Sherbo, 'Heber, Richard (1774–1833)', ODNB.

36. J. Ferriar, *The Bibliomania, an Epistle, to Richard Heber, Esq.*, London 1809, p. 3 – it opens: 'What wild desires, what restless torments seize / The hapless man, who feels the book-disease'; Dibdin 1809; T. F. Dibdin, *Bibliomania; or Book Madness: a Bibliographical Romance, in Six Parts*, London 1811.

37. T. F. Dibdin, *Bibliomania*, London 1842, p. 569.

38. Various attempts have been made to identify Dibdin's cast of characters. For a contemporary view, see the manuscript list in the 1811 edition of *Bibliomania* which belonged to the great collector Francis Douce (1757–1834), now Bodley, Douce D.240.

39. JRLUM, Eng. Ms. 71, fol. 32r (Spencer-Dibdin correspondence); JRLUM, Eng. MS. 69 ('Catalogue of [671] Aldines in Bibliotheca Spenceriana').

40. HHC, U DDSY/104/135–37;

41. *Bibliotheca Lindesiana: Catalogue of the Printed Books Preserved at Haigh Hall, Wigan*, Aberdeen 1910, i, col. viii.

42. E. Potten, 'The Rest of the Iceberg: Reassessing Private Book Ownership in the Nineteenth Century', *Transactions of the Cambridge Bibliographical Society*, xv, 3 (2014), pp. 125–50 (pp. 128–36).

43. Dibdin 1811, pp. 623–746.

44. I. Eller, *The History of Belvoir Castle*, London 1841, p. 280.

45. R. Alston, *Books Printed on Vellum in the Collections of the British Library*, London 1996, pp. 4–5.

46. E. Potter, 'To Paul's Churchyard to Treat with a Bookbinder', in R. Myers and M. Harris, *Property of a Gentleman: The Formation, Organisation and Dispersal of the Private Library, 1620–1920*, Winchester 1991, pp. 25–42 (p. 29).

47. *Historical Manuscripts Commission, The Manuscripts and Correspondence of James, First Earl of Charlemont. vol. II, 1784–1799*, London 1894, p. 45.

48. Bedfordshire and Luton Archives, I/118 (Bills and Receipts, Woburn Abbey).

49. Jensen 2011, p. 155.

50. Lister 1989, pp. 68–9; M. Lester, 'Spencer, George John, Second Earl Spencer (1758–1834)', ODNB.

51. Lister 1989, p. 68.

52. JRULM, Eng. MS. 65 ('Catalogue of Books at Althorp. 1792').

53. JRULM, Eng. MS. 72 ('Catalogus Cod. Saec. XV Impress. Qui in Bibliotheca Spenceriana Adservantur')

54. *The Althorp Attic Sale*, Christie's, London 7–8 July 2010, pp. 7, 18, 34–5, 172, 183.

55. Dibdin 1822, pp. 20–21.

56. Lister 1989, p. 80.

57. Dibdin 1822, p. 24.

58. Samuel Timmins, *Lord Spencer's Library: A Sketch of a Visit to Althorp*, Northampton 1870, p. 7.

59. Dibdin 1822, p. 26–7.

60. Dibdin 1822, pp. 27, 31–7.

61. N. Barker, *The Roxburghe Club: A Bicentenary History*, London 2012; N. Barker, *The Publications of the Roxburghe Club, 1814–1962*, Cambridge 1964.

62. A. N. L. Munby, *Connoisseurs and Medieval Miniatures*, Oxford 1972, p. 90.

63. De Ricci 1930, p. 115; WRO 6/1145.

64. Lister 1989, p. 68.

65. Lister 1989, p. 77; Dibdin 1814–15, iv, nos 838, 840 and 849.

66. C. Sykes, *The Big House: The Story of a Country House and its Family*, London 2004, pp. 107–10.

67. Fairfax-Blakeborough 1929, pp. 38–9.

68. *Catalogue of the Library of the Late Sir Mark Masterman Sykes* 1824, p. iii; B. Bloomfield (ed.), *A Directory of Rare Books and Special Collections in the United Kingdom and the Republic of Ireland*, 2nd edn., London 1997, p. 101; Fairfax-Blakeborough 1929, p. 172.

69. *Sledmere*, Norwich 2001, pp. 19–20; A. Bell, 'Sykes, Sir Mark Masterman, Third Baronet (1771–1823)', ODNB.

70. *A Catalogue of the Books in the Library of Ralph Willett, Esq., at Merly, in the County of Dorset*, London 1790 (sale prices from annotations in Bodley Mus. Bibl. 8°, 326); Lister 1989, p. 75.

71. V. Bemis, 'William Beckford', DLB, pp. 21–30.

72. Munby 1972, p. 9; G. Le. G. Norgate, 'Spencer, George, Fourth Duke of Marlborough' (1739–1817)', ODNB.

73. *A Catalogue of the Library at Attingham*, London 1809.

74. London, Sir John Soane's Museum, vol. 135: 'Antiquités judaïques et la guerre des Juifs', Bruges c.1478–80, for which see S. McKendrick, *Royal Manuscripts: The Genius of Illumination*, London 2011, pp. 204–5.

75. Lister 1989, p. 73.

76. J. Dearden, 'Thomas Johnes and the Hafod Press, 1803–10', *Book Collector*, xxii, 3 (Autumn 1973), pp. 315–36; G. Tyack, 'Nash, John (1752–1835)', ODNB.

77. De Ricci 1930, pp. 115–16; L. Morris, *Rosenbach Abroad: In Pursuit of Books in Private Collections*, Philadelphia 1988, p. 14.

78. H. George Fletcher (ed.), *The Wormsley Library: A Personal Selection by Sir Paul Getty*, London 1999, p. 114.

79. Illustrated in J. Cornforth, *The Search for a Style: Country Life and Architecture, 1875–1925*, London 1988, p. 118.

80. M. Purcell, 'Thorold, Sir John, Ninth Baronet (1734–1815)', ODNB; T. Knox, 'Sir John Thorold's Library at Syston Park, Lincolnshire', *Apollo*, September 1997, pp. 24–9; H. Thorold, *Lincolnshire Houses*, Norwich 1999, p. 173.

81. Bloomfield 1997, p. 634; N. Barker, *Bibliotheca Lindesiana*, London 1977.

82. *Bibliotheca Lindesiana* 1910, i, cols. vii–xii.

83. H. Brigstocke, 'Lindsey, Alexander William Crawford, Twenty-Fifth Earl of Crawford and Eighth Earl of Balcarres (1812–1880)', ODNB.

84. WRO 6/1145.

85. H. Summerson, 'The Lucys of Charlecote and their Library', *National Trust Studies* (1979), pp. 149–59, which is unduly dismissive of the nineteenth-century additions to the library and is usefully read in conjunction with C. Wainwright, *The Romantic Interior: The British Collector at Home, 1750–1850*, New Haven and London 1989, pp. 219, 225–32.

86. J. Collins, *A Short Account of the Library at Longleat House*, London 1980, pp. 24–9.

87. Munby 1972 pp. 122, 135.

88. A. Hare, *The Story of my Life*, London 1896, vi, p.121. I was unable to study the Ashburnham Library to the extent that I had hoped, owing to the arcane restrictions imposed in the new East Sussex Record Office, where it would have taken many days to order up and read the primary sources. Lord Ashburnham would surely have approved.

89. A. N. L. Munby, 'The Earl and the Thief', in A. N. L. Munby, *Essays and Papers*, London 1977, pp.175–91; see, too, A. N. L. Munby, 'The Triumph of Delisle: a Sequel', *Harvard Library Bulletin*, xvii, 3 (July 1969), pp.279–90.

90. Munby 1972 pp.120, 131–2, 135.

91. N. Barker, 'The Chatsworth Library', *Christie's Review of the Season* (1974), pp.300–14 (p.303); G. Jefcoate, 'Mr Cavendish's Librarian: Charles Heydinger and the Library of Henry Cavendish, 1783–1801', *Library & Information History*, xxxii, 1–2 (2016), pp.58–71.

92. Chatsworth, Chatsworth Library Catalogue [1813?], unreferenced; Devonshire House Library Catalogue [1813], unreferenced.

93. J. Lees-Milne, *The Bachelor Duke: A Life of William Spencer Cavendish, 6th Duke of Devonshire, 1790–1858*, London 1991, p.24.

94. William Spencer Cavendish, 6th Duke of Devonshire, *Handbook of Chatsworth and Hardwick*, London 1845, pp.71–4 (the Duke's own extra-illustrated copy is at Chatsworth, and I am grateful to have had access to it, and to the library and associated library records).

95. Barker 1974, pp.310–11; Lees-Milne, *The Bachelor Duke*, p.43; W. Cavendish 1845, p.71.

96. Barker 1974, p.311; Deborah Cavendish, Duchess of Devonshire, *Chatsworth; The House*, London 2002, p.151.

97. W. Cavendish 1845, p.71.

98. Barker 1974, p.310.

99. Lister 1989, pp.80–84.

100. Bloomfield 1997, p.623, and examination of the library; C. Hartley, 'The Library at Drum Castle', *Heritage Scotland*, v, 2 (Summer 1988), p.17.

101. J. Mulvagh, *Madresfield: The Real Brideshead*, London 2008, pp.225–7, and examination of the library; Fletcher 1999, pp.26–7.

102. MMBL, ii, pp.916–19.

103. B. Hillyard, 'Rosebery as Book Collector', *Journal of the Edinburgh Bibliographical Society*, vii (2012), pp.71–114.

104. Mount Stuart, Bute Collection, 8.B.03(B) (Mount Stuart Library Catalogue, 1896).

105. Mount Stuart, Bute Collection, B.A.02(B) ('A Catalogue of Printed Books in the Library at 5, Charlotte Square, Edinburgh' [1935]), B.8.B.10 ('Catalogue of the Library in the Billiard Room at Garrison in Millport, Isle of Cumbrae', 1910), MS. II.A.15(G) ('A Catalogue of Gaelic, Irish & Manx Books Collected by Donald Maclean' (1898).

106. T. Sadleir, 'An Eighteenth-Century Irish Gentleman's Library', *Book Collector*, 11, 2 (Autumn 1953), pp.173–6; *A Catalogue of the Library of the late Right Honourable Denis Daly, which will be Sold by Auction, on Thursday the First of May 1792, by James Vallance, at his Auction-Room, No. 6, Eustace-Street*, Dublin [1792] (photocopy of marked-up copy now PRONI T/2910), ESTC T3191.

107. P. Smith, 'Welbeck Abbey and the Fifth Duke of Portland', in M. Airs (ed.), *The Victorian Great House*, Oxford 2000, pp.147–64 (pp.156, 161).

108. J. Haythornthwaite, 'Elton Hall Library', *Library Association Rare Books Group Newsletter*, xxxi (May 1988), pp.14–17; *Catalogue of Nineteen Books of the Highest Importance from the Library of the Late Earl of Carysfort*, Sotheby, Wilkinson & Hodge, London 2 July 1923. I am grateful to Liam Sims for his comments on Elton.

109. Munby 1972, pp.82–116.

110. Quoted in Munby 1972, pp.86.

111. D. McKitterick, 'Sales from Wigan', *Book Collector*, lxi, 4 (Winter 2012), pp.581–4; 'Henry Tennyson Folkard, Librarian of Wigan Library, 1877–1916', *Past Forward*, xlii (April–July 2006), p.15.

112. A. West, *The Shakespeare First Folio: The History of the Book. Volume II: A New Worldwide Census of First Folios*, Oxford 2003.

113. CUL, Inc. I.A.1: [*Biblia Latina*] [Mainz c.1455].

Chapter Eight

1. Quoted in J. Lees-Milne, *The Bachelor Duke*, London 1991, p.23.

2. Chatsworth, DF4/2/2/8, pp.26–28; Lees-Milne 1991 p.97.

3. Lees-Milne 1991, p.97; *The Private Diary of Richard, Duke of Buckingham and Chandos*, London 1862, i, pp.2–3.

4. *The Diary of Humfrey Wanley, 1715–1726*, ed. C. and R. Wright, London 1966, i, p.154.

5. C. Blamires, 'Dumont, Pierre-Étienne-Louis (1759–1829)', ODNB.

6. J. Britton, *Bowood, and its Literary Associations*, [Norwich] 1854, p.7.

7. S. West, 'The Development of Libraries in Norfolk Country Houses, 1660–1830', PhD Thesis, University of East Anglia, 2000, pp.291–2.

8. A. Lister, 'The Althorp Library of Second Earl Spencer, now in the John Rylands University Library of Manchester: its Formation and Growth', *Bulletin of the John Rylands University Library of Manchester*, lxxi, 2 (Summer 1989), pp.67–88 (p.69); C. di Giorgio, 'Ocheda, Tommaso de', *Dizionario Biografico degli Italiani*, lxi (2013).

9. J. Lacaita, *Catalogue of the Library at Chatsworth*, London 1879; C. Lacaita, *An Italian Englishman: Sir James Lacaita, K.C.M.G*, London 1933, p.163.

10. Mount Stuart, Bute Collection, NS 340 ('Catalogue of the Library at Cardiff Castle' [1896]), MS. 217A ('Catalogue of the Tower Room Books at Cardiff Castle', 1909).

11. M. Purcell, 'Making History: the Library at Wallington', *National Trust Historic Houses and Collections Annual* (2014), pp.16–21 (p.18).

12. G. Goodwin, 'Hill, John Harwood (1809–1886)', ODNB.

13. Samuel Timmins, *Lord Spencer's Library: A Sketch of a Visit to Althorp*, Northampton 1870, pp.5, 12.

14. BL, Add. MS. 35628, fols. 16, 18 (letter from Plumptre to the 2nd Earl of Hardwicke, 1764), MS. 35,628, fol. 149 (letter from Plumptre to Hardwicke, 1772).

15. NAS, GD44/43/18/62 (Letter from Archibald Anderson to the Duke of Gordon, 1760).

16. NAS, GD44/43/62 (Letter from the Duke of Gordon to Mr Boys, 1772).

17. GA, D2700/QB4/1/20 (Diary of Richard Salter, 1848 to 1852).

18. D. Burnett, *Longleat: The Story of an English Country House*, London 1978, p.12.

19. *Antiquaries Journal*, lii (1972), pp.449–50.

20. LA, Goulding Papers 3/A/19.

21. J. Martin Robinson, *Requisitioned: The British Country House in the Second World War*, London 2014, p.77.

22. DLB, p.28.

23. Nicolas Barker, *Bibliotheca Lindesiana: The Lives and Collections of Alexander William, 25th Earl of Crawford and 8th Earl of Balcarres and James Ludovic, 26th Earl of Crawford and 9th Earl of Balcarres*, London 1977, *passim*.

24. WRO, CR/229/193 (Slip Catalogue of the Library at Ettington Park, 1867).

25. Quoted in T. Lloyd, 'Country House Libraries of the Eighteenth and Nineteenth Centuries', in P. Jones and E. Rees, *A Nation and its Books: A History of the Book in Wales*, Aberystwyth 1998, pp.135–46 (p.143).

26. LA, BNLW/2/6/5 (Bill from John Edward Martin to Lord Brownlow, 1847); I am grateful to Dunstan Roberts for this reference.

27. WSHC, 2657/H7/6; WRO, CRI36/V/91 ('Catalogue of the Arbury Library').

28. KHLC, U1590/C714/50 ('Papers of Instructions Relative to the New Catalogue of Chevening Library as Prepared by Mr Latter from Messrs. Hatchard, Piccadilly, 1856–7').

29. *Catalogue of the Library at Chevening*, London 1865.

30. Aberdeen University Library, MS. 3175/B2/76/1–2 (Slip Catalogue of the Library at Duff House).

31. *A Catalogue of the Books in the Goodwood Library, with an Alphabetical Index*, [Chichester] 1838; the print run for this catalogue was evidently very small indeed, and no copy is traceable via Copac, though there are copies at Goodwood.

32. CBS, D/LE/D845 (Letter from Thomas Osborne to Sir William Lee, 1764).

33. CornRO, DG/178 ('Catalogue of the Trelissick Library', 1885, and inserted notes); M. Purcell, 'Allnutt at Lanhydrock', *Bodleian Library Record*, xviii (2003–5), pp. 682–6.

34. Dorchester, Dorset History Centre, D/WLC/C269.

35. New York, Grolier Club, 08.28\D225\1910\Folio\vols. 1–2 ('Catalogue of the Library of the Earl of Dartmouth at Patshull' [1910]).

36. DevRO, 1148M/18/12.

37. StaffRO, D641/5/P(I)/5 ('Copy of Catalogue of Books in Library & Study belonging to Thos. Fitzherbert Esqre·, Swynnerton, June 20th 1832').

38. Bodley, MS. North e. 33 ('A Catalogue of the Books in the Library at Waldershare' [1767]).

39. Leicester, Leicestershire Record Office, DG7/3/137.

40. NNRO, MC 3/320/1 (E. H. Barker to Joseph Churchill); NAS, GD224/1040/60/24 (Letter from A. H. Bullen to Mr Stewart, 1895).

41. NAS, GD224/1040/34 (Notes about the Buccleuch libraries, 1851)

42. KLHC, U269/E/2/8 (Books missing at Knole, 1806 to 1824).

43. NUL, Ma 71/1 ('A Catalogue of His Grace the Duke of Kingston's Library at Thoresby, Nottinghamshire', 1771), Ma 71/2 ('A Catalogue of Her Grace the Duchess of Kingston's Library: to Which is Added, An Appendix, Containing an Account of the Books added to the Library since February 1771. Copied from the Catalogue Taken in 1771. With Improvements').

44. NLW, Chirk Castle Papers, A/29 (Chirk Library Catalogue, 1704).

45. For example Bodley MS. Eng. misc. e. 228 (Alphabetical Catalogue of the Library at Newnham Paddox Warwickshire, 1730), and

MS. Eng. misc. e. 229 (Library shelf-list for Newnham Paddox, 1752).

46. *Catalogus Bibliothecae Kingstonianæ*, [London 1727?], ESTC T123378; G. Pollard and A. Ehrman, *The Distribution of Books by Catalogue from the Invention of Printing to A.D. 1800*, Cambridge 1965, pp. 274–6.

47. T. Morell, *Catalogus Librorum in Bibliotheca Osterleiensi*, [London?] 1771 (ESTC n030998).

48. *Catalogue of the Library of the Earl of Bradford, Weston. Index of Subjects*, Weston 1887.

49. P. Morgan, 'Henry Cotton and W.H. Allnutt: two Pioneer Book-Trade Historians', in P. Isaac and B. McKay (ed.), *The Human Face of the Book Trade*, Winchester 1999, pp. 1–11 (pp. 5–11).

50. NLS, GD 224/657/10 ('Applications for the Situation, held by the Late Mr Stewart at Montagu House, September 1836').

51. PRONI, D/1071/H/B/J/56/1 (Letter from J. G. Jennings to the Marquess of Ava and Dufferin, n.d.).

Chapter Nine

1. H. von Pückler-Muskau, *Puckler's Progress: The Adventures of Prince Pückler-Muskau in England, Wales and Ireland, as Told in Letters to his Former Wife, 1826–9*, London 1987, pp. 85–6.

2. M. Berry, *Extracts of the Journals and Correspondence of Miss Berry, from the Year 1783 to 1852*, London 1865, ii, p. 402.

3. J. Cornforth, 'Books do Furnish a Living Room', *Country Life*, 13 December 2001, pp. 56–9.

4. C. Wainwright, 'The Library as Living Room', in R. Myers and M. Harris, *Property of a Gentleman: The Formation, Organisation and Dispersal of the Private Library*, Winchester 1991, p. 15; Cornforth 2001, pp. 56–9; J. Ciro, 'Country House Libraries in the Nineteenth Century', *Library History*, xviii (July 2002), pp. 89–98.

5. BLRS, I/118 (Sale of Contents of Ampthill House to the Dowager Lady Gowran).

6. DRO, D779B/F/103 ('An Inventory of the Household Furniture, Plate, Books &c. &c. of the late Robert Holden, Esquire of Darley Abbey in the County of Derby' [1808]).

7. S. West, 'The Development of Libraries in Norfolk Country Houses, 1660–1830', PhD Thesis, University of East Anglia, 2002, p. 295.

8. T. F. Dibdin, *Aedes Althorpianae; or an Account of the Mansion, Books, and Pictures, at Althorp*, London 1822, p. 31.

9. B. Askwith, *The Lytteltons: A Family Chronicle of the Nineteenth Century*, London 1975, p. 6.

10. Dibdin 1822, p. 26.

11. BLRS, L30/15/50/14 (Letter from Anne Robinson to Frederick Robinson, New Year's Eve, 1780).

12. BLRS, L30/15/50/24 (Letter from Anne Robinson to Frederick Robinson, 30 November 1781).

13. J. Byng, Viscount Torrington, *The Torrington Diaries*, London 1934–8, iii, p. 157.

14. J. Britton, *The History and Description, with Graphic Illustrations, of Cassiobury Park, Hertfordshire: the Seat of the Earl of Essex*, London 1837, plate [11].

15. HALS, D/ECP/F18 ('Catalogue of the Library at Cassiobury, Watford').

16. Pückler-Muskau 1987, p. 63.

17. E. Grant, *Memoirs of a Highland Lady*, Edinburgh 1988, i, pp. 293, 297.

18. M. Mansbridge, *John Nash: A Complete Catalogue*, Oxford 1991, pp. 49–50.

19. M. Girouard, *Life in the English Country House*, New Haven and London 1978, pp. 194–6.

20. BRO, D/EP6/F30 ('A General Inventory of Furniture, China, Glass &c. Belonging to Coleshill House, The Property of the Right Hon. the Earl of Radnor'). Some of the books in this room subsequently found their way to Montacute House in Somerset.

21. C. Lybbe Powys, *Passages from the Diaries of Mrs Philip Lybbe Powys, of Hardwick House, A.D. 1756–1808*, London 1899, pp. 197–8.

22. *Newhailes*, Edinburgh 2002, p. 26; I. Gow, '"The Most Learned Drawing Room in Europe": Newhailes and the Classical Scottish Library', in D. Mays (ed.), *Visions of Scotland's Past, Looking to the Future: Essays in Honour of John R. Hume*, Edinburgh 2000, pp. 81–96 (pp. 94–5).

23. NUL, Mi 1/23 ('Wollaton Hall Inventory', 1878).

24. CornRO, EN/2476/51; Esher is quoted in E. Diestelkamp, 'The National Trust Country House Scheme', in M. Airs (ed.), *The Twentieth-Century Great House*, Oxford 2002, pp. 75–100 (p. 84).

25. Huntingdonshire Archives, DC92 (Whitney Collection: Hinchingbrooke, c.1890); Caernarfon Gwynedd Record Office, XS/1077/7/6/2; for the contents of the Hinchingbrooke library, see Huntingdon Archives, Hinch/7/70 (Hinchingbrooke Library Catalogue 1904).

26. J. Bryant, *The Iveagh Bequest, Kenwood*, London 1990, pp. 15–22. The Kenwood library catalogue, apparently unknown to the author in 1990, is held by the Camden Local Studies and Archives Centre, but is unreferenced and uncatalogued. I am grateful to the staff there who found it for me.

27. T. F. Dibdin, *A Bibliographical, Antiquarian and Picturesque Tour in the Northern Counties of England, and in Scotland*, London 1838, ii, p. 944.

28. S. Jervis, 'The English Country House Library', in N. Barker (ed.), *Treasures from the Libraries of National Trust Country Houses*, New York 1999, pp. 13–34 (p. 23).

29. J. Newman, *Glamorgan, Mid Glamorgan, South Glamorgan and West Glamorgan (The Buildings of Wales)*, London 1995, p. 350.

30. Dibdin 1838, ii, p. 937.

31. J. Martin Robinson, *Arundel Castle, a Seat of the Duke of Norfolk, E. M.: A Short History and Guide*, Chichester 1994, p. 97.

32. M. Girouard, *The Victorian Country House*, London 1979, p. 69.

33. P. Bradley, *Flintham Hall, Nottinghamshire*, [Flintham? 2004], pp. [1], [3].

34. Pückler-Muskau 1987, p. 183.

35. R. Kerr, *The Gentleman's House*, London 1865, pp. 116–18; Girouard 1979, p. 69.

36. Kerr 1865, pp. 118–19.

37. Kerr 1865, pp. 188–9.

38. A. Cirket (ed.), 'The Earl de Grey's Account of the Building of Wrest House', *Publications of the Bedfordshire Historical Record Society, Miscellanea*, lix (1980) pp. 65–85 (pp. 72–5).

39. M. Purcell, *The Big House Library in Ireland: Books in Ulster Country Houses*, Swindon 2011a, p. 101.

40. Examples are too numerous to cite, but some of the more extreme examples include Springhill, County Londonderry (1950s), Belton House, Lincolnshire (1970s), and Kingston Lacy, Dorset, and Calke Abbey, Derbyshire (1980s), all of which have very large numbers of mostly nine-teenth – and twentieth-century books in store.

41. HRO, IIM49/208 (Catalogue of the Library at Hackwood, 1828).

42. *Catalogue of the Printed Books in the Library of His Grace the Duke of Portland at Welbeck Abbey, and in London*, London 1893.

43. R. Sackville-West, *Inheritance: The Story of Knole and the Sackvilles*, London 2010, p. 181.

44. Cornwall, Truro record Office, CY/1678 (Will of Sir James Tillie of Pentillie Castle, Pillaton, *c*. 1704).

45. M. Purcell and N. Thwaite, *The Libraries of Calke Abbey*, [London 2013], p. 9.

46. NT Sound Archive, Tape 268 (Canons Ashby). I am grateful to Amy Speckhart for this reference.

47. C. Rowell, *Turner at Petworth*, London 2002, pp. 108, 154.

48. HRO, 15M84/Z3/38: *Catalogue of the Library at Leigh Park*, S.l. 1842.

49. Inspection of the books, and see also B. Bloomfield (ed.), *A Directory of Rare Books and Special Collections in the United Kingdom and the Republic of Ireland*, London 1994, p. 633. For an earlier record of the Castle Fraser library, see Aberdeen, Aberdeen University Library, MS. 3470/1/3/2 ('Catalogue of Library Castle Fraser', n.d.).

50. HRO, 43M48/2017–18 ('Shelf Catalogue of Books in "Big" Library at Bramshill' [1898]); S. Lustig, 'Boswell, Margaret Montgomerie (1738?–1789)', ODNB.

51. DRO, D239/M/F/6808 (Letter to Sir H. Fitzherbert, 1824).

52. BRO, D/EWi/E40 (Catalogue of the Library at Sulham House, 1831).

53. NLS, MS. 9758 (Catalogue of the Kenmure Library, 1820); Bangor, Bangor University Archives and Special Collections BMSS/SHW (Library Catalogue of Sir Hugh Williams).

54. S. West, 'The Development of Libraries in Norfolk Country Houses, 1660–1830', PhD Thesis, University of East Anglia, 2000, p. 222.

55. S. Whatman, *The Housekeeping Book of Susanna Whatman, 1776–1800*, London 2000, pp. 39, 55; for Whatman see R. Brown, 'Whatman, Susanna (1753–1814)', ODNB.

56. BLRS, HW/87/191 (Richard How II to David Troup).

57. For an explanation of the dating, see M. Purcell, 'Libraries at Lacock Abbey', *National Trust Historic Houses & Collections Annual* (2012), pp. 36–43 (pp. 36–7).

58. W. Dean, *An Historical and Descriptive Account of Croome d'Abitot*, Worcester 1824, p. 50.

59. Byng 1934–8, iv, pp. 134–6.

60. Byng 1934–8, iii, p. 74, ii, p. 249.

61. C. Wainwright, *The Romantic Interior: The British Collector at Home, 1750–1850*, New Haven and London 1989, pp. 219, 225–32; W. Howitt, *Visits to Remarkable Places: Old Halls, Battle Fields, and Scenes Illustrative of Striking Passages in English History and Poetry*, London 1840, pp. 124–6.

62. *Audley End*, London 2002, pp. 11–12.

63. H. Repton, *Fragments on the Theory and Practice of Landscape Gardening*, London 1816, p. 210; M. Purcell, 'The Library at Sheringham Park', *Book Collector*, lxv, 1 (Spring 2016), pp. 71–82.

64. Repton 1816, p. 58.

65. S. West 2000, pp. 440–43.

66. C. Campbell Orr, 'Charlotte (1744–1818)', ODNB.

67. F. Parkes, *Domestic Duties; or, Instruction to Young Married Ladies*, London 1825, p. 381.

68. Grant 1988, i, p. 283.

69. Augusta, Lady Gregory, *Coole*, Dublin 1931, p. 2.

70. Gregory 1931, p. 17.

71. M. Ogilvy, Countess of Airlie, *Thatched with Gold: The Memoirs of Mabell, Countess of Airlie*, London 1962, pp. 25, 29.

72. GA, D5130/39 (Letter from Lady Prinn to Saunders and Ottley, 1842).

73. PRONI, D860/7/6 (*Regulations for the Lending Library, Ballykilbeg*, printed handbill, mid-nineteenth century).

74. For example, NT 3147296, J. Kemble, *The Farm House: a Comedy in Three Acts*, London 1789, ESTC T35363, illustrated in Purcell and Thwaite 2013, p. 21.

75. Quoted in Purcell and Thwaite 2013, p. 13.

76. J. Miller, *Fertile Fortune: The Story of Tyntesfield*, London 2003, p. 42.

77. Bodley, MS. Top. Oxon. *c*. 382 ('A Catalogue of the Earl of Abingdon's Libraries at Witham & Rycot', 1801), fol. 51r.

78. J. Brooks, 'Musical Monuments for the Country House: Music, Collection, and Display at Tatton Park', *Music and Letters*, xci, 4, pp. 513–35.

79. R. Williams, *Catalogue of the Castle Fraser Music Collection*, Aberdeen 1994.

80. G. Gifford, *A Descriptive Catalogue of the Music Collection at Burghley House, Stamford*, Aldershot [2002]; R. Langley, 'The Music', in T. Murdoch (ed.), *Boughton House: The English Versailles*, London 1992, pp. 175–7.

81. Rowell 2002, pp. 113, 115.

82. E. Stanley, 15th Earl of Derby, *The Diaries of Edward Henry Stanley, 15th Earl of Derby (1823–93) between 1878 and 1893: A Selection*, Oxford 2003.

83. R. Colt Hoare, *A Catalogue of Books Relating to the History and Topography of Italy*, London 1812; G. Mandelbrote and B. Taylor (eds), *Libraries within the Library: The Origins of the British Library's Printed Collections*, London 2009, p. 403.

84. Purcell 2012, pp. 36–43.

85. NT 3131817.

86. http://oxfordindex.oup.com/view/10.1093/ww/9780199540884.013.U187188 (accessed 26 March 2015).

87. L. Morris, *Rosenbach Redux: Further Book Adventures in England and Ireland*, Philadelphia 1989, pp. 36–50; N. Kissane (ed.), *Treasures from the National Library of Ireland*, Dublin 1994, pp. 11–13; W. Courtney, 'Shirley, Evelyn Philip (1812–1882)', ODNB; for the library interior at Lough Fea, see E. Shirley, *Lough Fea*, London 1869, and for the books, E. Shirley, *Catalogue of*

the Library at Lough Fea: an Illustration of the *History and Antiquities of Ireland*, London 1872.

88. NLI, MS, 19,708 9 (Catalogue of 'Irish Books Adare Library' [c.1870]).

89. A. Malcomson, *Virtues of a Wicked Earl: The Life and Legend of William Sydney Clements 3rd Earl of Leitrim*, Dublin 2009, pp. 349–51.

90. M. Purcell and W. Hale, 'Hibernica at Florence Court', *National Trust Historic Houses and Collections Annual* (2008), pp. 30–35; Purcell 2011a, pp. 75–86.

91. Purcell 2011a, pp. 95–114.

92. Quoted in T. Lloyd, 'Country-House Libraries of the Eighteenth and Nineteenth Centuries', in P. Jones and E. Rees, *A Nation and its Books: A History of the Book in Wales*, Aberystwyth 1998, pp. 135–46 (p. 135).

93. Purcell and Thwaite 2013, pp. 39–40.

94. NLW, Misc. vol. 67 ('A Catalogue of the Library at Llangibby Castle, Monmouthshire' [1953]).

95. D. Cannadine, 'Lord Strickland: Imperial Aristocrat and Aristocratic Imperialist', in D. Cannadine, *Aspects of Aristocracy*, New Haven and London 1994, pp. 109–29 (p. 124).

96. M. Purcell, 'Making History: the Library at Wallington', *National Trust Historic Houses and Collections Annual*, 2014, pp. 16–21; F. Stimpson, 'The Library at Wallington', *Book Collector*, lviii, 1 (Spring 2009), pp. 45–71; A. N. L. Munby, 'Macaulay's Library', in A. N. L. Munby, *Essays and Papers*, London 1977, pp. 121–40.

97. NT 3065025: Thucydides, *De Bello Peloponnesiaco Libri Octo*, Oxford 1696, Wing T1133, ESTC R38346.

Chapter Ten

1. P. Holden, '"One of the Most Remarkable Things in London": A Visit to the Lord Treasurer's Library in 1713 by Samuel Molyneux', *Electronic British Library Journal* (2010), article 10.

2. P. Holden (ed.), *The London Letters of Samuel Molyneux, 1712–13*, London 2011, pp. 43–4; J. Macky, *A Journey Through England*, London 1723, i, p. 194, ESTC T57749.

3. C. Tite, *The Manuscript Library of Sir Robert Cotton*, London 1994.

4. C. Woolgar, *The Great Household in Late Medieval England*, New Haven and London 1999), p. 80

5. M. Howard, *The Early Tudor Country House: Architecture and Politics, 1490–1550*, London 1989, p. 35.

6. E. Thompson, 'The Will and Inventory of Robert Morton, A.D. 1486–1488', *Journal of British Archaeological Association*, xxxiii (1877), pp. 308–30.

7. T. Fortescue, *A History of the Family of Fortescue*, London 1880, pp. 306, 310.

8. M. Guerci, 'The Construction of Northumberland House and the Patronage of its Original Builder, Lord Henry Howard, 1603–14', *Antiquaries Journal*, lxxxx (2010), pp. 341–400.

9. Hatfield, 'A Cattaloge of all Your Lordships Printed Books as they are Nowe Disposed in your Lordships Librarie taken this 26 of Januarie 1614' (i.e. 1615); 'A Catalogue of all the Printed Books in the Library of the Right Honble. William Earle of Salisbury at Salisbury House in the Strand' (1637); 'A Catalogue of all the Printed Books in the Library of the Right Honble. William Earle of Salisbury att Satlisbury House in the Strand' (1647) – all unreferenced.

10. *Historical Manuscripts Commission, Calendar of the Manuscripts of the Most Honourable the Marquis of Salisbury, Preserved at Hatfield House, Hertfordshire*, London 1883–1976, xxiv, pp. 148–52.

11. J. Lees-Milne, *The Bachelor Duke: A Life of William Spencer Cavendish, 6th Duke of Devonshire*, London 1991, pp. 195–6.

12. C. Sykes, *Private Palaces: Life in the Great London Houses*, London 1985, pp. 102–3.

13. Sykes 1985, p. 326.

14. C. Bailey, *The Secret Rooms*, London 2013, p. 162.

15. S. de Ricci, *Census of Medieval and Renaissance Manuscripts in the United States and Canada*, New York 1935–40, i, pp. 126–9; D. Dickinson, *Henry E. Huntington's Library of Libraries*, San Marino, CA 1995), pp. 102–3; J. Payne Collier, *A Catalogue Bibliographical and Critical of Early English Literature; Forming a Portion of the Library at Bridgewater House, the Property of the Rt. Hon. Lord Francis Egerton*, London 1837; W. Whiffen, 'Bridgewater House, St. James's', *Country Life*, 13 May 1949, pp. 1118–21.

16. M. Purcell, *The Big House Library in Ireland: Books in Ulster Country Houses*, Swindon 2011, p. 99.

17. J. Cornforth, *London Interiors from the Archives of Country Life*, London 2000, pp. 106–7.

18. Purcell 2011a, p. 29.

19. SRO, DD\WHH/127; New York, Grolier Club *08.26\Y65\1812\Folio ('Catalogue of Lord Hardwicke's London collection of Pamphlets', 1812).

20. J. Oldham, 'Murray, William, First Earl of Mansfield (1705–1793)', ODNB.

21. KHLC, U1590/U11; A. Hanham, 'Stanhope, James, First Earl Stanhope (1673–1721)', ODNB; *Catalogue of the Library at Chevening*, London 1865.

22. Hatfield, 'Catalogue of the Hatfield Library' (1712), unreferenced, and information supplied by Robin Harcourt-Williams.

23. J. Evelyn, *The Diary of John Evelyn*, Oxford 1955, iv, pp. 199–200.

24. NLI, MS. 2521 (Ormonde Inventories), fol. 29r.

25. H. Hamilton, *Selections from the Monymusk Papers (1713–1755)*, Edinburgh 1945, pp. xii, 1–8.

26. *A Catalogue of the Rich Houshold* [sic] *Furniture of the Right Honourable Henry Earl of Thomond, Deceas'd, which will Begin to be Sold at Auction on Monday the 25th Instant, at his Late Dwelling-House in Dover-Street, St James's*, [London] 25 January–4 February 1742; *A Catalogue of the Valuable Library of Books of the Right Honourable Henry Earl of Thomond, Deceas'd, Which Will Begin to be sold by Auction, on Friday the 5th of February, 1742*, [London] 5 February 1742.

27. PRONI, T.D. 4779 (photocopy of 'A Catalogue of the Library of the Earl of Macartney in Curzon Street, May-Fair', late eighteenth or early nineteenth century).

28. Ithaca, Cornell University Library, Wason MS. DS. M115 9 ('Catalogue of the books of the Right Honble. Lord MacCartney', 1786; microfilm, PRONI, MIC 395/1).

29. A. Murdoch, 'Campbell, Archibald, Third Duke of Argyll (1682–1761)', ODNB; *Catalogus Librorum A. C. D. A.* [i.e. Archibald Campbell, Duke of Argyll], Glasgow 1758, ESTC T28876.

30. JRLUM, BAG/5/3/7 ('A Catalogue of Lord John Murray's Books at Perth, London and Huntingtower', 1762).

31. Suffro, 941/77/1 ('Earl of Bristol's List of Book's London August 5th 1815'; TNA, C103/174 – Harvey v. Harvey [sic], Inventories, 1785, 1787).

32. Maidstone, Kent History and & Archive Centre, U269/E2/1 ('A Catalogue of My Lord of Dorsett's Books at Knole' [c.1651]).

33. Attingham Park, 'Catalogue of Lord Berwick's Books Attingham Park and Portman Square 1787'; Purcell 2011a, pp. 99–100.

34. WSRO, Goodwood MS. 430 ('Etat des Meubles et Effets qui se trouvent ... dans le Chateau d'Aubigny' [1763]), fols. 7r–10v.

35. Arundel, IN/65 (Inventory of Norfolk House, Worksop Manor and Arundel Castle, 1777, including library catalogues); *Plans, Elevations and Partial Measurements of Arundel Castle in Sussex ... Edited by Francis W. Steer*, [Arundel] 1976; J. Martin Robinson, 'The Library of the Duke of Norfolk', *Chichester and District Law Society*, ix (January 1985), pp. 21–7 (p. 21).

36. *Catalogue of Original XVIIIth Century Woodwork, Unique Marble Mantelpieces, ... Being the Remaining Contents of Norfolk House*, Christie, Manson & Woods, London 7 February 1938, pp. 94–5; Arundel, IN/61 ('Norfolk House,

NOTES TO PAGES 199–208 | 313

St James's Square, London: Inventory of the Contents of the Residence', 1924).

37. T. Murdoch (ed.), *Noble Households: Eighteenth-Century Inventories of Great English Houses: A Tribute to John Cornforth*, Cambridge 2006, pp. 233–6.

38. SHC, 58/15/148 ('William, Lord Huntingtower's Books in London' [1833]).

39. HRO, 21M57/2A2/10 (List of books belonging to the Earl of Normanton in his house at St Stephen's Green, Dublin, c.1810–11).

40. W. Nicolson, *The London Diaries of William Nicolson, Bishop of Carlisle, 1702–1718*, Oxford 1985, pp. 308, 312, 363, 503, 591.

41. M. Hunter (ed.), *From Books to Bezoars: Sir Hans Sloane and his Collections*, London 2012; S. Baker, *Catalogus Meadiana: sive Catalogus Librorum Richardi Mead*, [London] 1755, ESTC T1340; A. Guerrini, 'Mead, Richard (1673–1754)', ODNB.

42. K. Swift, 'The Formation of the Library of Charles Spencer, 3rd Earl of Sunderland (1674–1722): a Study in the Antiquarian Book Trade', D.Phil. Thesis, University of Oxford, 1987.

43. D. Adshead, *Wimpole: Architectural Drawings and Topographical Views*, [Swindon] 2007, p. 17; BL Add. MSS. 19746–57.

44. *The Minute-Books of the Spalding Gentlemen's Society, 1712–1755*, [Fakenham] 1981, p. 116. Aylesbury, Centre for Buckinghamshire Studies, D/D/3/1–6, confirm that Ellys was enlarging the London house in breach of his lease in the 1730s, knocking five separate dwellings together to produce a single large mansion, perhaps to accommodate the large numbers of books he was purchasing at the time. His librarian John Mitchell seems to have been resident in London, and was clearly not known personally to the Lincolnshire members of the Spalding Gentlemen's Society (*Minute-Books of the Spalding Gentlemen's Society, 1712–1755*, p. 22), who elected him as a compliment to Ellys, but got his Christian name wrong in their minute book.

45. W. and K. Smith, *An Architectural History of Towneley Hall, Burnley*, Burnley 2004, p. 79; B. Cook, 'Townley, Charles (1737–1805)', ODNB.

46. B. Hillyard, 'Ker, John, Third Duke of Roxburghe (1740–1804)', ODNB.

47. *Survey of London: Volume 10, St Margaret, Westminster Part 1: Queen Anne's Gate Area*, [London] 1926, pp. 130–31; G. Mandelbrote and B. Taylor, *Libraries within the Library: The Origins of the British Museum's Printed Collections*, London 2009, pp. 187–221, 321–40; F. Thompson, 'Grenville, Richard Plantagenet Temple-Nugent-Brydges-Chandos, Second Duke of Buckingham and Chandos', ODNB.

48. Aylesbury, Centre for Buckinghamshire Studies, D54/16 (2nd Duke of Buckingham to Thomas Grenville, 28 October 1845).

49. L. Morris, *Rosenbach Abroad: In Pursuit of Books in Private Collections*, Philadelphia 1988, pp. 12–33.

50. R. Bowdler, 'Dance, George, the Younger (1741–1825)', ODNB.

51. TNA, C112/186 ('A Catalogue of the Books at Chesterfield House which belonged to the Right Honble Philip Dormer, Earl of Chesterfield').

52. *Satires* (II, vi, 60–62): 'Now by reading ancient authors, now by sleep and hours of indolence / To lose in sweet oblivion the disquietudes of life'; *Private Palaces*, pp. 126–7.

53. J. Friedman, *Spencer House: Chronicle of a Great London Mansion*, London 1993, p. 218.

54. Sykes 1985, pp. 202–3.

55. M. Wanklyn (ed.), *Inventories of Worcestershire Landed Gentry, 1637–1786*, [Worcester?] 1998, pp. 189–96.

56. D. Vaisey (ed.), *Probate Inventories of Lichfield and District*, [Stafford] 1969, pp. 105–12.

57. Chatsworth, Compton Place Library Catalogue.

58. J. Millington, *William Beckford and his Tower*, Bath 1978, p. 2; W. Gregory, *The Beckford Family: Reminiscences of Fonthill Abbey and Lansdown Tower*, Bath 1887, p. 59; M. Bloch, *James Lees-Milne*, London 2009, pp. 289–90.

59. K. Armstrong, 'The Baikie Library at Tankerness House Museum, Kirkwall, Orkney', *Library Review*, xl, 1 (1991), pp. 37–44; the books are recorded in ESTC.

60. M. Girouard, 'The Country House and the Country Town', in G. Jackson-Stops (ed.), *The Fashioning and Functioning of the British Country House*, Washington 1989, pp. 305–28 (p. 307).

61. *A Select Set of Psalms and Hymns with a Choice Collection of Words and with Proper Tunes and Basses as they are Fitted to be Sung in the Parish Church of Grantham By John Hutchinson Clerk of the Parish*, [Grantham? 1756], ESTC T155509; *A Select set of Psalms and Hymns, with A Choice Collection of Words, with Proper Tunes and Basses, as they are Appointed to be Sung in the Parish Church of Grantham. By John Hutchinson, Late Clerk of the Parish*, Grantham 1792, ESTC T155508; I. Denson, *A Catalogue of the Hardy Trees, Shrubs, and Herbaceous Plants in the Botanic Garden Bury Saint Edmund's, by I. Denson, Curator*, [Bury St Edmunds] 1822.

62. J. Meredith, 'Letters between Friends: Lord Charlemont's Library and Other Matters', *Irish Architectural and Decorative Studies*, iv (2001), pp. 52–77 (pp. 56–8, 73); S. O'Reilly, 'Charlemont House: A Critical History', in E. Mayes and P. Murphy (eds), *Images and Insights*, Dublin

1993, pp. 42–54; S. O'Reilly, *The Casino at Marino*, Dublin 1991, pp. 6–8.

63. D. Griffin, *Leinster House, 1744–2000: An Architectural History*, Dublin 2000, pp. 44–45.

64. StaffRO, D615/E(H)/13 and D615/E(H)/62, marked-up copies of *Shugborough Hall, Near Stafford. Mr. George Robins is Honoured with Instructions to Announce for Unreserved Competition, on the Premises, on Monday, the 1st of August, 1842 and Thirteen Following Days, … the Splendid Property of Every Denomination Appertaining to Shugborough Hall* [G. Robins, London] 1842 and *A Catalogue of the Very Superior Furniture of Lichfield House, in Saint James' Square*, G. Robins [London] 1842. For Robins see R. Myers, 'Robins, George Henry (1777–1847)', ODNB.

65. N. Rodger, 'Anson, George, Baron Anson (1697–1762)', ODNB.

66. Cornforth 2004, p. 72.

67. BLRS, Grey MSS; L30/9a/2/3, quoted in J. Martin Robinson, *Shugborough*, London 1989, p. 33.

68. StaffRO, D615/E(H)/10 (Shugborough Inventory, 1773); *Shugborough Hall 1842*, pp. 138–9.

69. *Furniture of Lichfield House 1842*, pp. 8–9.

70. *Survey of London, Volumes 29 and 30, St James Westminster, Part 1*, London 1960, pp. 142–54; 'Historical Town Houses: Lichfield House, No. 15 St James's Square', *Architectural Review*, xxvii, 162 (May 1910), pp. 273–8.

71. StaffRO, D615/E(H)/14 (Bills and Accounts for the Furniture and Objets d'Art Purchased to Refurnish Shugborough, 1855–71).

72. D. Defoe, *A Tour through the Whole of Island of Great Britain*, New Haven and London 1991, p. 65.

73. R. Lloyd, *The Poetical Works*, London 1774, ESTC T94392, p. 43.

74. E. Chew, 'The Countess of Arundel and Tart Hall', in E. Chaney (ed.), *The Evolution of English Collecting: Receptions of Italian Art in the Tudor and Stuart Periods*, New Haven and London 2003, pp. 285–307.

75. J. Roundell, *Ham House: Its History and Art Treasures*, London 1904, pp. 133–4.

76. R. Wisker, 'Hyde, Jane, Countess of Clarendon and Rochester (c. 1672–1725)', ODNB.

77. E. Harris, *The Genius of Robert Adam*, New Haven and London 2001, pp. 78–80; illustrated in R. Adam, *The Works in Architecture*, London 1773–1822, iii, plate 3.

78. C. Campbell Orr, 'Lost Royal Libraries and Hanoverian Court Culture', in J. Raven (ed.), *Lost Libraries: The Destruction of Great Book Collections Since Antiquity*, London 2004, pp. 163–80 (p. 169).

79. M. Powell, 'The "Curious Books" in the Library at Strawberry Hill', in M. Snodin (ed.), *Horace Walpole's Strawberry Hill*, New Haven and London 2009, pp. 235–41; A. Hazen, *A Catalogue of Horace Walpole's Library*, New Haven and London 1969.

80. W. Lewis, *Collector's Progress*, London 1952.

81. J. Harris, *The Palladian Revival: Lord Burlington, his Villa and his Garden at Chiswick*, New Haven and London 1994, p 107.

82. P. Ayres, 'Burlington's Library at Chiswick', *Studies in Bibliography*, xlv (1992), pp. 113–27; Harris 1994, pp. 116, 178n.

83. Chatsworth, 'A Catalogue of the Earl of Burlington's Library at his Lordships Seat at Chiswick', 1742; Harris 1994, pp. 266, 268–70.

84. E. Harris, *Osterley Park, Middlesex*, London 1994, pp. 40–43.

85. Bodley Mus. Bibl. III, 8° 41, *A Catalogue of the Entire and Valuable Library of the Honourable Bryan Fairfax, Esq., One of the Commissioners of His Majesty's Customs, Deceased*, [John Prestage, London 1756], ESTC T187377. A contemporary manuscript note in this records the sale price, the date of March 1756, and the fact that all but twenty of the redundant printed sale catalogues were withdrawn. For Fairfax's other collections see *A Catalogue of the Genuine and Valuable Collection of Italian, Dutch, and Flemish Pictures of the Honourable Bryan Fairfax, Esq; Commissioner of His Majesty's Customs, … Likewise his Antique Marble, Verd Antique, Porphry Busts, Urns, Small Statues, Basso Relievos, Vases, Curious Bronzes, &c.*, J. Prestage, London 6–7 April 1756, ESTC T187377, and *A Catalogue of the Genuine and Valuable Collection of Greek, Roman and English Gold, Silver and Brass Coins, Medals and Medallions, of the Honourable Bryan Fairfax, Esq*, A. Langford, London 24 April 1751, ESTC T14347.

86. T. Morell, *Catalogus Librorum in Bibliotheca Osterleiensi*, [London?] 1771, ESTC N30998.

87. D. Lysons, *The Environs of London*, London 1792–6, ESTC T123547, ii, p. 216.

88. CUL, Inc.I.A.3a[3762] [*Biblia Latina*], [Mainz] 1462, ISTC ib00529000.

89. S. de Ricci, *English Collectors of Books and Manuscripts (1530–1930) and their Marks of Ownership*, Cambridge 1930, pp. 37–38.

90. PML, ChL1691, R. Lefèvre, *The Recuyell of the Historyes of Troye*, [Bruges] 1473 or 1474), ISTC il00117000; STC 15375, ESTC S109298.

91. PML, ChL1759, *The Dictes or Sayengis of the Philosophres*, Westminster 1477, ISTC id00272000; ChL1763, Christine de Pizan, *Morale Proverbes*, Westminster 1478, ISTC ic00473000; ChL1770, *Mirrour of the World*, Westminster 1481, ISTC im00883000; T. Malory,

Le Morte d'Arthur, Westminster 1485, ISTC im00103000; Virgil, *Eneydos*, Westminster 1490, ISTC iv00199000.

92. W. Hayes, *Portraits of Rare and Curious Birds, with their Descriptions, from the Menagery of Osterly Park, in the County of Middlesex*, London 1794[–1800], ESTC T129530.

93. S. Homer, 'The Osterley Menagerie', in T. Knox and A. Palmer (eds), *Aspects of Osterley*, London [2000], pp. 44–9 (p. 49).

94. Evelyn 1955, v, p. 206.

95. H. Snyder, 'Spencer, Charles, Third Earl of Sunderland (1675–1722)', ODNB; Swift 1987, p. 23; *Bibliotheca Sunderlandiana: Sale Catalogue of the Truly Important and Very Extensive Library of Printed Books Known as the Sunderland or Blenheim Library*, Puttick and Simpson, London 1881–3, i, pp. iii–viii.

96. Swift 1987, pp. 1–2, 6; the earliest extant catalogue of the Sunderland collection is JRULM, Eng. Ms. 62, which dates from the second quarter of the eighteenth century.

97. Swift 1987, pp. 9, 14.

98. J. Rocque, *A Plan of the Cities of London and Westminster*, [London] 1746, ESTC N5262.

99. Macky 1723,, i, p. 176, ii, p. 173.

100. BL, Blenheim MS. 61608, cited in Swift 1987, p. 37.

101. *A History of the County of Oxford: volume 12, Wootton Hundred (South) including Woodstock*, ed. Adlan Crossley and C. R. Elrington, London 1990, pp. 448–60.

102. W. Mavor, *New Description of Blenheim*, London 1789, ESTC T077052, pp. 76–80. 103. G. Murphy, 'Thomas, Vaughan (1775–1858)', ODNB.

104. Bodley, 259 d. 39, *Catalogue of the Books in the Library at Blenheim Palace, Collected by Charles, Third Earl of Sunderland*, Oxford 1872, manuscript note signed by W. H. Bliss and G. Parker, 1881.

105. M. Honeybone and Y. Lewis, 'Ellys, Sir Richard (1682–1742)', ODNB; Lysons 1792–6, ii, p. 228.

106. Oxford, Bodleian Library, MS. D.D. Dashwood, b.12/3/1a.

107. Aylesbury, Centre for Buckinghamshire Studies, D/D/3/1–6.

108. *Illuminated Manuscripts, Incunabula and Americana from the Famous Libraries of the Most Hon. the Marquess of Lothian*, Anderson Galleries, New York, 27–28 January 1932.

109. *The Minute-Books of the Spalding Gentlemen's Society, 1712–1755*; Diana and Michael Honeybone (eds), *The Correspondence of the Spalding Gentlemen's Society, 1710–61*, Woodbridge 2010.

110. E. Cannan, rev. R. Hayden, 'Gifford, Andrew (1700–1784)', ODNB; BL, c.188.a.17, *The Newe Testame[n]t as it was Written*, [Worms 1526?], STC 2824, ESTC S90891.

111. NT, Blickling Hall, NT 3031926: *Nouum Testamentum Omne*, Basel 1519; NT 3094690: *Biblia en Lengua Española* [Ferrara 1553].

112. NT, Blickling Hall, NT 3094722.5: *Vetus Testamentum Multipli Linguae Nunc Primo Impressum*, Alcalá de Henares 1514–17.

113. Cambridge, MA, Houghton Library, C 1195.1.5*, R. Ellys, *Fortuita Sacra*, Rotterdam 1727.

114. NT, Blickling Hall, NT 3094668: *The New Testament of our Lord and Saviour Jesus Christ. Translated into the Indian Language, and Ordered to be Printed by the Commissioners of the United Colonies in New England*, Cambridge, MA 1663, Wing B2748, ESTC W7783; NT, Blickling Hall, NT 3109892: *Catalogus Librorum Bibliothecae Collegij Harvardini quod est Cantabrigiae in Nova Anglia*, Boston 1723, ESTC W30259.

115. L. Cowie, *Henry Newman: An American in London, 1708–1743*, London 1956, pp. 193–94.

116. NT, Blickling, NT 3009526; *Gnomologia*, Paris 1512 (uncatalogued).

117. M. Maittaire, *Senilia, Sive Poetica Aliquot*, London 1742), ESTC T91003, pp. 69–71, 115–19.

118. EUL, La.II.90/1 (Letters from John Mitchell to Charles Mackie and letter dated 8 April 1731).

119. G. Mandelbrote and Y. Lewis, *Learning to Collect: The Library of Sir Richard Ellys (1682–1742)*, London 2004, p. 10.

120. H. M. Nixon, *Bookbindings from the Library of Jean Grolier*, London 1965, nos. 9, 13, 26, 95.

121. C. Wright (ed.), *The Diary of Humfrey Wanley*, London 1966, ii, pp. 352–3; the eighth-century Blickling Psalter is now New York, Pierpont Morgan Library, MS. M.776, and the Blickling Homilies, Princeton University Library, Scheide Library M.71.

122. *The Works of the Right Honourable Sir Chas. Hanbury Williams*, London 1822, i, pp. 47–50.

123. *Works of Hanbury Williams* 1822, i, pp. 47–50; L. Cowie, *Henry Newman: An American in London, 1708–43*, pp. 193–4.

124. Harvard, Houghton Library, C 1195.1.5*: R. Ellys, *Fortuita Sacra*, Rotterdam 1727, manuscript note by Thomas Hollis, transcribed in full in N. Barker, *Treasures from the Libraries of National Trust Country Houses*, New York 1999, p. 127.

125. Honeybone 2010, p. 116.

126. NRO, NRS 19373 42 A 4. The total figures break down as £30 30s. for packing, £55 1s. 3d. for packing cases and £62 14s. 5d. for carriage; W. Macray, *Annals of the Bodleian Library*, Oxford 1890, pp. 211–12.

127. NRO, MC 3/252, fol. IV; A. Laing and J. Maddison, 'Lord Hobart's Gallery', in A. Moore and C. Crawley, *Family and Friends: A Regional Survey of Portraits*, London 1992, pp. 39–45.

128. NRO, COL/13/34/35.

129. London, Sir John Soane's Museum, AL.46A (manuscript 'Observations of a Traveller in England Principally on the Seats and Mansions of the Nobility and Gentry …', attributed to William Fremen, d. 1749), pp. 120–22. I am grateful to David Adshead for drawing this reference to my attention.

130. NRO, NRS 14021.

131. NRO, MC 3/289, p. 23.

132. NRO, MC 3/320/1; T. F. Dibdin, *The Library Companion, or the Young Man's Guide and Old Man's Comfort in the Choice of a Library*, London 1824, p. 30; NRO, Colman Papers, unpublished typescript list, p. 71.

133. NRO, COL/13/222/12; G. Fisher and H. Smith, 'John Hungerford Pollen and his Decorative Work at Blickling Hall', *National Trust Year Book* (1975–6), pp. 112–19.

134. NRS, GD40/9/425/8/1.

Chapter Eleven

1. A. Pope, *An Epistle to the Right Honourable Richard, Earl of Burlington*, London 1731, ESTC T5700, p. 11.

2. F. O'Brien, *The Best of Myles: A Selection from 'Cruiskeen Lawn'*, London 1990, pp. 16–23.

3. D. Cavendish, Duchess of Devonshire, *Chatsworth: The House*, London 2002, p. 117.

4. *The Extraordinary Career of the 2nd Earl of Massereene, 1743–1805*, Belfast 1972, p. 46.

5. J. Martin, *Wives and Daughters: Women and Children in the Georgian Country House*, London 2004, p. 242.

6. W. Sherman, *Used Books: Marking Readers in Renaissance England*, Philadelphia 2008, p. 3.

7. M. Purcell, *The Big House Library in Ireland: Books in Ulster Country Houses*, Swindon 2011a, p. 102.

8. G. Trevelyan, *Marginal Notes by Lord Macaulay*, London 1907.

9. W. Lewis, *Horace Walpole's Library*, Cambridge 1958, pp. 23–5.

10. Mary, Countess Cowper, *Diary of Mary Countess Cowper, Lady of the Bedchamber to the Princess of Wales, 1714–1720*, London 1864, p. ix.

11. T. Tanselle, *Other People's Books: Association Copies and the Stories They Tell*, Chicago 2011, pp. 42–5.

12. M. Purcell, 'Making History: the Library at Wallington', *National Trust Historic Houses & Collections Annual* (2014), pp. 16–21; F. Stimpson, 'The Library at Wallington', *Book Collector*, lviii,

I (Spring 2009), pp. 45–72; F. Stimpson, '"I have Spent my Morning Reading Greek": the Marginalia of Sir George Otto Trevelyan', *Library History*, xxiii, 3 (August 2007), pp. 239–50.

13. M. Purcell, W. Hale and D. Pearson, *Treasures from the Library of Lord Fairhaven at Anglesey Abbey*, London 2014, p. 34.

14. I am grateful to Nicholas Pickwoad for this observation.

15. R. North, *The Lives of the Right Hon. Francis North, Baron Guilford, … Sir Dudley North, … and the Rev. Dr. John North*, London 1826, i, p. 19.

16. CALS, DET/3229/77 (Commonplace Book of Elizabeth Sykes, 1793).

17. NUL, Mi LM 31, Mi LM 34 (Manuscript notes on books in the hand of Sir Francis Willoughby, late sixteenth century); E. Rainey, 'The Library of Lord William Howard (1563–1640) from Naworth Castle', *Friends of the National Libraries Annual Report* (1992), pp. 22–3 (p. 22).

18. NUM, Mi LM 15/1 (Commonplace Book of Francis Willoughby the naturalist); KHLC, U269/F38/1 (Commonplace Book of Lady Rachel Fane).

19. E. Potten, '"A Great Number of Usefull Books": the Hidden Library of Henry Booth, 1st Earl of Warrington (1652–1694)', *Library & Information History*, xxv, 1 (March 2009), pp. 33–49.

20. M. McClain, *Beaufort: The Duke and his Duchess, 1657–1715*, New Haven and London 2001, p. 123.

21. *The Orrery Papers*, London 1903, ii, pp. 91, 267.

22. NUM, Mi LM 26 (Cassandra Willoughby, 'An Account of the Willoughbys of Wollaton', 1702), fol. 122r.

23. S. West, 'The Development of Libraries in Norfolk Country Houses, 1660–1830', PhD Thesis, University of East Anglia, 2000, pp. 66–7; M. Worsley, *Jottings*, York 2004, pp. 97–8.

24. C. Gascoygne-Cecil, Marchioness of Salisbury, *An Account of Life at Hatfield House, 1887–1903*, [Hatfield] 1930, p. 16.

25. NLS, MS. 5117–20.

26. ERCRO, DDCC/153/43A/3; DDCC/150/20 (Abstracts of books read by William Constable, mid-eighteenth century).

27. D. Defoe, *A Tour through the Whole Island of Great Britain*, New Haven and London 1991, p. 79.

28. D. Clifford (ed.), *The Diaries of Lady Anne Clifford*, Stroud 1990, pp. 41, 45, 52, 54, 61, 68, etc.; M. Purcell and N. Thwaite, *The Libraries at Calke Abbey*, London [2013], p. 21.

29. H. von Pückler-Muskau, *Tour of England, Ireland, and France, in the Year 1828 & 1829*, London 1832, iv, p. 364.

30. Quoted in I. Grundy, 'Lady Mary Wortley Montagu (bap. 1689, d. 1762)', ODNB.

31. J. Skinner, *Journal of a Somerset Rector*, Oxford 1984, pp. 120, 258.

32. Samuel Johnson and James Boswell, *To the Hebrides: Samuel Johnson's Journey to the Western Islands of Scotland and James Boswell's Journal of a Tour to the Hebrides*, ed. Ronald Black, Edinburgh 2007, pp. 98, 101, 136, 248, 369.

33. A. Hare, *The Story of My Life*, London 1896, iii, pp. 349–51.

34. T. F. Dibdin, *A Bibliographical, Antiquarian and Picturesque Tour in the Northern Counties of England and in Scotland*, London 1838, i, p. 242.

35. WSRO, PHA 5377 ('Catalogus Bibliothecae Petworthianae' [c.1690].

36. NLW, MS. 21244CC (Catalogue of the Libraries at Mostyn and Gloddaeth [1730].

37. D. Clarke, *Arthur Dobbs, Esquire 1689–1765*, London 1958, p. 97; WKC 7/85/14–15 (Letters from H. Repton to Mr Cobb, Felbrigg, 1782–3).

38. Suffro HA519/10; ERCRO, 150/59 ('Etat des livres prétes par Mr Constable à Mr de Villedeuil' [1796].

39. HHC, U DDSY/X2/1/6/108 (letter from J. L. Davis).

40. A. L. Rowse, *A Cornish Childhood*, London 1998, pp. 71–2.

41. G. Edwards, *From Crow-Scaring to Westminster: An Autobiography*, London 1922; F. Ketton-Cremer, *Felbrigg: The Story of a House*, London 1962, pp. 273–4. I am grateful to Merlin Waterson for these references.

42. E. Longley, 'Ledwidge, Francis Edward (1887–1917)', ODNB.

43. F. Willmoth, 'Moore, Sir Jonas (1617–1679)', ODNB.

44. D. Dean, 'Bryant, Jacob (bap. 1717, d. 1804)', ODNB.

45. *Bibliotheca Anglesiana, Sive Catalogus Variorum Librorum in Quavis Linguâ*, London, 1686, A2.

46. Quoted in C. Wright, 'The Dispersal of the Libraries in the Sixteenth Century', in F. Wormald (ed.), *The English Library before 1700*, London 1958, p. 156; Hatfield, 'A Catalogue of all the Printed Bookes in the Library of the Right Honble William Earle of Salisbury, at Salisbury House in the Strand' [1637], list of loans 'at the Latter Ende'.

47. *Historical Manuscripts Commission, Calendar of the Manuscripts of the Marquis of Bath*, Dublin 1907, ii, p. 77; J. Cooper, 'Godolphin, Sir William (b. in or before 1518, d. 1570)', ODNB.

48. KHLC, U269/E2/I ('A Catalogue of my Lord of Dorsetts Books' [c.1651]).

49. DEVRO, Z10/8/5 (Catalogue of the Library at Portledge [c.1683]).

50. NRS, DG3/5/17 (Letter from Countess of Perth to Countess of Eglinton, late seventeenth century).

51. NLS, MS. 6305 ('Catalogue of Books in the Library at Panmure', 1734).

52. NRO, MC 3/320/I.

53. NRS, GD44/53/42/16/27.

54. BLRS, HW87/181 (Letter from Richard How II to David Troup, eighteenth century).

55. LA, I Worsley 59, 1777 ('Catalogue of the Library of Sir Richard Worsley, Bart. of Appuldurcombe Park').

56. NRS, GD224/1063/I (Borrowing Register for Dalkeith Palace, 1795–1832); WSHC, 2057/H5/9 ('Wilton House Library: What Books Taken out, When Taken out, by Whom, and When Returned', 1772–1826); NLI, MS. 34,449 (Borrowers Register for the Library, Abbeyleix [1815–1916]; A. Malcomson, *The De Vesci Papers*, Dublin 2006, p.xiv.

57. Longford, St Mel's College, Catalogue of the Library of the Edgeworth Family, unreferenced, 1831 (=NLI Microfilm P. 7655).

58. NLI, MS. 34,449.

59. H. Slade, *Glamis Castle*, London 2000, p.87.

60. P. Cadell, 'Robertson, William (1740–1803)', ODNB.

61. Brodie Castle, Library Receipt Book (unreferenced).

62. *Memoir of Lady Warwick: also Her Diary*, London 1896, p.44.

63. NT, Felbrigg 1398606.

64. NRO, MC 3/535, 516x4 (Register of Books Borrowed from the Servants' Library at Blickling, 1869); I am grateful to Peter Hoare for the information on Hatfield, where a servants' library existed in 1855: the running number 123 on an extant book, Mottley's 1739 *History of Peter the Great*, suggests that it was substantial. At Hughenden, too, the evidence of a servants' library comes from extant books, for example NT 3085648, Mrs Elwood, *Memoirs of the Literary Ladies of England*, London 1843.

65. J. Fergus, 'Provincial Servants' Reading in the Late Eighteenth Century', in J. Raven, H. Small and N. Tadmor (eds), *The Practice and Representation of Reading in England*, Cambridge 1996, pp.202–25 (pp.222–3).

66. Purcell 2011b.

67. J. Medley, *The Catalogue of the Library*, Tyntesfield, in the County of Somerset, Bristol [1894].

68. Calke Abbey 5.a.71; *Rules for Calke Lending Library*, S.l., n.d..

Chapter Twelve

1. J. Nash, *The Mansions of England in the Olden Times*, London 1839–49; P. Mandler, *The Rise and Fall of the Stately Home*, New Haven and London 1997, pp.40–54.

2. These themes are explored in J. Mordaunt Crook, *The Rise of the Nouveaux Riches*, London 1999, especially pp.7–37.

3. See, too, A. Tinniswood, *The Long Weekend: Life in the English Country House, 1918–1939*, London 2016.

4. H. Heard, *William Armstrong: Magician of the North*, Newcastle 2011, p.123–5.

5. M. Girouard, *The Victorian Country House*, London 1979, pp.305–17 (p.306).

6. Mrs James de Rothschild, *The Rothschilds at Waddesdon Manor*, London 1979, p.18.

7. R. Kerr, *The Gentleman's House*, London 1864, p.116.

8. *Cragside*, London 1990, pp.11–13.

9. Heard 2011, p.216.

10. Heard 2011, pp.215–17.

11. C. Rowell, *Polesden Lacey, Surrey*, London 1999, pp.28, 58, 72–3; J. Lees-Milne, *Diaries, 1942–1945*, London 1998, p.115.

12. *Muckross House, Killarney, National Park*, [Killarney?] [c.2010?], p.11.

13. A. Scott, *Eccentric Wealth: The Bulloughs of Rum*, Edinburgh 2011, pp.5, 20.

14. Scott 2011, pp.158–9.

15. *Treasures of Fyvie*, Edinburgh [1985], p.19.

16. JRULM, Eng. MS. 1140 ('Longford Hall Library Catalogue. Compiled Christmas A.D. 1881').

17. J. Hodges, *Chateau Impney: The Story of a Victorian Country House*, S.l. 2009, pp.85, 100–1; A. Brooks and N. Pevsner, *Worcestershire: The Buildings of England*, New Haven and London 2007, pp.255–6.

18. M. Purcell, 'The Library at Penrhyn Castle', *Book Collector*, lix, 2 (Summer 2010), pp.241–50; M. Purcell, 'National Trust Libraries in Wales', *National Trust Historic Houses and Collections Annual* (2011b), pp.12–19 (p.19).

19. A. Laing, *In Trust for the Nation: Paintings from National Trust Houses*, London 1995, pp.94–5.

20. *Catalogue of Books Comprising the Property of Sir Francis Peel, Bt., the Property of Major and Mrs Disraeli, and Other Properties*, Sotheby's, London 22–23 February 1937, lots 404–579.

21. M. Spevack, 'The Library at Hughenden Manor', *Book Collector*, lix, 4 (Winter 2010), pp.547–80.

22. B. Bloomfield (ed.), *A Directory of Rare Books and Special Collections in the United Kingdom and the Republic of Ireland*, 2nd edn., London 1997, pp.683–4.

23. Quoted in R. Blake, *Disraeli*, London 1998, p.410.

24. J. Miller, *Fertile Fortune: The Story of Tyntesfield*, London 2003, pp.67–72.

25. Miller 2003, pp.114–15.

26. H. Meller, 'Knightshayes Court: Reconstructing a Victorian Library Room', *Library History*, xviii, 3 (November 2002), pp.235–40.

27. A. Quiney, *John Loughborough Pearson*, London 1979, pp.30–34.

28. Miller 2003 p.72.

29. J. B. Medley, *The Catalogue of the Library at Tyntesfield, in the County of Somerset*, [Bristol 1894]; NT 3139650, 'Library Entry-Book for Volumes Taken Out' [1894–1911].

30. M. Daunton, 'Gibbs, Henry Hucks, First Baron Alderton (1819–1907)', ODNB.

31. *A Catalogue of Some Printed Books and Manuscripts at St Dunstan's, Regent's Park, and Aldenham House, Herts, collected by Henry Hucks Gibbs*, London 1888; *Catalogue of the Aldenham Library: Mainly Collected by Henry Hucks Gibbs, First Lord Aldenham*, Letchworth 1914.

32. NT, Tyntesfield, NT 3143905: H. Gibbs, *The Game of Ombre*, London 1878.

33. T. Fry, *A Brief Memoir of Francis Fry, F.S.A. of Bristol*, S.l. 1887.

34. B. Quaritch Ltd, *A General Catalogue of Books Offered to the Public at Fixed Prices*, London 1887–97; A. Freeman, 'Quaritch, Bernard Alexander Christian (1819–1899)', ODNB.

35. Quoted in Mordaunt Crook 1999, p.5.

36. S. de Ricci, *A Hand-List of a Collection of Books and Manuscripts Belonging to the Right Hon. Lord Amherst of Hackney*, Cambridge 1906; A. Bell, 'Amherst, William Amhurst Tyssen-, First Baron Amherst of Hackney (1835–1909)', ODNB; R. Landon, 'Two Collectors: Thomas Grenville and Lord Amherst', in W. Kirsop (ed.), *The Commonwealth of Books: Essays and Studies in Honour of Ian Willison*, Clayton, Victoria 2007, pp.78–95 (pp.84–95).

37. J. Ing Freeman, 'Miller, William Henry (1789–1848)', ODNB; R. Pelik, *C. W. Dyson Perrins, D.C.L., J.P., D.L., F.S.A.: A Brief Account of his Life, his Achievements, his Collections and Benefactions*, Worcester 1983, pp.4–5.

38. *The Britwell Handlist*; for the sale catalogues, see de Ricci 1930, pp.109–13.

39. Pelik 1983, p.15; G. Warner, *Descriptive Catalogue of Illuminated Manuscripts in the Library of C. W. Dyson Perrins*, Oxford 1920; *The Dyson Perrins Collection: Catalogue of … Illuminated Manuscripts … which will be Sold by Sotheby & Co.*, Sotheby's, London 1958–60.

40. G. Barber, *The James A. de Rothschild Bequest at Waddesdon Manor, the National Trust: Printed Books and Bookbindings*, Waddesdon 2013, i, p.61.

41. Barber 2013, i, p.76.

42. Barber 2013, i, pp.51.

43. Barber 2013, i, pp.58, 69.

44. Barber 2013, i, pp.76–77.

45. Barber 2013, i, pp.52, 80.

46. *Catalogue des Livres français de la Bibliothèque de Baron Ferdinand de Rothschild à Waddesdon*, [London] 1897; D. McKitterick, *Old Books, New Technologies: The Representation, Conservation and Transformation of Books since 1700*, Cambridge 2013, pp.119–30.

47. L. Delaissé, J. Marrow and J. de Wit, *The James A. de Rothschild Collection at Waddesdon Manor: Illuminated Manuscripts*, [Fribourg] 1977, pp.10–11.

48. Barber 2013, w24, 29, 49, 77, 128, 139, 140, 171, 190, 194, 237, 296, 323, 366, 383, 389, 397, 513, 514, 515, 541, 566, 626, 646, 664 (Hamilton Palace), w153, 588, 592, 626, 690, 761 (Gosford), w466 (Apethorpe), w665 (Burton Constable), w104, 386, 702, 730 (Strawberry Hill), w491 (Syston), w412 (the Osterley Loggan).

49. Listed in *The Britwell Handlist*, pp.vii–xiv.

Chapter Thirteen

1. P. Mandler, *The Fall and Rise of the Stately Home*, New Haven and London 1997, p.118; A. Howkins, *Reshaping Rural England: A Social History*, London 1991, pp.138–40.

2. D. Cannadine, 'Aristocratic Indebtedness in the Nineteenth Century', in D. Cannadine, *Aspects of Aristocracy: Grandeur and Decline in Modern Britain*, New Haven and London 1994, pp.37–54 (p.50).

3. C. Bailey, *The Secret Rooms*, London 2013, p.164.

4. D. French, *Ishbel and the Empire: A Biography of Lady Aberdeen*, Toronto and Oxford 1988, p.299.

5. CBS, D56/7/47.

6. G. Worsley, 'Beyond the Powerhouse: Understanding the Country House in the Twenty-First Century', *Historical Research*, lxxviii, 201 (August 2005), pp.423–5 (p.429).

7. Massingberd, *Burke's Landed Gentry* (1972), introduction.

8. M. Ogilvy, Countess of Airlie, *Thatched with Gold: The Memoirs of Mabell, Countess of Airlie*, Leicester 1962, p.191.

9. J. Pearson, *Stags and Serpents: A History of the Cavendish Family and the Dukes of Devonshire*, London 1983, p.265.

10. M. Airs, 'Triumph against the Odds: the English Country House in the 20th Century', in M. Airs (ed.), *The Twentieth-Century Great House*, Oxford 2002, pp.1–14 (p.4).

11. http://webarchive.nationalarchives.gov. uk/20130217082231/http://www.hmrc.gov.uk/ history/taxhis3.htm> (accessed 29 March 2016).

12. *Bibliotheca Illustris: sive Catalogus Variorum in Quâvis Linguâ & Facultate …*, London 21 November 1687, Wing A801A, ESTC R282.

13. G. Mandelbrote, 'The Library of the Duke of Lauderdale (1616–82)', in C. Rowell (ed.), *Ham House*, New Haven and London 2013, pp.222–9.

14. KHLC, U120/Z4 ('A Catalogue of Sir Edward Filmer's Books', 1729).

15. J. Johnson, 'Brydges, James, First Duke of Chandos (1674–1744)', ODNB; *Wanstead House, Essex. Magnificent Furniture, Collection of Fine Paintings and Sculpture, Massive Silver & Gilt Plate, Splendid Library of Choice Books*, London 1822 (marked-up copy, Colchester, Essex Record Office, D/DU7).

16. *A Catalogue of the Duplicate Part of the Library of a Nobleman: Comprehending a Large Collection of Books of Natural History*, [R. Robson] London 1792, ESTC T150834; MMBL, ii, p.264.

17. For description of the libraries and their fittings, see H. Foster, *The Stowe Catalogue, Priced and Annotated*, London 1848, pp.xxxv–xxxviii, pp.56–7, 245–6; for the books, see *Catalogue of the Library Removed from Stowe House, Buckinghamshire*, Leigh & Sotheby, London 8 January 1848.

18. B. Disraeli, *Letters*, Toronto 1982–2014, v, p.52.

19. A. N. L. Munby, 'The Library', in *The Destruction of the Country House, 1875–1975*, London 1974, pp.106–11 (p.107).

20. Cardiff, Glamorgan Archives, DF/F/12 (will of Robert Jones of Fonmon, 1711).

21. Devro, 1706M/F2.

22. HALS, D/ECP/F18 ('Catalogue of the Library at Cassiobury, Watford. Bequeathed by the Will of the Rt. Hon. George Capel Coningsby, Earl of Essex, To go as Heirlooms with the Cassiobury Estate', 1839).

23. *The Settled Land Act*, 1882, 45 & 46 Vict., c. 38. The crucial clause is 37 (1): 'Where personal chattels are settled on trust so as to devolve with land until a tenant in tail by purchase is born or attains the age of twenty-one years, or so as otherwise to vest in some person becoming entitled to an estate of freehold of inheritance in the land, a tenant for life of the land may sell the chattels or any of them'. Under clause 37 (3) this provision could not be invoked without the permission of the Court of Chancery. The related legislation for Scotland is: *An Act to Amend the Law of Entail in Scotland*, 45 & 46 Vict., c. 53.

24. *An Act to Extend the Power of Sale Contained in the Resettlement of the Blenheim Settled Estates to the Sunderland Library; and for Other Purposes*, 43 & 44 Vict, c. 1.

25. H. Spencer-Churchill, *Blenheim and the Churchill Family: A Personal Portrait*, London 2005, pp.156–7; *Catalogue of the Books in the Library at Blenheim Palace, Collected by Charles, Third Earl of Sunderland*, Oxford 1872; *Bibliotheca Sunderlandiana: Catalogue of the Sunderland Library Removed from Blenheim Palace*, Puttick and Simpson, London 1881–3.

26. Munby 1974, p.108.

27. CBS, D-MH(addn)/1/29.

28. P. Lichfield, *Not the Whole Truth: An Autobiography*, London 1987, p.18.

29. M. Waterson, *The Country House Remembered: Recollections of Life Between the Wars*, London 1985, p.115.

30. JRULM, EGR4/6/5/4 (Letter from Stamford to the Revd Harry Gray).

31. *The Osterley Park Library: Catalogue of this Most Important Collection of Books, the Property of the Rt. Hon. the Earl of Jersey*, Sotheby, Wilkinson & Hodge, London 6 May 1885.

32. *Catalogue of an Important Portion of the Extensive and Valuable Library of the late Sir John Hayford Thorold, Bart*, Sotheby, Wilkinson & Hodge, London 12–20 December 1884.

33. For an overview of the palace and its demise, see I. Gow, *Scotland's Lost Houses*, London 2006, pp.27–33, and G. Walker, *Hamilton Palace: A Photographic Record*, Hamilton 1987).

34. *The Hamilton Palace Libraries. Catalogue … of the Beckford Library, Removed from Hamilton Palace …*, Sotheby, Wilkinson & Hodge, London 30 June & 11 December 1882, 2 July & 27 November 1883; *The Hamilton Palace Libraries. Catalogue of the Hamilton Library*, Sotheby, Wilkinson & Hodge, London 1–9 May 1884; *The Hamilton Palace Libraries. Catalogue of … Books Returned from the Sale of the Beckford & Hamilton Libraries, Having Been Bound Imperfect …*, Sotheby, Wilkinson & Hodge, London 8 July 1884.

35. S. Leslie, *Long Shadows*, London 1966, p.246.

36. Bodley, Hanson 121(3): *Catalogue of the Fine, Extensive and Valuable Library of the Rt. Hon. the Earl of Gosford, K.P. … To be Sold by Messrs Puttick and Simpson on Monday 21 April 1884*, Puttick and Simpson, London [1884].

37. *The Times*, 24 April 1884.

38. *Catalogue of the Clandon Library: in Which is Included the Collection of Books Formed by the Rt. Hon. Arthur Onslow, XXXIII Years Speaker of the House of Commons, Many Enriched with his Autograph Notes, The whole the Property of the the the Trustees of the Will of the Late Earl of Onslow*, Sotheby, Wilkinson & Hodge, London 20–21 March 1885.

39. *Catalogue of Valuable Old English Books and Manuscripts Selected from the Library of a Gentleman in the Country …*, Sotheby's, London 17–18 June 1904.

40. NorthRO, 1/9/7.

41. M. McLaggan, 'The Library of a Bibliomaniac Great-Grandfather', in R. Myers and M. Harris (ed.), *Bibliophily*, Cambridge 1986, pp. 121–37.

42. *Catalogue of a Choice Selected Portion of the Famous Library Removed from Sudbury Hall, Derbyshire, Including Illuminated and Other Manuscripts, and Rare Printed Books, the Property of Lieut. Lord Vernon, R.N.*, Sotheby, Wilkinson & Hodge, London 10 June 1918.

43. *Downing Hall, near Holywell. Catalogue of Sale of the Remainder of the Downing Library (formed by Thomas Pennant, the well-known Antiquary and Naturalist*, William Dew, Bangor 26–28 May 1913).

44. *Catalogue of the Renowned Library Removed from Ham House, Surrey*, Sotheby's, London 30–31 May 1938; M. Purcell, 'Clumber: the Rise and Fall of a Ducal Library', *Library & Information History*, xxxii, 1–2 (2016), pp. 88–99.

45. *Catalogue of Rare Books, the Property of W. R. Phelips, Esq. of Montacute House, Montacute, Somerset*, Knight, Frank & Rutley, London 17 November 1915, lots 1–124; further books from this library were sold in 1930: *Catalogue of Printed Books and a Few Manuscripts …*, Sotheby's, London 1930, lots 923–1042; *Catalogue of Books, Pictures and Furniture. By Order of the Executors; also the Property of a Gentleman, removed from Hastings; the Property of a Lady, and from Other Sources*, Knight, Frank & Rutley, London 14 January 1916.

46. *Catalogue of a Portion of the Valuable Library of a Noble* [i.e. the 13th Earl of Westmorland], Sotheby, Wilkinson & Hodge, London 13–15 July 1887; *Catalogue of Exceedingly Rare and Valuable Americana, with Some Important English Books & Manuscripts, Largely from the Library of Henry Percy (1564–1632) at Petworth House*, Sotheby's, London 23–24 April 1928.

47. Leslie 1966, p. 246.

48. M. Purcell, 'Libraries at Lacock Abbey', *National Trust Historic Houses & Collections Annual* (2012), pp. 36–43.

49. *Irish Times*, 19 December 1884, p. 5.

50. WSCH, 383/20.

51. *Catalogue of the Library Removed from Stourhead*, Sotheby, Wilkinson & Hodge, London 30 July–7 August 1883, p. 3; a second sale was held in 1887: *Catalogue of the Remaining Portion of the Library, Removed from Stourhead*, Sotheby, Wilkinson & Hodge, London 9–13 December 1887.

52. WSHC, 383/20 (Exchange of lawyers' letters, headed 'Stourhead Heir Looms', 1883); for the Wavendon books and their transfer to Stourhead, see WSHC, 383/17 ('Inventory of Books on the Premises, Wavendon House, Woburn, Beds', 1852).

53. WSHC, 383/20.

54. D. Green, *The Churchills of Blenheim*, London 1984, p. 116.

55. A. May, 'Philip Henry, Eleventh Marquess of Lothian (1882–1940)', ODNB.

56. *Illuminated Manuscripts, Incunabula, and Americana from the Famous Libraries of the Most Hon., the Marquess of Lothian, C.H., sold by his Order, Removed from Blickling Hall, Norfolk and Newbattle Abbey, Midlothian*, American Art Association, Anderson Galleries, New York 27–28 January 1932. For the background on Anderson Galleries, the American Art Society and New York art market in the 30s, see T. Norton, *100 Years of Collecting in America: The Story of Sotheby Parke Bernet*, New York 1984, pp. 14, 51; see, too, B. Boyce, *Collecting Blickling III: The Lothian Collection and the Book Sale of the Century*, S.l. 2013.

57. Leslie 1966, pp. 248–9; J. Butler, *Lord Lothian (Philip Kerr), 1882–1940*, London 1960, pp. 151–2; Norton 1984, p. 116.

58. James Lees-Milne, *Ancestral Voices*, London 1984, p. 112.

59. ESRO, BMV/A/10/109 ('Fire Place Inventory and Valuation, April 1939').

60. For the same room as it was in 1963, see Dublin, Irish Architectural Archive, 18/35, 710–11.

61. J. Martin Robinson, *Requisitioned: The British Country House in the Second World War*, London 2014, p. 44.

62. B. Bloomfield (ed.), *A Directory of Rare Books and Special Collections in the United Kingdom and the Republic of Ireland*, London 1994, p. 541; the Long Library in wartime is illustrated in Robinson 2014, pp. 46, 49.

63. WRO, CR1998/778/10; Lees-Milne 1984, p. 53.

64. CALS, DBC 2309/2/17; Robinson 2014, p. 25.

65. James Lees-Milne, *Diaries, 1942–1945*, London 1998, pp. 157–8.

66. M. Purcell, 'The Library at Lanhydrock', *Book Collector*, liv (2005), pp. 193–230 (p. 219); *Notes on Hatfield House*, S.l. 1886, pp. 9–10.

67. V. Murray, *Castle Howard: The Life and Times of a Stately Home*, London 1994, p. 221.

68. NT Sound Archive, Tape 183 (Blickling Hall); I am grateful to Amy Speckhart for this reference.

69. D. James, *The Gore-Booths of Lissadell*, Dublin 2004, p. 339.

70. F. Herrmann, 'The Role of the Auction Houses', in G. Mandelbrote (ed), *Out of Print and into Profit*, London 2006, pp. 3–34.

71. *Catalogue. Morval. … At the Above Mansion, the Whole of the Antique and Modern Furniture, Library of about 4,000 Vols. of Books*, Skardon and Sons, Plymouth 28–30 April & 1–4 May 1891; M. Purcell, 'From Bury to Bromham: Books at Canons Ashby', *National Trust Historic Houses and Collections Annual* (2010), pp. 18–25 (p. 24): a copy of the now very rare 1980 sale catalogue, annotated by Martin Drury, is in the files of the National Trust's Libraries Curator.

72. *Bodysgallen Hall, Llanrhos – Llandudno … Catalogue of the Important, Interesting, and Valuable Contents of this Historic Mansion*, Blomfield & Co., Llandudno 6–8 September 1967, pp. 30–34; *Stackpole Court, Pembrokeshire. Catalogue of the Important Three Days' Sale of Furniture & Effects …*, Strutt & Parker, London 19–21 November 1962.

73. HALS, D/EP/E80: *Panshanger, Hertford: Catalogue of the Part of the Library to be Sold by Auction upon the Premises on Wednesday, 9th September 1953*, Humbert & Flint [London 1953]; CALS, DBC 2309/2/7: *Catalogue of Sale of a Large Portion of the Valuable Period Furniture and Secondary Furnishings, Vale Royal*, Brown's, Chester 9–10 October 1946).

74. J. Bernasconi, *Inventory Work and Catalogues: A Concise Guide for the Compiler of Auction Catalogues of Furniture, Silver, etc., the Organisation of the Auction Sale and Inventories for Various Purposes*, London [1962?], p. 64.

75. *A Catalogue of a Collection of Books Relating to English & Foreign Literature forming the Library of Richard Brinsley Sheridan*, London 1884.

76. Munby 1974, pp. 106–7.

77. WSHC, 2057/H6/28, a marked-up copy of *Catalogue of Printed Books, Comprising the Property of Dr P. H. Plesch, the Property of the Late M. Fernand Vellut, and Other Properties*, Sotheby's, London 13–14 July 1964.

78. C. Edmonds, 'Exploration of Old Libraries', *The Athenaeum*, 16 May 1885.

79. NUL, Ma 7 1/5 ('Thoresby Library, Contents of Shelves', 1946).

80. http://www.quaritch.com/about/our-history/ (accessed 25 March 2016); *A General Catalogue of Books offered to the Public at the Affixed Prices by Bernard Quaritch*, London 1887–92.

81. F. Herrmann, 'Sotheby family (*per.* 1778–1861)', ODNB; see, too, his *Sotheby's: A Portrait of an Auction House*, London 1980.

82. Herrmann 2006, pp. 3–34 (pp. 17–21); for the library in better times, see Carlisle Archive Centre, DLONS/L/23/1/33 ('Catalogue of Books in the Library, Lowther' [1903]).

83. S. Markham, *A Book of Booksellers: Conversations with the Antiquarian Book Trade, 1991–2003*, London 2004, p. 243.

84. L. Farnham, *A Glance at Private Libraries*, Boston 1855, pp. 5–6.

85. S. de Ricci, *Census of Medieval and Renaissance Manuscripts in the United States and Canada*, New York 1935–40, i, p. 267; for the Warwick library, see WRO, CR1998/807/33 ('Catalogue of Books in Library & Cedar Lobby', 1914), and for the Shakespeare Library, Folger, W.a.254, 'Warwick Castle Library Shakespeare Collection: A Bibliographical Catalogue of the Books and Manuscripts Illustrating the Life and Works of William Shakespeare', 1890, and M.b.31: 'A Bibliographical Catalogue of the Books and Manuscripts Illustrating the Life and Works of William Shakespeare' (1889–90).

86. *The Huntington Library: Treasures from Ten Centuries*, San Marino, CA 2004, p. 12; James Thorpe, Robert R. Wark and Ray Allen Billington, *The Founding of the Henry E. Huntington Library and Art Gallery: Four Essays*, San Marino, CA 1969, p. 33.

87. *Huntington Library* 2004, p. 9; Thorpe et al. 1969, pp. 351, 36.

88. For correspondence on this sale, see WSRO PET/2974–95.

89. *The Athenaeum*, no. 4305 (30 April 1910), p. 524; D. Dickinson, *Henry E. Huntington's Library of Libraries*, San Marino, CA 1995, p. 67.

90. Leslie 1966, pp. 248–9.

91. W. Lewis, *Horace Walpole's Library*, Cambridge 1958, pp. 58–9.

92. Cambridge, MA, Houghton Library, *EC.A100.B659c.

93. *Supplement to the Census of Medieval and Renaissance Manuscripts in the United States and Canada*, New York 1962, pp. 226, 247, 367–8, 435.

94. A. West, *The Shakespeare First Folio: The History of the Book. Volume II: A New Worldwide Census of First Folios*, Oxford 2003, pp. 247–50, no. 145.

95. *Boston Globe*, 6 July 1953. I am grateful to Susan Hill Dolan of Castle Hill for a copy of this article.

96. K. Sinclair, *Descriptive Catalogue of Medieval and Renaissance and Western Manuscripts in Australia*, [Sydney] 1969, pp. 18–40; www.nla.gov.au/selected-library-collections/clifford-collection (accessed 12 March 2016); Bloomfield 1994, p. 57.

97. Pearson 1983, p. 285–7.

98. For details of the settlement, see D. Cavendish, Duchess of Devonshire, *Chatsworth: The House*, London 2002, pp. 232–5.

99. BL, Add. MS. 49598; W. Jackson, 'A Dibdinian Tour (1938)', in W. Jackson, *Records of a Bibliographer*, Cambridge, MA 1967, pp. 67–82 (p. 79); C. Wright, *The Diary of Humfrey Wanley*, London 1966, i, pp. 19, 42, 76–7, 106–7; C. Wright, 'The Benedictional of St Aethelwold', *British Museum Quarterly*, xxvii (1963), pp. 3–5.

100. Pearson 1983, p. 301; A. Cavendish, 11th Duke of Devonshire, *Accidents of Fortune*, Norwich 2004, p. 119.

101. WSHC, 2057/E2/10.

102. A. Cavendish 2004, p. 44.

103. Munby 1974, p. 107.

104. See, for example, M. Sroka, '"Forsaken and Abandoned": the Nationalization and Salvage of Deserted, Displaced, and Private Library Collections in Poland, 1945 to 1948', *Library & Information History*, xxviii, 4 (December 2012), pp. 272–88.

105. *Catalogue of Books and Manuscripts, also Autograph Letters & Historical Documents, Comprising the Property of the late W. Crambe Reid; … the Property of the late Horace W, Sandars; … the Property of the Countess of Ancaster; … the Property of Sir Henry Paston Bedingfeld, Bt. …*, Sotheby's, London 26 July 1922, lots 561–613.

106. *Catalogue of Valuable Printed Books, Autograph Letters and Historical Documents, etc. Comprising a Selection from the Library at Naworth Castle, Cumberland*, Sotheby's, London 27–28 October 1947).

107. *Catalogue of a Selected Portion of the Valuable Library at Wentworth Woodhouse, Rotherham the Property of the Rt. Honble. Earl Fitzwilliam, … The First Portion*, Sotheby's, London 1–2 March 1948; *Catalogue of a Selected Portion of the Valuable Library at Wentworth Woodhouse, Rotherham, the Property of the Rt. Honble Earl Fitzwilliam. The Second and Final Portion*, Sotheby's, London 26–28 April 1948; see, too, G. Jackson-Stops (ed.), *The Treasure Houses of Britain: Five Hundred Years of Private Patronage and Collecting*, Washington 1985, p. 407; H. George Fletcher (ed.), *The Wormsley Library: A Personal Selection by Sir Paul Getty*, London 1999, pp. 44–7.

108. Jackson 1967, p. 75.

109. *The Hurn Court Library: The Property of the Right Honourable the Earl of Malmesbury*, Sotheby's, London 9–10, 30–31 March & 27–28 April 1950).

110. *Catalogue of Valuable Printed Books, Autograph Letters, Historical Documents, etc., Comprising Travel Books with Coloured Plates on Ornithology, Botany, etc., the Property of the Lady Janet Douglas Pennant, removed from Penrhyn, Wales …*, Sotheby's, London 6 July 1953, lots 1–71; A. West 2003, no. 200.

111. *Catalogue of Valuable Printed Books, Autograph Letters and Historical Documents*, Sotheby's, London 14 October 1946.

112. NLI, MS. 35,542(1) (Materials relating to the Attack on Castlecomer House, 1798).

113. *An Act to Amend the Law Relating to the Occupation and Ownership of Land in Ireland and for other Purposes Relating thereto and to amend the Labourers (Ireland) Acts*, 3 Ed. 7, c. 37 [14 August 1903]; M. Purcell, *The Big House Library in Ireland: Books in Ulster Country Houses*, Swindon 2011a, pp. 16–17.

114. Leslie 1966, p 131.

115. NLI, MS. 35.263: *Catalogue of the Books in the Library of the Right Honorable [sic] Mervyn Richard, Lord Viscount Powerscourt*, S.l. [1907].

116. These events are helpfully summarised in M. Bence-Jones, *Twilight of the Ascendancy*, London 1993, a personal and elegiac account usefully read in conjunction with the more hard-headed analyses provided in T. Dooley, *The Decline of the Big House in Ireland*, Dublin 2001, and O. Purdue, *The Big House in the North of Ireland*, Dublin 2009.

117. NLI, MS. 36,378/7 ('Valuation of Household Furniture and Effects at Annaghmore', 1939).

118. Dooley 2001, pp. 172–3.

119. Dooley 2001, pp. 286–7.

120. Purdue 2009, pp. 145–9.

121. *The Times*, 22 January 1981.

122. *Irish Times*, 23 June 1919.

123. *Irish Times*, 23 February 1982.

124. Dooley 2001, p. 181.

125. D. Fitzpatrick, *Politics and Irish Life, 1913–1921: Provincial Experience of War and Revolution*, Dublin 1977, p. 56.

126. *Catalogue of a Collection of Important Books Selected from the Library at Carton, Co. Kildare*, Bennet and Son, Dublin 11 November 1925.

127. *Irish Times*, 6 June 1949.

128. *Irish Times*, 18 July 2011.

129. C. Smythe, 'Coole Library', *The Private Library*, vi, 2 (Summer 1973), pp. 75–82; A. Gregory, *Coole*, Dublin 1931, pp. 1–21.

130. K. Mulligan, *Ballyfin: The Restoration of an Irish House & Demesne*, London 2011, pp. 47–9, 73, 79.

131. For the contents of this library in its heyday, see NLI, MS. 38.628/7/(2) (Inventory of

the Books of the Earl of Wicklow at Shelton Abbey, *c.*1800), and for a final view of some of the contents, *Catalogue of a Selected Portion of the Library at Shelton Abbey, the Property of the Rt. Honble. the Earl of Wicklow*, Sotheby's, London 11–12 December 1950.

132. *Irish Times*, 29 April 1995, p.24, 18 November 1995, p.25 (the sale on 6 December); for the Clonbrock library in the nineteenth century, see NLI, MS. 19,947 (Library Catalogue, Clonbrock, County Galway, May 1807), MS19.949 (Library Catalogue, Clonbrock [1825?]) and NLI MS. 22,177 (Accounts from Booksellers sent to Luke Dillon, 2nd Lord Clonbrock, 1780–1826 and 1800–4), and P. Melvin, *Estates and Landed Society in Galway*, Dublin 2012, p.153.

133. *Irish Times*, 2 November 1976.

134. *Irish Times*, 28 June 1955, 19 November 1983.

135. *Catalogue of Printed Books, Comprising the Extensive Collection of Books on Ornithology and Natural History, the Property of the Revd. J. M. McWilliam …. Books on Art the Property of Mrs Thomas Lowinsky, the Property of the Late Franker Porter, Esq. Well-Bound Sporting Books and Others with Coloured Plates, Botanical Books, Nineteenth-Century Novels, etc, including the Property of Mrs. O. Hales Pakenham-Mahon, Strokestown Park, Co. Roscommon, Ireland …*, Sotheby's, London 1–3 December 1952, lots 587–708.

136. L. Morris, *Rosenbach Redux: Further Book Adventures in England and Ireland*, Philadelphia 1989, pp.26–35; P. Fox, *Trinity College Library, Dublin: A History*, Cambridge 2014, p.317.

137. James 2004, p.343–5; *Lissadell, Co. Sligo*, Christie's, London 25 November 2003, lots 84–5, 530–636.

138. PRONI, D4131/D/I/I (a box of documents relating to chattels at Lissadell, including correspondence and library shelf-lists from 1853 and 1951).

139. 'History Crumbles as Heiress is Gaoled', *Daily Telegraph*, 26 September 2002.

Chapter Fourteen

1. The designs, by George Trollope of London, are now StaffRO, D4893/A/B/2/v–xii.

2. J. Lees-Milne, *Diaries, 1942–45*, London 1998, pp.95–6.

3. V. Leatham, *Burghley: The Life of a Great House*, London 1992, p.203

4. A. Levin, *Raine and Johnnie: The Spencers and the Scandal of Althorp*, London 1993, p.223.

5. M. Purcell, 'The Country House Library Reassess'd:, Or Did the "Country House Library"

Ever Really Exist', *Library History*, xviii, 3 (November 2002), pp.157–74 (p.170).

6. J. McDonald, *Alnwick Castle: Home of the Duke and Duchess of Northumberland*, London 2012, p.67.

7. F. Cox, *Osterley Park Library*, [London?] 1926.

8. *Beaulieu: Beaulieu Abbey, Palace House, National Motor Museum*, Beaulieu [2013], p.4.

9. J. Martin Robinson, *The Architecture of Northern England*, London 1986, p.158.

10. *Croft Castle, Herefordshire*, London 2000, pp.9, 12.

11. A thousand volumes of books were sold jointly by W.J. Phillips of Aberaeron and Messrs Gurr, Johns and Co. (London) in October 1918. A catalogue was printed, priced at 6d (no copy traced) but the sale was advertised in the *Welsh Gazette*, 18 July 1918.

12. D. Vaisey, 'Obituary: W. O. Hassall', *The Independent*, 28 July 1994.

13. D. Cavendish, Duchess of Devonshire, *The House: A Portrait of Chatsworth*, London 1982, pp.76–84.

14. S. Markham, *A Book of Booksellers: Conversations with the Antiquarian Book Trade, 1991–2003*, London 2004, p.19.

15. R. Gascoyne-Cecil, 6th Marquess of Salisbury, *The Hatfield House Library: A Family Collection of over Four Hundred Years*, [New York 1967].

16. M. Worsley, *Jottings*, York 2004, pp.97–8; Leatham 1992, p.203.

17. BAL, PA 998/2(1–3) (Julian Bicknell, 'Preliminary and Alternative Designs for Fittings for the Library of Castle Howard').

18. BAL, 21564, CT570 (Roderick Gradidge in association with David Hicks, 'Easton Neston, Northamptonshire: Library created from a Sitting Room').

19. D. Cavendish 1982, p.162.

20. J. Cornforth, *The Search for a Style: Country Life and Architecture, 1897–1935*, London 1988, p.73.

21. J. Gretton, *Essays in Book-Collecting*, Dereham 1985, pp.41–7.

22. N. Major, *Chequers: The Prime Minister's Country House and its History*, London 1996, pp.138–41.

23. G. Pollard, 'Changes in the Style of Bookbinding, 1550–1830', *The Library* (1956), 5th series, xi, 2, pp.71–94 (p.73).

24. J. Bryant, *The Iveagh Bequest, Kenwood House*, London 1990, p.28.

25. I am grateful to Adam Nicolson for details.

26. Cornforth 1988, p.192.

27. A. Clark, *Diaries: Into Politics, 1972–1982*, London 2001, p.86.

28. T. Richardson, 'What Drives People to Steal Precious Books', *Financial Times*, 6 March 2009.

29. D. Drummond, 17th Earl of Perth, 'The Library at Stobhall', *Bulletin du Bibliophile* (1984), pp.301–6; 'The Earl of Perth' (Obituary), *Daily Telegraph*, 29 November 2002.

30. *The Wardington Library: Incunabula and the Wardington Hours*, Sotheby's, London 5 December 2006, pp.8–11.

31. K. Mulligan, *Ballyfin: The Restoration of an Irish House & Demesne*, [Tralee] 2011, pp.73, 113–16.

32. Dominic Winter, *A Gentleman's Library*, Dominic Winter Auctioneers, Swindon, 20 September 2012.

33. P. Minet, 'A Century of Innovation in Selling Books', in G. Mandelbrote (ed.), *Out of Print & Into Profit: A History of the Rare and Secondhand Book Trade in Britain in the Twentieth Century*, London 2006, pp.63–73 (p.71).

34. A. Hobson, 'Abbey, John Roland (1894–1969)', ODNB; A. Hobson and A. N. L. Munby, 'Contemporary Collectors xxvi: John Roland Abbey', *Book Collector*, x (1961), pp.40–48; A. Hobson, *Major Abbey's Bindings in the Saleroom*, London 1966.

35. H. George Fletcher (ed.), *The Wormsley Library: A Personal Selection by Sir Paul Getty, KBE*, 2nd edn., London 2007, pp.x–ix.

36. Robinson 1986, p.24.

37. C. O'Brien, 'Ralph Dutton and Ronald Fleming at Hinton Ampner House: Revivalist Tastes in Interior Decoration', *Apollo*, April 1997, pp.43–7; HRO 63M84/F9/6 ('Hinton Ampner House … Inventory & Valuation', 1946).

38. Y. Lewis, '"Appropriate for a County House?": Rebuilding Ralph Dutton's Library at Hinton Ampner', *National Trust Arts, Building & Collections Bulletin* (May 2013).

39. M. Purcell, W. Hale and D. Pearson, *Treasures from Lord Fairhaven's Library at Anglesey Abbey*, London 2013, pp.32–8.

40. *Punch*, 22 January 1947.

41. *Illuminated Manuscripts, Incunabula and Americana from the Famous Libraries of the Most Hon. The Marquess of Lothian, Sold by his Order, Removed from Blickling Hall, Norfolk and Newbattle Abbey, Midlothian*, Anderson Galleries, New York 27–28 January 1932. The Blickling Psalter (lot 1) and the Blickling Homilies (lot 2) are now in the Pierpont Morgan Library at the Scheide Collection, Princeton, respectively.

42. G. Jackson-Stops, 'The National Trust and the In Lieu System', in *Patronage Preserved: An Exhibition of Masterpieces Saved for Country Houses*, London 1991, pp.16–20 (pp.16–17).

43. *Magnificent Plate Books from the Library of the Earl of Bradford*, Sotheby's, London 15 March 2000, p.8.

44. J. Moore, 'Filling the Shelves at Montacute', *Library History*, xviii, 3 (November 2002), pp.153–6.

45. M. Bloch, 'Lady Anne Hill: Bookseller Wife of Heywood', *The Independent*, 31 January 2007.

46. Blickling, Correspondence file (J. Lees-Milne to M. O'Sullivan, 19 September 1946).

47. M. Drury, 'The Lily and the Boot: Early Days of the Historic Buildings Department', *Views*, 46 (Autumn 2009), pp.19–20; Belfast, PRONI, D/3839/B/14 (papers of the 8th Earl of Antrim).

48. *Fine Books from Famous Houses: An Exhibition of Printed Books and Manuscripts from National Trust Houses*, London 1958; E. Miller, 'The National Trust's Libraries', *National Trust*, xxviii (Autumn 1977), p.15.

49. M. Bence-Jones, *Ancestral Houses*, London 1984.

50. N. Barker, 'John Fuggles: Eccentric and Uproarious Libraries Adviser to the National Trust', *The Independent*, 19 November, 2002; J. Saumarez Smith, 'John Fuggles, Bibliomane', *Book Collector*, lxi (Winter 2012), pp.605–9.

51. J. Lees-Milne, *Holy Dread: Diaries, 1982–1984*, London 2001, pp.223–4.

52. N. Pickwood, 'Problems of Conservation', *Library Association Rare Books Group Newsletter*, xix (May 1982), pp.11–14.

53. P. Hoare, 'The Perils of Provenance: Serial Ownership, Bookplates and Obfuscation at Belton House', *Library History*, xviii, 3 (November 2000), pp.225–34; P. Hoare, 'An Icon of Gay Literature at Belton House', *National Trust Arts, Building & Collections Bulletin*, Summer 2007.

54. B. Bloomfield, 'Nicolas Barker. *Treasures from the Libraries of National Trust Country Houses*. New York: The Royal Oak Foundation and the Grolier Club, 1999' (Review), *Library History*, xvi, 2 (November 2000), pp.158–9.

55. NRS, ED/3/3R.

56. M. Swain, 'National Trust for Scotland in Crisis', *Country Life*, 10 August 2010.

57. NUL, MS. 328 (Annotated printed catalogue of the Library of Sir Thomas Foley, 1833).

58. B. Bloomfield (ed.), *A Directory of Rare Book and Special Collections in the United Kingdom and the Republic of Ireland*, 2nd edn., London 1997, p.590; *The Library of Thomas Percy, 1729–1811, Bishop of Dromore, Editor of the Reliques of Ancient English Poetry, Removed to Caledon House, Co. Tyrone in 1812, and now Sold by Order of the Trustees of the Caledon Estate and the Rt. Hon. the Earl of Caledon*, Sotheby's, London 23 June 1969, which covers only about a third of the collection.

59. P. Fox, *Trinity College Library, Dublin: A History*, Cambridge 2014, p.317.

60. N. Kissane (ed.), *Treasures from the National Library of Ireland*, Dublin 1994, pp.11–12; Bloomfield 1997, p.668.

61. O. Wright, 'Inside Whitehall. The Art of Claiming our Right to View Masterpieces', *The Independent*, 25 November 2013.

62. F. Russell, 'Preservation in Situ: the Role of the Auction House', in *Patronage Preserved: An Exhibition of Masterpieces Saved for Country Houses*, London 1991, pp.8–15 (p.11); the complex arrangements at Chatsworth are set out in D. Cavendish 1982, pp.233–5.

63. *Magnificent Plate Books from the Library of the Earl of Bradford*.

64. *Printed Books and Manuscripts from Beriah Botfield's Library at Longleat, Sold by Order of the Longleat Chattels Settlement*, Christie's, London 13 June 2002.

65. *Three Renaissance Masterworks from Chatsworth: Lots 50–52 to be Sold in the Old Master and British Paintings Evening Sale*, Sotheby's, London 5 December 2012.

66. *Magnificent Books, Manuscripts and Drawings from the Collection of Frederick, 2nd Lord Hesketh*, Sotheby's, London 7 December 2010; A. West, *The Shakespeare First Folio: The History of the Book*, Oxford 2003, ii, no. 44.

67. *Tew Park, Great Tew, Oxford: the Property of the Late Major Eustace Robb, Sold by Order of the Executors*, Christie's, London 27–29 May 1987.

68. *Magnificent Books, Manuscripts and Drawings from the Collection of Frederick, 2nd Lord Hesketh*.

69. N. Pevsner, *The Buildings of England: Oxfordshire*, London 1974, p.762; R. Strong, *The Roy Strong Diaries, 1967–1987*, London 1998, p.74.

70. G. Barker, 'Who's Laughing Now?', *Evening Standard*, 18 August 2004.

71. G. Worsley, 'Beyond the Powerhouse: Understanding the Country House in the Twenty-First Century', *Historical Research*, lxxviii, 201 (August 2005), pp.423–35.

72. H. Clifford, *Behind the Acanthus: The NADFAS Story*, London 2008, pp.67–76; J. Cornforth, *The Country Houses of England, 1948–1998*, London 1998, pp.253–4.

73. M. Evans, *A Catalogue of the Books at Fonmon Castle, Glamorgan*, Cardiff 1969; S. Pargeter, *Tatton Park Library Catalogue*, [Chester] 1977.

74. Hannah DeGroff, 'The Mental World of the Country House: the Textual Networks of the 3rd Earl of Carlisle', PhD Thesis, University of York (2013).

75. R. Stoddard, *Marks in Books, Illustrated and Explained*, Cambridge, MA 1985.

76. L. Jardine and A. Grafton, '"Studied for Action": how Gabriel Harvey read his Livy', *Past and Present*, cxxix, 1, pp.30–78.

77. D. Pearson, *Provenance Research in Book History*, London 1994; D. Pearson, *English Bookbinding Styles, 1450–1800*, London 2005.

78. D. Pearson, *Books as History*, London 2008.

Bibliography

Sale catalogues are listed separately at the end in chronological order.

Abbot, G., *The Case of Impotency as Debated in England*, London 1715, ESTC T76337

Adam, Robert, *The Works in Architecture*, London 1773–1822

Adam, William, *Vitruvius Scoticus: Being a Collection of Plans, Elevations, and Sections of Public Buildings, Noblemen's and Gentlemen's Houses in Scotland*, Edinburgh [1812?]

Adlam, Derek, *The Great Collector: Edward Harley, 2nd Earl of Oxford*, Welbeck 2013

Adshead, David, *Wimpole: Architectural Drawings and Topographical Views*, Swindon 2007

Airs, Malcolm, 'Triumph against the Odds: the English Country House in the 20th Century', in Malcolm Airs (ed.), *The Twentieth-Century Great House*, Oxford 2002, pp.1–14

Alexander, Jonathan, and Paul Binski (eds), *Age of Chivalry: Art in Plantagenet England, 1200–1400*, exh. cat., Royal Academy of Arts, London 1987

Alston, Robin, *Books Printed on Vellum in the Collections of the British Library*, London 1996

Ames, Joseph, *Typographical Antiquities: or, an historical account of the origin and progress of printing in Great Britain and Ireland*, London 1810–19

Anderson, Andrew H., 'The Books and Interests of Henry, Lord Stafford (1501–1563)', *The Library*, 5th series, XXI (1966), pp.87–144

The Architecture of Richard Morris (1767–1849) and William Vitruvius Morrison (1794–1838), Dublin 1989

Armstrong, Katherine A., 'The Baikie Library at Tankerness House Museum, Kirkwall, Orkney', *Library Review*, XL, 1 (1991), pp.37–44

Ascham, Roger, *The Scholemaster*, ed. D. C. Whimster, London 1934

Askwith, Betty, *The Lytteltons: A Family Chronicle of the Nineteenth Century*, London 1975

Atherton, Ian, 'Hassall, John (*bap.* 1571, *d.* 1654)', ODNB

Aubrey, John, *Aubrey's Brief Lives: Edited from the Original Manuscript and with a Life of John Aubrey*, London 1972

Audley End, London 2002

Ayres, Philip, 'Burlington's Library at Chiswick', *Studies in Bibliography*, XLV (1992), pp.113–27

Backhouse, Janet, *The Madresfield Hours: A Fourteenth-Century Manuscript in the Library of Earl Beauchamp*, Oxford 1975

—, 'Patronage and Commemoration in the Beaufort Hours', in K. Smith and C. Krinsky (eds), *Tributes to Lucy Freeman Sandler: Studies in Manuscript Illumination*, London 2007, pp.331–44

Bailey, Bruce, Nikolaus Pevsner and Bridget Cherry, *Northamptonshire: Buildings of England*, London 2013

Bailey, Catherine, *The Secret Rooms*, London 2013

Baird, Rosemary, *Goodwood: Art and Architecture, Sport and Family*, London 2007

Bankes, Viola, *A Dorset Heritage: The Story of Kingston Lacy*, London 1953

Barber, Giles, *Printed Books and Bookbindings: The James A. de Rothschild Bequest at Waddesdon Manor, the National Trust*, Aylesbury 2013

Barker, Godfrey, 'Who's Laughing Now?', *Evening Standard*, 17 August 2004

Barker, Nicolas, *The Publications of the Roxburghe Club, 1814–1962*, Cambridge 1964

—, 'The Chatsworth Library', *Christie's Review of the Season* (1974), pp.300–14

—, *Bibliotheca Lindesiana: The Lives and Collections of Alexander William, 25th Earl of Crawford and 8th Earl of Balcarres and James Ludovic, 26th Earl of Crawford and 9th Earl of Balcarres*, London 1977

—, 'The Books of Henry Howard, Earl of Northampton', *Bodleian Library Record*, XVIII, 2 (October 1990), pp.375–81

—, 'Books and Manuscripts', in Tessa Murdoch (ed.), *Boughton House: The English Versailles*, London 1992, pp.170–73

—, *Treasures from the Libraries of National Trust Country Houses*, New York 1999

—, 'John Fuggles: Eccentric and Uproarious Libraries Adviser to the National Trust', *The Independent*, 19 November 2002

—, *The Devonshire Inheritance: Five Centuries of Collecting at Chatsworth*, Alexandria, VA 2003, p. 95

—, *The Library of Thomas Tresham & Thomas Brudenell*, London 2006

—, *The Roxburghe Club: A Bicentenary History*, London 2012

Barnard, Toby, 'Learning, the Learned and Literacy in Ireland, c.1660–1760', in Toby Barnard, Dáibhí Ó Cróinín and Katharine Simms, '*A Miracle of Learning*'; *Studies in Manuscripts and Irish Learning: Essays in Honour of William O'Sullivan*, Aldershot 1997, pp. 209–35

—, 'From Imperial Schatzkammer to the Giant's Causeway: Collecting in Eighteenth-Century Ireland', *Irish Architectural and Decorative Studies*, VI (2003), pp. 141–61

—, *Making the Grand Figure: Lives and Possessions in Ireland, 1641–1770*, New Haven and London 2004

Barrett, Anthony A., 'Knowledge of Literary Classics in Roman Britain', *Britannia*, IX (1978), pp. 307–13

Batho, Gordon R., 'The Wizard Earl in the Tower', *History Today*, VI (1956), pp. 344–51

—, 'The Education of a Stuart Nobleman', *British Journal of Educational Studies*, V (1956–7), pp. 131–43

—, 'The Percies at Petworth, 1574–1632', *Sussex Archaeological Collections*, XCV (1957), pp. 1–27

—, 'Notes and Documents on Petworth House. 1574–1632', *Sussex Archaeology*, XCVI (1958), pp. 108–34

— (ed.), *The Household Papers of Henry Percy, Ninth Earl of Northumberland (1564–1632)*, London 1962

—, *Thomas Harriot and the Northumberland Household*, Oxford 1992

Bayly, Thomas, *Worcesters Apophthegmes: or witty sayings of the Right Honourable Henry (late) Marquess and Earl of Worcester*, London 1650, ESTC R204142, Wing W3535

Beale, Peter, '"My Books are the Great Joy of My Life": Sir William Boothby, Seventeenth-Century Bibliophile', *Book Collector*, XLVI, 2 (1997), pp. 356–62

Beaulieu: Beaulieu Abbey, Palace House, National Motor Museum, Beaulieu 2013

Bell, Alan, 'Amherst, William Amhurst Tyssen-, First Baron Amherst of Hackney (1835–1909)', ODNB

Bence-Jones, Mark, *Twilight of the Ascendancy*, London 1993

Bennett, N., 'Honywood, Michael (1596–1681)', ODNB

Bernard Quaritch Ltd, *A General Catalogue of Books Offered to the Public at Fixed Prices*, [Quaritch], London 1887–97

Bernasconi, J., *Inventory Work and Catalogues: A Concise Guide for the Compiler of Auction Catalogues of Furniture, Silver, etc., the Organisation of the Auction Sale and Inventories for Various Purposes*, London [1962?]

Berry, M., *Extracts of the Journals and Correspondence of Miss Berry, from the Year 1783 to 1852*, London 1865

Besson, A., 'Classification in Private Library Catalogues of the English Renaissance, 1500–1640', PhD Thesis, School of Library, Archive and Information Science, University College, London 1988

Betteridge, Robert L., 'The Library of the Dalrymples of Newhailes, *Journal of the Edinburgh Bibliographical Society*, VIII (2013)

Bibliotheca Lindesiana: Catalogue of the Printed Books Preserved at Haigh Hall, Wigan, Aberdeen 1910

Bibliotheca Norfolciana: Sive Catalogue Libb. Manuscriptorum & Impressorum Omni Arte & Lingua, quos Illustriss. Princips Henricus Dux Norfolciae, &c. Regiae Societatis Londiniensi … Donavit, London 1681, Wing N1230, ESTC R14407

Biddle, Martin, *Nonsuch Palace: The Material Culture of a Noble Restoration Household*, Oxford 2005

Binney, Marcus, *Lost Houses of Scotland*, London 2006

Binski, Paul, and Stella Panayotova (eds), *The Cambridge Illuminations: Ten Centuries of Book Production in the Medieval West*, London 2005

Birrell, T., 'Books and Buyers in Seventeenth-Century English Auction Sales', in R. Myers, M. Harris and G. Mandelbrote (eds), *Under the Hammer: Book Auctions since the Seventeenth Century*, New Castle, DE 2001, pp. 51–64

Blaess, Madeleine, 'L'Abbaye de Bordesley et les Livres de Guy de Beauchamp', *Romania*, LXXII (1957), pp. 511–18

Blake, Robert, *Disraeli*, London 1998

Bloch, Michael, 'Lady Anne Hill: Bookseller Wife of Heywood', *The Independent*, 31 January 2007

—, *James Lees-Milne*, London 2009

Bloomfield, Barry (ed.), *A Directory of Rare Books and Special Collections in the United Kingdom and the Republic of Ireland*, London 1994 & 1997 (2nd edn.)

—, 'Nicolas Barker. *Treasures from the Libraries of National Trust Country Houses*. New York:

The Royal Oak Foundation and the Grolier Club, 1999' (Review), *Library History*, XVI, 2 (November 2000), pp. 158–9

Booth, Henry, Earl of Warrington, *The Works of the Right Honourable Henry late L. Delamer and Earl of Warrington*, London 1694

Botfield, Beriah, 'The Holkham Library', *Miscellanies of the Philobiblon Society*, VI, 4 (1860–61), pp. 72–85

Bowden, Caroline M.K., 'Cecil [née Cooke], Mildred, Lady Burghey (1526–1589)', ODNB

Bowdler, Roger, 'Dance, George, the Elder (1741–1825)', ODNB

Bowett, Adam, 'The Engravings of Daniel Marot', *Furniture History*, XLIII (2007), pp. 85–100

Boyce, Brian P., *Collecting Blickling III: The Lothian Collection and the Book Sale of the Century*, S.l. 2013

Boynton, Lindsay (ed.), *The Hardwick Hall Inventories of 1601*, London 1971

—, *Appuldurcombe House, Isle of Wight*, London 1986

Brack, O. M., 'Osborne, Thomas (bap. 1704?, d. 1767)', ODNB

Bradley, P., *Flintham Hall, Nottinghamshire*, [Flintham?] 2004

Bramhall Hall, Stockport 2001

Brayman Hackel, Heidi, *Reading Material in Early Modern England*, Cambridge 2009

Brears, Peter, 'Wressle Castle: Functions, Fixtures and Furnishing for Henry Percy "The Magnificent", Fifth Earl of Northumberland, 1498–1527', *Archaeological Journal*, CLXVII (2010), pp. 55–114

Brenan, Gerald, *A History of the House of Percy from the Earliest Times down to the Present Century*, London 1902

Brett, Philip, 'Edward Paston … and His Musical Collection', *Transactions of the Cambridge Bibliographical Society*, IV (1964)

Brigstocke, Hugh, 'Lindsey, Alexander William Crawford, Twenty-Fifth Earl of Crawford and Eighth Earl of Balcarres (1812–1880)', ODNB

Britton, John, *The History and Description, with Graphic Illustrations, of Cassiobury Park, Hertfordshire: the Seat of the Earl of Essex*, London 1837

Brooks, Alan, and Nikolaus Pevsner, *Herefordshire: The Buildings of England*, London 2012

—, and Nikolaus Pevsner, *Worcestershire: The Buildings of England*, London 2007

Brooks, Jeanice, 'Musical Monuments for the Country House: Music, Collection, and Display at Tatton Park', *Music and Letters*, XCI, 4 (2010), pp. 513–35

Brown, Robert, 'Whatman [née Bosanquet], Susanna (1753–1814)', ODNB

Brundin, Abigail, and Dunstan Roberts, 'Book-Buying and the Grand Tour: the Italian Books at Belton House in Lincolnshire', *The Library*, 7th series, XVI, 1 (March 2015), pp. 51–79

Bryant, Julius, *The Iveagh Bequest, Kenwood House*, London 1990

Butler, James, *Lord Lothian Philip Kerr, 1882–1940*, London 1960, pp. 151–2

Butler, Marilyn, 'Austen, Jane (1775–1817)', ODNB

Byng, John, Viscount Torrington, *The Torrington Diaries, containing the tours through England and Wales of the Hon. John Byng, later fifth Viscount Torrington, between the years 1781 and 1794*, ed. C. Bruyn Andrews, 4 vols, London 1934–8

Byrne, Aisling, 'The Earls of Kildare and their Books at the End of the Middle Ages', *The Library*, 7th series, XIV, 2 (June 2013), pp. 129–53

St. Clare Byrne, M., and Gladys Scott Thomson, '"My Lord's Books": The Library of Francis, Second Earl of Bedford in 1584', *Review of English Studies*, VII, 28 (October 1931), pp. 385–405

Cadell, Patrick, 'Robertson, William (1740–1803)', ODNB

Cambers, Andrew, 'Readers' Marks and Religious Practice: Margaret Hoby's Marginalia', in John N. King (ed.), *Tudor Books and Readers: Materiality and the Construction of Meaning*, Cambridge 2010, pp. 211–31

Campbell, Colen, et al., *Vitruvius Britannicus*, London 1715–71

Cannadine, David, 'The Landowner as Millionaire: the Finances of the Dukes of Devonshire, c.1800–c.1926', *Agricultural History Review*, XXV (1977), pp. 77–97

—, 'Aristocratic Indebtedness in the Nineteenth Century' and 'Lord Strickland: Imperial Aristocrat and Aristocratic Imperialist', in David Cannadine (ed.), *Aspects of Aristocracy: Grandeur and Decline in Modern Britain*, New Haven and London 1994, pp. 37–54 and 109–29

Cannan, Edwin, rev. Roger Hayden, 'Gifford, Andrew (1700–1784)', ODNB

Carey, John, Maire Herbert, James Knowles, *Travelled Tales: The Book of Lismore at University College, Cork*, Cork 2011

Carley, James P., 'The Dispersal of the Monastic Libraries and the Salvaging of the Spoils', in Elisabeth Leedham-Green and Teresa Webber (eds), CHLBI, vol. I: To 1640, Cambridge 2006, pp. 265–91

Castell, Robert, *The Villas of the Ancients Illustrated*, London 1728, ESTC T50805

Castiglione, Baldassare, *The Covrtyer of Covnt Baldessar Castilio: diuided into foure books: very necessary and profitable for yonge gentilmen and gentilwomen abiding in court, palaice or place: done into Englyshe by Thomas Hoby*, London 1561, ESTC S122029, STC 4778

Catalogue of the Aldenham Library: Mainly Collected by Henry Hucks Gibbs, First Lord Aldenham, Letworth 1914

Catalogue of Books Printed in the XVth Century now in the British Museum [British Library], London 1908–2006

Catalogue of the Books in the Library at Blenheim Palace, Collected by Charles, Third Earl of Sunderland, Oxford 1872

Catalogue of the Books in the Library of the Right Honorable [sic] Mervyn Richard, Lord Viscount Powerscourt, S.l. [1907]

A Catalogue of a Collection of Books Relating to English & Foreign Literature forming the Library of Richard Brinsley Sheridan, London 1884

A Catalogue of the Library at Attingham, London 1809

Catalogue of the Library at Chevening, London 1865

Catalogue of the Library at Leigh Park, S.l. 1842

Catalogue des Livres français de la Bibliothèque de Baron Ferdinand de Rothschild à Waddesdon, London 1897

Catalogue of the Printed Books in the Library of His Grace the Duke of Portland at Welbeck Abbey, and in London, London 1893

A Catalogue of Some Printed Books and Manuscripts at St Dunstan's, Regent's Park, and Aldenham House, Herts, collected by Henry Hucks Gibbs, London 1888

Catalogus Bibliothecae Kingstonianae [London 1727?], ESTC T123378

Catalogus Librorum A.C.D.A. [i.e. Archibald Campbell, 3rd Duke of Argyll], Glasgow 1758, ESTC T28876

Cavanaugh, Susan Hagen, *A Study of Books Privately Owned in England: 1300 to 1450*, Part I, Ann Arbor, MI 1980

Cavendish, Andrew, 11th Duke of Devonshire, *Accidents of Fortune*, Norwich 2004

Cavendish, Deborah, Duchess of Devonshire, *The House: A Portrait of Chatsworth*, London 1982

—, *Chatsworth: The House*, London 2002

Cavendish, William Spencer, 6th Duke of Devonshire, *Handbook of Chatsworth and Hardwick*, London 1845, pp. 71–74

Cherry, Bridget, and Nikolaus Pevsner, *Devon: Buildings of England*, 2nd edn., New Haven and London 1989

Stanhope, Philip Dormer, Earl of Chesterfield, *The Letters of Philip Dormer Stanhope, Earl of Chesterfield*, London 1893

Chew, Elizabeth V., 'The Countess of Arundel and Tart Hall', in Edward Chaney (ed.), *The Evolution of English Collecting: Receptions of Italian Art in the Tudor and Stuart Periods*, Studies in British Art 12, New Haven and London 2003, pp. 285–307

Chippendale, Thomas, *The Gentleman and Cabinet-Maker's Director: Being a Large Collection of the most Elegant and Useful Designs of Household Furniture, in the Most Fashionable Taste*, 3rd edn., London 1762, ESTC T102007

Cirket, Alan F. (ed.), 'The Earl de Grey's Account of the Building of Wrest House', *Publications of the Bedfordshire Historical Record Society, Miscellanea*, LIX (1980) pp. 65–85

Ciro, Jeniffer, 'Country House Libraries in the Nineteenth Century', *Library History*, XVIII (July 2002), pp. 89–98

Clanchy, M. T., *From Memory to Written Record*, 2nd edn., Oxford 1993

Clark, Andrew (ed.), *Lincoln Diocese Documents, 1450–1544*, London 1914

Clark, Arthur, *Raglan Castle and the Civil War in Monmouthshire*, Chepstow 1953

Clark, Alan, *Diaries: Into Politics, 1972–1982*, ed. Ion Trewin, London 2001

Clark, J. W., *Libraries in the Medieval and Renaissance Periods*, Cambridge 1894

Clarke, Desmond, *Arthur Dobbs, Esquire 1689–1765*, London 1958

Clarke, John, *An Essay upon Study*, London 1731, ESTC T144041

Clarke-Maxwell, W., 'An Inventory of the Contents of Markeaton Hall. Made by Vincent Mundy, Esq., in the Year 1545', *Journal of the Derbyshire Archaeological and Natural History Society*, LI (1930), pp. 116–40

Clifford, David J. H. (ed.), *The Diaries of Lady Anne Clifford*, Stroud 1992

Clifford, Helen M., *Behind the Acanthus: The NADFAS Story*, London 2008

Coates, Alan (ed.), *A Catalogue of Books Printed in the Fifteenth Century now in the Bodleian Library*, Oxford 2005

Cochrane, John G., *Catalogue of the Library at Abbotsford*, Edinburgh 1838

Collard, Frances, 'A Design for Library Steps by Henry Keene', *Furniture History*, XXVI (1990), pp. 34–8

Collier, John Payne, *A Catalogue Bibliographical and Critical of Early English Literature; Forming a Portion of the Library at Bridgewater House, the Property of the Rt. Hon. Lord Francis Egerton*, London 1837

Collins, John, *A Short Account of the Library at Longleat House*, London 1980

Collinson, Patrick, Arnold Hunt and Alexandra Walsham, 'Religious Publishing in England', in CHBB, *vol. IV: 1557–1695*, John Barnard and D. F. McKenzie (eds), Cambridge 2002, pp. 29–66

Colvin, Howard, *The History of the King's Works*, London 1963–82

—, *Essays in English Architectural History*, London 1999

—, and Maurice James Craig (eds), *Architectural Drawings in the Library at Elton Hall*, Oxford 1964

—, and John Newman (eds), *Of Building: Roger North's Writings on Architecture*, Oxford 1981

Comenius, John Amos, *Orbis Sensualium Pictus*, Sydney 1967

Cook, B. F., 'Townley, Charles (1737–1805)', ODNB

Cook, Jean, and J. F. A. Mason (eds), *The Building Accounts of Christ Church Library, 1716–1779*, Oxford 1988

Cooper, J. P. D., 'Godolphin, Sir William (b. in or before 1518, d. 1570)', ODNB

Cooper, Nicholas, *Houses of the Gentry: 1480–1680*, New Haven and London 1999

Cooper, Thompson, *rev.* Adam Jacob Levin, 'Knowles, Thomas (1723–1802)', ODNB

Coral, Lenore, and A. N. L. Munby, *British Book Sale Catalogues, 1676–1800*, London 1977

Cornforth, John, *The Search for a Style: Country Life and Architecture, 1875–1925*, London 1988

—, 'Books do Furnish a Living Room', *Country Life*, 13 December 2001, pp. 56–9

—, *Early Georgian Interiors*, London 2004

Corrozet, Gilles, *Les Blasons domestiques*, Paris 1865

Courtenay, W. J., 'Bury, Richard (1287–1345)', ODNB

Cowell, Ben, 'Hardwick Hall in the Eighteenth Century', *Georgian Group Journal*, XVI (2008)

Cowie, Leonard W., *Henry Newman: An American in London, 1708–1743*, London 1956

Cowper, Countess Mary, *Diary of Mary Countess Cowper, Lady of the Bedchamber to the Princess of Wales, 1714–1720*, London 1864

Cox, F., *Osterley Park Library*, [London?] 1926

Cox, J. Charles, 'Norbury Manor House and the Troubles of the Fitzherberts', *Journal of the Derbyshire Archaeological and Natural History Society*, VII (January 1883), pp. 221–59

Cragside, London 1990

Croft, Pauline, 'Cecil, Robert, First Earl of Salisbury (1563–1612)', ODNB

Croft Castle, Herefordshire, London 2000

Crook, Joseph Mordaunt, *The Rise of the Nouveaux Riches*, 1999

Cruft, Kitty, John Dunbar and Richard Fawcett, *Borders: The Buildings of Scotland*, New Haven and London 2006

Cruickshank, Dan, *The Country House Revealed*, London 2011

Cust, Richard, 'Lucy, Sir Thomas (1583–1640)', ODNB

Darlington, John (ed.), *Stafford Castle: Survey, Excavation and Research, 1978–98*, Stafford 2001

Daunton, Martin, 'Gibbs, Henry Hucks, First Baron Alderton (1819–1907)', ODNB

Davies, John, *Antiquae Linguae Britannicae … Dictionarium Duplex*, London 1632, ESTC S12250, STC 6347

de Bury, Richard, *The Philobiblon: With an Introduction by Archer Taylor*, Berkeley 1948

DeGroff, H. J., 'Textual Networks and the Country House: the 3rd Earl of Carlisle at Castle Howard', PhD Thesis, University of York, December 2012

de Hamel, Christopher, *A History of Illuminated Manuscripts*, 2nd edn., London 1994

—, 'The Illuminated Manuscript Collection of Edmond de Rothschild', in R. Myers and M. Harris (eds), *Antiquaries, Book Collectors and the Circles of Learning*, Winchester 1996, pp. 129–51

—, 'Books in Society', in Nigel. J. Morgan and Rodney M. Thomson (eds), CHBB, *vol. II: 1100–1400*, Cambridge 2008, pp. 3–23

de Pisan, Christine, *The Book of Fayttes of Arms and of Chyualrye*, London 1489, STC 7269, ESTC S106571

de Voragine, Jacobus, *Thus Endeth the Legende Named in Latyn Legenda Aurea*, Westminster 1483 STC 24873, ESTC S541

Dean, Dennis R., 'Bryant, Jacob (bap. 1717, d. 1804)', ODNB

Dean, William, *An Historical and Descriptive Account of Croome d'Abitot*, Worcester 1824

Dearden, James A., 'Thomas Johnes and the Hafod Press, 1803–10', *Book Collector*, XXII, 3 (Autumn 1973), pp. 315–36

Defoe, Daniel, *A Tour Through the Whole Island of Great Britain*, New Haven and London 1991

Dekker, Elly, 'Uncommonly Handsome Globes', in Elly Dekker, *Globes at Greenwich: A Catalogue of Globes and Armillary Spheres in the National Maritime Museum, Greenwich*, Oxford 1999, pp. 87–136

Delaissé, L. M. J., James Marrow and John de Wit, *The James A. de Rothschild Collection at Waddesdon Manor: Illuminated Manuscripts*, Fribourg 1977

Denson, I., *A Catalogue of the Hardy Trees, Shrubs, and Herbaceous Plants in the Botanic Garden Bury Saint Edmund's, by I. Denson, Curator*, Bury St Edmunds 1822

Dent, John, *The Quest for Nonsuch*, London 1969

Stanley, Edward, 15th Earl of Derby, *The Diaries of Edward Henry Stanley, 15th Earl of Derby (1823–93) between 1878 and 1893: A Selection*, Oxford 2003

de Ricci, Seymour, *A Hand-List of a Collection of Books and Manuscripts Belonging to the Right Hon. Lord Amherst of Hackney*, Cambridge 1906

—, *English Collectors of Books & Manuscripts (1530–1930) and their Marks of Ownership*, Cambridge 1930

—, *Census of Medieval and Renaissance Manuscripts in the United States and Canada*, New York 1961

Description of Alnwick Castle, Alnwick 1818

Dibdin, Thomas Frognall, *The Bibliomania; or, Book-Madness; Containing Some Account of the History, Symptoms and Cure of this Fatal Disease. In an Epistle Addressed to Richard Heber, Esq.*, London 1809

—, *Bibliomania; or Book Madness: a Bibliographical Romance, in Six Parts*, London 1811

—, *Bibliotheca Spenceriana; or a Descriptive Catalogue of the Books Printed in the Fifteenth Century, and of Many Valuable First Editions, in the Library of George John, Earl Spencer*, London 1814–15

—, *The Bibliographical Decameron; or Ten Days Pleasant Discourse upon Illuminated Manuscripts*, London 1817

—, *A Bibliographical, Antiquarian and Picturesque Tour in France and Germany*, London 1821

—, *Aedes Althorpianae; or an Account of the Mansion, Books, and Pictures, at Althorp*, London 1822

—, *The Library Companion, or the Young Man's Guide and Old Man's Comfort in the Choice of a Library*, London 1824

—, *Bibliophobia, or Remarks on the Present Depression in the State of Literature and the Book Trade*, London 1832

—, *A Bibliographical, Antiquarian and Picturesque Tour in the Northern Counties of England and in Scotland*, London 1838

—, *Bibliomania*, London 1842

Dickinson, Donald D., *Henry E. Huntington's Library of Libraries*, San Marino 1995

Diestelkamp, Edward, 'The National Trust Country House Scheme', in M. Airs (ed.), *The Twentieth-Century Great House*, Oxford 2002, pp. 75–100

Disraeli, Benjamin, *Letters*, Toronto 1982–2014

Donaldson, Robert, 'Traquair House Library', *Bulletin du Bibliophile*, III (1984), pp. 321–5

Dooley, Terence, *The Decline of the Big House in Ireland*, Dublin 2001

Doran, Susan, 'Pickering, Sir William (1516/17–75)', ODNB

Doyle, A. I., 'English Books in and Out of Court from Edward III to Henry VII', in V. J Scattergood and J. W. Sherborne, *English Court Culture in the Later Middle Ages*, London 1983, pp. 163–81

Doyle, Kathleen, 'The Old Royal Library: "A Great Many Noble Manuscripts Yet Remaining"', in Scot McKendrick, John Lowden and Kathleen Doyle (eds), *Royal Manuscripts: The Genius of Imagination*, exh. cat., British Library, London 2011

Douglas, David Charles, *English Scholars*, London 1943

Drummond, D., 17th Earl of Perth, 'The Library at Stobhall', *Bulletin du Bibliophile* (1984), pp. 301–6

Drury, Martin, 'The Lily and the Boot: Early Days of the Historic Buildings Department', *Views*, 46 (Autumn 2009), pp. 19–20

Duffy, Eamon, *Marking the Hours: English People and their Prayers, 1240–1570*, New Haven and London 2006

Dugard, Thomas, *Death and the Grave: or, a Sermon Preached at the Funeral of that Honorable and Virtuous Ladie, the Ladie Alice Lucie*, London 1649, ESTC R6467, Wing D2453

Dutton, Ralph, *Hinton Ampner: A Hampshire Manor*, London 1969

'The Earl of Perth' (Obituary), *Daily Telegraph*, 29 November 2002

Eaton, Daniel, *The Letters of Daniel Eaton to the Third Earl of Cardigan, 1725–1732*, Kettering 1971

The Eaton Tourists, or A 'Colloquial Description' of the Hall, Grounds, Gardens, &c. at Eaton, the Seat of the Right Hon. Earl Grosvenor, Chester 1824

Edmonds, C., 'Exploration of Old Libraries', *The Athenaeum*, 16 May 1885

Edwards, A. S. G., 'Books owned by Medieval Members of the Percy Family', in M. Villalobos Hennessy, *Tributes to Kathleen L. Scott: English Medieval Manuscripts: Readers, Makers and Illuminators*, London 2009

Edwards, Edward, *Libraries and the Founders of Libraries*, London 1864

Edwards, George, *From Crow-Scaring to Westminster: An Autobiography*, London 1922

Eland, G., (ed.), *Purefoy Letters, 1735–1753*, 2 vols, London 1931

Eller, Irvin, *The History of Belvoir Castle*, London 1841

Ellys, Sir Richard, *Fortuita Sacra*, Rotterdam 1727

Mrs Elwood, *Memoirs of the Literary Ladies of England*, London 1843

Elzinga, J. G., 'Osborne, Peter (1521–1592)', ODNB

Emery, Anthony, *Greater Medieval Houses of England and Wales*, Cambridge 2000

Emmison, F. G., *Tudor Secretary: Sir William Petre at Court and Home*, London 1961

Evans, Sir John, 'Extracts from the Private Account Book of Sir William More, of Loseley, in Surrey, in the time of Queen Mary and of Queen Elizabeth', *Archaeologia*, XXXVI, 2 (January 1855), pp. 284–310

Evans, Margaret, *A Catalogue of the Books at Fonmon Castle, Glamorgan*, Cardiff 1969

Evans, Mark (ed.), *Art Collecting and Lineage in the Elizabethan Age*: The Lumley Inventory and Pedigree, London 2010

Evelyn, John, *The Diary of John Evelyn*, 6 vols, Oxford 1955

The Extraordinary Career of the 2nd Earl of Massereene, 1743–1805, Belfast 1972

Fairfax-Blakeborough, John, *Sykes of Sledmere: The Record of a Sporting Family and Famous Stud*, London 1929

Farnham, Luther, *A Glance at Private Libraries*, Boston 1855

Fehrenbach, R. J., 'Sir Roger Townshend's Books', in R. J. Fehrenbach and E. S. Leedham-Green (eds), *Private Libraries in Renaissance England: A Collection and Catalogue of Tudor and Early Stuart Book-Lists*, 2 vols, Binghamtown, NY 1992, vol. I, pp. 79–135

Fenlon, Jane, *Goods & Chattels: A Survey of Early Household Inventories in Ireland*, Dublin 2003

Fenning, Hugh (ed.), *The Fottrell Papers, 1721–39: an edition of the papers found on the person of Fr. John Fottrell, Provincial of the Dominicans in Ireland, at his arrest in 1739*, Belfast 1980

Fergus, Jan, 'Provincial Servants' Reading in the Late Eighteenth Century', in James Raven, Helen Small and Naomi Tadmor (eds), *The Practice and Representation of Reading in England*, Cambridge 1996, pp. 202–25

Ferriar, John, *The Bibliomania, an Epistle, to Richard Heber, Esq.*, London 1809

Fine Books from Famous Houses: An Exhibition of Printed Books and Manuscripts from National Trust Houses, London 1958

Firth, C. H., and R. S. Rait (eds), *Acts and Ordinances of the Interregnum*, London 1911

Fisher, Geoffrey, and Helen Smith, 'John Hungerford Pollen and his Decorative Work at Blickling Hall', in Gervase Jackson-Stops (ed.), *National Trust Year Book* (1975–6), pp. 112–19

Fitzpatrick, David, *Politics and Irish Life, 1913–1921: Provincial Experience of War and Revolution*, Dublin 1977

Fletcher, H. George (ed.), *The Wormsley Library: A Personal Selection by Sir Paul Getty*, 2nd edn., London 1999 & 2007

'Henry Tennyson Folkard, Librarian of Wigan Library', 1877–1916, *Past Forward*, XLII (April–July 2006), p. 15

Foot, Mirjam, *The Henry Davis Gift: A Collection of Bookbindings*, London 1978–2010

Forster, Henry Rumsey, *The Stowe Catalogue, Priced and Annotated*, London 1848

Fortescue, Thomas, Lord Clermont, *A History of the Family of Fortescue*, London 1880

Fox, Peter, *Trinity College Library, Dublin: A History*, Cambridge 2014

Francis, Jane, 'The Kedermister Library: an Account of its Origins and a Reconstruction of its Contents and Arrangement', *Records of Buckinghamshire*, XXXVI (1994), pp. 62–85

Freeman, Arthur, 'Quaritch, Bernard Alexander Christian (1819–1899)', ODNB

Freeman, Charles E., 'Elizabethan Inventories', *Publications of the Bedfordshire Historical Record Society*, XXXII (1952), pp. 92–156

Freeman, Janet Ing, 'Miller, William Henry (1789–1848)', ODNB

French, Doris, *Ishbel and the Empire: A Biography of Lady Aberdeen*, Toronto and Oxford 1988

Friends of the National Libraries: Annual Report (1991), pp. 17–19

Fry, Theodore, *A Brief Memoir of Francis Fry, F.S.A. of Bristol*, S.l. 1887

Furnivall, F., *The Petworth MS. of Chaucer's Canterbury Tales*, London 1868–84

Gage, John, *The History and Antiquities of Hengrave*, London 1822

Gameson, Richard, 'The Medieval Library (to c.1450)', in CHLBI, vol. I: To 1640, Elisabeth Leedham-Green and Teresa Webber (eds), Cambridge 2006, pp. 13–50

—, 'From Vindolanda to Domesday: the Book in Britain from the Romans to the Normans', in Richard Gameson (ed.), CHBB, vol. I: c.400–1100, Cambridge 2011, pp. 1–9

Gamon, Hannibal, *The Praise of a Godly Woman*, London 1627, STC 11458, ESTC S102888

Ganz, David, 'Anglo-Saxon England', in Elisabeth Leedham-Green and Teresa Webber (eds), CHLBI, vol. I: To 1640, Cambridge 2006, pp. 91–108

Gascoygne-Cecil, C., Marchioness of Salisbury, *An Account of Life at Hatfield House, 1887–1903*, [Hatfield] 1930

Gascoyne-Cecil, R., 6th Marquess of Salisbury, *The Hatfield House Library: A Family Collection of over Four Hundred Years*, [New York 1967]

Germain, Brice, *A New Description of Paris*, London 1687, Wing B4440, ESTC R3651

Gesta Abbatum Monasterii Sancti Albani, a Thoma Walsingham, Regnante Ricardo Secundo, Ejusdem Ecclesiae Praecentore, Compilata, ed. Henry Riley, 3 vols, London 1867–9

Gifford, Gerald (ed.), *A Descriptive Catalogue of the Music Collection at Burghley House, Stamford*, Aldershot 2002, pp.1–56

Gilbert, Christopher, *The Life and Work of Thomas Chippendale*, London 1978

Girouard, Mark, *Life in the English Country House*, London 1978

—, *The Victorian Country House*, London 1979

—, 'The Country House and the Country Town', in Gervase Jackson-Stops (ed.), *The Fashioning and Functioning of the British Country House*, Washington 1989, pp.305–28

—, *Elizabethan Architecture: Its Rise and Fall*, New Haven and London 2009

—, *Old Wardour Castle*, London 2012

Glenn, Virginia, 'George Bullock, Richard Bridges and James Wyatt's Regency Furnishing Schemes', *Furniture History*, XV (1979), pp.54–67

Goldfinch, John, 'Royal Libraries in the King's Library', in Kathleen Doyle and Scot McKendrick, *1000 Years of Royal Books and Manuscripts*, London 2013, pp.213–36

Gooch, Leo, *A Complete Pattern of Nobility: John, Lord Lumley (c.1534–1609)*, Rainton Bridge 2009

Goodall, John, *God's House at Ewelme*, Aldershot 2001

—, *Ashby de la Zouch Castle and Kirby Muxloe Castle*, 2nd edn., London 2011

—, *The English Castle*, New Haven and London 2011

Goodison, Nicholas, and John Hardy, 'Gillows at Tatton Park', *Furniture History*, VI (1970), pp.1–39

Gorhambury: Historic Home of the Grimston Family, Derby 1998

Gow, Ian, *The Scottish Interior*, Edinburgh 1992

—, '"The Most Learned Drawing Room in Europe?": Newhailes and the Scottish Classical Library', in D. Mays, M. Moss and M. Oglethorpe (eds), *Visions of Scotland's Paste: Looking to the Future: Essays in Honour of John R. Hume*, East Linton 2000, pp.81–96

—, *Scotland's Lost Houses*, London 2006

Grant, Elizabeth, *Memoirs of a Highland Lady*, Edinburgh 1988

Green, David Brontë, *The Churchills of Blenheim*, London 1984, p.116

Green, Richard F., 'King Richard II's Books Revisited', *The Library*, XXXI (1976), pp.235–9

Gregory, Lady Augusta, *Coole*, Dublin 1931

Gregory, William Henry, *The Beckford Family: Reminiscences of Fonthill Abbey and Lansdown Tower* Bath 1887

Gretton, John R., *Essays in Book-Collecting*, Dereham 1985

Griffin, David, Caroline Pegum and Elizabeth Mayes, *Leinster House, 1744–2000: An Architectural History*, Dublin 2000

Griffiths, William, *A Practical Treatise on Farriery*, Wrexham 1784, ESTC N20539

Grundy, Isobel, 'Lady Mary Wortley Montagu (bap. 1689, d. 1762)', ODNB

Guerci, Manolo, 'The Construction of Northumberland House and the Patronage of its Original Builder, Lord Henry Howard, 1603–14', *Antiquaries Journal*, LXXXX (2010), pp.341–400

Guerrini, Anita, 'Mead, Richard (1673–1754)', ODNB

Gunn, S. J., and P. G. Lindley, 'Charles Brandon's Westhorpe: an Early Tudor Courtyard House in Suffolk', *Archaeological Journal*, CXLV (1988), pp.272–89

Haddo House Library, [Aberdeen c.1920]

Hall, I. and E., *Burton Constable Hall: A Century of Patronage*, Hull 1991

Hallam, H., 'Lamport Hall Revisited', *Book Collector*, XVI, 4 (Winter 1967), pp.439–49

Ham House, Surrey, London 1995

Hamilton, H., *Selections from the Monymusk Papers (1713–1755)*, Edinburgh 1945

Hamilton, J., 'Hobbes's Study and the Hardwick Library', *Journal of the History of Philosophy*, XVI (1978), pp.445–53

Hamilton, J. S., 'Guy de Beauchamp (c.1272–1315)', ODNB, online edn., January 2008

Hanbury Williams, Charles, *The Works of the Right Honourable Sir Chas. Hanbury Williams*, London 1822

Hanham, A., 'Stanhope, James, First Earl Stanhope (1673–1721)', ODNB

A Handlist of Manuscirpts in the Library of the Earl of Leicester at Holkham Hall: Abstracted from the Catalogues of William Roscoe and Frederick Madden and annotated by Seymour De Ricci, [London] 1932

Hanna, Ralph, and Thorlac Turville-Petre (eds), *The Wollaton Manuscripts: Texts, Owners and Readers*, Woodbridge 2010

Hardwick, N. (ed.), *A Diary of the Journey through the North of England made by William and John Blathwayt of Dyrham Park in 1703*, [Bristol] 1972

Hare, A., *The Story of my Life*, London 1896

Harmsen, T., 'Hickes, George (1642–1715)', ODNB

Harris, E., *Osterley Park, Middlesex*, London 1994

—, *The Genius of Robert Adam: His Interiors*, London 2001

Harris, John, 'A Rare and Precious Room: the Kedermister Library, Langley, Buckinghamshire', *Country Life*, 1 December 1977, pp.1576–9

—, *The Palladian Revival: Lord Burlington, his Villa and his Garden at Chiswick*, New Haven and London 1994

Harris, Joseph, *The Description and Use of the Globes, and the Orrery*, London 1731, ESTC T113888

Harris, Kate, 'An Augustan Episode in the History of the Collections of Medieval Manuscripts at Longleat House', in A. Edwards, V. Gillespie and R. Hanna, *The English Medieval Book: Studies in Memory of Jeremy Griffiths*, London 2000, pp.233–47

Harris, P. R., *A History of the British Museum Library, 1753–1973*, London 1998

Hartwell, C., M. Hyde, E. Hubbard and N. Pevsner, *Cheshire: The Buildings of England*, London 2011

Hassall, W. O. (ed.), *A Catalogue of the Library of Sir Edward Coke*, London 1950

Hatfield House, Ipswich 2011

Hawkyard, A. D. K., 'Thornbury Castle', *Transactions of the Bristol and Gloucestershire Archaeological Society*, XCV (1997), pp.51–8

Hayes, William, *Portraits of Rare and Curious Birds, with their Descriptions, from the Menagery of Osterly Park, in the County of Middlesex*, London 1794[–1800], ESTC T129530

Haythornthwaite, J., 'Elton Hall Library', *Library Association Rare Books Group Newsletter*, XXXI (May 1988), pp.14–17

Hayward, Maria (ed.), *The 1542 Inventory of Whitehall: The Palace and its Keeper*, London 2004

Hazen, A. T., *A Catalogue of Horace Walpole's Library*, New Haven and London 1969

Hearn, K., 'A Question of Judgement: Lucy Harington, Countess of Bedford, as Art Patron and Collector', in E. Chaney (ed.), *The Evolution of English Collecting: Receptions of Italian Art in the Tudor and Stuart Periods*, London 2003, pp.221–39

Heard, H., *William Armstrong: Magician of the North*, Newcastle 2011, p.123–5

Heath, C., *Historical and Descriptive Accounts of the Ancient and Present of Ragland* [sic], Monmouth 1829

Hellinga, Lotte, *William Caxton and Early Printing in England*, London 2010

Herrmann, F., 'Sotheby family (*per.* 1778–1861)', ODNB

—, *Sotheby's: A Portrait of an Auction House*, London 1980

—, 'The Role of the Auction Houses', in G. Mandelbrote (ed), *Out of Print and into Profit*, London 2006, pp. 3–34

Hervey, Mary, *Letters of Mary Lepel, Lady Hervey*, London 1821

Higgitt, John, *The Murthly Hours: Devotion, Literacy and Luxury in Paris, England and the Gaelic West*, London 2000

Hillyard, B., 'Ker, John, Third Duke of Roxburghe, (1740–1804)', ODNB

—, 'Rosebery as Book Collector', *Journal of the Edinburgh Bibliographical Society*, VII (2012), pp. 71–114

Historical Manuscripts Commission: Calendar of the Manuscripts of the Most Honourable the Marquis of Salisbury, Preserved at Hatfield House, Hertfordshire, London 1883–1976

Historical Manuscripts Commission: Twelfth Report, Appendix, Part IV. The Manuscripts of His Grace the Duke of Rutland, G.C.B., Preserved at Belvoir Castle, London 1888

Historical Manuscripts Commission: The Manuscripts and Correspondence of James, First Earl of Charlemont. vol. II. 1784–1799, London 1894

Historical Manuscripts Commission: The Manuscripts of His Grace the Duke of Portland, Preserved at Welbeck Abbey, London 1897

Historical Manuscripts Commission: Report on the Manuscripts of His Grace the Duke of Portland Preserved at Welbeck Abbey, London 1901

Historical Manuscripts Commission: Report on the Manuscripts of the Earl of Verulam, Preserved at Gorhambury, London 1906

Historical Manuscripts Commission: Report on the Manuscripts of the Earl of Ancaster, Preserved at Grimsthorpe, Dublin 1907

Historical Manuscripts Commission: Calendar of the Manuscripts of the Marquis of Bath Preserved at Longleat, Dublin 1907

Historical Manuscripts Commission: Report on the Manuscripts of the Right Honourable Viscount de L'Isle, V. C., Preserved at Penshurst Place, Kent, London 1966

'Historical Town Houses: Lichfield House, No. 15 St James's Square', *Architectural Review*, XXVII, 162 (May 1910), pp. 273–8

'History Crumbles as Heiress is Gaoled', *Daily Telegraph*, 26 September 2002

Hoare, Peter, 'The Perils of Provenance: Serial Ownership, Bookplates and Obfuscation at Belton House', *Library History*, XVIII (2002), pp. 225–34

—, 'An Icon of Gay Literature at Belton House' *National Trust Arts, Building & Collections Bulletin*, Summer 2007

Hoare, R. Colt, *A Catalogue of Books Relating to the History and Topography of Italy*, London 1812

Hobson, Anthony, *Major Abbey's Bindings in the Saleroom*, London 1966

—, 'Abbey, John Roland (1894–1969)', ODNB

—, and A. N. L. Munby, 'Contemporary Collectors XXVI: John Roland Abbey', *Book Collector*, X (1961), pp. 40–48

Hodges, J., *Chateau Impney: The Story of a Victorian Country House*, S.l. 2009

Hofland, Barbara, *A Descriptive Account of the Mansions and Gardens of White Knights, … With Twenty-Three Engravings from Pictures … by T. C. Hofland*, London 1819

Holden, Paul, '"One of the Most Remarkable Things in London": A Visit to the Lord Treasurer's Library in 1713 by Samuel Molyneux', *Electronic British Library Journal* (2010)

—, (ed.), *The London Letters of Samuel Molyneux, 1712–13*, London 2011, pp. 43–4

Homer, Sarah, 'The Osterley Menagerie', in Timothy Knox and Anthea Palmer (eds), *Aspects of Osterley*, London 2000, pp. 44–9

Honeybone, D., and M. Honeybone (eds), *The Correspondence of the Spalding Gentleman's Society, 1710–1761*, Woodbridge 2010

Honeybone, M., and Y. Lewis, 'Ellys, Sir Richard, Third Baronet (1682–1742)', ODNB

Hope, W. H. St. John, 'The Last Testament and Inventory of John de Veer, Thirteenth Earl of Oxford', *Archaeologia*, LXVI (1915), pp. 275–348

Horrocks, H., *Newhailes*, Edinburgh 2004

Horton, S., and K. Oakes, *The Landmark Trust Handbook* Maidenhead 2003

Howard, D., *Lord Arundel and his Circle*, New Haven and London 1985

Howard, Maurice, *The Early Tudor Country House*, London 1987

Howarth, D., *Lord Arundel and his Circle*, New Haven and London 1985

Howitt, W., *Visits to Remarkable Places: Old Halls, Battle Fields, and Scenes Illustrative of Striking Passages in English History and Poetry*, London 1840

Hoyle, R. W., 'Percy, Henry Algernon, Fifth Earl of Northumberland, 1478–1527)', ODNB

Hunter, Michael (ed.), *From Books to Bezoars: Sir Hans Sloane and His Collections*, London 2012

The Huntington Library: Treasures from Ten Centuries, San Marino 2004

Hussey, Christopher, 'Caledon, Co. Tyrone', *Country Life*, 27 February and 6 March 1937

—, *English Country Houses: Early Georgian, 1715–1760*, London 1955

—, *The English Country Houses: Mid Georgian, 1760–1800*, London 1955

Hutton, Ronald, 'Maitland, John, Duke of Lauderdale (1616–1682)', ODNB

Huws, D., 'Sir Thomas Mostyn and the Mostyn Manscripts', in J. Carley and C. Tite, *Books and Collectors 1200–1700: Essays Presented to Andrew Watson*, London 1997, pp. 451–72

'The Inventory of Juliana de Leybourne, Countess of Huntyngdon', *Archaeologia Cantiana*, I (1858), pp. 1–8

'Inventory of the Plenishing of the House of The Binns at the date of the Death of General Thomas Dalyell', *Proceedings of the Society of Antiquaries of Scotland*, 5th series, X (1924), pp. 344–70

Irwin, Raymond, *The English Library: Sources and History*, London 1966

Isham, Gyles, *Lamport Hall: Past and Present*, Kettering 1985

Isham, T., *The Diary of Sir Thomas Isham of Lamport*, Farnborough 1971

Jack, Belinda, *The Woman Reader*, New Haven and London 2012

Jackson, W., 'A Dibdinian Tour (1938)', in W. Jackson, *Records of a Bibliographer*, Cambridge, MA 1967, pp. 67–82

Jackson-Stops, Gervase, 'Barons Court, Co. Tyrone' *Country Life*, 12, 19 and 26 July 1979

—, 'Thomas Hooper at Melford and Erddig', in Gervase Jackson-Stops (ed.), *National Trust Studies* (1981), pp. 69–83

—, *Hagley Hall: Seat of the Viscount Cobham*, Derby 1982

—, *The English Country House: A Grand Tour*, London 1984

— (ed.), *The Treasure Houses of Britain: Five Hundred Years of Private Patronage and Collecting*, Washington 1985

—, 'Most Learned Decoration', *Country Life*, 24 March 1988, pp. 120–23

—, 'A British Parnassus: Mythology and the Country House', in Gervase Jackson-Stops (ed.), *The Fashioning and Functioning of the British Country House*, Washington 1989, pp. 217–38

—, 'The National Trust and the In Lieu System', in *Patronage Preserved: An Exhibition of*

Masterpieces Saved for Country Houses, London 1991, pp. 16–20

James, Dermot, *The Gore-Booths of Lissadell*, Dublin 2004, p. 339

Jardine, Lisa, and Anthony Grafton, '"Studied for Action": how Gabriel Harvey read his Livy', *Past and Present*, CXXIX, (1990), 1, pp. 30–78

Jay, Emma, 'Queen Caroline's Library and its European Contexts', *Book History*, IX (2006), pp. 31–55

Jayne, Sears, *Library Catalogues of the English Renaissance*, Berkeley 1956

—, and Francis R. Johnson, *The Lumley Catalogue: The Catalogue of 1609*, London 1956

Jefcoate, Graham, 'Mr Cavendish's Librarian: Charles Heydinger and the Library of Henry Cavendish, 1783–1801', *Library & Information History*, XXXII, 1–2 (2016), pp. 58–71

Jenkins, Susan, '"An Inventory of His Grace the Duke of Chandos's Seat att Cannons Taken June the 19th 1725" by John Gilbert', *Walpole Society*, LXVII (2005), pp. 93–192

Jensen, Kristian, *Revolution and the Antiquarian Book: Reshaping the Past, 1780–1815*, Cambridge 2011

Jervis, Simon, 'The English Country House Library', in N. Barker (ed.), *Treasures from the Libraries of National Trust Country Houses*, New York 1999, pp. 13–33

John, W., and Kit Smith, *An Architectural History of Towneley Hall, Burnley*, Nelson 2004

Johnson, Joan, 'Brydges, James, First Duke of Chandos (1674–1744)', ODNB

Johnson, Samuel, and James Boswell, *To the Hebrides: Samuel Johnson's Journey to the Western Islands of Scotland and James Boswell's Journal of a Tour to the Hebrides*, ed. Ronald Black, Edinburgh 2007

Jones, J. Gwynfor, 'Wynn Family (*per. c. 1465–1678*)', ODNB

Joyce, Edmund, *Borris House, Co. Carlow, and Elite Regency Patronage*, Dublin 2013

Keiser, George R., 'Practical Books for the Gentleman', in Lotte Hellinga and J. B. Trapp (eds), CHBB, vol. III: *1400–1557*, Cambridge 1999, pp. 470–94

Kent, William, *Some Designs of Mr. Inigo Jones and Mr. Wm. Kent*, [London] 1744, ESTC T116216

Ker, Neil, 'Sir John Prise', *The Library*, 5th series, X, 1 (March 1955), pp. 1–24

—, *Medieval Libraries of Great Britain: A List of Surviving Books*, 2nd edn., London 1964

Kerr, Robert, *The Gentleman's House*, London 1864

Ketton-Cremer, Robert Wyndham, *Felbrigg: The Story of a House*, London 1986

Keynes, Simon, 'King Athelstan's Books', in M. Lapidge and H. Gneuss, *Learning and Literature in Anglo-Saxon England: Studies Presented to Peter Clemoes on the Occasion of his Sixty-Fifth Birthday*, Cambridge 1985, pp. 143–201

de Kind, Richard, 'The Roman portraits from the Villa of Lullingstone: Pertinax and his Father P. Helvius Successus', in T. Ganschow and M. Steinhart (eds), *Otium: Festschrift für Volker Michael Strocka*, Remshalden 2005, pp. 47–52

Kingsford, C. L., 'Two Forfeitures in the Year of Agincourt', *Archaeologia*, LXX (1920), pp. 71–100

—, 'Exeter House, formerly Leicester House and Exeter Inn', *Archaeologia*, LXXIII (1923), pp. 1–54

Kissane, Noel (ed.), *Treasures from the National Library of Ireland*, Dublin: Presented by the Boyne Valley Honey Company, 1994

Knox, Tim, 'Sir John Thorold's Library at Syston Park, Lincolnshire', *Apollo*, CXLVI (September 1997), pp. 24–9

—, '"A Mortifying Lesson to Human Vanity": Ralph Willett's Library at Merly House, Dorset', *Apollo* (July 2000), pp. 38–45

Kohl, Benjamin G., 'Tiptoft [Tibetot], John, First Earl of Worcester (1427–1470)', ODNB, online edn., September 2015

Laing, Alastair, *In Trust for the Nation: Paintings from National Trust Houses*, London 1995

Lancaster, H., 'Thynne, Thomas, First Viscount Weymouth (*bap. 1640, d. 1714*)', ODNB

Landon, R., 'Two Collectors: Thomas Grenville and Lord Amherst', in W. Kirsop (ed), *The Commonwealth of Books: Essays and Studies in Honour of Ian Willison*, Clayton, Victoria 2007, pp. 78–95

Langley, Robin, 'The Music', in T. Murdoch (ed.), *Boughton House: The English Versailles*, London 1992, pp. 175–7

Larsen, R. (ed.), *Maids & Mistresses: Celebrating 300 Years of Women and the Yorkshire Country House*, York 2004

Lauder, Sir John, *Journals of Sir John Lauder, Lord Fountainhall*, Edinburgh 1900

Leach, P., *James Paine*, London 1988

Leatham, Lady Victoria, *Burghley: The Life of a Great House*, London 1992

Lee, Brian North, 'Gentlemen and their Book-Plates', in Robin Myers and Michael Harris (ed.), *Property of a Gentleman: The Formation, Organisation and Dispersal of the Private Library, 1620–1920*, Winchester 1991, pp. 43–76

Leedham-Green, Elisabeth, and David McKitterick, 'Ownership: Private and Public Libraries', CHBB, IV, pp. 323–35

Lees-Milne, James, *English Country Houses: Baroque, 1685–1715*, London 1970

—, *Ancestral Voices*, London 1984

—, *The Bachelor Duke: A Life of William Spencer Cavendish, 6th Duke of Devonshire, 1790–1858*, London 1991

—, *Diaries, 1942–1945*, London 1998

—, *Holy Dread: Diaries, 1982–1984*, London 2001

Leland, John, *Itinerary*, London 1906–10

Leslie, Shane, 'The Shirley Library at Lough Fea, Carrickmacross in Co. Monaghan, Ireland', *Book Collectors' Quarterly*, 11, 6 (1932), pp. 1–9

—, *Long Shadows*, London 1966

Levin, A., *Raine and Johnnie: The Spencers and the Scandal of Althorp*, London 1993

Levine, J., *Between the Ancients and the Moderns: Baroque Culture in Restoration England*, New Haven and London 1999

Levy Peck, Linda, 'Uncovering the Arundel Library at the Royal Society: Changing Meanings of Science and the Fate of the Norfolk Donation', *Notes and Records of the Royal Society*, LII (1998), pp. 3–24

Lewin, P., 'Ross, Thomas (*bap. 1620, d. 1675*)', ODNB

Lewis, Wilmarth Sheldon, *Collector's Progress*, London 1952

—, *Horace Walpole's Library*, Cambridge 1958

Lewis, Yvonne, 'Sir Ralph Bankes (?1631–1677) and the Origins of the Library at Kingston Hall', *Library History*, XVIII, 3 (November 2002), pp. 215–23

—, '"Appropriate for a County House?": Rebuilding Ralph Dutton's Library at Hinton Ampner', *National Trust Arts, Building & Collections Bulletin* (May 2013)

Lichfield, Patrick, *Not the Whole Truth: An Autobiography*, London 1987

Lister, Anthony, 'Catalogus Bibliothecae Kingstonianae', *Book Collector*, XXXIII (1985), pp. 63–77

—, 'The Althorp Library of Second Earl Spencer, Now in the John Rylands University Library, Manchester, Its Formation and Growth', *Bulletin of the John Rylands University Library*, LXXI, 2 (1989), pp. 67–86

Lloyd, R., *The Poetical Works*, London 1774, ESTC T94392

Lloyd, Thomas, *Lost Houses of Wales: A Survey of Country Houses in Wales Demolished since c.1900*, London 1989

—, 'Country-House Libraries of the Eighteenth and Nineteenth Centuries', in P. Jones and E. Rees, *A Nation and its Books: A History of the Book in Wales*, Aberystwyth 1998, pp. 135–46

—, J. Orbach and R. Scourfield, *Pembrokeshire: The Buildings of Wales*, London 2004

Longley, E., 'Ledwidge, Francis Edward (1887–1917)', ODNB

Lustig, S., 'Boswell, Margaret Montgomerie (1738?–1789)', ODNB

Lyall, R. J., 'Books and Book Owners in Fifteenth-Century Scotland', in Jeremy Griffiths and Derek Pearsall, *Book Production and Publishing in Britain, 1375–1475*, Cambridge 2007

Lysons, Daniel, *The Environs of London*, London 1792–6, ESTC T123547

MacAodha, Breandan, 'The Big House in Western Ireland', in Jacqueline Genet (ed.), *The Big House in Ireland: Reality and Representation*, Dingle 1992, pp. 19–29

MacCaffrey, W., 'Cecil, William, First Baron Burghey (1520/21–1598)', ODNB

McCarthy, M., 'Soane's "Saxon" Room at Stowe', *Journal of the Society of Architectural Historians*, XLIV, 2 (May 1985), pp. 129–46

McClain, M., *Beaufort: The Duke and his Duchess, 1657–1715*, New Haven and London 2001

McCutcheon, E. (ed.), *Sir Nicholas Bacons's Great House Sententiae: The Latin Text, along with the First English Translation, and Introduction*, Honolulu 1977

McDonald, J., *Alnwick Castle: Home of the Duke and Duchess of Northumberland*, London 2012

MacDonald, R., *The Library of Drummond of Hawthornden*, Edinburgh 1971

McGibbon, D., and T. Ross, *The Castellated and Domestic Architecture of Scotland from the Twelfth to the Eighteenth Century*, Edinburgh 1887–92

MacGregor, Arthur, 'The Cabinet of Curiosities in Seventeenth-Century Britain', in O. Impey and A. MacGregor, *The Origins of Museums: The Cabinet of Curiosities in Sixteenth and Seventeenth-Century Europe*, Oxford 1985, pp. 155–8

McKendrick, Scot (ed.), *Royal Manuscripts: The Genius of Imagination*, London 2011

—, and Kathleen Doyle (eds), *Royal Illuminated Manuscripts: From King Athelstan to Henry VIII*, London 2011

McKitterick, David, *The Library of Sir Thomas Knyvett of Ashwellthorpe, c. 1539–1618*, Cambridge 1978

—, 'Sales from Wigan', *Book Collector*, LXI, 4 (Winter 2012), pp. 581–4

Macky, J., *A Journey through England, in Familiar Letters*, London 1723, ESTC T57749

McLaggan, M., 'The Library of a Bibliomaniac Great-Grandfather', in R. Myers and M. Harris (ed.), *Bibliophily*, Cambridge 1986, pp. 121–37

Macray, W. D., *Annals of the Bodleian Library*, Oxford 1890

Maddison, John, et al., *Blickling Hall, Norfolk*, London 1987

Maittaire, Michael, *Senilia, Sive Poetica Aliquot*, London 1742, ESTC T91003

Major, Norma, *Chequers: The Prime Minister's Country House and its History*, London 1996

Malcolm, Noel, *Aspects of Hobbes*, Oxford: Clarendon Press, 2002

—, 'Hobbes, Thomas' (1588–1679)', ODNB

Malcomson, A. P. W., *The De Vesci Papers*, Dublin 2006

—, *Virtues of a Wicked Earl: The Life and Legend of William Sydney Clements, 3rd Earl of Leitrim*, Dublin 2009

Mancinus, Dominicus, *Here Begynneth a Ryght Frutefull Treatyse, Intituled the Myrrour of Good Maners*, London 1518?, STC 17242, ESTC S103749

Mandelbrote, Giles, 'The Library of the Duke of Lauderdale (1616–1682)', in C. Rowell (ed.), *Ham House: Four Hundred Years of Collecting and Patronage*, New Haven and London 2013, pp. 222–31

—, and Yvonne Lewis, *Learning to Collect: The Library of Sir Richard Ellys (1682–1742)*, London 2004

—, and Barry Taylor, *Libraries within the Library: The Origins of the British Museum's Printed Collections*, London 2009

Mandelbrote, Scott, 'The English Bible and its Readers in the Eighteenth Century', in I. Rivers (ed.), *Books and their Readers in Eighteenth-Century England: New Essays*, London 2001, pp. 33–78

Mandler, Peter, *The Rise and Fall of the Stately Home*, New Haven and London 1997

Manly, John M., and Edith Rickerts, *The Text of the Canterbury Tales: Studied on the Basis of All Known Manuscripts*, Chicago 1940

Mansbridge, Michael, *John Nash: A Complete Catalogue*, Oxford 1991

Markham, Sheila, *A Book of Booksellers: Conversations with the Antiquarian Book Trade, 1991–2003*, London 2004

Marks, Richard, and Paul Williamson, *Gothic: Art for England, 1400–1547*, exh. cat., Victoria and Albert Museum, London 2003

Marot, Daniel, *Oeuvres du Sr. D. Marot, Architecte de Guillaume III. Roi de la Grande Bretagne, Contenant Plussieurs, Pensséz utile aux Architectes, Peintres, Sculpteurs, Orfeures & Jardiniers, & Autres*, The Hague 1703

Marsden, Jonathan, '"Far from Elegant, yet Exceedingly Curious": Neo-Norman Furnishings at Penrhyn', *Apollo*, CXXXVII, 374 (April 1993), pp. 263–70

Marshall, Pamela, *Wollaton Hall: An Archaeological Survey*, Nottingham 1996

Marshall, Peter, *Faith and Identity in a Warwickshire Family: The Throckmortons and the Reformation*, Stratford 2010

Martin, Joanna, *Wives and Daughters: Women and Children in the Georgian Country House*, London 2004

Massey, Owen, 'Notes on the Orrery Collection (2)', *Christ Church Library Newsletter*, V, 1 (Michaelmas 2008), pp. 6–8

Mathew, David, 'The Library at Naworth', in D. Woodruff (ed.), *For Hilaire Belloc: Essays in Honour of his 72nd Birthday*, London 1942, pp. 115–30

Mauchline, M., *Harewood House*, Ashbourne 1992

Mavor, William, *New Description of Blenheim*, London 1789, ESTC T077052

Maxwell Lyte, H., *The Lytes of Lytescary*, Taunton 1895

—, *A History of Dunster*, London 1909

May, A., 'Philip Henry, Eleventh Marquess of Lothian' (1882–1940)', ODNB

Meakin, H., *The Painted Closet of Lady Anne Drury*, Farnham 2013

Medley, John Bacon, *The Catalogue of the Library, Tyntesfield, in the County of Somerset*, Bristol [1894]

Meller, Hugh, 'Knightshayes Court: Reconstructing a Victorian Library Room', *Library History*, XVIII, 3 (November 2002), pp. 235–40

Mellerstain, Gordon, Berwickshire, Derby 1980

Melvin, P., *Estates and Landed Society in Galway*, Dublin 2012

Memoir of Lady Warwick: also Her Diary, London 1896

Meredith, J., 'Letters between Friends: Lord Charlemont's Library and Other Matters', *Irish Architectural and Decorative Studies*, IV (2001), pp. 52–77

Mertes, Kate, *The English Noble Household 1250–1600: Good Governance and Politic Rule*, Oxford 1988, pp. 18–21

Millar, S., *The Diaries of Sanderson Millar of Radway*, [Stratford-upon-Avon] 2005

Miller, Edward, 'A Collection of Elizabethan and Jacobean Plays at Petworth', *National Trust Studies* (1975), pp. 62–4

—, 'The National Trust's Libraries', *National Trust*, XXVIII (Autumn 1977), p. 15

Miller, James, *Fertile Fortune: The Story of Tyntesfield*, London 2003

—, 'Paston, Robert, First Earl of Yarmouth (1631–1683)', ODNB

Millington, J., *William Beckford and his Tower*, Bath 1978

Minet, P., 'A Century of Innovation in Selling Books', in G. Mandelbrote (ed.), *Out of Print & Into Profit: A History of the Rare and Secondhand Book Trade in Britain in the Twentieth Century*, London 2006, pp. 63–73

The Minute-Books of the Spalding Gentlemen's Society, 1712–1755, [Fakenham] 1981

Miscellanea Antiqua Anglicana; or a Select Collection of Curious Tracts Illustrative of the History, Literature, Manners and Biography of the English Nation, London 1816

Mitchell, R., 'A Renaissance Library: The Collection of John Tiptoft, Earl of Worcester', *The Library*, XVIII (1938), pp. 72–8

Moffat, B., 'Fraser, James (1645–1731)', ODNB

Montgomery-Massingberd, Hugh, *Great Houses of England and Wales*, London 1994

—, *Great Houses of Ireland*, London 1999

Moore, Andrew, *Norfolk & the Grand Tour*, Norwich 1985

—, *Dutch and Flemish Painting in Norfolk: A History of Taste and Influence, Fashion and Collecting*, London 1988

—, 'Fountaine, Sir Andrew (1676–1753)', ODNB

Moore, Jo, 'Filling the Shelves at Montacute', *Library History*, XVIII, 3 (November 2002), pp. 153–6

Morell, Thomas, *Catalogus Librorum in Bibliotheca Osteriensi*, [London?] 1771, ESTC N30998

Morgan, C., 'Herbert, Sir William (c. 1553–1593)', ODNB

Morgan, Nigel, 'Books for the Liturgy and Private Prayer', in CHBB, vol. II: 1100–1400, Nigel Morgan and Rodney Thomson (eds), pp. 291–316

—, and Paul Binski, 'Private Devotion: Humility and Splendour', in Binski and Panayotova 2005, pp. 163–76

Morgan, Paul, 'A 16th-Century Warwickshire Library: A Problem of Provenance', *Book Collector*, XXII, 3 (Autumn 1973), pp. 337–55

—, 'Frances Wolfreston and "Hor Bouks": a Seventeenth-Century Woman Book-Collector', *The Library*, 6th series, XI, 3 (September 1989), pp. 197–219

Morris, Leslie, *Rosenbach Abroad: In Pursuit of Books in Private Collections*, Philadelphia 1988

—, *Rosenbach Redux: Further Book Adventures in England and Ireland*, Philadelphia 1989

Morris, O., *The 'Chymick Bookes' of Sir Owen Wynne of Gwydir: An Annotated Catalogue*, Cambridge 1997

Moss, W., *Bindings from the Library of Robt. Dudley, Earl of Leicester, K.G.*, Sonning-on-Thames 1934

Muckross House, Killarney, National Park, [Killarney?] [c.2010?]

Mulligan, K., *Ballyfin: The Restoration of an Irish House & Demesne*, [Tralee] 2011

—, *South Ulster: The Counties of Armagh, Cavan and Monaghan: The Buildings of Ireland*, New Haven and London 2013

Mulvagh, J., *Madresfield: The Real Brideshead*, London 2008

Munby, A. N. L., 'The Triumph of Delisle: a Sequel', *Harvard Library Bulletin*, XVII, 3 (July 1969), pp. 279–90

—, *Connoisseurs and Medieval Miniature*, Oxford 1972

—, 'The Library', in *The Destruction of the Country House, 1875–1975*, London 1974, pp. 106–11

—, 'The Acquisition of Manuscripts by Institutional Libraries', in A. N. L. Munby, *Essays and Papers*, London 1977, pp. 67–81

—, 'The Earl and the Thief', in A. N. L. Munby, *Essays and Papers*, London 1977, pp. 175–91

Murdoch, A., 'Campbell, Archibald, Third Duke of Argyll (1682–1761)', ODNB

Murdoch, Tessa (ed.), *Noble Households: Eighteenth-Century Inventories of Great English Houses: A Tribute to John Cornforth*, Cambridge 2006

Murphy, G., 'Thomas, Vaughan (1775–1858)', ODNB

Murray, V., *Castle Howard: The Life and Times of a Stately Home*, London 1994

Myers, Alec Reginald (ed.), *The Household of Edward IV: The Black Book and the Ordinance of 1478*, Manchester 1959

Myers, Robin, 'Robins, George Henry (1777–1847)', ODNB

—, M. Harris and G. Mandelbrote (eds), *Under the Hammer: Book Auctions since the Seventeenth Century*, New Castle, DE 2001

Mynors, Charles, *Listed Buildings, Conservation Areas and Monuments*, London 2006

Nash, Joseph, *The Mansions of England in the Olden Times*, London 1839–49

Naudé, Gabriel, *Instructions Concerning Erecting of a Library*, London 1661, Wing N247, ESTC R8116

Neave, David, 'Wressle Castle', *Archaeological Journal*, CXLI (1984), pp. 58–60

Needham, Paul, *Twelve Centuries of Bookbindings, 400–1600*, New York 1979)

Newby Hall, S.l. 1982

Newhailes, Edinburgh 2002

Newman, J., *Glamorgan: The Buildings of Wales*, London 2004

Newton, E., *The House of Lyme: From its Foundation to the End of the Eighteenth Century*, London 1917

T. Nicholas, *Annals and Antiquities of the Counties and County Families of Wales*, London 1872

Nichols, J., *The Unton Inventories, Relating to Wadley and Faringdon, Co. Berks in the Years 1596 and 1620*, London 1841

Nicolson, William, *The English, Scotch and Irish Historical Libraries: Giving a Short View and Character of Most of Our Historians, Either in Print or Manuscript*, London 1736, ESTC T60243

—, *The London Diaries of William Nicolson, Bishop of Carlisle, 1702–1718*, Oxford 1985

Nixon, H. M., *Twelve Books in Fine Bindings from the Library of J. W. Hely-Hutchinson*, Oxford 1953

—, *Bookbindings from the Library of Jean Grolier*, London 1965

—, *Sixteenth-Century Gold-Tooled Bookbindings in the Pierpont Morgan Library*, New York 1971

—, 'Harleian Bindings', in *Studies in the Book Trade in Honour of Graham Pollard*, Oxford 1975, pp. 153–94

—, and M. Foot, *The History of Decorated Bookbinding in England*, 2nd edn. Oxford 1992

Norgate, G. Le G., 'Spencer, George, Fourth Duke of Marlborough' (1739–1817)', ODNB

North, R., *The Lives of the Right Hon. Francis North, Baron Guilford, … Sir Dudley North, … and the Rev. Dr. John North*, London 1826

Norton, T., *100 Years of Collecting in America: The Story of Sotheby Parke Bernet*, New York 1984

Notes on Hatfield House, S.l. 1886

Oakeshott, W., 'Sir Walter Raleigh's Library', *The Library*, 5th series, XXIII, 4 (December 1968), pp. 285–327

O'Brien, C., 'Ralph Dutton and Ronald Fleming at Hinton Ampner House: Revivalist Tastes in Interior Decoration', *Apollo* (April 1997), pp. 43–7

O'Brien, F., *The Best of Myles: A Selection from 'Cruiskeen Lawn'*, London 1990

O'Brien, K., 'The History Market in Eighteenth-Century England', in I. Rivers (ed.), *Books and their Readers in Eighteenth-Century England: New Essays*, London 2001, pp. 105–33

Ogilvy, Mabell, Countess of Airlie, *Thatched with Gold: The Memoirs of Mabell, Countess of Airlie*, ed. Jennifer Ellis, London 1962

Oldham, J., 'Murray, William, First Earl of Mansfield (1705–1793)', ODNB

Old Thorndon Hall, Chelmsford 1972

O'Reilly, Sean, *The Casino at Marino*, Dublin
1991

—, 'Charlemont House: A Critical History', in
E. Mayes and P. Murphy (eds), *Images and
Insights*, Dublin 1993, pp. 42–54

—, *Irish Houses and Gardens from the Archives of
Country Life*, London 1998

Orme, Nicholas, 'The Education of the Courtier',
in Vincent J. Scattergood and J. W. Sherborne,
English Court Culture in the Later Middle Ages,
London 1983, pp. 63–85

Ormrod, W. Mark, *Edward III*, New Haven and
London 2011

Orr, C. Campbell, 'Charlotte (1744–1818)', ODNB

—, 'Lost Royal Libraries and Hanoverian Court
Culture', in J. Raven (ed.), *Lost Libraries: The
Destruction of Great Book Collections Since
Antiquity*, London 2004

The Orrery Papers, London 1903

O'Shea, K., 'A Castleisland Inventory, 1590',
*Journal of the Kerry Archaeological and
Historical Society*, XV–XVI (1982–3), pp. 37–46

Otter, W., *The Life and Remains of Edward Daniel
Clarke*, London 1825

Ouy, Gilbert, 'Recherches sur la Librairie
de Charles d'Orléans', *Comptes rendus de
l'Académie des Inscriptions et Belles Lettres*
(1955), pp. 272–88

Ovenden, Richard, 'The Libraries of the
Antiquaries (c. 1580–1640) and the Idea of a
National Collection' CHLBI, vol. III, pp. 527–61

—, and S. Handley, 'Howard, Lord William
(1563–1640)', ODNB

Pächt, O., and J. J. Alexander, *Illuminated
Manuscripts in the Bodleian Library*, Oxford
1966–73

Paderni, Camillo, 'Extract of a Letter from
Camillo Paderni Keeper of the Museum
Herculaneum to Tho. Holles, Esq; Relating
to the Late Discoveries at Herculaneum',
Philosophical Transactions, XLVIII, I (1754),
pp. 821–5

Palladio, Andrea, *The Architecture of A. Palladio,
in Four Books … Revis'd, Design'd and Publish'd
by Giacomo Leoni*, London 1721, ESTC T22366

—, *The Four Books of Andrea Palladio's
Architecture* London 1738, ESTC T40073

Panayotova, Stella, *The Macclesfield Psalter*,
London 2008

Pantin, William Abel, 'Instructions for a Devout
and Literate Layman', in J. J. G. Alexander
and M. T. Gibson, *Medieval Learning and
Literature: Essays Presented to Richard William
Hunt*, Oxford 1976, pp. 398–422

Pargeter, S., *Tatton Park Library Catalogue*,
[Chester] 1977

Parkes, F., *Domestic Duties; or, Instruction to
Young Married Ladies*, London 1825

Parslow, Christopher, *Rediscovering Antiquity:
Karl Weber and the Excavation of Herculaneum,
Pompeii, and Stabiae*, Cambridge 1995

The Paston Letters AD 1422–1509, London 1900

Peacham, Henry, *Peacham's Compleat Gentleman,
1634*, Oxford 1906

Peacock, E. (ed.), 'The Inventories made for Sir
William and Sir Thomas Fairfax, Knights,
of Walton, and of Gilling Castle, Yorkshire,
in the Sixteenth & Seventeenth Centuries',
Archaeologia, XLVIII (1885), pp. 123–56

Pearson, David, *Provenance Research in Book
History*, London 1994

—, *English Bookbinding Styles, 1450–1800*, London
2005

—, *Books as History*, London 2008

Pearson, J., *Stags and Serpents: A History of the
Cavendish Family and the Dukes of Devonshire*,
London 1983

Peel, J., 'Croft, Sir Richard, Sixth Baronet
(1762–1818)', ODNB

Peignot, E., *Dictionnaire raisonné de Bibliologie*,
Paris 1802

Pelik, R., *C. W. Dyson Perrins, D.C.L., J.P.,
D.L., F.S.A.: A Brief Account of his Life, his
Achievements, his Collections and Benefactions*,
Worcester 1983, pp. 4–5

Penney, Christine, 'A Bishop and His Books',
Book Collector, LX, 3 (Autumn 2011),
pp. 401–16

Peter, Hugh, *The Full and Last Relationship of All
Things Concerning Basing House*, London 1645,
ESTC R200323, Wing P1702

Pevsner, Nikolaus, *Lancashire, 1: The Industrial
and Commercial South: The Buildings of
England*, London 1969

—, *The Buildings of England: Oxfordshire*, London
1974

—, and I. Richmond, *Northumberland: The
Buildings of England*, Harmondsworth 1992

—, and E. Williamson with G. Brandwood,
The Buildings of England: Buckinghamshire,
Harmondsworth 1994

Philip, Ian, 'Sir William Pickering and His
Books', *Book Collector*, V, 3 (Autumn 1956),
pp. 231–38

Piccope, G., *Lancashire and Cheshire Wills
and Inventories from the Ecclesiastical Court,
Chester: the First Portion*, Manchester 1854

Pickwoad, Nicholas, 'Problems of Conservation',
*The Library Association Rare Books Group
Newsletter*, XIX (May 1982), pp. 11–14

Piggott, S., *William Stukeley: An Eighteenth-
Century Antiquary*, London 1985

Plomer, H. M., 'A Cavalier's Library', *The Library*,
2nd series, V (1905), pp. 158–72

Plumptre, James, *James Plumptre's Britain: The
Journals of a Tourist in the 1790s*, London 1992

Pollard, Graham, 'Changes in the Style of
Bookbinding, 1550–1830', *The Library* (1956),
5th series, XI, 2, pp. 71–94

Pollock, L., *With Faith and Physick: The Life of
a Tudor Gentlewoman, Lady Grace Mildmay,
1552–1620*, London 1993

—, 'Grace Mildmay', ODNB

The Pomander of Prayer, London 1531, STC
25421.5, ESTC S4968

Porter, S., *The Blast of War: Destruction in the
English Civil Wars*, Stroud 2011

Potten, Edward, '"A Great Number of Usefull
Books": the Hidden Library of Henry Booth,
1st Earl of Warrington (1652–1694)', *Library
& Information History*, XXV, 1 (March 2009),
pp. 33–49

—, '"Bound in Vellum and Lettered": the Tatton
Park Library', in *National Trust Historic Houses
& Collections Annual* (2013), pp. 4–11 (pp. 5–7)

—, 'The Rest of the Iceberg: Reassessing Private
Book Ownership in the Nineteenth Century',
in *Transactions of the Cambridge Bibliographical
Society*, XV, 3 (2014), pp. 125–50

—, 'Beyond Bibliophilia: Contextualizing Private
Libraries in the Nineteenth Century', *Library
& Information History*, XXXI, 31, 2 (May 2015),
pp. 73–94

—, and James Rothwell, '"The Ewe-Lamb" of
Lyme Park Library: William Caxton's 1487
Missale ad Usum Sarum', in *National Trust
Historic Houses and Collections Annual* (2009),
pp. 42–7

Potter, E., 'To Paul's Churchyard to Treat with
a Bookbinder', in R. Myers and M. Harris
(ed.), *Property of a Gentleman: The Formation,
Organisation and Dispersal of the Private
Library, 1620–1920*, Winchester 1991, pp. 25–42

Powell, M., 'The "Curious Books" in the Library
at Strawberry Hill', in M. Snodin (ed.), *Horace
Walpole's Strawberry Hill*, New Haven and
London 2009, pp. 235–41

Powys, C. Lybbe, *Passages from the Diaries of Mrs
Philip Lybbe Powys*, London 1899

von Pückler-Muskau, Hermann, *Tour of England,
Ireland, and France, in the Year 1828 & 1829*,
London 1832

—, *Puckler's Progress: The Adventures of Prince
Pückler-Muskau in England, Wales and Ireland,
as Told in Letters to his Former Wife, 1826–9*,
London 1987

Pullen, G., 'The Harvington Library at Oscott',
Worcestershire Recusant, 1 (April 1963),
pp. 18–20

Purcell, Mark, '"A Relic of King Charles the Martyr?": the Juxon Bible at Chastleton', *Apollo* (April 2000), pp. 30–35

—, '"A Lunatick of Unsound Mind": Edward, Lord Leigh (1742–86) and the Refounding of Oriel College Library', *Bodleian Library Record*, XVII, 3–4 (Apr.–Oct. 2001), pp. 246–60

—, 'Books and Reading in Eighteenth-Century Westmorland: the Brownes of Townend', *Library History*, XVII, 2 (2001), pp 91–106

—, 'The Country House Library Reassess'd: or, Did the "Country House Library" Ever Really Exist', *Library History*, XVIII, 3 (November 2002), pp. 157–74

—, 'Thorold, Sir John, 9th Baronet (1734–1815)', ODNB

—, 'The Library at Lanhydrock', *Book Collector*, LIV (2005), pp. 195–230

—, 'From Bury to Bromham: Books at Canons Ashby', in David Adshead (ed.), *National Trust Historic Houses and Collections Annual* (2010), pp. 18–25

—, 'The Library at Penrhyn Castle', *Book Collector*, LIX, 2 (Summer 2010), pp. 241–50

—, *The Big House Library in Ireland: Books in Ulster Country Houses*, Swindon 2011

—, 'National Trust Libraries in Wales', in David Adshead (ed.), *National Trust Historic Houses & Collections Annual* (2011), pp. 12–19

—, 'Libraries at Lacock Abbey', in David Adshead (ed.), *National Trust Historic Houses & Collections Annual* (2012), pp. 36–43

—, 'Making History: the Library at Wallington', in David Adshead (ed.), *National Trust Historic Houses & Collections Annual* (2014), pp. 16–21

—, 'The Library at Sheringham Park', *Book Collector*, LXV, 1, (Spring 2016), pp. 71–82

—, 'Clumber: the Rise and Fall of a Ducal Library', *Library & Information History*, XXXII, 1–2 (2016), pp. 88–99

—, and J. Fishwick, 'The Library at Ickworth', *Book Collector*, LXI, 3 (September 2012), pp. 366–90

—, and William Hale, 'Hibernica at Florence Court', in David Adshead (ed.), *National Trust Historic Houses and Collections Annual* (2008), pp. 30–35

—, and Nicola Thwaite, *The Libraries of Calke Abbey*, [London 2013]

—, and Nicola Thwaite, 'Libraries at Hardwick' in David Adshead and David Taylor (eds), *Hardwick Hall: A Great Old Castle of Romance*, New Haven and London 2016, pp. 177–91

—, William Hale and David Pearson, *Treasures from the Library of Lord Fairhaven at Anglesey Abbey*, London 2014

Purdue, Olwen, *The Big House in the North of Ireland*, Dublin 2009

Quarrie, Paul, 'The Scientific Library of the Earls of Macclesfield', *Notes & Records of the Royal Society*, XX (2006), pp. 5–24

Quiney, R., *John Loughborough Pearson*, London 1979

Rainey, Elizabeth, 'The Library of Lord William Howard (1563–1640) from Naworth Castle', *Friends of the National Libraries Annual Report* (1992), pp. 20–22

Ramsay, Nigel, 'English Book Collectors and the Salerooms in the Eighteenth Century' in R. Myers, M. Harris and G. Mandelbrote (eds), *Under the Hammer: Books Auctions since the Seventeenth Century* (New Castle, DE 2001), pp 89–110

Raven, James, 'The Book Trades', in I. Rivers (ed.), *Books and their Readers in Eighteenth-Century England*, London 2001, pp. 1–34

—, H. Small and N. Tadmor, *The Practice and Representation of Reading in England*, Cambridge 1996

Rawcliffe, Carole, 'Somerset, John (d. 1454)', ODNB, online edn., January 2008

Rawlinson, Kent, '"In Chapel, Oratory or Other Suitable Places in Their Houses": Religious Routines and the Residences of Greater Medieval Households', in Malcolm Airs and Paul Barnwell (eds), *The Medieval Great House*, Donington 2011, pp. 171–99

Reed, M. (ed.), *Buckinghamshire Probate Inventories, 1661–1714*, Aylesbury 1988

—, 'Osterley Park in 1668: the Probate Inventory of Sir William Waller', *Transactions of the London and Middlesex Archaeological Society*, XLII (1991), pp. 115–29

Reeves, William, *Catalogue of the Library at Lough Fea in Illustration of the History and Antiquities of Ireland*, London 1872

The Regulation and Establishment of the Houshold [sic] of Henry Algernon Percy, the Fifth Earl of Northumberland, at his Castles of Wresill and Lekinfield in Yorkshire, London 1770, ESTC T131520

Reilly, R., 'Wedgwood, Josiah (1730–1795)', ODNB

Repton, H., *Fragments on the Theory and Practice of Landscape Gardening* London 1816

Richardson, G., *The New Vitruvius Britannicus*, London 1802

Richardson, J., 'Dibdin, Thomas Frognall (1776–1847)', ODNB

Richardson, T., 'What Drives People to Steal Precious Books', *Financial Times*, 6 March 2009

Richardson, W., 'John Boys (bap. 1571, d. 1625)', ODNB

Riden, Philip, and Dudley Fowkes, *Hardwick: A Great House and its Estate*, Chichester 2009

Ridgard, John (ed.), 'Medieval Framlingham: Select Documents, 1270–1524', *Suffolk Records Society*, XXVII (1985)

Roberts, Paul, *Life and Death in Pompeii and Herculaneum*, London 2013

Robinson, John Martin, *The Architecture of Northern England*, London 1986

—, *Shugborough*, London 1989

—, *A Guide to the Country Houses of the North West*, London 1991

—, *Arundel Castle, a Seat of the Duke of Norfolk, E.M.: A Short History and Guide*, Chichester 1994

—, *Arundel Castle, the Seat of the Duke of Norfolk, E.M.: A History and Guide*, Chichester 2011

—, *James Wyatt (1746–1813): Architect to George III*, New Haven and London 2012

Robinson, P., 'The Vernon Manuscript as a 'Coucher Book', in Derek Pearsall (ed.), *Studies in the Vernon Manuscript*, Cambridge 1990, pp. 15–28

Rocque, John, *A Plan of the Cities of London and Westminster*, [London] 1746, ESTC N5262

Rodger, N., 'Anson, George, Baron Anson (1697–1762)', ODNB

Rogers, David, *The Bodleian Library and its Treasures*, Henley 1991

Rogers, M., *Montacute House, Somerset*, London 1991

van Romburgh, S., 'Junius [Du Jon], Franciscus (1591–1677)', ODNB

5th Earl of Rothes, John, *A Relation of Proceedings Concerning the Kirk of Scotland, from August 1637 to July 1638*, Edinburgh 1830

de Rothschild, Mrs James, *The Rothschilds at Waddesdon Manor*, London 1979

Rothwell, James, *Dunham Massey, Cheshire*, London 2000

—, 'Dedicated to Books', in David Adshead (ed.), *National Trust Historic Houses and Collections Annual* (2010), pp. 56–61

Roundell, J., *Ham House: Its History and Art Treasures*, London 1904

Rowell, Christopher, *Polesden Lacey, Surrey*, London 1999

—, *Turner at Petworth*, London 2002

—, *Petworth: The People and the Place*, London 2012

—, (ed.), *Ham House: Four Hundred Years of Collecting and Patronage*, New Haven and London 2013

Rowse, A. L., *A Cornish Childhood*, London 1998

—, *Ralegh and the Throckmortons*, London 1961

Roy, I., 'The Libraries of Edward, 2nd Viscount Conway', *Bulletin of the Institute of Historical Research*, XLI, 103 (May 1968), pp.35–47

Rundle, David, 'Habits of Manuscript-Collecting: the Dispersals of the library of Humfrey, Duke of Gloucester', in James Raven, *Lost Libraries: The Destruction of Great Book Collections Since Antiquity*, London 2004, pp.106–23

Russell, F., 'Preservation in Situ: the Role of the Auction House', in *Patronage Preserved: An Exhibition of Masterpieces Saved for Country Houses*, Christie's, London 1991, pp.8–15

Rye, William B., *England as Seen by Foreigners in the Days of Elizabeth and James the First*, London 1865

Sackville-West, R., *Inheritance: The Story of Knole and the Sacvkvilles*, London 2010

Sadleir, T., 'An Eighteenth-Century Irish Gentleman's Library', *Book Collector*, II, 2 (Autumn 1953), pp.173–6

Sandler, Lucy Freeman, *The Lichtenthal Psalter and the Manuscript Patronage of the Bohun Family*, London 2004

Sands, F., 'The Art of Collaboration: Antonio Zucchi at Nostell Priory', *Georgian Group Journal*, XIX (2011), pp.106–19

Saunders, J., *Words and Phrases Legally Defined: Lexis Nexis*, London 1969–86

Scattergood, Vincent J., 'Two Medieval Book Lists', *The Library*, 5th series, XXIII (1968), pp.236–9

Schulz, Herbert C., *The Ellesmere Manuscript of Chaucer's Canterbury Tales*, San Marino, CA 1999

Scott, A., *Eccentric Wealth: The Bulloughs of Rum*, Edinburgh 2011

Scott, Geoffrey, 'The Throckmortons at Home and Abroad, 1680–1800', in P. Marshall and G. Scott (ed.), *Catholic Gentry in English Society: The Throckmortons of Coughton from Reformation to Emancipation*, Farnham 2009, pp.171–211

Scott-Fox, Charles, *Holcombe Court: A Bluett Family Tudor Mansion*, Exeter 2012

Scott-Warren, Jason, *Sir John Harington and the Book as Gift*, Oxford 2001

Seccombe, Thomas, 'Stearne, John (1660–1745)', ODNB

Seddon, P. R., 'Pierrepont, Henry, Marquess of Dorchester (1607–1680)', ODNB

A Select Set of Psalms and Hymns with a Choice Collection of Words and with Proper Tunes and Basses as they are Fitted to be Sung in the Parish Church of Grantham By John Hutchinson Clerk of the Parish, [Grantham? 1756] ESTC T155509

A Select set of Psalms and Hymns, with A Choice Collection of Words, with Proper Tunes and Basses, as they are Appointed to be Sung in the Parish Church of Grantham. By John Hutchinson, Late Clerk of the Parish, Grantham 1792, ESTC T155508

Selwyn, Pamela and David, '"The Profession of a Gentleman": Books for the Gentry and the Nobility (*c.* 1560 to 1640)', CHLBI, *vol. I: To 1640*, pp.489–519

Sherbo, A., 'Heber, Richard (1774–1833)', ODNB

Sherman, William, 'The Place of Reading in the English Renaissance: John Dee Revisited', in J. Raven, H. Small and N. Tadmor (eds), *The Practice and Representation of Reading in England*, Cambridge 1996, pp.62–76

—, *Used Books: Marking Readers in Renaissance England*, Philadelphia 2008

Shirley, E. P., *Lough Fea*, London 1869

—, *Catalogue of the Library at Lough Fea: an Illustration of the History and Antiquities of Ireland*, London 1872

Sider, David, *The Library of the Villa dei Papiri at Herculaneum*, Los Angeles 2005

Sinclair, K., *Descriptive Catalogue of Medieval and Renaissance and Western Manuscripts in Australia*, [Sydney] 1969

Skinner, John, *Journal of a Somerset Rector, 1803–1834*, ed. Howard and Peter Coombs, Oxford 1984

Slade, Harry Gordon, *Glamis Castle*, London 2000

Sledmere, Norwich 2001

Smith, A., *Sherborne Castle*, Shaftesbury 2011

Smith, D., 'Seymour, William, First Marquess and Second Duke of Somerset (1587–1660)', ODNB

Smith, Douglas, *Former People: The Last Days of the Russian Aristocracy*, London 2012

Smith, L., 'Boyle, Charles, Fourth Earl of Orrery (1674–1731)', ODNB

—, 'Boyle, John, Fifth Earl of Cork and Fifth Earl of Orrery (1707–1762)', ODNB

Smith, P., 'Welbeck Abbey and the Fifth Duke of Portland', in M. Airs (ed.), *The Victorian Great House*, Oxford 2000, pp.147–64

—, 'Lady Oxford's Alterations at Welbeck Abbey, 1741–55', *Georgian Group Journal*, XI (2001), pp.133–68

Smith, W. J. (ed.), *Herbert Correspondence: The Sixteenth and Seventeenth Century Letters of the Herberts of Chirbury, Powis Castle and Dolguog, formerly at Powis Castle in Montgomery*, Cardiff 1963

Smuts, R. Malcolm, 'Howard, Thomas, four-teenth Earl of Arundel, fourth Earl of Surrey, and first Earl of Norfolk (1585–1646)', ODNB

Snodin, Michael (ed.), *Sir William Chambers*, London 1996

Snyder, Henry L., 'Spencer, Charles, Third Earl of Sunderland (1675–1722)', ODNB

Spencer, Charles, *Althorp: The Story of an English House*, London 1998

Spevack, Marvin, 'The Library at Hughenden Manor', *Book Collector*, LIX, 4 (Winter 2010), pp.547–80

Sroka, M., '"Forsaken and Abandoned": the Nationalization and Salvage of Deserted, Displaced, and Private Library Collections in Poland, 1945 to 1948', *Library & Information History*, XXVIII, 4 (December 2012), pp.272–88

Stater, R., 'Hatton, Christopher, First Baron Hatton (*bap.* 1605, *d.* 1670)', ODNB

Steer, Francis, 'The Inventory of Arthur Coke of Bramfield', *Proceedings of the Suffolk Institute of Archaeology & History*, XXV (1951), pp.264–87

Stell, Philip (ed.), *Probate Inventories of the York Diocese, 1350–1500*, York 2006

Stevenson, D., 'Gordon, Sir Robert, of Gordonstoun, First Baronet (1580–1656)', ODNB

Stillman, D., *English Neo-Classical Architecture* London 1988

Stimpson, Felicity, '"I have Spent my Morning Reading Greek": the Marginalia of Sir George Otto Trevelyan', *Library History*, XXIII, 3 (August 2007), pp.239–50

—, 'The Library at Wallington', *Book Collector*, LVIII, I (Spring 2009), pp.45–72

Stoddard, R., *Marks in Books, Illustrated and Explained*, Cambridge, MA 1985

Stoker, D., 'Harley, Edward, Second Earl of Oxford and Mortimer (1689–1741)', ODNB

Stone, Lawrence, *The Crisis of the Aristocracy*, Oxford 1965

—, 'The Revival of Narrative: Reflections on a New Old History', *Past and Present*, LXXXV (1979), pp.3–24

Strachey, N., *Ickworth, Suffolk*, London 1998

Stratford, Jenny, *The Bedford Inventories: The Worldly Goods of John, Duke of Bedford, Regent of France (1389–1435)*, London 1993

Streeter, Burnett Hillman, *The Chained Library: A Survey of Four Centuries in the Evolution of the English Library*, London 1931

Suckling, A., *The History and Antiquities of the County of Suffolk*, London 1846–8

Suggett, Richard, *Houses & History in the March of Wales: Radnorshire, 1400–1800*, Aberystwyth 2005

Summerson, Henry, 'The Lucys of Charlcote and their Library', *National Trust Studies* (1979), pp.147–59

Survey of London: Volume 10, St Margaret, Westminster Part 1: Queen Anne's Gate Area [London] 1926

Survey of London: Volumes 29 and 30, St James Westminster, Part 1, London 1960

Swain, M., 'National Trust for Scotland in Crisis', *Country Life*, 10 August 2010

Swift, Katherine, 'The Formation of the Library of Charles Spencer, 3rd Earl of Sunderland (1674–1722): a Study in the Antiquarian Book Trade', D.Phil. Thesis, University of Oxford, 1987

Sykes, Christopher Simon, *Private Palaces: Life in the Great London Houses*, London 1985

—, *The Big House: The Story of a Country House and its Family*, London 2004

Tabor, S., 'The Bridgewater Library', in W. Baker and K. Womack (eds), *Pre-Nineteenth-Century British Book Collectors and Bibliographers*, Detroit 1999, pp. 40–50

Tanis, James, and Jennifer A. Thompson, *Leaves of Gold: Manuscript Illuminations from Philadelphia Collections*, Philadelphia 2001

Tanselle, G. Thomas, *Other People's Books: Association Copies and the Stories They Tell*, Chicago 2011

Taylor, Andrew, 'Into his Secret Chamber: Reading and Privacy in Late Medieval England', in James Raven, Helen Small and Naomi Tadmor, *The Practice and Representation of Reading in England*, Cambridge 1996, pp. 41–61

Thomas, P., 'Yorke, Philip, First Earl of Hardwicke (1690–1764)', ODNB

Thompson, E., 'The Will and Inventory of Robert Morton, A.D. 1486–1488', *Journal of the British Archaeological Association*, XXXIII (1877), pp. 308–30

Thompson, F., 'Grenville, Richard Plantagenet Temple-Nugent-Brydges-Chandos, Second Duke of Buckingham and Chandos', ODNB

Thornton, Dora, *The Scholar in His Study: Ownership and Experience in Renaissance Italy*, New Haven and London 1997

Thornton, Peter, *Seventeenth-Century Interior Decoration in England, France and Holland*, London 1978

Thorold, H., *Lincolnshire Houses*, Norwich 1999

Thorpe, Deborah, 'Writing and Reading in the Circle of Sir John Fastolf (d.1459)', PhD Thesis, University of York, 2011

Thorpe, James, Robert R. Wark and Ray Allen Billington, *The Founding of the Henry E. Huntington Library and Art Gallery: Four Essays*, San Marino, CA 1969

Timmins, Samuel, *Lord Spencer's Library: A Sketch of a Visit to Althorp*, Northampton 1870

Tinniswood, Adrian, *Belton House, Lincolnshire*, London 2006

Tite, Colin G. C., *The Manuscript Library of Sir Robert Cotton*, London 1994

Titler, R., 'Bacon, Sir Nicholas (1510–1579)', ODNB

Tomalin, M., 'The 1782 Inventory of Osterley Park', *Furniture History*, XXII (1986), pp. 107–35

Tomlin, Roger, 'The Book in Roman Britain', in Roger Gameson (ed.), CHBB, vol. 1: c.400–1100, Cambridge 2011, pp. 375–88

Treasures of Fyvie, Edinburgh [1985]

Trevelyan, George Otto, *Marginal Notes by Lord Macaulay*, London 1907

Turberville, A., *A History of Welbeck Abbey and its Owners*, London 1938–9

Turville-Petre, Thorlac, 'The Relationship of the Vernon and Clopton Manuscripts', in Derek Pearsall (ed.), *Studies in the Vernon Manuscript*, Cambridge 1990, pp. 29–44

von Uffenbach, Zacharias Conrad, *Oxford in 1710*, Oxford 1928

—, *London in 1710*, London 1934

Vaisey, David (ed.), *Probate Inventories of Lichfield and District*, [Stafford] 1969

—, 'Obituary: W. O. Hassall', *The Independent*, 28 July 1994

Vaulbert de Chantilly, Marc, 'Willett, Ralph (1719–1795)', ODNB

The Vernon Manuscript: A Facsmile of Bodleian Library, Oxford, MS. Eng. poet. a. 1, Cambridge 1987

Vernon, T., 'Inventory of Sir Henry Sharington: Contents of Lacock House, 1575', *Wiltshire Archaeological and Natural History Society Magazine*, LXIII (1968), pp. 72–82

Vitruvius Pollio, *Ten Books on Architecture*, Cambridge 1999

Vliegenthart, A., *Het Loo Palace: Journal of a Restoration*, Appeldoorn 2002

de Voragine, Jacobus, *Thus Endeth the Legende Named in Latyn Legenda Aurea*, Westminster 1483, STC 24873, ESTC S541

Waagen, Gustav, *Treasures of Art in Great Britain*, London 1854

Wagner, Bettina, 'Libri Impressi Bibliothecae Sancti Emmerammi: the Incunable Collections of St Emmeram, Regensburg, and its Catalogue of 1501', in K. Jensen (ed.), *Incunabula and their Readers: Printing, Selling and Using Books in the Fifteenth Century*, London 2003, pp. 179–277

Wainwright, Clive, *The Romantic Interior: The British Collector at Home, 1750–1850*, New Haven and London 1989

—, 'The Library as Living Room', in R. Myers and M. Harris, *Property of a Gentleman: The Formation, Organisation and Dispersal of the Private Library*, Winchester 1991

Walker, G., *Hamilton Palace: A Photographic Record*, Hamilton 1987

Wallis, H., 'The First English Globe: A Recent Discovery', *Geographical Journal*, CXVIII, 1951, pp. 275–90

Wallis, R., 'Jones, William (c.1675–1749)', ODNB

Wanklyn, Malcolm, 'Stratagems for Survival: Sir Robert and Sir Francis Throckmorton, 1640–1660', in Peter Marshall and Geoffrey Scott, *Catholic Gentry in English Society: The Throckmortons of Coughton from Reformation to Emancipation*, Farnham 2009, pp. 146–70

Warkentin, Germaine, 'The World and the Book at Penshurst: the Second Earl of Leicester (1595–1677) and His Library', *The Library*, 6th series, XX, 4 (December 1998), pp. 325–46

—, Joseph L. Black and William R. Bowen, *The Library of the Sidneys of Penshurst Place, Circa 1665*, Toronto 2013

Warner, G., *Descriptive Catalogue of Illuminated Manuscripts in the Library of C. W. Dyson Perrins*, Oxford 1920

Waterson, Merlin, *The Country House Remembered: Recollections of Life Between the Wars*, London 1985

—, *The National Trust: The First Hundred Years*, London 1994

Watson, Andrew G., *The Manuscripts of Sir Henry Savile of Banke*, London 1969

—, 'The Manuscript Collection of Sir Walter Cope (d. 1614)', *Bodleian Library Record*, XII, 4 (April 1987) pp. 262–97

Weber, S., 'Kent and the Georgian Baroque Style in Furniture: Domestic Commissions', in S. Weber (ed.), *William Kent: Designing Georgian Britain*, London 2013

Webster, Leslie, and Janet Backhouse (eds), *The Making of England: Anglo-Saxon Art and Culture*, London 1991

Weiss, R., 'The Library of John Tiptoft, Earl of Worcester', *Bodleian Quarterly Record*, VIII (1935–8), pp. 158–64

—, *Humanism in England During the Fifteenth Century*, Oxford 1957

—, 'The Private Collector and the Revival of Greek Learning', in Francis Wormald and Cyril E. Wright, *The English Library before 1700*, London 1958, pp. 112–35

West, A., 'Magnificae at Plane Regiae Domus Quae Vulgo Vocatur Nonesuch Brevis et Vera Descriptio', *Garden History*, XXVII, I (1999), pp. 168–78

—, *The Shakespeare First Folio: The History of the Book. Volume II: A New Worldwide Census of First Folios*, Oxford 2003

West, Susie, 'The Development of Libraries in Norfolk Country Houses, 1660–1830', PhD Thesis, University of East Anglia, 2000

—, 'Studies and Status Spaces in Seventeenth-Century Penshurst Place', *Transactions of the Cambridge Bibliographical Society*, XII (2002), pp. 266–92

—, 'An Architectural Typology for the Early Modern Country House Library, 1660–1720', *The Library*, 7th Series, XIV, 4 (2013), pp. 441–64

—, 'Life in the Library', in G. Perry, K. Retford, J. Vibert and H. Lyons, *Placing Faces: The Portrait in the Country House in the Long Eighteenth Century*, Manchester 2013, pp. 63–95

Whatman, S., *The Housekeeping Book of Susanna Whatman, 1776–1800*, London 2000

Whiffen, W., 'Bridgewater House, St. James's', *Country Life*, 13 May 1949, pp. 1118–21

Whitehead, J., 'An Inventory of the Goods and Chattels of Sir Richard Worsley of Appuldurcombe, A.D. 1566', *Papers and Proceedings of the Hampshire Field Club and Archaeological Society*, V (1904–6), pp. 277–95

Whitley, H., 'An Inventory of the Goods and Chattels of William Shelley of Michelgrove, 1585', *Sussex Archaeological Collections*, LV (1912), pp. 284–98

Widley, George, *The Doctrine of the Sabbath Handled in Foure Severall Bookes of Treatises*, London 1604, ESTC S119957, STC 256110

Wiggston, P., 'A Grain of Truth', *Architectural Heritage: The Journal of the Architectural Heritage Society of Scotland*, XII (2001), pp. 13–26

Willems, P., *Bibliotheca Fletcheriana: or the Extraordinary Library of Andrew Fletcher of Saltoun*, Wassenaar 1999

Willett, Ralph, *A Description of the Library at Merly in the County of Dorset*, London 1785, ESTC T88028

—, *A Catalogue of the Books in the Library of Ralph Willett, Esq., at Merly, in the County of Dorset*, London [1790], ESTC T08827

Williams, Frances, *Pleshey Castle, Essex (XII–XVI): Excavations in the Bailey, 1959–1963*, British Archaeological Reports 48, London 1977

Williams, R., *Catalogue of the Castle Fraser Music Collection*, Aberdeen 1994

Willmoth, F., 'Moore, Sir Jonas (1617–1679)', ODNB

Willoughby, Cassandra, *The Continuation of the History of the Willoughby Family*, Eton 1958

Winter, Dominic, *A Gentleman's Library*, Dominic Winter Auctioneers, Swindon 20 September 2012

Wisker, R., 'Hyde, Jane, Countess of Clarendon and Rochester (c.1672–1725)', ODNB

Woodbridge, K., *Landscape and Antiquity: Aspects of English Culture at Stourhead, 1718 to 1838*, Oxford 1970

Woolgar, C. M., *The Great Household in Late Medieval England*, New Haven and London 1999

Worsley, Giles, *England's Lost Houses*, London 2002

—, 'Beyond the Powerhouse: Understanding the Country House in the Twenty-First Century', *Historical Research*, LXXVIII, 201 (August 2005), pp. 423–35

Worsley, Marcus, *Jottings*, York 2004

Wotton, Sir Henry, *The Elements of Architecture*, London 1624, STC 26011, ESTC S120324

Wright, C. E., 'The Dispersal of the Libraries in the Sixteenth Century', in F. Wormald (ed.), *The English Library before 1700*, London 1958

—, 'Portrait of a Bibliophile VIII: Edward Harley, 2nd Earl of Oxford, 1689–1741', *Book Collector*, XI (1962), pp. 158–74

—, 'The Benedictional of St Aethelwold', *British Museum Quarterly*, XXVII (1963), pp. 3–5

Wright, O., 'Inside Whitehall. The Art of Claiming our Right to View Masterpieces', *The Independent*, 25 November 2013

Sale Catalogues (in chronological order)

Bibliotheca Angleseiana, Sive Catalogus Variorum Librorum in Quavis Linguâ, & Facultate Insignium, London 1682, ESTC R30816, Wing A3166

Bibliotheca Illustris: Sive Catalogus Variorum Librorum in Quâvis Linguâ & Facultate Insignium Ornatissimae Bibliothecae Viri Cujusdam Praenobilis ac Honoratissimi Olim Defuncti, London 1687, ESTC R282, Wing A801A

Bibliotheque de Feu [sic] Monseigneur de Lauderdale, London 1690, ESTC R43356, Wing L607

The English Part of the Library of the late Duke of Lauderdale, London 1690, ESTC R43357, Wing L611

Catalogus Variorum Librorum. Sive Bibliotheca Instructissima Doctimissi Cujusdam Genorosi Nuperrime Defuncti. Cui Praefigitur Bibliorum Polyglotton D. Ducis Lauderdaliensis, London [1691], ESTC R43369, Wing L610

Bibliotheca Instructissima ex Bibliothecis Duorum Doctissimorum Theologorum Londinen, Nuper Defunctorum, Compsita. Cui Adjicitur

Bibliotheca Manuscripta Lauderdaliana, Sive Catalogus Librorum Manuscriptorum, … & Alii Variis Linguis Facultatibusque Insig. Nondum Impressi, a Bibliotheca Ducis Lauderdaliana, London 1692, ESTC R221235, Wing L605

Catalogue of the Library of the Right Honourable the Earl of Yarmouth … Which Will be Sold … on Wednesday the Tenth of this Instant, April, 1734 … By Olive Payne, London 1734, ESTC T81780

A Catalogue of Greek, Roman and English Coins, Medallions and Medals, of the Right Honourable Edward Earl of Oxford, which will be Sold by Auction, by Mr Cock, at his House in the Great Piazza, Covent Garden, on Thursday March the 18th, 1741–2, [s.n. London] 1742, ESTC T30132

A Catalogue of the Rich Houshold [sic] Furniture of the Right Honourable Henry Earl of Thomond, Deceas'd, which will Begin to be Sold at Auction on Monday the 25th Instant, at his Late Dwelling-House in Dover-Street, St James's, [s.n., London] 25 January–4 February 1742

A Catalogue of the Valuable Library of Books of the Right Honourable Henry Earl of Thomond, Deceas'd, Which Will Begin to be sold by Auction, on Friday the 5th of February, 1742, [London] 1742

A Catalogue of the Genuine and Valuable Collection of Greek, Roman and English Gold, Silver and Brass Coins, Medals and Medallions, of the Honourable Bryan Fairfax, Esq;, A. Langford, London 24 April 1751, ESTC T14347

Catalogus Meadiana: sive Catalogus Librorum Richardi Mead, London 1755, ESTC T1340

A Catalogue of the Genuine and Valuable Collection of Italian, Dutch, and Flemish Pictures of the Honourable Bryan Fairfax, Esq; Commissioner of His Majesty's Customs, … Likewise his Antique Marble, Verd Antique, Porphry Busts, Urns, Small Statues, Basso Relievos, Vases, Curious Bronzes, &c., J. Prestage, London 6–7 April 1756, ESTC T187377

A Catalogue of the Entire and Valuable Library of the Honourable Bryan Fairfax, Esq., One of the Commissioners of His Majesty's Customs, Deceased, [John Prestage, London 1756], ESTC T187377

A Catalogue of the Entire Genuine Household Furniture and other Valuable Effects of the Hon. Henry Cecil, at Hanbury-Hall, in the County of Worcester, I. Tymbs, Worcester [1790]

A Catalogue of the Library of the late Right Honourable Denis Daly, which will be Sold by Auction, on Thursday the First of May 1792, by James Vallance, at his Auction-Room, No. 6, Eustace-Street, Dublin [1792], ESTC T3191

A Catalogue of the Duplicate Part of the Library of a Nobleman: Comprehending a Large Collection of Books of Natural History, [R. Robson] London 1792, ESTC T150834

White Knights Library. Catalogue of that Distinguished and Celebrated Library, Containing Numerous Very Fine and Rare Specimens from the Presses of Caxton, Pyson, and Wynkyn de Worde &c., London 1819

Wanstead House, Essex. Magnificent Furniture, Collection of Fine Paintings and Sculpture, Massive Silver & Gilt Plate, Splendid Library of Choice Books, T. Robins, London 1822

Catalogue of the Splendid, Curious and Extensive Library of the Late Sir Mark Masterman Sykes, London 1824

Shugborough Hall, Near Stafford. Mr. George Robins is Honoured with Instructions to Announce for Unreserved Competition, on the Premises, on Monday, the 1st of August, 1842 and Thirteen Following Days, … the Splendid Property of Every Denomination Appertaining to Shugborough Hall, [G. Robins, London] 1842

A Catalogue of the Very Superior Furniture of Lichfield House, in Saint James' Square, G. Robins, [London] 1842

Hughenden House, Bucks, Midway Between Oxford and London. A Catalogue of the Valuable Household Furniture, Rich China, and Glass, Fine Oil Paintings, Ancient Coins, Telescopes, Microscopes … Which will be Sold by Auction, without Reserve, by Alexander Davis, on Monday May 10th, 1847, and Five Following Days, … by Order of the Executors of the Late John Norris, Esq., Newbury [1847]

Catalogue of the Library Removed from Stowe House, Buckinghamshire, Leigh & Sotheby, London 8 January 1848

Bibliotheca Sunderlandiana: Sale Catalogue of the Truly Important and Very Extensive Library of Printed Books Known as the Sunderland or Blenheim Library, Puttick and Simpson, London 1881–3

The Hamilton Palace Libraries. Catalogue … of the Beckford Library, Removed from Hamilton Palace …, Sotheby, Wilkinson & Hodge, London 30 June and 11 December 1882, 2 July and 27 November 1883

Catalogue of the Library Removed from Stourhead, London: Sotheby, Wilkinson & Hodge, London 30 July–7 August 1883

Catalogue of the Fine, Extensive and Valuable Library of the Rt. Hon. the Earl of Gosford, K.P. … To be Sold by Messrs Puttick and Simpson on Monday 21 April 1884, Puttick and Simpson, London [1884]

The Hamilton Palace Libraries. Catalogue of the Hamilton Library, Sotheby, Wilkinson & Hodge, London 1–9 May 1884

The Hamilton Palace Libraries. Catalogue of … Books Returned from the Sale of the Beckford & Hamilton Libraries, Having Been Bound Imperfect …, Sotheby, Wilkinson & Hodge, London 8 July 1884

Catalogue of an Important Portion of the Extensive and Valuable Library of the late Sir John Hayford Thorold, Bart, Sotheby, Wilkinson & Hodge, London 12–20 December 1884

Catalogue of the Clandon Library: in Which is Included the Collection of Books Formed by the Rt. Hon. Arthur Onslow, XXXIII Years Speaker of the House of Commons, Many Enriched with his Autograph Notes, The whole the Property of the Trustees of the Will of the Late Earl of Onslow, Sotheby, Wilkinson & Hodge, London 20–21 March 1885

The Osterley Park Library: Catalogue of this Most Important Collection of Books, the Property of the Rt. Hon. the Earl of Jersey, Sotheby, Wilkinson & Hodge, London 6 May 1885

Catalogue of a Portion of the Valuable Library of a Nobleman [i.e the Earl of Westmorland, of Apethorpe], Sotheby's, London 13–15 July 1887

Catalogue of the Remaining Portion of the Library, Removed from Stourhead, Sotheby, Wilkinson & Hodge, London 9–13 December 1887

Catalogue of the Burton Constable Library of Printed Books, Collected Chiefly by William Constable, Esq., Sotheby, Wilkinson & Hodge, London 27–29 June 1889

Catalogue. Morval. … At the Above Mansion, the Whole of the Antique and Modern Furniture, Library of about 4,000 Vols. of Books, Skardon and Sons, Plymouth, 28–30 April and 1–4 May 1891

Catalogue of Valuable Old English Books and Manuscripts Selected from the Library of a Gentleman in the Country …, Sotheby's, London 17–18 June 1904

Downing Hall, near Holywell. Catalogue of Sale of the Remainder of the Downing Library (formed by Thomas Pennant, the well-known Antiquary and Naturalist, William Dew, Bangor, 26–28 May 1913

Catalogue of Rare Books, the Property of W. R. Phelips, Esq. of Montacute House, Montacute, Somerset, Knight, Frank & Rutley, London 17 November 1915

Catalogue of Books, Pictures and Furniture. By Order of the Executors; also the Property of a Gentleman, removed from Hastings; the Property of a Lady, and from Other Sources, Knight, Frank & Rutley, London 14 January 1916

Catalogue of a Choice Selected Portion of the Famous Library Removed from Sudbury Hall, Derbyshire, Including Illuminated and Other Manuscripts, and Rare Printed Books, the Property of Lieut. Lord Vernon, R.N., Sotheby, Wilkinson & Hodge, London 10 June 1918

A Catalogue of Valuable and Splendid Books from the Cassiobury Park Library, Hodgson, London 24 May 1922

Catalogue of Books and Manuscripts, Also Autograph Letters & Historical Documents, Comprising the Property of the late W. Crambe Reid; … the Property of the late Horace W, Sandars; … the Property of the Countess of Ancaster; … the Property of Sir Henry Paston Bedingfeld, Bt. …, Sotheby's, London 26 July 1922

A Catalogue of Valuable and Rare Books from the Extensive and Interesting Cassiobury Park Library, Hodgson, London 22 November 1922

A Catalogue of Rare Books and Tracts Mostly from the 16th and 17th Centuries, Selected from the Extensive and Valuable Cassiobury Park Library, Hodgson, London 30 November 1922

Catalogue of Nineteen Books of the Highest Importance from the Library of the Late Earl of Carysfort, Sotheby, Wilkinson & Hodge, London 2 July 1923

Catalogue of a Collection of Important Books Selected from the Library at Carton, Co. Kildare, Bennet and Son, Dublin 11 November 1925

Catalogue of Exceedingly Rare and Valuable Americana, with Some Important English Books & Manuscripts, Largely from the Library of Henry Percy, 9th Earl of Northumberland (1564–1632) at Petworth House, Sotheby's, London 23–24 April 1928

Catalogue of Printed Books and a Few Manuscripts …, Sotheby's, London 1930

Illuminated Manuscripts, Incunabula and Americana from the Famous Libraries of the Most Hon. The Marquess of Lothian, Sold by his Order, Removed from Blickling Hall, Norfolk and Newbattle Abbey, Midlothian, Anderson Galleries, New York 27–28 January 1932

Catalogue of Books Comprising the Property of Sir Francis Peel, Bt., the Property of Major and Mrs Disraeli, and Other Properties, Sotheby's, London 22–23 February 1937

Catalogue of Original XVIIIth Century Woodwork, Unique Marble Mantelpieces, … Being the Remaining Contents of Norfolk House, Christie, Manson & Woods, London 7 February 1938

Catalogue of the Renowned Library Removed from Ham House, Surrey, Sotheby's, London 30–31 May 1938

Catalogue of Sale of a Large Portion of the Valuable Period Furniture and Secondary Furnishings, Vale Royal, Brown's, Chester 9–10 October 1946

Catalogue of Valuable Printed Books, Autograph Letters and Historical Documents, etc. Comprising a Selection from the Library at Naworth Castle, Cumberland, Sotheby's, London 27–28 October 1947

Catalogue of a Selected Portion of the Valuable Library at Wentworth Woodhouse, Rotherham the Property of the Rt. Honble. Earl Fitzwilliam, … The First Portion, Sotheby's, London 1–2 March 1948

Catalogue of a Selected Portion of the Valuable Library at Wentworth Woodhouse, Rotherham, the Property of the Rt. Honble Earl Fitzwilliam. The Second and Final Portion, London: Sotheby, 26–28 April 1948

The Hurn Court Library: The Property of the Right Honourable the Earl of Malmsbury, Sotheby's, London 9–10 and 30–31 March, 27–28 April 1950

Catalogue of a Selected Portion of the Library at Shelton Abbey, the Property of the Rt. Honble. the Earl of Wicklow, Sotheby's, London 11–12 December 1950

Catalogue of Printed Books, Comprising the Extensive Collection of Books on Ornithology and Natural History, the Property of the Revd. J. M. McWilliam …. Books on Art the Property of Mrs Thomas Lowinsky, the Property of the Late Franker Porter, Esq. Well-Bound Sporting Books and Others with Coloured Plates, Botanical Books, Nineteenth-Century Novels, etc, including the Property of Mrs. O. Hales Pakenham-Mahon, Strokestown Park, Co. Roscommon, Ireland …, Sotheby's, London 1–3 December 1952

Catalogue of Valuable Printed Books, Autograph Letters, Historical Documents, etc., Comprising Travel Books with Coloured Plates on Ornithology, Botany, etc., the Property of the Lady Janet Douglas Pennant, removed from Penrhyn, Wales …, Sotheby's, London 6 July 1953

Panshanger, Hertford: Catalogue of the Part of the Library to be Sold by Auction upon the Premises on Wednesday, 9th September 1953, Humbert & Flint, [London 1953]

The Dyson Perrins Collection: Catalogue of … Illuminated Manuscripts … which will be Sold by Sotheby & Co., Sotheby's, London 1958–60

Stackpole Court, Pembrokeshire. Catalogue of the Important Three Days' Sale of Furniture & Effects …, Strutt & Parker, London 19–21 November 1962

Catalogue of Printed Books, Comprising the Property of Dr P. H. Plesch, the Property of the Late M. Fernand Vellut, and Other Properties, Sotheby's, London 13–14 July 1964

Bodysgallen Hall, Llanrhos – Llandudno … Catalogue of the Important, Interesting, and Valuable Contents of this Historic Mansion, Llandudno, Blomfield & Co., 6–8 September 1967

The Library of Thomas Percy, 1729–1811, Bishop of Dromore, Editor of the Reliques of Ancient English Poetry, Removed to Caledon House, Co. Tyrone in 1812, and now Sold by Order of the Trustees of the Caledon Estate and the Rt. Hon. the Earl of Caledon, Sotheby's, London 23 June 1969

Tew Park, Great Tew, Oxford: The Property of the Late Major Eustace Robb, Sold by Order of the Executors, Christie's, London 27–29 May 1987

Magnificent Plate Books from the Library of the Earl of Bradford, Sotheby's, London 15 March 2000

Printed Books and Manuscripts from Beriah Botfield's Library at Longleat, Sold by Order of the Longlear Chattels Settlement, Christie's, London 13 June 2002

The Wardington Library: Incunabula and the Wardington Hours, Sotheby's, London 5 December 2006

The Althorp Attic Sale, Christie's, London 7–8 July 2010

Magnificent Books, Manuscripts and Drawings from the Collection of Frederick, 2nd Lord Hesketh, Sotheby's, London 7 December 2010

Three Renaissance Masterworks from Chatsworths: Lots 50–52 to be Sold in the Old Master and British Paintings Evening Sale, Sotheby's, London 5 December 2012

Case.	Shelf.	Date Taken.	TITLE.	By whom Taken.	RETURNED.
II	2	July 20. 97.	William Blake.	Isabel Drury	July 23.
VII	3	Nov 3rd 97	Silvio Pellico	Austice W. Gibbs	Jan 21st /99
VII	2	Nov 10th 97	Oeuvres de P. Corneille .VI	Austice W. Gibbs	Mar 16th 98
XIV	4	Decr 8th 97	Latham's English Language	J.B. Medley	December 15th 1897
XIV	4	Dec 10th 97	Glossaries of dialects, Somerset &c	J.B. Medley	December 15th 1897
XI	8	Dic. 26 97	Chaucer Canterbury Tales	Evelyn Turney	4th January 1898
X	1	Dec. 27. 97	Sloane's Napoleon. vols I & IV	J.B. Medley	January 1. 1898
VII	6	Jan 3rd	The Talisman	Eustace & Gibbs	Jan 13
X	1	Jany 4. 98.	Sloane's Napoleon. Vol. III.	J.B. Medley	January 8th 1898.
VIII	9	Jany 4. 98	Plans to Siborne's Waterloo	J.B. Medley	January 8th 1898.
XI	3	May 1st 98	Poems by C. Rossetti	Corisande Briggs	May 3rd 1898
O.B.		July 15. 98.	Pepys's Diary. vol. 6.	J.B. Medley	July 17. 1898.
XV.	3	July 21. 98.	Macaulay's Essays Vol. I.	J.B. Medley	August 9. 1898
XI	3	August 4th 98	Coxe's Christian Ballads.	Corisande Briggs	August 6th 1898
XV	7	August 15th 98	Pedigree of Gibbs Family	Rev G.L. Master	Sept. 17. 1898.
II	3	August 30. 98	Pooley's Crosses of Somerset	J.B. Medley	October 13. 1898.
II	3	August 30. 98	Pooley's Crosses of Gloucestershire	J.B. Medley	October 13. 1898.
IV	3	October 17. 98	Greville Memoirs (Victoria) vol I.	J.B. Medley.	October 23. 1898.

[233] Borrower's register, Tyntesfield

Photographic and Copyright Credits

Index